CONTEMPORARY MARKETING

CONTEMPORARY MARKETING
THIRD EDITION

LOUIS E. BOONE
University of Central Florida

DAVID L. KURTZ
Eastern Michigan University

The Dryden Press
Hinsdale, Illinois

Copyright © 1980 by The Dryden Press
A division of Holt, Rinehart and Winston, Publishers
All rights reserved
Library of Congress Catalog Card Number: 79-51058
ISBN: 0-03-051391-X
Printed in the United States of America
0 032 987654321

Text and cover design by Stephen Rapley

Copy editing and cartoon research by Jo-Anne Naples
Indexing by Sheila Ary
Permissions by Mili Ve McNiece

To Anita, Bernice, Garret, Jo-Anne,
Nedah, and Stephen

PREFACE

The third edition of *Contemporary Marketing* retains the same conceptual framework of the first two editions. It is up-to-date, and it uses examples of recent origin. The book may be the most illustrative in the marketing field, with its hundreds of real-life examples, problem-solving questions, true case histories, and cartoons that emphasize key concepts. *Contemporary Marketing* relieves the student of the tedious, boring reading that traditionally has characterized the study of marketing.

Worldwide acceptance of the earlier editions demonstrates the correctness of its underlying philosophy: Both students and instructors want a learning/teaching package that makes the study of marketing interesting, realistic, and practical. Make no mistake—intellectual rigor has not been sacrificed. The text is conceptually sound, stressing all the major facets of marketing. But the authors believe that students who use *Contemporary Marketing* as their introductory text will regard it as one of the most interesting business administration textbooks they have ever encountered in a college classroom.

This revision has been based on numerous reviews by both users and nonusers of the earlier editions, as well as extensive marketing research by the publisher. The reviews showed that professors wanted additional coverage of international marketing and the marketing of services, as well as an integrating section that pulls together the various topics covered in the book. As a result of these inputs, the following changes have been made in this edition:

1. A separate chapter on international marketing has been included. This added coverage is indicative of the growing importance of world marketing and is a response to AACSB requirements.
2. Marketing of services is emphasized in Chapter 6. The added coverage points up the tremendous importance of this aspect of marketing.
3. Chapter 19 is the integrating mechanism for pulling together the marketing components into a strategy context. Instructors should find this chapter a major improvement over the previous edition.
4. The book is packed with new examples, illustrations, and cases. Included in the third edition are accounts of the marketing problems associated with Pop Rocks candy, Olde Frothingslosh beer, Perrier, Chelsea, and many more products. Among the new subjects covered are airline deregulation, the Foreign Corrupt Practices Act, teleshopping, and the shrinking U.S. household.

The third edition also retains many of the features that made the previous edition a unique book. Specifically:

1. Sexist language has been removed from the book. Women are portrayed in realistic contemporary circumstances rather than solely as the traditional homemaker/consumer goods shoppers characterized in most marketing textbooks. The authors are grateful to Barbara A. Pletcher of California State University, Sacramento, for her assistance in achieving this objective.
2. This volume is accompanied by the most comprehensive educational package ever produced for a marketing textbook. An entirely new supplement, *The Marketing Experience,* provides a hands-on, experiential approach to learning marketing concepts. Our comprehensive *Study Guide* for reinforcing text material has been carefully revised. The organizer includes a separate *Film Guide,* which offers a means of extending the learning situation. The instructor may also use the accompanying collection of cassette tapes featuring interviews with famous marketers. Additional instructional materials are available to the instructor and college or university.
3. The career appendix has been updated for the third edition. This material is designed to point out marketing career opportunities and to assist students in their search for challenging careers.
4. About 90 percent of the cases in the third edition are new or have been revised. They are all real cases featuring actual companies and the people who are involved and dealing with real situations. They are, we think, a marked improvement over the so-called armchair hypothetical cases.

Finally, we would like to extend our appreciation for the many suggestions from students and instructors that have been included in the third edition of the text. We shall be forever grateful to these people; they are the reason for our desire to develop a truly *teachable* textbook.

Louis E. Boone

David L. Kurtz

Orlando, Florida
Ypsilanti, Michigan
January 1980

ACKNOWLEDGMENTS

Most successful textbooks are the product of many people's work. *Contemporary Marketing* is no exception. This volume benefited from the efforts of numerous individuals.

First, we would like to acknowledge the many people whose works are cited here and/or whose works have pioneered development of the marketing discipline. Textbooks are, after all, merely a reflection of contemporary thought in a discipline. In this respect, marketing is blessed with a strong cadre of academicians and practitioners who are constantly seeking to improve and advance the discipline.

We are especially indebted to our reviewers, an able group of scholars and classroom teachers—professors who gave up their spare time to keep us on the right track in preparing this textbook. Our sincere appreciation is extended to the following people who have reviewed all or part of one or more of our editions:

Dub Ashton
University of Denver

Richard C. Becherer
Wayne State University

Howard B. Cox
Youngstown State University

Benjamin Cutler
Bronx Community College

Gordon Di Paolo
College of Staten Island

Jeffery T. Doutt
California State College, Sonoma

John W. Ernest
Los Angeles City College

Gary T. Ford
University of Maryland,
College Park

Jack E. Forrest
Middle Tennessee State University

James Gould
St. John's University

Donald Granbois
Indiana University

Ralph M. Gredeke
California State University,
Sacramento

John H. Hallaq
University of Idaho

Sanford B. Helman
Middlesex County College

John Ivancevich
University of Kentucky

Don L. James
Fort Lewis College

Bernard V. Katz
Oakton Community College

Harold Kellar
Baruch College, CUNY

Donald L. Knight
Lansing Community College

Paul James Londrigan
Charles Stewart Mott Community
College

Dorothy Maass
Delaware County Community
College

Robert D. Miller
Hillsborough Community College

J. Dale Molander
University of Wisconsin, Oshkosh

John F. Monoky
The University of Toledo

James R. Moore
Southern Illinois University,
Carbondale

Barbara Piasta
Somerset Community College

Constantine Petrides
Manhattan Community College

Barbara A. Pletcher
California State University,
Sacramento

Arthur E. Prell
Southern Illinois University,
Edwardsville

Gary Edward Reiman
City College of San Francisco

Lawrence M. Richard
Wayne State University

Arnold M. Rieger
College of Staten Island

Patrick J. Robinson
Robinson Associates

William C. Rodgers
Moorpark College

William H. Ronald
Miami-Dade College

Carol Rowey
Rhode Island Junior College

Bruce Seaton
Florida International University

Jack Seitz
Oakton Community College

Steven L. Shapiro
Queensborough Community
College

Dennis H. Tootelian
California State University,
Sacramento

We are especially indebted to Jim Langlas, Sharon Sliter, and Dinoo T. Vanier of San Diego State College, who prepared original materials for this volume; to Jo-Anne Naples, who did the editing and cartoon research; and to Stephen K. Keiser of the University of Delaware, Robert E. Stevens of Oral Roberts University, and Lynn J. Loudenback of Iowa State University, who prepared the *Study Guide.* They each contributed significantly to making this textbook a *teachable* addition to the marketing literature.

Our present and former colleagues at The University of Tulsa and Eastern Michigan University also deserve a special word of thanks. All have been generous in their encouragement and support of this project. Several have reviewed all or part of the volume. Former colleagues—James C.

Johnson of St. Cloud State University, James D. Goodnow of Roosevelt University, and Howard A. Thompson of Eastern Kentucky University—provided valuable guidance in several sections of this book.

Finally, the authors would like to express their thanks to the editorial staff of The Dryden Press. Their contributions are sincerely appreciated.

CONTENTS

PART ONE
THE CONTEMPORARY MARKETING ENVIRONMENT

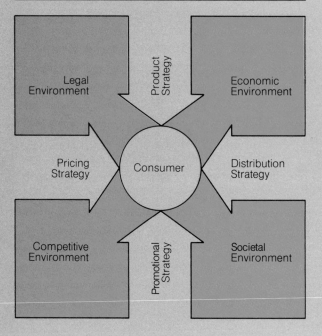

CHAPTER 1
THE MARKETING PROCESS: AN OVERVIEW

Key Terms

utility
marketing
seller's market
buyer's market
marketing concept
product strategy

distribution strategy
marketing channels
promotional strategy
pricing strategy
marketing mix

Learning Goals

1. To examine the evolution of the marketing process.
2. To recognize how the marketing concept has been widely accepted in business.
3. To analyze the four strategy elements of marketing: product, distribution, promotion, and pricing.
4. To identify the three basic reasons for students to study marketing.
5. To explain the alternative approaches to studying marketing.

1

Business organizations perform two basic operating functions; they produce goods or services, and they market them. This is true of all firms—from giant manufacturers such as General Electric and Xerox to neighborhood convenience stores. Production and marketing are the very essence of economic life in any society.

Production and Marketing Create Utility for the Consumer

Society allows businesses to operate only so long as they make a contribution to the members of society. By producing and marketing desired goods and services, businesses satisfy this societal commitment. They create what economists call **utility**—*the want-satisfying power of a product or service.*[1] There are four basic kinds of utility—form, time, place, and ownership.

Form utility is created when the business firm converts raw materials into finished products. Glass, steel, fabrics, rubber, and other components are combined to form a new Chevette or Fiesta. Cotton, thread, and buttons are converted into Arrow shirts. The creation of form utility is one of the production functions of the firm.

The three other kinds of utility—*time, place,* and *ownership*—are created by marketing. They appear when products are made available to consumers at convenient locations and at times when the consumers want to purchase them and when facilities are available for transferring title to the products at the time of purchase.

What Is Marketing?

All organizations must create utility if they are to survive. Miss Olde Frothingslosh does it for Pittsburgh Brewing. General Foods hopes Increda will do it in the bubble gum market. And AT&T, the communications giant, is just discovering the concept of marketing utilities.

Olde Frothingslosh

Pittsburgh Brewing was able to take a disc jockey's skit and convert it into a major marketing success. Back in the 1950s, a Pittsburgh disc jockey would use part of his show to satirize local personalities and happenings. One morning he created a British gentleman named Sir Reginald Frothingslosh who had been asked to develop "a new old ale, a pale, stale ale." The mythical brew was "Olde Frothingslosh," so light that "it floated on top of the foam. With the foam on the bottom, there were no more messy mustaches."

Pittsburgh Brewing, makers of Iron City beer, bought the disc jockey's rights in the pretend, beverage and in 1957 began producing the Olde Frothingslosh label as a Christmas business gift. The idea caught on, and the firm began to market some of its Iron City beer under the Olde Frothingslosh label every Christmas. By 1959, sales had reached eighty thousand cases.

Originally, the disc jockey appeared on the label as Sir Reginald. Later versions included a medieval dame and gentleman spoofing a British ale and two unsteady British lions having a beer while hanging over a coat of arms. Then, in 1965, Pittsburgh Brewing found a three hundred pound go-go dancer known as "The Blonde Bomber." Renamed "Miss Olde Frothingslosh," she began to make promotional visits to Pittsburgh taverns, where she would autograph the Olde Frothingslosh calendar and photographs that the firm used as promotional items.

Today, beer can collecting is a popular hobby, and Olde Frothingslosh is a must in any collection. In fact, Pittsburgh Brewing now produces it year round. The company also sells the popular promotional calendars it once gave away, and it has made available a bountiful supply of empty Olde Frothingslosh cans—at one dollar each. The three hundred pound Miss Olde Frothingslosh is still a major part of the brewery's promotional efforts.

Pittsburgh Brewing's marketing manager, Dan McCann, has explained the firm's marketing strategy this way: "It was a unique thing for us to do, and it gives us a chance to have people sample our regular product." McCann also has noted that the popularity of Olde Frothingslosh helps keep Pittsburghers from switching to a national brand and that it was a major asset in introducing the company's new light beer, Sierra.

Source: Adapted from "Pittsburgh Brewing Co.'s Olde Frothingslosh May Have 'the Foam at the Bottom,' but Its Profits Are at the Top: A Heady Story," *Sales & Marketing Management,* April 3, 1978, pp. 49–50, 52. Reprinted by permission from *Sales & Marketing Management* magazine. Copyright 1978. Photo courtesy of Pittsburgh Brewing Co.

General Foods is one of the most successful marketers in the United States. Consider its experiences with a recent product line.

General Foods Corporation

General Foods, the company that brought the under fifteen set Pop Rocks and Cosmic Candy, now has Increda Bubble Gum. Carbonated granule particles dissolve and pop in the chewer's mouth just as their predecessors did. Increda is aimed at the huge $1 billion gum market.

Pop Rocks and Cosmic Candy are candies, not gum. First introduced in 1976, these products became a national rage. Bootlegging of the candies to areas where they were not available became a major worry of General Foods.

Realizing that the candies were fads, the company would market a thirteen-week supply of one of them in a given area, wait nine months, and then introduce the other candy. As with most fads, initial sales were high, then dropped.

General Foods had a few problems with the celebrated candies. First, consumers protested that Cosmic Candy's original name—Space Dust—was much too close to Angel Dust, a drug. The candies also tended to lose their carbonation if they were left in over eighty degree temperatures. This prevented their year-round marketing.

The solution? Introducing Increda Bubble Gum as a twelve-month product. Once its carbonation is gone, the gum remains. Increda is priced at ten cents per packet and is available in pink, orange, and yellow. The success of the earlier candies has caused General Foods to take elaborate steps to protect the test areas where Increda would be first introduced. Fearing that bootleggers would rush in and buy their limited stocks for resale elsewhere before they could adequately evaluate Increda, management decided to skip the usual test market centers and go to smaller markets like Billings and Missoula, Montana, and Yakima, Washington.

Sources: Information from Nancy Giges, "GF Keeps Carbonated Gum Test Hush Hush to Avoid Bootleggers," *Advertising Age,* July 31, 1978, pp. 1, 60; and George Lazarus, "GF Bites the Bubble Gum Market," *Chicago Tribune,* October 25, 1978.

To create utility for consumers, organizations must listen carefully to what the marketplace is saying. Sometimes, this fact escapes even the largest firms. However, one of these firms—AT&T—is changing its attitude.

**AT&T Discovers
Marketing**

Many consumers do not realize that their monthly telephone bill accounts for less than half of the Bell System's business. AT&T's revenues are in excess of $36 billion, but only 43 percent comes from residential rates. Businesses account for 50 percent, directory advertising for 4 percent, and coin phones for 3 percent. For many years, AT&T was in the position of a regulated monopoly. But today the firm finds itself in a highly competitive communications market, particularly for its business customers. This situation is vastly different from when the company prided itself on good service but was never threatened by competition.

Competition took a $700 million chunk of the telephone market from AT&T last year alone. The PBX (switchboard) market has witnessed some sizable defections to foreign competitors. And even AT&T's private line customers have been buying specialized equipment provided by other firms. AT&T has good reason to fear firms like IBM, whose satellite business systems could skip the Bell network entirely in solving business communications problems.

Now AT&T is fighting back. The firm that long ignored marketing because it was protected by its monopolistic position has become an aggressive marketer. Six years ago, board chairman John De Butts announced that his goal was to "develop a marketing capability to match our technological capability."

The communications giant has since brought in marketing personnel from outside AT&T ranks and has set up a comprehensive sales program called the Bell Marketing System (BMS). Bell's 8,500 account executives (sales personnel) now specialize in the particular industries of their customers. They are backed by a substantial corps of technical support personnel, and they are evaluated on the basis of revenue performance.

As expected, many Bell employees still prefer to do things as they did in the monopolistic past. Perhaps AT&T's chief marketer, executive vice-president Kenneth J. Whelan, put it best: "It took us over 100 years before we discovered we could sell telephones in a color other than black." But times are changing at AT&T as Ma Bell enters the marketing era.

Source: Information from Thayer C. Taylor, "Can Ma Bell End Its Marketing Hang-up?" *Sales & Marketing Management,* May 1978, pp. 49–52, 54, 56.

**Marketing
Defined**

In order to standardize terminology in the field of marketing, an American Marketing Association committee developed a list of definitions for the major terms. First on the list was *marketing,* defined as "the performance of business activities that direct the flow of goods and services from producer to consumer or user."[2]

This definition is somewhat narrow because it emphasizes the flow of products that already have been produced. A broader and more descriptive view is that of the firm as an organized behavior system designed to generate outputs of value to consumers. Under this view, **marketing** is *the development and efficient distribution of goods and services for chosen consumer segments.* Profitability is achieved through creating customer satisfaction. Marketing activities begin with new product concepts and designs analyzed and developed to meet specific unfilled consumer needs—not with finished goods ready for shipment. In this way, the marketing system reflects consumer and societal needs.

The expanded conception of marketing activities permeates all organizational activities. It assumes that marketing effort will be in accordance with ethical business practices and that it will be effective from the standpoint of both society and the individual firm. It also emphasizes the need for efficiency in distribution, although the nature and degree of efficiency depend on the kind of business environment within which the firm operates. Finally it assumes that the consumer segments that will be satisfied through the firm's production and marketing activities have been selected and analyzed prior to production. In other words, the customer determines the marketing program.

Fifty years ago, most firms were production oriented. Manufacturers stressed production of quality products and then looked for people to purchase them. The Pillsbury Company of this period is an excellent example of a production oriented company. Here is how the company's board chairman, the late Robert J. Keith, described the Pillsbury of the early years:

We are professional flour millers. Blessed with a supply of the finest North American wheat, plenty of water power, and excellent milling machinery, we produce flour of the highest quality. Our basic function is to mill high-quality flour, and, of course (and almost incidentally), we must hire salesmen to sell it, just as we hire accountants to keep our books.[3]

The general attitude of this era was that a good product (defined in terms of physical quality) would sell itself. This production orientation dominated business philosophy for decades. Indeed, business success was often defined in terms of production victories.[4]

One explanation for the late emergence of the study of marketing is that time, place, and ownership utilities were not widely recognized until recent years. This is not to say, however, that marketing activities were nonexistent. Since people first created surpluses, they have wanted to exchange them for other needed items. One writer points out that "historical accounts of trade lead one to conclude that marketing has always existed. More than six thousand years of recorded history show the roots of both Western and Eastern civilizations to have included various forms of trade."[5]

Shift in Emphasis to Marketing and Consumer Orientation

Experience has shown that a firm's ability to produce a quality product is simply not enough for it to achieve success in a dynamic business environment; marketing effort is also required. For instance, advertising executive Mary Wells created an exciting new image for Braniff International by having its aircraft painted in bright colors and its flight attendants dressed in Pucci outfits.[6]

The old saying "if you make a better mousetrap, the world will beat a path to your door" is characteristic of a production orientation. Its implications are that a quality product will sell itself and that an effective production function is the key to high profits. But look at what happened to a firm that did actually produce a better mousetrap.

In 1956, the Pioneer Tool and Die Company produced a perfect mouse-trap from an engineering/production viewpoint. It was automatic, baitless, and odorless—a complex product about the size of an attaché case. The mouse was enticed to enter a hole, then proceed to a trap door. The rodents would follow a corridor onto a plank that would drop them into a water compartment, where they would drown. The product was truly innovative compared to the familiar wooden trap.

Pioneer produced 5,600 of these traps, but management abandoned the project after selling only 400. Its loss was $63,000. Apparently, consumers did not think the better mousetrap was worth its $29.95 price tag![7]

Pioneer failed in its new product venture because it forgot consumer constraints on purchase decisions. Consumers may view a new product as unique, well-designed, and possessing favorable features. But if the price is too high relative to the need satisfaction it provides, they will reject the item in the marketplace.

The moral of the mousetrap story is obvious. A quality product will not

Some "better mousetraps" rely on unsophisticated technology.

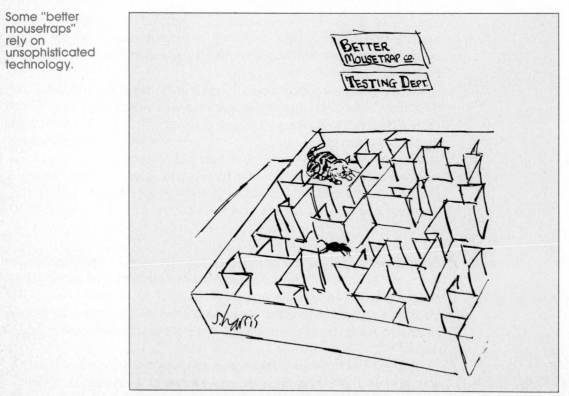

Source: Copyright © 1980 by Sidney Harris. Reprinted by permission.

be successful until it is effectively marketed, and marketing requires a thorough understanding of consumer needs. Paul Zinkann, Pioneer's president, explained this point well when he said, "Our big mistake was that nobody ever found out whether anyone wanted to buy a mousetrap as elaborate as ours for the original high retail price."[8]

Of course, Zinkann is not alone in his mistake. Inadequate consumer research is a leading cause of marketing failure. One company, however, avoided this error in an interesting way. The company had developed a dog shampoo with the unique advantage of using very little water, thereby saving the pet owner from an unplanned soaking. From a production and design viewpoint, the product was a major advance in dog shampoos. But, according to marketing research, dog owners did not trust the drier shampoo. They doubted whether it would actually clean their dogs as effectively as their previous brand. So the company included a tick-killing ingredient in order to convince consumers that the new shampoo was capable of doing a special job.[9]

To be successful, products require effective marketing based on a thorough understanding of what consumers want and need. Therefore, marketing is a primary function of any organization.

The Laser Beam Mousetrap

Joseph Sugarman is one of the nation's most successful mail-order merchandisers. He started JS&A National Sales Group with $12,000 in 1971, and by 1978 the company was generating almost $50 million in annual sales. But even Sugarman failed when he decided to test the better mousetrap adage. His attempt to market a $1500 mousetrap produced zero sales. Set on a walnut base, the contraption used a laser beam to trigger a spring-loaded wire trap. Sugarman's advertising claimed that the laser beam trap could be "handsomely displayed in any office, boardroom, or rodent-infested area."

Source: Information from Caesar Andrews, Jr., "Gadget Lover Hits Mail Order Jackpot Selling New Gadgets," *Wall Street Journal*, September 21, 1978, p. 18.

How, then, does marketing activity develop? The marketing function does not exist in subsistence level economies (those having an absolute minimum standard of living). It needs a production surplus in order to appear.

For example, assume the populace of a primitive society consists solely of Person A and Person B. Assume also that the only elements of their standard of living are food, clothing, and shelter. The two live in adjoining caves on a mountainside. They weave their own clothes and tend their own fields independently of each other. They are able to subsist even though their standard of living is minimal.

However, Person A is an excellent weaver but a poor farmer, while Person B is an excellent farmer but a poor weaver. In this situation, it will be wise for each to specialize in the line of work that each does best. The net result will be a greater total production of both clothing and food. In other words, specialization and division of labor will lead to a production surplus. But neither A nor B will be any better off until each *trades* the products of individual labor, thereby creating the exchange process.

Exchange is the origin of marketing activity. In fact, marketing has been described as "the process of creating and resolving exchange relationships."[10] When there is a need to exchange goods, the natural result is marketing effort on the part of the people involved.

Wroe Alderson, a leading marketing theorist, said, "It seems altogether reasonable to describe the development of exchange as a great invention which helped to start primitive man on the road to civilization."[11]

While the cave dweller example is simplistic, it does point up the essence of the marketing function. Complex industrial society may have a more complicated exchange process, but the basic concept is the same. Production is not meaningful until a system of marketing has been established. Perhaps publisher Red Motley's adage sums it up best: "Nothing happens until somebody sells something."[12]

Marketing Moves into the Twentieth Century

Although marketing had emerged as a functional activity within the business organization prior to the twentieth century, management's orientation remained with production for quite some time. In fact, what might be called industry's production era did not reach its peak until the early part of this century. The apostle of this approach to business operations was Frederick Taylor, whose *Principles of Scientific Management* was widely read and accepted at that time. Taylor's approach reflected his engineering background

The exchange process is the origin of marketing activity.

Source: Phil Frank/Chronicle Features.

by emphasizing efficiency in the production process. Later writers, such as Frank and Lillian Gilbreth, the originators of motion analysis, expanded on Taylor's basic concepts.[13]

On the practitioner's side, Henry Ford's mass production line was certainly an example of this orientation. Ford's slogan "they [customers] can have any color they want, as long as it is black" reflected a prevalent attitude toward marketing. Production shortages and intense consumer demand were the rule of the day. It is no wonder that production activities took precedence.

As personal income and consumer demand for goods and services dropped rapidly during the Great Depression of the 1930s, marketing was thrust into a more important role. Organizational survival dictated that managers pay closer attention to the markets for their products. This trend was halted by the outbreak of World War II, when rationing and shortages of consumer goods became commonplace. The war years, however, were an atypical pause in an emerging trend that was resumed almost immediately after the hostilities ceased. The marketing concept was about to be born.

New Way of Doing Business

What was the setting for the crucial change in management philosophy? Perhaps it can best be explained by the shift from a **seller's market**—*one with a shortage of goods and services*—to a **buyer's market**—*one with an abundance of goods and services.* When World War II ended, factories stopped manufacturing tanks and jeeps and started turning out consumer goods again—an activity that had for all practical purposes stopped in early 1942.

The advent of a strong buyer's market occasioned the need for a consumer orientation on the part of U.S. business. Goods had to be sold, not just produced. This realization has been identified as the emergence of the marketing concept. The recognition of this concept and its dominating role in business can be dated from 1952, when General Electric's annual report heralded a new management philosophy:

[The concept] introduces the marketing man at the beginning rather than at the end of the production cycle and integrates marketing into each phase of the business. Thus, marketing, through its studies and research, will establish for the engineer, the design and manufacturing man, what the customer wants in a given product, what price he is willing to pay, and where and when it will be wanted. Marketing will have authority in product planning, production scheduling, and inventory control, as well as in sales distribution and servicing of the product.[14]

In other words, marketing would no longer be regarded as a supplemental activity to be performed after the production process had been accomplished. For instance, the marketer would now play the lead role in product planning. Marketing and selling would no longer be synonymous. Business persons would first begin to realize that "marketing is as different from selling as chemistry is from alchemy, astronomy from astrology, chess from checkers."[15] Selling would be recognized as only one aspect of marketing. As a result, marketing would have a much expanded position in business organizations.[16]

Formally, the **marketing concept** is *a company-wide consumer orientation with the objective of achieving long-run profits.*[17] The key words are *company-wide consumer orientation.* All facets of the business must be involved with assessing and then satisfying customer wants and needs. The effort is not something to be left only to the marketers. Accountants working in the credit office and engineers employed in product design also play important roles.

The words *with the objective of achieving long-run profits* are used in order to differentiate the concept from policies of short-run profit maximization. The marketing concept is a modern philosophy for dynamic business growth. Since the continuity of the firm is an assumed part of it, company-wide consumer orientation will lead to greater long-run profits than will managerial philosophies geared to reaching short-run goals.

Organizational goals must be broadly defined and oriented toward consumer needs. Trans World Airlines, for example, has redefined its business aim from *air transportation* to *travel*. The firm now offers complete travel services, such as hotel accommodations, credit, and ground transportation, as well as air travel.[18]

Modifying the Marketing Concept

Industry has been responsive to the marketing concept as an improved method of doing business.[19] Since consideration of the consumer is now well accepted in most organizations, the relevant question has become: What should be the nature and extent of the concept's parameters?[20]

Some marketers argue that the concept should be substantially broadened to include many areas formerly not concerned with marketing efforts.[21] Others contend that the marketing concept has been extended too far.[22] Recent experience, for instance, has shown that many nonprofit organizations have accepted the marketing concept.[23] It is estimated that $3 billion is spent in nonprofit advertising annually.[24] The U.S. armed forces use advertising to recruit volunteers; the United Fund and other charitable groups have developed considerable marketing expertise; some police departments have used marketing inspired strategies to improve their public image; and marketing efforts are, of course, necessary in political campaigns.

It would be difficult to envision business returning to an era when engineering genius prevailed at the expense of consumer needs. It would be equally difficult to envision nonprofit organizations returning to a time when they lacked the marketing skills necessary to present their messages to the public. Marketing is a dynamic function, and it will no doubt be subject to continuous change.[25] But in one form or another it is playing a more important role in all organizations and in people's daily lives.

Introduction to the Marketing Variables

The starting place for effective marketing is the consumer. (Consumer behavior is treated in detail in Chapter 5.) Once a particular consumer group has been identified and analyzed, the marketing manager can direct company activities to profitably satisfy that segment.

Although thousands of variables are involved, marketing decision making can be conveniently classified into four strategies: (1) product, (2) distribution, (3) promotional, and (4) pricing.

Product strategy comprises *decisions about package design, branding, trademarks, warranties, guarantees, product life cycles, and new product development.* The marketer's concept of product strategy involves more than the *physical* product; it considers also the satisfaction of all consumer needs in relation to the good or service. **Distribution strategy** deals with *the physical distribution of goods and the selection of marketing channels.* **Marketing channels** are the *steps a good or service follows from producer to final consumer.* Channel decision making means establishing and maintaining the institutional structure in marketing channels. It involves retailers, wholesalers, and other institutional middlemen. **Promotional strategy** comprises *personal selling, advertising, and sales promotion tools.* The various aspects of promotional strategy must be blended together in order for the company to communicate effectively with the marketplace. **Pricing strategy,** one of the most difficult areas of marketing decision making, deals with *the methods of setting profitable and justified prices.* It is closely regulated and subjected to considerable public scrutiny.

The total package forms the **marketing mix**—*the blending of the four strategy elements of marketing decision making to satisfy chosen consumer segments.* Each of the strategies is a variable in the mix (see Figure 1–1). While this fourfold classification is useful in study and analysis, the total package (or mix) determines the degree of marketing success.

The Perrier Genius

Consider the marketing problems faced by Bruce Nevins. When he took over the Perrier business in the United States, few people were willing to pay for imported French water that tasted something like club soda. But Nevins was able to put together an effective marketing mix for his product. First, he positioned Perrier as the chic alternative to cocktails and soft drinks. He credits the success of this tactic to a new public awareness of the health problems caused by excessive consumption of alcohol and sugar.

Nevins was even able to get Perrier accepted at bars and cocktail lounges by people who chose not to drink alcoholic beverages. Nevins notes that many people have switched from "browns" (scotch and bourbon) to "whites" (gin and vodka) and then to wine. He says, "The next step is away from alcohol altogether. Which puts Perrier in a nice position."

Once Perrier was accepted on the cocktail circuit, Nevins shifted his attention to supermarkets. Perrier is stocked in the soft drink section and is offered in packages similar to those for soft drinks. A six-pack of 6½-ounce bottles goes for $2.39, a three-pack of 11-ounce bottles sells for $1.49, and a 23-ounce bottle is priced at $.79.

Nevins has obviously developed an effective marketing mix. He has promoted his product well, priced it in accordance with its chic appeal, and is using a distribution and packaging strategy designed to increase sales. The combination of these variables constitutes the marketing mix for Perrier. Nevins's success is evident, judging from the 90 million bottles of water he sells in the United States each year.

Source: Information from Bob Greene, "'Genius' Sells Water at $2.39 a Six-Pack," *Tulsa World,* November 11, 1978.

Marketing decisions are not made in a vacuum. That is, marketers cannot experiment with single variables while holding other factors constant. Instead, marketing decisions are made on the basis of the constant changes in the mix variables and the dynamic nature of environmental forces. To be successful, these decisions must take into account the four environments—competitive, legal, economic, and societal—in which they operate. The environmental factors are examined in Chapter 2, and the mix variables are

Figure 1–1
Elements of the
Marketing Mix

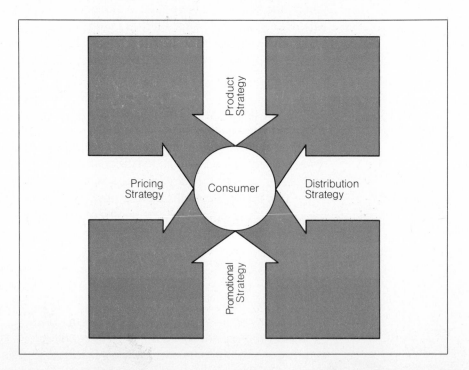

dealt with in Chapters 6 to 16. Each factor is introduced in one chapter, and its strategy implications are considered in the following chapters.

The Study of Marketing

In an era when relevance and practicality are often viewed as important criteria in evaluating any educational effort, this introductory chapter would be remiss if it did not address the following question: Why study marketing?

The response is that marketing is as relevant to contemporary life as any discipline currently existing. In one form or another, it is close to every person. Three of its most important concerns for students are:

1. Marketing costs may be the largest item in the personal budget. Numerous attempts have been made to determine these costs, and most estimates have ranged between 40 and 60 percent (with an approximate mean of 50 percent). Regardless of the exact cost, however, marketing is obviously a key item in any consumer's budget.

    However, the cost alone does not indicate the value of marketing. If someone says that marketing costs are too high, that person should be asked, "Relative to what?" The standard of living in the United States is in large part a function of the country's efficient marketing system. Looked at that way, the costs of the system seem reasonable. For example, marketing expands sales, thereby spreading fixed production costs over more units of output and reducing total output costs. Reduced production costs offset many marketing costs.

2. There is a good chance that individual students will become marketers. Marketing related occupations account for a significant portion of the nation's jobs. Indeed, marketing opportunities remained strong even during recent periods when one out of four graduates could not find jobs. History has shown that the demand for good marketers is not affected by cyclical economic fluctuations.

3. Marketing provides an opportunity to contribute to society as well as to an individual company. Marketing decisions affect everyone's welfare. Furthermore, opportunities to advance to decision-making positions come sooner in marketing than in most occupations. (Societal aspects of marketing will be covered in detail in later chapters.)

Approaches to the Study of Marketing

Table 1–1 outlines six approaches to the formal study of marketing. Commodity, functional, and institutional approaches are usually considered the traditional methods of study, while managerial, systems, and societal approaches are the most popular methods today.[26]

All the approaches to studying marketing have their merits, and all have been popular at one time or another. This textbook takes an integrated ap-

Table 1-1
Six Approaches to the Formal Study of Marketing

1. Commodity	Categorizes all goods and services and suggests an effective distribution system for each category.
2. Functional	Studies the eight basic functions of marketing: buying, selling, transporting, storing, grading, financing, entrepreneurial risk taking, and issuing marketing information.
3. Institutional	Concentrates on the independent institutions in a marketing channel, such as retailers and wholesalers.
4. Managerial	Is oriented toward a management and strategy viewpoint, focusing on the marketing manager's decision-making process.
5. Systems	Regards marketing as a functional element of the firm, which is a subset of the business system.
6. Societal	Views the marketing system from a macro viewpoint, exploring the various facets of the marketing-societal interface.

proach to studying the field. It considers the key concepts of each method at the practitioner's level, thereby maximizing exposure to the dynamic marketing system.

Summary

The two primary functions of any business organization are production and marketing. Traditionally, industry has emphasized production efficiency, often at the expense of marketing. Sometime after World War II, however, the *marketing concept* became the accepted business philosophy. The change was caused by the economy shifting from a seller's market to a buyer's market.

Marketing is the development and efficient distribution of goods and services for chosen consumer segments. Marketing decision making can be classified into four strategies: (1) product, (2) distribution, (3) promotional, and (4) pricing. These four variables together form the total marketing mix.

Marketing decisions must be made in a dynamic environment determined by competitive, legal, economic, and societal functions.

Three basic reasons for studying marketing are: (1) marketing costs may be the largest item in the personal budget; (2) there is a good chance individual students may become marketers; and (3) marketing provides an opportunity to contribute to society as well as to a company.

Six approaches to the study of marketing are commodity, functional, institutional, managerial, systems, and societal. This textbook follows an integrated approach in studying the field.

Questions for Discussion

1. Explain the following terms:

utility	distribution strategy
marketing	marketing channels
seller's market	promotional strategy
buyer's market	pricing strategy
marketing concept	marketing mix
product strategy	

2. Discuss the following statement: For a long time, most business people acknowledged only one line function—production.

3. What are the four types of utility? With which is marketing concerned?

4. Comment on the following statement: If you build a better mousetrap, the world will beat a path to your door.

5. Contrast the production era with the emergence of the marketing concept.

6. What did the General Electric annual report mean when it said it was introducing "the marketing man at the beginning rather than at the end of the production cycle"?

7. How would you explain marketing to someone not familiar with the subject?

8. Discuss the relationship between the major strategy elements in the marketing mix and the factors involved in the decision-making environment.

9. Discuss the following statement: Marketing costs are too high.

10. Describe the various approaches to the study of marketing. Illustrate how each approach can be used with a specific product.

11. What should be the parameters of the marketing concept?

12. Why is Olde Frothingslosh such a successful promotion for Pittsburgh Brewing?

13. What is the moral of the AT&T story that appears in the chapter?

14. Evaluate the marketing strategy for Perrier.

15. Why did Pioneer Tool and Die Company try to sell its new mousetrap at $29.95?

16. What are some other products that have failed because of poor marketing?

17. Jennifer Shannon is a recreation major at Center City College. She hopes eventually to direct a community recreation program involving sports leagues, youth camps, adult education classes, cultural programs, and other leisure-time activities. What does she need to know about marketing?

18. Prepare a brief report on marketing careers. Discuss it in class.

19. Assume that a recent series of traffic tragedies involving drunk drivers has led to a public protest in your community. You have been asked to explain how marketing can help a group crusading against drinking drivers. What will you say?

20. Write a one-page report on the views you held about marketing prior to enrolling in your marketing class. Discuss it with other class members; then, file it away until the end of the term. At that time, check to see if your thinking has changed.

Notes

1. The concept of utility is discussed in Dean S. Ellis and Lawrence W. Jacobs, "Marketing Utilities: A New Look," *Journal of the Academy of Marketing Science*, Winter 1976, pp. 21–26.

2. Committee on Definitions, *Marketing Definitions: A Glossary of Marketing Terms* (Chicago: American Marketing Association, 1960), p. 15.

3. Robert J. Keith, "The Marketing Revolution," *Journal of Marketing*, January 1960, p. 36.

4. An interesting analysis of the stages of business development is presented in Denis F. Healy, "What Next? Is the Marketing Orientation the Next Step in the Course of Organizational Evolution?" *Marquette Business Review*, Summer 1975, pp. 98–104.

5. Robert Bartels, *The Development of Marketing Thought* (Homewood, Ill.: Richard D. Irwin, 1962), p. 4.

6. This and other Braniff innovations are described in "Braniff Bucks the Headwinds," *Forbes*, October 15, 1975, p. 65.

7. The Pioneer Tool and Die Company story is from Lee Berton, "Firms Strive to Avoid Introducing Products That Nobody Will Buy," *Wall Street Journal*, March 6, 1967, pp. 1, 17.

8. Ibid., p. 1.

9. Roger Ricklefs, "Success Comes Hard in the Tricky Business of Creating Products," *Wall Street Journal,* August 23, 1978, p. 1.

10. Richard P. Bagozzi, "Marketing as an Organized Behavioral System of Exchange," *Journal of Marketing,* October 1974, p. 77. Further work by Bagozzi on this subject appears in "Marketing as Exchange," *Journal of Marketing,* October 1975, pp. 32–39, and "Marketing as Exchange: A Theory of Transactions in the Marketplace," *American Behavioral Scientist,* March–April 1978, pp. 535–536.

11. Wroe Alderson, *Marketing Behavior and Executive Action* (Homewood, Ill.: Richard D. Irwin, 1962), p. 292.

12. T. G. Povey, "Spotting the Salesman Who Has What It Takes," *Nation's Business,* July 1972, p. 70.

13. For a discussion of scientific management, see Claude S. George, *The History of Management Thought* (Englewood Cliffs, N.J.: Prentice-Hall, 1968), pp. 86–99.

14. *1952 Annual Report* (New York: General Electric, 1952), p. 21.

15. Theodore Levitt, *Innovations in Marketing* (New York: McGraw-Hill, 1962), p. 7.

16. The wide adoption of the concept was confirmed in Richard T. Hise, "Have Manufacturing Firms Adopted the Marketing Concept?" *Journal of Marketing,* July 1965, pp. 9–12.

17. This definition is offered in Lawrence A. Klatt, *Small Business Management* (Belmont, Calif.: Wadsworth Publishing, 1973), p. 157.

18. C. Glenn Walters, "Marketing Philosophy: Buried but Not Dead," *Mississippi Business Review,* December 1970, p. 6.

19. The current status of the marketing concept is explored in such articles as David Carson, "Gotterdammering for Marketing?" *Journal of Marketing,* July 1978, pp. 11–19; William S. Sachs and George Benson, "Is It Time to Discard the Marketing Concept?" *Business Horizons,* August 1978, pp. 68–74; Wayne Norvell, "Changing Attitudes toward Consumer Orientation in Making Marketing Decisions," *Pittsburgh Business Review,* June 1977, pp. 7–10; Jack L. Engledow, "Was Consumer Satisfaction a Pig in a Poke?" *Business Horizons,* April 1977, pp. 87–94; and William G. Nickels and Earnestine Hargrove, "A New Societal Marketing Concept," in *Contemporary Marketing Thought,* ed. Barnett A. Greenberg and Danny N. Bellenger (Chicago: American Marketing Association, 1977), p. 541.

20. An interesting discussion appears in Shelby D. Hunt, "The Nature and Scope of Marketing," *Journal of Marketing,* July 1976, pp. 17–28.

21. Definitive articles on the subject include Philip Kotler and Sidney J. Levy, "Broadening the Concept of Marketing," *Journal of Marketing,* January 1969, pp. 10–15; Leslie M. Dawson, "The Human Concept: New Philosophy for Business," *Business Horizons,* December 1969, pp. 29–38; and Sidney J. Levy and Philip Kotler, "Beyond Marketing: The Furthering Concept," *California Management Review,* Winter 1969, pp. 67–73.

22. This viewpoint is expressed in David J. Luck, "Broadening the Concept of Marketing—Too Far," *Journal of Marketing,* July 1969, pp. 53–55.

23. The use of marketing by nonprofit organizations is discussed in John D. Claxton, Thomas C. Kinnear, and J. R. Brent Ritchie, "Should Government Programs Have Marketing Managers?" *Michigan Business Review,* May 1978, pp. 10–16; Avraham Shama, "The Marketing of Political Candidates," *Journal of the Academy of Marketing Science,* Fall 1976, pp. 764–777; Leonard L. Berry and Bruce H. Allen, "Marketing's Crucial Role for Institutions of Higher Education," *Atlanta Economic Review,* July–August 1977, pp. 24–31; and Philip Kotler, "Strategies for Introducing Marketing into Nonprofit Organizations," *Journal of Marketing,* January 1979, pp. 37–44.

24. Noted in Bernice Finkelman, "Kotler Says: Growing Nonprofit Sector, Now 20% of Economy, Becoming Marketing-Conscious," *Marketing News,* January 15, 1974, p. 1.

25. See, for example, F. Kelly Shuptine and Frank A. Osmanski, "Marketing's Changing Role: Expanding or Contracting," *Journal of Marketing,* April 1975, pp. 58–66.

26. A good review of the traditional methods is contained in Harry L. Hansen, *Marketing: Text, Cases, and Readings,* rev. ed. (Homewood, Ill.: Richard D. Irwin, 1961), pp. 5–6.

CHAPTER 2
THE ENVIRONMENT
FOR MARKETING
DECISIONS

Key Terms

competitive
environment
legal environment
corrective advertising
economic
environment

inflation
stagflation
energy crisis
demarketing
societal environment

Learning Goals

1. To explain how marketing decisions must be made within an environmental framework.

2. To determine how competitive strategies influence the marketplace and are in turn influenced by competitors' strategies.

3. To examine the legal environment for marketing.

4. To illustrate how the economic environment affects marketing decisions.

5. To recognize the importance of the societal environment for marketing.

2

In 1911, while the Reynolds Tobacco Company was preparing to introduce the country's first mass marketed cigarette, President Theodore Roosevelt returned from a widely reported trip to Berlin. In honor of the occasion, young Richard S. Reynolds commissioned an artist to design a package for the new product. Reynolds wanted a picture of Germany's Kaiser Wilhelm in full regalia mounted on a white charger. The senior R. J. Reynolds rejected the proposal for Kaiser Wilhelm cigarettes, saying: "I don't think we should name a product after a living man. You never can tell what the damn fool might do." Instead, he chose the name *Camels*. Introduced in 1913, Camels captured 50 percent of the national market by 1921.[1]

What would have happened to Kaiser Wilhelm Cigarettes during the U.S. involvement in World War I is a matter for speculation only. This near disaster illustrates how important environmental factors are to marketing decisions. The marketer's product, channel, promotion, and pricing strategies must filter through various environmental factors before they reach their goal—the consumers who represent the firm's market target.

The environment for marketing decisions is actually four interacting environments: competitive, legal, economic, and societal. These factors are important because they provide the frame of reference within which marketing decisions are made.[2] However, they are not decision variables in the marketing process; instead, they are outside factors that influence marketing strategy.

Figure 2–1
Elements of the Marketing Mix as They Operate within an Environmental Framework

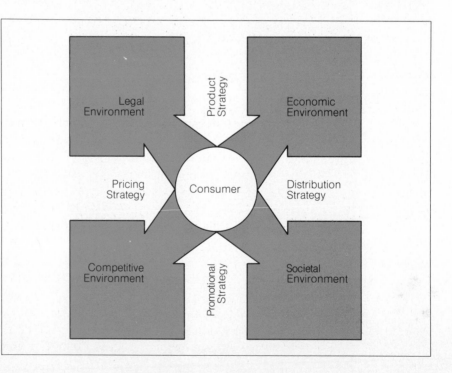

Even though marketing managers cannot direct them, they must take them into account when making marketing decisions. The strategy elements that can be directed—product planning, distribution, promotion, and pricing—are modified through pressures exerted by the uncontrollable environmental factors. Figure 2–1 illustrates these elements' influence on the consumer.

The dynamic nature of the environmental factors puts additional pressure on all levels of management to continually reevaluate marketing decisions in light of the contemporary business environment. Even modest environmental shifts can alter the results of marketing decisions. Ford Motor Company's failure to properly monitor environmental conditions contributed to the Edsel's demise—one of the most publicized product failures of all times.

Competitive Environment	*The interactive process that occurs in the marketplace* is referred to as the **competitive environment.** One firm's marketing decisions influence its market and are in turn affected by competitors' decisions. Miller Brewing's phenomenal success with its "Lite" beer led to a rush of competitors attempting to get part of a growing market segment—diet conscious beer drinkers.

The competitive environment often determines the success or failure of a product. Consider the case of Corfam, a leather substitute introduced by Du Pont during the 1960s. The product introduction was backed by a sizable advertising budget, which was cut back when management concluded that Corfam was a can't-miss product. But Corfam eventually had to be withdrawn after foreign shoe manufacturers invaded the U.S. market with genuine leather shoes that sold for less than Du Pont's substitute.[3]

Sporting goods provide another illustration of the importance of the competitive environment. Sports and recreation fads result in boom periods for the manufacturers of sports equipment. The manufacturers expand to meet the popular demand, excess supply soon develops, and some firms begin to cut prices. Then, other firms are forced to make similar reductions in order to remain competitive. Tensor metal tennis rackets, which once sold for $25, were available for $9 by the mid 1970s. Eventually, many of the marginal competitors are forced out of the industry, and production and marketing resume normal patterns—although the industry may be vastly restructured.[4]

Jogging and racquetball are among today's sports fads that have given rise to industries serving the participants. Twenty companies make running shoes or "training flats" for joggers. Racquetball courts dot the landscape of most suburban areas and smaller cities. Today, supplying racquetball equipment and accessories is a major industry. But the signs of change are already here. Joggers can now choose from 175 different models of jogging shoes.[5] And racquetball courts face increased competition in many major metropolitan areas. The competitive environment is a fact of life even in recreation and leisure activities.

Expanded Role of Competition

Through the years, the marketing system has become increasingly competitive. Traditional economic analysis views competition as a struggle among companies in the same industry or among substitutable products. Marketers, however, tend to accept the argument that all firms are competing for a limited amount of discretionary buying power. General Motors competes with Sears in the sale of automobile batteries and in auto repairs. Chrysler's Le Baron competes with a European vacation. Alcoa Aluminum competes with United States Steel.

Industry has also found numerous new uses for existing products, thereby expanding the arena of competition. While this trend forces business to reassess long-established marketing practices, it also opens new avenues of business opportunity. The popularity of running shoes among joggers has created a whole new class of leisure shoe manufacturers to compete with traditional shoe manufacturers.

Marketing: A Highly Visible Business Activity

While it is sometimes difficult to define the relationship between the competitive environment and the marketplace, it is easily recognized that marketing is the most visible of all business functions. No other one is exposed to public evaluation as continuously. In fact, to most consumers, the marketer is the company. An Eastern Airlines passenger's opinion of the airline is determined largely by his or her impression of the passenger agent and the flight service crew. A shopper's assessment of a store is significantly affected by its sales personnel.

Other functional activities, such as accounting, quality control, credit management, production, and engineering, are performed within the organization. Contact between people doing these jobs and the public is minimal. Marketing, by contrast, performs the bulk of its duties within full view of an often critical public. It is understandable, therefore, that marketing usually receives the brunt of the public's displeasure. Marketers know that, to a great extent, public acceptance of their activities sets the type of competitive environment in which they operate.

In the United States, favorable public opinion is crucial to marketing, since it is the authority that allows the competitive marketing system to operate. As an environmental factor, public opinion includes both the general public and the government in its role of licenser and sanctioner of marketing activities. In some countries, the competitive marketing process has been replaced by a state operated distribution system.

Marketers must always keep in mind that the general public grants them the license to practice their trade. Lack of this supportive framework assures the eventual failure of the firm, the system, or both.

Developing a Competitive Strategy

All marketers must develop an effective strategy for dealing with the competitive environment. Some compete in a broad range of product markets in many areas of the world. Others prefer to specialize in particular market segments such as those determined by geographical, age, or income factors. Essentially, the determination of a competitive strategy involves three questions:

1. Should the firm compete?
2. If so, in what markets?
3. How should it compete?

The first question should be answered on the basis of expected profit potential. If the expected profits are insufficient to pay an adequate return on the investment, the firm should consider moving into other lines of business. This decision should, of course, be continually reevaluated so as to avoid becoming tied to a market with declining profit margins.

In answer to the second question, the markets in which to compete should be those offering the greatest opportunity. Marketers have limited resources (sales personnel, advertising budgets, product development capability, and so on); they must therefore select only those markets in which they can do an effective job.

The third question requires marketers to make tactical decisions in setting up their comprehensive marketing strategies. Product, distribution, promotion, and pricing decisions are the major elements of these strategies.

Legal Environment

The **legal environment** for marketing decisions in the United States *is characterized by numerous, often vague, laws passed by a multitude of authorities.* These laws have been enacted at the federal, state, and local levels as well as by independent regulatory agencies. Their provisions often are confusing and poorly written and sometimes conflict with each other. The legal framework was constructed on a piecemeal basis, often in response to some popular issue.

The country has tended to follow a public policy of promoting a competitive marketing system. To maintain the system, competitive practices within it have been heavily regulated. Pricing and promotion are the most highly regulated areas of marketing.

Table 2–1 divides federal laws into two categories—those designed to

Table 2–1
Classification of Marketing Legislation

Maintenance of Competitive Environment	Regulation of Specific Marketing Activities
Sherman Antitrust Act (1890)	Pure Food and Drug Act (1906)
Clayton Act (1914)	Federal Trade Commission Act (1914)
Federal Trade Commission Act (1914)	Unfair Trade Laws (1930s)
Unfair Trade Laws (1930s)	Robinson-Patman Act (1936)
Celler-Kefauver Antimerger Act (1950)	Wheeler-Lea Act (1938)
Consumer Goods Pricing Act (1975)	Food, Drug, and Cosmetic Act (1938)
	Wool Products Labeling Act (1939)
	Fur Products Labeling Act (1951)
	Flammable Fabrics Act (1953)
	Kefauver-Harris Drug Amendments (1962)
	Fair Packaging and Labeling Act (1967)
	Consumer Credit Protection Act (1968)
	Fair Credit Reporting Act (1970)
	Environmental Protection Act (1970)
	Public Health Cigarette Smoking Act (1971)
	Consumer Product Safety Act (1972)
	Consumer Goods Pricing Act (1975)
	Equal Credit Opportunity Act (1975–1977)
	Fair Debt Collection Practices Act (1978)

maintain a competitive marketing system and those regulating specific marketing activities. A few laws fit both categories and appear in both columns.

Antitrust Legislation　　The *Sherman Antitrust Act* (1890) prohibits restraint of trade and monopolization. It subjects violators to civil suits as well as to criminal prosecution.[6] While the practices covered by the act were unlawful under common law and under several state acts passed in the previous decade, the Sherman Act was the first piece of federal legislation to clearly set out the maintenance of a competitive marketing system as national policy.

However, antitrust legislation has not been completely effective in eliminating abuses. A Department of Justice official once estimated that antitrust violations cost U.S. consumers $80 billion a year.[7]

The economic philosophy of the Sherman Act is in marked contrast to the philosophies of many foreign countries, where monopolies are openly encouraged by the government. In such cases, the government is usually attempting to foster productive efficiency that might be injured by excessive competition. Few nations have antitrust legislation even remotely comparable to that of the United States. As a result, foreign cartels (monopolies) used to have a distinct advantage over U.S. companies operating independently in international markets.

Because of this situation, the *Webb-Pomerene Export Trade Act* (1918) exempted voluntary export trade associations from the Sherman Act restric-

**Table 2–2
Ten Don'ts of
Antitrust**

*Warnings that companies most frequently issue to employees to keep them in
compliance with antitrust laws:*

1. *Don't* discuss with customers the price your company will charge others.
2. *Don't* attend meetings with competitors (including trade association gatherings)
   at which pricing is discussed. If you find yourself in such a session, walk out.
3. *Don't* give favored treatment to your own subsidiaries and affiliates.
4. *Don't* enter into agreements or gentlemen's understandings on discounts, terms
   or conditions of sale, profits or profit margins, shares of the market, bids or the
   intent to bid, rejection or termination of customers, sales territories or markets.
5. *Don't* use one product as bait for selling another.
6. *Don't* require a customer to buy a product only from you.
7. *Don't* forget to consider state antitrust laws as well as the federal statutes.
8. *Don't* disparage a competitor's product unless you have specific proof that your
   statements are true. This is an unfair method of competition.
9. *Don't* make either sales or purchases conditional on the other party making
   reciprocal purchases from or sales to your company.
10. *Don't* hesitate to consult with a company lawyer if you have any doubt about the
    legality of a practice. Antitrust laws are wide-ranging, complex, and subject to
    changing interpretations.

Source: "How to Avoid Antitrust," *Business Week,* January 27, 1975. Reprinted from the January 27, 1975, issue of *Business Week*
by special permission. Copyright © 1975 by McGraw-Hill, Inc., New York, NY 10020. All rights reserved.

tions—but only in their foreign trade dealings. (See Chapter 17 for more
details.) Exemptions of a similar nature have since been granted on the domestic front for the merger of the National and American football leagues
and for pollution control research carried on by automobile manufacturers.

The *Clayton Act* (1914) strengthened antitrust legislation by restricting
practices such as price discrimination, exclusive dealing, tying contracts,
and interlocking boards of directors where the effect "may be to substantially lessen competition or tend to create a monopoly." Later, the *Celler-
Kefauver Antimerger Act* (1950) amended the Clayton Act to include the
"purchase of assets" where the purchase would reduce competition.

Most companies go to considerable effort to avoid violations of the Sherman and Clayton acts. Many of them hold seminars on antitrust matters and
issue corporate guidelines in an attempt to prevent employee misunderstandings that could result in violations. *Business Week* has compiled a list
of antitrust warnings that firms typically issue to employees (see Table 2–2).

**Role of the
Federal Trade
Commission**

Another important aspect of the regulation of competition is the *Federal
Trade Commission Act,* which also became law in 1914. This act prohibited
"unfair methods of competition" and established the Federal Trade Commission (FTC) as an administrative agency to oversee the various laws dealing with business.

Since its early days, the FTC has assumed a large workload that continues to grow each year. Under the original act, it had to demonstrate injury to
competition before a court would declare a marketing practice unfair. The

Wheeler-Lea Act (1938), however, amended the Federal Trade Commission Act so as to ban deceptive or unfair business practices per se. At that point, the FTC no longer had to show injury to competition. The Wheeler-Lea Act was designed primarily to protect the consumer by preventing deceptive advertising and sales practices.

Armed with the Wheeler-Lea requirements, the FTC has assumed an activist role in protecting consumers. For example, it has adopted the concept of **corrective advertising,** under which *companies found to have used deceptive advertising are required to correct their earlier claims with new promotional messages.*[8]

One recent case involved STP Corporation. In that instance, the company was fined $500,000 and was required to spend another $200,000 on corrective advertising. The advertisements carried the headline "FTC Notice" and went on to tell about the "$700,000 settlement" and the FTC investigation into "certain allegedly inaccurate advertisements." The ad ran in all kinds of publications, among them the *Wall Street Journal,* the *New York Times,* the *Washington Post, Business Week, U.S. News & World Report, Esquire, Guns & Ammo,* and *People.*[9]

The FTC's position in this case was that STP had advertised that its oil treatment would cut oil consumption by 20 percent but that the company's tests of this feat were unreliable. The STP board chairman noted that the

Some consumers insist on verifying advertising claims.

"It's true—Gravely Flakes *do* make clothes blacker than black."

Source: *Wall Street Journal,* October 31, 1978, p. 18. Reprinted by permission of Sidney Harris.

firm has a policy of backing all advertising with valid information and that the tests in question had been conducted some time before.

The FTC generally has employed three procedures in carrying out its duties:

1. Conferences with the individuals or industries involved to secure voluntary compliance with its rules.
2. The consent method, under which the FTC secures the agreement of the firm or industry to abandon a practice the FTC deems unfair.
3. Formal legal action. (All FTC decisions can be appealed through the courts.)[10]

$285 — The Contribution of Federal Regulation to the Price of Your 1984 Car

According to the U.S. Department of Transportation, 1978 car prices included about $250, or about 5 percent of the total cost of the car, for federal safety requirements. Manufacturers claim the actual figure is double the government estimate. But that is only part of the financial impact of regulation. The government has already set other requirements for future automobiles. These include air bags or passive restraint systems, various fuel economy standards, and better bumpers. The government estimates that these requirements will add an extra $285 to the price of a 1984 car—and this figure assumes zero inflation. But the regulators add that the new fuel efficiency standards will save $750 in gasoline costs during the car's lifetime.

Source: Information from "Federal Rules to Add $285 to Cost of a Car by 1984, U.S. Finds," *Wall Street Journal*, June 19, 1978, p. 17.

Robinson-Patman Act

The *Robinson-Patman Act* (1936) was typical of depression era legislation. Known in some circles as the Anti-A&P Act, it was inspired by price competition from the developing grocery store chains. In fact, the law was originally prepared by the United States Wholesale Grocers Association. The country was in the midst of the Great Depression, and legislative interest was directed toward saving jobs. The developing chain stores were seen as a threat to traditional retailers and to employment. The Robinson-Patman Act was a government effort to reduce this threat.[11].

The act, which was technically an amendment to the Clayton Act, prohibited price discrimination that was not based on a cost differential. It also disallowed selling at an unreasonably low price in order to eliminate competition. The Clayton Act had applied only to price discrimination by geographic areas that injured local sellers.[12] The supporting rationale for the Robinson-Patman legislation was that the chain stores might be able to secure discounts from suppliers that were not available to the smaller, independent stores. As one writer expressed it: "The designers of the law, aiming to strengthen the precautionary element in antitrust and to afford greater equality of opportunities, thus gave consideration to the individual competitor as well as to competition in general."[13] The major defenses against charges of price discrimination are that it has been used in an attempt to meet competitors' prices and that it is justified by cost differences.

When a firm asserts that price differentials are used to meet competition in good faith, the logical question is: What constitutes good faith pricing behavior? The answer depends on the circumstances of each situation.

When cost differentials are claimed as a defense, the price differences must not exceed the cost differences resulting from selling to different classes of buyers.[14] A major difficulty of the defense is justifying the differences. Indeed, many authorities consider this area one of the most confusing in the Robinson-Patman Act.

The varying interpretations of the act certainly qualify it as one of the vaguest of marketing laws. For the most part, charges brought under the act are handled on a case by case basis. Marketers must therefore continually evaluate their pricing actions to avoid potential Robinson-Patman violations.

Unfair Trade Laws

Unfair trade laws are state laws requiring sellers to maintain minimum prices for comparable merchandise. Enacted in the 1930s, these laws were intended to protect small specialty shops, such as dairy stores, from the loss leader pricing of like products by chain stores. Typically, the retail price floor was set at cost plus some modest markup. While most of these laws remain on the books, they have become less important in the more prosperous years since the 1930s and are seldom enforced.

Removing Barriers to Competition

Fair trade is a concept that affected regulation of competitive activity for decades. In 1931, California became the first state to enact fair trade legislation. Most other states soon followed suit. Only Missouri, the District of Columbia, Vermont, and Texas failed to adopt such laws. *Fair trade laws* permitted manufacturers to stipulate a minimum retail price for a product and to require their retail dealers to sign contracts stating that they would abide by such prices.[15]

The basic argument behind the legislation was that a product's image, implied by its price, was a property right of the manufacturer, who should have the authority to protect the asset by requiring retailers to maintain a minimum price. Fair trade legislation can be traced to lobbying by organizations of independent retailers who feared chain store growth. The economic mania of the depression years was clearly evident in these statutes.

A U.S. Supreme Court decision holding fair trade contracts illegal in interstate commerce led to passage of the *Miller-Tydings Resale Price Maintenance Act* (1937). This law exempted interstate fair trade contracts from compliance with antitrust requirements. The states were thus authorized to keep these laws on their books if they so desired.

Over the years, fair trade declined in importance as price competition became a more important marketing strategy. The end of these laws occurred on March 11, 1976, when the *Consumer Goods Pricing Act* (1975) went into effect. This act halted all interstate usage of resale price maintenance, an objective long sought by consumer groups.

Toward an Activist Legal Environment

The first activist legislation dealing with a specific marketing practice was the *Pure Food and Drug Act* (1906), which prohibited the adulteration and misbranding of foods and drugs in interstate commerce. The bill was enacted because of the unsanitary meat-packing practices of Chicago stockyards. It was strengthened in 1938 by the *Food, Drug, and Cosmetic Act* and in 1962 by the *Kefauver-Harris Drug Amendments* (the latter instigated in response to the thalidomide tragedies).[16] Since that time, the Food and Drug Administration (FDA) has held increased regulatory authority in such matters as product development, branding, and advertising.

Another sphere of marketing's legal environment is the whole gamut of rules governing advertising and labeling. The *Wool Product Labeling Act* of 1939 (requiring that the kind and percentage of each type of wool be identified), the *Fur Product Labeling Act* of 1951 (requiring that the name of the animal from which the fur was derived be identified), and the *Flammable Fabrics Act* of 1953 (prohibiting the interstate sale of flammable fabrics) formed the original legislation in this area.[17] A more recent law—the *Fair Packaging and Labeling Act* passed in 1967—requires the disclosure of product identity, the name and address of the manufacturer or distributor, and information concerning the quality of the contents.[18] In 1971, the *Public Health Cigarette Smoking Act* restricted tobacco advertising on radio and television.

The *Truth-in-Lending* law deserves special attention. Formally known as *Title I of the Consumer Credit Protection Act* (1968), the statute requires disclosure of the annual interest rates on loans and credit purchases. The basic premise is that this information will make it easier for consumers to compare sources of credit. Various assessments of the law, however, suggest that many consumers pay relatively little attention to interest rates; furthermore, they often have limited alternative credit sources.

Other laws that may influence marketing practices are the *Fair Credit Reporting Act* and the *Environmental Protection Act,* both of which became law in 1970. The Fair Credit Reporting Act gives individuals access to credit reports prepared about them and permits them to change information that is incorrect. The Environmental Protection Act established the Environmental Protection Agency (EPA) and gave it the power to deal with major types of pollution. EPA actions, of course, have a large impact on the marketing system.

The *Consumer Product Safety Act* (1972) may have far-reaching effects on marketing strategy and on the environment in which marketers act. This legislation set up the Consumer Product Safety Commission, which has the authority to specify safety standards for most consumer products.

The *Equal Credit Opportunity Act* (1975–1977) banned discrimination in lending practices based on sex, marital status, race, national origin, religion, age, or receipt of payments from a public assistance program. The sex and marital status portions of the act went into effect in 1975, and the remaining portions became effective in 1977.

The *Fair Debt Collection Practices Act* (1978) outlawed harassing, deceptive, or unfair collection practices by debt-collecting agencies. In-house debt collectors such as banks, retailers, and attorneys are exempt, however. Misrepresentation of consumers' legal rights is an example of a specific practice that was banned by the act.[19]

The legal framework for marketing decisions is basically a positive environment in that it attempts to encourage a competitive marketing system employing fair business practices. What marketing's legalistic future will be, of course, is open to debate. It appears, however, that future marketing legislation will be more directly concerned with protecting consumer interests and will probably come from three sources: (1) state and local governments, (2) court decisions, and (3) regulations by administrative agencies such as the FTC and FDA. These sources, closely tied to consumer affairs, are likely to assume an active role in business legislation.[20]

Economic Environment	The **economic environment** is extremely complex. It *includes dynamic business fluctuations that tend to follow a four-stage pattern: (1) recession, (2) depression, (3) recovery, and (4) prosperity.* Four decades have passed since the Great Depression. Some economists are now arguing that government possesses new, sophisticated tools with which to prevent future depressions. If this is true, recessions will be followed by periods of recovery.

No marketer can disregard the economic climate, since the type, direction, and intensity of a firm's marketing strategy depend on it. In addition, marketers must be aware of the economy's relative position in the business cycle and how it will affect the position of the particular firm. Marketers must therefore study forecasts of economic activity.

By necessity, the type of marketing activity differs with each stage of the business cycle. Consumers are usually more willing to buy during prosperous times than when they feel economically threatened. For example, personal savings may climb during a downturn as consumers, fearing layoffs and slowdowns, cut back their expenditures for many nonessential products. Marketers must pay close attention to this relative willingness to buy. The aggressiveness of the marketing strategy and tactics often must depend on current buying intentions. For example, more aggressive marketing may be called for in periods of lessened buying interest.

While sales figures show cyclical variations, the successful firm has a rising sales trend line. The line depends on management's ability to foresee, correctly interpret, and reach new market opportunities. Effective forecasting and research are only partial solutions. Equally important is the intuitive awareness of potential markets that requires the ability to correctly delineate opportunities. The life-style concept is an example of where environmental forecasting is critical.

Life-style Concept

Life-style is simply the way people decide to live their lives. It concerns family, job, social activities, and consumer decisions. Changing life-styles are a variable that influences marketing. In the future, many people may choose to forego additional income in favor of increased leisure. Typical retirement ages may change drastically. Travel may become more important. These are all life-style decisions that will affect the economic environment for the competitive marketing system.

Inflation

Another economic factor that influences marketing strategy is inflation, which can occur during any stage in the business cycle. **Inflation** is a *rising price level that results in reduced purchasing power for the consumer.* That is, a person's money is devalued in terms of what it can buy. Traditionally, inflation has been more prevalent in foreign countries than in the United States. However, in the late 1970s, the United States has been experiencing double-digit inflation. This has led to widespread concern over public policy to stabilize price levels and over ways of adjusting personally to the reduced spending power.

Stagflation has been coined to describe a peculiar kind of inflation that characterized some of the U.S. economic experience in the 1970s. It is a situation that occurs when *an economy has high unemployment and a rising price level at the same time.* Marketing strategy is particularly difficult under this circumstance.[21]

Inflation affects marketing by modifying consumer behavior.[22] Modest increases in the general price level (often called creeping inflation) go largely unnoticed—except when current prices are well publicized. People have boycotted meat because of high prices even though food costs have increased far less than many other costs. But as purchasing power continues to decline, consumers become more conscious of inflation. The result is that they also become more price conscious. This consciousness can lead to three possibilities, all of them important to marketers. Consumers can (1) elect to buy now in the belief that prices will be higher later, (2) decide to reallocate their purchasing patterns, or (3) postpone a certain purchase.

The Energy Crisis

The term **energy crisis** refers to *the general realization that energy resources are not limitless.* This realization was first brought on by the 1973–1974 Arab oil embargo. Threatened by oil cutbacks, much of the industrialized world scrambled for ways of conserving energy. A Canadian division of Nashau Corporation even began labeling its promotional material: "Printed in U.S.A. to conserve Canadian raw material and energy."[23] In 1979, fuel shortages that began with civil turmoil in Iran led to long lines at gasoline stations. The shortages became painfully evident to everyone. Responses ranged from consumption restrictions like selling on alternative days according to odd and even license plate numbers to a search for synthetic fuel.

Certain facts have become evident about the energy crisis of the 1970s. First, this is not the first U.S. energy crisis and probably not the last. In 1872, for instance, a virus hit New England's horse population. About a quarter of the country's 15 million horses—the primary energy source of the day—were afflicted. Transportation lines ceased to operate. Homes were cold, and

Inflation can also create marketing opportunities.

Source: Copyright © 1980 by Sidney Harris. Reprinted by permission.

factories were shut down because there was no way to deliver coal. Trash was not collected. Mail delivery was stopped. When the crisis subsided, the nation began to shift to other energy sources.[24]

Second, the energy crisis of the 1970s is forcing business and society to rethink their current allocation of energy resources. Existing sources are being expanded, traditional sources (such as coal) are being rediscovered, and new sources are being sought. Perhaps of most importance is that attempts are being made to cut waste in energy usage. The reduced oil supplies have forced the industrialized free world to take steps necessary for its own self-preservation.

Third, the energy crisis has also affected marketing.[25] It has led to a whole assortment of other shortages, including even a once-heralded toilet paper shortage. As various shortages began to appear in crucial industrial areas, marketers were faced with an unusual question: How should limited supplies be allocated to customers whose demands exceeded the quantities available for distribution? At first, many marketers were not prepared to cope with such a situation. But the energy crisis and related shortages have forced marketers to come up with a range of strategy alternatives.

Demarketing: Dealing with Shortages

Shortages—whether temporary or permanent—can be caused by a number of factors. A brisk demand may exceed manufacturing capacity or the response time required to gear up a production line. A lack of raw materials, component parts, energy, or labor can bring them on. Regardless of the cause, shortages require marketers to reorient their thinking.[26]

Demarketing, a term that has come into general use in recent years, is *the process of cutting consumer demand for a product back to a level that can reasonably be supplied by the firm.* Some oil companies, for example, have publicized tips on how to cut gasoline consumption. Utility companies have encouraged homeowners to install more insulation in order to lower heating bills. Many cities have discouraged central business district traffic by raising parking fees and violation penalties.

Shortages also can force marketers to be allocators of limited supplies—a situation that is in sharp contrast to marketing's traditional objective of expanding sales volume. Shortages may require marketers to spread a limited supply over all customers so that none is completely satisfied or to back order for some customers so that others will be completely supplied. Thus shortages present marketers with a unique set of problems.

Societal Environment

The **societal environment** is the *marketer's relationships with society in general.* Such relationships have been on the decline since the mid-1960s. Opinion polls suggest that people have lost confidence in major corporations (although they maintain faith in the private enterprise system). These declines should, however, be viewed in perspective. All institutions have lost a degree of public confidence. In fact, polls show that government and labor unions are even less popular than business.[27] This result suggests that the public still views business as more competent to deal with its societal problems than are other major social and economic institutions.

The societal environment for marketing decisions has both expanded in scope and increased in importance. Today, no marketer can initiate a strategy without taking the societal environment into account—without developing an awareness of the manner in which it affects decisions.[28] One writer has succinctly pointed this out:

> The more educated society becomes, the more interdependent it becomes, and the more discretionary the use of its resources; the more marketing will become enmeshed in social issues. Marketing personnel are at the interface between company and society. In this position they have the responsibility not merely for designing a competitive marketing strategy, but for sensitizing business to the social, as well as the product, demand of society.[29]

Many marketers recognize societal differences among countries yet continue to assume that a homogeneous societal environment exists domestically. Nothing could be further from the truth. The United States is a mixed society composed of varied submarkets. These market segments can be classified by age, race, place of residence, sex, and numerous other determinants.

The black segment has historically been ignored by too many firms. In recent years, however, black consumers have been recognized as a distinct market. This market is particularly important in urban centers, where the bulk of the black population and its buying power is concentrated.

Sex is another increasingly important societal factor. The feminist movement has had a decided effect on marketing, particularly on promotion. Television commercials, for example, now feature women in nontraditional roles.[30]

Since societal variables change constantly, marketers must continually monitor their dynamic environment. What is taboo today may be tomorrow's greatest market opportunity. Consider the case of Kleenex. Prior to its introduction, the Puritan ethic engrained in U.S. society prohibited wastefulness. But Kimberly-Clark was able to show consumers the value of disposability, and Kleenex was launched.[31]

Because the societal variables affect the way consumers react to different products and marketing practices, they must be recognized by marketers. One of the most tragic—and avoidable—of all marketing mistakes is the failure to appreciate such differences in the domestic marketplace.

The rise of consumerism can be traced in part to the growing public concern with making business more responsible to its constituents. Consumerism (which is discussed in detail in Chapter 18) is an evolving aspect of marketing's societal environment. Certainly, the movement has led to more direct protection of consumer rights in such areas as product safety. This concern will undoubtedly be amplified in the years ahead.

Summary

The four specific environments for marketing decisions are competitive, legal, economic, and societal. These four are important to the study of marketing because they provide a framework within which marketing strategies are formulated. They are among the most dynamic aspects of contemporary business.

The competitive environment is the interactive process that occurs in the marketplace. A firm's marketing decisions influence the market and are in turn affected by competitors' strategies. The legal environment attempts to maintain competition as well as regulate specific marketing practices. The economic environment often influences the manner in which consumers will behave toward marketing appeals. The societal environment may become the most important to marketers. The matter of adapting to a changing societal environment has advanced to the forefront of marketing thought.

Questions for Discussion

1. Explain the following terms:

   competitive environment
   legal environment
   corrective advertising
   economic environment
   inflation

   stagflation
   energy crisis
   demarketing
   societal environment

2. List and briefly describe the four segments of the environment for marketing decisions.
3. Comment on the following statement: The dynamic nature of the contemporary business environment puts pressure on all levels of management to continually reevaluate marketing decisions.
4. Explain the relationship between the general public and the competitive marketing system.
5. Discuss the competitive environment for racquetball in your area. If no racquetball facilities exist, substitute tennis clubs, squash courts, swimming clubs, or any other sporting facilities.
6. Trace the FTC's evolution into an activist watchdog of marketing practices. Evaluate its degree of success.
7. How did the Great Depression influence marketing legislation?
8. Identify and evaluate the major defenses to the Robinson-Patman Act.
9. President Carter responded to high inflation by a program of voluntary price and wage controls supported by an extensive monitoring system. A mid-1978 Gallup Poll revealed that 53 percent of the public favored such controls. Comment on this issue. Defend your position with specific arguments for or against wage and price controls.
10. Canadian law requires all refrigerators to have labels indicating the number of kilowatt-hours they use. This requirement is designed to help Canadians pick energy efficient products. Similar legislation has been proposed for the United States. Do you favor a

program similar to the Canadian one? What are the advantages and disadvantages of such an effort?

11. Comment on the following statement: The legal framework for marketing decisions is basically a positive one.

12. How does inflation affect marketing activity?

13. Discuss the following statement: Marketing is becoming an activist business function since it is influencing the societal environment by contributing its tremendous ability to reach potential markets.

14. Can the consumerism movement be viewed as a rejection of the competitive marketing system? Defend your answer.

15. Research the most important state and local consumer protection regulations in your area. Discuss whether this legislation is accomplishing its original objectives.

16. In your opinion, are the benefits of government regulation of marketing activities worth the cost? Are there any factors that would cause you to change your opinion?

17. Would a gas station that sold gasoline to a city's police department for two cents per gallon less than to its other customers be in violation of the Robinson-Patman Act? Explain.

18. In post–World War I Germany, the exchange rate was 4.2 trillion marks to a U.S. dollar. While the U.S. double-digit inflation of the 1970s did not come close to Germany's earlier experience, many people in the United States did adjust their consumer behavior. Identify some of the steps they took to cope with inflation. Explain the role of the marketer during periods of rapid inflation.

19. How does one shop for credit? What role does the Truth-in-Lending Act play in the search?

20. Comment on the viewpoint expressed by Procter & Gamble's board chairman, Edward G. Harness:

> I have no quarrel with the citizenry, the bureaucrats, the legislators or the educators who say that corporations have a responsibility to society beyond the obligation to generate a fair return or profit for the investor. . . .
>
> However, I take real issue with the critics when they propose that corporations must put their other citizenship responsibilities ahead of their responsibility to earn a fair return for the owners. The only way in which corporations can carry their huge and increasing burden of obligations to society is for them to earn satisfactory profits. If we cannot earn a return on equity investment which is more attractive than other forms of investment, we die. I am not aware of any bankrupt corporations which are making important social contributions.[32]

Notes

1. See "The Reynolds Saga: The Sweet with the Bitter," *Forbes,* December 1, 1971, p. 32.

2. The importance of environmental factors is noted in C. Glenn Walters, D. Wayne Norvell, and Sam J. Bruno, "Is There a Better Way than 'Consumer Orientation'?" *Proceedings of the Southern Marketing Association,* ed. Henry W. Nash and Donald P. Robin, January 1976, pp. 79–81; and Michael E. Porter, "How Competitive Forces Shape Strategy," *Harvard Business Review,* March–April 1979, pp. 137–145.

3. Fred Danzig, "Du Pont's Corfam: What Went Wrong?" *Advertising Age,* April 5, 1971, pp. 6–7.

4. Competition in the sporting goods industry is described in "Repent at Leisure," *Forbes,* December 15, 1975, pp. 20–21.

5. The running shoe industry is described in Julie Salamon, "The Sky's the Limit for Pampered Feet of Today's Joggers," *Wall Street Journal,* July 20, 1977.

6. Marshal C. Howard, *Legal Aspects of Marketing* (New York: McGraw-Hill, 1964), contains an excellent review of antitrust legislation. See also Jerrold G. Van Cise, "For Whom the Antitrust Bell Tolls," *Harvard Business Review,* January–February 1978, pp. 125–130.

7. Reported in George E. Hartman, "Antitrust Violations, Costing U.S. Consumers $80 Billion a Year, Feed Inflationary Fires," *Marketing News,* October 15, 1974, p. 3.

8. Corrective advertising is discussed in William C. Rodgers, "The Corrective Advertising Remedy—Alternative Product and Consumer Interest Policy Dimensions," in *Proceedings of the Southern Marketing Association,* ed. Robert S. Franz, Robert M. Hopkins, and Al Toma, New Orleans, Louisiana, November 1978, pp. 109–111.

9. "Corrective Ads for STP Publicize Settlement Costs to Business Execs," *Advertising Age,* February 13, 1978, pp. 1, 106.

10. These methods are discussed in Vernon A. Mund, *Government and Business* (New York: Harper & Row, 1960), pp. 294–299.

11. The Robinson-Patman provisions have been the subject of considerable discussion in the marketing literature. A recent example is Roy O. Werner, "Robinson-Patman: Purchasing's Responsibility Still Unclear," *Journal of Purchasing and Materials Management,* Spring 1978, pp. 12–15.

12. See Lawrence X. Tarpey, "Buyer Liability under the Robinson-Patman Act: A Current Appraisal," *Journal of Marketing,* January 1972, pp. 38–42.

13. Howard, *Legal Aspects of Marketing,* p. 8.

14. Robert A. Lynn, "Is the Cost Defense Workable?" *Journal of Marketing,* January 1965, pp. 37–42. It has been pointed out that logistics cost evidence is the best justification under the Robinson-Patman Act. See J. L. Heskett, Robert M. Ivie, and Nicholas A. Glaskowsky, Jr., *Business Logistics* (New York: Ronald Press, 1964), p. 235.

15. The fair trade concept is reviewed in such articles as James C. Johnson and Louis E. Boone, "Farewell to Fair Trade," *MSU Business Topics,* Spring 1976, pp. 22–30; and L. Louise Luchsinger and Patrick M. Dunne, "Fair Trade Laws—How Fair?" *Journal of Marketing,* January 1978, pp. 50–54.

16. The Kefauver-Harris legislation is discussed in Paul Hugajab and George Tesar, "Some Issues in the Federal Regulation of Advertising," in *Proceedings of the Southwestern Marketing Association,* ed. John Swan and Robert C. Haring, Dallas, Texas, March 1978, p. 56.

17. Marshall C. Howard, "Textile and Fur Labeling Legislation: Names, Competition, and the Consumer," *California Management Review,* Winter 1971, pp. 69–80.

18. Dik Warren Twedt, "What Effect Will the 'Fair Packaging and Labeling Act' Have on Marketing Practices?" *Journal of Marketing,* April 1967, pp. 58–59. See also David M. Gardner, "The Package, Legislation, and the Shopper," *Business Horizons,* October 1968, pp. 53–58; and Warren A. French and Leila O. Shroeder, "Package Information Legislation: Trends and Viewpoints," *MSU Business Topics,* Summer 1972, pp. 39–44.

19. For information about the Equal Credit Opportunity Act, see John R. Nevin and Gilbert A. Churchill, Jr., "The Equal Credit Opportunity Act: An Evaluation," *Journal of Marketing,* Spring 1979, pp. 95–104; for information about the Fair Debt Collection Practices Act, see Richard A. Ryan, "Limits Put on Debt Collection," *Detroit News,* September 21, 1977.

20. An interesting discussion appears in Bernard A. Morin and Thomas L. Wheelan, "Status Report on Consumer Protection at the State Level," in *Contemporary Marketing Thought: 1977 Educators' Proceedings,* ed. Barnett A. Greenberg and Danny W. Bellenger (Chicago: American Marketing Association, 1977), p. 534.

21. See, for example, Fred W. Kniffen, " 'Stagflation' Pricing—Seven Ways You Might Improve Your Decisions," *Marketing News,* November 15, 1974.

22. This issue is explored in Zoher E. Shipchandler, "Inflation and Life Styles: The Marketing Impact," *Business Horizons,* February 1976, pp. 90–96.

23. "Business Bulletin," *Wall Street Journal,* April 11, 1974, p. 1.

24. The 1872 energy crisis is described in Jane Scherer, "Energy Crunch—1872," *PEN,* June 1974, pp. 21–22.

25. Interesting discussions of energy prospects and problems appear in William L. Shanklin, "The Energy Crisis and Consumer Behavior," *Atlanta Economic Review,* May–June 1978, pp. 23–32; and Terrell G. Williams, "Retailing and the Energy Crisis," *Review of Business,* November–December 1975, pp. 1–6, 8. See also two papers in the *Proceedings of the Southern Marketing Association,* ed. Henry W. Nash and Donald P. Robin, January 1976: Venkatakrishna V. Bellur, "Motorists' Attitudes toward the Energy Crisis," pp. 61–63; and Thomas L. Parkinson, "Consumer Energy Conservation Practices: Methods and Motivation," pp. 64–66.

26. Interesting articles related to this topic include Philip Kotler and Sidney J. Levy, "Demarketing, Yes, Demarketing," *Harvard Business Review,* November–December 1971, pp. 74–80; David W. Cravens, "Marketing Management in an Era of Shortages," *Business Horizons,* February 1974, pp. 79–85; A. B. Blankenship and John H. Holmes, "Will Shortages Bankrupt the Marketing Concept?" *MSU Business Topics,* Spring 1974, pp. 13–18; Philip Kotler, "Marketing during Periods of Shortages," *Journal of Marketing,* July 1974, pp. 20–29; Zohrab S. Demirdjian, "The Role of Marketing in an Economy of Affluence and Shortages," *Business and Society,* Spring 1975, pp. 15–21; and Nessim Hanna, A. H. Kizilbash, and

Albert Smart, "Marketing Strategy under Conditions of Economic Scarcity," *Journal of Marketing,* January 1975, pp. 63–67.

27. Seymour Martin Lipset, "How's Business? What the Public Thinks," *Public Opinion,* July–August 1978, pp. 41–47.
28. An interesting discussion appears in Charles W. Gross and Harish L. Verma, "Marketing and Social Responsibility," *Business Horizons,* October 1977, pp. 75–82.
29. Louis L. Stern, "Consumer Protection via Self-regulation," *Journal of Marketing,* July 1971, p. 53.
30. The changing roles of women portrayed in advertising are discussed in Robert A. Peterson and Roger A. Kerin, "The Female Role in Advertisements: Some Experimental Evidence," *Journal of Marketing,* October 1977, pp. 59–63; and William J. Lundstrom and Donald Sciplimpagli, "Sex Role Portrayals in Advertising," *Journal of Marketing,* July 1977, pp. 72–79.
31. The Kleenex story is told in Ronald D. Michman, "Culture as a Marketing Tool," *Marquette Business Review,* Winter 1975, pp. 177–184.
32. "Views on Corporate Responsibility," excerpts from a talk to Procter & Gamble management on December 8, 1977, by Edward G. Harness, Chairman of the Board, p. 6. Reprinted by permission.

PART TWO
IDENTIFYING CONSUMER NEEDS

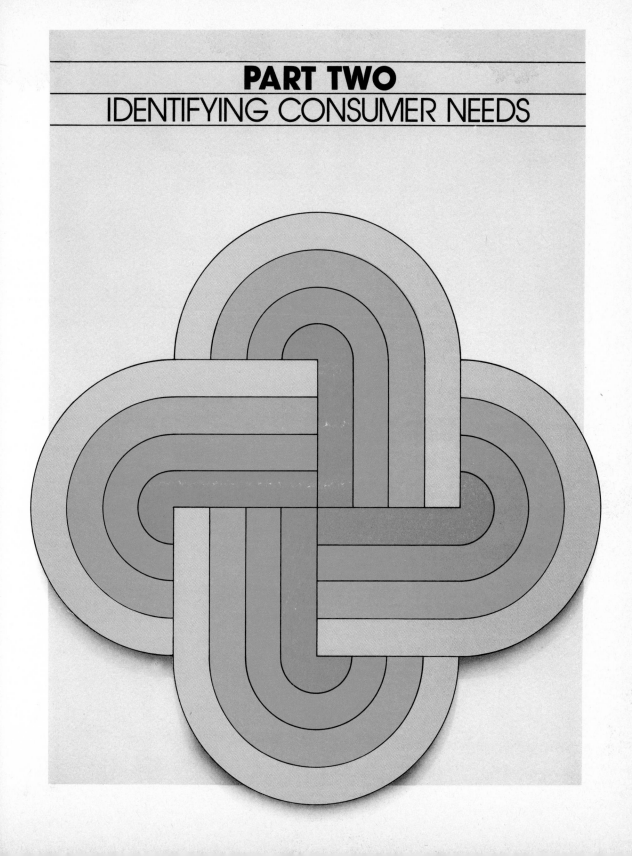

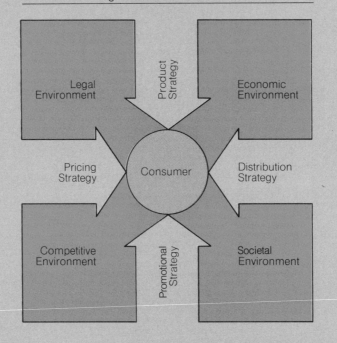

CHAPTER 3
MARKETING RESEARCH: INFORMATION FOR DECISION MAKING

Key Terms

marketing research
exploratory research
sales analysis
sales quota
marketing cost
analysis
secondary data

primary data
research design
focus group interview
marketing
information system
(MIS)
sales forecast

Learning Goals

1. To identify the different forms of marketing information.
2. To list the steps in the marketing research process.
3. To explain the types of primary data.
4. To identify the methods of collecting survey data.
5. To distinguish between marketing research and marketing information systems.
6. To explain the steps involved in developing a sales forecast.

3

Although Lever Bros. had successfully marketed Pepsodent toothpaste since 1944, by 1964 it was clear that changes were taking place in the marketplace. The firm conducted several surveys of toothpaste users that revealed young adults were dissatisfied with current offerings in two areas: tooth whitening and breath freshening. As a result of these studies, the idea of a combination toothpaste and mouthwash was born.

The idea was first tested among different age groups, including teens and young adults, and results were encouraging. Meanwhile, Lever Bros. scientists had invented a clear gel dentifrice base that appeared ideal in producing the effect of a mouthwash.

More than twenty-five varieties of product formulations were tested by groups of consumers under laboratory conditions, and several families were given samples to test at home. As a result, Close-Up was born.

The final step before introducing the product nationally was to test sales by distributing Close-Up in only a few cities. Different marketing expenditure plans, advertising and promotional approaches, and prices were tested.

Finally, the product was launched and proved successful by capturing 10 percent of the total market. Periodic surveys were continued in order to make certain that Close-Up was attracting the customers its marketers expected. Lever Bros. executives understand the importance of information in marketing decision making.[1]

The Scope of Marketing Research

The American Marketing Association defines **marketing research** as *"the systematic gathering, recording, and analyzing of data about problems relating to the marketing of goods and services."*[2] Marketing managers' main task is decision making. Managers earn their salaries by making effective decisions that enable their firms to solve problems as they arise and by anticipating and preventing future problems. Many times, though, they are forced to make decisions with inadequate information. Marketing research presents pertinent facts, analyzes them, and suggests possible action.

All marketing decision areas are candidates for marketing research investigations. As Table 3–1 indicates, marketing research efforts are commonly centered around developing sales forecasts for the firm's products, determining market and sales potential, designing new products and packages, analyzing sales and marketing costs, evaluating the effectiveness of the firm's advertising, and determining consumer motives for buying products.

Marketing research is a relatively new field. It traces its origin in the United States to 1911, when Charles C. Parlin was appointed manager of the commercial research division of the Curtis Publishing Company.[3] Much of the early research represented little more than written testimonials received from purchasers of the firm's products. One such testimonial, shown in Fig-

Research Activity	Percentage of Companies Conducting the Activity
Advertising Research	
Motivation research	48
Copy research	49
Media research	61
Studies of advertising effectiveness	67
Business Economic and Corporate Research	
Short-range forecasting (up to a year)	85
Long-range forecasting (over a year)	82
Plant and warehouse location studies	71
Export and international studies	51
Corporate Responsibility Research	
Consumers' "right-to-know" studies	26
Ecological impact studies	33
Studies of legal constraints on advertising and promotion	51
Social values and policies studies	40
Product Research	
New-product acceptance and potential	84
Competitive product studies	85
Product testing	75
Packaging research	60
Sales and Market Research	
Measurement of market potentials	93
Market share analysis	92
Determination of market characteristics	93
Sales analyses	89
Establishment of sales quotas, territories	75
Distribution channel studies	69
Test markets, store audits	54
Consumer panel operations	50

Source: Dik Warren Twedt, ed., *1978 Survey of Marketing Research* (Chicago: American Marketing Association, 1978), p. 41. Reprinted by permission.

ure 3–1, now hangs on the walls of the Henry Ford Museum.

Research became more sophisticated during the 1930s, but mistakes were still being made. The *Literary Digest* conducted a major national study of U.S. households selected at random from lists of telephone numbers and auto registration records and reported that Alf Landon—not Franklin D. Roosevelt—would be elected president. The fiasco resulted from a failure to realize that many voters (most of whom were apparently Democrats) did not have telephones in 1936.

The development of statistical techniques during the 1930s led to refinements in sampling procedures and greater accuracy in research findings. By

1978, the American Marketing Association reported that 87 percent of the nation's leading manufacturing firms had established formal marketing research departments. Although formal departments are mostly found in firms manufacturing consumer products, a substantial increase in the number of such departments has occurred in recent years in financial service concerns such as banks, savings and loan associations, other lending institutions, and insurance companies.[4] Total research expenditures in 1980 are estimated at more than $1 billion.

The Role of Information in the Decision Process

It has been said that the recipe for effective decisions is 90 percent information and 10 percent inspiration. Figure 3–2 separates the management decision process into a series of stages and indicates the type of information

Figure 3–1
A Testimonial from a Satisfied Customer

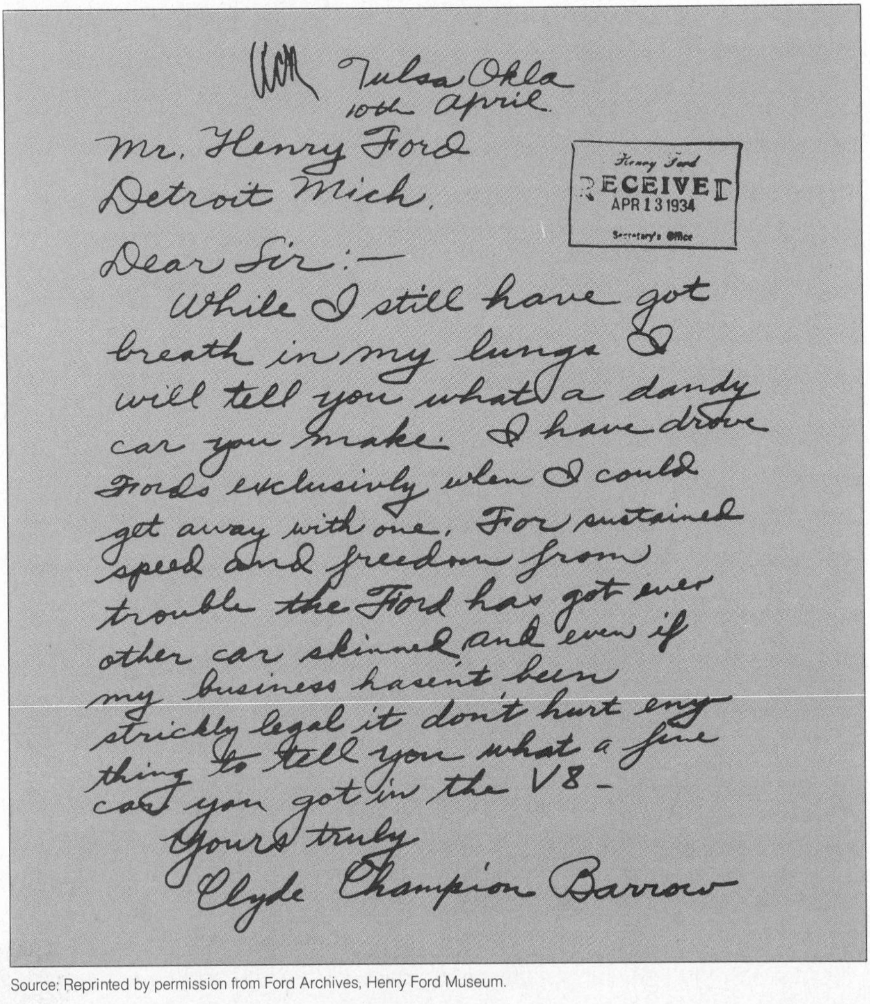

Tulsa Okla
10th April.

Mr. Henry Ford
Detroit Mich.

Henry Ford
RECEIVED
APR 13 1934
Secretary's Office

Dear Sir:—

While I still have got breath in my lungs I will tell you what a dandy car you make. I have drove Fords exclusivly when I could get away with one. For sustained speed and freedom from trouble the Ford has got ever other car skinned and even if my business hasent been strickly legal it don't hurt eny thing to tell you what a fine car you got in the V8—

Yours truly
Clyde Champion Barrow

Source: Reprinted by permission from Ford Archives, Henry Ford Museum.

Figure 3–2
Information Needs and the Management Process

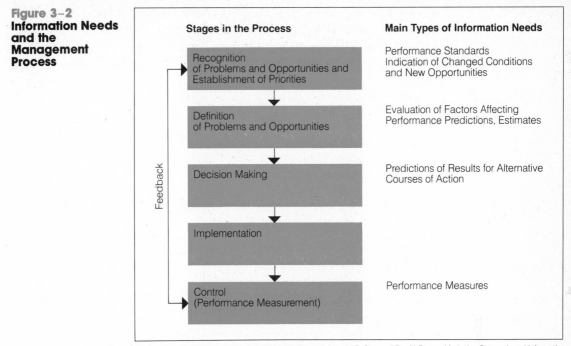

Source: Reprinted by permission from Robert D. Buzzell, Donald F. Cox, and Rex V. Brown, *Marketing Research and Information Systems* (New York: McGraw-Hill, 1969), p. 5.

that is crucial at each stage. Specific types of information are required to assist management at each stage of the decision-making process. The following hypothetical example describes the early stages of a decision process and illustrates how various types of information are used by management.

Delta Book Club

Delta Book Club is one of the leading book clubs in the country; its annual sales are in excess of $50 million. It competes with Book-of-the-Month Club in the general book market and, to varying degrees, with specialized book clubs such as the History Book Club, the Science Fiction Book Club, and the Executive Reading Program.

Although Delta's sales and profits have been increasing steadily since its formation in 1971, management has become concerned about the tremendous growth of a number of firms that rent best-selling books on cassette tapes. The rental companies have been in existence for only three years, but their sales have been phenomenal. This new marketing system for books has received considerable publicity, and Delta is concerned about whether it will affect the traditional mail-order sale of books.

At least one top management official at Delta is advocating the establishment of a separate division within the firm to market books in a cassette tape format. Other managers have favored the acquisition of one of the existing companies.

Delta is obviously facing a major decision. Its marketing research director has been asked to study the impact of cassette tape rentals on the existing book market and to forecast the sales for book rental companies over the next two years.

Delta's efforts illustrate some of the ways information is used at the early stages of the management process. The company probably learned of its problem (and potential opportunity) by reading about the cassette tape rental firms in a journal or magazine. It can now take steps to determine the actual impact of tape-recorded books and consumer attitudes toward the new book form.

Marketing Research Procedure

Most marketing research investigations begin with an awareness of a problem or opportunity. The first important task of the researcher is to define precisely this problem or opportunity.

Problem Definition Is Critical

By now, the reader may be thinking, "Everyone knows what the problem is. The task of the researcher is to determine methods of solving it. So why don't we eliminate step one?" The following hypothetical example should shed light on why this step is important.

What Happened to Wonderclean?

> Anne Stewart had been in Columbia Corporation's management development program for sixteen months when she received a two-month assignment in Columbia's marketing research department. Prior to this, she had worked with the sales representatives who called on wholesalers and supermarkets handling the firm's line of household cleaning products.
>
> After a month in the marketing research department, she had grown fond of her job, which consisted of updating company files of statistics released by the industry trade association and taking part in an occasional survey. But her attitude changed abruptly one morning when her boss entered her office and said: "Wonderclean isn't doing nearly as well as we expected. Find out why, and report back to me in two weeks."
>
> Anne Stewart was familiar with Wonderclean—the new product that was highly touted when she first joined Columbia. The reason for her change of attitude was her knowledge that any of a hundred factors could have affected the product's sales. She also recognized that defining the problem was to be the most important act to date in her career.

Exploratory Research Uncovers Causes

Marketing researchers are confronted with a number of problem *symptoms,* such as low sales. In order to solve a problem or enable a firm to take advantage of a potential opportunity, these researchers must search for *causes.* The purpose of this search is to gain understanding of the problem area and insight into it causes and effects.

Exploratory research consists of *discussing the problem with informed sources within the firm and with wholesalers, retailers, customers, and others outside the firm and examining secondary sources of information.** It also means evaluating internal company records, such as sales and profit analyses of the company's and its competitors' products. Table 3–2 lists the major topics for any exploratory research.

---

*Marketing researchers often refer to *internal* data collection as the *situation analysis* and to exploratory interviews with informed persons *outside* the firm as the *informal investigation.*

Table 3–2
Topics for the Exploratory Analysis

The Company and Industry	Sales Organization
1. Company objectives	1. Market coverage
2. The companies comprising the industry (size, financial power) and industry trends	2. Sales analysis by number of accounts per salesperson, size of account, type of account, and so on
3. Geographic locations of the industry	3. Expense ratios for various territories, product types, account sizes, and so on
4. The company's market share as compared with competitors'	4. Control procedures
5. Marketing policies of competitors	5. Compensation methods
The Market	**Pricing**
1. Geographic location	1. Elasticity
2. Demographic characteristics	2. Seasonal or special promotional price cuts
3. Purchase motivations	3. Profit margins of resellers
4. Product use patterns	4. Legal restrictions
5. Nature of demand	5. Price lines
Products	**Advertising and Sales Promotion**
1. Physical characteristics	1. Media employed
2. Consumer acceptance—strengths and weaknesses	2. Dollar expenditures as compared with competitors'
3. Package as a container and as a promotional weapon	3. Timing of advertising
4. Manufacturing processes, production capacity	4. Sales promotional materials provided for resellers
5. Closeness and availability of substitute products	5. Results from previous advertising and sales promotional campaigns
Marketing Channels	
1. Channels employed and recent trends	
2. Channel policy	
3. Margins for resellers	

Utilizing Internal Data

Valuable sources of information are contained in the business firm's records. Analysis of these records should provide a basis for obtaining an overall view of company efficiency and a clue to the problem under investigation.

The basis for analysis of internal data is traditional accounting data, provided by the accounting department and usually summarized on the firm's financial statements. Table 3–3 shows a simplified income statement.

Basic financial statements are often too broad to be very useful in marketing analysis. Where nondetailed accounts are used, their main contribution is that they assist the analyst in raising more specific questions. The income statement in Table 3–3 shows that the company earned a profit for the period involved and that selling expenses represent approximately 13 percent of sales.

Table 3–3
Income Statement for ABC Manufacturing Company

ABC Manufacturing Company
Income Statement
for the Year Ended December 31, 198–

Sales		$5,783,000
Cost of goods sold		3,291,000
Gross margin		$2,492,000
Expenses:		
Selling expenses	$753,000	
Other expenses	301,000	1,054,000
Profit before taxes		$1,438,000
Income taxes		719,000
Profit after taxes		719,000

$$\text{Cost/sales ratio} = \frac{\$753,000}{\$5,783,000} = 13\%.$$

Comparison of the 13 percent selling expense to sales ratio with previous years may hint at possible problems, but it will not specifically reveal the cause of the variation. To discover the cause, a more detailed breakdown is necessary.

Sales Analysis. Table 3–4 shows a typical breakdown of sales by territories. This kind of breakdown becomes part of an overall sales analysis. The purpose of the **sales analysis**—*the in-depth evaluation of a firm's sales*—is to obtain meaningful information from the accounting data.[5]

Easily prepared from company invoices stored on computer tapes, the sales analysis can be quite revealing for the marketing executive. As Table 3–4 shows, the sales force in Territory 4 has a much higher cost/sales ratio than the sales force in other territories.

In order to evaluate the performance of the salespeople in the five territories, the marketing executive must have a *standard of comparison.* Territory 4, for example, may be a large territory but with relatively few industrial centers. Consequently, the costs involved in obtaining sales will be higher than for other territories.

Table 3–4
Sales and Expense Analysis by Territory

Territory	Average Salary	Average Expenses	Total Sales Costs	Total Sales	Cost/ Sales Ratio
1	$23,600	$10,400	$34,000	$654,000	5.2%
2	21,900	12,800	34,700	534,000	6.5
3	27,200	13,100	40,300	790,000	5.1
4	25,700	12,300	38,000	180,000	21.1
5	24,200	11,700	35,900	580,000	6.2

Table 3–5
Sales Breakdown by Sales Representatives in Territory 4

Salesperson	Quota	Actual	Performance to Quota
Holtzman	$136,000	$128,000	94%
Thompson	228,000	253,000	111
Shapiro	118,000	125,000	106
Chandler	246,000	160,000	65
Total	$728,000	$666,000	91%

The standard by which actual and expected sales are compared typically results from a detailed sales forecast by territories, products, customers, and salespersons. Once the **sales quota**—*the level of expected sales by which actual results are compared*—has been established, it is a simple process to compare the actual results with the expected performance. Table 3–5 compares actual sales with the quota established for each person in Territory 4.

Even though Shapiro had the smallest amount of sales for the period, her performance was better than expected. However, the regional sales manager should investigate Chandler's performance since it resulted in the territory's failure to meet its quota for the period.

The Iceberg Principle. Territory 4 is a good illustration of the *iceberg principle.* The tip of the iceberg represents only one-tenth of its total size. The remaining nine-tenths lies hidden beneath the surface of the water. Summaries of data are useful, but the marketing researcher must be careful that they do not actually conceal more than they reveal. If the sales breakdown by salesperson for the territory had not been available, Chandler's poor performance would have concealed the unexpectedly high sales performances by Thompson and Shapiro.

Other Breakdowns. Other possible breakdowns for sales analysis include customer type, product, method of sale (mail, telephone, or personal contact), type of order (cash or credit), and size of order. Sales analysis is one of the least expensive and most important sources of marketing information, and any firm with data processing facilities should include it as part of its information system.

Marketing Cost Analysis. A second source of internal information is **marketing cost analysis**—*the evaluation of such items as selling costs, billing, warehousing, advertising, and delivery expenses in order to determine the profitability of particular customers, territories, or product lines.*

Marketing cost analysis requires a new way of classifying accounting data. *Functional accounts* must be established to replace the traditional natural accounts used in financial statements. These traditional accounts —such as salary—must be reallocated to the purpose for which the ex-

Table 3–6
Allocation of Marketing Costs

Marketing Costs	By Customer		By Territory		
	Large	Small	A	B	C
Advertising	$14,000	$ 30,000	$20,000	$10,000	$14,000
Selling	52,000	62,000	38,000	38,000	38,000
Physical distribution	33,000	26,000	28,000	14,000	17,000
Credit	400	2,600	1,600	600	800
Total	$99,400	$120,600	$87,600	$62,600	$69,800

penditure was made. A portion of the original salary account, for example, will be allocated to selling, inventory control, storage, billing, advertising, and other marketing costs. In the same manner, an account such as supply expenses will be allocated to the functions that utilize supplies.

The costs allocated to the functional accounts will equal those in the natural accounts. But instead of showing only total profitability, they can show the profitability of, say, particular territories, products, customers, salespersons, and order sizes. The most common reallocations are to *products, customers,* and *territories.* Table 3–6 shows how they can be made.

The marketing decision maker can then evaluate the profitability of particular customers and territories on the basis of the sales produced and the costs incurred in producing them.

Table 3–7 indicates that Territory B is the most profitable region and Territory A is unprofitable. Attention can now be given to plans for increasing sales or reducing expenses in this problem territory to make market coverage of the area a profitable undertaking. Marketing cost analysis is similar to sales analysis in that both provide warning signals of deviations from plans and allow the marketing executive the opportunity to explain and possibly correct the deviations.[6]

Secondary Data

An extremely important source of information for the marketing researcher is the use of **secondary**—*previously published*—**data.** In fact, so much in-

Table 3–7
Income Statement for Territories A, B, and C

	Territory			
	A	B	C	Total
Sales	$260,000	$200,000	$191,000	$651,000
Cost of sales	175,000	135,000	120,000	430,000
Gross margin	$ 85,000	$ 65,000	$ 71,000	$221,000
Marketing expenses	87,000	62,000	69,800	220,000
Contribution of each territory	($ 2,000)	$ 2,400	$ 1,200	$ 1,000

formation of this nature is available at little or no cost that the researcher faces the problem of being overwhelmed by it. In the era of the information explosion, one of the marks of a good researcher is the ability to select *pertinent* secondary data.[7]

Government Sources. The federal government is the nation's most important source of marketing data, and the most frequently used government data are *census data.* Although more than $1 billion was spent by the government in conducting the 1980 Census of Population, census information is available for use at no charge at local libraries, or it can be purchased on computer tapes at a nominal charge for instantaneous access. In fact, the Bureau of the Census produces seven censuses, briefly described in Table 3–8.

The 1980 census is so detailed for large cities that breakdowns of population characteristics are available by city block. Thus local retailers and shopping center developers can easily gather detailed information about

Table 3–8
Census Data Collected by the U.S. Bureau of the Census

Census of Population: Conducted once each decade, provides a count of all residents of the United States by state, city, and county and, in large cities, by census tract and city block. Data are also gathered on age, sex, race, citizenship, educational level, occupation, employment status, income, and family status.

Census of Housing: Since 1940, combined with the Census of Population to gather information regarding housing conditions, such as value of house, number of rooms, type of structure, race of occupants, and year house was built.

Census of Business: Includes information on retail trade, wholesale trade, and selected services; data broken down by counties and by large cities and including such facts as number of stores of a particular type, total sales, employment, and legal form of organization.

Census of Manufactures: Covers approximately 450 industries and reveals the value of products produced by industry, cost of materials and equipment, number of establishments, and wages paid.

Census of Agriculture: Gives data on number of farms, number of persons residing on farms (by age and sex), value of farm products sold, acreage of each major crop, number of tractors, number of livestock, and presence of electricity and running water for each county in the United States.

Census of Minerals: Includes data on employees, wages, quantities produced, cost of materials and supplies, types of equipment used, and hours worked in over 60 industries.

Census of Governments: Gives data every five years on number of public employees, payrolls, value of taxable property, and financial assets of state and local governments.

customers in the immediate neighborhood without spending the time or money to conduct a comprehensive survey.[8]

So much information is produced by the federal government that marketing researchers often purchase summaries such as the *Monthly Catalog of United States Government Publications,* the *Statistical Abstract of the United States,* the *Survey of Current Business,* and the *County and City Data Book.* Published annually, the *Statistical Abstract* contains a wealth of current data. The *Survey of Current Business,* updated monthly, focuses on a variety of industrial data. The *County and City Data Book,* typically published every three years, provides a variety of data for each county and each city of over 25,000 residents.

State and city governments are other important sources of information on employment, production, and sales activities. In addition, university bureaus of business and economic research often collect and distribute such information.

Private Sources. Numerous private organizations provide information for the marketing executive. For data on activities in a particular industry, trade associations are excellent sources. Advertising agencies continually collect information on the audience reached by various media. A wide range of illuminating and valuable data are found in the annual *Survey of Buying*

Figure 3–3
The Survey of Buying Power Provides Detailed Information for the Marketing Researcher

ILL. ESTIMATES — **SS** — EFFECTIVE BUYING INCOME 1978

METRO AREA / County / City	Total EBI ($000)	Median Hsld. EBI	A $8,000–$9,999	B $10,000–$14,999	C $15,000–$24,999	D $25,000 & Over	Buying Power Index
BLOOMINGTON - NORMAL	866,865	17,966	5.5	15.2	32.2	27.8	.0593
McLean	866,865	17,966	5.5	15.2	32.2	27.8	.0593
• Bloomington	320,476	16,702	6.5	16.2	31.2	24.3	.0275
• Normal	216,304	21,015	4.5	12.5	30.1	37.0	.0124
SUBURBAN TOTAL	330,085	17,890	5.0	15.6	34.5	26.5	.0194
CHAMPAIGN - URBANA - RANTOUL	1,146,369	16,355	6.5	17.4	31.0	23.8	.0793
Champaign	1,146,369	16,355	6.5	17.4	31.0	23.8	.0793
• Champaign	423,096	16,546	5.8	14.0	30.6	24.2	.0317
• Rantoul	141,964	13,787	10.0	30.1	29.5	14.0	.0105
• Urbana	232,947	14,819	6.4	17.6	25.3	24.1	.0147
SUBURBAN TOTAL	348,362	18,154	5.9	16.3	36.0	26.9	.0224
CHICAGO	54,252,265	20,101	4.4	13.2	31.7	34.2	3.6380
Cook	40,761,459	19,259	4.7	14.0	31.3	32.1	2.7076
Arlington Heights	666,138	29,187	1.5	4.8	23.7	65.0	.0398
Berwyn	398,585	19,240	4.3	13.5	34.0	30.5	.0263
• Chicago	21,140,781	15,990	6.1	17.1	30.7	22.8	1.4232
Chicago Heights	258,164	19,052	4.5	15.3	34.3	29.7	.0210
Cicero	468,926	18,285	4.5	15.5	37.5	24.6	.0287
Des Plaines	497,657	25,942	2.0	7.5	30.1	53.8	.0313
Evanston	731,946	21,867	4.6	13.2	26.6	41.5	.0439
Oak Lawn	513,738	25,224	2.2	7.2	31.5	50.8	.0375
Oak Park	613,891	22,073	3.9	12.1	28.8	41.4	.0369
Park Ridge	476,783	30,030	2.2	6.2	21.1	63.6	.0272
Skokie	764,776	28,939	1.6	6.2	24.4	61.5	.0529
Du Page	5,067,074	26,812	2.0	6.4	28.3	56.5	.3626
Elmhurst	424,538	27,516	2.2	6.2	25.4	59.0	.0300
Kane	1,999,897	21,148	3.9	11.9	36.1	35.2	.1375
Aurora	581,161	19,220	4.9	14.5	36.9	28.7	.0416
Elgin	483,975	20,035	4.6	13.3	34.6	31.6	.0378
Lake	3,466,277	22,829	3.5	10.8	31.0	43.0	.2326
North Chicago	196,242	18,297	4.2	19.5	35.7	28.1	.0110
Waukegan	468,854	18,695	5.3	15.2	35.7	27.4	.0390
McHenry	964,584	20,508	4.2	12.5	35.8	33.2	.0645
Will	1,992,974	19,241	3.7	13.5	40.9	27.0	.1332
Joliet	567,225	17,893	4.7	14.9	34.7	25.9	.0442
SUBURBAN TOTAL	33,111,484	23,560	2.8	9.5	32.5	45.0	2.2148
CHICAGO - GARY CONSOLIDATED AREA	58,802,499	20,165	4.3	13.0	32.0	34.3	3.9542
△ DANVILLE	763,560	18,277	5.1	12.8	31.7	28.6	.0491
Vermilion	763,560	18,277	5.1	12.8	31.7	28.6	.0491
• Danville	351,903	18,178	5.2	12.2	29.6	29.6	.0253
SUBURBAN TOTAL	411,657	18,351	5.1	13.3	33.7	27.8	.0238
DAVENPORT - ROCK ISLAND - MOLINE	2,740,308	19,026	4.6	13.0	34.8	29.3	.1843
Henry	399,131	17,838	5.5	13.6	34.3	25.9	.0249
Rock Island	1,290,992	19,864	4.3	12.2	34.0	32.6	.0841
• Moline	393,159	20,180	4.4	12.4	31.6	34.8	.0281
• Rock Island	397,230	19,090	5.0	12.1	29.8	32.6	.0247
Scott, Iowa	1,050,185	18,557	4.7	13.7	36.0	26.8	.0753
• Davenport	689,588	17,754	5.1	14.4	34.8	25.0	.0517
SUBURBAN TOTAL	1,260,331	19,414	4.3	12.6	37.3	29.2	.0798
DECATUR	958,618	18,271	5.3	13.3	34.6	26.8	.0664
Macon	958,618	18,271	5.3	13.3	34.6	26.8	.0664
• Decatur	713,708	17,750	5.7	13.3	32.5	26.6	.0536
SUBURBAN TOTAL	244,910	19,417	4.0	13.1	41.6	27.3	.0128
KANKAKEE	598,955	18,014	4.5	14.4	35.6	25.1	.0431
Kankakee	598,955	18,014	4.5	14.4	35.6	25.1	.0431
• Kankakee	224,107	17,388	4.8	14.5	33.0	25.5	.0200
SUBURBAN TOTAL	374,848	18,394	4.3	14.3	37.1	25.0	.0231

Source: "Survey of Buying Power," *Sales & Marketing Management,* July 23, 1979. Reprinted by permission from *Sales & Marketing Management* magazine. Copyright 1979.

Power published by *Sales and Marketing Management* magazine. Figure 3–3 illustrates the detailed information it collects for each of the states of the United States and the Canadian provinces.[9]

Several national firms also offer information to businesses on a subscription basis. The largest of these, A. C. Nielsen Company, collects data every two months on product sales, retail prices, display space, inventories, and promotional activities of competing brands of food and drug products. Its sample consists of approximately 1,600 supermarkets, 750 drugstores, and 150 mass merchandisers.

Market Research Corporation of America (MRCA) gathers information on consumer purchases of food and other household items from a panel of over 7,000 households throughout the United States. The panel (continuous sample) periodically gives MRCA a detailed list of all food and other household products purchased during a particular time. Viewed over a longer period of time, this information can be extremely useful in determining brand preferences, the effects of various promotional activities on retail sales in a particular region or among an age group, and the degree of brand switching that occurs with different products.

Planning Original Research: The Research Design

The use of secondary data offers two important advantages over the use of **primary data** *— data collected for the first time during a marketing research study:*

1. The assembly of previously collected data is almost always less expensive than the collection of primary data.
2. Less time is involved in locating and using secondary data.

The researcher must, however, be aware of two potential limitations to the use of secondary data: (1) that the data may be obsolete, and (2) that their classifications may not be usable in the study. Published information can quickly become obsolete. A marketing researcher analyzing the population of the Orlando, Florida, metropolitan market in early 1980 discovers that most of the 1970 census data are obsolete due to the influx of residents attracted by the development of Disney World.

Also, data may have been collected previously on the basis of county or city boundaries, but the marketing manager may require data broken down by city blocks or census tracts. In such cases, the marketing researcher may not be able to rearrange the secondary data in usable form and may have to begin collecting primary data.

Data collection should be preceded by a detailed **research design**— *"a series of advanced decisions that, taken together, comprise a master plan or model for the conduct of the investigation."*[10] By developing a comprehensive plan for performing the study, the researcher can control each step of

Table 3–9
Sixteen Steps in the Research Design

Questions Faced	Steps to Take or Choices
1. What is needed to measure the outcome of the alternative solutions?	1. Decide the subjects on which data are needed. 2. Examine the time and cost considerations.
2. What specific data are needed for that approach?	3. Write exact statements of data to be sought.
3. From whom are such data available?	4. Search and examine relevant secondary data. 5. Determine remaining data gaps.
4. How should primary data be obtained? 　a. What are the types of data? 　b. What general collection methods shall be used? 　c. How shall the sources be contacted? 　d. How may the data be secured from the sources? 　e. Shall there be a complete count of the population or a sample drawn from it? How chosen? 　f. How will the fieldwork be conducted?	6. Define the population from which primary data may be sought. 7. Determine the various needed facts, opinions, and motives. 8. Plan for obtaining data by survey, observational, or experimental methods. 9. If using a survey, decide whether to contact respondents by telephone, by mail, or in person. 10. Consider the questions and forms needed to elicit and record the data. 11. Decide on the coverage of the population: 　a. Choose between a complete enumeration or sampling. 　b. If sampling, decide whether to select from the whole population or restricted portions of it. 　c. Decide how to select sample members. 12. Map and schedule the fieldwork. 13. Plan the personnel requirements of the field study.
5. How will the data be interpreted and presented?	14. Consider editing and tabulating requirements. 15. Anticipate possible interpretation of the data. 16. Consider the way the findings may be presented.

Source: David J. Luck, Hugh G. Wales, and Donald Taylor, *Marketing Research*, 3rd ed., © 1970, p. 87. Adapted by permission of Prentice-Hall, Inc., Englewood Cliffs, New Jersey.

the investigation and avoid potential problems at its outset. Table 3–9 lists the steps involved in the research design.

Collecting Primary Data

As Table 3–9 indicates, the marketing researcher has three alternatives in the collection of primary data: observation, survey, or controlled experiment.

No single method is best in all circumstances, and any method may prove the most efficient in a particular situation.

The Observation Method. Observational studies are conducted by actually viewing the overt actions of the person being studied. They may take the form of a traffic count at a potential location for a fast-food franchise or a check of license plates at a shopping center to determine the area from which shoppers are attracted.

A. C. Nielsen's audimeter records the times television sets are turned on and the channels viewed. And in a famous study reported by Vance Packard, a special camera equipped with a telephoto lens recorded the number of consumer eye blinks per minute and, in some instances, allegedly indicated the mild hypnotic trance of a person "overcome" by the complexity of colors and packages on a supermarket shelf.[11]

How Nielsen Determines TV Viewership

The sample size is extremely small; the 1,200 Nielsen households represent a microscopic 0.00164 percent of the millions of homes with TVs. Yet the viewing habits of these persons determine the ratings of television network programs. And the ratings mean their success or cancellation.

More than that, high ratings mean more advertising dollars. A top-rated program like "Mork and Mindy" or "Laverne and Shirley" may charge $115,000 for a sixty-second commercial, while the lower ranked competing shows can ask only $85,000.

With so much at stake, it is not surprising that many persons in the entertainment industry criticize the rating system as inaccurately representing the viewing habits of 73 million U.S. households. But Nielsen executives argue forcefully that they have developed a representative sample. "We select the 1,200 homes based on the U.S. census data," explains Jerry Beman, Nielsen vice-president. "We lay a grid over the entire United States, analyzing the concentration of population and ending up with a scale model of the country. We eventually narrow down our selection to specific homes on specific blocks, and we approach the families. About 80 percent of them agree to cooperate. The entire selection process is very scientific and very expensive."

Each television receiver in the Nielsen households is attached to a recording device called an audimeter. This gadget is connected to the Nielsen computer with special telephone lines and produces a minute-by-minute record of the family's television viewing.

About 20 percent of the sample is changed each year. Five years is the maximum time permitted for participation, but moves reduce the average period to 3.5 years. Nielsen households receive an initial payment of $25, plus $1 a month and 50 percent of their television repair costs.

Nielsen representatives state that their ratings are accurate to within 1.7 percentage points. A program that, according to Nielsen, attracts 35 percent of the viewing audience could actually be attracting from 33.3 to 36.7 percent.

Source: Adapted by permission from Richard Trubo, "Who Really Runs TV? An Outfit Called Nielsen," *Detroit News,* March 12, 1978.

The Survey Method. Some information cannot be obtained through mere observation of overt consumer acts. The researcher must ask questions in order to obtain information on attitudes, motives, and opinions. The most widely used approach to collecting primary data is the survey method. Three kinds of surveys exist: telephone, mail, and personal interviews.

Telephone interviews are inexpensive and fast for obtaining small quantities of relatively impersonal information. Since many firms have leased WATS services (telephone company services that allow businesses to make unlimited long-distance calls for a fixed rate per state or region), a call to the farthest away state costs no more than an across-town interview.[12]

Telephone interviews account for an estimated 55 to 60 percent of all primary marketing research.[13] They are, however, limited to simple, clearly worded questions. They also have two other drawbacks. It is extremely difficult to obtain information on respondents' personal characteristics, and the survey may be prejudiced by the omission of households without phones and with unlisted numbers.

One survey reported that alphabetical listings in telephone directories excluded one-third of blacks with telephones and one-fourth of large-city dwellers and that they underrepresented service workers and separated and divorced persons. In addition, the mobility of the population creates problems in choosing names from telephone directories. As a result, a number of telephone interviewers have resorted to using digits selected at random and matched to telephone prefixes in the geographic area to be sampled. This technique is designed to correct the problem of sampling those with new telephone listings and those with unlisted numbers.[14]

Mail interviews allow the marketing researcher to conduct national studies at a reasonable cost. Whereas personal interviews with a national sample may be prohibitive in cost, the researcher can contact each potential respondent with the price of a postage stamp. Costs can be misleading, however. For example, returned questionnaires for such studies may average only 40 to 50 percent, depending on the length of the questionnaire and respondent interest. Also, some mail surveys include a coin to gain the reader's attention, which further increases costs.[15] Unless additional information is obtained from nonrespondents, the results of mail interviews are likely to be biased, since there may be important differences in the characteristics of respondents and nonrespondents. For this reason, follow-up questionnaires are sometimes mailed to nonrespondents, or telephone interviews are used to gather additional information.[16]

The Invisible-Ink Caper

"The Invisible-Ink Caper" was the name coined by the editor of the *National Observer* when he learned that a "confidential" eight-page survey mailed to three thousand of his newspaper's subscribers had been coded with invisible ink. The secret code was accidentally discovered by a Wisconsin subscriber who had put the questionnaire under ultraviolet light and had seen the code numbers pop into sight. The subscriber questioned the ethics of the practice in a letter to the *Observer* and asked for a public explanation of the procedure.

Editor Henry Gemmill learned that the invisible-ink code number on each questionnaire allowed the researchers to determine the name and address of each respondent. In a subsequent issue of the newspaper, Gemill wrote an editorial describing the incident and condemning it. He also printed a statement by the paper's general manager assuring readers it would not happen again.

The editorial reported that the use of secret coding was not uncommon. It named *Reader's Digest, Fortune, Business Week, Time,* and *Scientific American* as other publications using clandestine codes on their mail surveys. The marketing research director of *Newsweek* reported that the magazine had not used secret codes on questionnaires since 1969, when "we had a similar flap."

The leading book on mail surveys, *Professional Mail Surveys,* by Paul Erdos, mentions printing code numbers under the flap of the return envelope. Two other methods are putting the numbers under the postage stamp and cutting the paper in a certain way.

Why code mail questionnaires? A prime reason is cost. Coding allows the surveying company to determine by elimination who has not responded. Then, a second mailing can be made to those people—thereby eliminating the cost of sending unnecessary questionnaires and the annoyance to people who have already responded (as well as eliminating the possibility that respondents to the first mailing might complete the second questionnaire as well).

Some researchers print their codes in ink visible to everyone. Those who resort to secret codes, however, may find themselves facing federal prosecution. The FTC recently ruled that the use of such codes violates the Federal Trade Commission Act.[17]

Source: Most of this item is adapted with permission from Henry Gemmill, "The Invisible-Ink Caper," *National Observer,* November 1, 1975, p. 22. © Dow Jones & Company, Inc., 1975. All rights reserved.

Personal interviews are typically the best means of obtaining detailed information, since the interviewer has the opportunity to establish rapport with each respondent and can explain confusing or vague questions. Although mail questionnaires are carefully worded and often pretested to eliminate potential misunderstandings, such misunderstandings can occur anyway. When an employee of the U.S. Department of Agriculture accidentally ran into and killed a cow with his truck, an official of the department sent the farmer an apology and a form to be filled out. The form included a space for "disposition of the dead cow." The farmer responded, "Kind and gentle."[18]

Personal interviews are slow and are the most expensive method of collecting survey data. However, their flexibility coupled with the detailed information that can be collected often offset these limitations. The refusal to be interviewed and the increasing difficulty of hiring interviewers to call on respondents at night present problems in utilizing this technique.

Focus Group Interviews. Personal interviews are sometimes conducted on a group basis. Focus group interviews have been widely used in recent years as a means of gathering research information. In a **focus group interview,** *eight to twelve individuals are brought together in one location to discuss a subject of interest.* While the moderator typically explains the purpose of the meeting and suggests an opening discussion topic, he or she is interested in stimulating interaction among group members in order to develop the discussion of numerous points about the subject. Focus group sessions, which are often one to two hours long, are usually taped so the moderator can devote full attention to the discussion.[19]

Information is rarely gathered from all sources during a survey. If all sources are contacted, the results are known as a *census.* But unless the number of sources is small, the costs will be so great that only the federal government will be able to afford them—and it uses this method only once every ten years. Instead, researchers select a representative group called a sample. If this sample is chosen in such a way that every member has an equal chance of being selected, then the sample is a *simple random sample.* A simple random sample of students at Florida International University in Miami can be drawn by obtaining a list of names from the college registrar and assigning each a number, then selecting numbers on the list from a table of random numbers and questioning those selected.

A method of obtaining a random sample where population lists are unavailable is *area sampling.* Here, blocks instead of individuals are selected at random for the survey. Then, either everyone on the selected blocks is interviewed or respondents are randomly chosen from each designated block.

The Experimental Method. The final and least used method of collecting marketing information is that of *controlled experiments.* To date, the most common use of this method has been in test marketing.

Marketers face great risk in their efforts to gain acceptance for new

Personal interviewing is a major method of collecting survey data.

Source: *Detroit News,* October 17, 1978. © 1978 The Detroit News. Reprinted by permission.

products. They often attempt to reduce this risk by *test marketing*—introducing the product into a particular metropolitan area and then observing its degree of success. Frequently used cities include Columbus, Ohio; Peoria; Des Moines; and Phoenix. Consumers in the test market city view the product as any other new product since it is available in retail outlets and advertised in the local media. The test market city becomes a small-scale replica of the total market.

The marketing manager then compares actual sales with expected sales and projects the figures on a nationwide basis. If the test results are favorable, the risk of a large-scale failure is reduced. Many products fail at the test market stage; thus consumers who live in these cities may purchase products that no one else will ever buy.

The major problem with controlled experiments is that of controlling all variables in a real-life situation. The laboratory scientist can rigidly control temperature and humidity. But how can the marketing manager determine the effect of, say, varying the retail price through refundable coupons when the competition simultaneously issues such coupons?

Experimentation in this area will become more common as firms develop sophisticated competitive models for computer analysis. Simulation of market activities promises to be one of the great new developments in marketing.[20]

Interpretation of Research Findings

A number of marketing research books contain solutions to the many problems involved in surveying the public.[21] Among these problems are designing the questionnaires; selecting, training, and controlling the field interviewers; editing, coding, tabulating, and interpreting the data; presenting the results; and following up the survey.

It is crucial that marketing researchers and research users cooperate at every stage in the research design. Too many studies go unused because marketing management views the results as too restricted due to the lengthy discussion of research limitations or the use of unfamiliar terminology such as "levels of confidence" and "Type 1 errors."[22] Recommendations should always be included in the written report; and, where possible, an oral report should explain, expand on, or clarify the written one. This effort increases the possibility of management's positive use of the study.

Using Outside Research Agencies

While most large companies have their own marketing research departments, many smaller ones depend on independent marketing research firms to conduct their research studies. Even the largest firms typically rely on outside agencies to provide interviewers, and they often farm out some research studies to independent agencies. The decision on whether to conduct a study through an outside organization or internally is usually based on cost. Another consideration is the reliability and accuracy of the information collected by the outside agency.

Research is likely to be contracted to outside groups when the following requirements are met:

1. Problem areas can be defined in terms of specific research projects.
2. There is need for specialized know-how or equipment.
3. Intellectual detachment is necessary.[23]

For example, in-depth study of consumer motivations in the purchase of the firm's products may require the use of trained psychologists and of expertise not available within the firm. Also, the use of outside groups help ensure that the researcher is not conducting the study only to "prove" the wisdom of a favorite theory or package design. The most recent survey of marketing research by the American Marketing Association revealed that almost 50 percent of the responding firms' total marketing research budgets was spent for outside research.[24]

Marketing Information Systems: A New Era in Information Management	Many marketing managers discover that their information problems result from an overabundance—not a paucity—of marketing data. Their sophisticated computer facilities may provide them daily with printouts about sales in 30 market areas, about 100 different products, and about 6,400 customers. Managers sometimes solve the problem of too much information of the wrong kind in the wrong form by sliding the stack of printouts to the edge of the desk, where it quietly falls into the wastebasket. *Data* and *information* are not necessarily synonymous.

Obtaining *relevant* information appears simple enough. One can establish a systematic approach to information management by installing a planned marketing information system (MIS). Creating an effective MIS is, however, much easier said than done. A large number of firms have attempted to develop an MIS but have succeeded only in increasing the amount of irrelevant data.

The ideal **marketing information system** should be *a designed set of procedures and methods for generating an orderly flow of pertinent information for use in making decisions, providing management with the current and future states of the market, and indicating market responses to company and competitor actions.*[25]

A properly constructed MIS can serve as the nerve center for the company, providing instantaneous information suitable for each level of management. It can act as a thermostat, monitoring the marketplace continuously so that management can adjust its actions as conditions change.

The role of marketing information in a firm's marketing system can be illustrated with the analogy of how an automatic heating system works (see

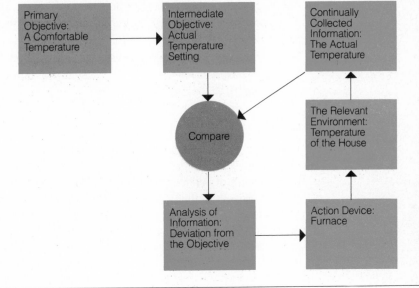

Source: Reprinted by permission from Bertram Schoner and Kenneth P. Uhl, *Marketing Research: Information Systems and Decision Making* (New York: Wiley, 1975), p. 10.

Figure 3–4). Once the objective of a particular temperature setting (say 68 degrees Fahrenheit) has been established, information about the actual temperature is collected and compared with the objective, and a decision based on this comparison is made. If the temperature drops below the established figure, the decision is to activate the furnace until the temperature reaches the established level. If the temperature is too high, the decision is to turn off the furnace.

Deviation from the firm's goals of profitability, improved return on investment, or greater market share may necessitate changes in price structures, promotional expenditures, package design, or other marketing alternatives. The firm's MIS should be capable of revealing such deviations and of suggesting changes that will result in attaining the established goals.

Marketing
Research and the
Marketing
Information System

Many marketing executives feel that their company does not need a marketing information system. Two arguments are most often given:

1. The size of the company operations does not warrant such a complete system.
2. The information provided by an MIS is already being supplied by the marketing research department.

These contentions arise from a misconception of the services and functions performed by the marketing research department. Marketing research has already been described as typically focusing on a specific problem or project; its investigations have a definite beginning, middle, and end.

Marketing information systems, on the other hand, are much wider in scope, involving the continual collection and analysis of marketing information. Figure 3–5 indicates the various information inputs—including marketing research studies—that serve as components of a firm's MIS.

Robert J. Williams, creator of the first marketing information system, explains the difference:

The difference between marketing research and marketing intelligence is like the difference between a flash bulb and a candle. Let's say you are dancing in the dark. Every 90 seconds you're allowed to set off a flash bulb. You can use those brief intervals of intense light to chart a course, but remember everybody is moving, too. Hopefully, they'll accommodate themselves roughly to your predictions. You may get bumped and you may stumble every so often, but you can dance along.

On the other hand, you can light a candle. It doesn't yield as much light, but it's a steady light. You are continually aware of the movements of other bodies. You can adjust your own course to the courses of the others. The intelligence system is a kind of candle. It's no great flash on the immediate state of things, but it provides continuous light as situations shift and change.[26]

Figure 3–5
Information Components of the Firm's Marketing Information System

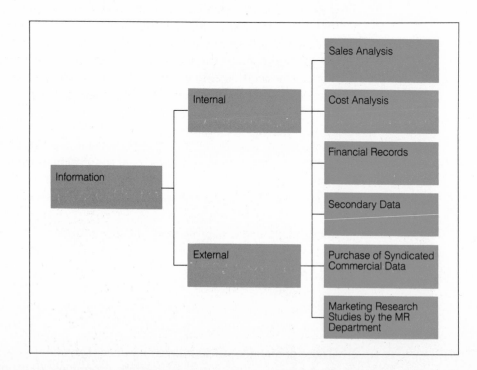

By focusing daily on the marketplace, the MIS provides a continuous systematic and comprehensive study of areas that indicate deviations from established goals. The up-to-the-minute data allow problems to be corrected before they adversely affect company operations.

Current Status of Marketing Information Systems

Marketing information systems have progressed a long way from the days when they were primarily responsible for clerical activities—and usually at an increased cost over the old method. Today, managers have available special computer programs, remote access consoles, better data banks, direct communication with the computer, and assignment of authority to the computer for review and referral. In some instances, the computer simulates market conditions and makes decisions based on the results of the model. But how does the marketer's information system relate to similar systems for decision makers in other functional areas?

Marketing information systems are major components of the firm's overall management information system—the information base for decision making in all functional areas. A recent survey of the 500 largest firms in the United States focused on the allocation of overall management information resources to each of the functional areas. A total of 202 responding companies indicated the approximate percentage of their total information system resources—including hardware, software, facilities, and personnel—allocated to four organizational functions: administration, finance, marketing, and production. Figure 3–6 shows their responses and their predictions of relative allocations for the next five years.

Although production and finance currently receive most of the management information system's resources, additional resources are expected to be devoted to marketing during the next five years.

Marketing research studies are important components of the total marketing information system.

"Hi, there."

Source: *Advertising Age*, December 26, 1977, p. 12. Reprinted with permission from the December 26, 1977, issue of *Advertising Age*. Copyright 1977 by Crain Communications, Inc.

**Figure 3–6
Current and
Future Allocation
of MIS Resources**

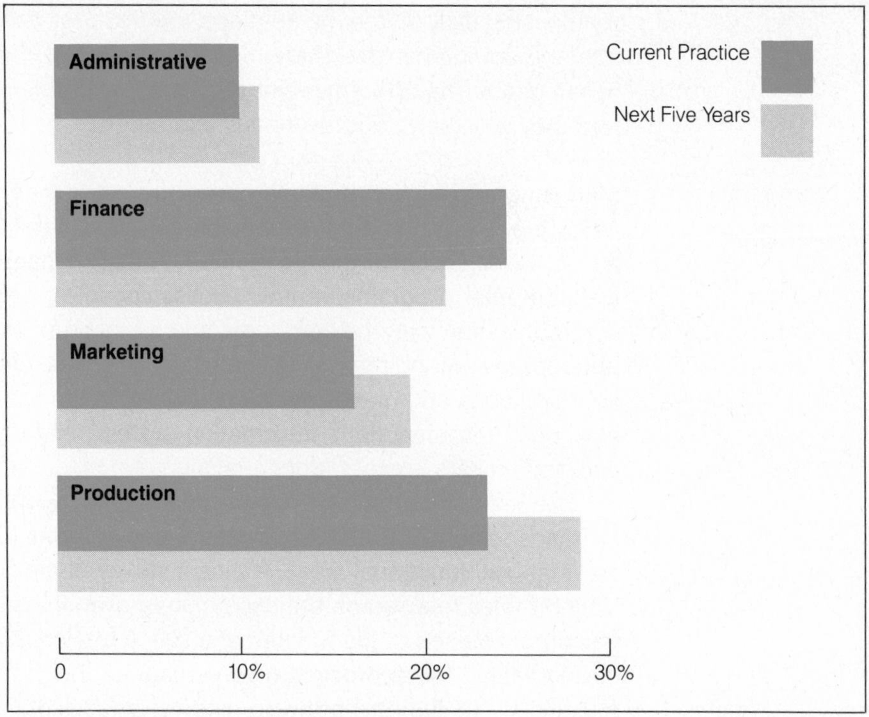

Source: Louis E. Boone and C. Richard Roberts, "MIS Development in American Industry: The Apex," unpublished working paper. © 1979; all rights reserved.

Two Examples of
Successful
Marketing
Information
Systems

Although only a few large companies currently have sophisticated computer-based marketing information systems, considerable attention is being focused on their contributions. By the end of the decade, most medium-sized companies will have established their own information systems.

Monsanto

Monsanto has designed one of the most advanced marketing information systems in operation. The system provides detailed sales analyses by product, sales district, type of mill, and end use. Consumer analyses are obtained from a continuing panel of 7,500 households representing a cross section of the national market. Information on purchase patterns by socioeconomic group is collected and analyzed to determine current buying trends.

Monsanto also collects survey data on the actions of competitors. In addition, its system generates short-, medium-, and long-range forecasts for the company and its industry. Short-term forecasts are developed for each of 400 products.

Monsanto and General Mills are two firms with a successful MIS in operation.

While the marketing information system is considered one part of the

Figure 3–7
The Marketing Information System at Mead Johnson

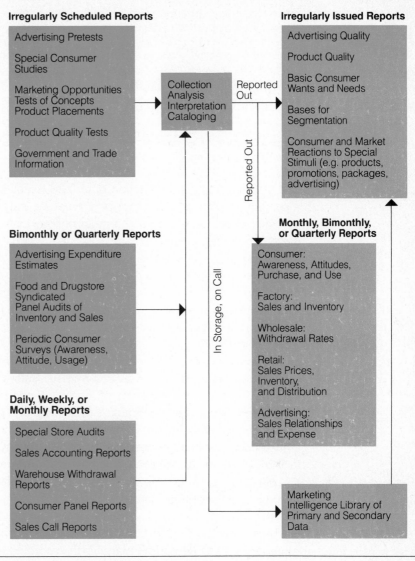

Irregularly Scheduled Reports
Advertising Pretests

Special Consumer Studies

Marketing Opportunities Tests of Concepts Product Placements

Product Quality Tests

Government and Trade Information

Bimonthly or Quarterly Reports
Advertising Expenditure Estimates

Food and Drugstore Syndicated Panel Audits of Inventory and Sales

Periodic Consumer Surveys (Awareness, Attitude, Usage)

Daily, Weekly, or Monthly Reports
Special Store Audits

Sales Accounting Reports

Warehouse Withdrawal Reports

Consumer Panel Reports

Sales Call Reports

Collection Analysis Interpretation Cataloging

Reported Out

Reported Out

In Storage, on Call

Irregularly Issued Reports
Advertising Quality

Product Quality

Basic Consumer Wants and Needs

Bases for Segmentation

Consumer and Market Reactions to Special Stimuli (e.g. products, promotions, packages, advertising)

Monthly, Bimonthly, or Quarterly Reports
Consumer: Awareness, Attitudes, Purchase, and Use

Factory: Sales and Inventory

Wholesale: Withdrawal Rates

Retail: Sales Prices, Inventory, and Distribution

Advertising: Sales Relationships and Expense

Marketing Intelligence Library of Primary and Secondary Data

Source: Lee Adler, "Systems Approach to Marketing," *Harvard Business Review,* May–June 1967, p. 11. Copyright © 1967 by the President and Fellows of Harvard College; all rights reserved.

overall information system, it must be carefully developed with inputs from users if it is to serve company decision makers. Figure 3–7, which depicts the components of Mead Johnson and Company's marketing information system, is a good illustration of decision information provided by a successful MIS.

General Mills

The General Mills computer supplies each zone, regional, and district manager with a daily teletype report on (1) the previous day's orders by brand and (2) current projections of monthly sales compared with the monthly total projected the week before. Each of 1,700 products is analyzed in terms of current profitability and projected annual profitability as compared with target projections made at the beginning of the year. "Problem" products requiring management attention are also listed in the daily report. A similar report looks for problem areas in each region and breaks down each problem by cause.

Sources: Information from "Marketing Management and the Computer," *Sales Management,* August 20, 1965, pp. 49–60. See also Leon Winer, "Effective Computer Use in Marketing Information Systems and Model Building," *Marketing: 1776–1976 and Beyond,* ed. Kenneth L. Bernhardt (Chicago: American Marketing Association, 1976), pp. 626–629.

Constructing an MIS

The first step in the construction of an MIS is obtaining the support of top management. Management not only must be truly enthusiastic about the potential of the system but also must believe that it is top management's place to oversee its development. Too often, technical staffs are left to build the system.

The next step involves a review and appraisal of the entire marketing organization and of the policies that direct it. The marketing managers' responsibilities must be clearly defined. If the system is to measure their performance against company plans, then each person's areas of accountability must be specified.

Once the organization is readied for the development of the system, its level of sophistication must be determined. Before this can be done, the company's needs and the costs of meeting those needs must be carefully considered. The ability of managers to develop and effectively use a sophisticated system must also be considered. Managers must be able to state their specific information needs. A questionnaire such as the one illustrated in Table 3–10 can be used to pinpoint specific information requirements.

Management must also be able to state explicitly its planning, decision-making, and control processes and procedures. An automated exception reporting system can be developed for the manager who states: "I always like to know about all situations in which sales, profits or market shares are running 4% or more behind plan. Furthermore, in any exceptional cases I also require the following diagnostic information: prices, distribution levels, advertising and consumer attitudes."[27]

Sales Forecasting

A vital form of marketing information is the **sales forecast**—*the estimate of company sales for a specified future period.* In addition to its use in marketing planning, the sales forecast also plays a critical role in production scheduling, financial planning, inventory planning, and procurement and in the determination of personnel needs. An inaccurate forecast will result in incorrect decisions in each of these areas.

Table 3–10
Sample Questionnaire for Determining Marketing Information Needs

1. What types of decisions are you regularly called upon to make?
2. What types of information do you need to make the decision?
3. What types of information do you regularly get?
4. What types of special studies do you periodically request?
5. What types of information would you like to get but are not currently receiving?
6. What information would you like to receive daily? weekly? monthly? yearly?
7. What magazines and trade journals would you like to receive regularly?
8. What types of data analysis programs would you like to receive?
9. What are four improvements you would like to see made in the present marketing information system?

Source: Philip Kotler, "A Design for the Firm's Marketing Nerve Center," *Business Horizons,* Fall 1966, p. 70. Copyright 1966 by the Foundation for the School of Business at Indiana University. Reprinted by permission.

The sales forecast is also an important tool for marketing control because it produces *standards* against which actual performance can be measured. Without such standards, no comparisons can be made; if there exists no criterion of success, there is also no definition of failure.

Sales forecasts are either short-run or long-run. Short-run forecasts usually include a period of up to one year, while long-run forecasts typically cover a longer period. Since both forecasts are developed in basically the same manner, and since more firms forecast sales for the coming year, short-run forecasting will be discussed here.

Steps in Sales Forecasting

Although sales forecasting methods vary, the most typical method begins with a forecast of general economic conditions and uses it to forecast industry sales and then to develop a forecast of company and product sales. This approach is termed the *top-down method.*[28]

Forecasting General Economic Conditions. The most common measure of economic output is *gross national product (GNP),* the market value of all final products produced in a country in a given year. Trend extension is the most frequently used method of forecasting increases in GNP. As Figure 3–8 shows, past data are plotted on a scatter diagram, and a trend line is drawn through the scattered points to produce the point where next year's expected GNP will be located. The trend line is usually developed by a statistical technique called the *least squares method.* This method utilizes a mathematical formula to plot a line in such a manner that the sum of the squared distances from each of the points on the diagram to the line is at a minimum.[29]

Input-Output Models as Aids in Economic Forecasting. During periods of steady growth, the trend extension method of forecasting produces satisfactory results. But it implicitly assumes that the factors contributing to the attainment of a certain level of output in the past will continue to operate in the same manner in the future. When conditions change, the trend ex-

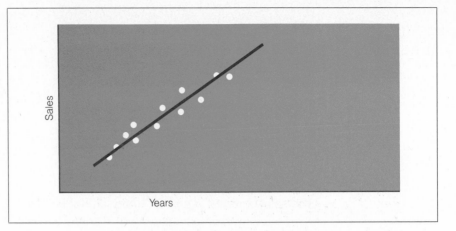

tension method often produces incorrect results. For this reason, forecast-ers are increasingly utilizing more sophisticated techniques and more complex mathematical models.

Input-output models, which depict the interactions of various industries in producing goods, are being developed by the U.S. Department of Com-merce and by private agencies. Since *outputs* (sales) of one industry are the *inputs* (purchases) of another, a change of outputs in one industry affects the inputs of other industries. Input-output models show the impact on sup-plier industries of increased production in a given industry and can be used to measure the impact of increased demand in any industry throughout the economy.

Since many federal agencies and other organizations develop regular forecasts of the GNP, a firm may choose to use their estimates. These fore-casts are regularly reported in such publications as the *Wall Street Journal* and *Business Week.*

Developing the Industry Sales Forecast. Once the economic forecast has been developed, the next step is developing an industry sales forecast. Since industry sales may be related to GNP or some other measure of the national economy, a forecast may begin by measuring the degree of this relationship and then applying the trend extension method to forecasting industry sales. More sophisticated techniques, such as input-output analy-sis or multiple regression analysis, may also be used.

Forecasting Company and Product Sales. Once the industry forecast has been done, the company and product forecasts are developed. They begin with a detailed sales analysis from company records for previous years. The firm's past and present market shares are reviewed, and product managers and regional and district sales managers are consulted about expected sales. Since an accelerated promotional budget or the introduction of new products may stimulate additional demand, the marketing plan for the coming year is also considered.

Like the sales analysis, the product and company forecast must evaluate many aspects of company sales: sales of each product; future trends; sales by customer, territory, salesperson, and order size; financial arrangements; and other aspects. Once a preliminary sales forecast has been developed, it is reviewed by the sales force and by the district, regional, and national sales managers.

New Product Sales Forecasting: A Difficult Assignment. Forecasting sales for new products is an especially hazardous undertaking, since no historical data are available. Companies typically employ consumer panels to obtain reactions to the products and probable purchase behavior. Test market data are also utilized.

Since few products are totally new, forecasters carefully analyze the sales of competing products that may be displaced by the new entry. A new type of fishing reel will compete in an established market with other reels. This *substitute method* provides the forecaster with an estimate of the size of the market and potential demand.

Summary

Information is vital for marketing decision making. No firm can operate without detailed information of its market. Information may take several forms: one-time marketing research studies, secondary data, internal sales and marketing cost analyses, and subscriptions to commercial information sources.

Marketing research, an important source of decision information, is defined as the systematic gathering, recording, and analyzing of data about marketing problems and opportunities. It involves the specific delineation of problems, research design, collection of secondary and primary data, interpretation of research findings, and presentation of results for use by management in decision making.

Sales forecasts are developed to help plan and control marketing, production, and financial operations. The most common approach to sales forecasting is to begin with a forecast of the national economy and use it to develop an industry sales forecast. That forecast is then used in developing a company and product forecast.

The scope of marketing information has broadened as an increasing number of firms have installed planned marketing information systems. Properly designed, the MIS will generate an orderly flow of decision oriented information as the marketing executive needs it. The number of firms with planned information systems will grow during the 1980s as more managers recognize their contribution to dealing with the information explosion.

Questions for Discussion

1. Explain the following terms:

    marketing research
    exploratory research
    sales analysis
    sales quota
    marketing cost analysis
    secondary data
    primary data
    research design
    focus group interview
    marketing information system (MIS)
    sales forecast

2. You have been asked to determine the effect on Gillette of Schick's introduction of a revolutionary new blade that is guaranteed to give a hundred nick-free shaves. Outline your approach to the study.

3. Suggest some useful breakdowns of sales analysis development for the following companies:
    a. a medium-sized company using catalogs to market its product lines
    b. an industrial firm operating throughout the United States and in twelve foreign countries
    c. a company that uses telephone solicitations, personal sales calls, and direct mail advertising to market a new type of liability insurance to individuals and small businesses
    d. a firm whose geographically dispersed sales force markets high-priced consumer products to young married couples and single-person households

4. Explain the iceberg principle as it relates to marketing decision making.

5. What advantages does the use of secondary data offer the marketing researcher? What potential limitations exist in using such data?

6. What type of marketing information can be obtained from the metropolitan chamber of commerce in your city (or a nearby city)?

7. Collect from secondary sources the following information:
    a. retail sales in El Paso, Texas, for last year
    b. number of persons over sixty-five in Buffalo, New York
    c. earnings per share for IBM last year
    d. bituminous coal production in the United States in a recent year
    e. consumer price index for a given month
    f. number of households earning more than $15,000 in Orlando, Florida

8. Distinguish among surveys, experiments, and observational methods of data collection.

9. Suggest several instances where an area sample rather than a simple random sample might be used in gathering primary data.

10. Illustrate each of the three methods for gathering survey data. Under what circumstances should each be used?

11. Under what circumstances would area sampling techniques be used?

12. What are the chief problems in using telephone interviews?

13. Why do marketing researchers sometimes resort to secretly coding mail questionnaires? What ethical issues are involved?

14. Under what circumstances should a firm use an outside marketing research firm to conduct research studies?

15. Frank Antonelli, the marketing vice-president of the Digital Time Company, refuses to involve himself with the activities of his marketing research staff. He explains that he has hired competent professionals for the research department, and he does not plan to meddle in their operation. Critically evaluate Antonelli's position.

16. Distinguish between marketing research and marketing information systems.

17. Explain the relationship between marketing information and the thermostat of a heating system.

18. A business executive has asked your assistance in setting up a new MIS for her firm. Describe how you would proceed with this task.

19. Discuss the advantages and shortcomings of basing sales forecasts on estimates developed exclusively by the company's sales force.

20. Assume that growth in industry sales will remain constant for the coming year. Forecast company sales for the coming year based on the following data:

Year	Sales
1	$1,600,000
2	1,750,000
3	1,700,000
4	1,900,000
5	2,900,000

What assumptions have you made in developing your forecast?

Notes

1. "Marketing-Oriented Lever Uses Research to Capture Bigger Dentifrice Market Shares," *Marketing News,* February 10, 1978, p. 9.
2. Committee on Definitions, *Marketing Definitions: A Glossary of Marketing Terms* (Chicago: American Marketing Association, 1960), p. 17.
3. For a detailed treatment of the historical development of marketing research, see Robert Bartels, *The Development of Marketing Thought* (Homewood, Ill.: Richard D. Irwin, 1962), pp. 106–124.
4. Dik Warren Twedt, ed., *1978 Survey of Marketing Research* (Chicago: American Marketing Association, 1978), pp. 10–13. See also Venkatakrishna V. Bellur, "Annual Expenditures and Types and Uses of Research by Firms Involved in Marketing Research," in *Proceedings of the Southern Marketing Association,* ed. Robert S. Franz, Robert M. Hopkins, and Al Toma, New Orleans, Louisiana, November 1978, pp. 459–462; and Yoram Wind and Daniel Gross, "Determination of the Size and Allocation of Marketing Research Budgets," in *Research Frontiers in Marketing,* ed. Subhash C. Jain (Chicago: American Marketing Association, 1978), pp. 57–61.
5. For a detailed treatment of sales analysis, see Charles Sevin, *Marketing Productivity Analysis* (New York: McGraw-Hill, 1965).
6. See Patrick M. Dunne and Harry I. Wolk, "Marketing Cost Analysis: A Modularized Contribution Approach," *Journal of Marketing,* July 1977, pp. 83–94.
7. C. R. Goeldner and Laura M. Dirks, "Business Facts: Where to Find Them," *MSU Business Topics,* Summer 1976, pp. 23–36.
8. See Manuel D. Plotkin, "Uses of Census Retail Sales Data for More Effective Marketing," *Atlanta Economic Review,* September–October 1976, pp. 3–8.
9. See Charles Waldo and Dennis Fuller, "Just How Good Is the 'Survey of Buying Power'?" *Journal of Marketing,* October 1977, pp. 64–66.
10. Robert Ferber et al., "The Design of Research Investigations," *Marketing Research Series,* no. 1 (Chicago: American Marketing Association, 1958), p. 5.
11. Vance Packard, *The Hidden Persuaders* (New York: David McKay, 1957).
12. See E. Laird Landon, Jr., and Sharon K. Banks, "Relative Efficiency and Bias of Plus-One Telephone Sampling," *Journal of Marketing Research,* August 1977, pp. 294–299.
13. "Many Researchers Prefer Interviewing by Phone," *Marketing News,* July 14, 1978, p. 8.
14. Reported in A. B. Blankenship, "Listed versus Unlisted Numbers in Telephone-Survey Samples," *Journal of Advertising Research,* February 1977, pp. 39–42. See also Roger Gates, Bob Brobst, and Paul Solomon, "Random Digit Dialing: A Review of Methods," in *Proceedings of the Southern Marketing Association,* New Orleans, Louisiana, November 1978, pp. 163–165; and Donald S. Tull and Gerald S. Albaum, "Bias in Random Digit Dialed Surveys," *Public Opinion Quarterly,* Fall 1977, pp. 389–395.
15. See James R. Harris and Hugh J. Guffey, Jr., "Questionnaire Returns: Stamps versus Business Reply Envelopes Revisited," *Journal of Marketing Research,* May 1978, pp. 290–293; Wesley H. Jones and Gerald Linda, "Multiple Criteria Effects in a Mail Survey Experiment," *Journal of Marketing Research,* May 1978, pp. 280–284; Thomas Vocino, "Three Variables in Stimulating Responses to Mailed Questionnaires," *Journal of Marketing,* October 1977, pp. 76–77; and John O. King and Donald D. Wilson, Jr., "The Influence of Personalization on Mail Survey Response Rates," *Arkansas Business & Economic Review,* Winter 1978, pp. 15–18.

16. See Marvin A. Jolson, "How to Double or Triple Mail-Survey Response Rates," *Journal of Marketing,* October 1977, pp. 78–81; Bruce J. Walker and Richard K. Burdick, "Advance Correspondence and Error in Mail Surveys," *Journal of Marketing Research,* August 1977, pp. 379–382; and Bruce Seaton and Ronald H. Vogel, "Language Effects on Response Rates to a Mail Questionnaire," in *Proceedings of the Southern Marketing Association,* November 1978, pp. 456–458.

17. "News Lines," *U.S. News & World Report,* October 9, 1978, p. 89.

18. "About That Cow," *Wall Street Journal,* June 28, 1972, p.1.

19. See Fred D. Reynolds and Deborah K. Johnson, "Validity of Focus-Group Findings," *Journal of Advertising Research,* June 1978, pp. 21–24; and Bobby J. Calder, "Focus Groups and the Nature of Qualitative Marketing Research," *Journal of Marketing Research,* August 1977, pp. 353–364.

20. See John R. Nevin, "Using Experimental Data to Suggest and Evaluate Alternative Marketing Strategies," in *Research Frontiers in Marketing*, ed. Subhash C. Jain (Chicago: American Marketing Association, 1978), pp. 207–211; and Chem L. Narayana and James F. Horrell, "Evaluation of Quality Factors in Marketing Experiments," *Journal of the Academy of Marketing Science,* Summer 1976, pp. 599–607.

21. Two excellent marketing research texts are Gilbert A. Churchill, Jr., *Marketing Research*, 2d ed. (Hinsdale, Ill.: Dryden Press, 1979); and Paul E. Green and Donald S. Tull, *Research for Marketing Decisions* (Englewood Cliffs, N.J.: Prentice-Hall, 1978).

22. See, for example, Jeffrey Gandz and Thomas W. Whipple, "Making Marketing Research Accountable," *Journal of Marketing Research,* May 1977, pp. 202–208; and Dwight L. Gentry and John Hoftyzer, "The Misuse of Statistical Techniques in Evaluating Sample Data," *Journal of the Academy of Marketing Science,* Spring 1977, pp. 106–112.

23. Bertram Schoner and Kenneth P. Uhl, *Marketing Research: Information Systems and Decision Making* (New York: Wiley, 1975), p. 199.

24. Twedt, *1978 Survey of Marketing Research,* p. 38.

25 Donald F. Cox and Robert E. Good, "How to Build a Marketing Information System," *Harvard Business Review,* May–June 1967, p. 147. See also Charles D. Schewe and William R. Dillon, "Marketing Information Systems Utilization: An Application of Self-concept Theory," *Journal of Business Research,* January 1978, pp. 67–79.

26. "Marketing Intelligence Systems: A DEW Line for Marketing Men," *Business Management,* January 1966, p.32.

27. Cox and Good, "How to Build a Marketing Information System," p. 152.

28. For an excellent short book on sales forecasting, see Roger K. Chisholm and Gilbert R. Whitaker, *Forecasting Methods* (Homewood, Ill.: Richard D. Irwin, 1971). See also Spyros Makridakis and Steven C. Wheelwright, "Forecasting: Issues and Challenges for Marketing Management," *Journal of Marketing,* October 1977, pp. 24–38.

29. For a thorough discussion of this technique and illustrations of its use, see Ya-lun Chou, *Probability and Statistics for Decision Making* (New York: Holt, Rinehart and Winston, 1972), chap. 8.

CHAPTER 4
IDENTIFYING MARKET TARGETS FOR CONSUMER AND INDUSTRIAL GOODS

Key Terms

market
consumer goods
industrial goods
market segmentation
Standard
Metropolitan
Statistical Area
(SMSA)
Standard
Consolidated
Statistical Area
(SCSA)

family life cycle
Engel's laws
Standard Industrial
Classification (SIC)
reciprocity

Learning Goals

1. To identify the four requirements that must be present in order for a market to exist.
2. To distinguish between consumer and industrial goods.
3. To identify the major recent population shifts and the age groups that will grow fastest during the 1980s.
4. To explain the use of the family life cycle in analyzing markets.
5. To show how market target decision analysis can be used in identifying specific market targets.

4

Successful marketers recognize the need to understand the characteristics of their market. Changes in these characteristics typically result in adjustments to marketing programs. The Chesapeake & Potomac Telephone Company makes careful projections of new household formations. One reason for doing this is that areas with large numbers of mobile young people may require more phone installers than do other areas. Westinghouse Health Systems, a division of Westinghose Electric Corporation, studies population trends to determine the demand for school buildings and hospitals. In the face of static enrollments, colleges and universities pay close attention to the age composition of the population. The increase in the number of working wives has resulted in shifts in retail store hours to accommodate after-work and weekend shopping.[1]

Marketing managers have two important tasks:

1. They must identify, evaluate, and select a *market target.*
2. They must develop and implement a *marketing mix* that satisfies the chosen market target.

There is no such thing as a single national market. In the United States, as in the rest of the world, literally hundreds of small market segments comprise the market arena. Before marketers can evolve effective strategies, they must pinpoint their market. Selection of this market target results from a careful analysis of the total market.

Once the market target has been chosen, the marketing manager develops the proper mix to satisfy it. The ingredients of this mix—product planning, appropriate marketing channels, promotional decisions, and pricing policies—are the subjects of Chapters 6 through 17. A number of environmental factors, discussed in Chapter 2, may also affect marketing decisions and must therefore be evaluated when such decisions are made. The subject of this chapter and the following one is the focal point of all marketing efforts—*the consumer.*

What Is a Market?   A market is people—but people alone do not make a market. The local car dealer is unimpressed by news that 60 percent of the marketing class raise their hands in response to the question: "Who wants to buy a new Pontiac Trans Am?" The next question is: "How many of them were waving green dollar bills in their outstretched hands?" A **market** *requires not only people and willingness to buy but also purchasing power and authority to buy.*

One of the first rules a successful salesperson learns is to determine who in an organization or household has the authority to make particular purchasing decisions. Without this knowledge, too much time can be spent convincing the wrong person that the product should be bought. A solitary male in a busy carpet store may be virtually ignored by the salespeople, who are aware that carpet purchases are typically made by the husband and wife together.

Differences between Consumer and Industrial Markets

Products are often classified as either consumer or industrial goods. **Consumer goods** are *products purchased by the ultimate consumer for personal use.* **Industrial goods** are *products purchased for use either directly or indirectly in the production of other goods for resale.* Most products bought by individual consumers—books, records, and clothes, for example—are consumer goods. Raw cotton and rubber, however, are generally purchased by manufacturers and are therefore considered industrial goods. Raw cotton will be made into cloth by, say, Burlington Industries, and rubber will be used in many products by B. F. Goodrich.

Sometimes the same product is destined for different uses. A set of tires purchased by a neighbor for her car is a consumer good. But a set of tires

Authority to buy is often shared by household members.

"I'm sorry, sir, but we don't sell wallpaper to gentlemen not accompanied by their wives."

Source: *Wall Street Journal,* September 6, 1978, p. 20. Reprinted by permission of the cartoonist, Leo Garel, and the *Wall Street Journal.*

purchased by American Motors for use on its Jeep is an industrial good, since it becomes part of another good destined for resale. Similarly, a typewriter purchased for a college student's Christmas present is a consumer good; the same typewriter purchased for use in a company's order processing department is an industrial good.* The key to proper classification of goods is the *determination of the purchaser* and the *reasons for the purchase.*

Segmenting Markets

The world is too large and filled with too many diverse people for any marketing mix to satisfy everyone. Unless the product is something aimed at the mass market—such as toothpaste, detergent, or deodorant—an attempt to satisfy everyone may doom a company to failure. (Indeed, even toothpastes are aimed at specific market segments. Stripe was developed for children, Crest focuses on tooth decay prevention, and Ultra Brite hints at enhanced sex appeal.)

The auto manufacturer that decides to produce and market one automobile to satisfy everyone will quickly encounter seemingly endless decisions to be made about color, styling, and engine size, for example. In its attempt to satisfy everyone, the firm may be forced to compromise in each of these areas and, as a result, may discover that it does not satisfy anyone *very well.* Other firms appealing to particular market segments—the youth market, the second car market, and others—may capture most of the car buying market by satisfying the needs of smaller, more homogeneous market targets. The *process of dividing the total market into several homogeneous groups* is called **market segmentation.**[2] Figure 4–1 shows several potential bases for this segmentation.

Consumer Goods Market

Four years ago, the world population passed the 4 billion mark. Only fifteen years had passed since the 3 billion mark had been reached in 1961. It took thirty-one years to reach 3 billion and over three hundred years to reach 2 billion. In contrast, forecasters predict the world population will reach 5 billion in 1989—just thirteen years after the 4 billion mark was reached.

The United States has attained one of the highest standards of living in the history of the world, but its population size is insignificant when compared with the rest of the world. Figure 4–2 shows how the United States is dwarfed by the tremendous populations of countries such as India and China. While fully one-fifth of the world's population lives in China, less than 6 percent resides in the United States.

But the choice of a successful market target requires *income* as well as *people.* With its very small percentage of the world population, the United

---

*Some marketers use the term *commercial good* to refer to industrial goods not directly used in producing other goods.

Figure 4-1
A Graphic Picture of a Market: Bases for Market Segmentation

The Product Market (Prospects for Purchase)			

Physical Attributes of the Market

Size of Market	Geographic Location	Demographic Description of Purchases	
Number of Units Sold Dollar Sales Share of Market Held by Each Competitor	Sales by Region Sales by County Size Sales by City Size Specific Locations Kinds of Stores Where Sales Are Made	Sex Age Income Occupation Marital Status	Number of Persons in Family Race Religion Education

Behavioral Characteristics of Purchasers

When Purchases Are Made	Reasons For Purchasing	Social-Psychological Classification	Purchasing Influences	How Buying Is Done
Month Week Season Day of Week	Obvious Utility Psychological Reasons Major and Minor Uses	Social Class Value Differences Introvert-Extrovert Others	Who Uses Product Who Buys Product Who Influences Buying	Impulse or Brand Request Unit Sizes Bought Number of Units Bought Frequency

Qualitative Dimensions of the Market
(Identification of Best Prospects by Focusing on Best Segments)

Heavy Users
Frequent Purchasers
Firm Intensions to Buy Soon
Good Brand Loyalty (If a Major Factor)
Favorable Attitudes toward Brand
Segmentation, Pinpointing Best Prospects (from Above)

Source: Jack Z. Sissors, "What Is a Market?" *Journal of Marketing,* July 1966, p. 21. Reprinted from the *Journal of Marketing* published by the American Marketing Association.

States possesses a third of the world's income. India has almost three times the United States' population, but its inhabitants' per capita income is $134 a year. Table 4–1 illustrates the great differences in per capita income distribution for the various countries of the world.

The U.S. population has grown from approximately 200 Europeans (and about 1 million Indians) in 1610 to 218 million people (including 800,000

Figure 4–2
**The World in
Proportion to
Population**

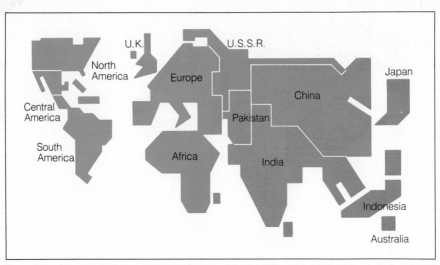

Source: Data used to create this figure are from *World Population Estimates, 1977* published by the Environmental Fund. © 1977 The Environmental Fund. Used with permission.

Indians) in 1980. *Zero population growth,* that point where live births equal the current death rate (between sixty and seventy births per thousand women of the childbearing ages of fifteen to forty-four), was reached in the United States during the mid-1970s. The birthrate increased at the end of the decade as large numbers of couples decided to have their first child after several years of marriage, but the rate is expected to decline again, beginning in the mid-1980s.[3] Should current birthrates continue, the U.S. population will reach 244 million in 1990 and 260 million in 2000.

Since zero population growth was achieved for several years during the 1970s, how did the U.S. population continue to grow? Population gains resulted from increased life expectancies, immigration, and increases in the number of women of childbearing years. Even if zero population growth is achieved during the 1980s, a constant population will not be a reality until late in the twenty-first century.

Geographic
Location of the U.S.
Population

The U.S. population, like that of the rest of the world, is not distributed evenly; it is concentrated in large metropolitan states, such as New York, Pennsylvania, California, Texas, Ohio, Michigan, and Illinois. Figure 4–3 illustrates this point by reducing Alaska, the largest state in land area, to diminutive size on the basis of its 1977 population of 421,000.

Not only do states vary widely in population density, but pronounced shifts are also evident. Population data for 1977 reveal that Arizona, Florida, Nevada, Alaska, Idaho, and Wyoming have experienced the most rapid growth since 1970, while the population of Rhode Island, New York, and the District of Columbia actually has declined. The figures indicate three major

Table 4–1
Per Capita Income for Selected Countries and Populations

Country	Per Capita Income	Population (in Millions)
North America		
United States	$7,933	217.9
Canada	6,741	23.4
Mexico	1,108	65.0
Cuba	937	9.6
Dominican Republic	909	5.2
Haiti	278	4.9
South America		
Argentina	1,584	26.5
Brazil	1,017	113.1
Venezuela	2,605	12.7
Europe		
United Kingdom	3,844	56.1
France	6,312	53.8
Italy	3,154	56.5
Portugal	1,239	9.8
Sweden	7,900	8.3
Turkey	681	42.0
Near East		
Israel	3,516	3.8
Egypt	341	38.9
Kuwait	11,455	1.1
Asia		
India	162	635.0
Japan	5,117	114.2
People's Republic of China	262	950.0
Philippines	389	45.0
Australia	5,835	13.9
Africa		
Chad	97	4.4
Angola	427	7.0
Liberia	463	1.8
Morocco	477	18.2
Mozambique	250	9.7

Source: *The Hammond Almanac* (Maplewood, N.J.: Hammond Almanac, 1979), pp. 504–709. Table permission Hammond Almanac, Maplewood, NJ.

population shifts: (1) shifts to the "sunbelt" states of the Southeast and Southwest, (2) continuing shifts from interior states to seacoast states, and (3) shifts to the West.

Population shifts have also occurred within states. The migration from the farm to the city has been in progress since 1800. The percentage of farm dwellers has now dropped below 5 percent. The twenty-five largest metro-

Figure 4-3
The United States in Proportion to Population

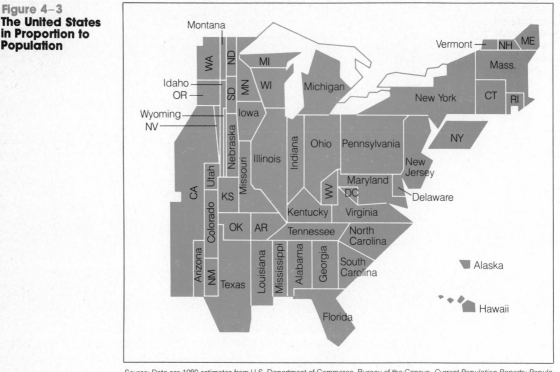

Source: Data are 1980 estimates from U.S. Department of Commerce, Bureau of the Census, *Current Population Reports: Population Estimates and Projections,* Series P-25, No. 735 (Washington, D.C.: Government Printing Office, October 1978), p. 4.

politan areas listed in Table 4-2 represent more than one-third of the population of the United States. Each of these metropolitan areas contains more inhabitants than the combined population of Wyoming (414,500) and Nevada (642,000).

The U.S. population ranks with the Australian and Canadian as the most mobile in the world. In an average year, approximately 40 million people in this country change their home address at least once. The average person moves twelve times in a lifetime as compared with eight times for the average English citizen and five times for the typical Japanese. Mobile home parks are appearing in every city, and more than 6 million people live in them.

New Definition of the City

The shift from farm to city has been accompanied recently by a shift to the suburbs. Recent population statistics report 96 million suburban residents, 28 million more than in central cities and 41 million more than in nonmetropolitan areas. The suburban areas with the greatest growth rates include Richland-Kennewick, Washington; Brownsville-Harlingen-San Benito, Texas; Rapid City, South Dakota; Fort Myers, Florida; and Santa Cruz, California.[4]

Table 4–2
The 25 Largest Metropolitan Areas Predicted for 1982

Rank	Metropolitan Area	Population (in Thousands)	Percent Change 1977–1982
1	New York	9,303	−2.1
2	Los Angeles–Long Beach	7,257	3.0
3	Chicago	7,082	0.9
4	Philadelphia	4,864	1.1
5	Detroit	4,283	−2.3
6	Boston	3,923	0.1
7	San Francisco–Oakland	3,286	2.8
8	Washington, D.C.	3,165	3.0
9	Houston	2,888	15.9
10	Dallas–Forth Worth	2,813	6.4
11	Nassau–Suffolk, New York	2,811	4.4
12	St. Louis	2,447	2.9
13	Baltimore	2,241	3.6
14	Pittsburgh	2,202	−3.6
15	Minneapolis–St. Paul	2,124	4.0
16	Anaheim–Santa Ana–Garden Grove	2,075	13.5
17	Atlanta	1,970	6.8
18	Newark, New Jersey	1,926	−2.7
19	San Diego	1,910	11.5
20	Cleveland	1,886	−3.3
21	Denver–Boulder	1,664	12.1
22	Miami	1,597	8.5
23	Tampa–St. Petersburg	1,575	10.0
24	Seattle–Everett	1,494	3.4
25	Riverside–San Bernardino–Ontario	1,464	12.3

Source: "Survey of Buying Power, Part II," *Sales & Marketing Management*, October 23, 1978, p. 14. Reprinted by permission from *Sales & Marketing Management* magazine. Copyright 1978.

The shift to the suburbs has been made primarily by middle-income families. It has resulted in radical changes in the cities' traditional patterns of retailing and has led to a disintegration of the downtown shopping areas of many cities. It has also made the traditional city boundaries almost meaningless.

To accommodate urban—and marketing—planners, the U.S. Bureau of the Census has developed an improved classification system for urban data. In urban areas, these data are now collected on the basis of a **Standard Metropolitan Statistical Area (SMSA)**—*an integrated economic and social unit containing one city of 50,000 inhabitants or "twin cities" with a combined population of at least 50,000.* The boundaries of the SMSA can cross state lines (as they do for the Duluth-Superior SMSA), but they must represent an integrated unit. The SMSAs shown in Figure 4–4 contain two-thirds of the population of the United States.

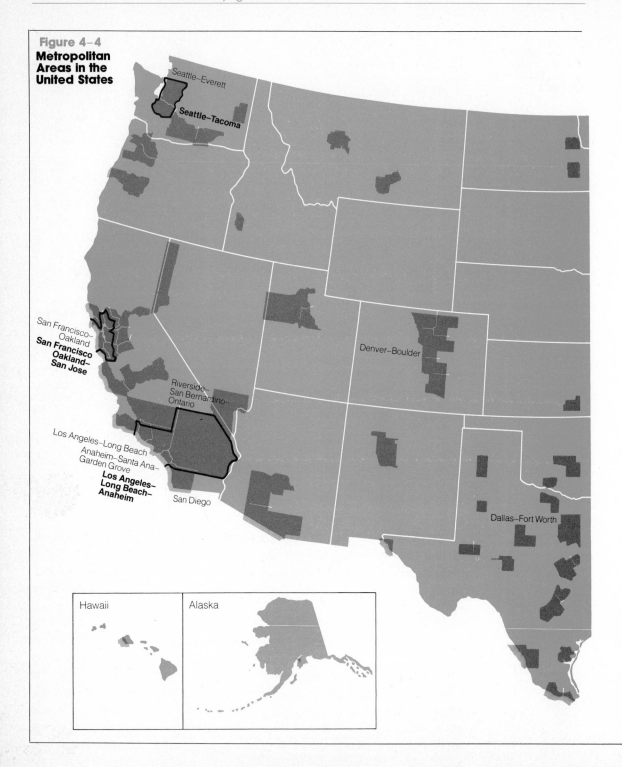

Figure 4-4
Metropolitan Areas in the United States

Seattle–Everett

Seattle–Tacoma

San Francisco–Oakland
San Francisco Oakland– San Jose

Denver–Boulder

Riverside–San Bernardino–Ontario

Los Angeles–Long Beach
Anaheim–Santa Ana–Garden Grove
Los Angeles–Long Beach–Anaheim

San Diego

Dallas–Fort Worth

Hawaii

Alaska

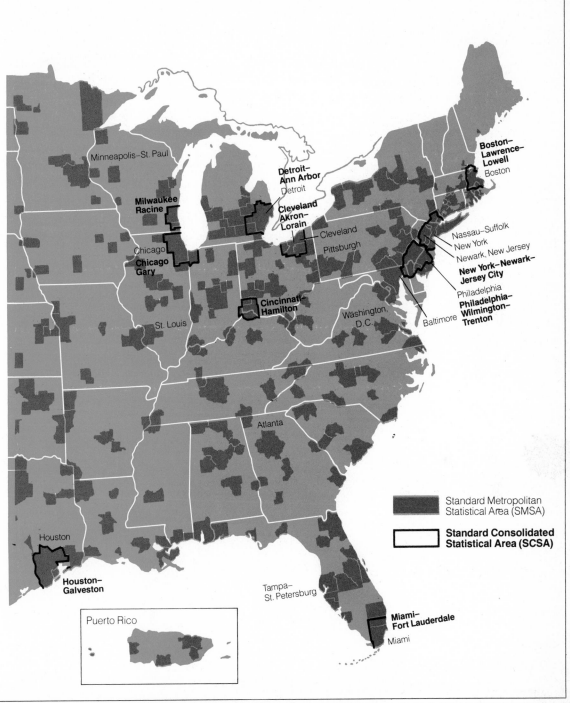

Minneapolis–St. Paul

Milwaukee Racine

Chicago

Chicago Gary

St. Louis

Houston

Houston– Galveston

Detroit– Ann Arbor
Detroit

Cleveland Akron– Lorain

Cleveland

Pittsburgh

Cincinnati– Hamilton

Washington, D.C.

Atlanta

Tampa– St. Petersburg

Boston– Lawrence– Lowell
Boston

Nassau–Suffolk
New York
Newark, New Jersey

New York–Newark– Jersey City

Philadelphia

Philadelphia– Wilmington– Trenton

Baltimore

Miami– Fort Lauderdale
Miami

Puerto Rico

Standard Metropolitan Statistical Area (SMSA)

Standard Consolidated Statistical Area (SCSA)

Source: U.S. Department of Commerce, Bureau of the Census, *County and City Data Book, 1977: A Statistical Abstract Supplement* (Washington, D.C.: Government Printing Office, 1978), pp. xiv-xv, xxv.

Figure 4–4 also reveals a concentration of population along the eastern sea-board, stretching from Boston to Washington, D.C. Another concentration of SMSAs is found along the shores of the Great Lakes and on the California coastline. In 1975, government statisticians gave formal recognition to these supercities by designating thirteen **Standard Consolidated Statistical Areas (SCSAs).** *Each SCSA contains an SMSA with a population of at least 1 million and one or more adjoining SMSAs that are related to it by high-density population centers and intermetropolitan commuting of workers.* The thirteen SCSAs shown in Figure 4–4 contain one-third of the population of the United States.

As the exodus to the suburbs continues, and as more industries follow their employees away from the central business districts, growth of the SCSAs will also undoubtedly continue. One large advertising agency coined the term *megalopolis* to describe these extensive urban-surburban strips of population and forecasted their continued growth. Projections for these areas are shown in Figure 4–5.

In the 1970s, a mild countertrend developed as young marrieds and married couples with no children at home abandoned suburban living in favor of the social and cultural attractions of major cities. Decaying sections of central cities are now being replaced by apartment towers and town houses, office buildings, and vertical "cities within cities" (buildings that contain apartments, shopping facilities, post offices, and so on) such as the John Hancock Center in Chicago.

**Figure 4–5
Projected
Growth of the
Megalopolis**

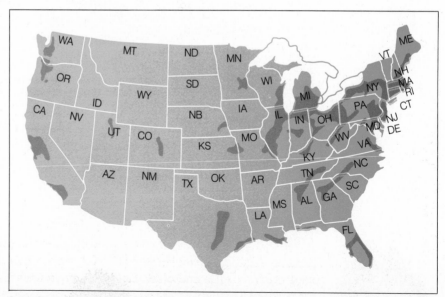

Source: Courtesy of J. Walter Thompson Company.

**The Rural Areas
Are Growing, Too**

By the mid 1970s, the nation's rural areas had reversed a population decline of one hundred years. While the growth rate of metropolitan areas doubled the rural rate during the 1960s, the nonmetropolitan areas grew by 5 percent during the 1970s. Also during this period, the total population grew by 3.8 percent, and the central cities declined by 1.6 percent. The following map shows the four fastest growing rural areas in the United States.

Fastest Growing Nonmetropolitan Regions

During a three-year period in which the total population increased by 3.2 percent, the Ozark-Ouachita population grew by 9.4 percent; the Upper Great Lakes region of Michigan, Wisconsin, and Minnesota by 8 percent; the Rocky Mountains from Idaho and Montana south to New Mexico by 7.1 percent; and the Southern Appalachian coalfields of southern West Virginia and eastern Kentucky by 6.3 percent.

   The reasons for this migration vary by region. Most of the recent growth in the Rockies has resulted from creation and expansion of retirement and recreation communities. Officials in one Kentucky county explain the population increase on the return of three groups of people: elderly natives who have found they can live more cheaply in the coal area, former mountaineers lured by the prospect that increased coal production will lead to jobs, and transplanted mountain people who are returning from the Northeast and northern Midwest. For others, rural living is simply an extension of the suburbs made possible by improved roads to the city. Still others seek to escape overcrowding, crime, pollution, and noise associated with the cities. For many of these pollster Louis Harris reflects their feelings with his statement, "Most Americans don't want more quantity of anything; but more quality in what they've got."[5]

Source: Adapted with permission from Richard Egan, "How Ya Gonna Keep 'Em in Metropolis," *National Observer*, May 31, 1975, p. 3.

Younger Middle-
Age Groups and
the Aged —
Growing Market
Segments

The population of the United States is expected to increase by 10 percent between 1980 and 1990, but this growth will be concentrated in two age groups—young to middle-age adults between thirty and forty-five and persons aged sixty-five and older. Both markets represent potentially profitable market targets.

The young middle-age adult segment includes family households with demands for such goods as homes, furniture, recreation, clothes, toys, and food. While this segment currently represents about one-fifth of the U.S. population, it will account for two-thirds of the growth in population during the 1980s.

Not so many years ago, there was no such thing as a *senior citizen* market, since few people reached old age. At present, however, one out of nine people is sixty-five or older. It is comforting for this year's retiree to learn that at age sixty-five his or her average life expectancy is at least another sixteen years. This increase also presents the marketing manager with a unique and potentially profitable market segment.[6]

Figure 4–6
Population Projections to 1990, by Age Groups

Population (in millions)		Change, 1980–1990
1980	1990	
Children and Teenagers		The absolute decline in the number of teenagers, which is more than offset by the slight increase in the number of babies and children under ten.
70.5	72.0	Up 2%
Young Adults, 20–29		Decline in the 20–29 age category in which people take their first jobs, marry, look for homes, start families, spend and borrow freely.
39.8	38.1	Down 4%
Younger Middle-Age Group, 30–44		Huge surge in the number of people in the younger middle-age group, where families climb the income ladder, spend on clothing and education for their children, move into larger homes, purchase larger autos.
43.0	57.5	Up 34%
Older Middle-Age Group, 45–64		Slight growth for the older middle-age group, where incomes tend to be highest and spending per person heaviest for such items as children's college education, travel, leisure, luxury goods, and services.
43.9	46.1	Up 5%
Persons 65 and Over		Sizable growth for 65 and older age category, which means increased demand for medical care, apartments, retirement homes, and luxuries such as travel, fashionable clothing, recreation, and books.
24.9	29.4	Up 18%

Source: U.S. Department of Commerce, Bureau of the Census, *Current Population Reports*, Series P-25, No. 704 (Washington, D.C.: Government Printing Office, July 1977), pp. 40, 50.

Market Target
Identifiable by
Age

Each age group in Figure 4–6 represents different consumption patterns, and each serves as the market target for several firms. Gerber traditionally has been extremely successful in aiming at the infant and children's market, and Geritol appeals primarily to older consumers (and attempts to reach them via commercials on the Lawrence Welk show). Table 4–3 lists some of the types of merchandise most often purchased by the various age groups.

Family Life Cycle

Using the concept of the **family life cycle,** the marketing planner combines the family characteristics of age, marital status, presence or absence of children, and ages of children in developing a marketing strategy. Six stages occur in the typical family life cycle:

1. Bachelor: Young single individual.
2. Young married couple with no children.
3. Full nest I: Young married couple with youngest child under six.
    Full nest II: Young married couple with youngest child six or over.
4. Full nest III: Older married couple with dependent children.
5. Empty nest: Older married couple with no children at home.
6. Solitary survivor: Older single or widowed person.

Table 4–3
Merchandise Purchased, by Consumer Age Groups

Age	Name of Age Group	Merchandise Purchased
0–5	Young children	Baby food, toys, nursery furniture, children's wear
6–19	Schoolchildren (including teenagers)	Clothing, sports equipment, phonograph records, school supplies, food, cosmetics, used cars
20–34	Young adult	Cars, furniture, houses, clothing, recreational equipment, purchases for younger age segments
35–49	Younger middle-aged	Larger homes, better cars, second cars, new furniture, recreational equipment
50–64	Older middle-aged	Recreational items, purchases for young marrieds and infants
65 and over	Senior adult	Medical services, travel, drugs, purchases for younger age groups

Table 4–4
An Overview of the Family Life Cycle

Bachelor Stage: Young Single People Not Living at Home	Newly Married Couples: Young, No Children	Full Nest I: Youngest Child under Six	Full Nest II: Youngest Child Six or Over
Few financial burdens	Better off financially than they will be in near future	Home purchasing at peak	Financial position better
Fashion opinion leaders		Liquid assets low	Some wives work
Recreation oriented	Highest purchase rate and highest average purchase of durables	Dissatisfied with financial position and amount of money saved	Less influenced by advertising
Buy basic kitchen equipment, basic furniture, cars, equipment for the mating game, vacations	Buy cars, refrigerators, stoves, sensible and durable furniture, vacations	Interested in new products	Buy larger-sized packages, multiple-unit deals
		Like advertised products	Buy many foods, cleaning materials, bicycles, music lessons, pianos
		Buy washers, dryers, TV, baby food, chest rubs and cough medicine, vitamins, dolls, wagons, sleds, skates	

Source: William D. Wells and George Gubar, "Life Cycle Concept in Marketing Research," *Journal of Marketing Research,* November 1966, p. 362. Reprinted from the *Journal of Marketing Research* published by the American Marketing Association.

The behavioral characteristics and buying patterns of families in each of the life cycle stages are described in Table 4–4.

Analysis of life cycle stages often gives better results than does reliance on only *individual* variables such as age. The buying patterns of the bachelor of twenty-five are much different from those of the young father of the same age. The full-nest family headed by parents who are fifty years old is a more likely prospect for *World Book Encyclopedia* than is the fifty-year-old solitary survivor.

Published data, such as census reports, are available for each of the family life cycle classifications. By using them, marketing planners can divide their markets into more homogeneous segments than would be possible if they were analyzing single variables.

The Shrinking U.S. Household

Slightly more than half the households in the United States are made up of only one or two persons. This development is in marked contrast to households that averaged 5.8 persons when the first census was taken in 1790.

The U.S. Department of Commerce cites several reasons for the trend toward smaller households. Among them are lower fertility rates, the tendency of young people to postpone marriage, the increasing desire among younger couples to limit the number of children, the ease and frequency of divorce, and the ability and desire of many young single adults and the elderly to live alone.

Full Nest III: Older Married Couples with Dependent Children	Empty Nest I: Older Married Couples, No Children Living with Them, Head in Labor Force	Empty Nest II: Older Married Couples, No Children Living at Home, Head Retired	Solitary Survivor, in Labor Force	Solitary Survivor, Retired
Financial position still better	Home ownership at peak	Drastic cut in income	Income still good but likely to sell home	Same medical and product needs as other retired group; drastic cut in income
More wives work	Most satisfied with financial position and money saved	Keep home		Special need for attention, affection, and security
Some children get jobs	Interested in travel, recreation, self-education	Buy medical appliances, medical care, products which aid health, sleep, and digestion		
Hard to influence with advertising	Make gifts and contributions			
High average purchase of durables	Not interested in new products			
Buy new, more tasteful furniture, auto travel, nonnecessary appliances, boats, dental services, magazines	Buy vacations, luxuries, home improvements			

More than 15 million people live alone today—more than one household in five. The single-person household has become an important market segment with a special title: *SSWD* (single, separated, widowed, and divorced). SSWDs buy 26 percent of all passenger cars but 50 percent of the Ford Mustangs and other specialty cars. They are also customers for single-serving food products, such as Campbell's Soup-for-One and Green Giant's single-serving casseroles.

Today, the average household size is 2.9 persons. And while married couple households continue to be dominant, they accounted for only 65 percent of all U.S. households in 1977, down from 71 percent in 1970.

Income and Expenditure Patterns

Markets were defined earlier as people and purchasing power. A common method of segmenting consumer markets is on the basis of income. Fashionable specialty shops stocking designer clothing make most of their sales to high-income shoppers. Other retailers aim their appeals at middle-income groups. Still others focus almost exclusively on low-income shoppers.

Income distribution in most countries is shaped like a pyramid, with a small percentage of households having high incomes and the majority of families earning very low incomes. As Figure 4–7 shows, this pattern was also true of the United States only a few decades ago. In 1955, more than half of all families earned less than $10,000. In recent years, however, the income pyramid has been overturned. By 1975, two-thirds of the U.S. households earned $10,000 or more. An estimated 30 percent of all U.S. families will have incomes of $25,000 or more by 1985, while only 22 percent will earn

Figure 4–7
Redistribution of Family Income, 1955–1985

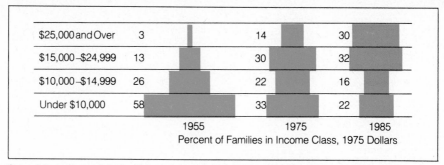

	1955	1975	1985
$25,000 and Over	3	14	30
$15,000–$24,999	13	30	32
$10,000–$14,999	26	22	16
Under $10,000	58	33	22

Percent of Families in Income Class, 1975 Dollars

Source: Data used by permission from Helen Axel, ed., *A Guide to Consumer Markets, 1977/1978* (New York: Conference Board, 1977), p.127.

less than $10,000. Higher incomes for the typical household should mean more discretionary spending power.

Household expenditures can be divided into two categories: basic purchases of essential household needs and other purchases that can be made at the discretion of the household members once the necessities have been purchased. Total discretionary purchasing power is estimated to have tripled since 1950.

How do expenditure patterns vary with increased income? More than a hundred years ago, a German statistician named Ernst Engel published three general statements—**Engel's laws**—based on his studies of spending behavior. According to Engel, *as family income increases:*

1. A smaller percentage of expenditures goes for food.
2. The percentage spent on housing and household operations and clothing remains constant.
3. The percentage spent on other items (such as recreation and education) increases.

Are Engel's laws still valid? Figure 4–8 supplies the answers. A steady decline in the *percentage* of total income spent for food, beverages, and tobacco occurs from low to high incomes. While high-income families spend a greater absolute amount on food purchases, their purchases represent a smaller percentage of their total expenditures than is true of low-income families. The second law is partly correct, since percentage expenditures for housing and household operations are relatively unchanged in all but the very lowest income group. The percentage spent on clothing, however, *increases* with increased income. As Figure 4–8 indicates, households earning less than $10,000 annually spend a smaller percentage of their income on clothing than do those earning more than $10,000. The third law is also true—with the exception of medical and personal care, which appears to decline in percentage expenditures with increased income.

Engel's laws provide the marketing manager with useful generalizations

Figure 4–8
Annual Family Expenditures by Income Groups

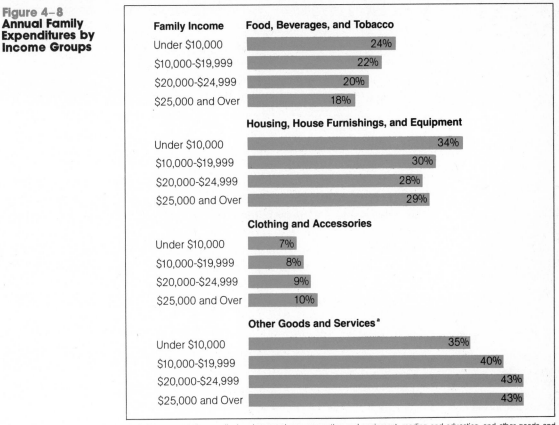

Family Income	Food, Beverages, and Tobacco
Under $10,000	24%
$10,000-$19,999	22%
$20,000-$24,999	20%
$25,000 and Over	18%

Housing, House Furnishings, and Equipment

Under $10,000	34%
$10,000-$19,999	30%
$20,000-$24,999	28%
$25,000 and Over	29%

Clothing and Accessories

Under $10,000	7%
$10,000-$19,999	8%
$20,000-$24,999	9%
$25,000 and Over	10%

Other Goods and Services[a]

Under $10,000	35%
$10,000-$19,999	40%
$20,000-$24,999	43%
$25,000 and Over	43%

[a]Includes transportation, medical and personal care, recreation and equipment, reading and education, and other goods and services.
Source: Adapted with permission from Helen Axel, ed., *A Guide to Consumer Markets 1977/1978* (New York: Conference Board, 1977), p. 173.

about the types of consumer demand that will evolve with increased income. They can also be useful for the marketer evaluating a foreign country as a potential market target.

Industrial Goods Market

The *industrial goods market* is made up of manufacturers, utilities, government agencies, contractors, mining firms, wholesalers, retailers, insurance and real estate firms, and institutions—such as schools or hospitals—that buy goods and services for use in producing other products for resale. This market accounts for about half of all the manufactured goods in the United States. The value added by manufacturing (the difference between the prices charged by manufacturers and the cost of their inputs) in 1976 totaled approximately $511 billion.

The industrial goods market has three distinctive characteristics—geographic market concentration, a relatively small number of buyers, and systematic buying procedures—that must be considered by marketing managers. This section examines several of the most important differences between the industrial and the consumer goods markets.[7]

Market Concentration

The market for industrial goods in the United States is much more concentrated geographically than is the market for consumer goods. Figure 4–9 shows the concentration in two areas, the East North Central and the Middle Atlantic. These areas account for over 50 percent of the value added by manufacturing in the United States.

The industrial market also concentrates on a limited number of buyers. Of the 312,000 firms in the United States, less than 2 percent of them—firms with 500 or more employees—are responsible for almost 50 percent of the total dollar value added by manufacturing and 42 percent of total employment in manufacturing. Four companies produce over two-thirds of the U.S. automobile tire output. One computer company, IBM, controls almost 70 percent of the electronic data processing market. Table 4–5 reflects the distribution of manufacturing firms in the United States.

The concentration of the industrial market greatly influences the marketing strategy used in serving it. Industrial marketers can usually make prof-

Figure 4–9
The United States in Proportion to Value of Manufactured Products

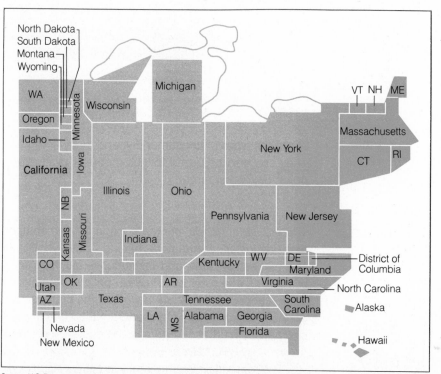

Source: U.S. Department of Commerce, Bureau of the Census, *Census of Manufactures Area Statistics* (Washington, D.C.: Government Printing Office, 1971), p. 39.

Table 4–5
Size Distribution of Manufacturing Firms

Number of Employees	Number of Establish-ments	Value Added by Manufacturing (in Millions)	Percentage of Establish-ments	Percentage of Value Added	Percent-age of Employees
1–4	112,289	$ 3,753	35.9	1.1	1.1
5–9	46,696	5,249	14.9	1.4	1.7
10–19	43,736	10,126	14.0	2.9	3.4
20–49	49,892	25,626	12.8	7.2	8.7
50–99	25,628	29,241	11.4	8.3	9.9
100–249	20,807	56,477	6.6	16.0	17.9
250–499	8,031	51,412	2.6	14.5	15.4
500–999	3,483	40,520	1.1	13.7	13.2
1,000–2,499	1,527	50,488	0.5	14.2	12.5
2,500 and over	582	73,109	0.2	20.7	16.2

Source: U.S. Department of Commerce, Bureau of the Census, *Census of Manufactures, 1967* (Washington, D.C.: Government Printing Office, 1971).

itable use of a sales force to provide regular personal contacts with a small, geographically concentrated market. Wholesalers are less frequently used, and the marketing channel for industrial goods is typically much shorter than for consumer goods. Advertising also plays a much smaller role in the industrial goods market.

SIC Codes Aid in the Analysis of Industrial Markets

The marketer focusing on the industrial market is aided by a wealth of information collected by the federal government, including number of firms, sales volume for each, and number of employees by industry, state, county, SCSA, and SMSA. The data are broken down by **Standard Industrial Classifications (SICs).** The SIC codes begin with *ten broad industry groups into which all types of businesses are divided:*

01–09   Agriculture, forestry, fishing
10–14   Mining
15–19   Contract construction
20–39   Manufacturing
40–49   Transportation and other public utilities
50–59   Wholesale and retail trade
60–67   Finance, insurance, and real estate
70–89   Services
90–93   Government—federal, state, local, and international
99   Others

Each major industry within these broad groups is assigned a separate two-digit number, and three- and four-digit numbers subdivide the industry into smaller segments. For example, the food and kindred products industry (code 20) can be subdivided into segments such as meat products (code 201) and dairy products (code 202). The meat products segment can then be

Industrial goods markets are concentrated in the East North Central and Middle Atlantic states.

"Hossman, I hate to tell you this, but the board has decided not to move to the Sun Belt."

Source: *New Yorker*, October 9, 1978, p. 39. Drawing by Ed Arno; © 1978 The New Yorker Magazine, Inc.

further divided into sausages and other prepared meat products (code 2013).

The SIC codes are helpful in analyzing the industrial market. The detailed information for each market segment provides industrial marketers with a comprehensive description of the activities of their potential customers on both a geographical and industrial basis.[8]

Buying Patterns of Industrial Purchasers

Most industrial firms have attempted to systematize their purchases by employing a professional consumer—the industrial purchasing agent. Unlike the ultimate consumer, the purchasing department devotes all its time and effort to making purchase decisions.

Where major purchases are involved, the negotiations may take several weeks or even months, and the buying decision may rest with a number of persons in the firm. The choice of a supplier for industrial drill presses, for example, may be made jointly by the production, engineering, and maintenance departments as well as by the purchasing agent. Each of these departments has a different point of view, and each must be taken into account in making a purchase decision.

The computer purchase decision shown in Figure 4–10 began with the department head in the calculations section. Next, the factory purchasing agent was informed. The agent then discussed company needs with salespeople representing three suppliers. The salespeople met with the calculations department head, who made a tentative decision to purchase from Supplier C. The decision was next considered by the associate research di-

Figure 4–10
The Decision to Purchase a Computer

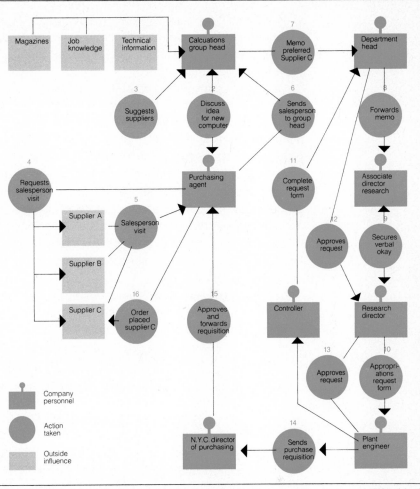

Source: "Who Really Makes the Purchasing Decision?" *Industrial Marketing*, September 1966, p. 79. Copyright 1966 by Advertising Publications, Inc., Chicago, Ill. Reprinted by permission.

rector, then the research director, the plant engineer, the controller, and the corporate director of purchasing. In all, the decision took two years from conception to order placement.

Many industrial goods are purchased for long periods of time on a contractual basis. Manufacturing operations require a continual supply of materials, and one- or two-year contracts with suppliers ensure this steady supply. Other industrial goods, such as conveyors, typewriters, and forklifts, generally last several years before replacement is necessary.[9]

Purchase decisions frequently are made on the bases of service, certainty of supply, and efficiency of the supplied products. These factors must be considered along with the prices quoted for the products.

Automobile manufacturers purchase steel, glass windows, spark plugs, and batteries as ingredients for their output. Since demand for these items is *derived* from the demand for consumer goods, most price changes do not substantially affect their sale. Price increases for paint have little effect on auto sales at General Motors, because paint represents a minute portion of the automobiles' total costs.

A highly controversial practice in a number of industries is **reciprocity,** *the extension of purchasing preference to suppliers who are also customers.* Reciprocal agreements were formerly used in industries involving homogeneous products with similar prices, such as the steel, chemical, rubber, paint, and petroleum industries. In times of shortages, a form of *reverse reciprocity* occasionally emerges as firms attempt to obtain crucial raw materials and parts to continue operations. Reverse reciprocity extends supply privileges to firms who provide needed supplies. While some reciprocal agreements still exist, both the Justice Department and the Federal Trade Commission view them as attempts to reduce competition. Federal intervention is common in cases where agreements are used systematically.[10]

The Government Market

The government—at all levels—is a sizable segment of the industrial market, since its expenditures represent one-third of the nation's gross national product. Total spending by government in 1976–1977 amounted to approximately $818 billion, with the federal government accounting for nearly 53 percent of the total. Table 4–6 indicates the major categories of expenditures by local, state, and federal governments.

Since most government purchases must, by law, be made on the basis of bids, government buyers develop specific descriptions of needed items for prospective bidders. For the federal government, most of the branded items (see Chapter 7 for details on branded goods) such as general purpose supplies, are purchased for all federal agencies by the General Services

Table 4–6 Selected Expenditures (in Millions) by Local, State, and Federal Governments: 1976–1977

Expenditures	Federal Government	State Government	Local Government
Total expenditures	$431,980	$191,238	$194,775
National defense and international relations	105,596	—	—
Postal service	14,641	—	—
Space research and technology	4,008	—	—
Education	18,041	64,037	76,064
Highways	6,431	17,496	9,275
Public welfare	34,424	32,779	12,499
Health and hospitals	9,860	12,607	11,522
Housing and urban renewal	5,126	353	3,234
Air transportation	2,402	235	1,139

Source: U.S. Department of Commerce, Bureau of the Census, *Governmental Finances in 1976–77*, Series GF77, no. 5 (November 1978), pp. 26–27.

Administration. The states generally have a comparable office for similar items.

Prospective government suppliers can learn of opportunities for sales by contacting the various government agencies. Most contracts are advertised by each agency, and information on bidding procedures can be obtained directly from the agency. Directories explaining procedures involved in selling to the federal government are available from the Government Printing Office, and most states provide similar information.[11]

Identifying Market Targets

So far, this chapter has examined the characteristics of the consumer and industrial markets with the objective of using these characteristics to identify and analyze potential market targets. The targets can be isolated by developing a cross-classification of the total market and selecting individual targets from the overall market. An example will show how market target decision analysis can be applied.[12]

The Market for Typewriters

Consider the decisions of a small firm wishing to analyze the market potential for a proposed line of typewriters. Because of limited financial resources, the company must operate on a regional basis. The grid in Figure 4–11 illustrates the first two decisions for the firm: choosing a geographic area and marketing the typewriters to the ultimate consumer. The typewriter company also could have chosen the industrial market. But to have done so would have required a separate marketing strategy, since each of the cells in Figure 4–11 represents unique markets with distinguishing characteristics.

The next steps involve the decision to market the typewriters to high-income households in the full nest II and III of the family life cycle, which in turn involves evaluating the market for typewriters as gifts for school-age children. Data can be gathered about the size of the market target in the eastern United States and the firm's predicted market share so that a final decision can be made.

The cross-classifications in Figure 4–12 can be further subdivided to

Figure 4–11
Market Target for Typewriters

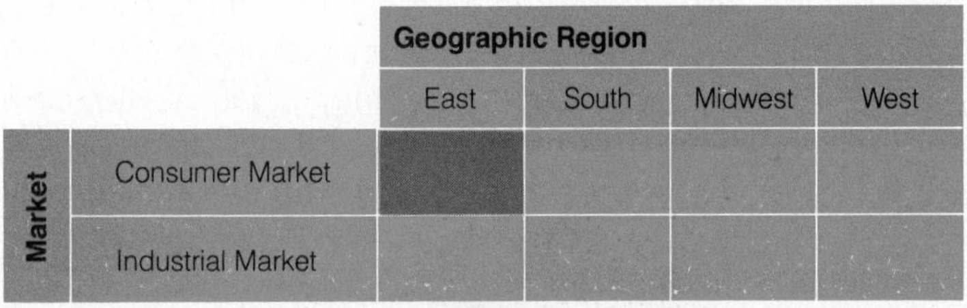

		Geographic Region			
		East	South	Midwest	West
Market	Consumer Market				
	Industrial Market				

Figure 4-12
Market Target for Typewriters to Consumers in the Eastern United States.

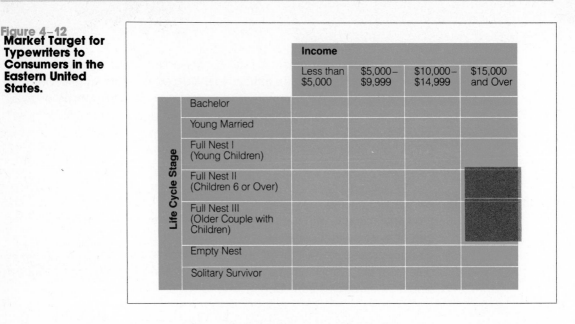

gather more specific data about the characteristics of the proposed market target. Such divisions are sometimes made intuitively, but usually the decisions are supported by concrete data.[13]

Summary

Markets are people with purchasing power and the authority to make purchase decisions. The total market can be divided into consumer and industrial markets. The ultimate consumer makes purchases for his or her own use, while the industrial purchaser buys products for use in making other products for resale.

The goal of the marketing manager in selecting a market target is to divide the total market into smaller homogeneous market segments. The most common variables for market segmentation are geographic location of population, urban-rural differences, age, stage in the family life cycle, income, and expenditure pattern. Industrial market segmentation can be accomplished on the bases of geographic location of the market, type of business (such as government, mining, manufacturing, services, institutions), size of firm, and buying pattern for different products.

Market target decision analysis allows marketing managers to isolate and evaluate potential target markets that can be profitably served by their firms. This vital first step permits the managers to gather pertinent information about a market target for use in accomplishing the second task—that of developing and implementing an effective marketing mix designed to satisfy the selected market target.

Questions for Discussion

1. Explain the following terms:

market

consumer goods

industrial goods

market segmentation

Standard Metropolitan Statistical Area (SMSA)

Standard Consolidated Statistical Area (SCSA)

family life cycle

Engel's laws

Standard Industrial Classification (SIC)

reciprocity

2. Identify the two-step process of developing a marketing strategy. Why is it essential that the steps be conducted in the proper sequence?

3. Explain why each of the four components of a market is necessary before a market can exist.

4. Toothpaste is a consumer good; iron ore is an industrial good. But what about automobiles—are they consumer goods or industrial goods? Justify your answer.

5. Based on data in Table 4–1, how would you expect consumer purchases in Portugal to differ from those in the United States?

6. Explain the concept of zero population growth.

7. What effect will a low birthrate have on future buying patterns? Which kinds of companies will benefit in the next ten years from a declining birthrate? Which will suffer?

8. Identify the major population shifts that have occurred in recent years. How do you account for these shifts?

9. What types of markets have been created in the past because of population mobility? What new markets are likely to develop in the next few decades because of this mobility?

10. How has the population shift from city to suburb affected the marketplace? What marketing changes do you anticipate from the growth of the megalopolis?

11. How do you account for the recent growth in the rural population?

12. List two products most likely to be purchased by persons in each stage of the family life cycle.

13. Identify the stages of the family life cycle. Which stage are you in? Which stage are your parents in?

14. Why is family life cycle analysis an improvement over market analysis by variables such as age or marital status?

15. Discuss the following statement: Based on Engel's laws, we should expect family expenditures for food to decline as income increases.

16. What are some major distinctions between the consumer and industrial markets?

17. Explain the use of SIC codes in industrial marketing.

18. Explain the following statement: Industrial demand is derived demand.

19. Why do purchasing agents tend to oppose reciprocity? Under what circumstances do the benefits of this practice outweigh its limitations?

20. Develop a market target decision analysis for home video recorders.

Notes

1. Reported in James C. Hyatt, "Demographers Finally Come into Their Own in Firms, Government," *Wall Street Journal*, July 19, 1978, p. 1.

2. For a thorough discussion of market segmentation, see Yoram Wind, "Issues and Advances in Segmentation Research," *Journal of Marketing Research*, August 1978, pp. 317–337. See also Fred W. Morgan, Jr., "Profitability Market Segmentation: Identifying the Heavy Users of Overdraft Checking," *Journal of Business Research*, May 1978, pp. 99–110; Thomas R. Wotruba and Joseph J. Vidali, "How Many Market Segments?" *Atlanta Economic Review*, September–October 1977, pp. 45–50; and Philip C. Burger and A. Venkatesh, "Market Segmentation: Some Unresolved Issues," in *Contemporary Marketing Thought*, ed. Barnett A. Greenberg and Danny N. Bellenger (Chicago: American Marketing Association, 1977), pp. 15–18.

3. "Delayed-Baby Boom: Its Meaning," *U.S. News & World Report*, February 20, 1978, pp. 39–41.

4. "Survey of Buying Power, Part II," *Sales & Marketing Management*, October 23, 1978, p. 11.

5. Quoted in "Americans on the Move," *Time*, March 15, 1976, p. 57.

6. See Betsy D. Gelb, "Exploring the Gray Market Segment," *MSU Business Topics*, Spring 1978, pp. 41–46; and Lynn W. Phillips and Brian Sternthal, "Age Differences in Information Processing: A Perspective on the Aged Consumer," *Journal of Marketing Research*, November 1977, pp. 444–457.

7. See J. S. Schiff, José Fernandez, and Leon Winer, "Segmentation as an Industrial Strategy," in Greenberg and Bellinger, *Contemporary Marketing Thought*, pp. 486–489; and Robert W. Haas, "Locating Industrial Customers," *Atlanta Economic Review*, September–October 1976, pp. 9–14.

8. For a description of the approximately four hundred SIC codes, see *Standard Industrial Classification Manual* (Washington, D.C.: Government Printing Office, 1972).

9. See James R. Cooley, Donald W. Jackson, Jr., and Lonnie L. Ostrom, "Relative Power in Industrial Buying Decisions," *Journal of Purchasing and Materials Management*, Spring 1978, pp. 18–20; E. H. Bonfield and Thomas W. Speh, "Dimensions of Purchasing's Role in Industry," *Journal of Purchasing and Materials Management*, Summer 1977, pp. 10–17; and Robert J. Dolan, "A Normative Model of Industrial Buyer Response to Quantity Discounts," in *Research Frontiers in Marketing*, ed. Subhash C. Jain (Chicago: American Marketing Association, 1978), pp. 121–125.

10. The history and current status of reciprocal agreements is summarized in E. Robert Finney, "Reciprocity: Gone but Not Forgotten," *Journal of Marketing*, January 1978, pp. 54–59. See also William J. Kehoe and Byron D. Hewett, "Reciprocity and Reverse Reciprocity: A Literature Review and Research Design," in *Proceedings of the Southern Marketing Association*, ed. Robert S. Franz, Robert M. Hopkins, and Al Toma, New Orleans, Louisiana, November 1978, pp. 481–483; and Monroe M. Bird, "Reverse Reciprocity: A New Twist to Industrial Buyers," *Atlanta Economic Review*, January–February 1976, pp. 11–13.

11. See John M. Rathmell, "Marketing by the Federal Government," *MSU Business Topics,* Summer 1973, pp. 21–28.

12. A similar analysis is suggested in Robert M. Fulmer, *The New Marketing* (New York: Macmillan, 1976), pp. 34–37; Philip Kotler, *Marketing Management* (Englewood Cliffs, N.J.: Prentice-Hall, 1976), pp. 141–151; and E. Jerome McCarthy, *Basic Marketing* (Homewood, Ill.: Richard D. Irwin, 1975), pp. 111–126.

13. A good example of this systematic approach to identifying a precise market target appears in Richard P. Carr, Jr., "Developing a New Residential Market for Carpeting: Some Mistakes and Successes," *Journal of Marketing*, July 1977, pp. 101–102.

CHAPTER 5
UNDERSTANDING CONSUMER BEHAVIOR

Key Terms

self-concept
consumer behavior
need
motive
perception
Weber's law
selective perception
subliminal perception
attitude

psychographics
learning
status
role
reference group
opinion leader
culture
subculture
cognitive dissonance

Learning Goals

1. To explain the self-concept and its components.
2. To identify the individual factors influencing consumer behavior.
3. To list the levels of the needs hierarchy.
4. To identify and briefly explain the components of the learning process.
5. To identify the environmental influences on consumer behavior.
6. To explain the determinants of reference-group influence on the individual.
7. To outline the simplified model of the consumer decision process.

5

The marketing concept, briefly stated, is: Find a need and fill it. The key to marketing success lies in locating unsatisfied consumers. These people may not be purchasing goods because the goods are currently unavailable, or they may be buying products that provide them with only limited satisfaction. In the latter case, they are likely to switch to new products that provide more satisfaction. Unsatisfied consumers should comprise the market targets for consumer oriented firms.

Extensive consumer research on the burgeoning headache remedy and antacid market led one major U.S. pharmaceutical firm to develop a new pill with the virtues of aspirin, Alka Seltzer, Bufferin, Excedrin, and similar tablets gulped down daily by tension-ridden people. The firm's product development department created the product with one advantage possessed by no other competitor—it could be taken without water.

The product, a cherry-flavored combination painkiller and stomach sweetener called Analoze, was tested for consumer acceptance. Samples were given to a panel of potential buyers, who compared it with competing products. They chose Analoze overwhelmingly.

Ads were then developed around the theme "works without water." The price was competitive, and the package design was eye-catching. Confident of success, the marketing vice-president gave Analoze its first real market test in four cities—Denver, Omaha, Phoenix, and Memphis—and sat back to await the positive results . . . and waited . . . and waited. Sales were virtually nil, and a few months later Analoze was withdrawn from the market.

What went wrong? In-depth research with headache sufferers revealed a ritual associated with pain relief. They swallowed (or dissolved) a pill and drank a glass of water. These people somehow associated water consumption with obtaining relief, and they were unwilling to spend money on a remedy that dissolved in the mouth.[1]

Demographic Market Segmentation Is Not Enough

The failure of Analoze did not result from a declining or otherwise inadequate market or from a lack of consumer income, education, or any of the other variables commonly used in segmenting markets. The product failed because the marketer did not take into account the psychology of the market.

Successful marketers attempt to understand the motivations of the individual consumers. Unfortunately, this task is perhaps the most difficult one in marketing. Marketing research studies can provide the following kinds of data for analyzing consumers' buying habits:

1. *Who* are the buyers?
2. *When* do they buy (time of day, seasonality of product sales)?
3. *Where* do they buy?

4. *What* do they buy?
5. *How* do they buy (how much and what type of sales—cash or credit)?

But answers to the question "*Why* do they buy (or not buy)?" are much more difficult to uncover.

Figure 5–1 depicts three layers of consciousness. The two outer areas are the conscious layers. The innermost layer consists of nonverbal, nonrational emotions.

Direct questioning can be used to obtain information about buying habits, but it will rarely uncover the basic motivations for purchasing a particular brand or patronizing a certain store—motivations residing in the middle and innermost layers. The consumer can easily verbalize the name of the supermarket last visited but almost invariably will come up with rationalizations when asked why he or she bought a particular brand. The reasons one man gave for purchasing a particular after-shave lotion were: "I like the tingle of the alcohol immediately after shaving in the morning" and "It helps heal minor nicks and cuts." But the real reason he bought the after-shave was that he had borrowed some from his roommate one morning, and a young woman at the office had murmured, "What a heavenly scent!" That afternoon, he purchased a quart.

Self-concept Theory

Individuals are physical and mental entities possessing multifaceted pictures of themselves. One young man may, for example, view himself as intellectual and self-assured and as a moderately talented athlete and a rising young business executive. People's actions, including their purchase decisions, are

Figure 5–1
Three Layers of Consciousness

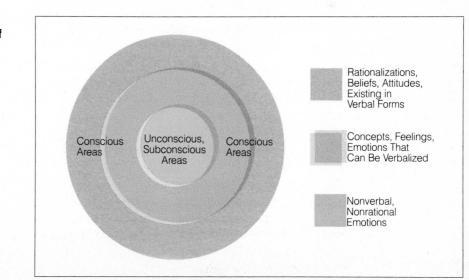

Conscious Areas

Unconscious, Subconscious Areas

Conscious Areas

Rationalizations, Beliefs, Attitudes, Existing in Verbal Forms

Concepts, Feelings, Emotions That Can Be Verbalized

Nonverbal, Nonrational Emotions

Figure 5–2
**Components of
Self-image**

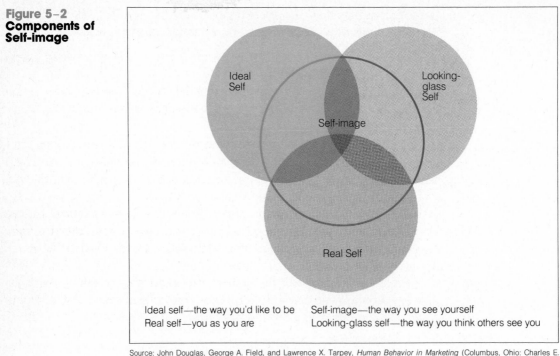

Ideal self—the way you'd like to be   Self-image—the way you see yourself
Real self—you as you are   Looking-glass self—the way you think others see you

Source: John Douglas, George A. Field, and Lawrence X. Tarpey, *Human Behavior in Marketing* (Columbus, Ohio: Charles E. Merrill Publishing, 1967), p. 65. Reprinted by permission.

dependent on their *mental conception of self*—their **self-concept.** And the response to direct questions like "Why do you buy Jovan cologne?" is likely to reflect this desired self-image.[2]

As Figure 5–2 indicates, the self has four components: real self, self-image, looking-glass self, and ideal self. The *real self* is an objective view of the total person. The *self-image*, the way individuals view themselves, may distort the objective view. The *looking-glass self,* the way individuals think others see them, may also be quite different from self-image, since people often choose to project a different image to others. The *ideal self* serves as a personal set of objectives, since it is the image to which the individual aspires.

In purchasing goods and services, people are likely to choose products that will move them closer to their ideal self-image. Those who see themselves as scholars are more likely than others to join literary book clubs. The young woman who views herself as a budding tennis star may become engrossed in evaluating the merits of graphite versus steel rackets and may view with disdain any cheaply made imports. The college graduate on the way up the organization ladder at a bank may hide a love for bowling and instead take up golf—having determined that golf is the sport for bankers. One writer used the self-concept idea to explain the failure of the Edsel. He claimed that potential Edsel purchasers were unsure of the car's image and faced the risk of moving away from their self-concept.[3]

Consumer Behavior as a Decision Process

Consumer behavior is *the acts of individuals in obtaining and using goods and services, including the decision processes that precede and determine these acts.*[4] This definition includes both the ultimate consumer and the purchaser of industrial goods. A major difference in the purchasing behavior of industrial consumers and ultimate consumers is that additional influences from within the organization may be exerted on the industrial purchasing agent.

The approach in this text is that of viewing consumer behavior as a *decision process* and the act of purchasing as merely *one point* in the process. To understand consumer behavior, the events that precede and follow the purchase act must be examined.

Consumer behavior results from individual and environmental influences. Consumers often purchase goods and services to achieve their ideal self-image and to project the self-image they want others to accept. Behavior is therefore determined by the individual's psychological makeup and the influences of others. This dual influence can be summarized as:

$$B = f(P, E).$$

Consumer behavior *(B)* is a function *(f)* of the interaction of consumers' *personal influences (P)* and the pressures exerted upon them by outside forces in the *environment (E).*[5] Understanding consumer behavior requires an understanding of the nature of these influences.

Individual Influences on Consumer Behavior

The basic determinants of consumer behavior include the individual's *needs, motives, perceptions,* and *attitudes.* The interaction of these factors with influences from the environment causes the consumer to act. Figure 5–3 presents a graphic picture of the interactions.

Needs and Motives

The starting point in the purchase decision process is the recognition of a felt need. A **need** is simply *the lack of something useful.* The consumer is typically confronted with numerous unsatisfied needs, but a need must be sufficiently aroused before it can serve as a motive to buy something.

Motives are *inner states that direct people toward the goal of satisfying a felt need.* The individual is *moved* (the root word for motive) to take action to reduce a state of tension and to return to a condition of equilibrium.

Although psychologists disagree on specific classifications, a useful theory of the hierarchy of needs has been developed by A. H. Maslow. Mas-

Figure 5–3
Basic Determinants of Consumer Behavior

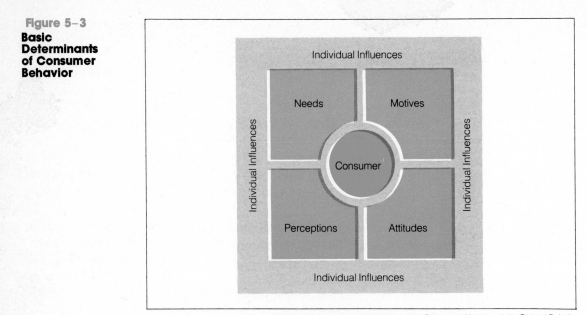

Source: C. Glenn Walters and Gordon W. Paul, *Consumer Behavior: An Integrated Framework* (Homewood, Ill.: Richard D. Irwin, 1970), p. 14. © 1970 by Richard D. Irwin, Inc. Reprinted by permission.

low's hierarchy is shown in Figure 5–4. His list is based on two important assumptions:

1. People are wanting animals whose needs depend on what they already possess. A satisfied need is not a motivator; only those needs that have not been satisfied can influence behavior.
2. People's needs are arranged in a hierarchy of importance. Once one need has been at least partially satisfied, another emerges and demands satisfaction.[6]

Figure 5–4
Hierarchy of Needs

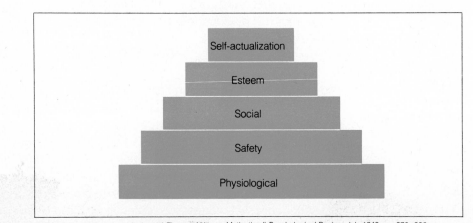

Source: Adapted from A. H. Maslow, "A Theory of Human Motivation," *Psychological Review*, July 1943, pp. 370–396.

Physiological Needs. The primary needs for food, shelter, and clothing that are present in all humans and must be satisfied before the individual can consider higher-order needs are *physiological needs*. A hungry person, possessed by the need to obtain food, ignores other needs. Once the physiological needs are at least partially satisfied, other needs enter the picture.

Safety Needs. The second-level *safety needs* include security, protection from physical harm, and avoidance of the unexpected. Gratification of these needs may take the form of a savings account, life insurance, the purchase of radial tires, or membership in a local health club.

Social Needs. Satisfaction of physiological and safety needs leads to the third level—the desire to be accepted by members of the family and other individuals and groups—the *social needs*. The individual may be motivated to join various groups, to conform to their standards of dress and behavior, and to become interested in obtaining status as means of fulfilling these needs.

Esteem Needs. The higher-order needs are more prevalent in developed countries, where a sufficiently high per capita income has allowed most

Successful products satisfy specific consumer needs.

"Then, too, of course, there's the damned human factor out there, and that, gentlemen, can be a wily little rascal."

Source: *New Yorker*, July 10, 1978, p. 31. Drawing by Ziegler; © 1978 The New Yorker Magazine, Inc.

families to satisfy the basic needs and to concentrate on the desire for status, esteem, and self-actualization. These needs, which are near the top of the ladder, are more difficult to satisfy. At the *esteem level* is the need to feel a sense of accomplishment, achievement, and respect from others. The competitive need to excel—to better the performance of others—is an almost universal human trait.

The esteem need is closely related to social needs. At this level, however, the individual desires not just acceptance but also recognition and respect. The person has a desire to stand out from the crowd in some way.

Self-actualization Needs. The top rung on the ladder of human needs is *self-actualization*—the need for fulfillment, for realizing one's own potential, for using one's talents and capabilities totally. Maslow defines *self-actualization* this way: "The healthy man is primarily motivated by his needs to develop and actualize his fullest potentialities and capacities. What man can be, he must be."[7]

Maslow points out that a satisfied need is no longer a motivator. Once the physiological needs are satiated, the individual moves on to higher-order needs. Consumers are periodically motivated by the need to relieve thirst or hunger, but their interests are most often directed toward satisfaction of safety, social, and other needs in the hierarchy.

Perception

Individual behavior resulting from motivation is affected by how stimuli are perceived. **Perception** is *the meaning that each person attributes to incoming stimuli received through the five senses.*

To perceive is { to see / to hear / to touch / to taste / to smell } some { thing / event / idea[8] }

Psychologists formerly assumed that perception was an objective phenomenon, that the individual perceived only what was there to be perceived. Only recently have researchers come to recognize that what people perceive is as much a result of what they want to perceive as of what is actually there. This does not mean that dogs may be viewed as pigeons or gasoline stations as churches. But a gas station with a national brand is perceived differently from an independent station. The Kharman Ghia and the Pontiac Grand Prix are both automobiles, but a study revealed that the Grand Prix is generally perceived to be a highly masculine automobile and the Kharman Ghia a feminine one.[9]

The perception of an object or event is the result of the interaction of two types of factors:

1. *Stimulus factors*—characteristics of the physical object, such as size, color, weight, or shape.
2. *Individual factors*—characteristics of the individual, including not only sensory processes but also past experiences with similar items and basic motivations and expectations.

Poison Labels – A Case of Misperception

Marketers of potentially dangerous products take numerous precautions to keep consumers from accidentally swallowing them—from child-resistant closures to warning labels. Yet, it is estimated that 2 million poisonings and more than four hundred deaths occur annually in the United States among children under five years of age.[10]

The skull and crossbones shown in the first box is the traditional symbol for poisonous products. But studies indicate that this symbol has lost most of its meaning. In fact, a group of nursery schoolchildren interpreted the label to mean "pirate food."

A proposed new warning symbol is shown in the second box. Mr. Yuk avoids the relationship of the skull and crossbones with pirates while denoting an unpleasant taste. Symbolic representations of danger are especially important in the case of young children, who cannot read written warnings.

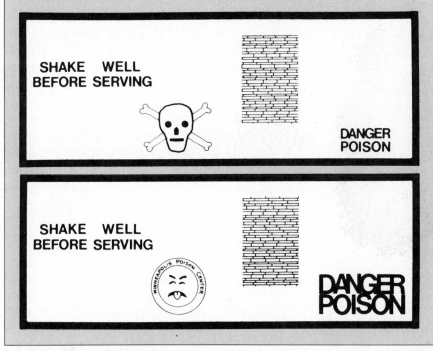

Source: Information from Kenneth C. Schneider, "Prevention of Accidental Poisoning through Package and Label Design," *Journal of Consumer Research*, September 1977, pp. 67–74. Labels courtesy of the journal.

The individual is continually bombarded with myriad stimuli, but most are ignored. In order to have time to function, people must respond selectively. The determination of which stimuli they do respond to is the problem of all marketers. How can the consumer's attention be gained so he or she will read the advertisement, listen to the sales representative, react to the point-of-purchase display?

Even though studies have shown that the average consumer is exposed to more than a thousand ads daily, most of these ads never break through people's perceptual screens. Sometimes breakthroughs are accomplished in the printed media through large-sized ads. Doubling the size of an ad increases its attention value by about 50 percent. Using color in newspaper ads—in contrast to the usual black and white ads—is another effective way of breaking through the reader's perceptual screen. However, the color ad must reach enough additional readers to justify the extra cost. Other methods using contrast are those of including a large amount of white space around the printed area or using white type on a black background.

In general, the marketer seeks to make the message stand out, to make it sufficiently different from other messages that it will gain the attention of the prospective customer. Menley & James Laboratories followed the practice of running hay-fever radio commercials for their Contac capsules only on days when the pollen count was above certain minimum levels. Each commercial was preceded by a live announcement of the local pollen count.

Analysis of audience reaction to television commercials shows either a sharp drop or a sharp rise in interest during the first five seconds. After that point, the audience will become only less interested, never more. The attention grabbing opening of commercials for American Express Travelers Cheques is: "You are about to witness a crime!" Viewers then watch a pick-pocket at work. The campaign showing the dangers of carrying cash reportedly helped American Express increase sales 28 percent.[11]

The relationship between the actual physical stimulus—such as size, loudness, or texture—and the corresponding sensation produced in the individual is known as *psychophysics*. It can be expressed as a mathematical equation:

$$\frac{\Delta I}{I} = k$$

where ΔI = the smallest increase in stimulus that will be noticeably different from the previous intensity.

I = the intensity of the stimulus at the point where the increase takes place.

k = a constant (that varies from one sense to the next).

In other words, *the higher the initial intensity of a stimulus, the greater the amount of the change in intensity that is necessary in order for a difference to be noticed.* The relationship, known as **Weber's law,** has some obvious implications in marketing. A price increase of $300 for a Mazda GLC is readily apparent to prospective buyers; the same $300 increase on a $25,000 Mercedes seems insignificant. A large package requires a much greater increase in size for the change to be noticeable than does a small package. People *perceive by exception,* and the change in stimuli must be sufficiently great to gain their attention.[12]

Cooking with Psychophysics

Commercials for Ragú Table Sauce, "ketchup's Italian cousin," summarized the distinctiveness of the new product offering the company was testing in Boston and Milwaukee. Ragú Foods was attempting to gain a share of the $650 million ketchup market—a market in which 97 percent of U.S. households are regular users and 44 percent purchase a bottle once a month.

Rather than compete head-on with such entrenched giants as Heinz, Hunt's, and Del Monte, Ragú decided to use a flank attack. Consumer research had uncovered a dissatisfied market segment comprised of users who considered the leading brands too bland or too sweet and who preferred a spicier sauce. From this research, the idea of "ketchup's Italian cousin" was born.

In order to develop a product with the just noticeable difference desired by this segment, Ragú Foods hired Mpi, a firm specializing in psychophysics. The company's list of clients includes Campbell Soup, PepsiCo, and Chesebrough-Pond's. Mpi conducted a series of taste tests, then used a computer to analyze the findings and construct a mathematical model to produce an "optimal sensory profile" for the ideal sauce. While some critics scoff at Mpi's ability to uncover the appropriate just noticeable difference for the chosen market target, Ragú Foods has several million dollars at stake.

Source: Information from Berkeley Rice. "Cooking with Psychophysics," *Psychology Today*, November 1978, pp. 80–84, 89, 122.

Selective Perception. Considerable light is shed by **selective perception** on the problem of getting consumers to try a product for the first time. The manufacturer bombards people with television and magazine advertising, sales promotion discounts and premiums, and point-of-purchase displays—often with little change in sales. Follow-up research shows that many consumers have no knowledge of the product or promotion. Why? Because this information simply never penetrated their *perceptual filters.* Consumers perceive incoming stimuli on a selective basis. To a large exent *they are consciously aware of only those incoming stimuli they wish to perceive.*

With such selectivity at work, it is easy to see the importance of the marketer's efforts to obtain a "consumer franchise" in the form of brand loyalty to a product. Satisfied customers are less likely to seek information about competing products. And even when it is forced on them, they are not as likely as others to allow it to pass through their perceptual filters. They simply tune out information that is not in accord with their existing beliefs and expectations.

Subliminal Perception. Is it possible to communicate with persons without their being aware of the communication? In other words, is there **subliminal perception**—*a subconscious level of awareness?* In 1957, the words "Eat popcorn" and "Drink Coca-Cola" were flashed on the screen of a New Jersey movie theater every five seconds at 1/300th of a second. Researchers reported that these messages, though too short to be recognizable at the conscious level, resulted in a 58 percent increase in popcorn sales and an 18 percent increase in Coca-Cola sales. After the findings were published, advertising agencies and consumer protection groups became intensely interested in subliminal perception.

Subliminal advertising is aimed at the subconscious level of awareness to avoid viewers' perceptual screens. The goal of the original research was to induce consumer purchasing while keeping consumers unaware of the source of their motivation to buy. Further attempts to duplicate the test findings, however, have invariably been unsuccessful.

Although subliminal advertising has been universally condemned (and declared illegal in California and Canada), it is exceedingly unlikely that it can induce purchasing except in those instances where the person is already inclined to buy. The reasons for this are:

1. Strong stimulus factors are required to even gain attention.
2. Only a very short message can be transmitted.
3. Individuals vary greatly in their thresholds of consciousness.[13] Messages transmitted at the threshold of consciousness for one person will not be perceived at all by some people and will be all too apparent to others. The subliminally exposed message "Drink Coca-Cola" may go unseen by some viewers, while others may read it as "Drink Pepsi Cola," "Drink Cocoa," or even "Drive Slowly."

Despite early fears, research has shown that subliminal messages cannot force the receiver to purchase goods that he or she would not consciously want.

Attitudes

Perception of incoming stimuli is greatly affected by attitudes about them. In fact, the decision to purchase a product is based on currently held attitudes about the product, the store, or the salesperson.

Attitudes are *a person's enduring favorable or unfavorable evaluations, emotional feelings, or pro or con action tendencies* in regard to some object or idea. They are formed over a period of time through individual experiences and group contacts and are highly resistant to change.

Since favorable attitudes are likely to be conducive to brand preferences, marketers are interested in determining consumer attitudes toward their products. Numerous attitude scaling devices have been developed, but the semantic differential is probably the most commonly used technique.[14]

Figure 5–5
Product Images of Brands X, Y, and Z

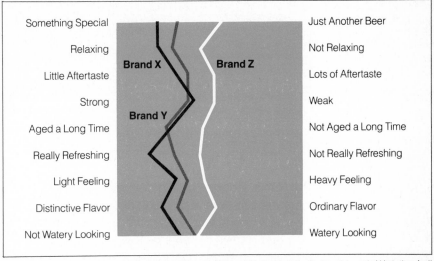

Source: Adapted from William A. Mindak, "Fitting the Semantic Differential to the Marketing Problem," *Journal of Marketing*, April 1961, pp. 28–33. Reprinted from the *Journal of Marketing* published by the American Marketing Association.

The *semantic differential* involves the use of a number of bipolar adjectives—such as new-old, reliable-unreliable, sharp-bland—on a seven-point scale. The respondent evaluates the product by checking a point on the scale between the extremes. The average rankings of all respondents then become a profile of the product.

A test comparing three unidentified brands of beer produced the profiles illustrated in Figure 5–5. Brands X and Y dominated the local market and enjoyed generally favorable ratings. Brand Z, a newly introduced beer, was less well-known and was reacted to neutrally.

Using the information provided by the profiles, weak areas in the image of any of the brands can be noted for remedial action. The semantic differential scale thus provides management with a more detailed picture of both the direction and the intensity of opinions and attitudes about a product than can be obtained through a typical research questionnaire. It supplies a comprehensive multidimensional portrait of brand images.

Producing Attitude Change. Given that a favorable consumer attitude is a prerequisite to marketing success, how can a firm lead prospective buyers to adopt this kind of attitude toward its products? The marketer has two choices: to attempt to change consumer attitudes, making them consonant with the product, or to first determine consumer attitudes and then change the product to match them.[15]

If consumers view the product unfavorably, the firm may choose to redesign it to better conform with their desires. It may make styling changes, vary ingredients, change package size, or switch retail stores.

Table 5–1
**Shopping Lists
Used in the Haire
Study**

Shopping List 1	Shopping List 2
1½ lbs. of hamburger	1½ lbs. of hamburger
2 loaves of Wonder Bread	2 loaves of Wonder Bread
Bunch of carrots	Bunch of carrots
1 can Rumford's Baking Powder	1 can Rumford's Baking Powder
Nescafé Instant Coffee	1 lb. Maxwell House coffee (drip grind)
2 cans Del Monte peaches	2 cans Del Monte peaches
5 lbs. potatoes	5 lbs. potatoes

Source: Mason Haire, "Projective Techniques in Marketing Research," *Journal of Marketing,* April 1950, pp. 649–656. Reprinted from the *Journal of Marketing* published by the American Marketing Association.

The other course of action—changing consumer attitudes—is much more difficult. A famous study of coffee drinkers revealed surprisingly negative attitudes toward those who serve instant coffee. Two imaginary shopping lists, shown in Table 5–1, were prepared and shown to a sample of a hundred homemakers. Half were shown List 1 and half List 2. Each respondent was then asked to describe the hypothetical shopper who purchased the groceries. The only difference in the lists was the instant versus the regular coffee.

The woman who bought instant coffee was described as lazy by 48 percent of the women evaluating List 1; but only 24 percent of those evaluating List 2 described the woman who bought regular coffee as lazy. Forty-eight percent described the instant coffee purchaser as failing to plan household purchases and schedules well; only 12 percent described the purchaser of regular coffee this way.

But consumer attitudes often change with time. The shopping list study was repeated twenty years later, and the new study revealed that much of the stigma attached to buying instant coffee had disappeared. Instead of describing the instant coffee purchaser as lazy and a poor planner, most respondents felt she was a working wife.[16] Nonetheless, General Foods took no chances when it introduced its new freeze-dried Maxim as a coffee that "tastes like *regular* and has the convenience of *instant.*"

Psychographics: A
New Technique in
Developing
Consumer Profiles

Chapter 4 described a number of segmentation variables for dividing broad groups of consumers into smaller, more homogeneous segments. These variables—income, population size and location, age, sex, and family life cycle stage, among others—are well-established tools for identifying and selecting market targets.

However, marketers have long recognized the need to develop fuller, more lifelike portraits of consumers for use in developing their marketing programs. In recent years, a new technique—psychographics—has been developed. It promises to be a better predictor of consumer purchase patterns than earlier techniques and to distinguish heavy users of a product from light users and nonusers.

Although definitions vary among researchers, **psychographics** generally means *psychological profiles of different consumers developed from quantitative research.* To create these profiles, consumers are asked to agree or disagree with several hundred statements dealing with a variety of activities, interests, and opinions. Some writers refer to these statements as *AIO statements.* Table 5–2 is an excerpt from a study of heavy users of eye makeup and shortening.

Hundreds of psychographic studies have been conducted on products and services ranging from beer to air travel. A study of female bank card users revealed the following profile:

The heavy user leads an active style of life; she belongs to social organizations and is concerned with her appearance. She perceives her role as homemaker as one of managing and purchasing in contrast to the traditional role of cleaning, cooking, and caring for children. She is liberal and liberated in her attitudes. She is a risk seeker, is innovative, and likes to try new things.[17]

Psychographic studies by General Foods identified the two types of dog owners most likely to purchase canned dog foods—the more expensive kind of food. The first type tended to regard dogs as baby substitutes. These consumers typically were women who lived in city apartments and owned very small dogs. The second group, the nutritionists, tended to be well-educated, to earn relatively high incomes, and to be willing to spend considerable amounts of money to keep their dogs healthy. General Foods kept these two types of consumers in mind when it introduced Cycle, the first dog food to come in four types to match the stages in a dog's life.[18]

The marketing implications of psychographic segmentation are considerable. Psychographic profiles produce rich descriptions of potential market targets and should help greatly in matching the image of the company and its product with the type of consumer using the product. Combined with demographics, psychographics can be an important tool for understanding the behavior of present and potential market targets.[19]

Learning

Marketing is as concerned with the process by which consumer decisions change over time as with describing those decisions at any one point. Thus the study of how learning takes place is important. **Learning** refers to *changes in behavior as a result of experience.*[20]

The learning process includes several components. The first component, *drive,* is *any strong stimulus that impels action.* Examples of drives are fear, pride, desire for money, thirst, pain avoidance, and rivalry.

Cues, the second component of the learning process, *are any objects*

Table 5–2
Profile of Heavy Users: Eye Makeup and Shortening

Heavy User of Eye Makeup	Heavy User of Shortening
Demographic Characteristics	
Young, well-educated, lives in metropolitan areas	Middle-aged, medium to large family, lives outside metropolitan areas
Product Use	
Also a heavy user of liquid face makeup, lipstick, hair spray, perfume, cigarettes, gasoline	Also a heavy user of flour, sugar, canned lunch meat, cooked pudding, catsup
Media Preferences	
Fashion magazines, *Tonight Show,* adventure programs	*Readers Digest,* daytime TV serials, family situation TV comedies

Activities, Interests, and Opinions
Agrees more than average with

"I often try the latest hairdo styles when they change."	"I love to bake and frequently do."
"An important part of my life and activities is dressing smartly."	"I save recipes from newspapers and magazines."
"I like to feel attractive to all men."	"I love to eat."
"I want to look a little different from others."	"I enjoy most forms of housework."
"I like what I see when I look in the mirror."	"Usually I have regular days for washing, cleaning, etc., around the house."
"I take good care of my skin."	"I am uncomfortable when my house is not completely clean."
"I would like to spend a year in London or Paris."	"I try to arrange my home for my children's convenience."
"I like ballet."	"Our family is a close-knit group."
"I like to serve unusual dinners."	"Clothes should be dried in the fresh air and out-of-doors."
"I really do believe that blondes have more fun."	"I would rather spend a quiet evening at home than go out to a party."

Disagrees more than average with

"I enjoy most forms of housework."	"My idea of housekeeping is once over lightly."
"I furnish my home for comfort, not for style."	"Classical music is more interesting than popular music."
"If it was good enough for my mother, it's good enough for me."	"I like ballet."
	"I'd like to spend a year in London or Paris."

Source: William D. Wells and Arthur D. Beard, "Personality and Consumer Behavior," in *Consumer Behavior,* Scott Ward and Thomas S. Robertson, eds., © 1973, pp. 195–196. Reprinted by permission of Prentice-Hall, Inc., Englewood Cliffs, N.J.

existing in the environment that determine the nature of the response to a drive. Examples of cues are a newspaper advertisement for a new French restaurant, an in-store display, and an Exxon sign on an interstate highway. For the hungry person, the shopper seeking a particular item, or the motorist needing gasoline, these cues may result in a specific response to satisfy a drive.

Responses are the individual's reactions to cues and drives. They include such reactions as purchasing a package of Gillette Trac II blades, dining at Burger King, or deciding to enroll at a particular college or university.

Reinforcement is the reduction in drive that results from a proper response. The more rewarding the response, the stronger becomes the bond between the drive and the purchase of that particular product. Should the purchase of Trac II blades result in closer shaves through repeated use, the likelihood of their purchase in the future is increased.

The concept of consumer learning and many of its components are illustrated in Table 5–3—an observation written in 1885.

Environmental Influences on Consumer Behavior

Thus far the chapter has concentrated on *individual* factors that affect consumer decisions. But people's lives are not dictated solely by their individual makeup. Rather, their behavior and, more specifically, their purchase actions are influenced to varying degrees by others. People are social animals, and often they buy goods and services that will enable them to project a favorable self-image to others. These influences may result from the family, from membership or reference groups, and from the individual's cultural environment.

Social Influences

Children's earliest awareness is of their membership in a very important group—the family. From this group they seek total satisfaction of their physiological and social needs. As they grow older, they join other groups—

Table 5–3
Hints to Advertisers . . . in 1885

The first time a man looks at an advertisement, he does not see it.
The second time he does not notice it.
The third time he is conscious of its existence.
The fourth time he faintly remembers having seen it before.
The fifth time he reads it.
The sixth time he turns up his nose at it.
The seventh time he reads it through and says, "Oh brother!"
The eighth time he says, "Here's that confounded thing again!"
The ninth time he wonders if it amounts to anything.
The tenth time he thinks he will ask his neighbor if he has tried it.
The eleventh time he wonders how the advertiser makes it pay.
The twelfth time he thinks perhaps it may be worth something.
The thirteenth time he thinks it must be a good thing.
The fourteenth time he remembers that he has wanted such a thing for a long time.
The fifteenth time he is tantalized because he cannot afford to buy it.
The sixteenth time he thinks he will buy it some day.
The seventeenth time he makes a memorandum of it.
The eighteenth time he swears at his poverty.
The nineteenth time he counts his money carefully.
The twentieth time he sees it, he buys the article . . .

Source: Quoted in Herbert E. Krugman, "An Application of Learning Theory to TV Copy Testing," *Public Opinion Quarterly* 26 (Winter 1962), pp. 626–634. Originally from Thomas Smith, *Hints to Intending Advertisers* (London, 1885).

Figure 5–6
Determinants of Consumer Behavior – Individual and Environmental

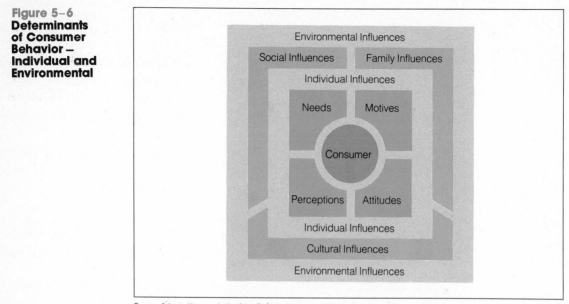

Source: Adapted by permission from C. Glenn Walters and Gordon W. Paul, *Consumer Behavior: An Integrated Framework* (Homewood, III.: Richard D. Irwin, 1970), p. 16.

neighborhood play groups, school groups, Scouts, Little League, and groups of friends, among others—from which they acquire both status and roles.

Status is *the relative position in the group of any individual member;* **roles** are *what the other members of the group expect of the individual who is in any particular position within the group.* Some groups (like the Scouts) are formal, and others (like friendship groups) are informal. Groups of either sort supply each member with both status and roles; in doing so, they influence the member's activities. Figure 5–6 shows how the social environment interacts with all other influences on the individual consumer.

Reference Groups. Group membership is not a prerequisite for group influence. In directing their purchase behavior, individuals often use **reference groups** as a basis for a decision:

Reference groups are *those with which an individual identifies to the point where the group becomes a standard, a norm, a point of reference for him.* In effect, the individual "refers" to such groups for his standards of behavior and even for his goals and personal values.[21]

Although a reference group can also be a membership group, it is not essential that the individual be a member in order for the group to serve as a point of reference. This concept helps explain the use of athletes in advertise-

**Figure 5–7
Classification of
Products and
Brands on the
Basis of
Reference Group
Influence**

	Reference Group Influence Relatively	
	Strong+	Weak−
Strong+	Cars Cigarettes Beer (Premium vs. Regular) Drugs	Clothing Furniture Magazines Refrigerator (Type) Toilet Soap
Brand or Type **Weak−**	Air-conditioners Instant Coffee TV (Black and White)	Soap Canned Peaches **Laundry Soap** **Refrigerator (Brand)** **Radios**

Source: Francis S. Bourne, *Group Influence in Marketing and Public Relations,* Foundation for Research on Human Behavior, copyright © 1956, p. 8. Reprinted by permission.

ments. Even though few racing fans possess the necessary skills, all can identify with the Indianapolis winner by injecting their engines with STP.

The extent of reference group influence varies widely. For the influence to be great, two factors must be present:

1. The item must be one that can be seen and identified by others.
2. The item must also be conspicuous; it must stand out, be unusual, and be a brand or product that not everyone owns.

Reference group influence for a variety of products and brands is shown in Figure 5–7. In the case of cars, a most conspicuous purchase, reference group influence is quite strong. Groups also exert a strong influence on the purchase of air-conditioners but not on the choice of particular brands. At the other extreme, there is negligible group influence on the purchase of canned peaches and soap, since these are typically products whose purchase is unknown to others.

Social Classes. Although people prefer to think of the United States as the land of equality, a well-structured class system does exist. Research conducted a number of years ago by W. Lloyd Warner revealed a six-class system within the social structure of both small and large cities. A description of the members of each class and an estimate of its population percentage is shown in Table 5–4.

Class membership is determined by occupation, source of income (not amount), education, family background, and dwelling area. Income is not a primary determinant; a pipefitter paid at union scale earns more than many college professors, but his or her purchase behavior may be quite different.

Table 5–4
The Warner Social
Class Hierarchy

Social Class	Membership	Population Percentage[a]
Upper-upper	Locally prominent families, third- or fourth-generation wealth. Merchants, financiers, or higher-level professionals. Wealth inherited. A great amount of traveling.	1.5
Lower-upper	Newly arrived in upper class—*"nouveau riche."* Not accepted by upper class. Executive elite, founders of large businesses, doctors, lawyers.	1.5
Upper-middle	Moderately successful professionals, owners of medium-sized businesses, and middle management. Status conscious. Child- and home-centered.	10.0
Lower-middle	Top of the average world. Nonmanagerial office workers, small business owners, and blue-collar families. "Striving and respectable." Conservative.	33.0
Upper-lower	Ordinary working class. Semiskilled workers. Income often as high as the next two classes above. Enjoy life. Live from day to day.	38.0
Lower-lower	Unskilled, unemployed, and unassimilated ethnic groups. Fatalistic. Apathetic.	16.0
	Total	100.0

[a]Estimates are based on Warner and Hollings's distributions in rather small communities. However, an estimate of social class structure for the United States approximates these percentages.
Source: Adapted with permission from Charles B. McCann, *Women and Department Store Advertising* (Chicago: Social Research, 1957).

Thus the line "A rich man is a poor man with more money" is wrong. Table 5–5 reveals far-reaching psychological differences between persons in the middle and lower classes.

Richard Coleman illustrates the behavior of three families, all earning less than $25,000 a year but all in decidedly different social classes. The upper-middle-class family in this income bracket—a young lawyer or college professor and family—is likely to spend its money in a prestige neighborhood, buy expensive furniture from high-quality stores, and join social clubs.

At the same time, the lower-middle-class family—headed by a grocery store owner or a sales representative—will probably purchase a good house in a less expensive neighborhood. It buys more furniture from less expensive stores and typically has a savings account at the local bank.

The lower-class family—headed by a truck driver or welder—spends less money on the house but buys one of the first new cars sold each year and owns one of the largest color television sets in town. It stocks its kitchen with appliances—symbols of security.[22]

Table 5–5
Psychological Differences between the Middle and Lower Social Classes

Middle Class	Lower Class
1. Pointed to the future.	1. Pointed to the present and past.
2. Viewpoint embraces a long expanse in time.	2. Lives and thinks in a short expanse of time.
3. More urban in identification.	3. More rural in identification.
4. Stresses rationality.	4. Essentially nonrational.
5. Has well-structured sense of the universe.	5. Has vague, unclear, and unstructured sense of the world.
6. Horizons vastly extended or not limited.	6. Horizons sharply defined and limited.
7. Greater sense of choice making.	7. Limited sense of choice making.
8. Self-confident, willing to take risks.	8. Very much concerned with security.
9. Immaterial and abstract in thinking.	9. Concrete and perceptive in thinking.
10. Sees self tied to national happenings.	10. World revolves around family and self.

Source: Adapted from Pierre D. Martineau, "Social Classes and Spending Behavior," *Journal of Marketing,* October 1958, p. 129. Reprinted from the *Journal of Marketing* published by the American Marketing Association.

Usage of the same product or service often varies among social classes. A study of commercial bank credit card holders, for example, uncovered class variations in how the cards were used. Lower-class families were more likely to use their credit cards for installment purchases, while upper-class families used them mainly for their convenience as a cash substitute.[23]

Role of the Opinion Leader. Each group usually contains a few members who can be considered **opinion leaders**—*trend setters.* These individuals are likely to purchase new products before others do and to serve as information sources for the others in the group.[24] Their opinions are respected, and they are often sought out for advice.

Elihu Katz and Paul Lazarsfeld have described the diffusion of information by opinion leaders as a two-step process of communication: "Ideas often proceed to flow from radio, television, and other mass media *to* opinion leaders and then from opinion leaders to the masses of the population."[25]

Because of the importance of opinion leaders in distributing information and advice, a number of companies have focused on likely opinion leaders as information outlets for new product introductions. When Ford introduced the Mustang, probable opinion leaders such as college newspaper editors, disc jockeys, and airline flight attendants were loaned Mustangs. In a similar attempt, Chrysler tried to generate conversation about its new Plymouth by offering 5,000 taxi drivers in 67 cities $5 if they would ask Chrysler "mystery riders" if they had seen the new Plymouth. Some restaurants and bars offer taxi drivers and bellhops meals and drinks at cost if they refer traveling executives and other out-of-towners to their establishments.[26]

The family represents one of the strongest sources of group influence on the individual consumer. Most people are members of two families during their lifetime—the family into which they are born and the one they eventually form as they marry and have children.

The establishment of a new household upon marriage results in new marketing opportunities. A new household means a new house or apartment and accompanying furniture. The need for refrigerators, vacuum cleaners, and, say, an original oil painting for the living room is dependent not on the number of persons comprising the household but on the number of households themselves.

Since the average household size is four persons, most milk is sold in half-gallons, most automobiles seat four or five, and most washing machines hold nine pounds of laundry. Nissan Motors has been able to greatly expand the market for its Datsun Z cars by adding a four-seat "2 + 2" series to meet the needs of family purchasers who are sports car enthusiasts.

A second market is established for parents who are left alone when children move away from home. These parents may find themselves with a four-bedroom "empty nest" and a half-acre of lawn to maintain. Lacking maintenance assistance from their children and no longer needing the large-sized house, they become customers for town houses, condominiums, and high-rise luxury apartments in the larger cities. Some become residents of St. Petersburg, Sun City, or other centers for retired persons. Others become market targets for medical insurance, travel, and hearing aids. Designing houses specifically for senior citizens is one effort to reach that market.

Traditional Family Roles. Traditionally, the wife has made the majority of the family purchases, and the husband has worked at a paying job most of the day. Even though the preferences of the children or the husband may have influenced her decisions, the wife usually has been responsible for food buying and for most of the clothing purchases. She has commonly purchased shirts and ties and even has made the final decision on her husband's suits.[27]

On the other hand, the husband traditionally has been the final authority on major purchases. Often, he has made the ultimate decision on whether the new refrigerator is to be a Westinghouse or Frigidaire—providing there are no major style differences in the two brands. Even where the decision has been shared, the husband generally has been concerned with an item's functional characteristics while the wife has evaluated its style and appearance.

James Myers and William Reynolds illustrate this use of implicit decision rules for the husband and wife in the purchase of a new car:

Often the family simply buys another car of the make previously owned. If the husband and wife disagree . . . a kind of "decision tree" comes into play. . . . If the husband and wife want to buy different makes, the ultimate purchase decision may depend on whether the two makes fall into the same or different price classes. In the first case, with both makes approximately the same price, the husband makes the decision on instrumental (functional) grounds. In the second case, the spouse favoring the *lowest price make* tends to win in the family decision process. In either case, once the decision is made, the husband then decides on such matters as engine and transmission options while the wife decides on color, trim and upholstery.[28]

Although an infinite variety of roles can be played by family members in household decision making, four role categories are often used: (1) *autonomic*—an equal number of decisions is made by each spouse, but each decision is individually made by one spouse or the other; (2) *husband dominant*; (3) *wife dominant*; and (4) *syncratic*—most decisions are jointly made by husband and wife.[29] Figure 5–8 shows the roles played by family members in the purchase of a number of products.

Changing Family Roles. Two forces are changing the wife's role as sole purchasing agent for most household items. First, a *shorter workweek* provides each wage-earning household member with more time for shopping. Second, there are a large number of *working wives.* In 1950, only one-fourth of married women were in the work force; by 1975, 44 percent were working wives. Over half of all married women with school-age children hold jobs outside the home.[30]

Studies of family decision making have shown that working wives tend to exert more influence in decision making than nonworking wives. The increased influence results from a combination of the feeling of liberation that comes from being a provider of family financial resources and the information and insights collected from persons outside the home. The result is a large number of joint decisions and an increase in night and weekend shopping.

Children's Roles in Household Purchasing. The role of the children in purchasing evolves as they grow older. Children's early influence is generally centered around toys to be recommended to Santa Claus and the choice of cereal brands. Younger children are also important to marketers of fast-food restaurants. Even though the parents may decide when to eat out, the children usually select the restaurant.[31]

As children gain maturity, they increasingly influence their clothing purchases. One study revealed that teenagers in the thirteen to fifteen age group spend an average of $12 per week. At sixteen to nineteen, their average weekly expenditures increase to $45. Teenage boys spend most of their

Figure 5–8
**Marital Roles in
25 Decisions**

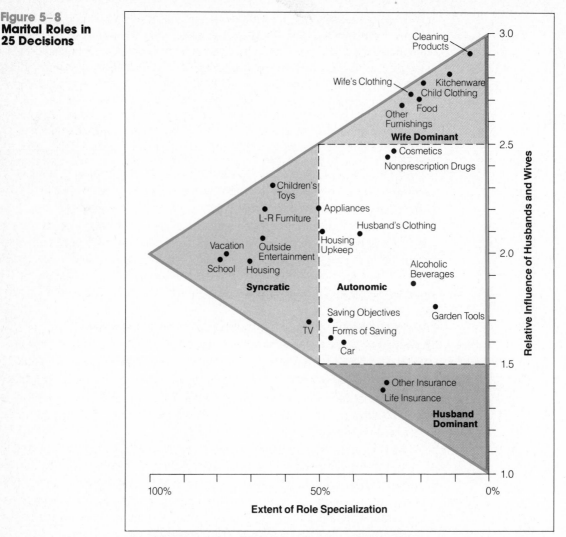

Source: Harry L. Davis and Benny P. Rigaux, "Perception of Marital Roles in Decision Processes," *Journal of Consumer Research*, June 1974, p. 57. Reprinted by permission.

funds on food, soft drinks, candy, gum, recreation, hobbies, movies, records, gasoline, and car accessories. Teenage girls spend most of their money on clothes and gifts.[32]

Cultural Influences

Culture, a more elusive term than *social class* or *reference group*, is *the complex of values, ideas, attitudes, and other meaningful symbols created by people to shape human behavior and the artifacts of that behavior as they are transmitted from one generation to the next.*[33] It is the completely learned and handed-down way of life that gives each society its own peculiar flavor.

The U.S. culture historically has been materialistic, an attitude derived from the Protestant ethic of hard work and the accumulation of traditional wealth. However, cultural values do change over time, and a number of Western core values are currently undergoing major shifts. Philip Kotler suggests that the following shifts are taking place in our core values:

From	To
Self-reliance	Government reliance
"Hard work"	The "easy life"
Religious convictions	Secular convictions
Husband-dominated home	Wife-dominated home
Parent-centered household	Child-centered household
Respect for the individual	Dislike of individual differences
Postponed gratification	Immediate gratification
Saving	Spending
Sexual chastity	Sexual freedom
Parental values	Peer-group values
Independence	Security[34]

The list in Table 5–6 is a useful summary of trends in U.S. cultural values.

As Joe Kent Kerby points out, language is an interesting cultural trait that changes within the space of a very few years. The word *rip-off* meant nothing in 1950, but it is widely used today to mean cheating, price-gouging, and other negative things. The meaning of the same word can also vary from

The head of household concept is less meaningful in the 1980s than it used to be.

"The head of the household? Oh, boy, are you gonna get me in trouble!"

Source: *Wall Street Journal*, November 15, 1977 © 1977. Reprinted by permission of the cartoonist, Brenda Burbank, and the *Wall Street Journal*.

Table 5–6
**Trends in U.S.
Values**

Trend	Manifestation
New romanticism	Desire to restore sentimentality, mystery and adventure to life
Novelty and change	Continuous search for new experiences and avoidance of sameness and repetition
Sensuousness	Emphasis on sensory experiences—touching, feeling, smelling
Mysticism	Search for new modes of spiritual experiences and beliefs
Introspection	Search for self-understanding
Physical self-enhancement	Expenditures of time, resources, and effort to maintain or enhance physical appearance and well-being
Personalization	Desire to express individuality
Physical health and well-being	Attention to diet, weight, and various aspects of physical well-being
Personal creativity	Widespread creativity in a variety of activities, hobbies, and leisure time
Meaningful work	Concern for work that is challenging and socially beneficial
Rejection of authority	Reluctance to accept the direction of authority
Female careerism	Rejection of homemaking as only career choice for women and increase in number of women in the labor force
Living for today	Rejection of traditional values of planning and saving
Blurring of the sexes	Decline in traditional distinctions between men and women
Liberal sexual attitudes	Relaxation of sexual prohibitions and deemphasis on "virtue," especially among women
Away from self-improvement	Rejection of the work ethic and a regard for "living what you are"
Return to nature	Concern for the natural and rejection of artificial ingredients

Source: *Yankelovich Monitor*, a service of Yankelovich, Skelly & White, Inc., 575 Madison Avenue, New York, NY 10022. Used by permission.

one section of the country to another. The word *dude* produces quite different images in New York and Montana.[35]

U.S. citizens have an unfortunate habit of stereotyping citizens of other countries or of using their own cultural backgrounds in relating to foreigners. But cultural differences do result in different attitudes, mores, and folkways. Consider how the examples below might influence marketing strategy:

A Goodyear advertisement demonstrated the strength of its "3T" tire cord by showing a steel chain breaking. When the commercial was shown in West Germany, however, it was perceived as an insult to steel chain manufacturers.[36]

The headline for a series of advertisements shown in Japan to introduce Seiko's new line of colored dial watches read as follows: "Like a Wind, I am the Color of a Bird." To people in the United States it was meaningless. But to Japanese consumers it meant something like: "This watch is light and delicate. It floats on your hand like a seedpod on the wind. Or a bird. A hummingbird with its jewel-like colors, the colors of the watch itself."[37]

Deodorant usage among men ranges from 80 percent in the United States to 55 percent in Sweden, 28 percent in Italy, and 8 percent in the Philippines.[38]

White is the color of mourning in Japan, and purple is associated with death in many Latin American countries.

Feet are regarded as despicable in Thailand. Athlete's foot remedies with packages featuring a picture of feet will not be well received.

Most U.S. hotels have eliminated the thirteenth floor.

In Ethiopia, the time required for a decision is directly proportional to its importance. This is so much the case that low-level bureaucrats attempt to elevate the prestige of their work by taking a long time to make decisions. U.S. citizens working in Ethiopia are innocently prone to downgrading their work in the local people's eyes by trying to speed things up.[39]

A marketing program that has been proven successful in the United States often cannot be applied directly in international markets because of cultural differences. Real differences do exist among different countries, and they must be known and evaluated by the international firm. When Helene Curtis introduced its Every Night shampoo line in Sweden, it renamed the product Every Day because Swedes usually wash their hair in the morning.[40]

Denture makers are aware of the impact of cultural differences on sales of false teeth. The people of Thailand are extremely fond of betel nuts, which stain their teeth black. For many years, once their original teeth wore out, they were replaced with black dentures. After World War II, however, fashions changed, and the Thais began using abrasives to scrub off the black stains. Abrasives are now popular items in Thailand. Scandinavians like greyish false teeth, mostly because nature has blessed them with naturally grey teeth. The Japanese select false teeth noticeably longer than their natural ones.[41]

World marketers face competition from firms in Germany, France, the Soviet Union, Japan, and a dozen other countries, as well as firms in the host nation. Therefore, they must become familiar with all aspects of the local population—including its cultural heritage. This can be accomplished by treating each country as having additional market segments that must be thoroughly analyzed prior to the development of a marketing plan for use in it.

Subcultures. Within each culture are numerous **subcultures**—*subgroups with their own distinguishing modes of behavior.* Any culture as heterogeneous as that existing in the United States is composed of significant subcultures based on factors such as race, nationality, age, rural-urban location, religion, and geographic distribution.

Inhabitants of the Southwest display a life-style that emphasizes casual dress, outdoor entertaining, and water recreation. Mormons refrain from buying tobacco and liquor. Orthodox Jews purchase kosher or other traditional foods. Blacks may exhibit interest in products and symbols of their African heritage.

Consumption Patterns of Black Shoppers

Blacks represent the largest racial/ethnic subculture in the United States. They account for 11 percent of the total population, far outdistancing the nation's second largest minority, the Spanish-speaking Americans. Several striking differences between the black and white populations are present. Almost 30 percent of blacks are below the poverty level, as defined by the U.S. Department of Commerce, compared to 10 percent of whites. Also, the black population is very young. The median age of the white population is 30 years; for blacks the median age is 24 years.

While marketers recognize that no group of 24 million people can be considered a homogeneous market segment for all products, a number of marketing studies have compared consumption patterns of blacks and nonblacks. The major findings are:

1. Blacks save more out of a given income than do whites with the same income.
2. Blacks spend more than whites at comparable levels for clothing and nonautomobile transportation; less for food, housing, medical care, and automobile transportation; and similar amounts for recreation and leisure, home furnishings, and equipment.
3. Blacks tend to own more higher-priced automobiles than comparable income white families.
4. Blacks appear to be more brand loyal than equivalent whites.
5. Black families purchase more milk and soft drinks, less tea and coffee, and more liquor than white families. In 1962, blacks accounted for almost half of all rum consumption in the United States, 41 percent of all gin, over half of all Scotch whiskies, and over 77 percent of the Canadian whiskies.
6. Black consumers react more favorably to advertisements with all black models or to integrated models than to advertisements with all white models. Whites appear to react to black models as favorably as to white models (or more so), although this varies by type of product and amount of prejudice. Black consumers *under the age of 30* appear to react unfavorably to advertisements with integrated settings.
7. Black grocery consumers tend to make frequent trips to neighborhood stores. This may be due to inadequate refrigeration and storage units and lack of transportation that would allow them to carry large amounts of groceries.
8. Black consumers tend to shop at discount stores as compared to department stores more than do comparable white consumers.

Source: These findings are summarized in James F. Engel, Roger D. Blackwell, and David T. Kollat, *Consumer Behavior*, 3rd ed. (Hinsdale, Ill.: Dryden Press, 1978), pp. 101–104.

Hispanics—Growing Market Targets. The alert marketing manager should recognize that subcultures may represent distinct market segments and should seek to increase the understanding of their motivations, needs, and attitudes. The U.S. Spanish-speaking population is increasing by more than one-half million a year and is becoming an increasingly important market segment. This is particularly true in metropolitan Miami, whose Cuban population of 430,000 is exceeded only by Havana's; Greater Los Angeles, whose 1.6 million Hispanic population is second only to Mexico City's; and New York, whose Puerto Rican population of 1.3 million is greater than San Juan's. Other concentrations of Spanish-speaking persons are found in the border states from Texas to California.

Marketers are focusing on these markets in several ways. In many communities, the sign *"Aquí se habla español"* (Spanish is spoken here) is displayed in store windows. Over 300 television and radio stations now broadcast all or a large portion of the time in Spanish. Procter & Gamble has hired Spanish-speaking salespeople to call on the 5,000 Spanish grocery stores (*bodegas)* and 750 drugstores *(farmacias)* in New York that cater to families of Puerto Rican origin.[42]

Integrating the Components of Consumer Behavior

Consumer behavior research has traditionally focused on such specific areas as attitudes, personality, and the influence of small groups on the individual. To see these fragments in their proper perspective, a conceptual model is needed. Such a model allows new research findings to be integrated properly in the search for a more complete explanation of why the individual behaves as he or she does.

The total model approach can be used in major buying situations (a first-time purchase of a new product or the purchase of a high-priced, long-lived article) and in routine purchases handled by the individual in a habitual manner (such as the purchase of a newspaper or a particular brand of chewing gum). Figure 5–9 represents a simplified schematic model of the consumer decision process.

The process begins when an unsatisfied basic determinant creates sufficient tension to motivate the consumer to take action. The tension may be the result of an internal biogenic need, such as hunger, or a need aroused by some external stimulus, such as an enticing advertisement or sight of the new product. Dissatisfaction with the present brand or product could also result in need arousal. Once the need is sufficiently aroused, the individual perceives a motive for taking action to satisfy it.

The individual is frequently aware of conflicting motives or competitive uses for his or her limited resources of time and money. The decision of a young man to buy a new motorcycle with a price tag of $1,800 could mean his foregoing of most of his planned fall wardrobe. He also may have some doubt about the reaction of his key reference group (his close friends or work associates) to the new means of transportation. And the weather may

Figure 5–9
The Consumer
Decision Process

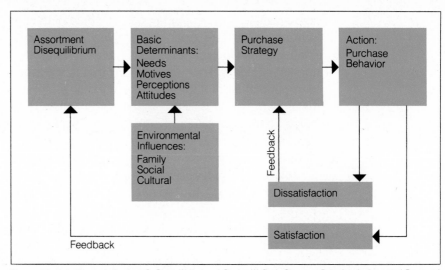

Source: Adapted with permission from C. Glenn Walters and Gordon W. Paul, *Consumer Behavior: An Integrated Framework* (Homewood, Ill.: Richard D. Irwin, 1970), p. 18.

prove too severe for him to derive enough benefits from the motorcycle to warrant the expenditure. Each of these conflicts must be resolved, or the decision process for the motorcycle will be halted at this point.

The individual's basic determinants and environmental influences operate simultaneously to affect buying behavior. Past experience, published information, and personality are also involved in evaluating a purchase decision.

In the formulation of purchase strategy, once a goal is recognized, both product and brand alternatives must be identified. In the case of the new motorcycle, available alternatives include the purchase of a used motorcycle, a second-hand car, or a ten-speed bicycle, riding with friends, or even walking. If one of the first three alternatives is chosen, the consumer must then choose from among several competing brands. The search for alternatives and the methods used in the search are influenced by such factors as (1) time and money costs, (2) the amount of information already possessed by the individual, and (3) the estimated perceived risk of making a wrong decision.

The individual looking at motorcycles may rely on his reference group for information. He may confer with other motorcycle owners. He may pay attention to advertisements or make several trips to motorcycle shops for demonstrations and additional information from sales clerks.

As the purchase action draws closer, the young man may exhibit what psychologists call the *approach-avoidance reaction* in his behavior. He may have convinced himself that he wants to buy the motorcycle, but the thought of withdrawing $1,800 from his savings may fill him with doubt. He may enter into a state of virtual panic before making the final decision, "almost" buying the motorcycle on several occasions before making the final plunge. These reactions are familiar to experienced salespeople, and they have developed such closing techniques as "no money down" and "buy now, pay later" to overcome this "terminal terror."

Postpurchase Behavior

The purchase act will result in satisfaction to the buyer—and a return to a condition of equilibrium—or dissatisfaction with the purchase. It is also common for consumers to experience some postpurchase anxieties. Leon Festinger refers to this *postpurchase doubt* as **cognitive dissonance.**[43]

Dissonance is a psychologically unpleasant state that occurs when there exists an imbalance among a person's *cognitions* (knowledge, beliefs, and attitudes). Consumers may, for example, experience dissonance after choosing a particular automobile over several alternative models when one or more of the rejected models have some desired features not available with the chosen one.

Festinger states that dissonance is likely to increase (1) as the dollar value of the purchase increases, (2) when the rejected alternatives have desirable features, and (3) when the decision is a major one. The consumer may attempt to reduce dissonance in a variety of ways. He or she may seek out advertisements and other information supporting the chosen alternative or seek reassurance from acquaintances who are satisfied purchasers of the product. The individual will also avoid information favoring the unchosen alternative. The Toyota purchaser is likely to read Toyota advertisements and to avoid Datsun and Volkswagen ads. The cigarette smoker may ignore the magazine articles reporting links between smoking and cancer.

Marketers can assist in reducing cognitive dissonance by providing informational support for the chosen alternative. Automobile dealers recognize "buyer's remorse" and often follow up purchases with a warm letter from the president of the dealership, who offers personal handling of any customer problems and includes a description of the quality of the product and the availability of convenient, top-quality service. General Motors provides Corvette purchasers with a subscription to a magazine filled with articles depicting the desirable life-style of Corvette owners.

A final method of dealing with cognitive dissonance is for the consumer to change opinions, thereby restoring the cognitive balance. In this instance, the consumer may ultimately decide that one of the rejected alternatives would have been the best choice and may decide to purchase it in the future.[44]

Should the purchase prove unsatisfactory, the consumer's purchase strategy must be revised to allow need satisfaction to be obtained. Whether satisfactory or not, feedback on the results of the decision process will serve as experience to be called upon in similar buying situations.

Summary

Understanding consumer behavior is the first step in formulating a marketing strategy. While Chapter 4 focused on demographic characteristics of the population, this chapter deals with the consumer as an individual. Consumer behavior is viewed as a problem-solving approach by which the consumer makes decisions and takes actions in order to satisfy felt needs.

Consumer behavior results from both individual and environmental influences. Individual influences include needs, motives, perceptions, and attitudes—the basic determinants in shaping the consumer's behavior. Other influences result from membership in social groups, family ties, and the broader attitudes and life-styles that result from membership in a particular culture or subculture. The simplified model of the consumer decision process shows the interactions of the basic determinants and the influences of forces from the individual's environment in shaping consumer behavior.

Market segmentation based on demographic factors is insufficient. It is also necessary to consider the consumer as an individual with basic motivations, attitudes, and life-styles. This difficult task must also be accomplished if the marketing concept is truly applied.

Questions for Discussion

1. Explain the following terms:

   self-concept   psychographics
   consumer behavior   learning
   need   status
   motive   role
   perception   reference group
   Weber's law   opinion leader
   selective perception   culture
   subliminal perception   subculture
   attitude   cognitive dissonance

2. Identify and briefly explain each of the components of the self-concept.
3. Relate each of the following to the appropriate component of the self-concept:
   a. "In two years I'll have the degree, a good job, and that bachelor pad!"
   b. "I'm outgoing, fun to be with, subscribe to *Gentlemen's Quarterly*. My friends see me as the personality kid!"
   c. "It's true that I'm outgoing and fun to be with, but I'm also much too hesitant when meeting people, especially older people."
   d. "Denise is a C student, has average athletic abilities, and is quite involved in the ecology movement."
4. What are the individual determinants of consumer behavior?
5. Explain the assumptions on which Maslow's hierarchy of needs is based.
6. Based on Maslow's hierarchy, which needs are being referred to in the following advertisements?
   a. "Never pick up a stranger!" (Prestone)
   b. "When you care enough to send the very best." (Hallmark)
   c. "Gatorade reaches the bloodstream fast!"
   d. "Country Club malt liquor is a step up from beer."
7. Explain the concept of psychophysics and its relationship to perception.
8. Explain and illustrate the two types of factors that determine whether perception will take place.
9. Why are techniques such as the semantic differential useful in measuring consumer attitudes?

10. What advantages do proponents of psychographics claim over traditional demographic segmentation?

11. Explain and illustrate each of the components of the learning process.

12. Discuss the following statement: Reference groups are sources of influence only for their members.

13. Identify and briefly explain each of the environmental influences on consumer behavior.

14. For which of the following products is reference group influence likely to be strong?
    a. digital watch
    b. skis
    c. shaving lather
    d. ten-speed bicycle
    e. portable radio
    f. cigarettes
    g. electric blanket
    h. contact lenses

15. List two products for which the following family members might be most influential:
    a. mother
    b. six-year-old child
    c. father
    d. teenage son
    e. teenage daughter
    f. two-year-old child

16. Discuss the following statement: A rich man is a poor man with money.

17. Distinguish between cultures and subcultures. Give several examples of subcultures, and specify your reasons for including each example.

18. Use the model of the consumer decision process in Figure 5–9 to explain what happened during and after the following decision. Make any assumptions that are necessary.

    Mark Washington, a senior at Memorial High School, faces the dilemma of choosing a college. He is a good student and has made all-state as a defensive end. His father is a graduate of a well-known eastern school and wants Mark to go there. Two universities that are major football powers have offered him athletic scholarships. One, located in his home town, is where his best friend has decided to go. After visiting both campuses, he decides to sign with the university located 1,200 miles away.

19. Relate the model of the consumer decision process to an industrial purchasing agent at General Mills who is buying pecans for use as a basic ingredient in the company's new cake mix.

20. Under what circumstances is cognitive dissonance most likely to occur?

Notes

1. Burt Schorr, "The Mistakes: Many New Products Fail Despite Careful Planning, Publicity," *Wall Street Journal,* April 5, 1961, pp. 1, 22.

2. See Corbett Gaulden, "Self and Ideal Self-images and Purchase Intentions," in *Proceedings of the Southern Marketing Association,* ed. Robert S. Franz, Robert M. Hopkins, and Al Toma, New Orleans, Louisiana, November 1978; and Terrence V. O'Brien, Humberto S. Tapia, and Thomas L. Brown, "The Self-concept in Buyer Behavior," *Business Horizons,* October 1977, pp. 65–74.

3. Richard H. Buskirk, *Principles of Marketing,* 3rd ed. (Hinsdale, Ill.: Dryden Press, 1970), pp. 139–140.

4. James F. Engel, Roger D. Blackwell, and David T. Kollat, *Consumer Behavior,* 3rd ed. (Hinsdale, Ill.: Dryden Press, 1978), p. 8.

5. See Kurt Lewin, *Field Theory in Social Science* (New York: Harper & Row, 1951), p. 62.

6. A. H. Maslow, *Motivation and Personality* (New York: Harper & Row, 1954).

7. Ibid., p. 382. See also George Brooker, "The Self-actualizing Socially Conscious Consumer," *Journal of Consumer Research,* September 1976, pp. 107–112.

8. Adapted from Paul T. Young, *Motivation and Emotion* (New York: Wiley, 1961), pp. 280–299.

9. Edward L. Grubb and Gregg Hupp, "Perception of Self, Generalized Stereotypes, and Brand Selection," *Journal of Marketing Research,* February 1968, pp. 58–63.

10. T. M. Deeths and J. T. Breeden, "Poisoning in Children—A Statistical Study of 1967 Cases," *Journal of Pediatrics,* February 1971, pp. 299–305.

11. Kenneth Roman and Jane Maas, *How to Advertise* (New York: St. Martin's Press, 1976), pp. 15–16.

12. Steuart Henderson Britt, "How Weber's Law Can Be Applied to Marketing," *Business Horizons,* February 1975, pp. 21–29.

13. See James H. Myers and William H. Reynolds, *Consumer Behavior and Marketing Management* (Boston: Houghton Mifflin, 1967), p. 14; J. Steven Kelly and Barbara M. Kessler, "Subliminal Seduction: Fact or

Fantasy?'' in *Proceedings of the Southern Marketing Association,* November 1978, pp. 112–114; and Joel Saegert, "Another Look at Subliminal Perception," *Journal of Advertising Research,* February 1979, pp. 55–57.

14. C. E. Osgood, G. J. Suci, and P. H. Tannenbaum, *The Measurement of Meaning* (Urbana: University of Illinois Press, 1957).

15. See Robert A. Westbrook and Joseph W. Newman, "An Analysis of Shopper Dissatisfaction for Major Household Appliances," *Journal of Marketing Research,* August 1978, pp. 450–466.

16. Frederick E. Webster, Jr., and Frederick Von Pechmann, "A Replication of the 'Shopping List' Study," *Journal of Marketing,* April 1970, pp. 61–63. See also George S. Lane and Gayne L. Watson, "A Canadian Replication of Mason Haire's 'Shopping List' Study," *Journal of the Academy of Marketing Science,* Winter 1975, pp. 48–59.

17. Joseph T. Plummer, "Life Style Patterns and Commercial Bank Credit Card Usage," *Journal of Marketing,* April 1971, pp. 35–41.

18. Peter W. Bernstein, "Psychographics Is Still an Issue on Madison Avenue," *Fortune,* January 16, 1978, p. 80.

19. For a thorough survey of previous psychographic studies and some case histories of the uses of psychographic research, see William D. Wells, "Psychographics: A Critical Review," *Journal of Marketing Research,* May 1975, pp. 196–213. See also Charles D. McCullough and Larry T. Patterson, "Demographic versus Psychographic Variables in Segmenting Markets," in *Proceedings of the Southern Marketing Association,* November 1978, pp. 97–100; William O. Bearden, Jesse E. Teel, Jr., and Richard M. Durand, "Media Usage, Psychographic, and Demographic Dimensions of Retail Shoppers," *Journal of Retailing,* Spring 1978, pp. 65–74; and Richard C. Becherer, Lawrence M. Richard, and James B. Wiley, "Predicting Market Behavior: Are Psychographics Really Better?" *Journal of the Academy of Marketing Science,* Spring 1977, pp. 75–84.

20. Learning is perhaps the most thoroughly researched field in psychology, and several learning theories have been developed. For a discussion of these theories, see Harold W. Berkman and Christopher C. Gilson, *Consumer Behavior* (Encino, Calif.: Dickenson Publishing, 1978), pp. 223–241.

21. Myers and Reynolds, *Consumer Behavior and Marketing Management,* pp. 173–174. See also John H. Murphy and William H. Cunningham, "Correlates of the Extent of Informal Friendship-Group Influence on Consumer Behavior," in *Research Frontiers in Marketing,* ed. Subhash C. Jain (Chicago: American Marketing Association, 1978), pp. 130–133.

22. See Richard P. Coleman, "The Significance of Social Stratification in Selling" and "Retrospective Comment," in *Classics in Consumer Behavior,* ed. Louis E. Boone (Tulsa, Okla.: PPC Books, 1977), pp. 288–302; and Richard P. Coleman and Lee Rainwater, *Social Standing in America: New Dimensions of Class* (New York: Basic Books, 1978).

23. John W. Slocum, Jr., and H. Lee Mathews, "Social Class and Income as Indicators of Consumer Credit Behavior," *Journal of Marketing,* (April 1970), pp. 69–74. See also Patrick E. Murphy, "The Effect of Social Class on Brand and Price Consciousness for Supermarket Products," *Journal of Retailing,* Summer 1978, pp. 33–45; and Harold W. Berkman and Christopher C. Gilson, "Social Class and Consumer Behavior: A Review for the 70s," *Journal of the Academy of Marketing Science,* Summer 1976, pp. 644–657.

24. See Danny N. Bellenger and Elizabeth C. Hirschman, "Identifying Opinion Leaders by Self-report," in *Contemporary Marketing Thought,* ed. Barnett A. Greenberg and Danny N. Bellenger (Chicago: American Marketing Association, 1977), pp. 341–344.

25. Elihu Katz and Paul F. Lazarsfeld, *Personal Influence* (New York: Free Press, 1957), p. 32.

26. Engel, Blackwell, and Kollat, *Consumer Behavior,* 3rd ed., pp. 295–296.

27. See Harry Davis, "Decision Making within the Household," *Journal of Consumer Research,* March 1976, pp. 241–260; and Donald J. Hempel, "Family Decision Making: Emerging Issues and Future Opportunities," in Greenberg and Bellenger, *Contemporary Marketing Thought,* pp. 428–431.

28. Myers and Reynolds, *Consumer Behavior and Marketing Management,* p. 243.

29. Engel, Blackwell, and Kollat, *Consumer Behavior,* 3rd ed., p. 152.

30. William Lazer and John E. Smallwood, "The Changing Demographics of Women," *Journal of Marketing,* July 1977, pp. 14–22; and Suzanne H. McCall, "Meet the 'Workwife,'" *Journal of Marketing,* July 1977, pp. 55–65. See also Rena Bartos, "What Every Marketer Should Know about Women," *Harvard Business Review,* May–June 1978, pp. 73–85; Mary Joyce, "The Professional Woman: A Potential Market Segment for Retailers," *Journal of Retailing,* Summer 1978, pp. 59–70; Myra H. Strober and Charles B. Weinberg, "Working Wives and Major Family Expenditures," *Journal of Consumer Research,* December 1977, pp. 141–147; and John Scanzoni, "Changing Sex Roles and Emerging Directions in Family Decision Making," *Journal of Consumer Research,* December 1977, pp. 185–187.

31. George J. Szybillo, Arlene K. Sosanie, and Aaron Tenenbein, "Should Children Be Seen but Not Heard?" *Journal of Advertising Research,* December 1977, pp. 7–13.

32. "Keeping Up . . . with Youth," *Parade,* December 11, 1977, p. 20. See also George P. Moschis, Roy L. Moore, and Lowndes F. Stephens, "Purchasing Patterns of Adolescent Consumers," *Journal of Retailing,* Spring 1977, pp. 17–26.
33. Engel, Blackwell, and Kollat, *Consumer Behavior,* 3rd ed., p. 65.
34. Philip Kotler, *Marketing Management* (Englewood Cliffs, N.J.: Prentice-Hall, 1976), p. 43. See also John I. Coppett, "The Consumption Ethic," *Business and Economic Perspectives,* Fall 1976, pp. 1–8.
35. Joe Kent Kerby, *Consumer Behavior* (New York: Dun-Donnelley Publishing, 1975), p. 569.
36. *Wall Street Journal,* March 9, 1977, p. 1.
37. Leon G. Schiffman and Leslie Lazar Kanuk, *Consumer Behavior* (Englewood Cliffs, N.J.: Prentice-Hall, 1978), p. 390.
38. "'Personal Care Items' Global Outlook Good," *Advertising Age,* April 1, 1974, p. 28.
39. Edward T. Hall, "The Silent Language in Overseas Business," *Harvard Business Review,* May–June 1960, p. 89.
40. Patricia L. Layman, "In Any Language, the Beauty Business Spells Success," *Chemical Week,* September 17, 1975, p. 26.
41. N. R. Kleinsfield, "This Is One Story with Teeth in It—False Ones, That Is," *Wall Street Journal,* August 18, 1975, p.1.
42. "Hispanics Push for Bigger Role in Washington," *U.S. News & World Report,* May 22, 1978, pp. 58–61. See also William G. Zikmund, "A Taxonomy of Black Shopping Behavior," *Journal of Retailing,* Spring 1977, pp. 61–72.
43. Leon Festinger, *A Theory of Cognitive Dissonance* (Stanford, Calif.: Stanford University Press, 1958), p. 3.
44. See Robert J. Connole, James D. Benson, and Inder P. Khera, "Cognitive Dissonance among Innovators," *Journal of the Academy of Marketing Science,* Winter 1977, pp. 9–20; David R. Lambert, Ronald J. Dornoff, and Jerome B. Kernan, "The Industrial Buyer and the Postchoice Evaluation Process," *Journal of Marketing Research,* May 1977, pp. 246–251; and William H. Cummings and M. Venkatesan, "Cognitive Dissonance and Consumer Behavior: A Review of the Evidence," *Journal of Marketing Research,* August 1976, pp. 303–308.

PART THREE
PRODUCT STRATEGY

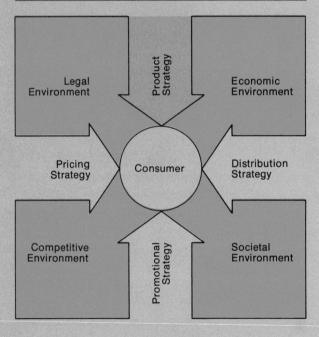

CHAPTER 6
INTRODUCTION TO PRODUCT STRATEGY

Key Terms

product
warranty
product life cycle
adoption process
consumer innovator
diffusion process
consumer goods
industrial goods
convenience goods

impulse goods
shopping goods
specialty goods
raw materials
supplies
goods-services
continuum
services

Learning Goals

1. To explain the concept of the product life cycle.
2. To identify the determinants of the speed of the adoption process.
3. To explain the methods for accelerating the speed of adoption.
4. To identify the classifications for consumer goods and to briefly describe each category.
5. To identify the types of industrial goods.
6. To explain the key distinguishing features of services.

6

This chapter considers the first element of the firm's marketing mix—the product. Since the marketing mix is designed to satisfy market targets, an appropriate starting place in its development is the careful analysis of the firm's products and services.

Planning efforts begin with the choice of products to offer the market target. Pricing structures, marketing channels, and promotional plans—the other variables of the marketing strategy—are all based on product planning. In a very real sense, the sole economic justification of the firm's existence is the production and marketing of want satisfying products.

What Is a Product?

The easiest way to respond to the question "What is a product?" is by example. The newly purchased long-playing album is a flat, black, circular pressing of vinyl in a cardboard cover. The vinyl record contains narrow grooves that produce pleasant sounds on a phonograph. But the buyer knows that the purchase is more than just an accumulation of paper, vinyl, and pleasant sounds. It is also the satisfaction that the record collection itself contains the best-selling album of the last two years.

The newlyweds' first washing machine is much more than a collection of nuts and bolts, a motor, and an enamel-covered metal box that washes clothes. It is also a respected brand name, an unconditional one-year warranty at a store with trained service personnel, and the ability to spread payments over a twelve-month period. And its features and color are esthetically pleasing.

Marketing managers must realize that people purchase more than the physical features of products. They also are buying *want satisfaction*. Most drivers know very little about the gasoline they purchase. If they bother to analyze it, they discover that it is almost colorless and emits a peculiar odor. However, most people do not think of gasoline as a product at all; to them, it is a tax—a payment they must make periodically for the privilege of driving their cars on the streets and highways. And they see the service station attendant as a tax collector.

Quality Is the Hallmark of Maytag Products

Maytag's television commercials feature the Maytag repairer as "the loneliest person in town," and their products prove it. Twenty-five years ago, the firm's late president set a standard of ten years of trouble-free operation for automatic clothes washers. Since then, Maytag has become renowned for product quality. And sales continue to increase even though the washer commands a premium of roughly $70 at retail over competitors' washers.

Some products have no physical ingredients. A razor cut by the local hair stylist produces only well-groomed hair. A tax counselor produces only advice. Therefore, a broader view of products must also include services. A **product** is *a bundle of physical, service, and symbolic attributes designed to produce consumer want satisfaction.*

The Warranty: An Important Product Component

An important feature of many products is the product **warranty**—*the guarantee to the buyer that the manufacturer will replace the product or refund its purchase price if it proves defective during a specified period of time.* Warranties increase consumer purchase confidence and are often an important means of stimulating demand. The manufacturer of Zippo lighters offers a lifetime guarantee, promising to repair or replace any damaged or defective Zippo lighter regardless of age. This warranty is one of the most important features of the firm's marketing strategy.

The *Magnuson-Moss Warranty Act* gives the Federal Trade Commission power to develop regulations affecting warranty practices for any product costing more than $15 that is covered by a written warranty. While the act does not require firms to give warranties, it is designed to assist the consumer in comparison shopping among competing products. Warranties

Should assembly be part of the broader definition of products?

"Would you assemble the easy-to-assemble kit you brought me last year?"

Source: *Wall Street Journal,* December 20, 1974. Reprinted by permission of the cartoonist, Joseph Serrano, and the *Wall Street Journal.*

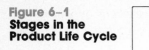

Figure 6–1
Stages in the
Product Life Cycle

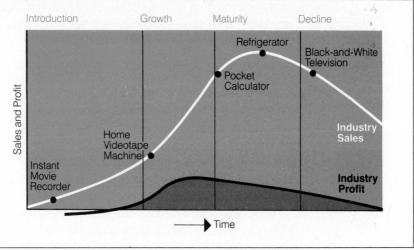

must be easy to read and understand, and firms offering them must also establish informal mechanisms for handling buyer complaints.[1]

Product Life Cycle

From their initial appearance to their death, products—like humans—pass through a series of stages. While humans progress from infancy to childhood to adulthood to retirement to death, *products progress through four stages—introduction, growth, maturity, and decline—before their death;* this progression is known as the **product life cycle.** The cycle is depicted in Figure 6–1, and each of its four stages is discussed in the following sections.

Stages of the Cycle

The firm's objective in the early stages of the product life cycle is to stimulate demand for the new market entry.

Introductory Stage. Since the product is not known to the public, promotional campaigns stress information about its features. They also may be directed toward middlemen in the channel to induce them to carry the product. In this phase, the public is acquainted with the merits of the product and begins to accept it.

As Figure 6–1 indicates, losses are common during the introductory stage due to heavy promotion and extensive research and development expenditures. But the groundwork is being laid for future profits. Firms expect to recover their costs and begin earning profits when the new product moves into the second phase of its life cycle—the growth stage.

Growth Stage. Sales volume rises rapidly during the growth stage as new customers make initial purchases and early ones repurchase it. Word-of-mouth and mass advertising induce hesitant buyers to make trial purchases. More than a half million videotape machines were sold in the United States in 1978—four times the number sold the previous year. These machines, currently in the growth stage, are in 10 percent of all U.S. homes.

As the firm begins to realize substantial profits from its investment during the growth stage, it attracts competitors. Success breeds imitation, and other firms rush into the market with competitive products in search of profit.

Maturity Stage. Industry sales continue to grow during the early part of the maturity stage, but eventually they reach a plateau as the backlog of potential customers is exhausted. By this time, a large number of competitors have entered the market, and profits decline as competition intensifies.

In the maturity stage, differences among competing products diminish as competitors discover the product and promotional characteristics most desired by the market. Heavy promotional outlays emphasize subtle differences among competing products, and brand competition intensifies.

For the first time, available products exceed industry demand. Companies attempting to increase their sales and market share must do so at the expense of competitors. As competition intensifies, the competitors tend to cut prices in an attempt to attract new buyers. Even though a price reduction may be the easiest method of inducing additional purchases, it is also one of the simplest moves for competitors to duplicate. Reduced prices result in decreased revenues for all firms in the industry unless the price cuts produce enough increased purchases to offset the loss in revenue on each item sold.[2]

Decline Stage. In the final stage of the product's life, innovations or shifting consumer preferences bring about an absolute decline in industry sales. The safety razor and electric shaver replace the straight razor, skateboards replace Pet Rocks and hermit crabs as the latest fad, and the black-and-white television is exchanged for a color set. As Figure 6–2 indicates, the decline stage of the old product is also the growth stage for the new market entry.

Industry profits decline and in some cases actually become negative as sales fall and firms cut prices in a bid for the dwindling market. Manufacturers gradually begin to leave the industry in search of more profitable products.

The Year the Undershirt Died

Products move from the maturity to the decline stage of their life cycles for a variety of reasons. Typically, a new product with more attractive features relegates the current offering to an early death. Although recent sales declines have led industry representatives to wonder aloud whether the bottom has fallen out of the underwear market, no undergarment has moved so rapidly from the maturity to the decline stage as the undershirt. And few products have experienced sales decreases for such bizarre reasons.

The year was 1934, and the movie that reportedly caused the decline was *It Happened One Night.* One scene showed Clark Gable taking off his shirt to reveal a bare chest. Undershirt sales are said to have dropped 75 percent that year.

Source: Information from "The Story, If Brief, Is Men's Underwear, and It's Full of Holes," *Wall Street Journal,* June 3, 1975, p. 1.

Utilizing the Concept

The major advantage of the product life cycle concept is that it provides insight about developments at the various stages of the product's life. Knowledge that profits follow a predictable pattern through the stages and that promotional emphasis must shift from product information in the early stages to brand promotion in the later ones should allow the marketing decision maker to improve planning.

The length of the life cycle and of each of its stages varies considerably. A new shoe fashion may have a total life span of one calendar year, with an introductory stage of two months. But the automobile has been in the maturity stage for more than twenty years. Marketing managers may be able to extend the product life cycle if they take action early in the maturity stage. Products such as Jell-O, nylon, and Scotch tape have been given extended lives through marketing moves designed (1) to increase the frequency of use by present customers, (2) to add new users, (3) to find new uses for the products, and (4) to change package sizes, labels, or product quality.[3]

Figure 6–3 depicts how the development of new uses for nylon succeeded in extending the life of this synthetic fiber. Nylon was originally used by the military in the production of parachutes, thread, and rope. It next revolutionized the women's hosiery industry and has since been used in

Figure 6–2
Overlap of Life Cycles for Products A and B

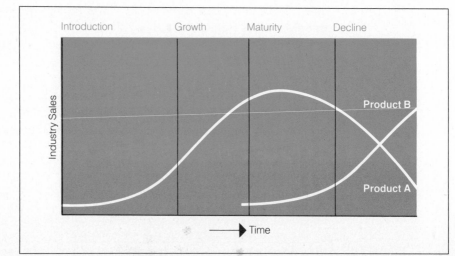

Figure 6–3
Hypothetical Life Cycle for Nylon

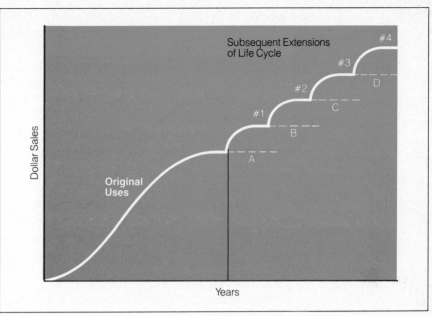

Source: Theodore Levitt, "Exploit the Product Life Cycle," *Harvard Business Review*, November–December 1965, pp. 81–94. Copyright © 1965 by the President and Fellows of Harvard College; all rights reserved. Reprinted by permission.

Product life cycles for fads are very short.

Source: Copyright © 1980 by Sidney Harris. Reprinted by permission.

producing men's stretch socks, sweaters, panty hose, body stockings, tires, carpets, and ball bearings, to name only a few products.

Tide, the synthetic detergent introduced nationally in 1947, continues to sell well in 1980. But more than fifty modifications of packaging, cleaning performance, sudsing characteristics, esthetics, and physical properties have been made during its lifetime.[4] Church & Dwight had been marketing Arm & Hammer baking soda for more than 125 years when a decision to emphasize new uses for the product revitalized its sales. Six months after its promotion as a refrigerator deodorant, an estimated 70 percent of the nation's refrigerators contained a box of Arm & Hammer baking soda!

Consumer Adoption Process

Consumers also make decisions about the new product offering. In the **adoption process,** *potential consumers go through a series of stages from learning of the new product to trying it and deciding to purchase it regularly or to reject it.* These stages in the consumer adoption process can be classified as:

1. *Awareness.* Individuals first learn of the new product but lack information about it.
2. *Interest.* They begin to seek out information about it.
3. *Evaluation.* They consider whether the product is beneficial.
4. *Trial.* They make a trial purchase in order to determine its usefulness.
5. *Adoption.* If the trial purchase is satisfactory, they decide to make regular use of the product.[5]

Knowledge of the adoption process allows the marketing manager to facilitate the movement of potential consumers to the adoption stage. Once the manager learns that a large number of potential purchasers of a new ultrasonic oven are at the interest stage, purchases may be stimulated by the company's allowing a thirty-day rental with an option to buy. S. C. Johnson & Sons introduced *Agree* shampoo by mailing 45.7 million samples to households in the United States and Canada. Total cost of the mailing was $14 million. By reducing the risk of evaluation and trial, the marketing manager can move the consumer quickly through the stages leading to adoption.

Adopter Categories

Some people purchase a new product almost as soon as it is placed on the market. Others wait for additional information and rely on the experiences of the first purchasers before making trial purchases. **Consumer innovators** — *first purchasers* — are likely to be present in each product area. Some families are first in the community to buy color television sets. Some doctors are first to prescribe new drugs, and some farmers plant new hybrid seeds much earlier than their neighbors. Some people are quick to adopt new fashions, and some drivers make early use of automobile diagnostic centers.

A number of investigations analyzing the adoption of new products have resulted in the identification of five categories of purchasers based on relative time of adoption. These categories, shown in Figure 6–4, are innovators, early adopters, early majority, late majority, and laggards.

The **diffusion process** is *the acceptance of new products and services by the members of a community or social system.* Figure 6–4 shows this process as following a normal distribution. A few people adopt at first; then the number of adopters increases rapidly as the value of the innovation is apparent. The rate finally diminishes as fewer potential consumers remain in the nonadopter category.

Since the categories are based on the normal distribution, standard deviations are used to partition them. Innovators are the first 2.5 percent to adopt the new product; laggards are the last 16 percent to do so. Excluded from Figure 6–4 are the nonadopters—those who never adopt the innovation.

Identifying the First Adopters

Locating first buyers of new products is an enticing thought for the marketing manager. If they can be reached early in the product's development or introduction, they can serve as a test market—evaluating the products and making suggestions for modifications. Since early purchasers are often opinion leaders, from whom others seek advice, their attitudes toward new products are quickly communicated to others. Acceptance or rejection of the innovation by these purchasers can help indicate the expected success of the new product.

Unfortunately, first adopters of one new product are not necessarily first adopters of other products or services. A large number of research studies have, however, established some general characteristics possessed by most first adopters.

Figure 6–4
Categories of Adopters on the Basis of Relative Time of Adoption

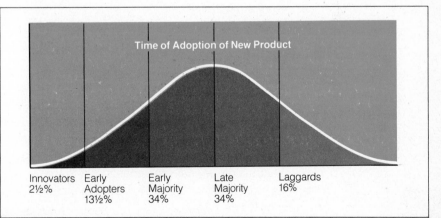

Time of Adoption of New Product

| Innovators 2½% | Early Adopters 13½% | Early Majority 34% | Late Majority 34% | Laggards 16% |

Source: Reprinted with the permission of Macmillan Publishing Company, Inc., from *Communications of Innovations: A Cross Cultural Approach* by Everett M. Rogers and Floyd F. Shoemaker (p. 182). Copyright © 1971 by the Free Press, a division of the Macmillan Company.

First adopters tend to be younger, to have a higher social status, to be better educated, and to enjoy a higher income than others. They are more mobile than later adopters and change both their jobs and home addresses more often. They are also more likely to rely on impersonal information sources than are later adopters, who depend more on promotional information from the company and word-of-mouth communications.

What Determines the Rate of Adoption?

Frisbees progressed from the product introduction stage to the market maturity stage in a period of six months. But it took the U.S. Department of Agriculture thirteen years to convince corn farmers to use hybrid seed corn—an innovation capable of doubling corn yields. The adoption rate is influenced by five characteristics of the innovation:

1. *Relative advantage*—the degree to which the innovation appears superior to previous ideas. The greater the relative advantage—manifested in terms of lower price, physical improvements, or ease of use—the faster the adoption rate.
2. *Compatibility*—the degree to which the innovation is consistent with the values and experiences of potential adopters. The failure of Analoze, the waterless pain remedy discussed in Chapter 5, resulted largely from consumers' unwillingness to accept a product whose use was contradictory to expected directions for use.
3. *Complexity.* The more difficult the new product is to understand or use, the longer it will take to be generally accepted in most cases.
4. *Divisibility*—the degree to which the innovation can be used on a limited basis. First adopters face two types of risk, financial losses and ridicule by others, if the new product proves unsatisfactory. The option of sampling the innovation on a limited basis allows these risks to be reduced and generally accelerates the rate of adoption.
5. *Communicability*—the degree to which the results of using the product are observable or communicable to others. If the superiority of the innovation can be displayed in a tangible form, the adoption rate can be increased.[6]

These five characteristics can be used to some extent by the marketing manager in accelerating the rate of adoption. Product complexity must be overcome by informative promotional messages. Products should be designed to emphasize their relative advantages and, whenever possible, should be divisible for sample purchases. If divisibility is physically impossible, in-home demonstrations or trial placements in the home can be used. Positive attempts must also be made to ensure compatibility of the innovation with the adopters' value systems.

These actions are based on extensive research studies of innovators in agriculture, medicine, and consumer goods. They should pay off in increased sales by speeding up the rate of adoption in each of the adopter categories.

A Method for Classifying Products

The output of two firms may vary from candy to forklift trucks. One company may specialize in high-quality perfumes, while another markets a line of floor wax. Different strategies must be employed to successfully market these different products.

Chanel stresses subtle promotions in prestige media such as the *New Yorker* and *Vogue* magazines and markets its perfumes through department stores and specialty shops. Hershey markets its candy products through candy wholesalers to thousands of supermarkets, variety stores, discount houses, and vending machine companies. Its marketing objective is to saturate the market and to make its candy as convenient as possible for potential buyers to purchase. A firm manufacturing and marketing forklifts may use sales representatives to call on industrial buyers and ship its product either directly from the factory or from regional warehouses.

Even though the variety of products and marketing strategies seems endless, it is possible to divide the products into subgroups and develop several generalizations about the marketing strategy to be employed for each. In Chapter 4, a distinction was made between consumer goods and industrial goods. As explained there, **consumer goods** are *products destined for use by the ultimate consumer,* and **industrial goods** are *products used directly or indirectly in producing other goods for resale.* These two major categories can be broken down further.

Characteristics of Consumer Goods

Although a number of classification systems have been suggested, the system most often used is based on *consumer buying habits.* The three categories of consumer goods are convenience goods, shopping goods, and specialty goods.[7]

Convenience Goods. *The products that the consumer wants to purchase frequently, immediately, and with a minimum of effort* are called **convenience goods.** Milk, bread, butter, eggs, and beer (the staples of the twenty-four-hour convenience food stores) are all convenience goods. So are newspapers, chewing gum, magazines, M&M's, and the items found in most vending machines.

Convenience goods are usually sold by brand name and are low-priced. Many of them—such as bread, milk, and gasoline—are staple items, and the consumer's supply must be constantly replenished. In most cases, the buyer has already decided to buy a particular brand of gasoline or candy or to buy at a particular store and spends little time deliberating about the purchase decision. He or she purchases an item through habit when supply is low. *Products of this sort purchased on the spur of the moment and in such instances are referred to as* **impulse goods.**

The consumer rarely visits competing stores or compares price and quality in purchasing convenience goods. The possible gains from such comparisons are outweighed by the costs of acquiring the additional information. This does not mean, however, that the consumer is destined to remain permanently loyal to one brand of cigarettes, beer, or candy. People continually receive new information from radio and television advertisements, billboards, and word-of-mouth communications. Since the price of most convenience goods is low, trial purchases of competing brands or products are made with little financial risk, and often new habits are developed.

Since the consumer is unwilling to expend much effort in purchasing convenience goods, the manufacturer must strive to make them as convenient as possible. Newspapers, cigarettes, and candy are sold in almost every supermarket, variety store, service station, and restaurant. Where retail outlets are physically separated from a large number of consumers, the manufacturer constructs small stores in the form of vending machines and places them in spots that are convenient for its customers (such as office buildings and factories). Even though Coca-Cola distributors feel that most people prefer their soft drink over Pepsi-Cola, they also know that they will not leave the building in search of a Coke if the vending machine is completely stocked with Pepsi. They must protect this fragile loyalty by ensuring that their product is equally available.

Retailers usually carry several competing brands of convenience products and are unlikely to promote any particular one. The promotional burden, therefore, falls on the *manufacturer,* which must advertise extensively to develop consumer acceptance of its product. The Coca-Cola promotional program consists of radio and television commercials, magazine ads, billboards, and point-of-purchase displays in stores. These efforts to motivate the consumer to choose Coke over competing brands are a good example of a manufacturer's promotion designed to stimulate consumer demand.

Shopping Goods. In contrast with convenience goods, **shopping goods** *are purchased only after the consumer has made comparisons of competing goods in competing stores on bases such as price, quality, style, and color.* The purchaser of shopping goods lacks complete information prior to the shopping trip and gathers information during it.

A woman intent on adding a new dress to her wardrobe may visit many stores, try on a number of dresses, and spend days making the final choice. She may follow a regular route from store to store in surveying competing offerings and ultimately will select the dress that most appeals to her. New stores carrying assortments of shopping goods must ensure that they are located near other shopping goods stores so that they will be included in shopping expeditions.

Shopping goods are typically more expensive than convenience goods and are most often purchased by women. In addition to women's apparel, shopping goods include such items as jewelry, furniture, appliances, shoes, and used automobiles.

Some shopping goods, such as children's shoes, are considered *homogeneous*; that is, the consumer views them as essentially the same. Others, such as furniture and clothing, are considered *heterogeneous*—essentially different. Price is an important factor in the purchase of homogeneous shopping goods, while quality and styling are relatively more important in the purchase of heterogeneous goods.[8]

Brands are often less important for shopping than for convenience goods. Of greater importance are the physical attributes of the product, its price and styling, and even the retail store that handles it. Although apparel companies spend large amounts of money promoting their brands, consumers know that the brand is inside the garment and are more impressed with how the garment looks and fits than with the hidden label.

Since buyers of shopping goods expend some effort in making their purchases, manufacturers utilize fewer retail stores than for convenience goods. Retailers and manufacturers work closely in promoting shopping goods, and retail purchases are often made directly from the manufacturer or the representative rather than the wholesaler. Fashion merchandise buyers for department stores and specialty shops make regular buying trips to regional and national markets in New York, Dallas, and Los Angeles. Buyers for furniture retailers often go directly to the factories of furniture manufacturers or visit furniture trade shows.

Specialty Goods. The specialty goods purchaser is well aware of what he or she wants and is willing to make a special effort to obtain it. The nearest Leica camera dealer may be twenty miles away, but the camera enthusiast will go there to obtain that camera. The purchase of high-quality stereo components may require a special trip to a nearby city.

A **specialty good** *possesses some unique characteristics that cause the buyer to prize that particular brand.* For these products, the buyer possesses complete information prior to the shopping trip and is unwilling to accept substitutes.

Specialty goods are typically high-priced and are frequently branded. Since consumers are willing to exert considerable effort to obtain them, fewer retail outlets are needed. Mercury outboard motors and Porsche sports cars may be handled by only one or two retailers for each 100,000 people.

The three-way classification system allows the marketing manager to gain additional information for use in developing a marketing strategy. Once the new food product has been classified as a convenience good, insights are gained about marketing needs in branding, promotion, pricing, and distribution methods.

But the classification system also poses problems. The major problem is that it suggests a neat, three-way series of demarcations into which all products can easily be fitted. Some products do fit neatly into one of the classifications, but others fall into the grey areas between each category.

How should a new automobile be classified? It is expensive, sold by brand, and handled by a few exclusive dealers in each city. But before classifying it as a specialty good, other characteristics must be considered. Most new-car buyers shop extensively among competing models and auto dealers before deciding on the best deal. A more effective way to utilize the classification is to consider it a continuum representing degrees of effort expended by the consumer (as in Figure 6–5).[9] If this is done, the new-car purchase can be located between the categories of shopping and specialty goods but nearer the specialty goods end of the continuum.

A second problem with the classification system is that consumers differ in their buying patterns. One person will make an unplanned purchase of a new Chevette, while others will shop extensively before purchasing a car. But an impulse purchase by one buyer does not make the Chevette a convenience good.

Some smokers will shop extensively to locate the store carrying their favorite brand at the lowest price. The advertising agency for Camel cigarettes (a typical convenience good) has attempted to create an impression of the product as a specialty good with a promotional campaign built around the theme "I'd walk a mile for a Camel." Goods are classified by the purchase patterns of the *majority of buyers.*

The three-way classification of consumer goods is based on consumer purchase patterns of securing a particular product. The system can be extended to retail stores by considering the reasons consumers shop at particular stores. Thus retail stores can also be classified as convenience stores, shopping stores, and specialty stores. By cross-classifying the product and store

**Figure 6–5
Continuum of
Product
Classification**

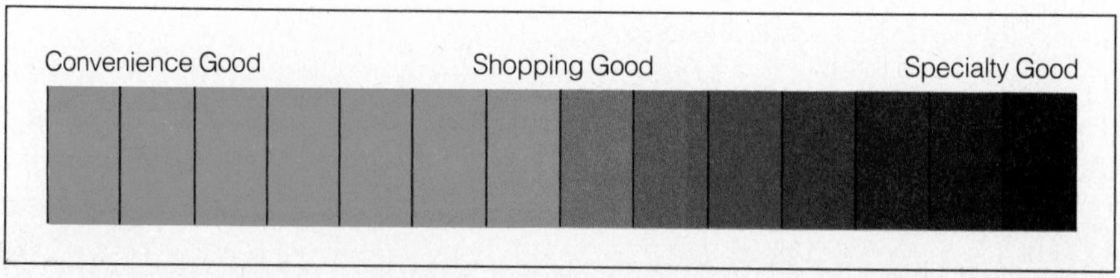

Convenience Good   Shopping Good   Specialty Good

classifications, a three-by-three matrix representing nine possible types of consumer purchase behavior is created (see Figure 6–6).

Behavior patterns in each cell can be described as:

1. *Convenience store–convenience good.* The consumer purchases the most readily available brand of the product at the nearest store.
2. *Convenience store–shopping good.* The consumer chooses a product from among the assortment carried by the most accessible store.
3. *Convenience store–specialty good.* The consumer purchases his or her favorite brand from the nearest store carrying it.
4. *Shopping store–convenience good.* The consumer is indifferent to the brand purchased; shopping is done among competing stores to secure the best services or price.
5. *Shopping store–shopping good.* The consumer makes comparisons among store-controlled factors and factors associated with the product or brand.
6. *Shopping store–specialty good.* The consumer purchases only a favorite brand but shops among a number of stores to obtain the best service or price for it.
7. *Specialty store–convenience good.* The consumer trades at only a specific store and is indifferent to the brand purchased.
8. *Specialty store–shopping good.* The consumer trades at only a specific store and chooses a product from among the assortment carried by it.
9. *Specialty store–specialty good.* The consumer has a strong preference for both a particular store and a specific brand.

This matrix gives a realistic picture of how people buy. The most exclusive specialty store carries handkerchiefs, and many supermarkets have gourmet food departments. The cross-classification system should help the retailer develop appropriate marketing strategies to satisfy particular market segments. The retailer who chooses cells 8 and 9 must seek to develop an image of exclusiveness and a good selection of widely accepted competing brands.

**Figure 6–6
A Matrix of
Consumer
Purchase
Behavior**

Goods	Stores		
	Convenience	Shopping	Specialty
Convenience			
Shopping			
Specialty			

The same retailer must also have an assortment of specialty goods, such as high-fashion clothing and expensive perfumes.[11]

As with consumer goods, industrial goods can be subdivided into categories—installations, accessory equipment, fabricated parts and materials, raw materials, and industrial supplies. But a different basis must be used in classifying industrial goods.

While the consumer goods classification system is based on consumer buying habits, this kind of basis is not used for industrial goods. Purchasers of each type of industrial product exhibit fairly uniform buying patterns, so another system must be used to classify the goods they buy. Industrial buyers are professional consumers; their job is to make effective purchase decisions. The purchase decision process involved in buying supplies of flour for General Mills is very much like that used in buying the same supplies for Pillsbury. Thus the classification system for industrial goods is based on *product uses* rather than consumer buying patterns.

Installations. *Specialty goods of the industrial market* are called *installations.* Included in this classification are major capital assets, such as factories and heavy machinery or new planes for National Airlines and diesel locomotives for the Illinois Central Railroad.

Since installations are relatively long-lived and involve large sums of money, their purchase represents major decisions for the company. Consequently, negotiations often extend over a period of several months and involve numerous decision makers. In many cases, technical expertise must be provided by the selling company. When custom-made equipment is involved, representatives of the selling firm must work closely with the buyer's engineers and production personnel to design the most feasible product for the firm.

Price is almost never the deciding factor in the purchase of installations. The purchasing firm is interested in the product's performance over its useful life. The firm wants minimum down time and fast, efficient service. Any period of nonuse during which the installation is being repaired also means the nonproductivity of employees who continue to be paid even though they cannot work until the installation is functioning again.

Since most of the factories of firms purchasing installations are geographically concentrated, the selling firm places its promotional emphasis on well-trained salespeople who often have a technical background. Most installations are sold directly from manufacturer to user. Even though a sale may be made on a one-time basis, contracts often call for regular product servicing during the life of the contract. In the case of extremely expensive installations, such as computer equipment, some firms lease the installations rather than sell them outright and assign personnel directly to the lessee to operate the equipment.

Accessory Equipment. Fewer decision makers are usually involved in purchasing *accessory equipment—capital items that are usually less expensive and shorter-lived than installations*. While quality and service are still important, the firm is likely to be much more price-conscious than for installations. Accessory equipment includes such products as typewriters, portable drills, hand tools, small lathes, and adding machines. Although these goods are considered capital items and are depreciated over several years, their useful life is generally much less than for installations.

Because of the need for continuous representation and the more widespread geographic dispersion of accessory equipment purchasers, wholesalers—often called *industrial distributors*—are used to contact potential customers in each geographic area. Technical assistance is usually not necessary, and the manufacturer of accessory equipment can effectively utilize wholesalers in marketing the firm's products. Advertising is also a more important component of the manufacturer's promotional mix than of the installation producer's.

Fabricated Parts and Materials. While installations and accessory equipment are used in producing the final product, *fabricated parts and materials are the finished industrial goods that actually become part of the final product.* Champion spark plugs make the new Chevrolet complete; batteries are often added to Mattel toys; tires are included with Checker taxis. Some fabricated materials, such as flour, undergo further processing before producing a finished product.

Purchasers of fabricated parts and materials need a regular, continuous supply of uniform quality goods. These goods are generally purchased on contract for a period of one year or more. Direct sale is common, and satisfied customers often become permanent buyers. Wholesalers sometimes are used for fill-in purchases and in handling sales to smaller purchasers.

Raw Materials. *Farm products*—such as wheat, cotton, soybeans, cattle, pigs, milk and eggs—and *natural products*—such as copper, iron ore, lumber, and coal—constitute **raw materials.** They are similar to fabricated parts and materials in that they are used in producing the final products.

Since most raw materials are graded, the purchaser is assured of standardized products with uniform quality. As is true of fabricated parts and materials, direct sale of raw materials is common, and sales are typically made on a contractual basis. Wholesalers are increasingly being utilized in the purchase of raw materials from foreign suppliers.

Price is seldom a deciding factor, since it is often quoted at a central market and is virtually identical among competing sellers. Purchasers buy from the firms they consider most able to make deliveries of raw materials in the amount and of the quality required.

Supplies. If installations represent the specialty goods of the industrial market, then operating supplies are the convenience goods. **Supplies** are *regular expense items necessary in the daily operation of the firm, but not part of the final product.*

Supplies are sometimes called *MRO items* because they can be divided into three categories: *m*aintenance items, such as floor-cleaning compounds, brooms, and light bulbs; *r*epair items, such as nuts and bolts used in repairing equipment; and *o*perating supplies, such as pencils and stationery, lubricating oil, and heating fuel.

The regular purchase of operating supplies is a routine part of the purchasing agent's job. Wholesalers are commonly used in the sale of supplies due to the items' low unit prices, small sales, and large number of potential buyers. Since supplies are relatively standardized, price competition is frequently heavy. However, the purchasing agent spends little time in making purchase decisions. He or she frequently places telephone or mail orders or makes regular purchases from the sales representative representing the local office supply wholesaler.

Services: Intangible Products[12]

Both industrial buyers and ultimate consumers are frequent purchasers of services as well as goods. Services—ranging from necessities such as electric power and medical care to luxuries such as foreign travel, backpacking guides, ski resorts, and tennis schools—now account for almost half of the average consumer's total expenditures. While *products* was defined to include both tangible and intangible items earlier in the chapter, differences do exist between tangible products and intangible services. In addition, services account for two-thirds of the private (nongovernment) labor force; they are therefore important enough to require careful analysis.

The Difficulty of Defining Services

Services are difficult to define. Marketers have traditionally considered them simply another form of goods, so little attention has been given them until recently. It is also difficult to distinguish between certain kinds of goods and services. Personal services, such as hair styling and dry cleaning, are easily recognized as services; but they represent only a small part of the total service industry.

Some firms provide a combination of goods and services to their customers. Wackenhut Corporation, a protection specialist, markets alarms and closed-circuit TVs (goods) in addition to uniformed guards and trained dogs (services). An optometrist may give eye examinations (a service) and sell contact lenses and eyeglasses (goods). Some services are an integral part of the marketing of physical goods. For example, a Burrough's computer sales representative may emphasize the firm's service capabilities at minimizing machine down time. These illlustrations suggest that some method of alleviating definitional problems in the marketing of services is needed.

One useful method is the utilization of a product spectrum, which shows that most products have both goods and services components. Figure 6–7 presents a **goods-services continuum**—*a method for visualizing the differences and similarities of goods and services.*[13] A tire is a pure good, although the service of balancing may be sold along with it or included in the total price. Hair styling is a pure service. In the middle ranges of the continuum are products with both goods and services components. The satisfaction that results from dining in an exclusive restaurant is derived not only from the food and drink but also from the services rendered by the establishment's personnel.

While it is difficult, if not impossible, to describe all the services available to consumer and industrial purchasers, a general definition can be developed. **Services** are *intangible tasks that satisfy consumer and industrial user needs when efficiently developed and distributed to chosen market segments.*

Classifying Consumer and Industrial Services

Literally thousands of services are offered to consumer and industrial users. In some instances, they are provided by specialized machinery with almost no personal assistance (such as an automated car wash). In other cases, they are provided by skilled professionals with little reliance on specialized equipment (such as accountants and management consultants). Figure 6–8 provides a means of classifying services based on the following two factors:

Figure 6–7
The Goods-Services Continuum

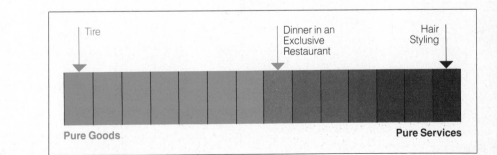

Tire / Dinner in an Exclusive Restaurant / Hair Styling
Pure Goods / Pure Services

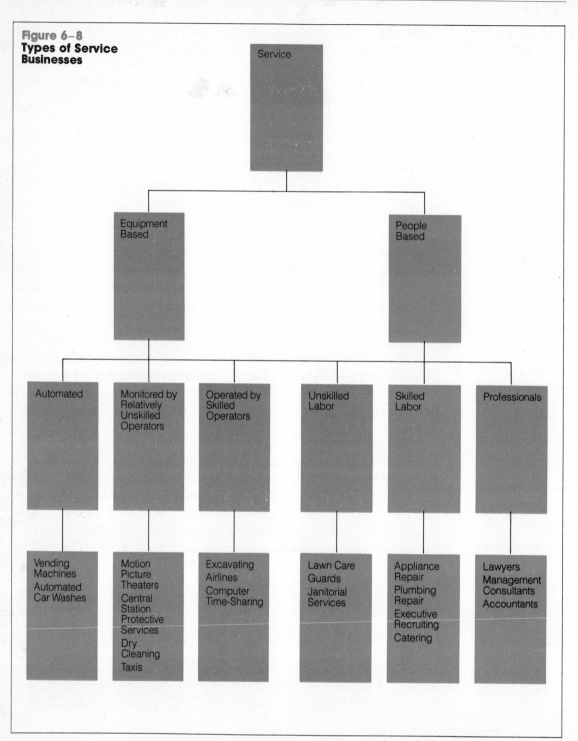

Figure 6–8
Types of Service Businesses

Service

Equipment Based

People Based

Automated

Monitored by Relatively Unskilled Operators

Operated by Skilled Operators

Unskilled Labor

Skilled Labor

Professionals

Vending Machines
Automated Car Washes

Motion Picture Theaters
Central Station Protective Services
Dry Cleaning
Taxis

Excavating
Airlines
Computer Time-Sharing

Lawn Care
Guards
Janitorial Services

Appliance Repair
Plumbing Repair
Executive Recruiting
Catering

Lawyers
Management Consultants
Accountants

(1) degree of reliance on equipment in providing the service, and (2) degree of skill possessed by the people who provide the service.

Features of Services

The preceding discussion suggests that services are varied and complex. Following are the four key features of services that have major marketing implications:

1. Services are intangible.
2. They are perishable.
3. Their standardization is difficult.
4. Buyers are often involved in their development and distribution.

Intangibility. Services do not have tangible features that appeal to consumers' senses of sight, hearing, smell, taste, and touch. They are therefore difficult to demonstrate at trade fairs, to display in retail stores, and to illustrate in magazine advertisements. They are nearly impossible to sample, and they cannot make use of many other forms of sales promotion. Consequently, imaginative personal selling is usually essential in marketing services.

Furthermore, buyers are often unable to judge the quality of a service prior to purchase. Because of this, the reputation of the service's vendor is often a key factor in a buyer's decision.

Perishability. The utility of most services is short-lived; therefore, they cannot be produced ahead of time and stored for periods of peak demand. Vacant seats on an airplane, idle dance instructors, and unused electrical generating capacity represent economic losses that can never be recovered. Sometimes, however, idle facilities during slack periods must be tolerated so the firm will have sufficient capacity for peak periods. Electric and gas utilities, resort hotels, telephone companies, and airlines all face the problem of perishability.

Difficulty of Standardization. It is often impossible to standardize offerings among sellers of the same service or even to assure consistency in the services provided by one seller. No two hair styles from the same beautician are identical. Although standardization is often desirable, it occurs only in the case of equipment based firms such as those offering automated banking services, automated car washes, and computer time sharing. Creative marketing is needed to adapt nonstandardized services to the unique needs of individual customers.

Involvement of Buyers. Buyers often play major roles in the marketing and production of services. The hair stylist's customer may describe the desired style and make suggestions at several stages during the styling process. Different firms often want unique blends of insurance coverage, and the final policy may be developed after several meetings between the purchaser and the insurance agent. Although purchaser specifications also play a role in the creation of major products such as installations, the interaction of buyer and seller at both the production and distribution stages is a common feature of services.

Personal contact between salespeople and customers occurs in the marketing of goods as well as services; however, service representatives play an even more important role. One writer described it this way:

With service retailing there is a change in the sequence of events that occur— the sale must be made before production and consumption take place. Thus the truism that all customer contact employees are engaged in personal selling is much more real for the service firm than for the goods firm. With goods, the physical object can carry some of the selling burden. With services, contact personnel *are* the service. Customers, in effect, perceive them to be "the product." They become the physical representation of the offering. The service firm employees are both factory workers *and* salespersons because of the simultaneous production and consumption of most services.[14]

Summary

A critical variable in the firm's marketing mix is the products it plans to offer its market target. The best price, most efficient distribution channel, and most effective promotional program cannot gain continuing purchases of an inferior product.

Consumers view products not only in physical terms but more often in terms of expected want satisfaction. The broad marketing conception of a product encompasses a bundle of physical, service, and symbolic attributes designed to produce this want satisfaction.

All products pass through the four stages of the product life cycle: introduction, growth, maturity, and decline. Consumers also go through a series of stages in adopting new product offerings: initial product awareness, interest, evaluation, trial purchase, and adoption or rejection of the product.

Although first adopters of new products vary among product classes, several common characteristics have been isolated. First adopters are often younger, better educated, and more mobile, and they have higher incomes and higher social status than later adopters.

The rate of adoption for new products depends on five characteristics: (1) relative advantage, the degree of superiority of the innovation over the previous product; (2) compatibility, the degree to which the new product or idea is consistent with the value system of potential purchasers; (3) complexity of the new product; (4) divisibility, the degree to which trial purchases on a small scale are possible; and (5) communicability, the degree to which the superiority of the innovation can be transmitted to other potential buyers.

Products are classified as either consumer or industrial goods. Consumer goods are used by the ultimate consumer and are not intended for resale or further use in producing other products. Industrial goods are used either directly or indirectly in producing other products for resale.

Differences in consumer buying habits can be used to further classify consumer goods into three categories: convenience goods, shopping goods, and specialty goods. Industrial goods are classified on the basis of product uses. The five categories in the industrial goods classification are installations, accessory equipment, fabricated parts and materials, raw materials, and industrial supplies.

Almost half of all personal consumption expenditures go to the purchase of services—intangible tasks that satisfy consumer and industrial user needs when efficiently developed and distributed to chosen market segments. The marketing of services has many similarities to the marketing of goods, but there are also significant differences. The key features of services are their intangibility and perishability, the difficulty of standardizing them, and the involvement of buyers in their development and distribution.

Once the firm's products have been classified, the marketing manager is provided with a number of insights in making decisions about distribution channels, price, and promotion—the three other variables of the marketing mix.

Questions for Discussion

1. Explain the following terms:

product	convenience goods
warranty	impulse goods
product life cycle	shopping goods
adoption process	specialty goods
consumer innovator	raw materials
diffusion process	supplies
consumer goods	goods-services continuum
industrial goods	services

2. Justify the inclusion of services in the definition of *product*.
3. Select a specific product in each stage of the product life cycle (other than those shown in Figure 6–1). Explain how the marketing strategies vary by life cycle stage for each product.
4. Suggest several means by which the life cycle of a product (such as Scotch tape) can be extended.
5. Identify and briefly explain the stages in the consumer adoption process.
6. Describe each of the determinants of the rate of adoption.
7. Choose a newly introduced product with which you are familiar and make some positive suggestions to accelerate its adoption rate.
8. Suggest some practical uses for currently known facts about the consumer innovator.
9. Home burglar alarm systems using microwaves are the fastest growing product in the

home security market. Such systems operate by filling rooms with microwave beams, which set off alarms when an intruder intercepts one of them. What suggestions can you make to accelerate the rate of adoption for this product?

10. Why is the basis used for categorizing industrial goods different from that used for categorizing consumer goods?

11. Of what possible value is a classification scheme that allows an automobile tire to be both a consumer and an industrial good?

12. What determines whether a product is a consumer good or an industrial good?

13. Compare a typical marketing mix for convenience goods with a mix for specialty goods.

14. Give two illustrations from your own experience of each of the following kinds of goods: convenience goods, shopping goods, and specialty goods. Justify your classifications.

15. Explain how a suit can be a convenience good for one person, a shopping good for a second, and a specialty good for a third. Does this fact of life destroy the validity of the consumer goods classification? Support your answer.

16. Classify the following consumer goods:
    a. furniture
    b. Adidas tennis shoes
    c. felt-tip pen
    d. swimsuit
    e. Datsun sports car
    f. Binaca breath freshener
    g. *People* magazine
    h. original oil painting

17. Identify a retail store and at least two specific items carried by that store that appear to match cells 4, 6, and 9 in the matrix that comprises Figure 6–6.

18. Classify the following products into the appropriate industrial goods category. Briefly explain your choice for each product.
    a. calculators
    b. land
    c. light bulbs
    d. wool
    e. paper towels
    f. nylon
    g. airplanes
    h. tires

19. How will the marketing mix for installations differ from the mix for raw materials? Support your answer with specific illustrations.

20. Identify and explain the key features of services.

Notes

1. *Warranties: There Ought to Be a Law* (Washington, D.C.: Government Printing Office, 1978).

2. Students of economics will recognize this situation as exemplifying elasticity of demand. For a discussion of the concept of elasticity, see Edwin G. Dolan, *Basic Economics*, 2d ed. (Hinsdale, Ill.: Dryden Press, 1980).

3. See David R. Rink, "A Theoretical Extension of the Product Life Cycle Concept," *Pittsburgh Business Review,* December 1977, pp. 12–19; and Charles R. Wasson, "The Importance of the Product Life Cycle to the Industrial Marketer," *Industrial Marketing Management,* August 1976, pp. 299–308.

4. "Good Products Don't Die, P&G Chairman Declares," *Advertising Age,* November 1, 1976, p. 8. See also Ben M. Enis, Raymond LaGarce, and Arthur E. Prell, "Extending the Product Life Cycle," *Business Horizons,* June 1977, pp. 46–56.

5. Everett M. Rogers and F. Floyd Shoemaker, *Communication of Innovations* (New York: Free Press, 1971), pp. 135–157. See also Thomas S. Robertson, *Innovative Behavior and Communication* (New York: Holt, Rinehart and Winston, 1971); David F. Midgley and Grahame R. Dowling, "Innovativeness: The Concept and Its Measurement," *Journal of Consumer Research,* March 1978, pp. 229–242; James W. Taylor, "A Striking Characteristic of Innovators," *Journal of Marketing Research,* February 1977, pp. 104–107; and F. Kelly Shuptine, "Identifying Innovative Behavior Patterns Using Canonical Analysis," *Journal of Business Research,* September 1977, pp. 249–260.

6. For a more thorough discussion of the speed of the adoption process, see Rogers and Shoemaker, *Communication of Innovations,* pp. 135–157.

7. This three-way classification of consumer goods was first proposed by Melvin T. Copeland. See his *Principles of Merchandising* (New York: McGraw-Hill, 1924), chaps. 2–4. For a more recent discussion of this classification scheme, see Marvin A. Jolson and Stephen L. Proia, "Classification of Consumer Goods—A Subjective Measure?" in *Marketing: 1776–1976 and Beyond* (Chicago: American Marketing Association, 1976), pp. 71–75.

8. For an early discussion of the distinctions between homogeneous and heterogeneous shopping goods,

see E. J. McCarthy, *Basic Marketing* (Homewood, Ill.: Richard D. Irwin, 1964), pp. 398–400. See also Harry A. Lipson and John R. Darling, *Marketing Fundamentals* (New York: Wiley, 1974), p. 244.

9. A similar classification scheme has been proposed by Leo Aspinwall, who considers five product characteristics in classifying consumer goods—*replacement rate, gross margin* (the difference between cost and selling price), *adjustment* (the necessary changes made in a goal to satisfy precisely the consumer's needs), *time of consumption* (the time interval during which the product provides satisfaction), and length of consumer *searching time.* See Leo V. Aspinwall, "The Characteristics of Goods Theory," in *Four Marketing Theories* (Boulder: Bureau of Business Research, University of Colorado, 1961).

10. This section is adapted from Louis P. Bucklin, "Retail Strategy and the Classification of Consumer Goods," *Journal of Marketing,* January 1963, pp. 50–55, published by the American Marketing Association.

11. See Leon G. Schiffman, Joseph F. Dash, and William R. Dillon, "The Contribution of Store-Image Characteristics to Store-Type Choice," *Journal of Retailing,* Summer 1977, pp. 3–12; and Eric N. Berkowitz, Terry Deutscher, and Robert A. Hansen, "Retail Image Research: A Case of Significant Unrealized Potential," in *Research Frontiers in Marketing,* ed. Subhash C. Jain (Chicago: American Marketing Association, 1978), pp. 62–66.

12. Some of the information in this section is from Eugene M. Johnson, "The Selling of Services" in *Handbook of Modern Marketing,* ed. Victor P. Buell (New York: McGraw-Hill, 1970), pp. 12–110 to 12–120.

13. A goods-services continuum is suggested in G. Lynn Shostack, "Breaking Free from Product Marketing," *Journal of Marketing,* April 1977, p. 77. See also John M. Rathmell, "What is Meant by Services?" *Journal of Marketing,* October 1966, pp. 32–36.

14. William R. George, "The Retailing of Services—A Challenging Future," *Journal of Retailing,* Fall 1977, pp. 89–90. See also Richard B. Chase, "Where Does the Customer Fit in a Service Operation?" *Harvard Business Review,* November–December 1978, pp. 137–142.

CHAPTER 7
ELEMENTS OF
PRODUCT STRATEGY

Key Terms

undifferentiated marketing
differentiated marketing
concentrated marketing
product line
product manager
venture team
test marketing
brand
brand name
trademark
generic name
brand recognition
brand preference
brand insistence
generic product

Learning Goals

1. To compare the three basic strategies for matching markets with product offerings.
2. To explain the reasons most firms develop a line of related products rather than a single product.
3. To identify and explain the four organizational arrangements for new-product development.
4. To list the stages in the product development process.
5. To identify the characteristics of a good brand name.
6. To describe the major functions of the package.
7. To explain the functions of the Consumer Product Safety Commission.

7

Chapter 6 dealt with the broad marketing conception of products as sources of consumer satisfaction. The president of a large tool manufacturing company had this meaning in mind when he reported to his audience at the annual stockholders' meeting that "last year we sold over a million quarter-inch bits to people who didn't want to buy them. They all wanted quarter-inch *holes*."

Chapter 6 also dealt with the impact of the product life cycle on the firm's marketing strategy and developed a classification method for both consumer and industrial goods. This chapter will focus on the other elements of a firm's product marketing strategy: the product market matching process, product line planning, the introduction of new products, the deletion of products from the product line, and product identification in the form of brands, trademarks, packaging, and product safety. Each of the decision variables represents an important area of responsibility for the marketing manager.

Product Market Matching Strategies

At the very core of the firm's strategies is the objective of matching product offerings to customers' needs. A successful match is vital to the market success of the firm.

Three basic product market strategies for achieving consumer satisfaction are available. *Firms that produce only one product and market it to all customers with a single marketing mix practice* **undifferentiated marketing.**[1] *Those that produce numerous products with different marketing mixes designed to satisfy smaller market segments practice* **differentiated marketing.** *Firms that concentrate all marketing resources on a small segment of the total market practice* **concentrated marketing.** These product market strategies are illustrated in Figure 7–1.

Figure 7–1
Three Product Market Strategies

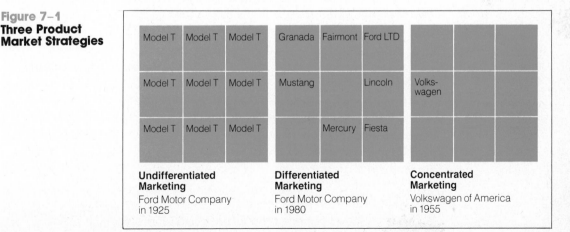

Model T	Model T	Model T
Model T	Model T	Model T
Model T	Model T	Model T

Granada	Fairmont	Ford LTD
Mustang		Lincoln
	Mercury	Fiesta

| Volkswagen | | |

Undifferentiated Marketing
Ford Motor Company in 1925

Differentiated Marketing
Ford Motor Company in 1980

Concentrated Marketing
Volkswagen of America in 1955

Undifferentiated Marketing

The policy of undifferentiated marketing was much more common in the past than it is today. Henry Ford built the Model T and sold it for one price to everyone. Realizing that people had different tastes, he agreed to paint the car any color they wanted "as long as it is black."

Although marketing managers recognize the existence of numerous segments in the total market, they generally ignore minor differences and focus on the broad market. To reach the general market, they use mass advertising, mass distribution, and broad themes.

One immediate gain from the strategy of undifferentiated marketing is the efficiency resulting from longer production runs that is not possible under a strategy of differentiated marketing. Henry Ford's major claim to fame is his mass production and marketing of a simple, well-designed product. The undifferentiated marketing strategy simplified Ford's production operations. It also minimized inventories, since neither Ford nor its affiliated automobile dealers had to contend with optional equipment and numerous color combinations.

However, there are dangers inherent in the strategy of undifferentiated marketing. A firm that attempts to satisfy *everyone* in the market faces the threat of competitors who sell specialized products to smaller segments of the total market and better satisfy each of these segments. Indeed, firms using a strategy of differentiated marketing or concentrated marketing may enter the market and capture sufficient small segments to make the strategy of undifferentiated marketing unworkable.

A firm using undifferentiated marketing may also encounter problems in foreign markets. The Campbell Soup Company suffered heavy losses in attempting to market tomato soup in the United Kingdom before discovering that the British prefer a bitterer taste. Another U.S. firm, Corn Products Company, discovered real differences in U.S. and European soup preferences when it failed in an attempt to market Knorr dry soups in the United States. Although dry soups are commonly purchased by Europeans, the U.S. homemaker prefers liquid soup, apparently because of the inconvenience associated with the fifteen- to twenty-minute cooking time for dry soups.

Differentiated Marketing

The company employing a strategy of differentiated marketing is still attempting to satisfy a large part of the total market; but instead of marketing one product with a single marketing program, it markets a number of products designed to appeal to individual parts of the total market. As Figure 7–1 indicates, Ford now offers Fairmonts, Mustangs, Granadas, LTDs, and Thunderbirds to various segments of the new-car market. The firm's objective is to produce a greater number of total sales and to develop more product loyalty in each of the submarkets. It does this by providing a marketing mix designed to serve the needs of each market target rather than inducing the segments to purchase one product designed for everyone.

Most firms practice differentiated marketing. Procter & Gamble markets Tide, Dash, Duz, Cheer, Bold, Gain, Oxydol, Bonus, and other detergents to meet the desires of detergent buyers. Lever Brothers offers two brands of complexion soap, Dove and Lux, and two brands of deodorant soap, Lifebuoy and Phase III.

By providing increased satisfaction for each of numerous market targets, the company with a differentiated marketing strategy can produce more sales than are possible with undifferentiated marketing. In general, however, the costs of differentiated marketing strategy are greater than those of an undifferentiated strategy. Production costs usually rise because additional products mean shorter production runs and increased setup time. Inventory costs rise due to added space needs for the products and increases in necessary recordkeeping. Promotional costs also increase as unique promotional mixes are developed for each market segment.

Even though the costs of doing business are typically greater under a differentiated marketing strategy, consumers are usually better served through the provision of products specifically designed to meet the needs of smaller segments. Also, a firm wishing to employ a single marketing strategy for an entire market may be forced to choose a strategy of differentiated marketing instead. If competitors appeal to each market target in the total market, the firm must also use this approach in order to remain competitive.

Concentrated Marketing

Rather than attempting to market its product offerings to the entire market, a firm may choose to focus its entire effort on profitably satisfying a smaller market target. This strategy of concentrated marketing is particularly appealing to new, small firms that lack the financial resources of their competitors.

Perhaps the most famous example of a firm practicing the concentrated marketing strategy is Volkswagen of America. For twenty years, the Volkswagen beetle was symbolic of a product specifically designed and marketed to buyers wanting economy and practical performance in their transportation. Rolls Royce is famous throughout the world for producing and marketing the ultimate in expensive, luxury automobiles.

Concentration on a segment of the total market often allows a firm to maintain a profitable operation. Fisher-Price has developed an enviable image in the toy industry because of its reputation as a high-quality manufacturer and marketer of children's toys.

Concentrated marketing, however, poses dangers as well. Since the firm's growth is tied to a particular segment, changes in the size of the segment or in the customers' buying patterns may result in severe financial problems. Sales may also drop if new competitors appeal to the same market segment.

Choosing a
Strategy

Although most business firms adopt the strategy of differentiated marketing, there is no single best strategy. Any of the three alternatives may prove to be best in a particular situation. The basic determinants of a product market strategy are company resources, product homogeneity, stage in the product life cycle, and competitive strategies.

A concentrated marketing strategy may be a necessity for a firm with *limited resources*. Small firms, for example, may be forced to choose small market targets because of limitations in financing, size of sales force, and promotional budgets.

On the other hand, an undifferentiated marketing strategy should be used for *products perceived by consumers as relatively homogeneous*. Marketers of grain sell their products on the basis of standardized grades rather than individual brand names. Some petroleum companies use a strategy of undifferentiated marketing in distributing their gasoline to the mass market.

The firm's product market strategy may also change *as the product progresses through the various stages of its life cycle*. During the introduction and growth stages, an undifferentiated marketing strategy may be useful as the firm attempts to develop initial demand for the product. In the later stages, competitive pressures may result in modified products and marketing strategies aimed at smaller segments of the total market.

A final factor affecting the choice of a product market strategy is the *strategies used by competitors*. A firm may find it unfeasible to use an undifferentiated marketing strategy if its competitors are actively cultivating smaller segments. Competition usually forces each firm to adopt the differentiated marketing strategy.

Product Line
Planning

Instances of firms whose output consists of a single product are rare today. Most firms offer the public a **product line**—*a series of related products.* The 3M Company started operations in 1900 with a single product—sandpaper. Today, it manufactures thousands of products. Several factors account for the inclination of firms to develop a complete line rather than concentrate on a single product.

Desire to Grow. A company places definite limitations on its growth potential when it concentrates on a single product. In 1979, Kellogg accounted for approximately 42 percent of the cold cereal market with Rice Krispies, Corn Flakes, Sugar Frosted Flakes, Special "K," Raisin Bran, Froot Loops, Sugar Smacks, Sugar Pops, Product 19, Apple Jacks, Frosted Mini Wheats, Cocoa Krispies, and Country Morning. Had the company been satisfied with merely producing and marketing corn flakes, its market share would have been 5 percent.

Firms often introduce new products to offset seasonal variations in the sales of their current products. Since the majority of soup purchases are made during the winter months, the annual sales curve for the Campbell Soup Company resembles a graph of the economic history of the United States. In an attempt to generate additional sales during the warmer months, when their soup was purchased primarily by persons recovering from illnesses, Campbell's management once test marketed a line of fruit soups designed to be served chilled. Sales results in the test market cities indicated that the country was apparently not yet ready for fruit soup.

Optimum Use of Company Resources. By spreading the costs of company operations over a series of products, it may be possible to reduce the average costs of all products. The Texize Company started with a single household cleaner—and learned painful lessons about marketing costs when a firm has only one major product. Management rapidly added such products as K–2r and Fantastick to the line. The company's sales representatives can now call on middlemen with a series of products at little more than the cost of a single product. In addition, Texize's advertising produces benefits for *all* products in the line. Similarly, production facilities can be used economically in producing related products. Finally, the expertise of all the firm's personnel can be applied more widely to a line of products than to a single one.

Increase of Company Importance in the Market. Consumers and middlemen often expect a firm that manufactures and markets small appliances to also offer related products under its brand name. The Maytag Company offers not only washing machines but also dryers, since consumers often demand matching appliances. Gillette markets not only razors and blades but also a full range of grooming aids, including Foamy shave cream, Right Guard deodorant, Gillette Dry Look hair spray, and Super Max hair dryers.

The company with a line of products is often more important to both the consumer and the retailer than is the company with only one product. Shoppers who purchase a tent often buy related items such as tent heaters, sleeping bags and air mattresses, camping stoves, and special cookware. Recognizing this tendency, the Coleman Company now includes in its product line dozens of items associated with camping. The firm would be little-known if its only product were lanterns.

Exploitation of the Product Life Cycle. As its output enters the maturity and decline stages of the product life cycle, the firm must add new products if it is to prosper. The regular addition of new products to the firm's line helps ensure that it will not become a victim of product obsolescence. The development of stereophonic sound in the 1950s shifted high-fidelity phonographs from the maturity stage to the decline stage. But companies such as RCA, Magnavox, and Zenith began to develop new products utilizing stereo.

Introduction of New Products

Business has been compared with bicycling: In both, you either keep moving or you fall down. New and profitable products are the life blood of the business firm. But new-product introductions are also probably the most risky of the decision maker's responsibilities. A Gallagher research report concluded that two out of three consumer products in the past ten years have failed. An A. C. Nielsen study showed a failure rate of 53 percent, and a Conference Board study of 125 firms established the *median* consumer product failure rate at 40 percent.[2]

As Figure 7–2 indicates, dozens of new-product ideas are required to produce even one successful product. The management consulting firm of Booz, Allen & Hamilton surveyed a total of fifty-one companies and reported its findings in the form of the product decay curve depicted in Figure 7–2. Of every fifty-eight ideas produced in these firms, only twelve passed the preliminary screening test designed to determine whether they were compatible with company resources and objectives. Of these twelve, only seven showed sufficient profit potential in the business analysis phase. Three survived the development phase, two made it through the test marketing stage, and only one, on the average, was commercially successful. Thus, of fifty-eight ideas, less than 2 percent resulted in a successful product.

Figure 7–2
Decay Curve of New-Product Ideas

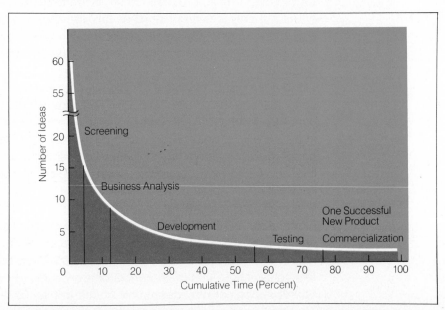

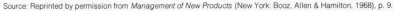

Source: Reprinted by permission from *Management of New Products* (New York: Booz, Allen & Hamilton, 1968), p. 9.

At this point, the question "What is a new product?" may be raised. New products are not always the major innovations such as digital watches or the Polaroid camera. They may merely involve a packaging innovation, such as pump dispensers, with the same ingredients as in the previous product. Or they may be an imitation of competitive products, new only to the company. The correct answer to the question "What is a new product?" appears to be "Products new to either the company or its customers."

Organizing for
New-Product
Introduction

An important prerequisite for efficient product innovations is an organizational arrangement designed to stimulate and coordinate new-product development. The development of successful products is a specialized task and requires the expertise of many departments.[3] A company that delegates new-product development responsibility to the engineering department often discovers that engineers sometimes design good products from a design standpoint but bad ones in terms of consumer needs. The major criticism of many new products is that they contain more quality than the consumer really wants to buy. Most of the successful medium- and large-sized companies employ one or more of the following alternatives in locating organizational responsibility for new-product development: (1) new-product committees, (2) new-product departments, (3) product managers, or (4) venture teams.

New-Product Committees. The most common organizational arrangement for new-product development is the new-product committee. Such a committee is typically composed of representatives of top management in areas such as marketing, finance, manufacturing, engineering, research, and accounting. Committee members are concerned less with the conception and development of new-product ideas than with reviewing and approving new-product plans.

Since the committee members are key executives in the functional areas, their support for any new-product plan is likely to result in its approval for further development. However, new-product committees tend to be slow in making decisions and conservative in their views, and sometimes they compromise so members can get back to their regular company responsibilities.

New-Product Departments. To overcome the limitations of new-product committees, a number of firms have established a separate, formally organized department responsible for all phases of the product's development within the firm, including screening decisions, development of product specifications, and coordinating product testing. One study of manufacturing firms revealed that 86 percent of the surveyed companies had established new-product departments.[4]

A formally organized new-product department makes new-product development a permanent, full-time activity. The head of the department has substantial authority and usually reports to the president or to the top marketing officer.

Product Managers. For decades, product managers have been used in department stores, where they have complete responsibility for marketing a limited line of goods. However, except in a few firms—such as Johnson & Johnson and Procter & Gamble—where they are called brand managers, the product manager concept is a relatively new one for many manufacturing firms.

The typical **product manager** *is assigned one product or product line and is given complete responsibility for determining objectives and establishing marketing strategies for it.* The manager sets prices, develops advertising and sales promotion programs, and works with sales representatives in the field. Although the product manager has no line authority over the field sales force, the objective of increasing sales for the brand is the same, and the manager attempts to help the salespeople accomplish their task.[5]

A Typical Product Manager under Thirty

Joe Antonelli graduated from California State University at Long Beach eight years ago with a major in political science. His grades improved from average at California State to above average in Arizona State University's MBA program. After graduation two years later, he accepted a position with a large consumer goods manufacturer.

Joe's first assignment was as brand manager of a liquid sugar substitute. Although he reported directly to the marketing vice-president, Joe was completely in charge of the product and made the decisions for an optimal promotional mix of the product, its price, its distribution channels, and even its chemical content.

Although Joe experienced difficulty in identifying with the product (he was a six-footer who weighed 160 pounds), his marketing efforts resulted in a market share increase of more than two percentage points in a fifteen-month period. He also averaged fifty hours per week on the job.

Joe's salary increased from an initial $17,000 annually to $19,000 after the first year. In less than a year, he was promoted to product manager of a more important part of the firm's business. His new job involved responsibility for all of the firm's cake mix and frosting line. Another raise of $3,000 accompanied this promotion.

The job was both stimulating and challenging. In effect, Joe ran a miniature company within the larger firm, dealing with all the problems and making all the decisions for a one-product firm. His next promotion placed him in charge of a group of six product managers.

In multiproduct companies such as Colgate-Palmolive, Kimberly-Clark, and Procter & Gamble, product managers are key people in the marketing departments. They provide individual attention to each product, while the firm as a whole has a single sales force, marketing research department, and advertising department that all product managers can utilize.

In addition to primary responsibility for successfully marketing a particular product or product line, the product manager is often responsible for new-product development, the creation of new-product ideas, and recommendations for improving existing products. These suggestions become the basis for proposals submitted to top management.

Using a product manager to develop new products is open to one of the same criticisms as using new-product committees for that purpose—that new-product development may get secondary treatment because of the manager's time commitments on existing products. Although a number of extremely successful new products have resulted from ideas submitted by product managers, it cannot be assumed that the skills required for marketing an existing product line are the same as those required for successfully developing new products.

Venture Teams. An increasingly common technique for organizing new-product development is the use of venture teams.[6] One-third of the hundred largest U.S. industrial firms utilize venture teams, and at least twenty of these teams have been established within the last twelve years.

The **venture team** concept is *an organizational strategy for developing new-product areas through combining the management resources of technological innovations, capital, management, and marketing expertise.*[7] Like new-product committees, venture teams are composed of specialists from different areas of the organization: engineering representatives for expertise in product design and the development of prototypes; marketing staff members for development of product concept tests, test marketing, sales forecasts, pricing, and promotion; and financial accounting representatives for detailed cost analyses and decisions concerning the concept's probable return on investment.

Unlike committees, venture teams do not disband after every meeting. Their members are assigned the project as a major responsibility, and the teams possess the authority necessary to both plan and carry out a course of action.

As a means of stimulating product innovation, the team is typically *separated from the permanent organization and linked directly with top management.* The Cudahy Packing Company moved its three-member venture team from its Phoenix headquarters to a suite of offices in New York City. Since the venture team manager reports to the division head or the chief administrative officer, communications problems are minimized and high-level support is assured.

The venture team usually begins as a loosely organized group of members with a common interest in a new-product idea. The members often are given time during the workday to devote to the venture. If the team comes up with viable proposals, it is formally organized as a task force within a venture department or reporting to a vice-president or the chief executive officer.

The criteria that must be met include prospective return on investment, uniqueness of the product, existence of a well-defined need, degree of the product's compatibility with existing technology, and strength of patent protection. Although the organization is considered temporary, the actual life span of venture teams is flexible, often extending over a number of years. When the commercial potential of new products has been demonstrated, the products may be assigned to an existing division, become a division within the company, or serve as the nucleus of a new company.

The flexibility and authority of the venture team allows large firms to develop the maneuverability of smaller companies. Venture teams established by Colgate-Palmolive have already broadened the base of the toiletries and detergents manufacturer into such products as freeze-dried flowers. Such teams also serve as an outlet for innovative marketing by providing a mechanism for translating research and development ideas into viable products:

> The venture team with its single mission, unstructured relationships, insulation from the daily routine, and entrepreneurial thrust is an organizational concept uniquely suited to the task of product innovation. For many companies whose future depends as much on the successful launching of new products as the successful marketing of existing ones, the venture-team concept offers a promising mechanism for more innovative marketing and the growth which it makes possible.[8]

Development of New Products

Once the firm has organized for new-product development, it can establish procedures for evaluating new-product ideas. The product development process involves six stages—new-product idea generation, screening, business analysis, product development, test marketing, and commercialization. At each stage, management faces the decision to (1) abandon the project, (2) continue to the next stage, or (3) seek additional information before proceeding further.[9]

New-Product Idea Generation. New-product development begins with ideas that emanate from many sources: the sales force, customers who write letters asking "Why don't you . . . ," marketing employees, research and development (R&D) specialists, competitive products, retailers, and inventors outside the company. It is important for the firm to develop a system for stimulating new ideas and for rewarding persons who develop them.[10]

Screening of New-Product Ideas. The first, crucial stage involves separating ideas with potential from those incapable of meeting company objectives. This is an important point in the product development process, since any product ideas that go beyond this stage will cost the firm time and money.[11]

Business Analysis. Product ideas surviving the initial screening are subjected to a thorough business analysis. The analysis involves an assessment of the potential market, its growth rate, and the likely competitive strength of the new product. Decisions must be made about the compatibility of the proposed product with such company resources as financial support for necessary promotion, production capabilities, and distribution facilities. The consideration of the product idea prior to its actual development is often referred to as *concept testing*.[12]

Those product ideas with profit potential are converted into a physical product. The conversion process is the joint responsibility of the development engineering department, which turns the original concept into a product, and the marketing department, which provides feedback on consumer reactions to product designs, packages, colors, and other physical features. Numerous changes may be necessary before the original mock-up is converted into the final product.

Product development requires close coordination between marketing and production.

"For generations we've used wool and grasscloth, but for true colors and durability, we now find there's nothing like Acrilan."

Source: Copyright © 1980 by Sidney Harris. Reprinted by permission.

The series of tests, revisions, and refinements should result ultimately in the introduction of a product with a great likelihood of success. Some firms obtain the reactions of their own employees to proposed new-product offerings. Employees at Levi Strauss test new styles by wearing them and reporting back on the various features. Thom McAn asks its workers to report regularly over an eight-week testing period on shoe wear and fit.

But occasional attempts to be the first with a new product result in the product's premature introduction. Kellogg and several other cereal makers experienced this problem several years ago when they all failed in their attempts to introduce freeze-dried fruit cereal. In the rush to be first on the market with the new offering, they did not perfect the product. The small, hard pellets of real fruit took too long to reconstitute in the bowl, and millions of bowls of cereal went into garbage cans.[13]

Test Marketing. To determine consumer reactions to its product under normal shopping conditions, many firms test market their new product offerings. Up to this point, consumer information has been obtained by submitting free products to consumers, who then give their reactions. Other information may come from shoppers asked to evaluate competitive products. But test marketing is the first point where the product must perform in a real-life environment.

As described in Chapter 3, **test marketing** is *the selection of a specific city or television coverage area considered reasonably typical of the total market and the introduction of the product—with a total marketing campaign—in this area.* If carefully designed and controlled, such a test allows management to develop estimates of what sales will be on a full-scale introduction.[14]

Some firms omit the test marketing stages and move directly from product development to full scale production. They cite two problems with test marketing:

1. Competitors who learn about the test marketing often disrupt the test by reducing the price of their products in the test area or by increasing their promotional outlays.
2. Test marketing a new product communicates company plans to competitors prior to the product's introduction. Kellogg discovered a new product with suspected sales potential by learning of the test marketing of a new fruit-filled tart designed to be heated in the toaster and served for breakfast. Kellogg rushed a similar product into full-scale production and became the first national marketer of the product they named Pop Tarts.

A decision to skip the test marketing stage should be based on the high likelihood of the product's success. The costs of developing a new detergent

Sabotage in the Supermarket

Many competitors have been known to disrupt test market results through price cuts, free sample offers, use of coupon offers, special dealer allowances, and the like. But Edward Buxton lists several other steps sometimes used by unethical competitors to discourage new product tests.

They'll take other steps, too, that are not so open. For example, sending in salesmen who, while supposedly checking stock, will rearrange the new brand into bottom-shelf positions. Rearranging gambits are varied. Some will see that his competitor has moved in a handsome new stand-up rack neatly stacked with his stack products. The wily competitor will, if unobserved, remove the top few rows of merchandise and put in his own. Or maybe it's a jumble display, a full bin of his competitor's products at a choice end-of-the-aisle location. The alert competitive salesman will sprinkle his own wares over the top of this bin. Another trick often used in the dairy cabinets is to rearrange a competitive milk brand so that the fresh milk is always up front. Customarily, when a driver salesman leaves off new milk in the morning, he will put yesterday's leftovers up front so that they will move out before turning bad. By pushing these to the back again, the competitor may succeed in getting some customers to buy sour milk under his rival's label. Another dairy-case trick: the competitive salesman will wear a special ring with a pin sticking out of the setting. As he stocks his own milk, his wrist will snap left and right as he punches tiny holes in the paper containers of his rival's brand. Grocers hate "leakers." The brand is dropped after a few such days.

Source: Excerpted from Edward Buxton, *Promise Them Anything* (New York: Stein & Day, 1972), pp. 88–89.

from idea generation to national marketing have been estimated at $10 million! Even though a firm experiences losses on any product that passes the initial screening process but is not introduced, it is still much better off stopping as soon as it discovers that the product cannot succeed rather than being faced with a national failure—such as Corfam, with losses of more than $100 million.

Commercialization. The few product ideas that survive all the steps in the development process are ready for full-scale marketing. Marketing programs must be established, outlays for necessary production facilities must be made, and the sales force, middlemen, and potential customers must become acquainted with the new product.

Systematic planning of all phases of new-product development and introduction can be accomplished through the use of such scheduling methods as the *Program Evaluation and Review Technique (PERT)* and the *Critical Path Method (CPM).* These techniques, developed originally by the U.S. Navy in connection with construction of the Polaris missile and submarine, map out the sequence in which each step must be taken and show the time allotments for each activity. Detailed PERT and CPM flowcharts (examined in detail in Chapter 19) coordinate all activities involved in the development and introduction of new products.

As Table 7–1 indicates, new-product development and introduction can take many years. A study of the elapsed time between initial development and full-scale introduction of forty-two products revealed a time lag ranging from one year for Gerber strained baby food to fifty-five years for television.

Table 7–1
Elapsed Time between Initial Development and Full-scale Introduction

Product	Years
Strained baby food	1
Filter cigarettes	2
Frozen orange juice	2
Polaroid Land Camera	2
Dry dog food	4
Electric toothbrush	4
Plastic tile	6
Roll-on deodorant	6
Stripe toothpaste	6
Liquid shampoo	8
Fluoride toothpaste	10
Freeze-dried instant coffee	10
Penicillin	15
Polaroid Color-pack Camera	15
Xerox electrostatic copier	15
Transistors	16
Minute rice	18
Instant coffee	22
Zippers	30
Television	55

Source: Adapted from Lee Adler, "The Lag in New Product Development," *Journal of Marketing,* January 1966, pp. 17–21, published by the American Marketing Association.

Since the time needed for orderly development of new products can be longer than expected, the planning horizon for new-product ideas may have to be extended five to ten years into the future.[15]

Product Deletion Decisions

While many firms devote a great deal of time and resources to the development of new products, the thought of eliminating old ones is painful for many executives. Often, sentimental attachments to marginal products with declining sales prevent objective decisions to drop them.

If waste is to be avoided, product lines must be pruned, and old, marginal products must eventually be eliminated. This decision is typically faced in the late maturity and early decline stages of the product life cycle. Periodic reviews of weak products should be conducted in order to prune them or justify retaining them.

In some instances, a firm will continue to carry an unprofitable product so as to provide a complete line of goods for its customers. Even though most supermarkets lose money on bulky, low unit-value items such as salt, they continue to carry it to meet shopper demand.

Shortages of raw materials have prompted some companies to discontinue the production and marketing of previously profitable items. Du Pont dropped Zerex antifreeze from its product line, and Alcoa discontinued its Alcoa aluminum foil due to raw material shortages.

In other cases, profitable products are dropped because of a failure to fit into the firm's existing product line. The introduction of automatic washing machines necessitated the development of low-sudsing detergents. Monsanto produced the world's first detergent of this sort—All—in the 1950s. All was an instant success, and Monsanto was swamped with orders from supermarkets throughout the nation. But the Monsanto sales force was primarily involved in marketing industrial chemicals to large-scale buyers, and the company would need a completely new sales force to handle the product. Nine months after the introduction of All, Procter & Gamble introduced the world's second low-sudsing detergent—Dash. The Procter & Gamble sales force handled hundreds of products and could spread the cost of contacting dealers over all of them. Monsanto had only All. Rather than attempting to compete, Monsanto sold All in 1958 to Lever Brothers, a Procter & Gamble competitor that had a marketing organization capable of handling it.

Product Identification

Manufacturers identify their products with brand names, symbols, and distinctive packaging. So also do large retailers such as Sears, Roebuck (Craftsman tools) and A&P Food Stores (Ann Page products). Almost every product distinguishable from another contains a means of identification for the buyer. Even a five-year-old can distinguish a Chiquita brand banana from a Dole one. The California Fruit Growers Exchange literally brands its oranges with the name *Sunkist*. The purchasing agent for a construction firm can turn over an ordinary sheet of aluminum and find the name and symbol for Alcoa. Choosing the means of identifying the firm's output is often a major decision for the marketing manager.

Brands, Brand Names, and Trademarks

A **brand** is *a name, term, sign, symbol, design, or some combination used to identify the products of one firm and to differentiate them from competitive offerings.* A **brand name** is *that part of the brand consisting of words or letters that comprise a name used to identify and distinguish the firm's offerings from those of competitors.*[16] It is, therefore, that part of the brand which can be vocalized. A **trademark** is *a brand that has been given legal protection; the protection is granted solely to the brand's owner.* Thus the term *trademark* includes not only the pictorial design but also the brand name. Some 400,000 trademarks are currently registered in the United States.

For the consumer, brands allow repeat purchases of the same product, since the product is identified with the name of the firm producing it. The purchaser thus can associate the satisfaction derived from a carbonated cola beverage with the brand name Coca-Cola.

"Nipper" Comes Home

Source: Information from George Lazarus, "RCA Corp. Going Back into the Doghouse," *Chicago Tribune*, October 31, 1978. Trademark used with permission of RCA Corporation.

For the marketing manager, the brand serves as the cornerstone of the product's image. Once consumers have been made aware of a particular brand, its appearance becomes further advertising for the firm. Shell Oil's symbol is instant advertising to motorists who view it while driving.

Well-known brands also allow the firm to escape some of the rigors of price competition. Although any chemist will confirm that all brands of aspirin contain the same amount of the chemical acetylsalicylic acid, Bayer has developed so strong a reputation that it can successfully market its aspirin at a higher price than competitive products. Well-known gasoline brands typically sell at slightly higher prices than independent brands because many purchasers feel that they are marketing higher quality gasoline.

What Constitutes a Good Brand Name? Good brand names are easy to pronounce, recognize, and remember. Short names like Busch, Gleem, Dash, and Kodak meet these requirements. Multinational marketing firms face a particularly acute problem in selecting brand names; an excellent brand name in one country may prove disastrous in another. When Standard Oil decided to reduce its number of gasoline brands from three (Esso, Enco, and Humble) to one, company officials ruled out Enco, because in Japanese the word means "stalled car." The ultimate choice was Exxon— a unique, distinctive name.

Datsun is a good Japanese brand name, but it is an unfortunate choice for the United States. Some people pronounce the "a" in Datsun like the "a" in "hat," and others pronounce it like the "o" in "got." But changing the name of an automobile to meet the needs of one country is an almost impossible task. Every language has "o" and "k" sounds, and "okay" has become an international word. Every language also has a short "a," so that Coca-Cola and Texaco are good brands in any country. An advertising campaign for E-Z washing machines, however, failed in the United Kingdom, because the British pronounce "z" as "zed."

The brand name should give the buyer the right connotation. Country

Club malt liquor presents favorable images of leisure life-styles. The Crafts-man name used on the Sears line of quality tools also produces the desired image. Accutron suggests the quality of the high-priced and accurate time-piece sold by Bulova. But what can the marketing manager for a jam and jelly preserve company named Smuckers do? The decision was to poke fun at this improbable name in a promotional campaign built around the theme "With a name like Smuckers it has to be good!"

Research conducted several years ago by the Cities Service Company revealed that a large number of gasoline buyers vaguely associated the brand name Cities Service with some type of public utility. In addition, the name was too long to display on billboards. Cities Service decided to change its name to a five-letter word beginning with CIT. After considering several hundred possibilities, its management selected the name CITGO and en-closed it in a new three-tone red triangle. The total cost of changing the brand name was approximately $20 million. Cities Service sales increased 11 percent the following year, compared with an industry average of 6 per-cent. Credit for the marked sales improvement was given to a revitalized marketing program, but the new, modern brand CITGO was the visible sym-bol of the changing company.

The brand name must be legally protectable. The *Lanham Act* (1946) states that registered trademarks must not contain words in general use—such as *automobile* or *suntan lotion*. These *generic words* are actually de-scriptive of a particular type of product and thus cannot be granted exclu-sively to any company.

When a unique product becomes generally known by its original brand name, the brand name may be ruled a descriptive **generic name**; if this oc-curs, the original owner loses exclusive claim to it. As Figure 7–3 indicates, the generic names *nylon, aspirin, escalator, kerosene,* and *zipper* were once brand names. Other generic names that used to be brand names are cola, yo-yo, linoleum, and shredded wheat.

There is a difference between brand names that are legally generic and those that are generic in the eyes of many consumers. *Jell-o* is a brand name owned exclusively by General Foods. But to most grocery purchasers, the name *Jell-o* is the descriptive generic name for gelatin desserts. Legal brand names—among them *Formica, Xerox, Thermopane, Kodak, Frisbee, Styro-foam, Coke, Kleenex, Scotch tape, Fiberglas, Band-Aid,* and *Jeep*—are often used by consumers as descriptive names. *Xerox* is such a well-known brand name that it is frequently used as a verb. British and Australian consumers often use the brand name *Hoover* as a verb for vacuuming.

To prevent their brand names from being ruled descriptive and available for general use, most owners take steps to inform the public of their exclu-sive ownership of the name. Eastman Kodak developed a series of advertise-ments around the theme "If it isn't an Eastman, it isn't a Kodak." Coca-Cola

Nylon
Aspirin
Escalator
Kerosene
Zipper
Addressograph®

Sometimes a company's product becomes so well known that its name becomes generic.

It's not going to happen to Addressograph, no sir. Even though some of our competitors have lately fallen into the unfortunate habit of using variations of our trademark to describe their equipment.

For 82 years, no one's beat us in offering you the broadest, best line of addressing equipment. We make the addresser you need. We always will. And now we've added folders and inserters, too.

So the next time their salesman tells you he's got something that's "just like Addressograph", please help us protect our good name. Tell him that as far as you're

concerned "there's nothing like Addressograph."

Then call your nearby AM Representative. He'll show you why you're right. Or write: Dept. M., 1800 W. Central Rd., Mt. Prospect, Ill. 60056.

We make you look better on paper.

 ADDRESSOGRAPH MULTIGRAPH
MULTIGRAPHICS DIVISION

NOTE: Nylon, Aspirin, Escalator, Kerosene, and Zipper—all once registered trademarks—are now generic dictionary words. "Addressograph" remains a registered and protected trademark of Addressograph Multigraph Corp., as it has been since 1906.

Source: Photo courtesy of A. M. Addressograph.

uses the ® symbol for registration immediately after the name *Coca-Cola* and *Coke* and sends letters to newspapers, novelists, and others who use Coke with a lower-case first letter informing them that the name is owned by Coca-Cola.[17] These companies face the dilemma of attempting to retain exclusive rights to a brand name when it is generic to a large part of the market.

Since any dictionary name may eventually be ruled generic, some companies create new words for their brand names. Names such as Tylenol, Keds, Rinso, and Kodak have been created by their owners.

Measuring Brand Acceptance. Brands vary widely in consumer familiarity and acceptance. While a boating enthusiast may insist on a Mercury outboard motor, one study revealed that 40 percent of U.S. homemakers could not identify the brands of furniture in their own homes. Brand acceptance can be measured in three stages: brand recognition, brand preference, and brand insistence.

Brand recognition is *a company's first objective for its newly introduced products—to make them familiar to the consuming public.* Often, this is achieved through offers of free samples or discount coupons for purchases. Several new brands of toothpaste have been introduced on college campuses in the free sample kits called Campus Pacs. Once consumers have used a product, it moves from the unknown to the known category, and its probability of being repurchased is increased—provided the consumer is satisfied with the trial sample.

Brand preference, the second stage of brand acceptance, is the situation where, *based on previous experience with the product, consumers will choose it rather than its competitors—if it is available.* Although the students in a classroom may prefer Coca-Cola as a means of quenching their thirst, almost all of them will quickly switch to Pepsi-Cola or Seven-Up when they discover the vending machine has no Cokes and the nearest supply is two buildings away. Companies with products at the brand preference stage are in a favorable position for competing in their industry.

Brand insistence, the last stage in brand acceptance, is where *consumers will accept no alternatives and will search extensively for the product.* A product at this stage has achieved a monopoly position with the particular group of consumers. Although brand insistence is the goal of many firms, it is seldom achieved. Only the most exclusive specialty goods attain this position with a large segment of the total market.

What Brand Strategy Should Be Used? Brands can be classified as family brands or individual brands. A *family brand* is one brand name used for several related products. Norton Simon markets hundreds of food products under the Hunt brand. General Electric has a complete line of kitchen appliances under the GE name. Johnson & Johnson offers parents a line of baby powder, lotions, plastic pants, and baby shampoo under one name.

On the other hand, manufacturers such as Procter & Gamble market hundreds of *individual brands*, such as Tide, Cheer, Crest, Gleem, Oxydol, and Dash. Each item is known by its own brand name rather than by the name of the company producing it or by an umbrella name covering similar items. Individual brands are more expensive to market, since a new promotional program must be developed to introduce each new product to its market target.

The use of family brands enables promotional outlays to benefit all products in the line; that is, the effect of the promotion is spread to each of the products. A new addition to the Heinz line gains immediate recognition because the family brand is well-known. Use of family brands also facilitates the task of product introduction to the customer and to the retailer. Since supermarkets stock an average of nearly 10,000 items, they are reluctant to add new products unless they are convinced of potential demand. A marketer of a new brand of turtle soup would have to promise the supermarket chain buyer huge advertising outlays for promotion and evidence of consumer buying intent before getting the product into the stores. With approximately 85 percent of the market, Campbell Soup could merely add the new flavor to its existing line and secure store placements much easier than could another company with individual brand names.

Family brands should be used only when the products are of similar quality, or the firm will risk harming its product image. Use of the Mercedes brand name on a new, less expensive auto might severely tarnish the image of the other models in the Mercedes product line.

Individual brand names should also be used for dissimilar products. Campbell Soup once marketed a line of dry soups under the brand name Red Kettle. Large marketers of grocery products—such as Procter & Gamble, General Foods, and Lever Brothers—employ individual brands to appeal to unique market segments. These brands also enable the firm to stimulate competition within the organization and to increase total company sales. Consumers who do not want Tide can choose Dash or Oxydol rather than purchase a competitor's brand.

National Brands or Private Brands? Most of the brands mentioned in this chapter have been manufacturers' brands—commonly termed *national brands.* But, to an increasing extent, large wholesalers and retailers operating over a regional or national market are placing their own brands on the products they market. The brands offered by wholesalers and retailers are usually called *private brands.*[18] Sears, Roebuck, the nation's largest retailer, sells its own brands—Kenmore, Coldspot, Craftsman, DieHard, and Harmony House. A&P shelves are filled with such company brands as Ann Page, Jane Parker, Sultana, and Iona. In total, A&P brands represent 30 percent of all products in the average A&P supermarket.

Private brands allow large retailers such as Sears, Safeway, and J. C. Penney to establish an image and to maintain control over the products they handle. Quality, price, and availability of products become the responsibility of the retailer or wholesaler who develops a line of private brands.

Even though the manufacturers' brands are largely presold through national promotional efforts, the wholesaler and retailer can easily lose customers when the same products are available in competing stores. But only Sears handles the Kenmore line of appliances. By eliminating the promotion costs of the manufacturers' brands, the dealer can usually offer a private brand at a price lower than that for the competing national brands.

Generics—New Form of Private Brands. One result of the continuing worldwide inflation and subsequent rising prices for consumer goods has been the introduction of **generic products**—*food and household staples characterized by plain labels, little or no advertising, and no brand names.* Generic products were first sold in Europe, where their prices were as much as 30 percent below brand name products. By 1979, they had captured 40 percent of total volume in European supermarkets.

This new version of private brands is rapidly becoming accepted in the United States. Surveys indicate that both professional, college-educated consumers and lower-income, blue-collar consumers are heavy purchasers of generics. Canned vegetables are the most commonly purchased generic product, followed by fruits and paper goods. Shoppers are indicating a willingness to forego the known quality levels of regular brands in exchange for the lower prices of the generics.[19]

Battle of the Brands. Competition between manufacturers' brands and the private brands offered by wholesalers and large retailers has been called the *battle of the brands.* Although the battle appears to be intensifying, the marketing impact varies widely among industries. One survey showed that private brands represented 36 percent of the market in replacement tires but only 7 percent in portable appliances. Private brands account for 52 percent of shoe sales but only 15 percent of gasoline sales.

The growth of private brands has paralleled the growth of chain stores in the United States, most of which has occurred since the 1930s. Chains that use their own brands become customers of the manufacturer, which places the chains' private brand names on the products it produces.

Such leading manufacturers as Westinghouse, Armstrong Rubber, and Heinz are obtaining larger and larger percentages of their total income through selling private label goods. Private label sales to Sears and other major customers account for two-thirds of Whirlpool's sales.

Polaroid recently began manufacturing private label instant cameras for Sears. Witco Chemical Company, the nation's largest producer of private brand detergents, recently introduced its own brand—Active. This brand now competes with Witco brands sold by Safeway, Jewel, and other retailers, which puts Witco in the position of competing with its own customers.[20] Although some manufacturers refuse to produce private brand goods, most regard such production as reaching another segment of the total market.

It is clear that great inroads have been made on the dominance of the manufacturers' national brands. Private brands and generics have proven that they can compete with national brands and have often succeeded in causing price reductions on the national brands to make them more competitive.

Packaging

The package is a vital part of the total product. It offers physical protection for the product while simultaneously promoting it on the store shelf. It must accomplish these tasks at a reasonable cost.

The importance of packaging can be inferred from the size of the industry. The U.S. packaging industry is comparable in size with the automobile and meat-packing industries. Approximately $50 billion is spent annually on packaging. With about 1 million workers, the package making industry is one of the nation's largest industrial employers.

For some products, packaging is a major cost. For example, it represents the largest single item in the cost of producing a can of beer. In the case of the single-serving packets of sugar found on restaurant tables, packaging accounts for 70 percent of the total cost.

A third packaging objective is convenience.[21] Pump dispenser cans facilitate the use of products ranging from whipped cream to insect repellant. Pop-top cans provide added convenience for soft drinks, beer, and other food products. The six-pack carton, first introduced by Coca-Cola in the 1930s, can be carried with minimum effort by the food shopper.

Packaging can play an important role for the retailer in preventing pilferage. At the retail level, pilferage is estimated to cost retailers $9 million each day. Bubble packages with oversized cardboard backing usually are too large to fit in a shoplifter's pocket or purse.

A growing number of firms are designing packages intended for reuse. Peanut butter and jelly jars have long been used as glasses. Bubble bath is purchased in plastic animal containers. During the holiday season, bourbon is often packaged in attractive decanters. Even laundry bleach comes in a plastic container designed for further use.

The Metric System's Effects on Packaging

Steadily and without much fanfare, the United States is adopting the *metric system*—the standard of weights and measures based on the decimal system of ten and its multiples and used throughout most of the world. Seven-Up now comes in half liter and liter bottles as a substitute for pints and quarts. Some canned and packaged foods list metric equivalents to ounces and pounds on their labels. Mustangs equipped with 2.3 liter engines are being powered by motors designed entirely in metric measurements.

While many people fail to understand the new system—and laugh at stories about a Miss America measuring 91-66-91 and Reggie Jackson hitting a 112-meter home run—preparations are already underway to equip the next generation with a working knowledge of metrics. Twenty-five states, the District of Columbia, and several territories have already begun to prepare classwork in metrics. In California, all elementary school math texts must include metrics. Many major league baseball clubs have marked their stadiums in both feet and meters. At Metropolitan Stadium, home of the Minnesota Twins, the distance from home plate to the left-field foul pole is indicated by two numerals painted on the stands: 330 (for feet) and 100 (for meters.)

International marketers are making the switch to enable them to compete in a metric world. Such firms as Caterpillar Tractor, John Deere, International Harvester, and IBM have been using metrics for years in their foreign trade. The switch to metrics should increase export sales by small U.S. firms that cannot afford to produce two sets of products for different markets.

Refusal to convert to the metric system would eventually isolate U.S. manufacturers from the rest of the industrialized nations. The only countries that have not already begun to convert to metrics are Brunei, Burma, Liberia, the Yemen Arab Republic, and the Yemen People's Democratic Republic.[22]

Labeling

Although in the past the label was often a separate item applied to the package, most of today's plastic packages contain it as an integral part of the package. Labels perform both promotional and informational functions. A **label** in most instances contains *the brand name or symbol, the name and address of the manufacturer or distributor, the product composition and size, and the recommended uses for the product.*

Consumer confusion and dissatisfaction over such incomprehensible sizes as giant economy size, king size, and family size led to the passage of the *Fair Packaging and Labeling Act* (1966). The act requires adequate in-

Labeling of food products is a government requirement as well as a marketing tool.

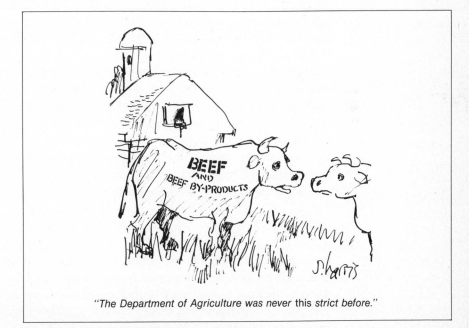

"The Department of Agriculture was never this strict before."

Source: Copyright © 1980 by Sidney Harris. Reprinted by permission.

Figure 7–4
**Product Label
with Specified
Nutritional
Contents**

Source: Reprinted by permission of Del Monte.

formation concerning the package contents and a package design that facilitates value comparisons among competitive products.

Food and Drug Administration regulations require that the nutritional contents be listed on the label of any food product to which a nutrient has been added or for which a nutritional claim has been made.[23] Figure 7–4 is a label showing nutritional ingredients.

Voluntary packaging and labeling standards have also been developed in a number of industries. As a result, the number of toothpaste sizes was reduced from fifty-seven to five and the number of dry detergent sizes from twenty-four to six. In other industries—such as drug, food, fur, and clothing—federal legislation has been enacted to force the companies to provide information and to prevent misleading branding. The marketing manager in such industries must be fully acquainted with these laws and must design packages and labels in compliance with them.

Product Safety

If the product is to fulfill its mission of satisfying consumer needs, it must, above all, be safe. Manufacturers must design their products in such a way as to protect not only children but all consumers who use them. Packaging can play an important role in product safety. Aspirin bottle tops have been made child-proof (and virtually parent-proof) by St. Joseph's and Bayer since

1968. This safety feature has reduced by two-thirds the number of children under five years of age swallowing accidental doses of aspirin.

Prominent safety warnings on the labels of such potentially hazardous products as cleaning fluids and drain cleaners inform users of the dangers of these products and urge them to store the products out of the reach of children. Changes in product design have reduced the dangers involved in the use of such products as lawn mowers, hedge trimmers, and toys.

Federal and state legislation has long played a major role in promoting product safety.[24] Many of the piecemeal federal laws passed over a period of fifty years were unified by the *Consumer Product Safety Act* (1972). The act created what has become one of the nation's most powerful regulatory agencies—the Consumer Product Safety Commission (CPSC). The new agency has assumed jurisdiction over every consumer product except food, automobiles, and a few other products that are already regulated by other agencies.

The CPSC has the authority to ban products without a court hearing, order the recall or redesign of products, and inspect production facilities; and it can charge managers of accused companies with criminal offenses.[25] Within four years after its creation, it has assembled a staff of nine hundred and spent approximately $157 million. Its national toll-free ''hot line''(800-638-8326) received more than thirty thousand consumer inquiries and complaints in the four-month period following its installation. Research on consumer accidents produced the twenty most dangerous products list shown in Table 7–2.

The CPSC has been active in developing and enforcing rules designed to reduce these injuries:

Already the CPSC is enforcing rules about aspirin bottles, refrigerator-door latches, children's pajamas, and the distance between the slats of cribs. It has issued warnings about such disparate products as mobile homes (they seem to abound in fire hazards), tricycles (they tip over), and sandals made of water-buffalo hide imported from India (they can give you a rash). In the near future the commission is likely to publish edicts governing the design or use of swimming-pool slides, aluminum electrical wiring, architectural glass, book matches, power lawn mowers, and pacifiers. In time, virtually every sector of the American economy will feel the impact of this extraordinary regulatory enterprise.[26]

Product Liability: A Growing Concern for Marketers

A parallel development to the increased concern for product safety has been the tremendous increase in product liability suits. The number of claims against producers or retailers of allegedly unsafe or defective products has jumped from 50,000 in 1960 to more than a million in 1977. While many of these claims are settled out of court, others are decided by juries who have sometimes awarded multimillion-dollar settlements.

Table 7–2
The Twenty Most Dangerous Consumer Products

Rank	Item
1	Bicycles and bicycle accessories
2	Stairs, steps, ramps, and landings
3	Football
4	Baseball
5	Playground equipment
6	Non-glass tables
7	Beds
8	Chairs, sofas, and sofa beds
9	Liquid fuels
10	Power lawn mowers
11	Swimming pools
12	Nails, tacks, and screws
13	Basketball
14	Bleaches, cleaning agents, and caustic compounds
15	Floors and flooring materials
16	Bathtubs and showers
17	Skateboards
18	Glass doors, windows, and panels
19	Miscellaneous household chemicals
20	Toboggans, sleds, snow discs, and snow tubing

Rankings are determined by multiplying the estimates of the number of injuries for a product category by the average severity of these injuries. Injuries to persons fourteen or under, an accident-prone group, are given a 2.52 weighting. The estimates represent product involvement in injuries but do not indicate a cause-effect relationship between the product and the injury.
Source: U.S. Consumer Product Safety Commission, *1979 Annual Report: Fiscal Year 1978* (Washington, D.C.: Government Printing Office, 1979), p. 47–59.

Between 1971 and 1976, the average amount sought rose from $476,000 to $1.7 million. In 1978, a jury awarded a judgment of $128.5 million against Ford Motor Company in a case involving a Pinto accident. A judge later reduced the total to $6.1 million, but Ford appealed.

Not only have marketers stepped up efforts to ensure product safety, but product liability insurance has become an essential ingredient in any new or existing product strategy. Premiums for this insurance have risen at an alarming rate, and in some cases coverage is almost impossible to obtain. A Detroit producer of components for pleasure boats discovered that its liability insurance premiums had increased from $2,500 in 1975 to $160,000 in 1977—even though the insurance company had never paid a claim on the firm's behalf. Several manufacturers of football helmets discontinued production in recent years due to the unavailability of the insurance.[27]

Efforts are underway in several states to exempt companies from liability for injuries or property loss resulting from misuse of the products or customer negligence. Such an exemption would have protected the retailer who recently paid damages to two men hurt by a lawn mower they held up to trim a hedge.

CPSC activities and the increased number of liability claims have prompted companies to voluntarily improve their safety standards. Product safety standards are currently being increased for such products as gas ranges, power hedge trimmers, and toys. For many companies, safety has become a vital ingredient of the broad definition of product.

Summary

Marketing managers have three alternatives in matching their product offerings with the needs of their chosen market target. They can employ undifferentiated marketing and attempt to reach the entire market with a single marketing strategy; they can practice differentiated marketing and design unique marketing strategies for each segment of the total market; or they can choose to satisfy one segment of the total market through a strategy of concentrated marketing. Selection of the most appropriate product market matching strategy results from a careful analysis of such factors as company resources, degree of product homogeneity, stage in the product life cycle, and strategies employed by competitors.

Product market strategy typically involves a line of related products. Firms usually produce several related products rather than a single product in order to achieve the objectives of growth, optimum use of company resources, and increased company importance in the market.

New-product organizational responsibility in most large firms is assigned to new-product committees, new-product departments, product managers, or venture teams. New-product ideas evolve through six stages before their market introduction: (1) new-product idea generation, (2) screening, (3) business analysis, (4) product development, (5) test marketing, and (6) commercialization.

While new products are added to the line, old ones may face deletion from it. The typical causes for product eliminations are unprofitable sales and failure to fit into the existing product line.

Product identification may take the form of brand names, symbols, distinctive packaging, and labeling. Effective brand names should be easy to pronounce, recognize, and remember; they should give the right connotation to the buyer; and they should be legally protectable. Brand acceptance can be measured in three stages: brand recognition, brand preference, and, finally, brand insistence. Marketing managers must decide whether to use a single family brand for their product lines or to use an individual brand for each product.

The package must provide protection, convenience, and economy while achieving the company's promotional goals. The label is also an important promotional and informational part of the package.

Product safety has become an increasingly important component of the total product concept. This change has occurred as a result of voluntary attempts by product designers to reduce hazards and of stricter requirements established by the Consumer Product Safety Commission.

This chapter concludes the analysis of problems and activities in developing the right products for the market target. The next four chapters deal with the subject of marketing channels—getting the right product to the market target.

Questions for Discussion

1. Explain the following terms:

undifferentiated marketing	brand name
differentiated marketing	trademark
concentrated marketing	generic name
product line	brand recognition
product manager	brand preference
venture team	brand insistence
test marketing	generic product
brand	

2. Which product market matching strategy would you recommend for each of the following:
   a. a large firm marketing an extensive line of breakfast cereals on a national scale
   b. a small firm marketing a new perfume with a new fragrance and a pump dispenser
   c. a medium-sized firm marketing a line of "king-size" men's clothing through a chain of eighty-seven retail stores in ten eastern states
   d. a large firm marketing a new camera capable of developing its own film in under ten seconds

3. Discuss the following statement: Undifferentiated marketing, differentiated marketing, concentrated marketing—none of these strategies is inherently superior. Each may be best in a given situation.

4. Why do most business firms market a *line* of related products rather than a single product?

5. Evaluate the alternative organization arrangements for new-product introductions. Which organizational arrangement seems best? Defend your answer.

6. Why has the product manager concept proven so popular among multiproduct firms in recent years?

7. A firm's new-product idea suggestion program has produced a design for a portable car washer that can be attached to a garden hose. Outline a program for deciding whether the product should be marketed by the firm.

8. Contrast the screening and business analysis stages of the new-product development process.

9. What is the chief purpose of test marketing? What potential problems are involved in it?

10. Under what circumstances might a firm choose to retain an unprofitable product?

11. Give an example of each of the following:
    a. brand
    b. brand name
    c. trademark
    d. family brand
    e. individual brand
    f. national brand
    g. private brand

12. List the characteristics of a good brand name. Illustrate each characteristic with an appropriate brand name.

13. Distinguish between generic names and brand names.
14. Identify and briefly explain each of the three stages of brand acceptance
15. Why do so few brands reach the brand insistence stage of brand accept
16. What are the chief advantages of using family brands?
17. Under what circumstances should individual brands be used?
18. What criteria should a retailer or wholesaler use in deciding whether to develop a line of private brand merchandise?
19. What are the physical functions of the package? Give examples to illustrate how the package can be an effective promotional tool.
20. Explain the chief functions of the Consumer Product Safety Commission. What steps can it take to protect consumers from defective and hazardous products?

Notes

1. This strategy has also been called *product differentiation.* See Wendell R. Smith, "Product Differentiation and Market Segmentation as Alternative Marketing Strategies," *Journal of Marketing,* July 1956, pp. 3–8. The terms *undifferentiated marketing, differentiated marketing,* and *concentrated marketing* were suggested by Philip Kotler. See his *Marketing Management,* 3d ed. (Englewood Cliffs, N.J.: Prentice-Hall, 1976), pp. 151–154.
2. Reported in James R. Tindall, "Quaker Oats' 3-Stage New Product Formula," *Marketing Times,* March–April 1978, p. 7. See also C. Merle Crawford, "Marketing Research and the New Product Failure Rate," *Journal of Marketing,* April 1977, pp. 51–61.
3. See James Rothe, Michael Harvey, and Walden Rhines, "New Product Development under Conditions of Scarcity and Inflation," *Michigan Business Review,* May 1977, pp. 16–22.
4. *Management of New Products* (New York: Booz, Allen & Hamilton, 1968), p. 20.
5. See Dilip Phadnis, "Training a New Product Manager," *Product Marketing,* April 1977, pp. 35–38.
6. This discussion is based on Richard M. Hill and James D. Hlavacek, "The Venture Team: A New Concept in Marketing," *Journal of Marketing,* July 1972, pp. 44–50.
7. See Richard M. Hill and James D. Hlavacek, "Learning from Failure: Ten Guidelines for Venture Management," *California Management Review,* Summer 1977, pp. 5–16; Dan T. Dunn, Jr., "The Rise and Fall of Ten Venture Groups," *Business Horizons,* October 1977, pp. 32–41; and William W. George, "Task Teams for Rapid Growth," *Harvard Business Review,* March–April 1977, pp. 71–80.
8. Hill and Hlavacek, "The Venture Team," p. 50.
9. For an excellent treatment of the product development process, see Robert D. Hisrich and Michael P. Peters, *Marketing a New Product* (Menlo Park, Calif.: Benjamin/Cummings Publishing, 1978); Richard T. Hise, *Product/Service Strategy* (New York: Mason/Charter Publishers, 1977); A. Edward Spitz, *Product Planning,* 2d ed. (New York: Mason/Charter Publishers, 1977); and Chester R. Wasson, *Dynamic Competitive Strategy and Product Life Cycles* (Austin, Texas: Austin Press, 1978).
10. See Eric von Hippel, "Successful Industrial Products from Customer Ideas," *Journal of Marketing,* January 1978, pp. 39–49; and James L. Ginter and W. Wayne Talarzyk, "Applying the Marketing Concept to Design New Products," *Journal of Business Research,* January 1978, pp. 51–66.
11. See William B. Locander and Richard W. Scamell, "Screening New Product Ideas—A Two Phase Approach," *Research Management,* March 1976, pp. 14–18.
12. See Edward M. Tauber, "Forecasting Sales prior to Test Market," *Journal of Marketing,* January 1977, pp. 80–84.
13. Reported in Edward Buxton, *Promise Them Anything* (New York: Stein & Day, 1972), p. 101.
14. For a discussion of the problems involved in test marketing and the conditions under which tests should be conducted, see Jay E. Klompmaker, G. David Hughes, and Russell I. Haley, "Test Marketing in New Product Development," *Harvard Business Review,* May–June 1976, p. 128.
15. Lee Adler, "Time Lag in New-Product Development," *Journal of Marketing,* January 1966, p. 17.
16. Committee on Definitions, *Marketing Definitions: A Glossary of Marketing Terms* (Chicago: American Marketing Association, 1960), pp. 9–10.
17. John Koten, "Mixing with Coke over Trademarks Is Always a Fizzle," *Wall Street Journal,* March 9, 1978, p. 1.
18. See E. B. Weiss, "Private Label? No, It's Now 'Presold'—Wave of Future," *Advertising Age,* September 30, 1974, p. 27.
19. See Diana Sperberg, "Generics Sell 40 Percent of Total Volume in European Supermarkets," *Product Marketing,* September 1978, p. 12; Robert H. Ross and Frederic B. Kraft, "Consumer Evaluation of Generic Products: A Preliminary Investigation," paper presented at the Southwestern Marketing Association,

Houston, Texas, March 16, 1979; and Charles G. Burck, "Plain Labels Challenge the Supermarket Establishment," *Fortune,* March 26, 1979, pp. 70–76.

20. Robert E. Weigand, "Fit Products and Channels to Your Markets," *Harvard Business Review,* January–February 1977, p. 95.

21. See Robert W. Shoemaker, "Consumer Decisions on Package Size," in *Research Frontiers in Marketing,* ed. Subhash C. Jain (Chicago: American Marketing Association, 1978), pp. 152–157.

22. The metric system is discussed in Paul N. Keaton and Lawrence P. Ettkin, "American Industry Inches (Centimeters) toward Metric," *Business Horizons,* December 1977, pp. 59–61; and "Rising Backlash against Switch to Metrics," *U.S. News & World Report,* November 13, 1978, p. 77.

23. Dorothy Cohen, "The Legal Environment for Marketing," in *Review of Marketing 1978,* ed. Gerald Zaltman and Thomas V. Bonoma (Chicago: American Marketing Association, 1978), p. 398.

24. See Brian T. Ratchford, "Banning Unsafe Products: A Framework for Policy Analysis," in *Contemporary Marketing Thought,* ed. Barnett A. Greenberg and Danny N. Bellenger (Chicago: American Marketing Association, 1977), pp. 362–365; and Walter Guzzardi, Jr., "The Mindless Pursuit of Safety," *Fortune,* April 9, 1979, pp. 54–64.

25. For a discussion of steps involved in the recall of defective and hazardous products, see Mary C. Harrison, "Product Recall Guidelines for Small Businesses," in *Proceedings of the Southern Marketing Association,* ed. Robert S. Franz, Robert M. Hopkins, and Al Toma, New Orleans, Louisiana, November 1978, pp. 271–274.

26. Paul H. Weaver, "The Hazards of Trying to Make Consumer Products Safer," *Fortune,* July 1975, p. 133.

27. See *The Product Liability Crisis* (Lansing, Mich.: Michigan Product Liability Council, 1978); "When Firms Get Sued for 'Faulty' Goods," *U.S. News & World Report,* May 22, 1978, pp. 93–95; and William I. Trombetta, "Products Liability, Foreseeability, and the Product Planner," *Marquette Business Review,* Summer 1977, pp. 74–81.

PART FOUR
DISTRIBUTION STRATEGY

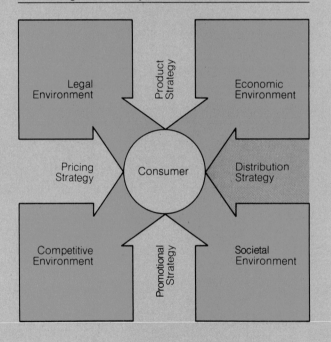

CHAPTER 8
INTRODUCTION TO
CHANNEL STRATEGY

Key Terms

marketing channel
middleman
wholesaling
retailer
facilitating agency
intensive distribution
selective distribution
exclusive distribution
exclusive dealing
agreement

closed sales
territories
tying agreement
missionary
salesperson
vertical marketing
system (VMS)
franchise

Learning Goals

1. To list the types of utility created by marketing channels.
2. To identify the major marketing channels for consumer and industrial goods.
3. To explain the factors that determine the optimum marketing channel for a product or service.
4. To identify and discuss the three degrees of intensity of marketing coverage.
5. To explain the three major types of vertical marketing systems.

8

Chapters 6 and 7 examined the problems and activities involved in designing the right products for the firm's market target. This chapter deals with getting the product to the consumer. Samsonite luggage is made in Colorado, Mazda RX-7s come from Japan, avocados grow in California, and Timex watches are assembled in Little Rock, Arkansas. Since very few consumers live next door to the factory, some method must be devised to bridge the gap between producer and consumer—to provide the latter with a convenient means of obtaining the products he or she wishes to buy. This, essentially, is the function of **marketing channels**—*the paths that goods, and title to them, follow from producer to consumer.*[1] In moving goods to a convenient location, channels provide time, place, and ownership utility.

Time Utility: Products Available *When* the Consumer Wants to Buy. Production and marketing problems are reduced substantially under a system of *job-order production.* In such a system the consumer places an order and returns several weeks or months later to claim the finished product. The firm has a minimal inventory of finished products and few marketing risks. However, except for major purchases of installations with unique specifications and large government contracts, few products are purchased on a job-order basis. *Speculative production*—production based on the firm's estimate of the demand for its product—is the rule, not the exception, in the business world of the 1980s.

Color television sales increase markedly on the Friday before the Super Bowl game or the opening game of the World Series. But the appliance store manager also recounts sadly that the purchasers are not at all receptive to home delivery of the set on the following Monday. The sale of each set is, in fact, contingent on its installation in the purchaser's home by noon the following day. Too many of these sales cannot be consummated, however, because the store manager has no time to place the orders with suppliers.

The annual toy fair takes place in New York City each March. Toy buyers for the nation's department stores, toy shops, variety stores, and discount stores visit the fair and make their decisions on toys to stock for the coming Christmas season. This lead time is required to produce the necessary quantities of each toy and to transport the toys to each purchaser's store.

In the same manner, swimwear for the coming spring and summer has already been produced in the cold months of December and January and is en route to retail stores throughout the nation. Swimwear manufacturers' success or failure depends on consumer reactions to new colors, styles, and fabrics decided on months earlier. But the swimsuits are ready in the store for the first warm day in March or April that customers decide to shop for them.

Place Utility—Products Available *Where* the Consumer Wants to Buy. Products in the manufacturer's warehouse are of no value to the consumer. Since few consumers are willing to seek out the manufacturer (except in the case of factory outlet stores), thousands of retail stores have been established to provide goods in locations convenient to consumers. These stores, along with vending machines, mail-order catalogs, and telephone sales, are a means of conveniently supplying products to the consumer.

Ownership Utility—Exchanging *Title* to the Products. Marketing channels also provide a means for title to be transferred from manufacturer to buyer. The purchaser can obtain physical possession of *and* title to the product at the retail store.

Some Necessary Definitions. Any discussion of marketing channels must supply an explanation of its terminology. A **middleman** is *a business firm operating between the producer and the consumer or industrial purchaser.* The term therefore includes both wholesalers and retailers.

Wholesaling is *the activities of persons or firms who sell to retailers, other wholesalers, and industrial users but do not sell in significant amounts to ultimate consumers.* The terms *jobber* and *distributor* are considered to be synonymous with *wholesaler* in this book.

Confusion can result from the practices of some firms that operate both wholesaling and retailing operations. Sporting goods stores, for example, often maintain a wholesaling operation in marketing a line of goods to high schools and colleges as well as operating retail stores. For the purposes of this text, it is simpler to conceive of such operations as two separate institutions.

A second source of confusion is the misleading practice of some retailers who claim to be wholesalers. Such stores may actually sell at wholesale *prices* and can validly claim to do so. However, *stores that sell products purchased by individuals for their own use and not for resale are* by definition **retailers**, not wholesalers.

Channel Alternatives Available to the Marketing Manager

A cursory look at the literally hundreds of marketing channels in everyday use should be sufficient to convince the marketing manager that there is no such thing as a best marketing channel. Best for Electrolux vacuum cleaners may be direct from manufacturer to consumer through a sales force of 7,000 men and women. Best for frozen french fries may be from food processor to agent middleman to merchant wholesaler to supermarket to consumer. Instead of searching for a best channel for all products, the marketing manager must analyze alternative channels in the light of consumer needs in order to determine an optimum channel (or channels) for the firm's products.[2]

Even when the proper channels have been chosen and established, the marketing manager's channel decisions are not ended. Channels, like so many of the other marketing variables, *change;* today's ideal channel may prove disastrous in a few years.

Until the 1960s, the typical channel for beer was from brewery to local distributor (wholesaler) to local pubs, since most beer was consumed in these retail outlets. But the majority of the beer purchases of the 1980s are made at the local supermarket, and the channel for Busch, Coors, Stroh's, Schlitz, and Miller Lite must change to reflect these changes in consumer buying patterns.

Manufacturer to Consumer or Industrial User. The simplest, most direct marketing channel is not necessarily the best, as is evidenced by the relatively small percentage of the dollar volume of sales that moves along this route. Less than 5 percent of all consumer goods move from producer to consumer. Dairies, Tupperware, Avon cosmetics, and numerous mail-order houses are examples of the firms whose products move directly from manufacturer to ultimate consumer. Almost all services, however, utilize this channel.*

Manufacturer owned channels — a common alternative.

Source: Copyright ©1980 by Sidney Harris. Reprinted by permission.

*Producers of some services do utilize agent middlemen. For example, airlines use travel agents, and many insurance companies market their programs through independent agents.

Direct channels are much more important to the industrial goods market. Most major installations and accessory equipment—and even fabricated parts and raw materials—are marketed through direct contacts between seller and buyer.

Manufacturer to Wholesaler to Retailer to Consumer or Industrial User.
The traditional marketing channel is from manufacturer to wholesaler to retailer to user (see Figure 8–1). It is the method used by literally thousands of small manufacturers that produce limited lines of products and by small retailers. Small companies with limited financial resources utilize wholesalers as immediate sources of funds and as a means to reach the hundreds of retailers who will stock their products. Small retailers rely on wholesalers as *buying agents* to ensure a balanced inventory of goods produced in various regions of the world.

The wholesaler's sales force is responsible for reaching the market with the manufacturer's output. Many manufacturers also use sales representatives, who call on retailers and help merchandise the manufacturer's line. These representatives serve as sources of market information for manufacturers, but do not actually sell the product.

Figure 8–1
Typical Channels in the Marketing of Consumer and Industrial Goods

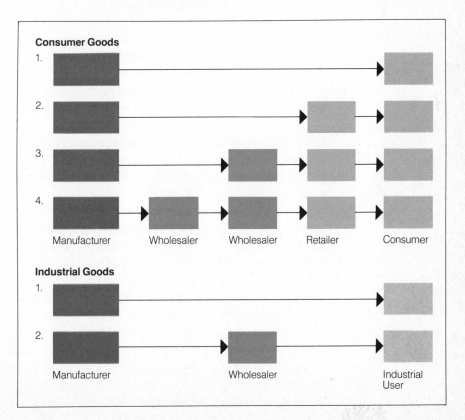

In the industrial market, *industrial distributors* are normally used. These wholesalers are involved in the marketing of small accessory equipment and operating supplies, such as building supplies, office supplies, and small hand tools.[3]

Manufacturer to Agent to Wholesaler to Retailer to Consumer. Where products are produced by a large number of small companies, a unique middleman—the agent—performs the basic function of bringing buyer and seller together. *Agents* are, in fact, wholesaling middlemen, but they differ from the typical wholesaler in that *they do not take title to the goods.* They merely represent the manufacturer or the regular wholesaler (who does take title to the goods) in seeking a market for the manufacturer's output or in locating a source of supply for the buyer. Chapter 9 will consider two types of wholesaling middlemen—*merchant wholesalers,* who take title to the goods that they handle, and *agent wholesaling middlemen,* who do not take title to the goods.

Agents are used in such industries as canning and frozen food packing. In these industries, many producers supply a large number of geographically scattered wholesalers. The agent wholesaling middleman performs a service by bringing buyers and sellers together.

Manufacturer to Agent to Wholesaler to Industrial User. Similar conditions often exist in the industrial market, where small producers attempt to market their offerings to large wholesalers. The agent wholesaling middleman, often called a *manufacturers' representative,* serves as an independent sales force in contacting the wholesale buyers.

Manufacturer to Agent to Industrial User. Where the unit sale is small, merchant wholesalers must be used to cover the market economically. By maintaining regional inventories, they achieve transportation economies by stockpiling goods and making the final small shipment over a small distance. Where the unit sale is large and transportation accounts for a small percentage of the total product cost, the manufacturer to agent to industrial user channel is usually employed. The agent wholesaling middlemen become, in effect, the company's sales force.

Multiple Channels—A Common Occurrence Today. An increasingly common phenomenon is the use of more than one marketing channel for similar products. Armour & Company's Dial soap is distributed to grocery wholesalers, who deliver it to food stores, which sell it to consumers. But a second marketing channel also exists; large retail chains and motels buy the soap directly from the manufacturer. A&P's Eight O'Clock coffee is marketed through a number of independent retailers (such as Flickinger in

Buffalo and Southland's 7-11 chain of convenience stores) in addition to being sold to A & P retail outlets.[4]

Firestone automobile tires are marketed through even more channels. They are distributed to (1) General Motors, where they serve as a fabricated part for new Chevrolets; (2) Firestone-owned retail outlets; (3) tire jobbers, who sell them to retail gas stations; and (4) franchised Firestone outlets. Each channel enables the manufacturer to serve a different market.

Facilitating Agencies – Providing Specialized Services for Channel Members	A number of important channel functions are performed by **facilitating agencies**—*marketing research firms, transportation and storage companies, advertising agencies, insurance companies, and financial institutions.* These agencies *provide specialized assistance for the regular channel members*—manufacturers, wholesalers, and retailers—*in moving products from producer to consumer.*

Facilitating agencies perform a number of special services. Insurance companies assume some of the risks involved in transporting the goods; marketing research firms supply information; financial institutions provide the necessary financing; advertising agencies help sell the goods; and transportation and storage firms store and physically move the goods. In some instances, the major channel members perform these services.

Facilitating agencies are not, however, involved in directing the flow of goods and services through the channel. Figure 8–2 illustrates the total distribution channel, with the channel members in brown boxes and facilitating agencies in gray ones.

Factors Affecting Channel Choice	What makes a direct channel best for the Fuller Brush Company? Why do operating supplies often go through both agents and merchant wholesalers before being purchased by the industrial firm? Why do some firms employ multiple channels for the same product? The firm must answer many such questions in determining its choice of marketing channels. The choice is based on an analysis of the consumer, the type of firm, the product's characteristics, and considerations of the firm's environment. Each factor can be of critical importance, and the factors are often interrelated.

The Consumer	A major determinant of channel structure is *whether the product is intended for the consumer or the industrial market.* Industrial purchasers usually prefer to deal directly with the manufacturer (except for supplies or small accessory items), but most consumers make their purchases from retail stores. Products for both industrial users and consumers are sold through more than one channel.

The geographic location and the needs of the firm's potential market

Figure 8–2
**Channel Members
and Facilitating
Agencies in the
Marketing
Channel**

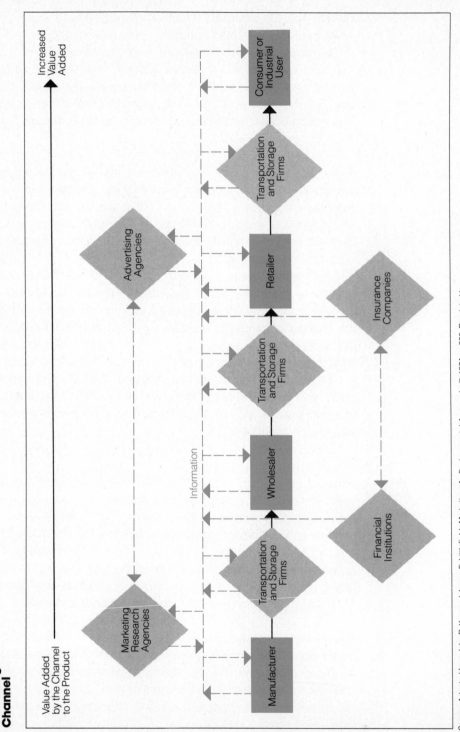

Value Added
by the Channel
to the Product

Increased
Value
Added

Source: Adapted from John R. Kerr and James E. Littlefield, *Marketing: An Environmental Approach,* © 1974, p. 305. Reprinted by permission of Prentice-Hall, Inc., Englewood Cliffs, N.J.

affect channel choice. Direct sales are possible where the firm's potential market is concentrated in a few regions. Since industrial production tends to be concentrated this way, direct contact is possible. A small number of potential buyers also increases the feasibility of direct channels. Consumer goods are purchased by households everywhere. Since these households are numerous and geographically dispersed, and since they purchase a small volume at a given time, middlemen must be employed to market products to them.

Shifts in consumer buying patterns also influence channel decisions. The desire for credit, the growth of self-service, the increased use of mail-order houses, and the greater willingness to purchase from door-to-door salespeople all affect a firm's marketing channel.

Characteristics of the Product

Product characteristics also play a role in determining optimum marketing channels. *Perishable products* such as fresh produce and fruit and fashion products with short life cycles *typically move through relatively short channels* directly to the retailer or the ultimate consumer. The National Biscuit Company distributes its Nabisco products from the bakery to retail shelves. Each year, Hines & Smart Corporation ships some 5 million pounds of live lobsters in specially designed styrofoam containers directly to restaurants and hotels throughout North America.

Complex products, such as custom-made installations or computer equipment, are typically sold by the manufacturer to the buyer. As a general rule, *the more standardized the product, the longer the channel.* Standardized goods usually are marketed by wholesalers. Also, products requiring regular service or specialized repair service usually avoid channels employing independent wholesalers. Automobiles are marketed through a franchised network of regular dealers whose employees receive regular training on how to properly service their cars.

Another generalization about marketing channels is that *the lower the unit value of the product, the longer the channel.* Convenience goods and industrial supplies with typically low unit prices are frequently marketed through relatively long channels. Installations and more expensive industrial and consumer goods employ shorter, more direct channels.

Characteristics of the Manufacturer

Companies with adequate resources—financial, marketing, and managerial—are less compelled to utilize middlemen in marketing their products. A financially strong manufacturer can hire its own sales force, warehouse its products, and grant credit to retailers or consumers. A weaker firm must rely on middlemen for these services (although some large retail chains purchase all of the manufacturer's output, thereby bypassing the independent wholesaler). Production oriented firms may be forced to utilize the marketing expertise of middlemen to replace the lack of finances and management in their organization.

A firm with a *broad product line* is usually able to market its products directly to retailers or industrial users, since its sales force can offer them a variety of products. Larger total sales allow the selling costs to be spread over a number of products and make direct sales feasible. The single-product firm often discovers that direct selling is an unaffordable luxury.

The manufacturer's *need for control over the product* also influences channel selection. If aggressive promotion at the retail level is desired, the manufacturer will choose the shortest available channel. For new products, the manufacturer may be forced to implement an introductory advertising campaign before independent wholesalers will handle the items.

Environmental Considerations

Some firms are forced to develop unique marketing channels because of *inadequate promotion of their products by independent middlemen.* Avon's famous shift to house-to-house selling was prompted by intense competition with similar lines of cosmetics. This radical departure from the traditional channel resulted in sales of $1.6 billion in 1977 by the firm's 1 million neighborhood sales women. Similarly, Honeywell discovered that its Concept 70 home security system was being inadequately marketed by the traditional channel of wholesaler to retailer and switched to a direct-to-home sales force.

Legal considerations may affect the manufacturer's desire to limit the number of middlemen handling the product. General Motors' attempt to prevent its California dealers from "bootlegging" its new automobiles to independent dealers was ruled illegal by the United States Supreme Court.

The nature and extent of competition is a third environmental factor. An industry made up of a large number of competitors with similar products often experiences intense competition, particularly at the retail level. This competition often leads to the purchase of effective eye-level retail shelf space (through additional discounts to the retailer) to ensure adequate market coverage.

Determining the Intensity of Market Coverage

Adequate market coverage for some products could mean one dealer for each fifty thousand people. Procter & Gamble defines adequate coverage for Crest toothpaste as almost every supermarket, discount store, drugstore, and variety store, plus many vending machines. Figure 8–3 illustrates the degrees of market exposure along a continuum with three general categories—intensive distribution, selective distribution, and exclusive distribution.

Figure 8–3
Degrees of
Market Coverage

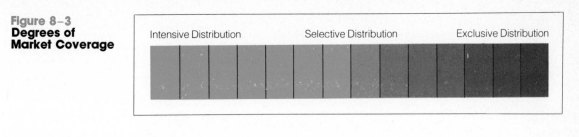

Intensive Distribution   Selective Distribution   Exclusive Distribution

Intensive
Distribution

Manufacturers of convenience goods who attempt to provide saturation coverage of their potential markets are the prime users of **intensive distribution.** Soft drinks, cigarettes, candy, and chewing gum are available in convenient locations to enable the purchaser to buy with a minimum of effort.

Bic pens can be purchased in more than two hundred thousand retail outlets in the United States. The American Time Company uses an intensive distribution strategy for its Timex watches. Consumers can buy a Timex in many jewelry stores, the traditional retail outlet for watches. In addition, they can find Timex in discount houses, variety stores, department stores, discount stores, hardware retailers, and drugstores.

Mass coverage and low unit prices make the use of wholesalers almost mandatory for such distribution. An important exception to this generalization is Avon Products, which sells directly to the consumer through a nationwide network of neighborhood saleswomen. These women purchase directly from the manufacturer at 60 percent of the retail price and service a limited area with cosmetics, toiletries, jewelry, and toys. (see page 208)

Selective
Distribution

As the name implies, **selective distribution** involves *the selection of a small number of retailers to handle the firm's product line.* By limiting the number of retailers, the firm can reduce its total marketing costs while establishing better working relationships within the channel. Cooperative advertising (where the manufacturer pays a percentage of the retailer's advertising expenditures and the retailer prominently displays the firm's products) can be utilized for mutual benefit, and marginal retailers can be avoided. Where product service is important, dealer training and assistance are usually forthcoming from the manufacturer. Finally, price cutting is less likely, since fewer dealers are handling the firm's line.

Exclusive
Distribution

When manufacturers grant exclusive rights to a wholesaler or retailer to sell in a geographic region, they are practicing **exclusive distribution**—an extreme form of selective distribution. The best example of exclusive distribution is the automobile industry. For example, a city of one hundred thousand will have a single Toyota dealer or one Cadillac agency. Exclusive dealership

**How Avon Breaks
the Rules**

Analysis of consumer and product characteristics would lead most marketing students to predict that a company such as Avon Products would use middlemen in distributing its 1,400 products. Yet Avon markets directly to the consumer through an army of 1 million bell ringers to more than 85 million households in the United States, Canada, and sixteen foreign countries. In the United States, Avon holds 85 percent of the door-to-door market for cosmetics and toiletries and approximately 20 percent of the total $5 billion market.

The Avon system consists of five levels. At the top is a general manager who oversees one of seven branches across the country and two regional managers. Each regional manager supervises eight divisional managers, and each divisional manager keeps tabs on eighteen district managers. Each district manager recruits, trains, and works with an average of 150 bell-chiming Avon saleswomen.

A part-time independent businesswoman, as Avon likes to describe her, the Avon saleswoman receives no company benefits, puts up a $10 "appointment fee" when she starts, and pays for most of her promotional materials. These include samples, demonstration kits, small customer brochures, and paper bags for packaging. An order of bags costs $1.50, and kits are $3 or $4 (some as much as $8 or $10). The work year is divided into twenty-six preplanned, two-week selling campaigns built around individual campaign brochures that are prepared months in advance.

The saleswoman is typically twenty-five to forty-four years old, has two children, and lives in a middle- or lower-income neighborhood. She works fifteen hours a week covering her two hundred family territory and visits thirty families per campaign. She earns about $1,400 a year (before expenses) on the $3,500 worth of products she sells. For every $100 in retail sales that she generates during a campaign, she gets a 40 percent commission. Sales of less than $100 bring 25 percent. For each saleswoman she helps recruit, she receives $7.50.

Since most Avon saleswomen work only for a little spare cash, turnover runs more than 100 percent a year. While almost half of all saleswomen have been with the company for more than a year and one-third for more than three years, the rest work for only a few months.

Sources: Information from "Troubled Avon Tries a Face-Lifting," *Business Week,* May 11, 1974, pp. 98–106; and "Money Isn't Everything," *Forbes,* April 16, 1979, p. 145.

arrangements also occur in the marketing of some major appliances and in fashion apparel.

Some market coverage may be sacrificed through a policy of exclusive distribution, but this loss is often offset by the development and maintenance of an image of quality and prestige for the products and the reduced marketing costs associated with a small number of accounts. Manufacturer and retailer cooperate closely in decisions concerning advertising and promotion, inventory to be carried by the retailer, and prices.

The Legal Problems of Exclusive Distribution. The use of exclusive distribution presents a number of potential legal problems in three areas—exclusive dealing agreements, closed sales territories, and tying agreements. While none of these practices is necessarily illegal, all may be ruled illegal if they result in reduced competition or tend to create a monopoly situation.

Exclusive Dealing Agreements—Prohibiting Middlemen from Handling Competitors' Products. An **exclusive dealing agreement** *prohibits a middleman* (either a wholesaler or, more typically, a retailer) *from handling competing products.* Manufacturers of high-priced shopping goods, specialty goods, and accessory equipment often require such agreements as assurance by the middleman of total concentration on the firm's product line. These contracts are considered violations of the Clayton Act if the manufacturer's or the dealer's sales volume represents a substantial percentage of total sales in the market or sales area. The courts have ruled that sellers who are just entering the market can use exclusive dealing agreements as a means of strengthening their competitive position. But the same agreements are considered violations of the Clayton Act when used by firms with sizable market shares, since competitors may be barred from the market because of the agreements.

Closed Sales Territories—Restricting the Geographic Coverage of Middlemen. Manufacturers with **closed sales territories** *restrict the geographic territories for each of their distributors.* Although the distributors may be granted exclusive territories, they are prohibited from opening new facilities or marketing the manufacturer's products outside their assigned territories. The legality of closed sales territories is determined by whether the restrictions decrease competition. If competition is lessened, they are considered to be violations of the Federal Trade Commission Act and of provisions of the Sherman Act and the Clayton Act.

The legality of closed sales territories is also affected by whether they are horizontal or vertical. *Horizontal* territorial restrictions involve agreements among retailers or wholesalers to avoid competition among products from the same manufacturer. Such agreements have consistently been declared illegal. However, the U.S. Supreme Court recently ruled that *vertical* territorial restrictions—those between the manufacturer and the wholesaler or retailer—*may* be legal. While the ruling was not entirely clear-cut, such agreements are likely to be legal in cases where the manufacturer is a relatively small part of the market. In such cases, the restrictions may actually increase competition among competing brands. The wholesaler or retailer faces no competition from other dealers carrying the manufacturer's brand and can therefore concentrate on effectively competing with other brands.[5]

Tying Agreements—Forcing Middlemen to Handle the Entire Product Line. The third legal question of exclusive dealing involves the use of **tying agreements**—*agreements that require a dealer who wishes to become the exclusive dealer for a manufacturer's products to also carry other of the manufacturer's products in inventory.* In the clothing industry, for example, such an agreement may require the dealer to carry a line of less popular clothing in addition to the fast-moving items.

Tying agreements are considered violations of the Sherman Act and the Clayton Act when they lessen competition or create monopoly situations by keeping competitors out of major markets. For this reason, the International Salt Company was prohibited from selling its salt as a tying product with the lease of its patented salt-dispensing machines for snow and ice removal. The Supreme Court ruled that such an agreement unreasonably eliminated competition among sellers of salt.

Tying agreements continue to be common in franchising operations. One study estimated that over 70 percent of all franchisees are required to purchase at least some of their operating supplies from the franchisors.[6]

Conflict and Cooperation in the Marketing Channel	Although the marketing channel must be viewed and organized as a systematic cooperative effort if operating efficiencies are to be achieved, channel members often operate as separate, independent, and even competitive forces. Too often, marketing institutions within the channel view the channel as extending only one step forward or backward. They think in terms of suppliers and customers rather than of vital links in the total channel.

The necessary leadership in the marketing channel typically is the responsibility of the most powerful link in the distribution channel (the dominant and controlling member), who is often referred to as the *channel captain.* Historically, the role of channel captain was performed by the manufacturer or wholesaler, since retailers tended to be small and localized. However, retailers are increasingly assuming the leadership as large chains take on the traditional wholesaling functions and even dictate product design specifications to the manufacturer.[7]

Channel conflict can arise from a number of sources:

A manufacturer may wish to promote a product in one manner . . . while his retailers oppose this. Another manufacturer may wish to get information from his retailers on a certain aspect relating to his product, but his retailers may refuse to provide this information. A producer may want to distribute his product extensively, but his retailers may demand exclusives. A supplier may force a product onto its retailers, who dare not oppose, but who retaliate in other ways, such as using it as a loss leader. Large manufacturers may try to dictate the resale price of their merchandise; this may be less or more than the price at which the retailers wish to sell it. Occasionally a local market may be more competitive for a retailer than is true nationally. The manufacturer may not recognize the difference in competition and refuse to help this channel member. There is also conflict because of the desire of both manufacturers and retailers to eliminate the wholesaler.[8]

The basic antidote to channel conflict is effective cooperation among channel members. However, channels usually have more harmonious relationships than conflicting ones; if they did not, the channels would have ceased to exist long ago. Cooperation is best achieved by considering all channel members as part of the same organization. Achievement of this cooperation is the prime responsibility of the channel captain.

A manufacturer who assumes the role of channel captain may use **missionary salespersons**—*special representatives who help wholesalers and retailers become familiar with the firm's products.* In addition, the missionary salespeople can help the channel members develop effective promotional ideas and sales contests, create store layout designs, and generally act as management consultants for the other channel members. Retailer channel captains can perform a vital role in supplying the wholesaler and manufacturer with information about consumer purchases and reactions to various components of the manufacturer's marketing mix.

Vertical Marketing Systems[9]	The traditional marketing channel has been described as a "highly fragmented network in which vertically aligned firms bargain with each other at arm's length, terminate relationships with impunity, and otherwise behave autonomously."[10] This potentially inefficient system of distributing goods is gradually being replaced by **vertical marketing systems (VMS)**—*"professionally managed and centrally programmed networks preengineered to achieve operating economies and maximum impact."*[11] VMS produce economies of scale through their size and by eliminating duplicated services. As Table 8–1 indicates, three types prevail—corporate, administered, and contractual.

Corporate System. When there is single ownership of each stage of the marketing channel, a *corporate vertical marketing system* exists. A reported 50 percent of all Sears, Roebuck products are purchased from manufacturers in which the nation's largest retailer has an equity interest. Holiday Inn owns a furniture manufacturer and a carpet mill. Hart, Schaffner & Marx owns a retail chain of over two hundred men's clothing stores.

Administered System. Channel coordination is achieved through the exercise of economic and "political" power by a dominant channel member in an *administered vertical marketing system.* Magnavox obtains aggressive promotional support from its retailers because of the strong reputation of its brand. Although the retailers are independently owned and operated, they cooperate with the manufacturer because of the effective working relationships built up over the years.

Table 8-1
Three Types of Vertical Marketing Systems

Type of System	Description	Examples
Corporate	Channel owned and operated by a single organization	Hart, Schaffner & Marx Firestone Sherwin-Williams A&P
Administered	Channel dominated by one powerful member who acts as channel captain	Magnavox General Electric Kraftco Corning Glass
Contractual	Channel coordinated through contractual agreements among channel members	*Wholesaler Sponsored Voluntary Chain:* IGA Western Auto Stores Associated Druggists Sentry Hardware *Retail Cooperative:* Associated Grocers *Franchise Systems:* McDonald's Red Carpet Real Estate Century 21 Real Estate AAMCO Transmissions Coca-Cola bottlers

Contractual System. The most significant form of vertical marketing is the *contractual vertical marketing system*, which accounts for nearly 40 percent of all retail sales. Instead of the common ownership of channel components that characterized the corporate VMS or the relative power of a component of an administered system, the contractual VMS is characterized by formal agreements among channel members. In practice, there are three types of agreements.

The *wholesaler sponsored voluntary chain* represents an attempt by the independent wholesaler to preserve a market for the firm's products by strengthening the firm's retailer customers. In order to enable the independent retailers to compete with the chains, the wholesaler enters into a formal agreement with a group of retailers whereby the retailers agree to use a common name, have standardized facilities, and purchase the wholesaler's products. The wholesaler often develops a line of private brands to be stocked by the members of the voluntary chain.

A common store name and similar inventories allow the retailers to achieve cost savings on advertising, since a single newspaper ad promotes all the retailers in the trading area. IGA Food Stores, with a membership of approximately 5,000 stores, is a good example of a voluntary chain. Mc-

Kesson & Robbins Drug Company has established a large voluntary chain in the retail drug industry.

A second type of contractual VMS is the *retail cooperative,* which is established by a group of retailers who set up a wholesaling operation to better compete with the chains. The retailers purchase shares of stock in a wholesaling operation and agree to buy a minimum percentage of their inventory from the firm. The members may also choose to use a common store name and develop their own private brands in order to carry out cooperative advertising. Retail cooperatives have been extremely successful in the grocery industry, accounting for one-fifth of all retail grocery sales.

A third type of contractual VMS is the **franchise**—*an agreement whereby dealers (franchisees) agree to meet the operating requirements of a manufacturer or other franchisor.* The dealers typically receive a variety of marketing, management, technical, and financial services in exchange for a specified fee.[12]

Although franchising attracted considerable interest beginning in the late 1960s, the concept is as old as the automobile industry. The soft drink industry is another example of a franchise, but in this case the contractual arrangement is between the manufacturer and the wholesale bottler.

The franchising form that has created the most excitement in retailing during the past fifteen years has been *the retailer franchise system sponsored by the service firm.* McDonald's is an excellent example of such a franchise operation. The company brings together suppliers and a chain of hamburger outlets. It provides a proven system of retail operation (the operations manual for each outlet weighs several pounds) and lower prices through its purchasing power on meat, buns, napkins, and necessary supplies. In return, the franchisee pays a fee of about $150,000 for the use of the McDonald's name and a percentage of gross sales. Other familiar examples are Hertz, Century 21 and Red Carpet real estate agencies, Arby's, Pizza Hut, Howard Johnson's, and Weight Watchers. Franchises account for one-third of all retail sales in the United States.

McDonald's has almost five thousand restaurants in operation and has upgraded its facilities to better serve its customers. The early McDonald's outlets offered a severely restricted menu and little or no seating. Their 1980 counterparts provide an expanded breakfast and luncheon selection and seating capacity for one hundred to three hundred diners. These efforts are aimed at obtaining even more of the $50 billion spent annually in U.S. restaurants. One out of every three meals in the United States is eaten in restaurants, and the rate is expected to grow to one out of two within the next five years. Table 8–2 lists the ten largest fast-food restaurants in the United States.

Fast-food franchising has already proven itself in the international market. In Tokyo, London, Rome, and Paris, McDonald's hamburgers are con-

Table 8–2
The Ten Largest Fast-Food Restaurants

Rank	Company	1978 Sales (in Millions)	Percent Change since 1977	Percent of Market[a]
1	McDonald's	$ 3,838.0	18.7	18.7
2	Kentucky Fried Chicken	1,205.0	4.3	5.7
3	Burger King	1,130.7	27.4	5.3
4	International Dairy Queen	823.0	12.0	3.9
5	Wendy's International	783.3	84.0	3.7
6	Pizza Hut	724.7	22.0	3.4
7	Sambo's	538.6	18.9	2.5
8	Hardee's	460.8	19.3	2.2
9	Jack in the Box	430.0	2.4	2.0
10	Howard Johnson's	425.0	6.3	2.0
	Total for top 10	$10,369.1	17.9	48.8

[a]Based on Commerce Department figures for fast-food restaurants that franchise.
Source: John C. Maxwell, Jr., "Fast-Food Sales May Grow 20% in '79," *Advertising Age,* September 10, 1979, p. 46. Reprinted with permission from the September 1979 issue of *Advertising Age.* Copyright 1979 by Crain Communications Inc. and John C. Maxwell, Jr. Data courtesy of John C. Maxwell, Jr. Figures given are for U.S. domestic sales.

sumed daily. Kentucky Fried Chicken has opened more than five hundred restaurants outside the United States in locations as diverse as Manila and Munich, Nice and Nairobi. In some countries, adjustments to U.S. marketing plans have been made to match local needs. Although their menu is rigidly standardized in the United States, McDonald's executives approved the addition of wine to the menu in French outlets. Kentucky Fried Chicken also substituted french fries for mashed potatoes to satisfy its Japanese customers.[13]

"Welcome to Hamburger University!"

Since the typical McDonald's outlet generates annual sales of approximately $500,000 and produces earnings before taxes of around $70,000, it is not surprising that the home office receives thousands of requests for franchises each year. Only about 10 percent of them are accepted.

McDonald's guards its leading position in the fast-food business carefully and takes every possible step to ensure the success of each new outlet. Although it closed three stores in Holland, the McDonald's success story is being repeated in Canada, Australia, Germany, and Japan. One of the first requirements for the new franchisee is a series of courses at Hamburger U., McDonald's training center in Oak Brook, Illinois, a suburb of Chicago. In order to earn a "Bachelor of Hamburgerology, with a minor in french fries," the franchisee must take courses covering everything from how to scrape a grill to how to keep books. Thorough grounding in the McDonald's system allows each new franchisee to apply techniques that have been proven successful in more than three thousand instances.

Source: Information from Max Boas and Steve Chain, *Big Mac: The Unauthorized Story of McDonald's* (New York: E. P. Dutton, 1976).

The infatuation with the franchising concept and the market performance of franchise stocks lured dozens of newcomers into the market. Lacking experience and often with a well-known name as their sole asset, many of these firms (among them Broadway Joe's and Minnie Pearl's) quickly disappeared.[14]

Franchising has revolutionized the fast-food industry.

Source: "Funky Winkerbean" by Tom Batiuk. ©1979 Field Enterprises, Inc. Courtesy Field Newspaper Syndicate.

Whether corporate, administered, or contractual, vertical marketing systems are already a dominant factor in the consumer goods sector of the U.S. economy. An estimated 64 percent of the available market is currently in the hands of retail components of VMS.

Summary

Marketing channels bridge the gap between producer and consumer. By making products available when the consumer wants to buy and at a convenient location and by arranging for transfer of title to the goods, marketing channels create time, place, and ownership utility.

The marketing manager faces a host of alternative channels for the firm's products—from contacting the consumer directly through catalog sales or the use of salespersons to using a variety of independent wholesaling middlemen and retailers. In fact, manufacturers of similar products often utilize multiple channels. The choice of optimum channels is based on careful analysis of the firm's market target, characteristics of the manufacturer, product characteristics, and a number of environmental factors.

The degree of intensity of market coverage for products may vary from a single dealer in a given territory (exclusive distribution) to the use of a few dealers (selective distribution) to a total saturation of the market using every dealer who will agree to handle the products (intensive distribution). Exclusive distribution policies may present legal problems, since the concept of limiting the number of dealers who can handle a firm's output has overtones of restraint of trade.

Cooperation among channel members is essential for efficient distribution. The channel captain, the dominant member of the channel, typically assumes the responsibility for obtaining cooperation from channel members. Although channel captains have traditionally been manufacturers or wholesalers, large retailers are increasingly assuming this role in the marketing channel.

The need for channel cooperation has resulted in the development of vertical marketing systems (VMS). Whether formed through single ownership of each stage in the marketing channel, through contractual relationships among channel members, or through voluntary cooperation, these systems have proven effective and efficient in managing the operations of the marketing channel.

Questions for Discussion	1. Explain the following terms:

1. Explain the following terms:

marketing channel	exclusive distribution
middleman	exclusive dealing agreement
wholesaling	closed sales territories
retailer	tying agreement
facilitating agency	missionary salesperson
intensive distribution	vertical marketing system (VMS)
selective distribution	franchise

2. Explain and illustrate each of the utilities provided by marketing channels.
3. What types of products are most likely to be distributed through direct channels?
4. Which marketing channel is the "traditional" channel? Give some reasons for its frequent use.
5. Refer to the classifications of consumer and industrial goods in Chapter 6. Suggest a best channel for each type. Defend your answer.
6. Explain and illustrate the major factors affecting choice of marketing channels.
7. Which degree of intensity of market coverage is appropriate for each of the following:
   a. *Time* magazine
   b. Catalina swimwear
   c. Irish Spring soap
   d. Johnson outboard motors
   e. Scotch brand cellophane tape
   f. Kawasaki motorcycles
   g. Steuben glassware
8. Why would manufacturers choose more than one channel for their products?
9. Under what conditions is a manufacturer most likely to bypass independent wholesalers and market the firm's products directly to the retailer?
10. Why would any manufacturer deliberately choose to limit market coverage through a policy of exclusive coverage?
11. Why would manufacturers favor the use of tying agreements?
12. Under what circumstances are sales territory restrictions likely to be illegal?
13. Under what circumstances is the retailer likely to assume the role of channel captain? When will the manufacturer typically fulfill this role?
14. Why have retailers only recently begun to assume the role of channel captain?
15. In what ways could the use of multiple channels produce channel conflict?
16. Explain and illustrate each type of vertical marketing system.
17. What is the basic distinction between retail cooperatives and voluntary chains?
18. What conditions are necessary for an administered VMS to prove effective?
19. What advantages does franchising offer the small retailer?
20. One generalization of channel selection mentioned in the chapter was that low unit value products require long channels. How can you explain the success of a firm (such as Avon) that has a direct channel for its relatively low unit value products?

Notes

1. Committee on Definitions, *Marketing Definitions: A Glossary of Marketing Terms* (Chicago: American Marketing Association, 1960), p. 10. Some authors limit the definition to the route taken by the title to the goods, but this definition also includes agent wholesaling middlemen who do not take title but who do serve as an important component of many channels.
2. See Mary A. Higby, *An Evaluation of Alternative Channels of Distribution* (East Lansing: Michigan State University, 1977).
3. See Frederick E. Webster, Jr., "The Role of the Industrial Distributor in Marketing Strategy," *Journal of Marketing,* July 1976, pp. 10–16.
4. Robert E. Weigand, "Fit Products and Channels to Your Markets," *Harvard Business Review,* January–February 1977, p. 97.
5. Michael B. Metzger, "Schwinn's Swan Song," *Business Horizons,* April 1978, pp. 52–56. See also Dorothy Cohen, "The Legal Environment for Marketing," in *Review of Marketing 1978,* ed. Gerald Zaltman and Thomas V. Bonoma (Chicago: American Marketing Association, 1978), pp. 395–397.
6. Shelby D. Hunt and John R. Nevin, "Tying Agreements in Franchising," *Journal of Marketing,* July 1975, pp. 20–26.
7. See James R. Brown and Gary L. Frazier, "The Application of Channel Power: Its Effects and Connotations," in *Research Frontiers in Marketing,* ed. Subhash C. Jain (Chicago: American Marketing Association, 1978), pp. 266–270; and Bruce J. Walker and Donald W. Jackson, Jr., "The Channels Manager: A Needed New Position," in *Proceedings of the Southern Marketing Association,* ed. Robert S. Franz, Robert M. Hopkins, and Al Toma, New Orleans, Louisiana, November 1978, pp. 325–328.
8. Bruce Mallen, "A Theory of Retailer-Supplier Conflict, Control, and Cooperation," *Journal of Retailing,* Summer 1963, p. 26. Reprinted by permission. See also J. Steven Kelly and J. Irwin Peters, "Vertical Conflict: A Comparative Analysis of Franchisees and Distributors," in *Contemporary Marketing Thought,* ed. Barnett A. Greenberg and Danny N. Bellenger (Chicago: American Marketing Association, 1977), pp. 380–384; William G. Zikmund and Ralph F. Catalanello, "Managing Channel Conflict through Channel Development," *Journal of the Academy of Marketing Science,* Fall 1976, pp. 801–813; and Michael Pearson and John F. Monoky, "The Role of Conflict and Cooperation in Channel Performance," in *Marketing: 1776–1976 and Beyond,* ed. Kenneth L. Bernhardt (Chicago: American Marketing Association, 1976), pp. 240–244.
9. This section is based on Bert C. McCammon, Jr., "The Emergence and Growth of Contractually Integrated Channels in the American Economy," in *Marketing and Economic Development* (Chicago: American Marketing Association, 1965), pp. 496–515. Used by permission.
10. Ibid., p. 496.
11. See Bert C. McCammon, Jr., "Perspectives for Distribution Programming," in *Vertical Marketing Systems,* ed. Louis P. Bucklin (Glenview, Ill.: Scott, Foresman, 1970), pp. 32–51.
12. See Donald W. Hackett, *Franchising: The State of the Art* (Chicago: American Marketing Association, 1977), for an excellent treatment of franchising.
13. See Donald W. Hackett, "U.S. Franchise Systems Abroad—The Second Boom," in *Marketing: 1776–1976 and Beyond,* ed. Kenneth L. Bernhardt (Chicago: American Marketing Association, 1976), pp. 253–256.
14. Shelby D. Hunt, "Franchising: Promises, Problems, Prospects," *Journal of Retailing,* Fall 1977, pp. 71–84.

CHAPTER 9
MARKETING INSTITUTIONS: WHOLESALING

Key Terms

wholesaler
wholesaling
middleman
sales branch
public warehouse
sales office
trade fair
merchandise mart
merchant wholesaler
broker

rack jobber
cash-and-carry
wholesaler
truck wholesaler
drop shipper
commission
merchant
auction house
selling agent
manufacturers' agent

Learning Goals

1. To identify the functions performed by marketing institutions.
2. To distinguish between wholesaling and retailing.
3. To explain the channel options available to a manufacturer who desires to bypass independent wholesaling middlemen.
4. To identify the conditions under which a manufacturer is likely to assume wholesaling functions rather than use independents.
5. To distinguish between merchant wholesalers and agents and brokers.
6. To identify the major types of merchant wholesalers and instances where each type might be used.
7. To describe the major types of agents and brokers.

9

The steps that goods follow on the way to the consumer or industrial user are made up of marketing institutions—wholesalers and retailers. Only 3 percent of the dollar volume of all goods sold to the ultimate consumer is made directly from the manufacturer. Therefore, the bulk of all products sold pass through these institutions.

An increasing number of consumers are complaining about the high cost of goods. They point most often at wholesalers and retailers—those middlemen who allegedly drive prices up through their high profits. Discount stores have been advertising that their prices are lower because they buy directly from the manufacturer and eliminate the middlemen and their profits. Chain stores are increasingly assuming the functions of wholesalers and independent retailers, which allows them to bypass the middlemen also.

Are these complaints and claims valid? Are the wholesalers and the small retailers anachronisms doomed to a swift demise? This chapter and the next one will analyze the functions and costs of both institutions so the answers to these important questions can be developed individually.

What Are the Functions of Marketing Institutions?

A marketing institution can continue to exist only so long as it fulfills a need by performing a required service. Its death will be slow but inevitable if other channel members discover that they can survive without it. What functions are performed by the marketing institution that consists of wholesalers and retailers?

Convenient Product Storage

Wholesalers and retailers store products at locations convenient to customers. Manufacturers ship products from their warehouses to numerous wholesalers, who then ship smaller quantities to retail outlets convenient to purchasers. A large number of wholesalers and most retailers assume the inventory function (and cost) for the manufacturer. They benefit through the convenience afforded by local inventories. The manufacturer benefits through reduced cash needs, since its products are sold directly to the retailer or wholesaler.

At the wholesale level, costs are reduced through making large purchases from the manufacturer. The wholesaler receives quantity discounts from the manufacturer and has lower transportation costs because economical carload or truckload shipments are made to the wholesaler's warehouses. At the warehouse, the wholesaler divides the goods into smaller quantities and ships them to the retailer over a shorter distance (but at a higher rate) than would be the case if the manufacturer filled the retailer's order directly from a central warehouse.

Costs are often lower when retailers or wholesalers represent many manufacturers to a single customer. As Figure 9–1 indicates, the number of transactions between manufacturers and their customers can be markedly reduced by introducing a middleman (a wholesaler or retailer), and reduced market contacts can lead to lower marketing costs.

Figure 9–1
The Reduction of the Number of Necessary Contacts between Manufacturers and Their Customers by Middlemen

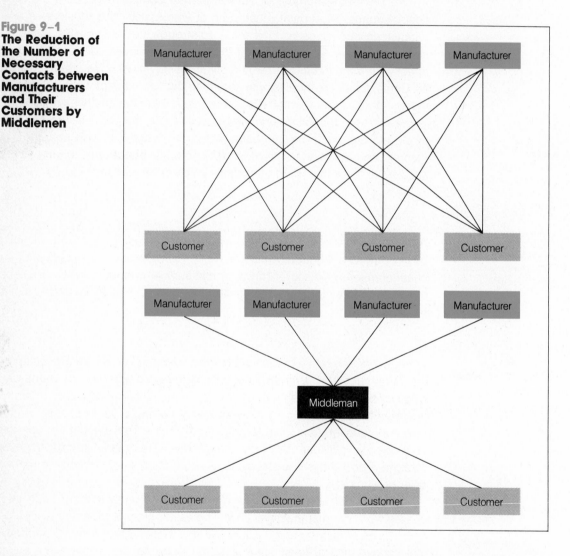

Because of their central position between the manufacturer and the consumer, wholesalers and retailers serve as important information links. Wholesalers provide their retail customers with useful information about new products. Both retailers and wholesalers supply manufacturers with information about the market reception of their product offerings.

Marketing Middlemen – Vital Cogs in the Magazine Industry

Magazines are distributed through two channels—customer subscriptions and single-copy sales at supermarkets, chain stores, convenience stores, drugstores, and newsstands. As the subscription channel becomes more expensive due to high postal rates (which have risen almost 400 percent in four years), the single-copy channel becomes increasingly important.

But every year, millions of magazines are returned unsold; $200 million worth of them—more than total industry profits—go into the shredder. Magazine wholesalers are working to provide the information necessary to reduce the number of unsold copies.

Ten national wholesalers are responsible for moving more than 33,000 titles from the publishers to about 500 local wholesalers in small regions throughout the nation. The local wholesalers supply copies to the various retail outlets. Speed is essential. As one local wholesaler stated, "*TV Guide* prints one day and within 36 hours is stocked in more than 150,000 establishments."

In an attempt to reduce the number of unsold copies that some people have labeled "a conspiracy to deforest Canada," the magazine wholesalers provide publishers with a detailed breakdown of their returns and sellouts by area and magazine type. This information should help publishers regulate the number of magazines shipped to a given area and select the proper combination for the demographics of the area. In addition, publishers such as *Cosmopolitan* are providing wholesalers with specific marketing information to help them promote sales. Cooperation between publishers and their marketing intermediaries is aimed at achieving the goal of a 95 percent sellout.

Source: Bernice Kanner, "Wholesalers—Vital Cog in Magazine Machinery," *Advertising Age*, October 16, 1978, p. 30. Adapted with permission from the October 16, 1978, issue of *Advertising Age*. Copyright 1978 by Crain Communications, Inc.

Middlemen are often blamed for increasing food prices.

"*If* you're not making any money, the packer isn't making any money and the rancher isn't making any money, then the cows must have a bundle stashed away."

Source: *Wall Street Journal*, June 22, 1976. Reprinted by permission of *The Wall Street Journal* and Bo Brown.

Wholesalers and retailers also serve a financing function. Wholesalers often provide retailers with goods on credit, which means that the retailers can minimize their cash investment in inventory and pay for most of the goods as they are sold. This allows them to benefit from the principle of *leverage,* whereby a minimum amount spent on goods inflates the return on investment (ROI). A retailer with an investment of $1 million and profits of $100,000 will realize an ROI of 10 percent. But if the necessary invested capital can be reduced to $800,000 through credit from the wholesaler, and if the $100,000 profits can be maintained, the retailer's ROI increases to 12.5 percent.

Retailers often perform the same financing function for their customers. Most department stores and other specialty shops offer thirty-day free charge accounts for their regular customers. However, financing costs are so high that many retailers have converted to *revolving charge accounts.* Under this system, the credit customer pays an interest rate of 15 to 18 percent for credit charges after the thirty-day free period. Revolving charge accounts keep cash-paying customers from having to absorb a portion of the store's credit charges in the prices of its products and allow charge customers to enjoy the benefits of credit purchases—at a price. The cost of credit is equally high for the wholesalers, who usually attempt to induce their retail customers to pay bills promptly through a cash discount policy. Wholesalers typically quote rates of 2/10, net 30, which allows customers to realize a discount of 2 percent from the bill for payment within a ten-day period.

Wholesalers of industrial goods provide similar services for the purchasers of their goods. In the steel industry, middlemen (referred to as metal service centers) currently market one-fifth of all steel shipped by U.S. mills. One such center, the Earle M. Jorgensen Company in Los Angeles, stocks 6,500 items for sale to many of the 50,000 major metal users who buy in large quantities directly from the steel mills but who turn to service centers for quick delivery of special orders.

While an order from the mills may take ninety days for delivery, a service center can usually deliver locally within twenty-four to forty-eight hours. In order to attract business from key customers, such as AMF, which makes bicycles locally, Jorgensen carries inventory for them without demanding a contract. The cost and the risk of maintaining the stock are assumed by the service center in order for it to provide overnight delivery service for its customers.[1]

It is apparent from a quick review of the functions performed by middlemen that a manufacturer can bypass them by assuming the functions they perform. Manufacturers can establish networks of regional warehouses, maintain large sales forces to provide market coverage, serve as sources of information, and assume the financing function. They can also attempt to push

Table 9–1
Median Net Profits of Selected Wholesalers

Kind of Business	Net Profit as a Percentage of Net Sales[a]
Automotive parts and supplies	3.03
Beer, wine, and alcoholic beverages	1.59
Clothing and furnishings, men's and boys'	2.05
Confectionary	1.18
Dairy products	1.42
Drugs, drug proprietaries, and sundries	1.61
Electrical appliances, TV sets, and radios	1.97
Footwear	1.91
Furniture and home furnishings	1.67
Groceries, general line	0.80
Hardware	2.25
Meats and meat products	0.62
Paper and paper products	1.92
Petroleum and petroleum products	0.90
Tires and tubes	2.33
Tobacco and tobacco products	0.64

[a] After provision for federal income taxes
Source: "The Ratios of the Wholesalers," *Dun's Review,* October 1978, pp. 133–136. Reprinted with the special permission of *Dun's Review,* October 1978. Copyright 1978, Dun & Bradstreet Publications Corporation.

the responsibility through the channel on to the retailer or ultimate purchaser. Large retailers who choose to perform their own wholesaling operations face the same choice.

A key marketing principle is: *Marketing functions must be performed by some member of the channel; they can be shifted, but they cannot be eliminated.* The potential gain for the manufacturer or retailer is summarized in Table 9–1. If the manufacturer or retailer can perform the wholesale functions as efficiently as the independent wholesaler, the potential savings are indicated by the wholesaler's net profits. If a manufacturer decides to bypass the meat and meat products wholesaler, the potential saving is about two-thirds of 1 percent. This saving can be used to lower retail prices, increase the manufacturer's profits, or both.

The most revealing information in Table 9–1 is the low profit rate earned by most wholesalers. Four types of wholesalers (tobacco and tobacco products, petroleum and petroleum products, meats and meat products, and groceries) earned less than 1 percent, while the group with the highest profit as a percentage of sales (automotive parts and supplies wholesalers) earned 3.03 percent.

Wholesaling Middlemen

As defined in Chapter 8, wholesaling involves the activities of persons or firms who sell to retailers and other wholesalers or to industrial users but not in significant amounts to ultimate consumers. While the term **wholesaler** usually applies only to *wholesaling middlemen who take title to the products* *they handle,* the broader term **wholesaling middlemen** describes *not only middlemen who assume title to the goods that they handle but also agents and brokers who perform important wholesaling activities without taking title to the goods.*

The most recent Census of Wholesale Trade lists nearly 370,000 wholesaling establishments with total sales of $695 billion. Wholesaling middlemen are concentrated in the Middle Atlantic and East North Central states. The New York City metropolitan area alone accounts for 18 percent of all wholesale trade.

Although many types of wholesalers perform all the middleman functions discussed earlier, their major function is probably buying large amounts of goods and routing small orders to retailers, thereby realizing substantial savings in transportation costs. Figure 9–2 diagrams the major types of wholesaling middlemen.

Manufacturer Owned Facilities

Increasing amounts of products are being marketed directly by manufacturers through company owned facilities—for several reasons. Some products are perishable; some require complex installation or servicing; others need aggressive promotion; still others are high unit value goods that the manufacturer can sell profitably to the ultimate purchaser. Among the industries that have shifted from the use of independent wholesaling middlemen to the use of company owned channels are paper, paint, lumber, construction materials, piece goods, and apparel manufacturers.[2] More than 50 percent of all industrial goods are sold directly to users by manufacturers, and slightly more than one-third of all products are marketed through manufacturer owned channels.[3]

Figure 9–2
Major Types of Wholesaling Middlemen

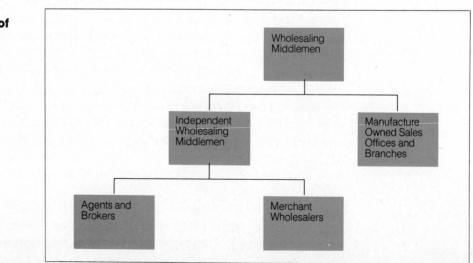

Sales Branches and Offices. The basic distinction between a company's sales branches and sales offices is that **sales branches** *carry inventory and process orders to customers from available stock.* Branches duplicate the storage function of independent wholesalers and serve as offices for sales representatives in the territory. They are prevalent in the marketing of commercial machinery and equipment, petroleum products, motor vehicles, and chemicals.

Since warehouses represent a substantial investment in real estate, small manufacturers and even large firms developing new sales territories may choose to use **public warehouses**—*independently owned storage facilities.* For a rental fee, manufacturers can store their goods in any of the more than ten thousand public warehouses in the United States for shipment by the warehouses to customers in the area. Warehouse owners will package goods into small quantities to fill orders and will even handle billing for manufacturers. Public warehouses can also provide a financial service for manufacturers by issuing warehouse receipts for inventory. These receipts can be used by manufacturers as collateral for bank loans.

Sales offices, by contrast, *do not carry stock but instead serve as regional offices for the firm's sales personnel.* Maintenance of sales offices in close proximity to the firm's customers helps reduce selling costs and improve customer service. The listing of a firm in the local telephone directory often results in new sales for the local representative. Many buyers prefer to telephone the office of a supplier rather than take the time to write to distant suppliers.

Other Outlets for the Manufacturer's Products. In addition to using a sales force and regionally distributed sales branches, manufacturers often market their products through trade fairs and merchandise marts. **Trade fairs** (or **trade exhibitions**) are *periodic shows where manufacturers in a particular industry display their wares for visiting retail and wholesale buyers.* The New York City toy fair and the High Point, North Carolina, furniture show are annual events for both manufacturers and purchasers of toys and furniture. **Merchandise marts** *provide space for permanent exhibitions where manufacturers rent showcases for their product offerings.* The largest is the Chicago Merchandise Mart, which is two blocks long, a block wide, and twenty-one floors high. Over a million items are on display there. Retail buyers can compare the offerings of dozens of competing manufacturers and make most purchase decisions in a single visit to a trade fair or merchandise mart.

Independent Wholesaling Middlemen

As Table 9–2 indicates, independent wholesaling middlemen account for 87 percent of the wholesale establishments and approximately two-thirds of the wholesale sales in the United States.

**Table 9–2
Wholesale Trade
by Type of
Operation**

Type of Operation	Number of Establishments	Sales (in Billions)	Percentage of Total Sales
Merchant wholesalers	289,974	$353.9	50.9
Manufacturers' sales branches and offices	47,197	255.7	36.8
Agents and brokers	32,620	85.6	12.3
Total wholesale trade	369,791	$695.2	100.0

Source: *1972 Census of Wholesale Trade, Establishment Size and Firm Data* (Washington, D.C.: Government Printing Office, 1976), pp. 1–7.

Merchant Wholesalers. Independent wholesaling middlemen can be divided into two categories—**merchant wholesalers** (who *take title to the goods*) and agents and **brokers** (who *may take possession of the goods but not title*). Merchant wholesalers account for slightly more than 50 percent of all sales at the wholesale level, and their sales are projected to reach the $1 trillion mark by 1985.[4] As Figure 9–3 indicates, they can be further classified as full or limited function wholesalers.

Full Function Merchant Wholesalers. A complete assortment of services for retailers and industrial purchasers is provided by *full-function merchant wholesalers*. These wholesalers store merchandise in convenient locations, thereby allowing their customers to make purchases on short notice and to minimize their inventory requirements. They also usually maintain sales forces to call regularly on retailers, make deliveries, and extend credit to qualified buyers. In the industrial goods market, full function merchant

**Figure 9–3
Classification of
Independent
Wholesaling
Middlemen**

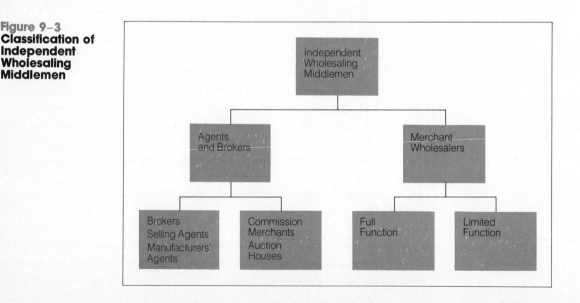

**The World's
Largest
Wholesaler**

If the *Guinness Book of World Records* had a category for wholesalers, Super Valu Stores would easily claim the title of the largest in the world. The Hopkins, Minnesota, based giant recorded sales of $2.6 billion for the fiscal year ending in 1978.

Super Valu is a typical merchant wholesaler and offers its retail grocery customers a range of services, including accounting, merchandising, site location, store design, and financing. For a fee that seldom exceeds a few hundred dollars, Super Valu will assist a retail customer in analyzing everything from market share, cash flow, and current profit position to proposed store locations. Retail stores can even obtain a daily printout of individual department performance compared with expectations.

Super Valu has developed standards of performance through experience and uses them to point out trouble spots. For instance, in larger stores, soaps, towels, and other dry goods take up a substantial amount of selling space, but average a gross profit of only 16 percent. By comparison, an in-store bakery chalks up average gross profits of 72 percent, a deli delivers 37 percent, and a large meat department produces 22 percent.

Super Valu not only serves 1,864 independent food retailers but has diversified through the direct ownership of 36 supermarkets, 65 Mr. Quik convenience food stores, and several nonfood chains. Its continued growth (sales have doubled over the past five years) and razor-thin profit margin (less than 1 percent of sales) are strong evidence that this wholesale giant is playing an important role in the food marketing channel.

Sources: Most recent data from *1978 Factbook* (Hopkins, Minn.: Super Valu Stores, 1978). Other information from "How to Boost Profits without Boosting Prices," *Business Week,* March 31, 1973, p. 101. See also Joseph S. Coyle, "Inside the World's Largest Wholesaler," *Progressive Grocer*, September 1975, pp. 62–67.

wholesalers (often called industrial distributors) usually market machinery, inexpensive accessory equipment, and supplies.

Full function merchant wholesalers prevail in industries where retailers are small and carry large numbers of relatively inexpensive items, none of which is stocked in depth. The hardware, drug, and grocery industries have traditionally been serviced by them.

A unique type of service wholesaler emerged after World War II as supermarkets began to stock high profit margin nonfood items. Since the supermarket managers generally possessed no knowledge of such products as toys, housewares, paperback books, records, and health and beauty items, the **rack jobber** provided the necessary expertise. This wholesaler *supplies the racks, stocks the merchandise, prices the goods, and makes regular visits to refill the shelves.* In essence rack jobbers rent space from retailers on a commission basis. They have expanded into drug, hardware, variety, and discount stores.

Since full function merchant wholesalers perform a large number of services, their costs are sometimes as high as 20 percent of sales. Attempts to reduce the costs of dealing with these wholesalers have led to the development of a number of limited function middlemen.

Limited Function Merchant Wholesalers. There are three types of limited function merchant wholesalers—cash-and-carry wholesalers, truck wholesalers, and drop shippers. **Cash-and-carry wholesalers** are appropriately named, since they *perform most wholesaling functions—with the exception of financing and delivery.* They first appeared on the marketing scene in the grocery industry during the depression era of the 1930s. In an attempt to reduce costs, retailers began driving to wholesalers' warehouses, paying cash for their purchases, and making their own deliveries. By eliminating the delivery and financing functions, cash-and-carry wholesalers were able to reduce their operating costs to approximately 9 percent of sales.

Although feasible for small stores, this kind of wholesaling is generally unworkable for large-scale supermarkets. Chain store managers are unwilling to perform the delivery function, and cash-and-carry these days is typically one department of a regular full service wholesaler. The cash-and-carry wholesaler has proven successful, however, in the United Kingdom, where six hundred such operations produce over $1 billion a year in sales.

Truck wholesalers (or **truck jobbers**) *market perishable food items such as bread, tobacco, potato chips, candy, and dairy products.* They make regular deliveries to retail stores as well as performing the sales and collection functions. They also aggressively promote their product lines. The high costs of operating delivery trucks and the low dollar volume per sale mean relatively high operating costs of 15 percent.

The **drop shippers** *receive orders from customers and forward them to producers, who ship directly to the customers.* Although drop shippers take title to the goods, they never physically handle or even see them. Since they perform no storage or handling function, their operating costs are a relatively low 4 to 5 percent of sales.

Drop shippers operate in fields where products are bulky and customers make their purchases in carload lots. Transportation and handling costs represent a substantial percentage of the total cost of such products as coal and lumber. Drop shippers do not maintain an inventory of these products, thereby eliminating the expenses of loading and unloading carload shipments. Their major service is the development of a complete assortment of customers. Since various types and grades of coal and lumber are produced by different companies, drop shippers can assemble a complete line to fill any customer's order.

Agents and Brokers. Even though some merchant wholesalers do not take physical possession of goods, all of them take title. A second group of independent wholesaling middlemen—the *agents and brokers*—may or may not take possession of the goods, but they never take title. They normally perform fewer services than the merchant wholesalers and are typically involved in bringing together buyers and sellers. Agent wholesaling middlemen can be classified into five categories—commission merchants, auction houses, brokers, selling agents, and manufacturers' agents.

Commission Merchants. **Commission merchants**, who predominate in the marketing of agricultural products, *take possession when the producer ships goods such as grain, produce, and livestock to a central market for sale. They act as the producer's agents and receive an agreed upon fee when the sale is made.* Since customers inspect the products, and since prices fluctuate, commission merchants are given considerable latitude in making decisions. The owner of the goods may specify a minimum price, but the commission merchant will sell them on a "best price" basis. The merchant's fee is deducted from the price and remitted to the original owner.

Auction Houses. A valuable service in markets such as used cars, livestock, antiques, tobacco, works of art, fur, and fruit is performed by the agent wholesaling middlemen known as **auction houses.** They *bring buyers and sellers together in one location and allow potential buyers to inspect the merchandise before purchasing it.* Auction houses' commissions for their services are often based on the sale price of the goods. Sotheby, Parke, Bernet of New York and London is a well-known auction house specializing in works of art.

Brokers. The task of *brokers* is to bring buyers and sellers together. Brokers operate in industries characterized by a large number of small suppliers and purchasers—real estate, frozen foods, and used machinery, for example. They represent either the buyer or the seller in a given transac-

Brokers bring buyers and sellers together.

"Do you ever try to explain to your kid that you spend all day buying and selling things that you don't have?"

Source: *Wall Street Journal.* Reprinted by permission of Sidney Harris.

tion, but not both. Brokers receive a fee from the client when the transaction is completed. Since the only service they perform is negotiating for exchange of title, their operating expense ratio can be as low as 2 percent.

Because brokers operate on a one-time basis for sellers or buyers, they cannot serve as an effective marketing channel for manufacturers seeking regular, continuing services. A manufacturer who seeks to develop a more permanent channel utilizing agent wholesaling middlemen must evaluate the use of the selling agent or the manufacturers' agent.

Selling Agents. For small, poorly financed, production oriented manufacturers, **selling agents** may prove the ideal marketing channel. These wholesaling middlemen have often been referred to as independent marketing departments, since they *can be responsible for the total marketing program of a firm's product line.* Typically, selling agents have full authority over pricing decisions and promotional outlays, and often they provide financial assistance for the manufacturer. The manufacturer can concentrate on production and rely on the expertise of the selling agent for all marketing activities.

Selling agents are common in the textile, coal, and lumber industries. The latest Census of Business lists 1,722 of them—with total sales of approximately $6.5 billion and operating expenses averaging 3.2 percent of sales.

Manufacturers' Agents. While manufacturers may utilize only one selling agent, they often use a number of **manufacturers' agents**—*independent salespeople who work for a number of manufacturers of related but noncompeting products and who receive commissions based on a specified percentage of sales.* Although some commissions are as high as 20 percent of sales, they usually average between 6 and 7 percent. Unlike selling agents, who may be given exclusive world rights to market a manufacturer's product, manufacturers' agents operate in a specified territory.[5]

Manufacturers' agents reduce their selling costs by spreading the cost per sales call over a number of different products. An agent in the plumbing supplies industry, for example, may represent a dozen manufacturers.

Manufacturers develop their marketing channels through the use of manufacturers' agents for several reasons. First, when they are developing new sales territories, the costs of adding salespeople to "pioneer" the territory may be prohibitive. Agents, who are paid on a commission basis, can perform the sales function in these territories at a much lower cost.

Second, firms with unrelated lines may need to employ more than one channel. One line of products may be marketed through the company's sales force. Another may be marketed through independent manufacturers' agents. This is particularly common where the unrelated product line is a recent addition and the firm's sales force has had no experience with it.

Finally, small firms with no existing sales force may turn to manufacturers' agents in order to have access to their market. A newly organized firm producing pencil sharpeners may use office equipment and supplies agents to reach retailers and industrial purchasers.

The importance of selling agents has declined since 1940 because of manufacturers' desire to better control their marketing programs. Nonetheless, the volume of sales by manufacturers' agents doubled over the period 1939 to 1972, and it is now *one-fourth of all sales by agent wholesaling middlemen.* In 1972, the nation's 16,000 agents accounted for more than $23 billion in sales.

Costs of the Wholesaling Middlemen

Costs of the various wholesaling middlemen are calculated as a percentage of total sales. Table 9–3 shows the costs for each major category. The major conclusion to be drawn from the table is that expense variations result from differences in the number of services provided by each middleman. The highest cost ratios are for merchant wholesalers and manufacturers' sales branches because both provide such services as maintenance of inventories, market coverage by a sales force, and transportation. Brokers perform only one service—bringing buyers and sellers together; as a consequence, they have the lowest expense ratios. Of course, these ratios are averages and will vary among firms within each category, depending on the actual services provided.

Independent Wholesaling Middlemen – A Durable Marketing Institution

Many marketing observers of the 1920s felt that the end had come for the independent wholesaling middlemen as chain stores grew in importance and attempted to bypass them. Over the ten-year period 1929 to 1939, the independent wholesalers' sales volume did indeed drop, but it has increased

Table 9–3
Operating Expenses as Percentages of Sales by Wholesaling Middlemen

Type of Wholesaling Middleman	Operating Expenses as Percentage of Net Sales
Merchant wholesalers	13.9
Manufacturers' sales branches	11.0
Manufacturers' sales offices	4.1
Agents and brokers	4.2
Brokers	3.2
Manufacturers' agents	7.1
Selling agents	3.2
Commission merchants	3.8
Auction houses	2.5

Source: *1967 Census of Business* (Washington, D.C.: Government Printing Office, 1970), pp. 1–9.

Table 9–4
Wholesale Trade by Type of Operation: 1929 to 1972

Type of Operation	Percentage of Total Sales		
	1929	1967	1972
Merchant wholesalers	54.0	52.5	50.9
Manufacturers' sales branches and offices	24.2	34.2	36.8
Agents and brokers	21.8	13.3	12.3

Petroleum bulk station and assembler percentages are combined with merchant wholesaler data for 1929 and 1967 for comparison with 1972 data.
Sources: 1929 and 1967 data from James R. Moore and Kendall A. Adams, "Functional Wholesaler Sales Trends and Analysis," in *Combined Proceedings* (Chicago: American Marketing Association, 1976), p. 402. Reprinted with permission. 1972 data from *1972 Census of Wholesale Trade, Establishment Size and Firm Data* (Washington, D.C.: Government Printing Office, 1976), pp. 1–7.

since then. Table 9–4 shows how the relative shares of total wholesale trade have changed since 1929.

While the period from 1929 to the present has seen the decline in importance of agents and brokers and the increase in importance of company owned channels, it is also true that independent wholesaling middlemen are far from obsolete. In fact, they are responsible for nearly two-thirds of all wholesale trade. Their continued importance is evidence of their ability to adjust to changing conditions and changing needs. Their market size proves their ability to continue to fill a need in many marketing channels.

Summary

Wholesalers are one of the two major institutions that make up a firm's marketing channel. They are persons or firms who sell to retailers and other wholesalers or to industrial users but who do not sell in significant amounts to ultimate consumers. The three types of wholesaling middlemen are manufacturer owned facilities, merchant wholesalers, and agents and brokers. Merchant wholesalers take title to the goods they handle. Agents and brokers may take possession of the goods but do not take title. Merchant wholesalers include full function wholesalers, rack jobbers, cash-and-carry wholesalers, truck wholesalers, and drop shippers. Commission merchants, auction houses, brokers, selling agents, and manufacturers' agents are classified as agent wholesaling middlemen because they do not take title to goods.

The operating expenses of wholesaling middlemen vary considerably, depending on the number of services provided and the costs involved. The services include storage facilities in conveniently located warehouses, market coverage by a sales force, financing for retailers and manufacturers, market information for retailers and manufacturers, transportation, and, specifically for retailers, management services, retail sales training, and merchandising assistance and advice.

While the percentage of wholesale trade by manufacturer owned facilities has increased since 1929, independent wholesaling middlemen continue to account for 87 percent of all wholesale establishments and nearly two-thirds of total wholesale trade. They accomplish this by continuing to provide desired services to manufacturers and retailers.

Questions for Discussion

1. Explain the following terms:

wholesaler	rack jobber
wholesaling middleman	cash-and-carry wholesaler
sales branch	truck wholesaler
public warehouse	drop shipper
sales office	commission merchant
trade fair	auction house
merchandise mart	selling agent
merchant wholesaler	manufacturers' agent
broker	

2. Distinguish between a wholesaler and a retailer.
3. In what ways do wholesaling middlemen assist manufacturers? How do they assist retailers?
4. Explain how wholesaling middlemen can assist retailers in increasing their return on investment.
5. Distinguish between sales offices and sales branches. Under what conditions might each type be used?
6. Explain the strength of wholesale volume through manufacturers' sales offices and branches even though the percentage of total wholesale sales through brokers and selling agents has been declining.
7. What role does the public warehouse play in marketing channels?
8. Distinguish merchant wholesalers from agents and brokers.
9. Which major type of wholesaling middleman represents the most frequently used marketing channel? Which major type is least often used?
10. Comment on the following statement: Drop shippers are good candidates for elimination. All they do is process orders. They don't even handle the goods.
11. Why is the operating expense ratio of the merchant wholesaler higher than that for the typical agent or broker?
12. Complete the following table:

	Operating Expense Ratio		
Type of Wholesaling Middleman	High (over 10%)	Medium (5–10%)	Low (under 5%)
Full function merchant wholesaler			
Cash-and-carry wholesaler			
Truck wholesaler			
Drop shipper			
Broker			
Manufacturers' agent			
Selling agent			

13. Why does the truck wholesaler have a relatively high operating expense ratio?
14. Match each of the following industries with the most appropriate wholesaling middleman:

    ____ groceries   a. drop shipper
    ____ potato chips   b. truck wholesaler
    ____ coal   c. auction house
    ____ grain   d. manufacturers' agent
    ____ antiques   e. full function merchant wholesaler
                              f. commission merchant

15. In what ways are commission merchants and brokers different?
16. The term *broker* also appears in the real estate and securities fields. Are these brokers identical to the agent wholesaling middlemen described in this chapter?
17. Distinguish between a manufacturers' agent and a selling agent.
18. Why do commission merchants, unlike most other agents and brokers, take possession of the products they market?
19. Under what conditions would a manufacturer utilize manufacturers' agents for a marketing channel?
20. What type of firm is likely to utilize selling agents?

Notes

1. Marilyn Wellemeyer, "Middlemen of Metal," *Fortune,* March 1977, pp. 163–165.
2. James R. Moore and Kendell A. Adams, "Functional Wholesaler Sales Trends and Analysis," in *Combined Proceedings,* ed. Edward M. Mazze (Chicago: American Marketing Association, 1976), pp. 402–405.
3. Louis P. Bucklin, *Competition and Evolution in the Distributive Trades* (Englewood Cliffs, N.J.: Prentice-Hall, 1972), p. 214.
4. Benson Shapiro, "Improve Distribution with Your Promotional Mix," *Harvard Business Review,* March–April 1977, p. 116.
5. For a profile of the typical manufacturers' agent, see Stanley D. Sibley and Roy K. Teas, "Agent Marketing Channel Intermediaries' Perceptions of Marketing Channel Performance," in *Proceedings of the Southern Marketing Association,* ed. Robert S. Franz, Robert M. Hopkins, and Al Toma, New Orleans, Louisiana, November 1978, pp. 336–339.

CHAPTER 10
MARKETING INSTITUTIONS: RETAILING

Key Terms

retailing
single line store
limited line store
supermarket
specialty store
general merchandise
store
department store
mass merchandiser

discount house
hypermarket
chain store
planned shopping
center
scrambled
merchandising
wheel of retailing
teleshopping

Learning Goals

1. To distinguish between single line and limited line stores and general merchandise retailers.
2. To identify the major types of mass merchandisers.
3. To explain the types of nonstore retailing.
4. To distinguish between chain and independent retailers and to identify several industries dominated by chains.
5. To contrast the three types of planned shopping centers.

10

In 1976, W. T. Grant Company made retailing history. When the final liqui-dation sales were completed, the chain had the dubious distinction of being the largest collapse in retailing history. Two years earlier, in 1974, Grant's (as the company was known) ranked as the seventeenth largest U.S. retailer, with sales of almost $1.8 billion. But that same year, its 1,188 retail stores had a combined loss of $177 million!

Grant's problems could be traced back to the mid-1960s, when it watched such competitors as F. W. Woolworth Company and S. S. Kresge Company begin huge expansion programs and broaden their variety store merchandise lines. Grant's followed by opening 410 large stores, each over 50,000 square feet, between 1967 and 1973. During that same time, it en-larged another 36 stores and closed 307 smaller ones. It also decided to become a general merchandise retailer.

The old W. T. Grant had been a retailing operation with an image of limited price items in small wares, wearing apparel, and soft goods. The new Grant's could not decide whether to emulate K mart or follow Sears and Penney. As a result, it took a position somewhere between the two. New emphasis was placed on big-ticket items such as major appliances, furniture, television sets, and power tools. Grant's put its own brand name on these products and immediately ran into consumer acceptance problems.

Addition of big-ticket items meant that Grant's had to provide credit for its customers. Bad debts soared because of over-lenient credit. "If a cus-tomer's breath fogged a mirror, the customer was given instant credit," a Grant's president reported. Also, the rapid expansion required major financ-ing, and the new stores placed too great a strain on Grant's management resources. Finally, a general downturn in the economy was taking place.

In a futile final attempt to save the chain, a consumer survey was con-ducted. It revealed that shoppers did not want to buy major appliances from Grant's. They perceived the store as a variety store. The blurred image had produced staggering losses in both the major appliance and furniture oper-ations.

Although new management at Grant's took drastic steps to reduce losses by closing large numbers of stores, replacing its credit operation with Visa and Master Charge credit cards, and eliminating the furniture and major appliance operations, a federal bankruptcy court ordered its liquidation. By the end of 1979, W. T. Grant Company was only a memory.[1]

What Is Retailing?   Retailing is the end of the marketing channel for the consumer goods man-ufacturer. Whether the manufacturer has established a company owned chain of stores or uses several of the nearly 2 million retail stores in the United States, the success of the entire marketing strategy rides with the decisions of consumers in the retail store.

Retailing consists of *all the activities involved in the sale of products and services to the ultimate consumer for his or her own use.* It involves not only sales in retail stores but also telephone and mail-order sales, vending machine sales, and direct house-to-house solicitations. As Table 10–1 indicates, 97.5 percent of the $459 billion retail sales in 1972 were made in retail stores. The other three retailing methods account for a total of 2.5 percent.

The First U.S. Retailers

Early retailing can be traced to the establishment of trading posts such as the Hudson Bay Company and to pack peddlers who literally carried their wares to outlying settlements. But the first important retail institution in the United States was the *general store*—a general merchandise store stocked to meet the needs of a small community or rural area. Here, customers could buy clothing, groceries, feed, seed, farm equipment, drugs, spectacles, and candy.

The basic needs that caused the general store to develop also doomed it to a limited existence. Since the storekeeper attempted to satisfy the needs of customers for all types of goods, he or she (many storekeepers were women) carried a small assortment of each good. As communities grew,

**Table 10–1
Retail Trade by
Type of Operation**

Type of Operation	Number of Establishments	Sales (in Billions)	Percentage of Total Sales
Building materials, hardware, garden supply, and mobile home dealers	83,842	$ 23.8	5.2
General merchandise	56,245	65.1	14.2
Department stores	7,742	51.1	11.1
Variety stores	21,852	7.3	1.6
Other	26,651	6.7	1.5
Food stores	267,352	100.7	21.9
Automobile dealers	121,369	90.0	19.6
Gasoline service stations	226,459	33.7	7.3
Apparel and accessory stores	129,201	24.7	5.4
Furniture, home furnishings, and equipment stores	116,857	22.5	4.9
Eating and drinking places	359,524	36.9	8.0
Drugstores and proprietary stores	51,542	15.6	3.4
Other retailers[a]	338,359	34.4	7.5
Nonstore retailers	162,121	11.6	2.5
Mail-order houses	7,982	4.6	1.0
Automatic merchandising machine operators	12,845	3.0	0.7
Direct selling	141,294	4.0	0.9
Total retail trade	1,912,871	$459.0	100.0

[a]Includes liquor, jewelry, and sporting goods stores and florists.
Source: U.S. Department of Commerce, Bureau of the Census, *Census of Retail Trade, 1972, Establishment and Firm Size* (Washington, D.C.: Government Printing Office, 1976).

new stores specializing in specific product lines, such as groceries, hardware, dry goods, and drugs, appeared. The general stores could not compete, and their owners either converted them into more specialized limited line stores or closed them. But general stores in some rural areas still do fill a need. Today, a few thousand such stores are still operating, mostly in rural areas of the South and West.

Types of Retail Facilities	Retailing operations are remarkable illustrations of the marketing concept in operation. The development of retail innovations can be traced to attempts to better satisfy particular consumer needs. As Chapter 6 pointed out, retail stores, like products, can be categorized as convenience, shopping, and specialty.

As consumers demand different satisfactions from retailers, new institutions emerge to meet this demand. The supermarket appeared in the early 1930s in response to consumer desires for lower prices. Today, convenience food stores meet consumers' desires for convenience in purchasing and late hour availability. Discount houses reflect consumers' demands for lower prices and their willingness to give up services. Department stores meet the demands of their clientele with a wide variety of products and services. Vending machines, door-to-door retailing, and mail-order retailing offer the ultimate in buyer convenience. Planned shopping centers provide a balanced array of consumer goods and services and include parking facilities for their customers. The nation's 2 million retailing establishments are involved in developing specific marketing mixes designed to satisfy chosen market targets.[2]

Single Line and Limited Line Stores	*A large assortment of one line of products or a few related lines of goods are offered in* **single line** *and* **limited line stores.** Their development paralleled the growth of towns when the population grew sufficiently to support them. These operations include such retailers as furniture stores, hardware stores, grocery stores, appliance stores, and sporting goods stores. Examples of single line and limited line stores are Lionel Leisure City and Toys "R" Us (toys); Levitz, John Lawhon, J. Homestock, and Wickes (furniture); Tandy Radio Shack and Playback (home electronics); Handy Dan and Handy Man (home repair products); Brain Factory (electronic calculators); and Lerner Shops (clothing).

These retailers cater to the needs of people who want to select from a complete line in purchasing a particular product. The marketing vice-president of Toys "R" Us summarized the limited or single line retailer's strategy this way: "Sears can show customers three types of footballs, but we can show them forty."[3] Most retailers are in the single line or limited line category.

The Supermarket. Supermarkets offer low prices through a policy of self-service. Prior to the 1920s, food purchases were made at full service grocery stores. Store personnel filled orders (often from customers' shopping lists), delivered goods, and often granted credit to their customers. Supermarkets exchanged these services for lower prices and quickly revolutionized food shopping in the United States and much of the world.[4]

Supermarkets are *large-scale departmentalized retail stores offering a variety of food products such as meats, produce, dairy products, canned goods, and frozen foods in addition to various nonfood items. They operate on a self-service basis and emphasize low prices and adequate parking facilities.* Supermarket customers typically shop once or twice a week and make fill-in purchases between each major shopping trip. In 1972, the 25,000 U.S. supermarkets represented only about one-tenth of the nation's food stores; yet their sales accounted for 68 percent of all food sales. The largest supermarket chains in the United States are Safeway, Kroger, Lucky Stores, Jewel, A&P, Winn-Dixie, and Food Fair.

With a razor-thin profit margin (averaging only about 1 percent of sales after taxes) supermarkets compete through careful planning of retail displays in order to sell a large amount of merchandise each week and thereby keep a low investment in inventory. Product location is studied carefully in order to expose the consumer to as much merchandise as possible (and increase impulse purchases). In an attempt to fight the fast-food threat—the tendency of consumers to eat many of their meals outside the home—supermarkets have begun to install their own delicatessens. In Florida, the Publix supermarkets sell fried chicken by the bucket. Supermarkets General of New Jersey has even established cafeterias and snack shops in factories.[5]

Supermarkets carry nonfood products such as toys, toiletries, magazines, records, and small kitchen utensils for two reasons: (1) consumers have displayed a willingness to buy such items in supermarkets, and (2) supermarket managers like their profit margin, which is higher than that for food products. Nonfood sales account for almost one-fourth of all supermarket sales.

Inside a Soviet Supermarket

The construction of "bedroom" suburbs around large Russian cities has prompted Soviet planners to introduce a Western food retailing mainstay—the supermarket. Some twelve supermarkets have been built among the massive multistory apartment buildings that house the 4 million residents of Leningrad, for example.

Viewed from the outside, the typical Soviet supermarket appears little different from its U.S. counterpart. Large windows cover the front of a number of checkout lanes, and cash registers can be seen inside.

Once inside, a number of differences are evident. The total number of different products in stock is only about two thousand—one-fifth of what a comparable U.S. supermarket would have. Competing brands are almost nonexistent, and different brands of a food item indicate its quality or variety. Far more space is used for stocking each item. Twelve feet of space is used for stocking sardines; more than seven hundred bottles of champagne are on the shelves.

Packaging on the whole is unattractive by Western standards. Pictures of product contents in use are very rare. Weight, date of manufacture, and price are printed on each package. Mineral water, beer, and an apple-lemon flavored soft drink are mingled on the same shelf, and only the embossed print on the bottle cap indicates which is which.

Prices tend to be higher than those in the United States. Even vodka carries a $4.75 price tag for a pint bottle.

Nonfood items are also present. Toys are stocked at relatively high prices; stuffed animals, for example, from $13 to $20. Kitchenware (with some electrical appliances) and cleaning supplies are also on the shelves.

Missing from the supermarket are frozen foods. Few canned vegetables are carried, and bath soap is sold only in drugstores.

Store hours are from 8 A.M. to 10 P.M. six days a week. Female employees are used almost exclusively. The manager of the store receives a relatively high base salary of $400 per month and is eligible for bonuses based on store sales. She is also supplied with a car for her own use.

Comparison shopping among competing food stores is pointless, since all stores charge the prices set by a committee of the state organization called *Gastronome*. This organization also makes such decisions as where to locate various items in the store and what markdowns to use. Advertising is limited to weekly notices in the Leningrad papers listing new stores and seasonal buys. Store displays are also insignificant, consisting primarily of merchandise location signs, a few posters, and prices on displays and shelves.

Sources: Adapted from Howard W. Barnes, "AMAer Finds Soviets Have Long Lines, Little Service, 19¢ Bread, 700 Bottles of Champagne on the Shelf," *Marketing News*, September 12, 1975, pp. 1, 6; and David J. Luck and Daniel B. Bosse, "AMAers Tour Showplace Soviet Supermarket," *Marketing News*, September 12, 1975, pp. 7, 9. Reprinted from *Marketing News* published by the American Marketing Association. Photo courtesy of Warren N. Cordell.

Specialty Stores

Only part of a single line of products is typically handled in a **specialty store.** However, this part is stocked in considerable depth for the store's customers. Specialty stores include meat markets, men's and women's shoe stores, bakeries, furriers, and millinery shops. Although some are operated by chains, most are run as independent small-scale operations. They are perhaps the greatest stronghold of independent retailers, who can develop expertise in providing a very narrow line of products for their local market.

Specialty stores should not be confused with specialty goods. These stores typically carry convenience and shopping goods. The label *specialty* comes from their practice of handling a specific, narrow line of merchandise.

General Merchandise Retailers

The general store, described earlier in this chapter, is a good example of the **general merchandise store**—*a store that carries a wide variety of product lines, all of which are stocked in some depth.* Included in this category of retailers are department stores, variety stores, and many discount houses. In 1972, general merchandise retailers accounted for one-seventh of all retail sales. Even though the nation's 22,000 variety stores accounted for only 1.6

Variety, Width, and Depth in Retail Product Mixes

Retailers, like manufacturers and wholesalers, develop a product mix designed to attract the customers who comprise their market target. In analyzing retail product mixes, it is useful to consider three dimensions of retailers' merchandise assortments: variety, width, and depth.

Variety refers to the number of product lines carried by the retailer. Department stores, discount houses, drug retailers, and catalog stores all handle a wide number of lines. The typical catalog retailer carries lines of jewelry, small appliances, toys, sporting goods, sound systems, household accessories, records, luggage, candy, toiletries, and even clothing. Such a retailer appeals to a larger potential market than a competitor that specializes in, say, leather goods. In addition, the potential for unplanned purchases in other merchandise lines is increased for the retailer offering a variety of lines.

Width (or breadth) refers to complementary products within a merchandise line. Jewelry stores, bakeries, meat markets, and shoe stores typically carry a number of complementary items in their respective product lines. Customers are attracted to such stores because of the wide assortments of goods available.

Depth refers to the number of sizes, colors, and other characteristics carried in a single product line. A men's clothing store stocking Izod sweaters in twelve colors, five sizes, and V-neck and crew neck offers its customers considerable depth in this product line.

Most retailers compete on the bases of the variety, width, and depth of their merchandise. Some retailers, such as department stores, feature all three dimensions in their merchandise assortments. Discount houses tend to offer a variety of merchandise lines, but they often stock only the popular sizes and best-selling complementary items. Single-line and limited-line retailers such as Peaches (record stores) and Emerald City (waterbeds) specialize in a narrow line of products stocked in considerable depth.

percent of total retail sales, department stores represented a little over 11 percent of all retail sales. The major institutions in the general merchandise retailing category—department stores and discount houses—will be examined in greater detail.

Department Stores—One-Stop Shopping Centers. The **department store** is actually a series of limited line and specialty stores under one roof. By definition, it is *a large retail firm handling a variety of merchandise that includes men's and boy's wear, women's wear and accessories, household linens and dry goods, home furnishings, appliances, and furniture.* It serves the consumer by acting as a one-stop shopping center for almost all personal and household items.

A distinguishing feature of the department store is indicated by its name. The entire store is organized around departments for the purpose of providing service, promotion, and control. A general merchandising manager is responsible for the store's product planning. Reporting to the manager are the buyers who manage each department. These buyers typically run the departments almost as independent businesses; they are given considerable discretion in merchandising and layout decisions. Acceptance of the retailing axiom that well-bought goods are already half-sold is indicated by the department manager's title of *buyer.* Buyers, particularly those in charge of high fashion departments, spend a considerable portion of their time deciding on the inventory to be carried in their departments.

The department store has been the symbol of retailing since the construction in 1863 of the nation's first department store—the A. T. Stewart store in New York City. Almost every urban area in the United States has one or more department stores associated with its downtown area and its major shopping areas. Macy's Herald Square store in New York City is the world's largest department store; it contains over 2 million square feet of space and produces gross sales of approximately $200 million each year. An average of 150,000 customers each day buys at least one of its 400,000 items available in 168 selling departments.

Figure 10–1 illustrates the impact of department stores in major U.S. cities. Many of these cities can even be identified by reference to their major department store. The impact of department stores on urban life is not confined to the United States. European shoppers associate London with Harrod's, Paris with Au Printemps, and Moscow with GUM. Myer is the dominant department store in both Melbourne and Sydney, Australia.

Department stores are known for offering their customers a wide variety of services, such as charge accounts, delivery, gift wrapping, and liberal return privileges. In addition, some 50 percent of their employees and 40 percent of their floor space are devoted to nonselling activities. As a result, they

Figure 10–1
Major U.S. Department Stores

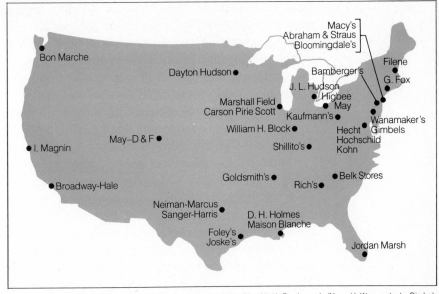

Answers: Filene (Boston); Macy's, Abraham & Straus, Bloomingdale's (New York); Bamberger's (Newark); Wanamaker's, Gimbels (Philadelphia); Kaufmann's (Pittsburgh); G. Fox (Hartford); J. L. Hudson (Detroit); Marshall Field, Carson Pirie Scott (Chicago); Higbee, May (Cleveland); Shillito's (Cincinnati); William H. Block (Indianapolis); Dayton Hudson (Minneapolis); Hecht, Hochschild Kohn (Baltimore/Washington, D.C.); Belk Stores (Charlotte); Rich's (Atlanta); Goldsmith's (Memphis); D. H. Holmes, Maison Blanche (New Orleans); Jordan Marsh (Miami); Foley's, Joske's (Houston); Neiman-Marcus, Sanger-Harris (Dallas); May–D & F (Denver); Broadway-Hale (Los Angeles); I. Magnin (San Francisco); Bon Marche (Seattle).

have relatively high operating costs, averaging between 45 and 60 percent of sales.

Department stores have displayed a willingness to adapt to changing consumer desires. They have added bargain basements and expanded parking facilities in attempts to compete with discount operations and suburban retailers. They have also followed the movement of the population to the suburbs by opening major branches in outlying shopping centers.[6] And they have attempted to revitalize downtown retailing in many cities by modernizing their stores, extending store hours, attracting the tourist and convention trade, and focusing on the residents of the central cities.

Mass Merchandisers. Mass merchandising has made major inroads on department store sales during the past two decades by emphasizing lower prices for well-known brand name products, high turnover of goods, and reduced services. **Mass merchandisers** *often stock a wider line of products than department stores, but they usually do not offer the depth of assortment in each line.* Major types of mass merchandisers are discount houses, hypermarkets, and catalog retailers.

Discount Houses—Limited Services and Lower Prices. The birth of the modern **discount house** came at the end of World War II, when a New York

Company named Masters discovered that a large number of customers were willing to shop at *a store that charges lower than usual prices and does not offer such traditional retail services as credit, sales assistance by clerks, and delivery.* Soon, retailers throughout the country were following the Masters formula, either changing over from their traditional operation or opening new stores dedicated to discounting. At first, the discount stores sold mostly appliances, but they have spread into furniture, soft goods, drugs, and even food. Over 12 percent of all retail stores today operate as discount houses.

Discount operations had existed before World War II, but the early discounters usually sold goods from manufacturers' catalogs; they kept no stock on display and often limited potential customers. The new discounters operated large stores, advertised heavily, emphasized low prices for well-known brands, and were open to the public. Elimination of many of the "free" services provided by traditional retailers allowed these operations to keep their markups 10 to 25 percent below those of their competitors. Consumers had become accustomed to self-service by shopping at supermarkets, and they responded in great numbers to this retailing innovation. Conventional retailers such as Kresge and Woolworth joined the discounting practice by opening their own K mart and Woolco stores. Currently, about 38 cents of every dollar spent by U.S. consumers is spent in a discount store.[7]

As discount houses move into new product areas, a noticeable increase in the number of services offered is evident. Carpets are beginning to appear on discounters' floors, credit is increasingly available, and many discounters are quietly dropping *discount* from their name. Although they still offer fewer services than other retailers, discounters' operating costs are increasing as they become similar to the traditional department stores. Some have even moved into the "best" shopping areas. Discount shoppers can now patronize Korvettes at its prestigious Fifth Avenue location in New York City.

Hypermarkets—Shopping Centers in a Single Store. A relatively recent retailing development has been the introduction of **hypermarkets**—*giant mass merchandisers who operate on a low-price, self-service basis and carry lines of soft goods and groceries.* The hypermarket began in France and has since spread to Canada and the United States. Meijer's Thrifty Acres in suburban Detroit has 220,000 square feet of selling space (eleven to fifteen times that of the average supermarket) and more than forty checkout counters. It sells food, hardware, soft goods, building materials, auto supplies, appliances, and prescription drugs; and it has a restaurant, a beauty salon, a barbershop, a branch bank, and a bakery.[8] By pricing inventory between 10 and 15 percent below normal retail, the average hypermarket has an annual sales volume of $35 million. More than a thousand of these super-stores are currently in operation.

Catalog Retailers—Cutting Costs with a Catalog, a Showroom, and a Warehouse. One of the major growth areas in retailing during the past decade has been that of catalog retailing.[9] *Catalog retailers* mail catalogs to their customers and operate from a showroom displaying samples of each product handled by them. Orders are filled from a backroom warehouse. Price is an important factor for catalog store customers, and low prices are made possible by few services, storage of most of the inventory in the warehouse, reduced shoplifting losses, and the handling of products that are not very likely to become obsolete, such as luggage, small appliances, gift items, sporting equipment, toys, and jewelry. Major catalog retailers include Service Merchandise, Giant Stores, Vornado, Zale, and Gordon Jewelry Corporation. (Mail-order catalog retailing is discussed in the next section.)

Nonstore Retailing

A number of retail sales are not made in stores. Goods are often sold door-to-door, in mail-order houses, and by automatic vending machines. These kinds of sales account for 2.5 percent of all retail sales.

House-to-House Retailing. One of the oldest marketing channels was built around direct contact between the seller and customer at the home of the customer—*house-to-house retailing.* This channel provides maximum convenience for the consumer and allows the manufacturer to control the firm's marketing channels. It is a minor part of the retailing picture, with less than 1 percent of all retail sales.[10]

House-to-house retailing is used by a number of merchandisers, such as manufacturers of bakery and dairy products, newspapers, and potato chips. Firms emphasizing product demonstrations also tend to use this channel. Among them are companies that sell vacuum cleaners (for example, Electrolux), household brushes (Fuller Brush Company), encyclopedias (World Book), and insurance. Some firms, such as Tupperware, use a variation called *party-plan selling,* where a customer hosts a party to which several neighbors and friends are invited. During the party, a company representative makes a presentation of the products. The host receives a commission based on the amount of products sold. Table 10–2 lists the ten largest direct sales retailers.

The house-to-house method of retailing appears to be a low-cost method of distribution. No plush retail facilities are required, no investment in inventory is necessary, and most house-to-house salespeople operate on a commission basis. However, the method is actually an extremely high-cost

Rank	Company and Products	1977 Sales (in Millions)
1	Avon Products (cosmetics)	$1,600
2	Electrolux (vacuum cleaners)	500
3	Tupperware Home Parties (food containers)	350
4	Amway (household products)	300
5	World Book–Childcraft International (encyclopedias, books)	250
6	Shaklee (food supplements)	200
7	Home Interiors & Gifts (decorative accessories)	200
8	C. H. Stuart (jewelry, crafts, decorative accessories)[a]	150
9	Stanley Home Products (household products)	150
10	Kirby (vacuum cleaners)	100

[a]Parent company of Sarah Coventry, Caroline Emmons, Artcraft Concepts, and Gateway Home Decorators.
Source: Estimates by Direct Selling Association. Reprinted from "How the 'New Sell' Is Raking in Billions," *U.S.News & World Report*, May 8, 1978, p. 74. Copyright 1978 U.S. News & World Report, Inc.

approach to distribution. Markups average 50 to 60 percent as compared with 25 to 30 percent for in-store retailing. High travel costs, nonproductive calls, and the limited number of contacts per day result in high operating expenses.

Mail-Order Retailing. The customers of *mail-order retailing merchandisers* can order merchandise by mail, by telephone, or by visiting the mail-order desk of a retail store. Goods are then shipped to the customer's home or to the local retail store.

Vending
machines – one
form of nonstore
retailing.

"Room service here."

Source: *New Yorker*, March 27, 1978, p. 40. Drawing by Leo Cullum, © 1978 The New Yorker Magazine, Inc.

Mail-order selling began in 1872, when Montgomery Ward issued its first catalog to rural midwestern families. That catalog contained only a few items, mostly clothing and farm supplies. Sears, Roebuck soon followed Ward's lead, and mail-order retailing became an important source of goods in isolated settlements.

Even though mail-order sales represent only 1 percent of all retail sales, they are an important channel for consumers who desire convenience and a large selection of colors and sizes. In 1980, more than 2 billion catalogs were mailed. Sears, which currently holds 44 percent of the mail-order market, mails 300 million catalogs annually. Mail-order houses offer a wide range of products—from novelty items (Spencer Gifts) to hunting and camping equipment (L. L. Bean) to an eighteenth century Chinese screen priced at $60,000 (Horchow). Many mail-order catalog houses also generate retail sales by having consumers buy from retail outlets of their catalog stores.

Automatic Merchandising. Maximum convenience is provided by *automatic vending machines*—the true robot stores—for a wide range of convenience goods. These machines account for 25 percent of all soft drink sales, 16 percent of cigarette sales, and 20 percent of candy bar sales in the United States.[11] Approximately 6 million vending machines are currently in operation throughout the country.

While automatic merchandising is important in the retailing of some products, it represents less than 1 percent of all retail sales. Its future growth is limited by such factors as the cost of the machines and the necessity for regular maintenance and repair. In addition, automatically vended products are confined to convenience goods of standard sizes and weights that have a high turnover rate. Prices for many products purchased in vending machines are higher than store prices for the same products.

Worms in the Vending Machine

Forgetting the live bait no longer need ruin a fishing trip. Franko's Live Bait has solved the problem with vending machines. Insert from $1.25 to $3 and out pops a can containing a dozen nightcrawlers. Push another button for a can of forty redworms. Other cans may contain forty "mighty mealies" or even live minnows. All of Franko's bait carries a thirty-day guarantee of life and involves no messy handling or odors.

The new product line is the creation of Frank Kartesz, a thirty-eight-year-old mathematics teacher in Rockwood, Pennsylvania. An avid angler, Kartesz says he got fed up having to wait for the local bait store to open each morning before he could go fishing. After extensive testing, he and his brother developed a substance that could sustain live bait in cans for up to six months. Sales have been brisk. In 1978, some 35 million worms were sold from 152 vending machines in taverns and restaurants.

Source: Information from George Getschow, "Fishermen Discover Vending Machines for Buying Worms," *Wall Street Journal*, June 28, 1978, p. 37.

**The Impact of
Chain Stores on
Retailing**

Chain stores are *groups of retail stores that are centrally owned and managed and that handle the same lines of products.* The concept of chain stores is certainly not new. The Mitsui chain was operating in Japan in the 1600s. One of the largest retail chains in the United States, the Great Atlantic & Pacific Tea Company (A&P), began in 1859.

The major advantage possessed by chain operations over independent retailers is economies of scale. Volume purchases through a central buying office allow such chains as Safeway, Kroger's, and Food Fair to obtain lower prices than independents. Since chains may have thousands of retail stores, specialists in layout, sales training, and accounting systems can be used to increase efficiency. Advertising can also be effectively used; a single advertisement for Sears, Roebuck in a national magazine covers every Sears store in the United States.

Chains account for 31 percent of all retail stores, and their dollar volume of sales amounts to approximately one-third of all retail sales. At the present time, chains dominate four fields. They account for approximately 90 percent of all department stores sales, almost 80 percent of all variety store sales, 54 percent of all food store sales, and almost 45 percent of all retail shoe store sales.[12] Table 10–3 lists the ten largest retailers in the United States.

Sears, Roebuck is nearly twice the size of the country's next largest retailer. It accounts for just under half of all catalog sales, 3.5 percent of all nonfood retail sales, and fully 1 percent of the nation's gross national product. One out of every three U.S. families now carries a Sears credit card, and three of four adults shop at Sears every year.[13] It is appropriate that the company headquarters are located in the 110-story Sears, Roebuck Tower in Chicago, the tallest building the the United States.

Many of the larger chains have expanded their operations to the rest of

**Table 10–3
The Ten Largest
Retailers in the
United States**

Rank	Company	Sales (in Thousands)	Net Income as Percent of Sales
1	Sears, Roebuck	$17,946,336	5.1
2	Safeway Stores	12,550,569	1.2
3	K mart	11,812,810	2.9
4	J. C. Penney	10,845,000	2.5
5	Kroger	7,828,071	1.1
6	Great Atlantic & Pacific Tea	7,288,577	0.1
7	F. W. Woolworth	6,102,800	2.1
8	Federated Department Stores	5,404,621	3.7
9	Montgomery Ward	5,013,514	2.4
10	Lucky Stores	4,658,409	1.7

Source: "The Fortune Directory of the Fifty Largest Retailing Companies," *Fortune*, July 16, 1979, p. 164–165. Reprinted by permission from the Fortune Directory; © 1979 Time Inc.

the world. Sears now has branch stores in Spain, Mexico, and South America. Safeway operates supermarkets in Germany, the United Kingdom, and Australia. J. C. Penney has retail operations in Belgium and Italy. Direct retailers such as Avon and Tupperware have sales representatives in Europe and South America. Japanese consumers can shop at more than three hundred 7-11 stores.

Reactions by Independent Retailers

Even though most retailers are small, independent operators, the larger-sized chains dominate a number of fields. The U.S. retailing structure can be characterized as having a large number of small stores, many medium-sized stores, and a small number of large stores. Even though only about 4 percent of all stores have annual sales of $1 million or more, they account for more than half of all retail sales in the United States. As Table 10–4 indicates, about 25 percent of all stores in the United States have sales of less than $20,000 each year.

Independents have attempted to compete with chains in a number of ways. Some were unable to do so efficiently and went out of business. Oth-

Table 10–4
Retail Trade in the United States by Number of Establishments and Sales Volume

	Establishments			Sales Volume		
	Number	Percent	Cumulative Percent	Amount (in Billions)	Percent	Cumulative Percent
Total for all stores	1,912,871			$459.0		
Establishments operated entire year, total	1,709,555	100.0		$427.6	100.0	
With annual sales of:						
$5 million or more	9,239	.5	.5	89.7	21.0	21.0
$2 million to $4.99 million	26,781	1.6	2.1	81.1	19.0	40.0
$1 million to $1.99 million	38,313	2.2	4.3	53.8	12.5	52.5
$500,000 to $999,999	70,800	4.1	8.4	48.8	11.4	63.9
$300,000 to $499,999	106,494	6.2	14.6	40.5	9.5	73.4
$100,000 to $299,999	449,862	26.3	40.9	77.7	18.2	91.6
$50,000 to $99,999	304,135	17.8	58.7	22.0	5.1	96.7
$30,000 to $49,999	188,387	11.1	69.8	7.4	1.7	98.4
$20,000 to $29,999	127,342	7.4	77.2	3.1	0.7	99.1
$10,000 to $19,999	170,719	10.0	87.2	2.4	0.6	99.7
Less than $10,000	217,483	12.8	100.0	1.2	0.3	100.0

Source: U.S. Department of Commerce, Bureau of the Census, *Census of Retail Trade, 1972, Establishment and Firm Size* (Washington, D.C.: Government Printing Office, 1976), pp. 1–8.

ers have joined retail cooperatives, wholesaler sponsored voluntary chains, or franchise operations, described in Chapter 8. Still others have remained in business by exploiting their advantages of flexibility in operation and knowledge of local market conditions. The independents continue to represent a major part of U.S. retailing.[14]

Planned Shopping Centers

A pronounced shift of retail trade away from the traditional downtown retailing districts and toward **planned shopping centers** has been developing since 1950. These *planned retailing centers* have followed population shifts to the suburbs and have focused on correcting many of the problems of shopping in the downtown business districts. Acres of parking and locations away from downtown traffic congestion appeal to suburban shoppers. Additional hours for shopping during the evenings and on weekends facilitate family shopping.

There are three types of planned shopping centers. The smallest and most common is the *neighborhood shopping center,* which is typically composed of a supermarket and a group of smaller stores such as a drugstore, a laundry and dry cleaner, a small appliance store, and perhaps a beauty shop and barbershop. The *community shopping center* is larger and includes a branch of a local department store and a variety store. The largest planned center is the *regional shopping center,* a giant shopping district of at least 400,000 square feet of shopping space typically built around one or two major department stores and as many as a hundred smaller stores. Planned centers appear to be replicas of downtown retailing districts, but they are different in two important ways:

The center is organized and controlled by a single management to create an integrated approach to accommodate vehicular traffic. For every foot of selling space, three or four feet of parking space is provided. Secondly, this same management directs its attention toward developing an equally integrated and homogeneous marketing approach. Whereas the traditional central business district was an agglomeration of retailers joined by their individual decisions to rent adjacent space, the tenants of planned regional centers are selected with almost as much care as the names in a social register. The aim is to form a set of stores that will complement each other in the quality of the merchandise offerings and to cover the range of merchandise that the market could be expected to desire.[15]

Planned shopping centers account for about 45 percent of all retail sales.

Scrambled Merchandising

A second fundamental change in retailing has been the steady deterioration of clear-cut delineations of retailer types. Anyone who has attempted to fill a prescription recently has been exposed to the concept of **scrambled merchandising**—*the practice of carrying dissimilar lines in an attempt to gen-*

erate added sales volume. The drugstore carries not only prescription and proprietary drugs but also gifts, hardware, housewares, records, magazines, grocery products, garden supplies, and even small appliances. Gasoline retailers now market bread and milk, and supermarkets carry antifreeze.

Many supermarkets fill prescriptions and stock such nonfood items as portable televisions, cameras, stereo equipment, citizen band radios, and clothing such as jeans and T-shirts. Customers can use bank credit cards for payment.[16] The best-selling product in dollar volume in drugstores is Polaroid Polacolor II film for instant movies. Other photographic materials—Kodacolor II and Polaroid SX-70 films and Sylvania flash cubes—also are among the top ten drugstore sellers.[17] Two-thirds of all toothpaste purchases are made in supermarkets; and about one-fourth of all retail stores are at least partially involved in selling tires, batteries, and other automobile parts and accessories.[18]

Scrambled merchandising was born out of retailers' willingness to add dissimilar merchandise lines in order to satisfy consumer demands for one-stop shopping. It complicates manufacturers' channel decisions, because attempts to maintain or increase their market share will, in most instances, mean that they will have to develop multiple channels to reach the diverse retailers handling their products.

The Wheel-of-Retailing Hypothesis and Retail Change

M. P. McNair attempted to explain the patterns of change in retailing through what has been termed the **wheel of retailing.** According to this hypothesis, *new types of retailers gain a competitive foothold by offering lower prices to their customers through the reduction or elimination of services. Once they are established, however, they add more services, and their prices gradually rise. Then they become vulnerable to a new low-price retailer who enters with minimum services*—and the wheel turns.

Most of the major developments in retailing appear to fit the wheel pattern. Early department stores, chain stores, supermarkets, discount stores, hypermarkets, and catalog retailers all emphasized limited service and low prices. For most of these retailers, price levels gradually increased as services were added.

There have been some exceptions, however. Suburban shopping centers, convenience food stores, and vending machines were not built around low-price appeals. However, the wheel pattern has been present often enough in the past that it should serve as a general indicator of future developments in retailing.[19]

Future Trends in Retailing[20]

A number of trends that will greatly affect tomorrow's retailer are currently emerging. Cable television is likely to revolutionize many retail practices by the early 1990s, when it is expected to be in 50 percent of U.S. homes. The cable will make **teleshopping** possible. That is, *consumers will be able to order merchandise that has been displayed on their television sets.* Such remote shopping is likely to be especially common for products where sight, feel, smell, and personal service are not important when ordering the merchandise.[21] One such system already in operation is called Qube; it is a Warner Communications cable network connected to some 30,000 homes in Columbus, Ohio. The system allows instant two-way sales communications between retailers and consumers about products for sale.[22] Video telephones offer the same promise, but their introduction is likely to be delayed because of high costs involved in making them available.

Retail executives believe that catalog stores, direct mail, discount houses, hypermarkets, and telephone selling are likely to offer major growth opportunities. Discounting is expected to grow to 25 percent of the total general merchandise sales volume. Furniture warehouse retailers such as Levitz and Wickes are regarded as major threats to established furniture outlets. In addition, grocery, drug, and other limited line retailers are likely to generate new competition for the consumer's general merchandise business.

A renewed emphasis on the pleasurable aspects of shopping is another trend that should accelerate in the next few years. Department stores are expected to place increased emphasis on in-house boutiques and specialty shops, which will allow them to provide more individualized service and to appeal to specific kinds of customers.

The future of the specialty stores appears bright; their share of the gen-

The Universal Product Code is designed to reduce retailing costs.

Source: *Wall Street Journal*, October 25, 1978. Reprinted by permission of the cartoonist, Nick Hobart, and the *Wall Street Journal*.

The Computerized Checkout

The latest application of the computer in supermarkets is the computerized checkout. The printed lines appearing on nearly every consumer product, called the *Universal Product Code,* are actually magnetic symbols that can be "read" by the optical scanning device of a computer. As cashiers pass each item over the electronic reader, the computer instantly displays and records the sale and gives the customer a detailed receipt. It also provides supermarket managers with a detailed analysis of daily sales. This information allows the managers to tailor merchandise to the demands of a particular area and to try out new products and determine how well they are selling.

Although the system is expensive (between $100,000 and $150,000 per store) and is opposed by both the retail clerks union (which fears job losses) and consumer groups (which fear shopper exploitation if supermarkets stop marking prices on individual items), many supermarket chain executives argue that the new system is a worthwhile investment. Only a few hundred of the nation's 33,000 supermarkets have the devices in operation, but complete conversion to the new system would probably save about $100 million in food costs a year, since the system is faster and more accurate than the methods currently in use.

Source: Computerized checkouts are described in Roger B. May, "As Costs Fall and Incentives Rise, Supermarkets Begin to Install Computer Checkouts on Counters, "*Wall Street Journal*, June 13, 1978, p. 40.

eral merchandise market is expected to increase to 48 percent by the mid-1980s. However, the *number* of small, independent specialty stores is expected to continue to decline. Those that survive will become stronger and will generate the increase in sales volume.

Summary

Retailers are the end of the marketing channel. Retail stores, which account for 97 percent of total retail sales in the United States, can be divided into three categories: *general merchandise retailers,* such as department stores, variety stores, and mass merchandisers such as discount houses, hypermarkets, and catalog retailers—all handling a wide variety of products; *limited line or single line stores,* which compete by carrying a large assortment of one or two lines of products; and *specialty stores,* which carry a large assortment of only part of a single line of products.

Nonstore retailing includes house-to-house retailing, mail-order retailing, and automatic merchandising machines. These methods provide maximum consumer convenience and represent 2.5 percent of all retail sales.

Chains are groups of retail stores that are centrally owned and managed and that handle the same lines of products. Chain stores dominate retailing in four fields: department stores, variety stores, food stores, and shoe stores. They account for approximately one-third of all retail sales.

A pronounced shift in retailing away from the downtown business districts to planned suburban shopping centers has taken place. These shopping centers account for 45 percent of all retail sales.

The changes in retailing practices and the development of new retailing forms reflect retailers' attempts to keep up with changing consumer demands. Retailers are a vital institution in the firm's marketing channel.

Questions for Discussion

1. Explain the following terms:

   retailing
   single line store
   limited line store
   supermarket
   specialty store
   general merchandise store
   department store
   mass merchandiser

   discount house
   hypermarket
   chain store
   planned shopping center
   scrambled merchandising
   wheel of retailing
   teleshopping

2. Why, in this era of super-stores and mass merchandising, have general stores survived?
3. Identify each of the three major categories of retail stores. Give an example of each in your city.
4. How are limited line and specialty stores able to compete with such general merchandise retailers as department stores and discount houses?
5. Why have supermarkets increased the number of nonfoods stocked in their stores?
6. Identify the major types of general merchandise retailers.
7. Give reasons for the success of discount retailing in the United States.
8. Identify and briefly explain each of the types of nonstore retailing operations.
9. Explain the party plan approach to house-to-house retailing. In what other product lines might this technique be successful?
10. Why has mail-order retailing, a holdover from the nineteenth century, continued to exist as a separate form of retail selling?
11. In what fields are chain stores dominant? Explain their success in these fields.
12. What advantages do chain stores possess over independent retailers?
13. Chain stores offer their customers the benefit of economies of scale; yet independent retailers account for over two-thirds of all retail sales. Explain.
14. A few food stores in every city continue to offer credit and delivery service. How can they survive the competition of the chain stores and independent supermarkets, with their lower prices?
15. Comment on the following statement: Planned shopping centers are replicas of the downtown retailing districts.
16. Why has the practice of scrambled merchandising become so common in retailing?
17. What problems for the manufacturer result from the practice of scrambled merchandising?
18. List several examples of the wheel of retailing in operation. List examples that do not conform to the wheel hypothesis.
19. In 1978, A&P decided to resume its previous practice of offering trading stamps to its customers. Explain this decision in terms of the wheel of retailing hypothesis.
20. What changes would you predict for retailing as a result of the development of the video telephone? Which retailers are likely to be affected most by this innovation?

Notes

1. The W. T. Grant story is chronicled in "How W. T. Grant Lost $175 Million Last Year," *Business Week,* February 24, 1975, pp. 74–76; Stanley Slom and Karen Rothmyer, "W. T. Grant Co. Files Bankruptcy Petition, Marketing Failure of its Turnaround Efforts," *Wall Street Journal,* October 3, 1975, p. 24; Stanley H. Slom, "Hard-Nosed Salesman Shuts Stores, Cuts Jobs to Save W. T. Grant," *Wall Street Journal,* December 4, 1975, p. 1; and "Dividing What's Left of Grant's," *Business Week,* March 1, 1976, p. 21.
2. For a discussion of the different types of consumers and the services each type expects from retailers, see Louis E. Boone, David L. Kurtz, James C. Johnson, and John A. Bonno, "'City Shoppers and Urban Identification' Revisited," *Journal of Marketing,* July 1974, pp. 67–69. See also W. Thomas Anderson, Jr., William H. Cunningham, and John H. Murphy, "Retail Consumer Typologies and Market Segmentation: Strategic Implications," in *Contemporary Marketing Thought,* ed. Barnett A. Greenberg and Danny N. Bellenger (Chicago: American Marketing Association, 1977), pp. 302–307; and Phillip B. Niffenegger and Patrick D. McElya, "Consumer Purchase Orientation and Race: Replication and Extension," in Greenberg and Bellenger, *Contemporary Marketing Thought,* pp. 350–354.

3. "Sears' Identity Crisis," *Business Week,* December 8, 1975, p. 54.

4. See Thomas J. Stanley and Murphy A. Sewell, "Predicting Supermarket Trade: Implications for Marketing Management," *Journal of Retailing,* Summer 1978, pp. 13–22. See also Danny N. Bellenger, Thomas J. Stanley, and John W. Allen, "Trends in Food Retailing," *Atlanta Economic Review,* May–June 1978, pp. 11–14.

5. Christy Marshall, "Supermarkets Fight Fast-Food Challenge," *Advertising Age,* October 30, 1978, pp. 30, 34. See also Robert H. Williams, John J. Painter, and Herbert R. Nichols, "A Policy-Oriented Typology of Grocery Shoppers," *Journal of Retailing,* Spring 1978, pp. 27–42.

6. See Eleanor G. May and Malcolm P. McNair, "Department Stores Face Stiff Challenge in Next Decade," *Journal of Retailing,* Fall 1977, pp. 47–58. The department store shopper is described in Melvin R. Crask and Fred D. Reynolds, "An In-Depth Profile of the Department Store Shopper," *Journal of Retailing,* Summer 1978, pp. 23–32.

7. "Business Bulletin," *Wall Street Journal,* October 26, 1978, p. 1.

8. Marcia Ming, "There'll Be More Thrifty Acres," *Detroit News,* October 1, 1978. See also Ronald S. Rubin and Donald A. Fuller, "The Hypermarket: A Challenge to the Supermarket?" in *Proceedings of the Southwestern Marketing Association,* ed. John E. Swan and Robert C. Haring, Dallas, Texas, March 1978, p. 38.

9. The growth of catalog retailing is described in Joseph Barry Mason and Morris L. Mayer, *Modern Retailing: Theory and Practice* (Dallas: Business Publications, 1978), pp. 54–55. See also Louis E. Boone and James C. Johnson, *Marketing Channels* (Tulsa, Okla.: PPC Books, 1977), pp. 489–494.

10. See Peter L. Gillett, "In-Home Shoppers—An Overview," *Journal of Marketing,* October 1976, pp. 81–88.

11. "Vendors Pull Out All Stops," *Business Week,* August 15, 1970, pp. 52–54.

12. U.S. Department of Commerce, Bureau of the Census, *Statistical Abstract of the United States,* 97th ed. (Washington, D.C.: Government Printing Office, 1976), p. 773.

13. "Mail-Order Marketer Sears Grows to an Institution 'Where America Shops,'" *Marketing News,* April 21, 1978, pp. 1, 16.

14. See "Those Mom-and-Pop Stores Are Still Going Strong," *U.S. News & World Report,* July 24, 1978, pp. 59–62; and "We Know Our Territory," *Forbes,* November 13, 1978, pp. 86–87.

15. Louis P. Bucklin, *Competition and Evolution in the Distributive Trades* (Englewood Cliffs, N.J.: Prentice-Hall, 1972), p. 108. See also William O. Bearden, "Determinant Attributes of Store Patronage: Downtown versus Outlying Shopping Centers," *Journal of Retailing,* Summer 1977, pp. 29–38; and Danny N. Bellenger, Dan H. Robertson, and Barnett A. Greenberg, "Shopping Center Patronage Motives," *Journal of Retailing,* Summer 1977, pp. 29–38.

16. "Home-Baked Bread, Anyone? TV Sets? Blue Jeans?" *Forbes,* May 15, 1977, pp. 144–148.

17. "Business Bulletin," *Wall Street Journal,* March 30, 1978, p. 1.

18. William R. Davidson, "Changes in Distributive Institutions," *Journal of Marketing,* January 1970, p. 8. See also William R. Davidson, "Changes in Distributive Institutions: A Reexamination," *Canadian Marketer,* Winter 1975, pp. 7–13.

19. For a complete discussion of the wheel of retailing hypothesis, see Stanley C. Hollander, "The Wheel of Retailing," *Journal of Marketing,* July 1960, pp. 37–42. See also Dillard B. Tinsley, John R. Brooks, Jr., and Michael d'Amico, "Will the Wheel of Retailing Stop Turning?" *Akron Business and Economic Review,* Summer 1978, pp. 26–29.

20. This section is adapted from Raymond A. Marquardt, James C. Makens, and Robert G. Roe, *Retail Management: Satisfaction of Consumer Needs,* 2d ed. (Hinsdale, Ill.: Dryden Press, 1979), pp. 28–31. See also J. Barry Mason and Morris L. Mayer, "Retailing Executives View the 1980s," *Atlanta Economic Review,* May–June 1978, pp. 4–10; and Leonard L. Berry and Ian H. Wilson, "Retailing: The Next Ten Years," *Journal of Retailing,* Fall 1977, pp. 5–28.

21. Malcolm P. McNair and Eleanor G. May, "The Next Revolution of the Retailing Wheel," *Harvard Business Review,* September–October 1978, pp. 81–91.

22. "Retailers Shake a Staid Old Image," *U.S. News & World Report,* October 23, 1978, p. 84.

CHAPTER 11
MANAGEMENT OF PHYSICAL DISTRIBUTION

Key Terms

physical distribution systems

customer service standards

tariffs

class rate

commodity rate

storage warehouse

distribution warehouse

break-bulk center

make-bulk center

EOQ (economic order quantity) model

materials handling

unitizing

containerization

Learning Goals

1. To explain the role of physical distribution in an effective marketing strategy.

2. To describe the objective of physical distribution.

3. To list the three concepts that make up the physical distribution concept.

4. To identify and compare the major elements of a physical distribution system.

5. To relate the major transportation alternatives to such factors as speed, dependability, and cost.

11

A California producer of cut flowers had a plan designed to broaden the market for his flowers. He would market them in department stores and supermarkets rather than in flower shops. But two problems stood between him and his goal: (1) convincing the retailers that they could handle the flowers with a minimum of floor space, and (2) providing the retailers with fresh and timely assortments of flowers in order to maintain high turnover.

The first problem was solved through the design of a special case to hold trays of cut flowers. The compact case minimized the use of floor space and maximized the store display. The second problem was solved by air freight shipment and a special container that cooled the blossoms as they were cut in the fields, held trays of flowers in different quantities, and was easy to handle. Physical distribution technology thus made it possible to deliver freshly cut flowers to almost any store in the United States in twenty-four hours or less.[1]

What Is Physical Distribution?

The cut flower producer recognized the importance of physical distribution to the success of his marketing program. So does Bharat Jashanmal, who is responsible for stocking a supermarket in Doha, Qatar, on the oil-rich Persian Gulf. Every week, Flying Tiger Line flies 100,000 pounds of fresh produce, fresh and frozen meat, dairy products, and assorted dry goods from Seattle to Qatar. Even though Jashanmal admits that Seattle is a long way to go for a head of lettuce, he argues that the range and availability of goods as well as competitive prices more than compensate for the cost of shipping them 10,000 miles.[2]

While the previous distribution chapters have concentrated on the flows of title and use rights, payments, products, and information, this chapter focuses specifically on the flows of physical goods. Improving customer service through more efficient physical distribution is an important aspect of any firm's marketing strategy. In addition, this improvement of efficiency means substantial cost savings. Almost 50 percent of all marketing costs result from physical distribution activities.

Physical distribution is *the broad range of activities concerned with efficient movement of finished products from the end of the production line to the consumer.*[3] These activities include freight transportation, warehousing, materials handling, protective packaging, inventory control, plant and warehouse site selection, order processing, market forecasting, and customer service.

Why has the distribution function of marketing taken on such importance in recent years? Why is it referred to as the "last great frontier for increased marketing efficiency"?[4] Why is management consultant Peter F. Drucker calling it the most exciting area of business today?[5]

Answers to these questions can be found in the history of U.S. business. Starting with the industrial revolution in the early 1800s, businesses emphasized efficient production, stressing their ability to decrease production costs for each unit they produced. By the early 1900s, production began to catch up with demand, and firms started to recognize the importance of sales. However, physical distribution was still basically ignored.

During World War II, the Allied military forces effectively used logistics, mathematical models, and systems analysis to ensure that the right war materials were at the proper place at the correct time.[6] (The term *logistics* is used interchangeably with *physical distribution* in this chapter.) These techniques were not immediately applied to business problems, however. Instead, U.S. firms turned their attention to the pressing job of filling the unprecedented demand for goods and services that existed at the end of the war. Not until the recessions of the 1950s did marketing managers begin to reexamine their physical distribution network. The 1958 recession and profit squeeze created an environment in which marketers began to search in earnest for effective cost control systems. Almost spontaneously, many firms came to realize that physical distribution was a major cost item that had never been carefully studied and coordinated.

In addition to the economic climate of the 1950s, four other basic business trends stimulated the search for increased efficiency in physical distribution. First, *transportation costs were increasing rapidly.* Traditional methods of distribution were becoming more costly, and marketing managers began to realize that corrective action was needed to offset the rising expenses. In 1978, U.S. industry spent over $200 billion on transportation of goods, more than $125 billion to warehouse them, more than $75 billion in inventory carrying charges, and nearly $20 billion to administer and manage physical distribution. Total physical distribution costs amounted to over $420 billion—more than 20 percent of the nation's gross national product!

Second, *production efficiency had reached a point where it was becoming difficult to effect significant cost savings in this area.* Most of the "fat" had been removed from production, while physical distribution was still untouched.

Third, *a fundamental change in inventory-stocking practices occurred.* At one time, inventory was typically held at about 50/50 between distributors and retailers. But advances in inventory control methods had changed that ratio to 90/10 by 1950. This change meant that greater emphasis had to be placed on dependable movement of products.

Fourth, *the product lines of many companies were proliferating.* As firms attempted to apply the newly accepted marketing concept of giving customers the exact products they desired, a steady stream of additions to product lines appeared. Prior to the 1950s, products such as typewriters, light bulbs, appliances, and tissue paper were largely functional in nature; differences among them were structural. Today, however, IBM can no longer stock only the standard black or grey electric typewriter with pica type. Its sales representatives must be able to match the typewriter color with the office decor, and the type face must support the image the purchasing company wants to project. As product proliferation continues, an increasing burden is placed on the physical distribution function, since, from a logistical point of view, each product variation is a new product that requires its own inventory system and transportation planning.

Applying the Systems Concept to Physical Distribution

The study of physical distribution is one of the classic examples of the systems approach to business problems. **Systems** are *a set of objects with relationships between the objects and between their attributes.*[7] From a company point of view, the systems approach means that the firm's broad objectives can be accomplished only by recognizing the mutual interdependence of the basic functional areas of the firm (marketing, production, and finance). The same reasoning can be applied to physical distribution. The logistics manager must balance each functional area of physical distribution so that no single area is stressed to the point where it becomes detrimental to the overall functioning of the department.[8]

The Objective of Physical Distribution

What are the firm's "broad objectives"? In other words, what is the goal of a physical distribution system? The goal is to produce a specified level of customer service while minimizing the costs involved in physically moving and storing the product from its production point to the point where it is ultimately purchased. Marketers must first agree on the necessary level of customer service, then seek to minimize the *total* costs of moving the product to the consumer or industrial user.

To achieve the objective, the physical distribution manager must use three basic systems concepts that are vital to effective logistics management: (1) the total cost approach, (2) the avoidance of suboptimization, and (3) cost trade-offs.

Total Cost Approach

The premise that all relevant factors in physically moving and storing products should be considered as a whole and not individually forms the basis of the *total cost approach*. A number of vital functions must be considered: (1) transportation, (2) warehousing, (3) warehouse location, (4) inventory control systems, (5) materials handling, (6) internal information flows, (7) customer service standards, and (8) packaging. All these functions must be considered as a whole when attempting to meet customer service levels at minimum cost.

Avoidance of Suboptimization

To completely understand the total cost approach, it is necessary to consider the second basic physical distribution concept—suboptimization. *Suboptimization* is a condition where the manager of each physical distribution function attempts to minimize costs, but, due to the impact of one physical distribution task on the others, the results are less than optimal. Why does suboptimization prevail in physical distribution? The answer lies in the fact that each separate logistics activity is judged by its ability to achieve certain management objectives, some of which are at cross-purposes with other objectives. Sometimes, departments in other functional areas take actions that cause the physical distribution area to operate at less than full efficiency.

Suboptimization in Action

The production department attempts to minimize the cost of production per unit of output. To achieve its goal, it operates long production runs with as few changeovers as possible. The result of this action is excess inventory and the added cost of holding this inventory.

The marketing department desires to give the finest customer service possible in order to maximize sales. The effect of this policy is to encourage a maximum of inventory in the field so that orders can be received by customers as soon as possible. Again, the cost of holding inventory tends to be relatively high.

The traffic department is judged on its ability to minimize the cost of transportation per unit shipped. But transport costs decrease on a per unit basis as larger shipments are made. In one case, the traffic manager insisted that all salespersons hold orders from customers who were known to order at random intervals in relatively small quantities. The orders were to be held until enough of them were accumulated to send a carload shipment to the customer's market area.

The results were impressive. Transport costs on a per unit basis declined dramatically. However, the marketing department was less than pleased. Why? Because the company was gaining a reputation for sporadic delivery of orders, and the net effect was a gradual erosion of the firm's market position.[9]

One purchasing department attempted to minimize the cost per unit of its purchases. It ordered goods in large numbers to take advantage of quantity discounts. As a result, the company incurred excessive inventory and material handling costs.

The traffic manager of a consumer goods producing company in eastern Canada was determined to reduce transport costs. Trucks were used to haul the product from the Toronto plant to a branch warehouse at the rate of 30 cents per hundred pounds. By negotiating with a railroad, the traffic manager was able to get the rate of 25.5 cents per hundred pounds. This 4.5 cent difference amounted to a savings of $4,150 annually.

However, the rail transport took three days, while the truck transport had taken eight hours. The difference in time meant that an additional $112,500 in inventory was needed to cover the three additional days of lead time before an order arrived. The firm valued its inventory holding costs at 15 percent per year; it therefore incurred an increased inventory cost of $16,900 a year. The reduced freight costs ended up costing the firm $12,750 in increased overall distribution costs. As soon as general management became aware of this situation, the firm's products were back in trucks.[10]

Cost Trade-offs

The third fundamental concept of physical distribution is that of *cost trade-offs*. This approach assumes that some functional areas of the firm will experience cost increases while others will have cost decreases. The result will be the minimization of total physical distribution costs. At no time will the established level of customer service be sacrificed.[11]

Cost Trade-offs at Gillette, Singer, and Xerox

> Gillette, the world's largest producer of safety razors, was faced with an ever increasing assortment of products due to its expansion into a broad range of toiletries. To offer good customer service, Gillette began shipping goods by air freight; but this proved to be an expensive form of distribution. Through a detailed study of its distribution system, Gillette discovered that its problem was inefficient order processing. By simplifying the paperwork involved, the firm was able to reduce the time required to process new orders. It was then able to return to lower-cost surface transportation and still meet previous delivery schedules. The cost trade-off here was that the order processing costs increased and transportation costs decreased; the net result was that total logistics costs decreased.
>
> Singer had a policy of shipping its sewing machines once a month to its retail stores. The company now ships four times a month. George L. Cwik, assistant manager of the transportation services department, stated, "We pay higher LTL [less-than-truckload] rates, but this is more than offset by lower inventories in the stores." The lower inventory is particularly important to Singer, since many of its 1,600 sewing centers are in comparatively high-rent districts. The company now can devote less of its expensive floor space to inventory. In this case, the trade-off involved greater transportation costs versus lowered inventory costs.
>
> Xerox needs to carry a large inventory of supplies for its office machines. The company used to maintain forty warehouses that stocked paper, chemicals, and machine parts. A study by Xerox revealed that 80 percent of the inventory items were "slow movers."[12] The company therefore decided to consolidate its slow selling products at one location and to air freight them to customers as needed. The cost trade-off—higher transportation costs for lower inventories—is reported to have saved Xerox millions of dollars annually.[13]

The integration of these three basic concepts—the total cost approach, the avoidance of suboptimization, and cost trade-offs—forms what is commonly referred to as the *physical distribution concept*.[14] The uniqueness of this concept is not in the individual functions, since each function was performed prior to the concept's inception. Rather, it stems from the integration of all the functions into a unified whole whose objective is providing an established level of customer service at the lowest possible distribution costs.

Organizational Considerations

The integration of physical distribution functions into a unified system is a very difficult organizational problem. In most companies, before the physical distribution concept is recognized, the logistics functions are dispersed throughout the organization. Figure 11–1 illustrates the organizational structure of a typical company.

Unifying the physical distribution activities involves shifting functions from the other departments to form the new logistics division. However, de-

Figure 11–1
Physical Distribution Organization in a Typical Manufacturing Company

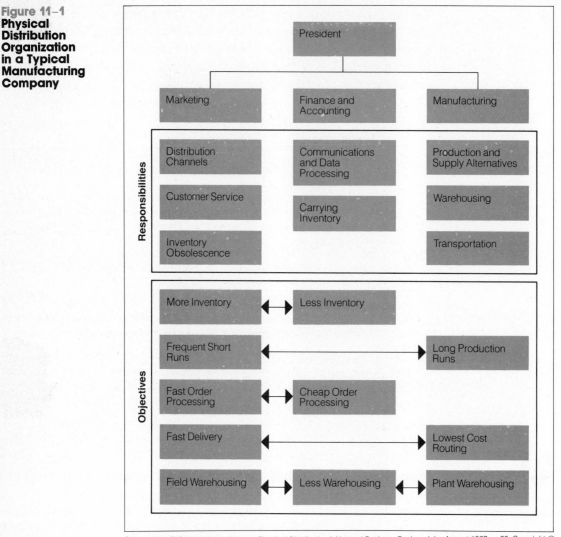

partments may be reluctant to give up their jurisdiction over procedures. Too often, when a new physical distribution department is finally established, the traffic manager receives the title of director of physical distribution. But in effect the person does little more than he or she previously did. The firm has a physical distribution department, but in name only. Such an outcome is all too common. Management pays lip service to the physical distribution concept, but it fails to take the necessary organizational steps to implement the program.

Suppose, however, that the firm wants to reorganize its functional areas into a truly unified physical distribution department. How should it accomplish this formidable task? Donald B. Bowersox offers insight into this problem:

Development of a physical distribution organization is initially staff oriented rather than line. The relative newness of the physical distribution concept renders a need for substantial work of a staff nature prior to line reorganization. Thus, the separation of physical distribution staff activities from traditional departments offers a convenient way to initiate and evaluate organizational change. Under this arrangement the staff initiates research and development of distribution activities while the old functional departments handle the line operations.[15]

After staffs from the other functional areas have specified the operating procedures for the new department, their line counterparts make the switch into the department. When this is accomplished, the firm is in a position to realize the benefits of the physical distribution concept.

The question of whether the physical distribution department should be centralized or decentralized remains. The trend is clearly in the direction of *centralized* physical distribution management. Since transport costs decrease on a per unit basis as the shipment size increases, shipments should be consolidated whenever possible. Freight shipments by separate operating divisions do not allow these cost savings. As a result, freight consolidation has been an important factor in the movement to centralization.

Another force encouraging a centralized department is the need to be near the firm's central computer facilities. This need is most important, since the physical distribution concept is made feasible only with the aid of the computer. The computer systematically keeps track of the thousands of details involved in any logistics operation: applicable tariff rates, daily inventory levels at each warehouse, and individual order processing.

Customer Service Standards

Customer service standards are *the quality of service that the firm's customers will receive.* For example, a customer service standard for one firm might be that 60 percent of all orders will be shipped within forty-eight hours after they are received, 90 percent in seventy-two hours, and all within ninety-six hours.

The level of customer service to be provided is an important marketing decision. Inadequate customer service may mean dissatisfied customers and loss of future sales. The chief role of the physical distribution department in determining customer service levels is to point out the costs involved in providing proposed standards. A conflict may arise when sales representatives make unreasonable delivery promises to their customers in order to obtain sales. In many cases, however, the need for additional inventory or the use of premium-cost transportation raises costs so high that the order proves unprofitable.

In an attempt to increase its share of the market, a major manufacturer of highly perishable food items set a 98 percent service level; that is, 98 percent of all orders were to be shipped the same day they were received. To meet this extremely high level of service, the firm leased warehouse space in 170 different cities and kept large stocks in each location. The large inventories, however, often meant the shipment of dated merchandise. Customers interpreted this practice as evidence of a low-quality product—or poor "service."[16]

Elements of a Physical Distribution System

Establishment of acceptable levels of customer service provides the physical distribution department with a standard by which actual operations can be compared. The physical distribution system should be designed to achieve this standard by minimizing the total costs of the following components: (1) transportation, (2) warehouses and their location, (3) inventory control, (4) order processing, and (5) materials handling. Relative costs for each component are illustrated in Figure 11–2.

Figure 11–2 Where the Physical Distribution Dollar Goes

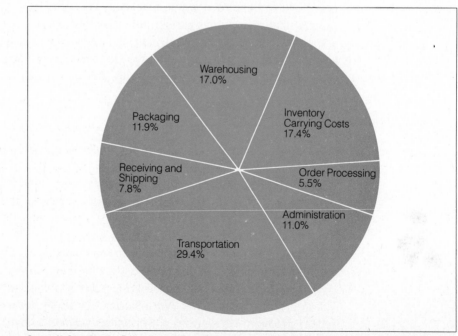

Source: *Air Cargo from A to Z* (Washington, D.C.: Air Transport Association of America, 1971), p. 5. Reprinted by permission.

Transportation
Considerations

The transportation system of the United States is a regulated industry, much the same as the telephone and electric industries. In fact, the courts have often referred to the transport modes as public utilities. The railroads were first regulated under the Interstate Commerce Act of 1887. This act established the first regulatory body in the United States, the Interstate Commerce Commission (ICC). The ICC regulates the railroads, pipelines, motor carriers, and inland water carriers. The Civil Aeronautics Board regulates U.S. air carriers, and the Federal Maritime Commission regulates U.S. ocean carriers.

In general, the regulation of all the transportation modes includes a provision that the rate charged must be "just and reasonable." *Just* means that the rate must be fair to the shipper in relationship to what other shippers pay for moving similar commodities under approximately the same conditions. *Reasonable* implies that the carrier should be allowed to earn a fair return on the firm's investment. The services offered by the carriers are also regulated. Finally, the right to enter into the business of transportation is restricted in most instances. Permission must usually be obtained from the appropriate regulatory body before a new carrier is allowed to compete in the industry.

Rate Determination. One of the most difficult problems facing the physical distribution manager who must choose a transportation service is determining the correct rate or cost of the service. The complexity results from **tariffs**—*the books (referred to as official publications) that are used to determine shipping charges.* Tariffs take on the force and effect of statutory law when they are filed with the appropriate regulatory body. There are literally thousands of tariff books, and their number is growing at a fantastic rate. One tariff expert has estimated that there are 43 trillion rates on file with the ICC in tariff books. If they were stacked one on top of another, they would be three times as tall as the Empire State Building *with* its TV antenna.

A final indication of the complexity of tariffs is the fact that an entire profession—freight bill auditing—has developed merely to detect mistakes made in trying to determine proper freight charges. Freight bill auditing companies independently check each company's ability to determine the correct freight rate. After a shipper has paid the freight rate, he or she turns over the paid bills to the freight auditor, who then checks to ensure that the lowest rate has been paid. If an overpayment is discovered, the freight auditor generally receives 50 percent of it as payment for the service.

There are two basic freight rates: class and commodity. The **class rate** is *the "standard" rate,* since one can be found for every commodity moving between any two destinations. Of the two rates, the class rate is the higher. The **commodity rate** *is sometimes called a special rate, since it is given by carriers to shippers as a reward for either regular use or large quantity ship-*

ments. It is used extensively by the railroads and the inland water carriers. One study showed that between 90 and 95 percent of all rail shipments were traveling under commodity rates.[17]

The Controversy over Deregulation

A currently popular topic is that of excess government regulation of transportation. The subject has been a regular item in newspapers, magazines, and television news programs since President Carter signed the Airline Deregulation Act of 1978. The act, which ended forty years of federal protection for the airlines, marked the first time in decades that the government had deregulated an entire industry.

The act will end the Civil Aeronautics Board's powers over routes and air fares by 1983 and will abolish the agency entirely in 1985. In the interim, the board's authority will be gradually reduced. Carriers can choose new routes and can cut their fares by half or raise them by 5 percent on routes where they control less than 70 percent of the traffic. The result is crowded airports, marked increases in the number of air travelers, added competition on some routes, loss of service (other than by commuter airlines) for some cities previously served by the major airlines, and improved profits for the carriers.

Some critics of the Interstate Commerce Commission are questioning the need to set rates and impose entry restrictions for the trucking industry—an industry in which some 17,000 firms currently operate. Others favor attempts to deregulate the nation's railroads. They argue that the benefits—discounted fares and increased profits—produced by deregulation of the airline industry could be gained in other industries as well.

Source: Airline deregulation is described in Rush Loving, Jr., "How the Airlines Will Cope with Deregulation," *Fortune*, November 20, 1978, pp. 38–41.

Classes of Carriers. Freight carriers are classified as common, contract, and private. *Common carriers,* sometimes called the backbone of the transportation industry, are for-hire carriers who serve the general public. Their rates and services are regulated, and they cannot conduct their operations without the appropriate regulatory authority's permission. They exist for all the modes of transport.

Contract carriers are for-hire transporters who do not offer their services to the general public. Instead they establish specific contracts with certain customers and operate exclusively for a particular industry (most commonly the motor freight industry). These carriers are subject to much less regulation than are common carriers.

Private carriers are not-for-hire carriers. Their operators transport products only for a particular firm and cannot solicit other transportation business. Since the transportation they provide is solely for their own use, there is no rate or service regulation.

Modal Considerations

The physical distribution manager has five major transportation alternatives: railroads, motor carriers, water carriers, pipelines, and air carriers. Figure 11–3 indicates the percentage of total ton-miles shipped by each major mode. A ton-mile is referred to as moving one ton of freight one mile. Thus a three-ton shipment moved eight miles equals twenty-four ton-miles.

Figure 11–3
Intercity Ton-Miles by the Various Transport Modes

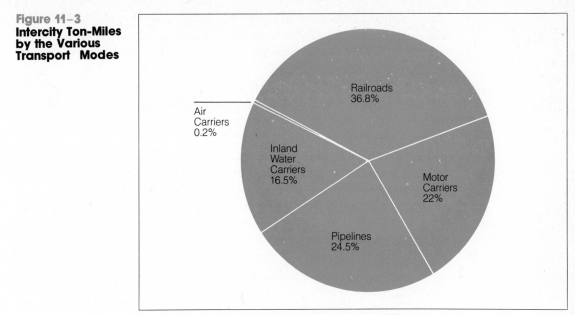

Source: U.S. Interstate Commerce Commission, *Transport Economics* 5 (1978), p. 2.

The water carriers' percentage has remained generally stable over the years, while the railroads have experienced a significant decrease and the pipelines and motor carriers have experienced substantial increases. Air carriers are dwarfed by the other transportation alternatives, accounting for less than 1 percent of all shipments.

Railroads. The largest transporter of freight (as measured by ton-miles) continues to be the railroads by about a 1.5 to 1 margin over their nearest competitors. They are the most efficient mode for the movement of bulk commodities over long distances. In 1977, coal alone made up about one-fifth of the total rail carloadings in the United States. In addition, mineral products account for almost one of every two loaded rail cars.[18] The railroads have launched a drive in recent years to improve their service standards and capture a larger percentage of manufactured and other high-value products. To accomplish their goal, they have introduced a number of innovative concepts. One service innovation is run-through trains, which are scheduled to bypass completely any congested terminals. The Chicago and North Western Railroad and the Union Pacific offer a run-through train from Chicago to Los Angeles. Known as the *Super Van*, this train consistently covers the 2,050 miles in under fifty-two hours.

Railroads are also making extensive use of unit trains to provide time and cost savings for their customers. Unit trains are used exclusively by a single customer, which receives lower rates than others for each shipment.

Unit coal trains are operated by the Burlington Northern Railroad for electricity utility companies in the Midwest. The railroad hauls a trainload of low-sulphur coal from Montana or Wyoming to the generating plants and then returns empty for another run.

The U.S. railroad system recognizes that the marketing concept also applies to its industry, and it is stressing improved service for its shippers. In response to the need for a more efficient method of transporting popular compact cars, the Southern Pacific Railroad invented a new rail car called Vert-a-Pac. This car hauls thirty Chevettes on their "noses" in a vertical position. The new rail car has lowered the shipping costs per auto significantly. It handles about a dozen more automobiles per rail car than does the standard auto car rack, and it decreases damage and pilferage.

Railroads are the largest transporter of the nation's output.

"I traveled by railroad all through their good years and I think it's only fair to stick with them when the going is tough."

Source: Reproduced by permission of the cartoonist, Bo Brown, and the *Wall Street Journal*.

Motor Carriers. The trucking industry has shown dramatic growth over the past decades. Its prime advantage over the other modes is its relatively fast, consistent service for both large and small shipments. Motor carriers concentrate on manufactured products, while railroads haul more bulk and raw material products. Motor carriers therefore receive greater revenue per ton shipped than do railroads. In 1978, the former received 9.3 cents per ton-mile while the latter earned 2.4 cents.

Trucking's primary appeal to shippers is superior service, and the industry is working diligently to maintain this advantage. The TIME-DC trucking company is currently running schedules that just a few years ago would have seemed impossible. It used to take seven to ten days for a coast-to-coast truckload shipment. TIME-DC now offers its Yellowbird service between New York–New Jersey and Southern California in sixty-nine hours, with delivery made the third morning after departure.

Water Carriers—Slow but Inexpensive. There are basically two types of water carriers—the inland or barge lines and the ocean deep-water ships. Barge lines are efficient transporters of bulk commodities. A typical lower Mississippi River barge line may be more than a quarter mile in length and two hundred feet wide.

Ocean-going ships operate on the Great Lakes, between United States port cities, and in international commerce. Water carrier costs average 0.4 cents per ton-mile.

Water Transportation – When Time Is Not Critical

The waterways of the United States provide an inexpensive source of transportation for thousands of producers and customers. Their cost savings must, however, be balanced with the slow delivery characteristic of this mode of transport. The following are illustrations of typical waterways' travel time for the mileage involved:

☐ Pittsburgh–New Orleans, 1,851 miles: Upstream 14 days and 2 hours; downstream 8 days and 18 hours.

☐ St. Louis–Houston (via New Orleans), 1,458 miles: Upstream 11 days and 4 hours; downstream 6 days and 12 hours.

☐ Cincinnati–New Orleans, 1,380 miles: Upstream 10 days and 19 hours; downstream 6 days and 7 hours.

☐ Minneapolis–New Orleans, 1,731 miles: Upstream 12 days and 12 hours; downstream 7 days and 22 hours.

☐ Chicago–New Orleans, 1,418 miles: Upstream 11 days and 8 hours; downstream 6 days and 7 hours.

☐ Pittsburgh–Brownsville (via New Orleans), 2,542 miles: Upstream 18 days and 21 hours; downstream 12 days and 8 hours.

Source: Adapted by permission from "Coming: Stiffer Waterway Rates," *Distribution Worldwide,* June 1976, pp. 50–53.

Pipelines. Even though the pipeline industry is second only to the railroads in number of ton-miles transported, many people are barely aware of their existence. Pipelines are extremely efficient transporters of natural gas and oil products, as evidenced by their average revenue per ton-mile of a little less than 0.3 cents. Oil pipelines carry two types of commodities—crude (unprocessed) oil and refined products, such as gasoline and kerosene. There is also a slow but steady growth in the use of "slurry" pipelines. In this method of transport, a product such as coal is ground up into a powder, mixed with water, and transported in suspension through the pipeline.[19]

Air Carriers—Fast but Expensive. The use of air carriers has been growing significantly. In 1961, U.S. airlines flew about 1 billion ton-miles. By 1978, this figure had jumped to 5 billion ton-miles. However, air freight is still a relatively insignificant percentage of the total ton-miles shipped, amounting to one-fifth of 1 percent in 1980.

Because of air freight's relatively high cost, it is used primarily for valuable or highly perishable products. Typical shipments are of watches, computers, furs, fresh flowers, high-fashion clothing, and live lobsters.[20] Air carriers often offset their higher transportation costs with reduced inventory holding costs and faster customer service.

Table 11–1 ranks the five transport modes on several bases.[21]

Table 11–1
Comparing the Transport Modes

| Factor | Rank | | | | |
	1	2	3	4	5
Speed	Air carriers	Motor carriers	Railroads	Water carriers	Pipelines
Dependability in meeting schedules	Pipelines	Motor carriers	Railroads	Water carriers	Air carriers
Cost	Water carriers	Pipelines	Railroads	Motor carriers	Air carriers
Frequency of shipments	Pipelines	Motor carriers	Air carriers	Railroads	Water carriers
Availability in different locations	Motor carriers	Railroads	Air carriers	Water carriers	Pipelines
Flexibility in handling products	Water carriers	Railroads	Motor carriers	Air carriers	Pipelines

Source: Based on a discussion in James L. Heskett, Nicholas A. Glaskowsky, Jr., and Robert M. Ivie, *Business Logistics* (New York: Ronald Press, 1973), pp. 113–118. Used with permission.

Freight Forwarders—Transportation Middlemen. *Freight forwarders* are considered transportation middlemen because their function is to consolidate shipments in order to get lower rates for their customers. The transport rates on less-than-truckload (LTL) and less-than-carload (LCL) shipments are often twice as high on a per unit basis as are the rates on truckload (TL) and carload (CL) shipments. Freight forwarders charge less than the higher rates but more than the lower rates. They make their profit by paying the carriers the lower rates. By consolidating shipments, they offer their customers two advantages—lower costs on small shipments and faster delivery service than is available from the LTL and LCL shippers.

Supplemental Carriers. The physical distribution manager can also use a number of auxiliary or supplemental carriers that specialize in transporting small shipments. These carriers include bus freight services, United Parcel Service, and the U.S. Postal Service.

Intermodal Coordination. The various transport modes often combine their services to give shippers the service and cost advantages of each mode. The most widely accepted form of coordination is *piggyback*—railroad transportation between cities of a truck trailer carried on a rail flatcar. The motor carrier delivers and picks up the shipment.

The combination of truck and rail services generally gives shippers faster service and lower rates than either mode would individually, since each method is used where it is most efficient. Shipper acceptance of piggybacking has been tremendous. In 1955, fewer than 200,000 piggyback rail cars were shipped. By 1976, more than 1.3 million cars were involved. Piggyback shipments are expected to account for 40 percent of all rail traffic by 1995.

Another form of intermodal coordination is *birdyback*. Here, motor carriers deliver and pick up the shipment, and air carriers take it over the long distance. Not to be outdone, motor carriers and water carriers have developed a form of intermodal coordination called *fishyback*.

Warehouses and Their Location

There are two types of warehouses—storage and distribution. **Storage warehouses** *store products for moderate to long periods of time in an attempt to balance supply and demand for producers and purchasers.* They are used most often by firms whose products are characterized by seasonal supply or demand.

Distribution warehouses are *places to assemble and redistribute products.* They are used to keep the products on the move as much as possible. Many distribution warehouses or centers achieve an operational objective of having the goods physically in the warehouse less than one day.

To save on transportation costs, manufacturers have developed central distribution centers. A manufacturer located in Atlanta with customers in the Illinois, Wisconsin, and Indiana area could send each customer a direct shipment. But if each customer places small orders, the transportation charges for the individual shipments will be relatively high. A feasible solution is to use a "break-bulk point," probably Chicago in this case. As Figure 11–4 illustrates, *consolidated shipments are sent to a central distribution center, and then smaller shipments are made for delivery to the individual customers in the area.* Such centers have logically been named **break-bulk centers.**

An alternative distribution center—the **make-bulk center**—*brings together shipments going to one point from others and consolidates them into one shipment.* For example, a giant retailer such as Safeway Stores may have several satellite production facilities in a given area. Each plant can send shipments to a storage warehouse in Kansas City. However, this may result in an excessive number of small, expensive shipments. Therefore, a make-bulk distribution center is created in Los Angeles, as illustrated in Figure 11–4. Each supplier sends its shipment to the Los Angeles make-bulk point, and all shipments bound for Kansas City are consolidated into more economical shipments. The top five distribution center cities in the United States, as measured by the total number of break-bulk distribution centers, are Chicago, Los Angeles–Long Beach, the New York City area, Dallas–Fort Worth, and Atlanta.

Figure 11–4
Use of Break-Bulk and Make-Bulk Centers

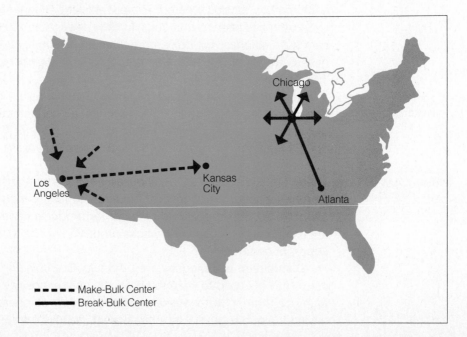

Chicago

Los Angeles

Kansas City

Atlanta

- - - - - Make-Bulk Center
———— Break-Bulk Center

Automated Warehouses. Warehouses lend themselves well to automation, with the computer as the heart of the operation. An outstanding example is the Aerojet-General Industrial Systems Division warehouse in Frederick, Maryland. This huge warehouse is operated entirely by a single employee who gives instructions to the facility's governing computer. The computer operates the fully automated materials handling system and generates all the necessary forms.[22]

Although automated warehouses may cost as much as $10 million, they can provide major savings to high-volume distributors such as grocery chains. Some current systems can select 10,000 to 300,000 cases per day of up to 3,000 different items. They can "read" computerized store orders, choose the correct number of cases, and move them in the desired sequence to loading docks. These warehouses reduce labor costs, worker injuries, pilferage, fires, and breakage; and they assist in inventory control.

Location Factors. A major decision each company must make is the number and location of its storage facilities. While this is a complex problem, the two general factors involved are (1) warehousing and materials handling costs and (2) delivery costs from the warehouse to the customer. The first costs are subject to economies of scale; therefore, on a per unit basis, they decrease as volume increases. Delivery costs, on the other hand, increase as the distance from the warehouse location to the customer increases.

The two cost items are diagrammed in Figure 11–5. The asterisk in the figure marks the ideal area of coverage for each warehouse. This model

**Figure 11–5
Factors
Influencing the
Number of
Warehouses**

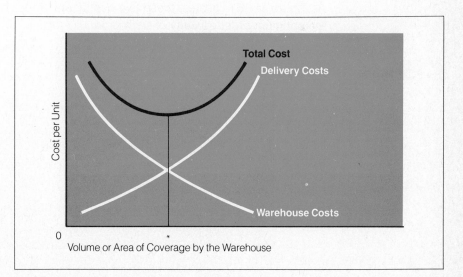

helps determine the proper number of warehouses if decentralization is desired.

The specific location of the firm's warehouses is another complicated problem. Factors that must be considered include (1) local, county, and state taxes; (2) local, county, and state laws and regulations; (3) availability of a trained labor force; (4) police and fire protection; (5) access to the various transport modes; and (6) the attitude of the community toward the proposed warehouses.

Inventory Control Systems

Inventories have been referred to as the graveyards of U.S. businesses. The title is often earned because this little-known and unglamorous aspect of business is generally regarded as unimportant and is therefore basically ignored—with deadly results.

Many marketing managers fail to see the significant expense involved in holding inventory over a period of time. Most current estimates of inventory holding costs are 25 percent per year. This means that $1,000 of inventory held for a single year costs the company $250. Inventory costs include such expenses as storage facilities, insurance, taxes, handling costs, opportunity costs for funds invested in inventory, and depreciation and possible obsolescence of the goods in inventory.

Inventory control analysts have developed a number of techniques to help the physical distribution manager effectively control inventory. The most basic is the **EOQ (economic order quantity) model.** This technique *emphasizes a cost trade-off between* two fundamental costs involved with inventory: *inventory holding costs* that increase with the addition of more inventory and *order costs* that decrease as the quantity ordered increases. As Figure 11–6 indicates, these two cost items are traded off to determine the optimum order quantity of each product.

Figure 11–6
The EOQ Model

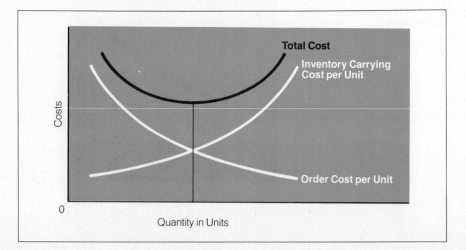

Order Processing

Like customer service standards, order processing is a quasi-logistics function. The physical distribution manager is concerned with this activity because it directly affects the firm's ability to meet its customer service standards. If a firm's order processing system is inefficient, the company may have to compensate by using costly premium transportation or increasing the number of field warehouses in all major markets.

The EOQ point in Figure 11–6 is the point where total cost is minimized. By placing an order for this amount as needed, inventory costs are minimized.

Materials Handling Systems

All the activities associated in moving products within the manufacturer's plants, warehouses, and transportation company terminals are called **materials handling.** These activities must be thoroughly coordinated for both intra- and intercompany activities. The efficiency of plants and warehouses is dependent on an effective system.

Two important innovations have been developed in the area of materials handling. One is known as **unitizing**—*combining as many packages as possible into one load,* preferably on a pallet (a platform, generally made of wood, on which products are transported). This can be accomplished by using steel bands to hold the unit in place or by shrink packaging. Shrink packages are constructed by placing a sheet of plastic over the unit and then heating it. When the plastic cools, it shrinks and holds the individual packages securely together. Unitizing has the advantages of requiring little labor

Materials handling is an important component of the firm's physical distribution system.

"They're a heck of a nice outfit to do business with!"

Source: © *Seaway Review*, the Great Lakes Press. Used with permission.

per package, promoting fast movements, and minimizing damage and pilferage.

The second innovation is **containerization.** *Containerized cargo is a combination of several unitized loads.* It is typically eight feet wide, eight feet high and ten, twenty, thirty, or forty feet long. Its containers allow ease of intertransport mode changes. A container of oil rig parts, for example, can be loaded in Tulsa and trucked to Kansas City, where it can be placed on a high-speed run-through train to New York City. There, it can be placed on a ship and sent to Saudi Arabia.

Containerization also markedly reduces the time involved in loading and unloading ships. Container ships can often be unloaded in less than twenty-four hours—a task that otherwise can take up to two weeks. In-transit damage is also reduced, since individual packages are not handled en route to the purchaser.

International Physical Distribution

The United States has experienced rapid growth in international trade since World War II. Exports have grown at an average rate of 7 percent a year, while imports have increased even faster. In 1978, U.S. merchandise exports totaled approximately $137 billion. Total imports for 1978 amounted to $173 billion.[23] This unparalleled growth of international commerce has placed new responsibilities on physical distribution departments.

A major problem facing international marketers is the flood of paperwork involved in exporting products. Over a hundred different international trade documents representing more than a thousand separate forms must be completed for each international shipment. The result is that an average export shipment requires approximately thirty-six employee hours for documentation and twenty-seven employee hours for importing a shipment. Paperwork alone equals 7 percent of the total value of U.S. international trade.[24] Many physical distribution departments are not large enough to employ international specialists, and they subcontract the work to *foreign freight forwarders*, intermediaries who specialize in foreign physical distribution.

The major impetus to exporting has been the advent of containerization and container ships. One shipping company currently has container ships that can make a round trip between New York, Bremerhaven, and Rotterdam in fourteen days. Only four days are needed for crossing the Atlantic and another six for three port calls. This speed allows U.S. exporters to provide competitive delivery schedules to European markets.

Summary

Physical distribution includes the activities of transportation, warehousing, materials handling, inventory control, order processing, and customer service. It has been called the "last great frontier of increased marketing efficiency" because its potential for reduced costs and improved customer service has been recognized only in the past two decades.

The physical distribution department is one of the classic examples of the systems approach to business problems. Three basic concepts of the systems approach—the total cost approach, the avoidance of suboptimization, and cost trade-offs—combine to form the *physical distribution concept.*

The goal of a physical distribution department can be stated as follows: to produce a specified level of customer service while minimizing the costs involved in physically moving and storing the product from its production point to the point where it is ultimately purchased.

The physical distribution manager has available five transportation alternatives: railroads, motor carriers, water carriers, pipelines, and air freighters. Intermodal transport systems are also available and are increasingly being used.

Other elements of the physical distribution department include warehousing and warehouse location, inventory control systems, materials handling systems, customer service standards, and order processing. Efficient international physical distribution allows U.S. firms to compete effectively in foreign markets.

Physical distribution, by its very nature, involves keeping track of thousands of details, such as transport rates, inventory locations, and customer locations. The computer is a necessary and invaluable tool for the logistics manager.

Questions for Discussion

1. Explain the following terms:

   physical distribution
   systems
   customer service standards
   tariffs
   class rate
   commodity rate
   storage warehouse
   distribution warehouse

   break-bulk center
   make-bulk center
   EOQ (economic order quantity) model
   materials handling
   unitizing
   containerization

2. Why was physical distribution one of the last areas in most companies to be carefully studied and improved?

3. Outline the basic reasons for the increased attention to physical distribution management.

4. What is the basic objective of physical distribution?

5. What is the most effective organization for physical distribution management? Explain.

6. Why did the railroads lose a large percentage of the total ton-miles transported since World War II?

7. Suggest the most appropriate method of transportation for each of the following products and defend your choices:

   a. iron ore   b. Dash detergent

        c. heavy earth-moving equipment   e. orchids

        d. crude oil   f. lumber

8. Discuss the relative advantages of public versus private warehouses.

9. Develop an argument for the increased use of intermodal coordination.

10. What factors should be considered in locating a new distribution warehouse?

11. Are the inventory holding costs discussed in this chapter realistic? Explain.

12. Who should be ultimately responsible for determining the level of customer service standards? Explain.

13. Discuss the basic strengths and weaknesses of each mode of transport.

14. Which mode of transport do you believe will experience the greatest ton-mile percentage growth during the 1980s? Why?

15. Under what conditions would you recommend the construction of a fully automated warehouse? When would an automated warehouse be inappropriate?

16. Under what circumstances are freight forwarders used?

17. What is meant by *transportation deregulation*? Is it in the best interests of the country? Explain.

18. Comment on the following statement: The popularity of physical distribution management is a fad; ten years from now it will be considered a relatively unimportant function of the firm.

19. Discuss the similarities of and differences between domestic and international physical distribution.

20. Discuss the basic cost factors involved in the EOQ formula. Does the basic EOQ formula consider all relevant costs? Explain.

Notes

1. Reported in Bert Rosenbloom, *Marketing Channels: A Management View* (Hinsdale, Ill.: The Dryden Press, 1978), pp. 244–245; based on a description in Edward W. Smykay, *Physical Distribution Management*, 3d ed. (New York: Macmillan, 1973), p. 38.

2. Stanley H. Slom, "It Seems Like a Long Way to Go for a Head of Lettuce," *Wall Street Journal*, March 13, 1978,

3. *General Information Pamphlet* (Chicago: National Council of Physical Distribution Management, 1971).

4. See Thomas W. Speh and Michael D. Hutt, "The Other Half of Marketing: Lost or Found?" in *Proceedings of the Southern Marketing Association,* ed. Robert S. Franz, Robert M. Hopkins, and Al Toma, New Orleans, Louisiana, November 1978, pp. 332–335.

5. See Roy D. Voorhees and Merril K. Sharp, "The Principles of Logistics Revisited," *Journal of Transportation,* Fall 1978, pp. 69–84.

6. See Donald J. Bowersox, "The Logistics of the Last Quarter of the 20th Century," *Journal of Business Logistics* 1 (1978), pp. 1–17; and James C. Johnson and Donald T. Berger, "Physical Distribution: Has It Reached Maturity?" *International Journal of Physical Distribution* 7 (1977), p. 36.

7. Arthur D. Hall, *A Methodology for Systems Engineering* (Princeton, N.J.: Van Nostrand–Reinhold, 1963), p. 60.

8. Colin Barrett, "The Machine and Its Parts," *Transportation and Distribution Management,* April 1971, p. 3.

9. Donald J. Bowersox, Edward W. Smykay, and Bernard J. LaLonde, *Physical Distribution Management*, rev. ed. (New York: Macmillan, 1968), p. 6.

10. F. R. Denham, "Making the Physical Distribution Concept Pay Off," *Handling and Shipping,* October 1967.

11. William D. Perrault, Jr., and Frederick A. Russ, "Improving Physical Distribution Decisions with Trade-off Analysis," *International Journal of Physical Distribution* 7 (1977), pp. 117–127.

12. This finding, often called the "20–80" rule, is typical of many firms, both large and small. The rule states that for many companies 20 percent of the product line accounts for 80 percent of total sales.

13. "New Strategies to Move Goods," *Business Week*, September 24, 1966, pp. 112–114, 119–120.

14. See George A. Gecowitz, "The Physical Distribution Concept," *Dun's Review,* August 1978, p. 63.

15. Donald J. Bowersox, "Emerging Patterns of Physical Distribution Organization," *Transportation and Distribution Management,* May 1968, pp. 53–56. See also James C. Johnson and Donald F. Wood, *Contemporary Physical Distribution* (Tulsa, Okla.: PPC Books, 1977), pp. 431–446.

16. Robert E. Sabath, "How Much Service Do Customers Really Want?" *Business Horizons,* April 1978, pp.

26–32. See also Douglas M. Lambert and James R. Stock, ''Physical Distribution and Consumer Demands,'' *MSU Business Topics,* Spring 1978, pp. 49–56.

17. Charles A. Taff, *Management of Physical Distribution and Transportation,* 5th ed. (Homewood, Ill: Richard D. Irwin, 1972), p. 324.

18. *Yearbook of Railroad Facts* (Washington, D.C.: Association of American Railroads, 1979), pp. 26, 36.

19. Martin T. Farris and David L. Shrock, ''The Economics of Coal Slurry Pipelines: Transportation and Non-transportation Factors,'' *Transportation Journal,* Fall 1978, pp. 45–57.

20. See ''Air Freight: How It Works, What It Costs,'' *Administrative Management,* September 1978, pp. 28–29; and ''Why Nobody Is Rushing into Airfreight,'' *Business Week,* November 6, 1978, pp. 190–192.

21. For a discussion of how shippers evaluate transport modes, see James R. Stock and Bernard J. LaLonde, ''The Purchasing Approach to Transportation Mode Selection,'' *Journal of Purchasing and Materials Management,* Spring 1978, pp. 2–5.

22. ''The Ultimate in Automation,'' *Transportation and Distribution Management,* January 1970, p. 38.

23. Council of Economic Advisers, *Economic Report of the President* (Washington, D.C.: Government Printing Office, 1979), p. 297.

24. ''Reducing Paperwork,'' *Transportation and Distribution Management,* November 1971, p. 15.

PART FIVE
PROMOTIONAL STRATEGY

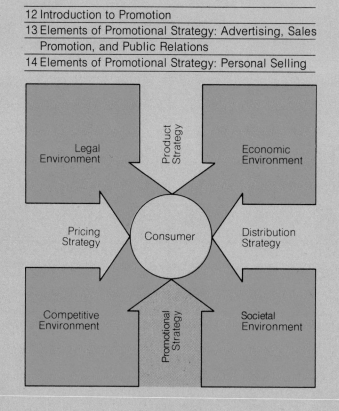

CHAPTER 12
INTRODUCTION TO
PROMOTION

Key Terms

promotion
marketing
communications
personal selling
advertising
sales promotion

public relations
pulling strategy
pushing strategy
task objective
method
direct-sales results
test

Learning Goals

1. To explain the relationship of promotional strategy to the process of communication.
2. To identify the chief components of the promotional mix.
3. To analyze the variables used in determining the optimum promotional mix.
4. To list the objectives of promotion.
5. To compare the methods of developing a promotional budget.

12

Gillette is usually the dominant firm in the shaving supplies market in each of the two hundred nations in which it competes. In the United States, the firm enjoys a 58 percent market share. But everything is not perfect at Gillette's Boston headquarters.

A diversification attempt failed when Gillette gave up on digital watches and pocket calculators, decided not to expand its only line of smoke detectors, and sold its Buxton leather products line to Beatrice Foods. Gillette's new strategy is to concentrate on the areas of its greatest strength, and this requires changes in the firm's promotional strategy.

Gillette, a longtime advertiser on sports programs, had switched to prime time advertising in an attempt to reach the various market targets of its diversified product lines. The firm's new strategy has required a reversal of this trend, and Gillette is back as a major sponsor of sports broadcasting. Other promotional changes are also taking place. In sharp contrast to its cautious approach in the past, Gillette is using aggressive promotional claims. A promotional budget of more than $31 million has been approved in an attempt to increase the firm's share of the U.S. razor blade market beyond the 60 percent mark.

Gillette has also ended its practice of investing the bulk of its promotional budget in new products at the expense of existing products. The practice was based on the belief that most new-product sales would simply *cannibalize* (take sales away from) sales of existing ones, so promotion of existing products was unproductive.

Gillette's Atra razor is the new market entry. Trac II, a razor introduced in 1971, now leads the industry. The Atra ads emphasize its unique feature, a pivoting shaving head that follows the shape of the face. Trac II is being promoted by point-of-purchase displays, discounts, and the like. Joseph A. Marino, Gillette's marketing vice-president, sums up the promotional strategy this way: "With Atra, we want to entice people to try a superior razor; with Trac II promotions, we want to move blades."

The management at Gillette knows that even the most dominant firm in the industry must develop a viable promotional strategy if it is to remain the leader. For Gillette this means several strategy shifts. First, it returned to its original advertising plan, and second, it developed a strategy that would allow it to promote both existing and new products simultaneously.[1]

Promotion is *the function of informing, persuading, and influencing the consumer's purchase decision.* Many business people consider it the most critical variable in the marketing process. The dynamic nature of promotion also makes it one of the most difficult and interesting areas of marketing decision making.

**Marketing
Communications**

Promotional strategy is closely related to the process of *communications*—the transmission of a message from a sender to a receiver. **Marketing communications,** then, are *the messages that deal with buyer-seller relationships.* The term *marketing communications* is a broader one than promotional strategy since it includes word-of-mouth and other forms of unsystematic communication. A planned promotional strategy, however, is certainly the most important part of it.

Figure 12–1 shows a generalized communications process.[2] The *sender* is the source of the communications system, since he or she seeks to convey a *message* (a communication of information or advice or a request) to a *receiver* (the recipient of the communication). The message must accomplish three tasks in order to be effective:

1. It must gain the attention of the receiver.
2. It must be understood by both the receiver and the sender.
3. It must stimulate the needs of the receiver and suggest an appropriate method of satisfying those needs.[3]

**Figure 12–1
A Generalized
Communications
Process**

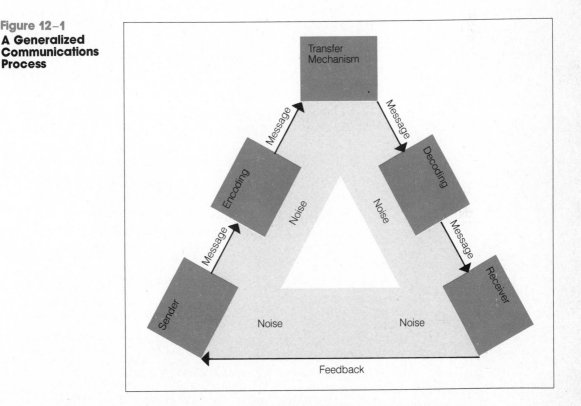

Encoding is the translation of the message into understandable terms and its transmittal through a communications medium. *Decoding* is the receiver's interpretation of the message. The receiver's response, known as *feedback*, completes the system. Throughout the process, *noise* can interfere with the transmission of the message.

In Figure 12–2 the marketing communications process is applied to promotional strategy. The marketing manager is the sender in the system. The message is encoded in the form of sales presentations, advertisements, displays, or publicity releases. The *transfer mechanism* for delivering the message may be a salesperson, a public relations channel, or the advertising media. The decoding step involves the consumer's interpretation of the sender's message. This aspect is often the most troublesome in marketing communications since consumers do not always interpret promotional messages the same as their senders do.

General Motors' attempt to market its Chevrolet Nova through its Puerto Rican dealers produced only laughter, since in Spanish *no va* means "it

Figure 12–2
The Process of Marketing Communications

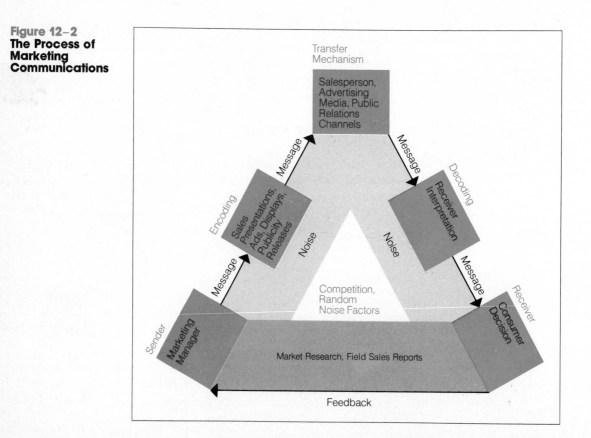

Some
communication
is nonverbal.

"We can't say it outright, Forbes, so here's where you come in. We want you to imply,
with a look, shrug, nuance, or whatever, that our competitor's product stinks."

Source: *TV Guide*, January 24, 1970. Reprinted by permission of Sidney Harris.

does not go." GM quickly changed the car's name to Caribe ("savage") in
Puerto Rico.

Information about consumer decisions is fed back to the marketing
manager in the form of marketing research or field sales reports. The noise
element is usually represented by competitive promotional messages transmitted over the same communications channel or random noise factors
such as a telephone ringing during a television commercial.

The Promotional Mix

The components of the promotional mix are personal selling and nonpersonal selling (including advertising, sales promotion, and public relations).[4]

Personal selling and advertising are the most significant elements, usually accounting for the bulk of a firm's promotional expenditures. However,
all factors in the promotional mix contribute to efficient marketing communications. A detailed discussion of each element is presented in the chapters
that follow. A brief definition of each will be given here in order to set the
framework for the discussion of promotion.

Personal Selling

Personal selling is *a seller's promotional presentation conducted on a person-to-person basis with the buyer.* It is a direct, face-to-face form of promotion. Selling is the original form of promotion. Today, several million people are engaged in it.

Nonpersonal Selling

Nonpersonal selling is divided into advertising, sales promotion, and public relations. Advertising is usually regarded as the most important form.

Advertising is *a nonpersonal sales presentation usually directed to a large number of potential customers.* It involves mass media such as newspapers, television, radio, magazines, and billboards. Business has come to realize the tremendous potential of this form of promotion, and during recent decades, advertising has become increasingly important in marketing. Mass consumption makes it particularly appropriate for products that rely on sending the same promotional message to large audiences.

Sales promotion includes *"those marketing activities other than personal selling and advertising, and publicity, that stimulate consumer purchasing and dealer effectiveness, such as displays, shows and expositions, demonstrations, and various nonrecurrent selling efforts not in the ordinary routine."*[5] More than $35 billion is spent annually on various types of sales promotion.[6]

Public relations is *a firm's communications and relationships with its various publics.* These publics include customers, suppliers, stockholders, employees, the government, the general public, and the society in which the firm operates. Public relations programs can be either formal or informal. Every organization, whether or not it has a formalized (organized) program, needs to be concerned about its public relations.

Publicity for a company's products or affairs is an important part of an effective public relations effort. In comparison to personal selling, advertising, and sales promotion, expenditures for public relations are usually low in most firms. However, this indirect promotional channel remains an important method of reaching potential customers since it hits audiences in a manner not obtainable by other methods of promotion.

Developing an Optimal Promotional Mix

The most critical promotional problem facing the marketing manager is that of the proper mix of the four methods outlined in the preceding section. The discussion here will be limited to advertising and personal selling, since they are the primary ingredients of promotional strategy.

The decision to emphasize personal selling or advertising depends primarily on (1) the type of goods (industrial or consumer) and (2) the relative value of the product.

Table 12–1 shows the relative use of advertising and personal selling as determined by these factors. The relative use of advertising is high for low-

**Table 12–1
Relative Use of
Advertising and
Personal Selling**

	Relative Use of	
Type of Product	Advertising	Personal Selling
Low-value consumer goods	High	Low
High-value consumer goods	High	High
Low-value industrial goods	Moderate	High
High-value industrial goods	Low	High

value consumer goods, then declines somewhat as personal selling plays a larger role in the promotion of higher-priced consumer goods. But both forms are used extensively. The explanation for advertising's dominance of promotional strategy for low-unit-value consumer goods is simple: The cost of selling has risen tremendously in recent years. The cost of an industrial sales call, for example, is now estimated to be $96.79.[7]

As a result, it has become unprofitable to promote lower-value goods through this medium. Advertising, by contrast, permits a low promotional expenditure per sales unit, since it reaches mass audiences. For low-value consumer products such as chewing gum, soft drinks, and snack foods, advertising is the only feasible means of promotion.

Industrial goods, whose average value is high, are more amenable to personal selling as the chief promotional channel. Table 12–1 shows that advertising in industrial markets is limited mostly to products with relatively low value, such as industrial supplies.

Timing

Timing is another factor to consider in the development of a promotional strategy. Figure 12–3 shows the relative importance of advertising and selling in the different time periods of the purchase process. During the pretransactional period (prior to the actual sale), advertising is usually more important than personal selling. It is often argued that one of the primary advantages of a successful advertising program is that it assists the salesperson in approaching the prospect. Selling becomes more important than advertising during the transactional phase of the process. In most situations, personal selling is the actual mechanism of closing the sale. In the posttransactional stage, advertising regains primacy in the promotional effort. It serves as an affirmation of the customer's decision to buy a particular good or service as well as a reminder of the product's favorable characteristics and performance.

Promotional Strategy – Pull or Push

Essentially, two promotional policies are employed: a pulling strategy and a pushing strategy. A **pulling strategy** is *a promotional effort by the seller to stimulate final user demand; this demand exerts pressure on the distribution channel.* The plan is to build consumer demand for the product that is

**Figure 12–3
Relative
Importance of
Advertising and
Selling at Each
Stage of the
Purchase Process**

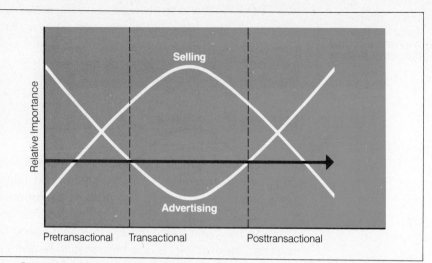

Source: Reprinted by permission from Harold C. Cash and W. J. E. Crissy, "The Salesman's Role in Marketing," *Psychology of Selling*, vol. 12, Personnel Development Associates, P.O. Box 586, Fairfield, Iowa 52556.

recognizable to channel members, who will then seek to fill the void. Advertising and sales promotion are the most commonly used elements of promotion in a pulling strategy.

By contrast, a **pushing strategy** relies more heavily on personal selling. Here, the objective is *the promotion of the product to the members of the marketing channel* rather than to the final user. The objective can be accomplished through cooperative advertising allowances, trade discounts, and other dealer supports. While the two strategies are presented as alternative policies, most companies depend on a mixture of them.

Some marketers use an aggressive pulling strategy.

"And this is Rocketman reminding you that if you don't buy CocoFlakes, I don't want you watching my program anymore!"

Source: *Milwaukee Journal, Sunday Magazine*, April 9, 1972. Reprinted by permission of Sidney Harris.

Objectives of Promotion	Determining the precise objectives of promotion has always been a perplexing problem for management. In 1961, the Association of National Advertisers suggested that promotional strategy be oriented toward achieving clearly stated communications objectives that are measured.[8]

What specific tasks should promotion accomplish? The answer to this question seems to be as varied as the sources consulted. Generally, however, the following can be considered objectives of promotion: (1) to provide information, (2) to increase demand, (3) to differentiate the product, (4) to accentuate its value, and (5) to stabilize sales. |
| **Providing Information** | The traditional function of promotion has been to inform the market about the availability of a particular product. Indeed, many promotional efforts are still directed at providing product information to potential customers. An example is the typical health insurance advertisement appearing in the Sunday newspaper. Its content emphasizes informative features, such as the rising cost of hospital care.

R & S Liquors of Chicago once employed an interesting twist in its retail price advertisements. The firm listed its entire inventory in newspaper advertisements that looked like stock market quotations. A bottle selling for $5.50 appeared as 5½. Bottled-in-bond whiskies appeared in the "bond market," and French wines were called "bourse listings."[9] |
Stimulating Demand	The primary objective of most promotional efforts is to increase the demand for a good or service. The Gillette example at the beginning of the chapter pointed out that the firm's promotional strategy for its Trac II razor is to sell more blades to people who have already purchased a razor. Gillette attempts to accentuate demand through discounts, in-store displays, and other promotional techniques.
Differentiating the Product	Product differentiation is often an objective of the firm's promotional effort. *Homogeneous demand,* represented by the horizontal line in Figure 12–4, means that consumers regard the firm's output as being no different from that of their competitors. In this case, the individual firm has no control over such marketing variables as price. A *differentiated demand* schedule, by contrast, permits more flexibility in marketing strategies such as price changes.
Accentuating the Value of the Product	Promotion can provide more ownership utility to buyers, thereby accentuating the value of a product. The good or service may then be able to command a higher price in the marketplace. For example, status-oriented advertising may allow some retail clothing stores to command higher prices than

Figure 12–4
**Product
Differentiation**

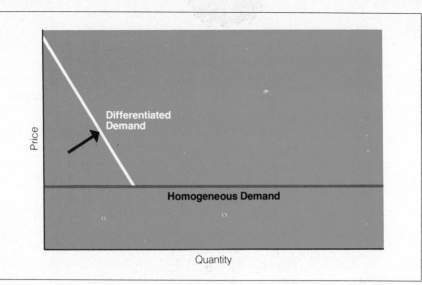

Source: *Markets and Marketing: An Orientation,* by Lee E. Preston (Glenview, Ill.: Scott, Foresman, 1970), p. 196. Copyright © 1970 by Scott, Foresman and Company. Reprinted by permission of the publisher.

others. The demand curve for a prestige store may be less responsive to price differences than that for a competitor without a quality reputation. The responsiveness to price differences is shown in Figure 12–5.

Stabilizing Sales

A company's sales are not uniform throughout the year. Fluctuations can be caused for cyclical, seasonal, or irregular reasons. Reducing these variations

Figure 12–5
**Promotion Can
Accentuate the
Value of the
Product**

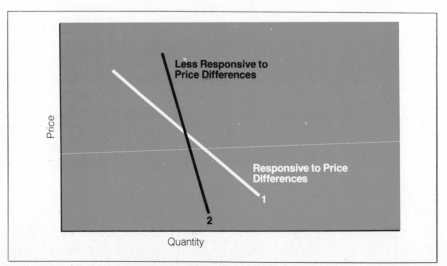

Source: *Markets and Marketing: An Orientation,* by Lee E. Preston (Glenview, Ill.: Scott, Foresman, 1970), p. 196. Copyright © 1970 by Scott, Foresman and Company. Reprinted by permission of the publisher.

The Value of a Good Promotional Theme — The Hallmark Example

A survey by R. H. Bruskin Associates of New Brunswick, New Jersey, asked 2,531 people to rate advertising slogans in terms of truthfulness. Eleven major promotional themes were shown to the respondents, who rated them true, partially true, or untrue. Hallmark Cards' "when you care enough to send the very best" ranked highest with a 62 percent true rating. Hallmark has apparently gotten good value for its slogan, which has been around since 1944.

   The Hallmark theme was followed closely by "Kodak makes your pictures count" with a 60 percent true rating. Zenith's "the quality goes in before the name goes on" was third with a 49 percent true ranking.

Source: Adapted from "Adbeat," *Advertising Age*, October 24, 1977, p. 94. Reprinted by permission from the October 24, 1977, issue of *Advertising Age*. Copyright 1977 by Crain Communications, Inc.

is often an objective of the firm's promotional strategy. Lee E. Preston states:

Advertising that is focused on such attitudinal goals as "brand loyalty" and such specific sales goals as "increasing repeat purchases" is essentially aimed at stabilizing demand. The prominence of such goals in the current literature and in advertising planning discussions suggests that stabilizing demand and insulating the market position of an individual firm and product against unfavorable developments is, in fact, one of the most important purposes of promotional activity at the present time.[10]

Budgeting for Promotional Strategy

Promotion budgets can differ not only in amount but also in composition. Industrial firms generally invest a larger proportion of their budgets for personal selling than for advertising, while the reverse is often true for producers of consumer goods.

   A simple model showing the productivity of promotional expenditures is shown in Figure 12–6. In terms of sales revenue, initial expenditures on promotion usually result in increasing returns. Some economies are also associated with larger promotional expenditures. These economies result from factors such as the cumulative effect of promotional expenditures. As more promotional inputs are added, however, marginal productivity begins to decrease.[11] Eventually, the firm reaches negative returns on its promotional expenditures.

   For example, an initial expenditure of $40,000 may result in the sale of 100,000 product units for a consumer goods manufacturer. An additional $10,000 expenditure may sell 30,000 more units of the item, and a further $10,000 may produce another 35,000 unit sale. The cumulative effect of the expenditures has been increasing returns on the promotional outlays. However, as the advertising budget moves from $60,000 to $70,000, the marginal productivity of the additional expenditure may fall to 28,000 units. At some later point, the return may actually become negative, as competition intensifies, markets become saturated, and effective media opportunities are exhausted.

**Figure 12–6
Promotion-Sales
Curve**

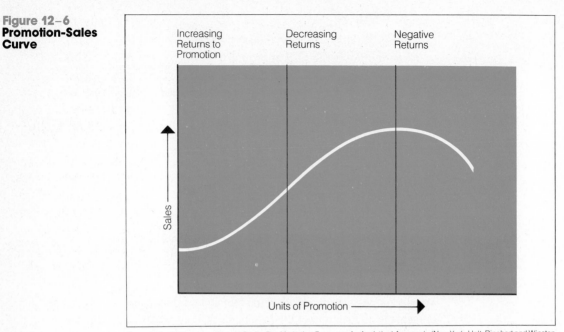

Source: John C. Narver and Ronald Savitt, *The Marketing Economy: An Analytical Approach,* (New York: Holt, Rinehart and Winston, 1971), p. 294. Reprinted by permission of the authors.

To test the thesis that advertising expenditures have a saturation point, Anheuser-Busch once quadrupled its advertising budget in several markets. After three months, the company's distributors demanded an advertising cut. Many claimed that beer consumers had come into their stores saying, "Give me anything *but* BUD." [12]

Developing a
Budget

Figure 12–6 suggests that the optimal method of allocating a promotion budget is to expand it until the cost of each additional increment equals the marginal revenue received from it. In other words, the most effective allocation procedure is to increase promotional expenditures until each dollar of promotion expense is matched by an additional dollar of profit. This procedure—called *marginal analysis*—maximizes the input's productivity. The difficulty arises in identifying this optimal point, which requires a precise balancing of marginal expenses for promotion and the resulting marginal receipts.

The more traditional methods of allocating a promotional budget are by percentage of sales, fixed sums per unit, meeting the competition, and task objectives. [13]

Percentage of sales is the most common way of allocating promotion budgets. The percentage can be based on either past (such as the previous year) or forecasted (current year) sales. While the simplicity of the plan is appealing, it is not an effective way of achieving the basic promotional objectives. Arbitrary percentage allocations, whether applied to historical or future sales figures, fail to allow the required flexibility.

The *fixed sum per unit* approach differs from percentage of sales in only one respect; it applies a predetermined allocation to each sales or production unit. The allocation can also be set on either a historical or a forecasted basis. Automobile manufacturers often use this budgeting method.

Another traditional approach is simply *to match competitors' outlays — to meet competition —* on either an absolute or a relative basis. But keeping up with the Joneses usually leads to a status quo situation. Meeting the competition's budget does not necessarily relate to the objectives of promotion and therefore is inappropriate for most contemporary marketing programs.

The **task objective method** of developing a promotional budget is based on a sound evaluation of the firm's promotional objectives and is therefore better attuned to modern marketing practices. It involves two sequential steps:

1. The organization *must define the particular goals the firm wants the promotional mix to accomplish —* for example, a 5 percent increase in market share, a 10 percent rise in gross sales, or a 3 percent addition to net profit (or, more likely, a combination of several items). The key is to quantitatively specify the objectives to be accomplished. They then become an integral part of the promotional plan.
2. The organization *must determine the amount (as well as type) of promotional activity required to accomplish each of the objectives.* The sum of these units becomes the firm's promotion budget.

A crucial assumption underlies the task objective approach—that the productivity of *each promotional dollar* is measurable. If, for example, it is known that each dollar spent on promotion yields $20 in sales revenue, then it will be a relatively simple task to divide 20 into the sales increase projected in the statement of objectives. The result is the amount the organization should spend on promotion. Other goals, such as profitability and market share, are also easily calculated. A study by the Marketing Science Institute found that many firms do not keep adequate records of promotional expenditures and do not attempt to test alternative promotional efforts.[14]

Promotional budgeting is always difficult. But recent research studies and more frequent use of computer-based models make it less difficult than it has been in the past.

Measuring the
Effectiveness of
Promotion

It is widely recognized that part of a firm's promotional effort is ineffective. John Wanamaker, a successful nineteenth century retailer, is said to have observed: "I know half the money I spend on advertising is wasted; but I can never find out which half."

Measuring the effectiveness of promotional expenditures has become an important research question, particularly among advertisers. Studies aimed at this measurement dilemma face several major obstacles, among them the difficulty of isolating the effect of the promotion variable.

Most marketers prefer to use a **direct-sales results test** to measure the effectiveness of promotion. This test *ascertains for each dollar of promotional outlay the corresponding increase in revenue*. The primary difficulty is controlling the other variables operating in the marketplace. A $1.5 million advertising campaign may be followed by an increase in sales of $20 million. However, the increase may be due more to a sudden price hike by the leading competitor than to the advertising expenditure.

The marketer cannot conduct research in a controlled environment common to other disciplines. The difficulty in isolating the effects of promotion cause many to abandon all attempts at measurement. Others, however, turn to indirect evaluation, concentrating on quantifiable factors such as recall (how much is remembered about specific products or advertisements) and readership (the size and composition of the audience). The main problem here is that it is difficult to relate the variables to changes in sales volume. Another problem is the high cost of research in promotion. To assess the effectiveness of promotional expenditures accurately requires a significant investment.

Integrating the Promotional Plan	One task that has always plagued marketing managers is how to best integrate the promotional plan. In far too many cases, the elements of personal selling and nonpersonal selling have been employed in an uncoordinated fashion. The result has been a duplication of efforts, and in some cases the various elements have worked at cross-purposes. The promotional plan should be directed toward a complete integration of all aspects of the marketing program. How can this best be accomplished?

Marketing Science Institute's study of promotional decision making resulted in a decision-making process known as *adaptive planning and control sequence (APACS)*. APACS provides an analytical framework of eight steps for reaching promotional decisions:

1. Define the problem and set objectives.
2. Appraise the overall situation.
3. Determine tasks and identify the means of accomplishing them.
4. Identify alternative plans and mixes.
5. Estimate expected results.
6. Review decisions by management.
7. Get feedback of results and postaudit.
8. Adapt program if required.[15]

Figure 12–7 shows the development of an integrated promotion plan for chosen consumer segments. Regional planning is often desirable.[16] The marketing manager sets the goals and objectives of the firm's promotional strategy in accordance with corporate objectives and the goals of the marketing organization.[17] Then, based on these goals, the various elements of the strategy—personal selling, advertising, sales promotion, and public relations—are formulated in a coordinated promotion plan. Budgeting, of course, is one of the most important aspects of the procedure.

The coordinated promotional strategy then becomes an integral part of the total marketing program for reaching the selected consumer segments. Finally, the feedback mechanism, in such forms as marketing research and field sales reports, closes the system by suggesting modifications for improvement.

In Defense of Promotion

Promotion has often been the target of criticisms such as:

"Promotion contributes nothing to public welfare."
"Most advertisements and sales presentations insult my intelligence."
"Promotion 'forces' consumers to buy products they do not want
 and do not need."
"Advertising and selling are economic wastes."
"Promotional programs are usually unethical."

Although the list is far from complete, it represents the types of complaints that have been presented. Consumers, public officials, and marketers agree

Figure 12–7
Integrating the Promotional Plan into the Total Marketing Program

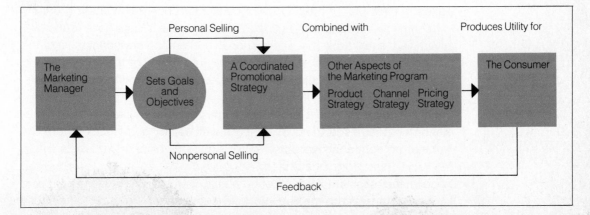

that too many of these complaints are true. Some salespeople do use uneth-ical sales tactics. Some product advertising is directed at consumer groups that can least afford to purchase the particular item. Many television com-mercials do contribute to the growing problem of cultural pollution.

While promotion can certainly be criticized on many counts, it plays a crucial role in modern society. This point is best explained by looking at promotion's business, economic, and social importance.

Business Importance

Promotional strategy has become increasingly important to both large and small business enterprises. The long-term rise in outlays for promotion is well documented and attests to management's faith in the ability of promo-tional efforts to produce additional sales. It is difficult to conceive of a firm that does not attempt to promote its product or service in some manner or another. Most modern institutions simply cannot survive in the long run with-out promotion.

Nonbusiness enterprises have also recognized the importance of pro-motion. The attempt by the armed services to increase enlistments is based on a substantial advertising campaign stressing the advantages of a military career. Religious organizations have acknowledged the importance of pro-moting their product. Even labor organizations have used promotional chan-nels to make their viewpoints known to the public at large. In fact, it is rea-sonable to say that promotion now plays a larger role in business (including nonprofit organizations) than it ever has in the past.

Economic Importance

If for no other reason than its employment of several million people, promo-tion has assumed a degree of economic importance.[18] Moreover, effec-tive promotion has allowed society to derive benefits not otherwise available. For example, the criticism that promotion costs too much fails to consider the effect of promotion on other categories of expenditures.

Promotion strategies that increase the number of units sold permit econ-omies in the production process, thereby lowering the production costs as-signed to each unit of output. Lower consumer prices allow these products to become available to more people. Similarly, researchers have found that advertising subsidizes the informational content of newspapers and the broadcast media.[19] In short, promotion pays for many of the enjoyable and educational aspects of contemporary life, as well as lowering product costs.

Social Importance

Criticisms such as "most promotional messages are tasteless" and "pro-motion contributes nothing to society's well-being" sometimes ignore the fact that no commonly accepted set of standards or priorities exists within our social framework. The United States is a diverse economy characterized by consumer segments with differing needs, wants, and aspirations. What is tasteless to one group may be informative to another. Promotional strategy is faced with an averaging problem that escapes many of its critics. The one generally accepted standard in a market society is freedom of choice for the consumer. Customer buying decisions eventually determine what is acceptable practice in the marketplace.

Promotion has become an important factor in the campaigns to achieve societal objectives such as physical fitness and the elimination of drug abuse. It performs an informative and educative task that makes it extremely important in the functioning of modern society.

Summary

This chapter has provided an introduction to promotion, the third variable in the marketing mix. Promotional strategy is closely related to the marketing communications system, which includes the functions of sender, message, encoding, transfer mechanism, decoding, receiver, feedback, and noise. Its major components are personal selling and nonpersonal selling (advertising, sales promotion, and public relations). Each of these elements is discussed fully in the two chapters that follow.

Developing an effective promotional strategy is a complex matter. The elements of promotion are related to the type and value of the product being promoted as well as to the timing of the promotional effort. Personal selling is used primarily for industrial goods, higher value items, and during the transactional phase. Advertising, by contrast, is used primarily for consumer goods, lower value items, and during the pretransactional and posttransactional phases.

A pushing strategy, which relies on personal selling, attempts to promote the product to the members of the marketing channel rather than to the ultimate user. A pulling strategy concentrates on stimulating user demand primarily through advertising and sales promotion.

The five basic objectives of promotion are to (1) provide information, (2) increase demand, (3) differentiate products, (4) accentuate the value of the product, and (5) stabilize sales. There are several problems involved in promotional budgeting and in measuring the effectiveness of promotional expenditures. The coordination of the entire promotional effort can be accomplished by the eight-stage adaptive planning and control sequences.

The target of much criticism, promotion does have great value on business, economic, and social levels.

Questions for Discussion

1. Explain the following terms:

promotion	public relations
marketing communications	pulling strategy
personal selling	pushing strategy
advertising	task objective method
sales promotion	direct-sales results test

2. Relate promotional strategy to the process of communications.
3. Why is promotion considered one of the more difficult aspects of marketing decision making?
4. Compare the five basic objectives of promotion. Cite specific examples of each.
5. Perhaps the most critical promotional question facing the marketing manager concerns *when* to use each of the components of promotion. Comment on this statement, relating your response to the goods classification, product value, and the timing of the promotional effort.
6. Prepare a critique of a promotional campaign employed by a firm with which you are familiar.
7. Discuss the productivity of promotion.
8. Discuss why it is difficult to measure the effectiveness of promotional efforts.
9. Explain why the task objective method is considered the best way to allocate a promotional budget. What are the advantages and disadvantages of each of the alternative allocation methods?
10. In too many instances, promotional programs have led to a duplication of efforts or have worked at cross-purposes. How would you correct this situation?
11. Why is promotion so often the target of critics? How would you answer the complaints?
12. Relate the generalized communications process to the promotion of a new computer.
13. What mix of promotion variables would you use for each of the following:
    a. a management consulting service
    b. car batteries
    c. ladies' sports outfits
    d. industrial drilling equipment
    e. lawn mowers
    f. customized business forms
14. Develop a hypothetical promotion budget for the following—ignoring dollar amounts by using percentage allocations to the various promotion variables (such as 40 percent to personal selling, 50 percent to advertising, and 10 percent to public relations):
    a. Avis Rent-a-Car
    b. Ramada Inns
    c. a manufacturer of industrial chemicals
    d. Prudential Insurance Company
15. Develop a plan for measuring the effectiveness of a current advertising campaign with which you are familiar.
16. The Ridge Tool Company of Elyria, Ohio, recently honored a promotional deal that it ran in a 1931 issue of *Popular Science*. The ad had offered a wrench for 20 cents. Ridge Tool sent the wrench, which now sells for $4.20, and even returned the customer's 20 cents. How could an action of this type fit into Ridge Tool's overall promotional strategy?
17. The Justice Bedding Company of Chepachet, Rhode Island, has developed a product it believes is better than an electric blanket. What type of promotional strategy would you devise for Justice Bedding's new electric mattress?
18. Many professionals, such as physicians, attorneys, and dentists, are now allowed to promote their services through media advertising. What effect is this likely to have on the practices of those professionals who advertise?
19. Develop a promotional strategy to expand the membership of a campus organization to which you belong or with which you are familiar.
20. Consider the Gillette case that appears in this chapter. In what other ways could the firm promote Atra and Trac II?

Notes

1 "Gillette Renews Its Love for Television Sports," *Business Week,* October 23, 1978, pp. 142, 147.
2. Similar communication processes are suggested in David K. Berlo, *The Process of Communications* (New York: Holt, Rinehart and Winston, 1960), pp. 23–38; and Thomas S. Robertson, *Innovative Behavior and Communication* (New York: Holt, Rinehart and Winston, 1971), p. 122. See also Claude Shannon and Warren Weaver, *The Mathematical Theory of Communication* (Urbana: University of Illinois Press, 1949), p. 5; and Wilbur Schramm, "The Nature of Communication between Humans," in *The Process and Effects of Mass Communication,* rev. ed. (Urbana: University of Illinois Press, 1971), pp. 3–53.

3. Schramm, "Nature of Communication," pp. 3–53. Other communication models are discussed in two articles by C. A. Maile and A. H. Kizilbash: "A Marketing Communications Model," *Business Horizons,* November 1977, pp. 77–84; and "A Communications Model for Marketing Decisions," *Journal of the Academy of Marketing Science,* Winter 1977, pp. 48–56. See also Michael L. Rothschild, "Marketing Communications in Nonbusiness Situations," *Journal of Marketing,* Spring 1979, pp. 11–20.

4. An excellent discussion of sales promotion appears in Roger A. Strang, "Sales Promotion—Fast Growth, Faulty Management," *Harvard Business Review,* July–August 1976, pp. 115–124.

5. Committee on Definitions, *Marketing Definitions: A Glossary of Marketing Terms* (Chicago: American Marketing Association, 1960), p. 20.

6. "Let's Drop the Cinderella Attitude," *Marketing and Sales Promotion* (special report of *Sales & Marketing Management*), n.d., p. 2.

7. Estimated by McGraw-Hill's Research Laboratory of Advertising Performance and reported in "Industrial Newsletter," *Sales & Marketing Management,* August 1978, p. 32.

8. Richard H. Colley, *Defining Advertising Goals* (New York: Association of National Advertisers, 1961).

9. Joe Cappo, "R&S Going to Stocks to Market Inventory," *Chicago Daily News,* October 9, 1975.

10. From *Markets and Marketing: An Orientation* by Lee E. Preston (Glenview, Ill.: Scott, Foresman, 1970), p. 198. Copyright © 1970 by Scott, Foresman and Company. Reprinted by permission of the publisher.

11. Determination of the correct advertising frequency is examined in Herbert E. Krugman, "What Makes Advertising Effective?" *Harvard Business Review,* March–April 1975, pp. 96–103.

12. Charles G. Burck, "While the Big Brewers Quaff, the Little Ones Thirst," *Fortune,* November 1972, p. 107.

13. An excellent discussion of budgeting for promotion is included in S. Watson Dunn and Arnold M. Barban, *Advertising: Its Role In Modern Marketing,* 4th ed. (Hinsdale, Ill.: Dryden Press, 1978), pp. 266–285. See also Gary L. Lilien, Alvin J. Silk, Jean-Marie Chaffray, and Murdidhar Rao, "Industrial Advertising Effects and Budgeting Practices," *Journal of Marketing,* January 1976, pp. 16–24; William A. Staples and Robert W. Sweadlow, "A Zero Base Approach to Advertising Planning," in *Proceedings of the Southern Marketing Association,* ed. Robert S. Franz, Robert M. Hopkins, and Al Toma, New Orleans, Louisiana, November 1978, pp. 315–317; Michael Etgar and Meir Schneller, "Advertising in a Multiproduct Firm," in *Contemporary Marketing Thought*, ed. Barnett A. Greenberg and Danny N. Bellenger (Chicago: American Marketing Association, 1977), p. 527; and Joseph A. Bellizzi, A. Frank Thompson, and Lynn J. Loudenback, "Promotional Activity and the U.S. Business Cycle," in *Proceedings of the Southwestern Marketing Association,* ed. Robert C. Harvey, G. Edward Kiser, and Ronnie D. Whitt, Houston, Texas, 1979, pp. 27–28.

14. Reported in *Marketing Science Institute Briefs,* December 1975, p. 1.

15. Patrick J. Robinson and David J. Luck, *Promotional Decision-Making: Practice and Theory* (New York: McGraw-Hill, 1964), pp. 3–4. An interesting discussion of the APACS process appears in Martin L. Bell, *Marketing: Concepts and Strategy,* 2d ed. (Boston: Houghton Mifflin, 1972), pp. 780–781.

16. The need for regional promotional strategies is pointed out in Martin R. Schlissel, "Effective Promotional Strategy through Decentralization," *Journal of the Academy of Marketing Science,* Spring 1973, pp. 59–66.

17. A similar type of hierarchy is suggested in James U. McNeal and Jerome B. Kernan, "Multi-Stage Coordination of Promotion," *Southern Journal of Business,* October 1966, pp. 18–21.

18. The economic effects of advertising are explored in Jean-Jacques Lambin, "What Is the Real Impact of Advertising?" *Harvard Business Review,* May–June 1975, pp. 139–147.

19. Francis X. Callahan, "Does Advertising Subsidize Information?" *Journal of Advertising Research,* August 1978, pp. 19–22.

CHAPTER 13
ELEMENTS OF PROMOTIONAL STRATEGY: ADVERTISING, SALES PROMOTION, AND PUBLIC RELATIONS

Key Terms

advertising
demographics
psychographics
positioning
comparative
advertising
product advertising
institutional
advertising
pretesting

posttesting
retail advertising
cooperative
advertising
sales promotion
specialty advertising
public relations
publicity

Learning Goals

1. To explain advertising's current status and historical development.
2. To list the steps in advertising planning, the basic types of advertisements, and the various advertising media.
3. To explain the organization of the advertising function, the creation of advertisements, and the status of retail advertising.
4. To identify the principal methods of sales promotion.
5. To describe the role of public relations and publicity in the firm's promotional strategy.

13

Campbell Soup had never used separate advertisements for its markets until the "give-me-the-Campbell's life" campaign was begun.[1] Campbell's targeted its efforts at people who typically ate casual meals, including retirees and career couples. One extensively used commercial had a young husband putting together a soup and sandwich dinner while awaiting his wife's arrival from work. The advertisement was designed to reach a previously neglected market—families where both adults worked. Segmenting the soup market this way had a positive effect on Campbell's sales.

In Chapter 13, a continuation of Chapter 12, the nonpersonal elements of promotion—advertising, sales promotion, and public relations—will be examined. These elements play a crucial role in the promotional strategies used by most organizations today.

Advertising

President Franklin D. Roosevelt is reputed to have said: "If I were starting my life over again, I am inclined to think I would go into the advertising business in preference o almost any other."[2] As a matter of fact, President Roosevelt probably would have made an excellent advertising executive. His use of persuasive radio "fireside chats" certainly exemplifies the definition of advertising given earlier. **Advertising** is *a nonpersonal sales presentation usually directed to a large number of potential customers.*

Today's widespread markets make advertising an important part of business. Advertising and related expenditures have risen faster than gross national product and most other economic indicators since World War II. Furthermore, about 200,000 people are employed in advertising, according to an American Association of Advertising Agencies estimate.[3]

Seven companies—Procter & Gamble, General Motors, General Foods, Sears, K mart, Bristol-Myers, and Warner-Lambert—spent over $200 million for advertising in 1977. Table 13–1 ranks the nation's top advertisers. The United States accounts for about 57 percent of the world's total advertising expenditures. This means that nearly $157 is spent on advertising each year for each person in the United States.[4]

Advertising expenditures vary among industries and companies. Cosmetics companies are often cited as examples of firms that spend a high percentage of their funds on advertising and promotion. Chicago consultants Schonfeld & Associates studied over a thousand firms and industries and calculated their average advertising expenditures as a percentage of both sales and gross profit margin. Estimates for selected industries are given in Table 13–2. There are wide differences among industries, as shown in the table. Advertising spending can range from zero in an industry like iron and steel foundries to a third of the firm's gross profit margin in a retail mail-order house.

Table 13-1
Twenty Leading Advertisers

Company	Media Total	Magazines	Newspapers	Network Television	Spot Television	Network Radio	Outdoor
1. Procter & Gamble	$460,000,000	$21,442,300	$5,830,400	$235,251,300	$114,625,700	—	—
2. General Motors	312,000,000	44,029,400	47,504,900	90,699,500	26,748,300	$2,915,100	$5,777,200
3. General Foods	300,000,000	29,026,800	6,271,300	143,312,800	71,987,700	833,800	203,700
4. Sears, Roebuck	290,000,000	41,344,700	—	80,226,900	22,072,200	5,143,400	86,900
5. K mart	210,000,000	4,955,600	—	5,240,300	15,126,000	2,101,500	1,900
6. Bristol-Myers	203,000,000	23,316,200	2,970,500	114,414,700	18,952,700	—	14,700
7. Warner-Lambert	201,000,000	785,900	884,900	62,098,300	20,158,600	4,191,600	670,600
8. Ford Motor	184,000,000	25,351,600	26,835,600	66,085,400	28,033,700	1,007,100	1,116,100
9. Philip Morris	184,000,000	48,232,800	53,123,300	31,756,100	10,375,900	—	22,488,500
10. American Home Products	171,000,000	5,928,600	2,210,400	108,428,700	35,250,500	2,765,800	—
11. R. J. Reynolds	164,686,100	59,558,900	59,044,700	5,148,400	4,842,800	—	33,552,300
12. General Mills	160,500,000	15,764,000	3,690,600	82,535,000	44,253,800	876,300	67,800
13. Richardson-Merrell	148,771,000	3,654,200	198,300	34,275,500	7,981,000	382,700	—
14. Unilever	145,000,000	7,160,800	3,574,700	68,418,300	35,926,600	—	—
15. Mobil	142,772,470	4,624,300	5,820,600	7,334,900	27,834,900	168,000	75,000
16. AT&T	131,968,200	10,459,100	9,966,500	28,963,100	28,276,700	14,100	740,700
17. Norton Simon	127,115,000	14,872,700	5,758,300	29,440,700	12,506,400	196,700	2,370,800
18. Chrysler	127,100,000	18,000,000	2,500,000	33,000,000	17,700,000	1,000,000	500,000
19. PepsiCo	124,000,000	1,510,600	1,683,200	35,141,100	40,305,100	—	694,000
20. RCA	124,000,000	16,747,300	14,343,400	16,142,100	11,133,800	66,600	326,800

Figures are estimated by *Advertising Age.*
Source: Adapted from "Marketing Profiles of 100 Leading Advertisers," *Advertising Age,* August 28, 1978, pp. 29–210. Reprinted with permission from the August 28, 1978, issue of *Advertising Age.* Copyright 1978 by Crain Communications Inc.

Industry in general has become somewhat advertising oriented as other elements of promotion have grown relatively more expensive. But advertising's future potential remains a matter of conjecture, although it may be determined by the environmental framework within which it operates. The role of advertising in U.S. society attracts considerable public interest today. (See Chapter 18 for more information on the subject.)

Historical Development[5]

Some form of advertising of products has probably existed since the development of the exchange process. Most early advertising was vocal; criers and hawkers sold various products, made public announcements, and chanted advertising slogans like the once familiar:

One-a-penny, two-a-penny, hot-cross buns
One-a-penny, two for tuppence, hot-cross buns.

Criers were common in colonial America. The cry of "Rags! Any rags? Any wool rags?" filled the streets of prerevolutionary Philadelphia.

Signs were also used in early advertising. Most were symbolic in their

Table 13-2
Estimates of Advertising to Sales and Advertising to Gross Profit Margin, by Industry

Industry	Advertising as a Percentage of Net Sales	Advertising as a Percentage of Gross Profit Margin
General building contractors	0.8	5.5
Meat products	1.2	7.7
Dairy products	1.7	11.6
Bakery products	1.6	3.8
Beer, alcoholic beverages, and soft drinks	5.1	14.8
Cigarets	6.2	14.7
Floor covering mills	1.3	4.5
Household furniture	1.7	7.2
Chemicals and allied products	1.9	5.0
Soaps, detergents, and cosmetics	10.4	19.1
Petroleum refining	0.6	3.0
Glass containers	5.9	16.1
Iron and steel foundries	0.0	0.0
Farm and garden machinery and equipment	1.1	4.3
Household appliances	3.9	12.9
Motor vehicles and car bodies	1.6	8.0
Photographic equipment and supplies	1.9	4.6
Jewelry-precious metals	5.6	12.4
Toys and amusement sport goods	5.2	16.3
Telephone communication	0.5	1.3
Retail-department stores	2.9	9.9
Retail-auto dealers and gas stations	2.1	8.9
Retail-women's ready to wear	2.0	12.1
Retail-eating places	2.9	15.4
Retail-mail order houses	13.4	27.9
Hotel-motels	2.5	11.2
Service-motion picture theatres	3.7	30.5

Source: "Estimates of '78 Advertising to Sales and Advertising to Gross Profit Margin by Industry," *Advertising Age,* July 23, 1979, p. 40. Reprinted by permission of Schonfeld & Associates Inc., 120 S. LaSalle Street, Chicago, Illinois.

identification of products or services. In Rome, a goat signified a dairy, a mule driving a mill signified a bakery, and a boy being whipped signified a school.

Later, the development of the printing press greatly expanded advertising's capabilities. A 1710 advertisement in the *Spectator* billed one dentifrice as "the Incomparable Powder for cleaning of Teeth, which has given great satisfaction to most of the Nobility and Gentry in England." Colonial newspapers like Benjamin Franklin's *Gazette* also featured advertising. Indeed, many newspapers carried it on their first page. Most of these advertisements would be called "classified ads" today. Some national advertisers also began to use newspaper advertising at this time. For instance, Pierre Lorillard was an early promoter of his tobacco products.

Volney Palmer organized the first advertising agency in the United States in 1841. George P. Rowell was another early advertising agent. Originally, these agencies simply sold advertising space. Services like advertising research, copywriting, and planning came later. Claude C. Hopkins used a large-scale consumer survey concerning home-baked beans before launching a campaign for Van Camp's Pork and Beans in the early 1900s. Hopkins claimed that home-baked beans were difficult to digest and suggested that consumers try Van Camp's beans. He advocated the use of "reason-why copy" to show why people should buy the product.

Some early advertising promoted products of questionable value, such as patent medicines. As a result, a reformist movement in advertising developed during the early 1900s, and some newspapers began to screen their advertisements. Magazine publisher Cyrus Curtis began rejecting certain types of advertising, such as medical copy that claimed cures and alcoholic beverage advertisements. And in 1911, the forerunner of the American Advertising Federation drew up a code for improved advertising.

These improvements established the springboard for a growth in advertising that many of the industry's forefathers thought impossible. In this regard, an interesting story is told about the founder of the J. Walter Thompson Agency:

At noon on a summer day in 1916 a media representative called at the J. Walter Thompson agency and found that his luncheon date was tied up with a client and would not be able to see him. He was about to leave, . . . when he found himself being clapped on the back by the normally aloof Commodore Thompson himself. To his amazement, Thompson invited him to lunch at the Duane Hotel across Madison Avenue and even bought the first round of drinks. He then made a gleeful announcement: "Congratulate me, Joe! I just sold the business to the Resor boys. They don't know it, but the advertising agency business has seen its best days!"[6]

The moral of the story is obvious. Today, the J. Walter Thompson agency has annual billings of over a billion dollars.

One identifying feature of advertising after 1900 has been its concern for researching the markets that it attempts to reach. Originally, advertising research dealt primarily with media selection and the product. Then, advertisers became increasingly concerned with determining the appropriate **demographics**—*characteristics such as the age, sex, and income level of potential buyers.* Now, understanding consumer behavior has become an important aspect of advertising strategy. *Behavioral influences on purchase decisions*—often called **psychographics**—can be useful in describing potential markets for advertising appeals. These influences include such factors as life-style and personal attitudes. Increased knowledge in these areas has led to improved advertising decisions.

The emergence of the marketing concept, with its emphasis on a company-wide consumer orientation, saw advertising take on an expanded role as marketing communications assumed greater importance in business. Advertising provides an efficient, inexpensive, and fast method of reaching the much sought-after consumer. Its extensive use now rivals that of personal selling. Advertising has become a key ingredient in the effective implementation of the marketing concept.

Advertising Objectives

The objectives of advertising were traditionally stated in terms of direct sales goals. A better approach, however, is to view advertising as having communications objectives that seek to inform, persuade, and remind potential customers of the product. Advertising seeks to condition the consumer to have a favorable viewpoint toward the promotional message. The goal is to improve the likelihood that the customer will buy a particular product. In this sense, advertising is an excellent example of the close relationship between marketing communications and promotional strategy.

Burger King's promotional campaigns offer an illustration of advertising's communications objectives. Initially, the hamburgers offered at most fast-food outlets were small, so Burger King advertised that its burgers were bigger. As the industry matured, nearly all the competition began to stress that its hamburgers were big. But, at this point, many people objected to prefabricated hamburgers, so Burger King switched to its well-known "Have It Your Way" theme. The company has adopted communications goals to meet its market.[7]

Advertising Planning

Advertising planning begins with effective research. Its results allow management to make strategic decisions that are translated into tactical areas such as budgeting, copywriting, scheduling, and the like. Finally, there is feedback for measuring the effectiveness of the advertising. The elements of advertising planning are shown in Figure 13–1.

There is a real need for following a sequential process in advertising decisions. Novice advertisers are often overly concerned with the technical aspects of advertisement construction and ignore the more basic steps, such as market analysis. The type of advertisement employed in any particular situation is related in large part to the planning phase of this process.

Positioning[8]

One of the most widely discussed strategies in advertising is the concept of **positioning**, which involves *the development of a promotional strategy aimed at a particular segment of the market.* While advertising experts continue to debate its effectiveness and origin, positioning is being used by an increasing number of firms. The strategy is applicable primarily to products that are not the leaders in their particular fields. These products are apparently more successful if their advertising concentrates on specific market segments rather than attacking dominant brands. The specialization is best accomplished through an advertising strategy or theme that positions them in the specified market segments.

Figure 13–1
Elements of Advertising Planning

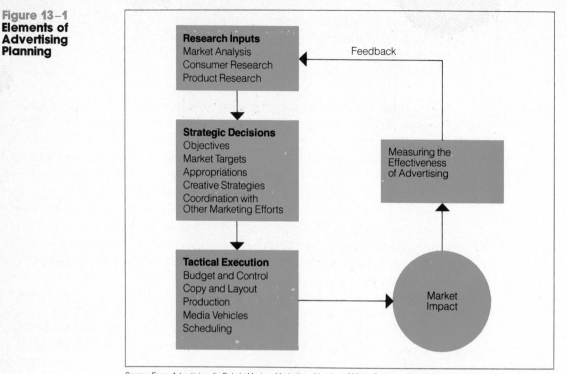

Source: From *Advertising: Its Role in Modern Marketing,* 4th ed., p. 206, by S. Watson Dunn and Arnold Barban. Copyright © 1978 by Dryden Press, a division of Holt, Rinehart and Winston. Reprinted by permission of Holt, Rinehart and Winston.

Wasko Denture Clinic: Call 333-3 . . .

Dr. Stanley Wasko has gone on Philadelphia television to advertise his denture work. He has also expanded his staff to handle the additional business. The Philadelphia dentist says his dentures sell for $155, compared to $450 for those from other dentists in the "city of brotherly love."

Certainly, many of the barriers to advertising by professionals have fallen. But opinions vary on advertisements like those produced by Dr. Wasko. Some say that advertising makes professional services more available to all consumers and that it tends to lower prices. Others argue that advertising lowers the quality of professional services and destroys their ethical status.

To date, most advertisements have come from the two fields with the largest number of practitioners—law and dentistry. Most of the advertisements have been produced by the advertisers themselves. Oddly enough, advertising by these people often lacks the professional quality most consumers expect of commercials. In fact, Roger P. Brosnahan, who chairs the American Bar Association's commission on advertising, said:

We've found that the most effective ads were done by professionals. Advertising is a specialized field that calls for specialists. Lawyers who do their own advertising will probably waste their time and money because they won't adequately determine what they're trying to inform the public of, and they can't define the market. [9]

Source: Information from "Ads Start to Take Hold in the Professions," *Business Week*, July 24, 1978, pp. 122, 124. Photo courtesy of Wasko Studios and Bernie Cleff/Business Week Magazine. © 1979 Bernie Cleff.

With the image of being a mixer for older people's drinks, 7–Up was missing the primary market for soft drinks—children, teenagers, and young adults. So the firm used its now well-known UnCola campaign to first identify the product as a soft drink and then position it as an alternative to cola. In another classic promotional campaign, Avis positioned itself against Hertz with the theme, "Avis is only number two in rent-a-cars, so why go with us? We try harder."

Comparative Advertising

Comparative advertising, another strategy to consider in the planning phase, *makes direct promotional comparisons with leading competitive brands.* The strategy usually is employed by firms that do not lead the market.[10] Market leaders prefer not to acknowledge that there are competitive products. Procter & Gamble and General Foods, for instance, devote little of their huge promotional budgets to comparative advertising. But many firms do use it. About 10 percent of all television advertisements make comparisons to competitive products. Examples are plentiful:

Suave antiperspirant will keep you just as sweet as Ban Ultra Dry does—and for a lot less.

Volkswagen's Dasher picks up speed faster than a Mercedes and has a bigger trunk than a Rolls.

Nationwide, more Coca-Cola drinkers prefer the taste of Pepsi.[11]

A recent Opel campaign (described on page 310) may prove to be a classic of comparative advertising.

Marketers who contemplate comparative advertising should take precautions to assure that they can back their claims. In the Opel campaigns, General Motors went beyond EPA data to run its own tests. The comparison advertising trend has produced several lawsuits, so practitioners must be especially careful when employing this technique.

Types of Advertisements

Essentially, there are two basic types of advertisements—product and institutional. Each can be subdivided into informative, persuasive, and reminder categories.

Product advertising is the type normally thought of when the subject of advertising comes up in a conversation. It deals with *the nonpersonal selling of a particular good or service.* **Institutional advertising,** by contrast, is concerned with *promoting a concept, an idea, a philosophy, or the goodwill of an industry, company, or organization.* It is often closely related to the public relations function of the enterprise.[12] An example of institutional ad-

How the Opel Came in Second — and Won

Buick's Japanese-made Opel was in trouble. It was eleventh in sales among the twelve imported cars in its price class (Renault was last), and by the end of 1976, its U.S. sales had fallen by half. "We found ourselves with an inventory of about 20,000 cars, and were selling only 1,000 a month," says George Frink, director of marketing at Buick. "You could say we were headed for disaster."

Frink knew what had to be done—somehow he had to get people who were shopping for an import to take a look at the Opel. And the way to do it, he decided, was to run an ad campaign comparing the Opel with four leading imports—the Toyota Corolla, Datsun B-210, VW Rabbit, and Subaru DL—on the basis of measurable things, such as fuel economy and performance. Though a lot of supporting data from the Environmental Protection Agency was already available on some of these points, Buick bought ten models of each make that it was challenging in order to run tests of its own. This it did at the huge General Motors proving grounds in Mesa, Arizona.

It took time to devise tests that would clearly be both fair and meaningful. And once the tests got going, the necessity for absolute accuracy made things move slowly. By February, Frink was getting nervous. He wanted the ad campaign to run before summer, which experience has shown to be the best selling season for imports. Before the final tests were made—i.e., before he even knew how the Opel was going to finish—Frink slipped the first of five ads into newspapers nationwide, boldly announcing the "Five Car Showdown."

Judging by the results of the first showdown, Opel might just as well have stayed in the starting gate. The first tests were for quietness and roominess. And in these respects, "Opel finishes third to VW and Toyota," flashed the headline of the ad. It added: "Drats!"

By the end of the campaign in May, however, the Opel had placed a respectable second overall, behind VW's Rabbit. The folks at Buick were ecstatic, and so were the folks who bring out the Rabbit. Eager to spread the gospel according to Opel, VW ran its own ad—a "thank you" to Opel for proclaiming that the Rabbit was the best car tested.

Buick spent about $4 million on the Opel Showdown, and it was worth it. Opel's share of the market more than doubled, to 1.9 percent, compared with 13 percent for VW. The percentage may seem slim, but Buick is now selling all the Opels that it gets, and that's a happier situation than the one it confronted just a year ago.

Source: Reprinted by permission from Aimee L. Morner, "It Pays to Knock Your Competition," *Fortune*, February 13, 1978, p. 106. Opel ad courtesy of General Motors.

vertising by a state appears in Figure 13–2. The National Coal Association also has used institutional advertising (see Figure 13–3).

Informative Product Advertising. Informative product advertising seeks to develop initial demand for a product. It tends to characterize the promotion of any new type of product since the objective is often simply to announce its availability. Figure 13–4 shows that informative advertising is usually used in the introductory stages of the product life cycle. In fact, it was the

**Figure 13–2
An Example of
Institutional
Advertising Used
by the State of
Washington**

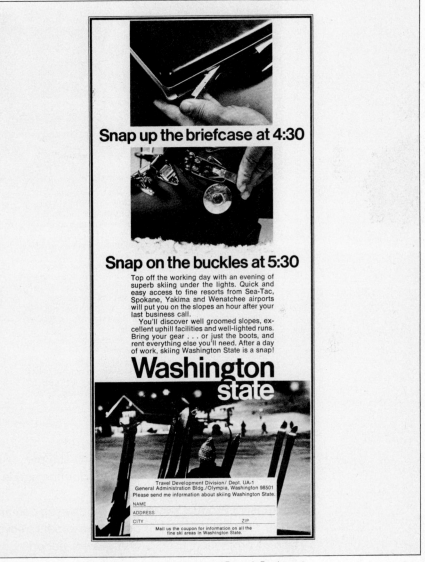

Source: Courtesy of Washington State Department of Commerce and Economic Development.

Figure 13–3
An Example of Institutional Advertising Used by the National Coal Association

The game we can't afford to play

America has been playing a game with energy resources. We've been importing nearly half the oil we use from foreign countries and paying dearly for it—$32 billion last year. This has drained our economy and promoted inflation.

We've been demanding more natural gas than our limited supplies can deliver. This situation can only worsen as demands increase.

We thought that nuclear power might rescue us in the near future. But this has not been in the cards. And we're still waiting for a breakthrough in solar technology.

America has failed to fully use its most abundant domestic resource. We've limited the use of coal, while a supply that will last for centuries sits under our noses.

What should we call this game we've been playing—hesitation, indecision, blindness? What are we waiting for? Our country can't afford to wait

any longer. We need to use coal now.

Write for our free booklet, The Energy Answer. National Coal Association, 1130 17th Street, N.W., Washington, D.C. 20036.

Coal
America's
Ace in the Hole
SM

Source: Reprinted by permission of the National Coal Association and Richard Newman Associates, Inc.

original approach to advertising: Early shippers used to post bulletins announcing the arrival of a ship and listing the goods it carried.

Persuasive Product Advertising. To develop demand for a particular product or brand is the goal of persuasive product advertising—a competitive type of promotion used in the growth period and to some extent in the maturity period of the product life cycle (see Figure 13–4). The increased

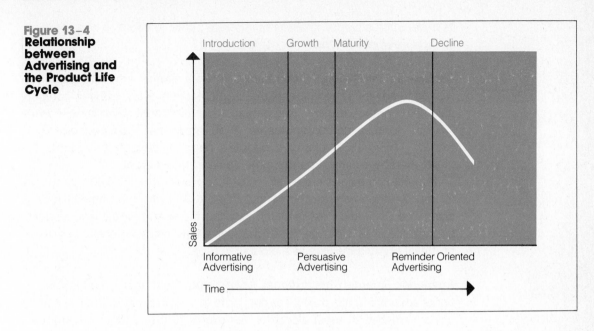

competition that has characterized all marketplaces in recent years even forced Hershey Foods Corporation, a long-time hold-out, to finally begin to advertise.

Reminder Oriented Product Advertising. The goal of reminder oriented product advertising is to reinforce previous promotional activity by keeping the product name in front of the public. It is used in the maturity period as well as throughout the decline phase of the product life cycle.

Dewar's profiles of young, active people are an example.[13] Each profile gives the person's age, profession, most memorable book read, favorite quotation, and, of course, preference for Dewar's Scotch. The campaign has been running since 1969, primarily because of the extensive reader interest in the profiles that appear in mass circulation magazines. The people are real, and their only compensation is five cases of Dewar's Scotch. By using this advertising method, Dewar's has kept its name in front of consumers and has climbed to second place in scotch sales.

Informative Institutional Advertising. Baltimore uses the slogan "Balti-More than You Know" to overcome its low-key image and to point out the harbor city's many advantages.[14] Baltimore wants to build up its economic base by attracting new industry and major conventions. Informative institutional advertising is part of its image building plan.

Another example of this type of institutional advertising is the local United Fund's listing of all the agencies and organizations that benefit from its drive. Such advertising seeks to increase public knowledge of a concept, political viewpoint, industry, or company.

Persuasive Institutional Advertising. When a firm or advertising agency wishes to advance the interests of a particular institution within a competitive environment, it often uses persuasive institutional advertising. For instance, Honda's campaign theme "You meet the nicest people on a Honda" (1964–1967) changed people's negative stereotype of motorcyclists, thereby greatly expanding the demand for its product.

Not all campaigns are as successful as Honda's. A $200,000 campaign to improve the image of the potato chip industry ran into immediate criticism. The St. Louis Post-Dispatch assailed the snack food's lack of nutritional value, then went on to say that the potato chip campaign was like a portrayal of Attila the Hun as a pioneer in urban renewal.[15]

Reminder Oriented Institutional Advertising. Reminder oriented institutional advertising has objectives similar to those of reminder oriented product advertising. In most elections, for example, the nominee's early persuasive (issue directed) advertising is replaced by reminder oriented advertising during the closing weeks of the campaign. The media abound with examples of this type of institutional advertising. FMC Corporation's theme "Suddenly the world sees a future for coal" represents a corporate effort to remind the public of the importance of this vital ore.

Media Selection

One of the most important decisions in developing an advertising strategy is the selection of the media to be employed. A mistake at this point can cost a company literally millions of dollars in ineffectual advertising. Media strategy must achieve the communications goals mentioned earlier.

Research should identify the market target to determine its size and characteristics and then match the target with the audience and the effectiveness of the available media. The objective is to achieve adequate media coverage without advertising beyond the identifiable limits of the potential market. Finally, alternative costs should be compared to determine the best possible media purchase.

There are numerous types of advertising media, and the characteristics of some of the more important ones will be considered here. The advantages and disadvantages of each are shown in Table 13–3.

Newspapers. About 30 percent of total advertising revenues, the largest share received by any of the media, is spent on advertising in newspapers. The primary advantages of newspapers are flexibility (advertising can be varied from one locality to the next), community prestige (newspapers have

Table 13–3
Advantages and Disadvantages of the Various Advertising Media

Media	Advantages	Disadvantages
Newspapers	Flexibility Community prestige Intense coverage Reader control of exposure Coordination with national advertising Merchandising service	Short life span Hasty reading Poor reproduction
Magazines	Selectivity Quality reproduction Long life Prestige associated with some Extra services	Lack of flexibility
Television	Great impact Mass coverage Repetition Flexibility Prestige	Temporary nature of message High cost High mortality rate for commercials Evidence of public lack of selectivity
Radio	Immediacy Low cost Practical audience selection Mobility	Fragmentation Temporary nature of message Little research information
Outdoor advertising	Communication of quick and simple ideas Repetition Ability to promote products available for sale nearby	Brevity of the message Public concern over esthetics
Direct mail	Selectivity Intense coverage Speed Flexibility of format Complete information Personalization	High cost per person Dependence on quality of mailing list Consumer resistance

Source: Based on S. Watson Dunn and Arnold Barban, *Advertising: Its Role in Modern Marketing,* 4th ed. (Hinsdale, Ill.: Dryden Press, 1978), pp. 535–606.

a deep impact on the community), intense coverage (in most places 90 percent of the homes can be reached by a single newspaper), reader control of exposure to the advertising message (unlike time media, readers can refer back to newspapers), coordination with national advertising, and merchandising services (such as promotional and research support). The disadvantages are a short life span, hasty reading (the typical reader spends only twenty to thirty minutes on the newspaper), and poor reproduction.[16]

Magazines. Magazines, which are divided into such diverse categories as consumer, farm, and business publications, account for about 7 percent of all advertising. The primary advantages of magazine advertising are selectivity of market targets, quality reproduction, long life, the prestige associated with some magazines, and the extra services offered by many publications. The primary disadvantage is that magazines lack the flexibility of newspapers, radio, and television.

Television. Television has been the fastest growing advertising medium ever. With about 18 percent of total advertising volume, it is now second to newspapers. Television advertising can be divided into three categories: network, national, and local. Columbia Broadcasting System, National Broadcasting Company, and American Broadcasting Company are the three national networks. Their programs usually account for a substantial portion of the total television advertising expenditures. A national "spot" is nonnetwork broadcasting used by a general advertiser. Local advertising spots, used primarily by retailers, consist of locally developed and sponsored commercials. Television advertising offers the advantages of impact, mass coverage, repetition, flexibility, and prestige. Its disadvantages include relinquishing control of the promotional message to the telecaster (who can influence its impact), high costs, high mortality rates for commercials, some public distrust, and a lack of selectivity.

Radio. Advertisers using the medium of radio can also be classified as network, national, and local. Radio accounts for 5 to 6 percent of total advertising volume. Its advantages are immediacy (studies show most people regard radio as the best source for up-to-date news), low cost, flexibility, practical and low-cost audience selection, and mobility. Its disadvantages include fragmentation (New York City, for instance, has twenty-nine AM and FM stations), the temporary nature of the message, and less research information than for television.

Impact is a primary advantage of advertising.

Source: Reprinted by permission of Chronicle Features.

Who Has Ever Heard of Bonnie Herman?

Bonnie Herman is rumored to make more than $200,000 a year as a singer. Her voice is heard by millions daily, and her songs are hummed and whistled by countless people. But almost no one has ever heard of Bonnie Herman. This is not surprising because she is a jingle singer—the voice of commercials for United Airlines, Coca-Cola, McDonald's, Cheerios, and numerous other products. Jingle singers must be able to change pitch, tune, and rhythm quickly, since they often do several different commercials in a single day. Bonnie and her counterparts must also learn to cope with the lack of recognition accorded them. But most jingle singers feel that the security and high earnings are well worth the price. Despite their obscurity, people like Bonnie Herman are vital parts of the advertising industry.

Source: Adapted from Philip Revzin, "For Jingle Vocalists, There Isn't Any Fame—But There Is Money," *Wall Street Journal,* August 13, 1975, pp. 1,6. Reprinted by permission of *The Wall Street Journal,* © Dow Jones & Company, Inc., 1975. All rights reserved.

Outdoor Advertising. Posters (commonly called billboards), painted bulletins or displays (such as those that appear on the walls of buildings), and electric spectaculars (large, illuminated, sometimes animated, signs and displays) make up outdoor advertising. This form of advertising has the advantages of communication of quick and simple ideas, repetition, and the ability to promote products that are available for sale nearby. Outdoor advertising is particularly effective in metropolitan and other high-traffic areas. Disadvantages of the medium are the brevity of its message and public concern over esthetics. The Highway Beautification Act of 1965, for instance, regulates outdoor advertising near interstate highways.

Direct Mail. Sales letters, postcards, leaflets, folders, broadsides (larger than folders), booklets, catalogs, and house organs (periodical publications issued by organizations) are all forms of direct mail advertising. The advantages of direct mail are selectivity, intensive coverage, speed, format flexibility, complete information, and the personalization of each mailing piece. Direct mail purchasers also tend to be consistent buyers.[17] Disadvantages of direct mail are its high cost per reader, its dependence on the quality of the mailing list, and some people's annoyance with it. This situation led the Direct Mail/Marketing Association in 1971 to establish its Mail Preference Service. This consumer service sends out name-removal forms to people who do not wish to receive direct mail advertising. It also provides add-on forms for those who like to receive a lot of mail (see Figure 13–5). By mid-1978, over 200,000 households had sent in forms.[18]

Assessing the Effectiveness of an Advertisement[19]

Advertising represents a major outlay for many firms, so it is imperative for them to determine whether a chosen campaign is accomplishing their promotional objectives. The determination of advertising effectiveness, however, is one of the most difficult undertakings in marketing. It consists of two primary elements—pretesting and posttesting.

Figure 13–5
An Advertisement Used by the Direct Mail/Marketing Association

There are 3 ways to deal with advertising mail:

1. You can just throw it all out, the good with the bad, without reading it.

2. Or you can mail the coupon below and get taken off many mailing lists.

3. Or you can decide for yourself which mail to read, which offers to accept.

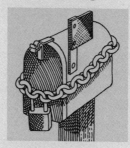

"Just some more advertising." It's easy to say that, and toss a piece of mail, unopened and unread, into the wastebasket. But people who never read advertising mail could be missing out on some pleasant surprises.

When you do take a few moments to open your advertising mail, you might find discount coupons to use at your local store…or a money-saving subscription offer for a magazine you've been buying at newsstand price…or a big sweepstakes you may enter without buying anything…or a valuable free gift you can keep just for trying a product.

Chances are that most of the advertising in your mailbox nowadays comes directly from manufacturers, publishers or retailers you've long trusted. Check over their colorful catalogs and brochures. You'll find top-brand products, fully described, with free-trial privileges you don't often get at stores, as well as money-back guarantees.

Of course it's your choice to toss out all advertising mail unopened. But then you'll never know what really worthwhile opportunities you may have missed.

If you'd like to get less advertising mail, there's a simple way to stop most of it from ever reaching your mailbox. The Direct Mail Marketing Association, which represents 1700 companies who advertise and sell by mail, has set up a Mail Preference Service for your convenience.

Just fill in the coupon below, checking the box marked "Name-Removal," and mail it to us at the address shown. We'll promptly send you a simple form. When the form is completed and returned the companies participating in this program will remove your name from their mailing lists. About 90 days after returning the Name-Removal Form, you should notice what will become a substantial reduction in the amount of mail advertising you receive.

There's no way we can stop all advertising mail from reaching you—but we will do our best. Participating companies are glad to extend this courtesy.

To most people, shopping by mail is like being in a big store. Many items are on display. Some you pass by quickly. Others look more interesting, so you stop, examine, compare, and perhaps buy. But the choice is always yours.

You may even want to receive more mail about certain hobbies or interests of yours. If so, check the box marked "Add-On" below. Mail Preference Service will send you a form allowing you to have your name added to mailing lists of companies in the areas of interest you specify—from cooking and gardening to books, travel, sports and many others. Then you can take even greater advantage of the extra opportunities you find only in mail advertising.

Mail Preference Service
DIRECT MAIL/MARKETING ASSOCIATION
6 East 43rd Street, New York, N.Y. 10017

☐ I want to receive *more* advertising mail on the subjects that interest me most. Please send me an ADD-ON Form.

☐ I want to receive *less* advertising mail. Please send me a NAME-REMOVAL Form.

Name _____
    (please print)
Address _____
City _____ State _____ Zip _____

Source: Courtesy of Direct Mail/Marketing Association, Inc., 6 East 43rd Street, New York, NY 10017.

Pretesting

Pretesting is *assessing the advertisement's effectiveness before it is actually used.* It includes a variety of evaluative methods. To test magazine advertisements, the ad agency Batten, Barton, Durstine & Osborn cuts ads out of advance copies of magazines and then "strips in" the ads it wants to test. Interviewers later check the impact of the advertisements on the readers who receive free copies of the revised magazine.

McCann-Erickson, another ad agency, uses a "sales conviction test" to evaluate magazine advertisements. Interviewers ask heavy users of a particular item to pick which of two alternative advertisements would "convince" them to purchase it.

Potential radio and television advertisements are often screened by consumers who sit in a studio and press two buttons—one for a positive reaction to the commercial, the other for a negative one. Sometimes, proposed ad copy is printed on a postcard that also offers a free product; the number of cards returned is viewed as an indication of the copy's effectiveness. "Blind product tests" are also often used. In these tests, people are asked to select unidentified products on the basis of available advertising copy. Mechanical means of assessing how people read advertising copy are yet another method. One mechanical test uses an eye camera to photograph how people read ads; its results help determine headline placement and advertising copy length.

Posttesting

Posttesting is *the assessment of advertising copy after it has been used.* Pretesting is generally a more desirable testing method than posttesting because of its potential cost savings. But posttesting can be helpful in planning future advertisements and in making adjustments to current advertising programs.

In one of the most popular posttests, the *Starch Readership Report,* interviewers ask people who have read selected magazines about whether they have read various ads in them. A copy of the magazine is used as an interviewing aid, and each interviewer starts at a different point in the magazine. For larger ads, respondents are also asked about specifics such as headlines and copy. All readership, or recognition, tests assume that future sales are related to advertising readership.

Unaided recall tests are another method of posttesting advertisements. Here, respondents are not given copies of the magazine but must recall the ads from memory. Gallup and Robinson require people to prove they have read a magazine by recalling one or more of its feature articles. The people who remember particular articles are given cards with the names of products advertised in the issue. They then list the ads they remember and explain what they remember about them. Finally, the respondents are asked about their potential purchase of the product. A readership test concludes the Gallup and Robinson interview. Burke Research Corporation uses telephone interviews the day after a commercial appears on television in order to test brand recognition and the effectiveness of the advertisement.

Inquiry tests are another popular posttest. Advertisements sometimes offer a free gift, generally a sample of the product, to people who respond to the advertisement. The number of inquiries relative to the cost of the advertisement is then used as a measure of effectiveness. *Split runs* allow advertisers to test two or more ads at the same time. Under this method, a publication's production run is split in two; half the magazines use Advertisement A, and half use Advertisement B. The relative pull of the alternatives is then determined by inquiries.

Regardless of the exact method used, marketers must realize that pretesting and posttesting are expensive and must therefore plan to use them as effectively as possible.

Organization of the Advertising Function

While the ultimate responsibility for advertising decisions often rests with top marketing management, the organization of the advertising function varies among companies. A producer of a technical industrial product may be served by a one-person operation primarily concerned with writing copy for trade publications. A consumer goods company, on the other hand, may have a large department staffed with advertising specialists.[20]

The advertising function is usually organized as a staff department reporting to the vice-president (or director) of marketing. The director of advertising is the department's liaison with the rest of the company. The department's technical competence is important, but so is its ability to relate well to the rest of the organization. The major tasks typically organized under advertising include advertising research, art, copywriting, media analysis, and, in some cases, sales promotion.

Advertising Agencies

Many major advertisers make use of independent advertising agencies. There are several advantages to such an arrangement. Agencies provide a degree of creativity and objectivity that is difficult to maintain in a corporate advertising department. In some cases, they also reduce the cost of advertising, since they do not have many of the fixed expenses associated with internal advertising departments.

Figure 13–6 shows the organization chart for a large advertising agency. While the titles may vary from agency to agency, the major operational responsibilities can be classified as creative services, account management, research, and promotional services.

J. Walter Thompson Company is the largest advertising agency in the

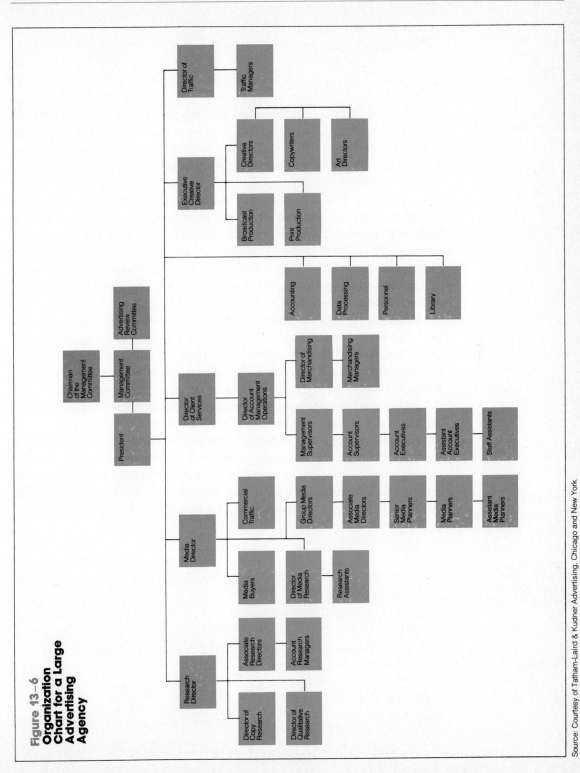

**Figure 13–6
Organization
Chart for a Large
Advertising
Agency**

Source: Courtesy of Tatham-Laird & Kudner Advertising, Chicago and New York.

United States, with worldwide billings of over $1 billion. Table 13–4 shows the ten leading U.S. advertising agencies ranked in terms of their world billings.

Creation of an Advertisement

The final step in the advertising process is the development and preparation of an advertisement that flows logically from the promotional theme selected. The advertisement's association with other company products and its continuity are the major factors to be considered in its preparation.

Sometimes related products are an advantage, and sometimes they are not. Taster's Choice by Nestlé leads Maxim by General Foods even though Maxim was the first freeze-dried coffee on the market. One explanation is that General Foods did not attempt to maximize its early advantage by going after regular coffee drinkers. General Foods apparently feared that Maxim's sales would cut into the sales of its regular coffee, Maxwell House. Nestlé, by contrast, attacked this market directly by advertising that a jar of Taster's Choice is about the equivalent of two pounds of regular coffee.[21]

What should an advertisement accomplish? Regardless of the exact appeal chosen, an advertisement should gain attention and interest, inform and/or persuade, and eventually lead to buying action. Gillette Company had a chimpanzee shave a man's face in a commercial. After tests in Indianapolis and Dallas, someone at the company observed: "Lots of people remembered the chimp, but hardly anyone remembered our product. There was fantastic interest in the monkey, but no payoff for Gillette."[22]

An advertisement that fails to gain the receiver's attention and then hold the person's interest is ineffectual. Thus information and persuasion is the second factor to consider when creating an advertisement. Health insurance advertisements typically specify the features of a policy and use testimonials in an attempt to persuade prospects. But stimulating buying action with an

Table 13–4 Top Ten U.S. Advertising Agencies in World Billings

Rank	Agency	Amount (in Millions)
1	J. Walter Thompson	$1,476.5
2	McCann-Erickson	1,404.5
3	Young & Rubicam	1,359.5
4	Ogilvy & Mather International	1,003.7
5	BBDO International	890.0
6	Ted Bates	890.0
7	Leo Burnett	865.1
8	SSC&B	840.5
9	Foote, Cone & Belding	740.3
10	D'Arcy-MacManus & Masius	698.8

Source: "629 Agencies Rack Up $3.46 Billion Income," *Advertising Age*, March 14, 1979, p. 1. Reprinted with permission from the March 14, 1979, issue of *Advertising Age*. Copyright 1979 by Crain Communications, Inc.

ad is often difficult since the ad cannot actually close the sale. Furthermore, many advertising managers fail to suggest how the receiver of the ad can effect a purchase if he or she so desires. This is a shortcoming that should be eliminated.

Celebrity Testimonials: Advantages and Pitfalls[23]

Gregory Peck was worth a million dollars to Traveler's Insurance. The Wool Bureau paid Jack Benny the same amount, and GAF and TWA paid another million dollars each for Henry Fonda and Peter Sellers, respectively. A service station operator from Plains, Georgia, has made considerable money for promoting beer and other products. But Frank Sinatra may have the best deal. He got a six-figure check for permitting Ford Motor Company to play part of "The Best Is Yet to Come" as background music to a commercial; Ford also agreed to use Sinatra's daughter in one commercial. These firms all invested in name talent to promote their offerings.

For many years, celebrities often did not want to be associated with commercials. There were exceptions, of course—like Joan Bennett advertising Chesterfield Cigarettes in 1942—but for the most part, stars stayed away from product endorsements. Glenn Ford's recent Buick commercials were his first, and Steve McQueen has appeared in only one commercial—a motorcycle advertisement. Even then, McQueen stipulated that the ad be used only in Japan.

Things are different now. Many celebrities openly seek advertising assignments, and their fees often are more reasonable than in the past. A local bank, for example, paid only $15,000 plus production costs for an Ed McMahan commercial. In other cases, celebrities have cut their fees after leaving the public spotlight. Joe Namath trimmed his fee 50 percent to $50,000 after his playing career was over.

The primary advantage of using big-name personalities is that they may improve product recognition in a promotional environment filled with hundreds of competing thirty-second commercials. (Advertisers use the term *clutter* to refer to this situation.) Of course, the celebrity must be a credible source of information for the item being sold.

There are also some disadvantages to using stars to sell a product. Some celebrity advertisements simply do not succeed. This is particularly true when there is no reasonable relationship between the celebrity and the product. Another problem is that some event will make the commercial meaningless or cast a negative image on it. Miller Brewing had already completed a commercial showing New York Yankees owner George Steinbrenner and his manager, Billy Martin, when Martin made some derogatory remarks about his boss and was fired. The Miller commercial—which had Steinbrenner firing Martin in a bar—was rereleased when Steinbrenner rehired Martin in 1979 and was viewed as particularly timely.

Advertisers are not the only ones with potential problems. The Federal Trade Commission has announced a policy of assessing financial liability to any celebrity who makes a false product claim. The new rule was first enforced against singer Pat Boone, who promoted Acne-Statin, a skin preparation sold as an acne cure. The FTC alleged that some of the product claims were false. Boone, while noting that his daughters did use Acne-Statin as claimed and that he believed the product claims, signed a consent decree in which he agreed to stop promoting the product and to pay up to $5,000 of any refunds that might be ordered. As a result of the Boone case, it now seems likely that name personalities will insist that advertisers reimburse any damages assessed as the result of a commercial.

Retail Advertising

Retail advertising is *all advertising by stores that sell goods or services directly to the consuming public.*[24] While accounting for a sizable portion of total annual advertising expenditures, retail advertising is not always effective. One study showed that consumers were often suspicious of retail price advertisements. Source, message, and shopping experience seemed to affect consumer attitudes toward these advertisements.[25]

The basic problem is that store managers are usually given the responsibility of advertising as an added task to be performed along with their normal functions. Advertising agencies are rarely used. The result is that advertising is often relegated to a secondary activity in retail stores. The basic step in correcting this deficiency is to give one individual both the responsibility and the authority for developing an effective retail advertising program.

Cooperative Advertising

One aspect of retail advertising—cooperative advertising—deserves special attention. **Cooperative advertising** is *a sharing of advertising costs between the retailer and the manufacturer or vendor.* It resulted initially from the media practice of offering lower rates to local advertisers than to national advertisers. Later, cooperative advertising was seen as a method of improving dealer relations. From the retailer's viewpoint, it permits a store to secure advertising that it would not otherwise have.

Sales Promotion

The second type of nonpersonal selling is sales promotion. This type of selling is so varied that many find it difficult to comprehend or define it clearly. Sales promotion is *a category of nonpersonal selling efforts designed to supplement and extend the other aspects of promotional strategy.*

Methods of Sales Promotion

Firms that wish to use sales promotion have various methods from which to choose—point of purchase advertising; specialty advertising; trade shows; samples, coupons, and premiums; contests; and trading stamps.

More than one of these options may be used in a single promotional strategy, but probably no promotional strategy has ever used all in a single program. While they are not mutually exclusive, the promotions are generally employed on a selective basis.

Point of Purchase Advertising. Point of purchase advertising refers to displays and other promotions located near where a buying decision is actually made. The in-store promotion of consumer goods is a common example. Such advertising can be useful in supplementing a theme developed in another area of promotional strategy. A life-size display of a celebrity used in television advertising could be a very effective in-store display. Another example is the L'eggs store displays that completely altered the pantyhose industry.

Specialty Advertising. Specialty advertising is *a sales promotion medium that utilizes useful articles carrying the advertiser's name, address, and advertising message to reach the target consumers.*[26] The origin of specialty advertising has been traced to the Middle Ages, when wooden pegs bearing the names of artisans "were given to prospects to be driven into their walls and to serve as a convenient place upon which to hang armor."[27] Examples of contemporary advertising specialties carrying the firm's name include calendars, coffee mugs, pens, matchbooks, personalized business gifts of modest value, ash trays, balloons, yardsticks, and key rings. The Internal Revenue Service defines items worth less than $4 and imprinted with the name of the donor's company as advertising specialties rather than gifts. These items are not subject to the $25 per person annual business gift limitation.[28]

Advertising specialties help reinforce previous or future advertising

Gulf Metals Industries

When Gulf Metals Industries of Houston added aluminum and copper bits to its vast selection of products, the sales department sought an effective way to bring the new products to the attention of purchasing agents in the foundry industry.

The challenge was to highlight the bits so they would stand out from the rest of the company's products—as well as those of competitors—during the introduction period. The sales department turned to specialty advertising to accomplish the mission.

Playing on the idea of "two bits," Gulf Metals embedded two clusters of the new copper and aluminum bits alongside a U.S. Quarter in a clear plastic paperweight.

The highly distinctive gift-reminders were delivered either by the salesperson or through the mail. Once in the purchasing agents' offices, these conversation piece specialties served to remind the recipients again and again of the Gulf Metals sales message. An entire year's production capacity of the new metal bits was sold during the first two months of the campaign.

Source; Adapted from "Gulf Metals Finds Little Bits Count," *Specialty Advertising Report* 7, no. 3, p. 2. Reprinted by permission of Specialty Advertising Association International.

and sales messages. In one survey of recipients of such items, 59 percent of the respondents reported an enhanced image of the specialty advertiser.[29] The Gulf Metals story describes how one firm successfully employed a unique advertising specialty.

Trade Shows. To influence channel members and resellers in the distribution channel, it has become a common practice for sellers to participate in *trade shows.* These shows are often organized by an industry's trade association and may be part of the association's annual meeting or convention. Vendors serving the particular industry are invited to the show to display and demonstrate their products for the association's membership. An example is the professional meetings attended by college professors in a given discipline. Here, the major textbook publishers exhibit their offerings to the channel members in their marketing system. Shows are also used to reach the ultimate consumer. Home and recreation shows, for instance, allow businesses to display and demonstrate home care, recreation, and other consumer products to the entire community.

Samples, Coupons, and Premiums. The distribution of samples, coupons,

Premiums do not always lead to consumer satisfaction.

"So what if I am overdrawn? That toaster of yours didn't work either."

Source: *Wall Street Journal,* March 21, 1974, p. 12. © 1974. Reprinted by permission of the cartoonist, Bo Brown, and the *Wall Street Journal.*

and premiums is probably the best-known sales promotion technique. *Sampling* is the free distribution of a product in an attempt to obtain future sales for it. The distribution may be done on a door-to-door basis, by mail, via demonstrations, or by inclusion in packages containing other products. Sampling is especially useful in promoting new products.

Coupons offer a discount, usually some specified price reduction on the next purchase of a product. They are redeemable at retail outlets, which receive a handling fee. Mail, magazine, newspaper, and package insertions are the standard methods of distributing coupons.

Premiums are gift items given free with the purchase of another product. They have proved effective in getting consumers to try new products or different brands. Premiums should be related to the purchased item. For instance, the service department of a car dealership might offer its customers ice scrapers. Premiums are also used to obtain direct mail purchases. The value of premium giveaways runs into billions of dollars each year.

Contests. Firms often sponsor contests to attract additional customers, offering substantial cash or merchandise prizes to call attention to their products. In recent years, however, various rulings and legal restrictions have placed limitations on the use of contests. As a result, companies probably should employ specialists in developing this kind of sales promotion.

Trading Stamps. A sales promotion technique similar to premiums is *trading stamps.* These stamps are used to obtain a gift in addition to the product being purchased.[30] Whether the consumer benefits depends on the relative price levels of the goods offered. Trading stamps originally appeared in the last two decades of the nineteenth century. They are now distributed by grocery stores, gas stations, savings and loan associations, and mail-order houses. The extent of their usage seems to depend on factors such as relative price levels, location of redemption centers, and legal restrictions.

Public Relations

The previous chapter defined **public relations** as *the firm's communications and relationships with its various publics,* including customers, suppliers, stockholders, employees, the government, and the society in which it operates. Public relations expenditures are small relative to those for personal selling, advertising, and even sales promotion. Nonetheless, public relations does provide an efficient indirect communications channel for promoting products.

For instance, After Six, the tuxedo manufacturer, once rushed a pair of size 42 trousers to Buddy Hackett via a commercial airliner. Hackett's own pants had been ruined, and he had five nights remaining in a Gaithersburg,

Maryland, nightclub engagement. A hurried call to After Six put a company vice-president in action, and the trousers arrived a few hours later—without a bill. Buddy Hackett has voluntarily plugged After Six ever since the firm saved his act at Gaithersburg.[31]

The public relations program has broader objectives than the other aspects of promotional stategy. It is concerned with the prestige and image of all parts of the organization. Examples of nonmarketing oriented public relations objectives are a company's attempt to gain favorable public opinion during a long strike and an open letter to Congress published in a newspaper during congressional debate on a bill affecting a particular industry. While public relations departments are not always located in the marketing organization, their activities do have an impact on promotional strategy.

Publicity

The part of public relations that is most directly related to promoting a company's products or services is **publicity.** Since it is designed to familiarize the general public with a product's characteristics and advantages, publicity is an information activity of public relations.

Some publicity is used to promote a company's image or viewpoint, but a significant amount provides information about products, particularly new ones. Publicity releases covering products are typically sent to media editors for possible inclusion in news stories. Many consumers accept information in a news story more readily than they accept it in an advertisement.

Publicity releases are sometimes used to fill voids in a publication and other times are used in regular features. In either case, publicity releases are a valuable supplement to advertising.

Some critics have asserted that the publication of product publicity is directly related to the amount of advertising revenue coming from a firm. But this is not the case at most respected newspapers and magazines. The story is told that some years ago a Greyhound executive was enraged at a cartoon appearing in a Chicago newspaper that told of a character having numerous problems on a bus trip. The executive threatened to cancel future advertisements in the newspaper unless the cartoon strip was stopped or changed immediately. The newspaper's curt reply was, "One more such communication from you and the alternative of withdrawing your advertising will no longer rest with . . . Greyhound."[32]

Today, public relations has to be considered an integral part of promotional strategy even though its basic objectives extend far beyond just attempting to influence the purchase of a particular good. Public relations programs—and especially their publicity—make a significant contribution to the achievement of promotional goals.

Summary

Advertising, sales promotion, and public relations—the nonpersonal selling elements of promotion—are not twentieth century phenomena. Advertising, for instance, can trace its origin to very early times. Today, these elements of promotion have gained professional status and are vital aspects of the business scene.

Advertising, a nonpersonal sales presentation usually directed to a large number of potential customers, seeks to achieve communications goals rather than direct sales objectives. It strives to inform, persuade, and remind potential consumers of the product or service being promoted.

Advertising planning starts with good research, which permits the development of a strategy. Tactical decisions about copy and scheduling are then made. Finally, advertisements are evaluated, and appropriate feedback is provided to management. There are six basic types of advertising: (1) informative product advertising, (2) persuasive product advertising, (3) reminder oriented product advertising, (4) informative institutional advertising, (5) persuasive institutional advertising, and (6) reminder oriented institutional advertising.

One of the most vital decisions in developing an advertising strategy is the selection of the media to be employed: For a particular marketplace, which would be the best—newspapers, magazines, television, radio, outdoor advertising, or direct mail, or a combination of all of them?

The major tasks of advertising departments are advertising research, art, copywriting, media analysis, and sales promotion. Many advertisers use independent advertising agencies to provide them with the creativity and objectivity missing in their own organizations and to reduce the cost of advertising. The final step in the advertising process is developing and preparing the advertisement.

The principal methods of sales promotion are point of purchase advertising; specialty advertising; trade shows; samples, coupons, and premiums; contests; and trading stamps.

Public relations and publicity play major roles in developing promotional strategies.

Questions for Discussion

1. Explain the following terms:

advertising	posttesting
demographics	retail advertising
psychographics	cooperative advertising
positioning	sales promotion
comparative advertising	specialty advertising
product advertising	public relations
institutional advertising	publicity
pretesting	

2. Why do some firms and industries spend more than others for advertising? What generalizations can you draw from Tables 13–1 and 13–2?

3. Trace the historical development of advertising.

4.   Describe the objectives or goals of advertising.
5.   Discuss the process of advertising planning.
6.   List and discuss the six basic types of advertising. Cite examples of each type.
7.   Discuss the relationship between advertising and the product life cycle.
8.   Comment on the following statement: One of the most vital decisions in developing an advertising strategy is the selection of the media to be employed.
9.   What are the advantages and disadvantages associated with using each of the advertising media?
10. Discuss the organization of the advertising function. Consider all the major activities associated with advertising.
11. Why is retail advertising so important today?
12. List and discuss the principal methods of sales promotion.
13. Pick a candidate who ran for political office during a recent election. Assume that you were in charge of advertising for this person's campaign. Develop an advertising strategy for your candidate. Select a campaign theme and the media to be employed. Finally, design an advertisement for the candidate.
14. What specialty advertising items would be appropriate for the following:
     a. an independent insurance agent
     b. a retail carpet store
     c. Bethlehem Steel Company
     d. an interior decorator
15. Several states now have government operated lotteries. How should the state agencies involved advertise their lottery tickets?
16. *Cooperative advertising* refers to a sharing of advertising costs between the retailer and the manufacturer or vendor. From society's standpoint, should this kind of advertising be prohibited on the ground that it leads to manufacturer domination of the distribution channel? Defend your answer.
17. Sweden's business practices court ordered a U.S. advertising agency and its client, a Swedish insurance company, to stop using models identified in a commercial as other people. The court decided that the practice misled buyers. What is your opinion of the Swedish ruling?
18. Research suggests that the best placement for an advertisement in a magazine or newspaper is at the beginning or end of the publication. Why is this true?
19. What do most of your friends think about the role of advertising in contemporary society? Why do you think they hold these beliefs?
20. Now that you have studied this chapter, what is your opinion of advertising and its role in contemporary society?

Notes

1.   Ellen Graham, "Advertisers Take Aim at a Neglected Market: The Working Woman," *Wall Street Journal,* July 5, 1977.
2.   Quoted in S. Watson Dunn and Arnold M. Barban, *Advertising: Its Role in Modern Marketing,* 4th ed. (Hinsdale, Ill.: Dryden Press, 1978), p. 5.
3.   Ibid., pp. 16–17.
4.   Reported in "World Ads Set at $59 Billion," *Advertising Age,* November 6, 1978, p. 43.
5.   This section follows the discussion in Dunn and Barban, *Advertising,* pp. 19–41.
6.   Leo Bogart, *Strategy in Advertising* (New York: Harcourt Brace Jovanovich, 1967), p. 1.
7.   The Burger King story is told in E. E. Norris, "Your Surefire Clue to Ad Success: Seek Out the Consumer's Problem," *Advertising Age,* March 17, 1975, p. 44.
8.   See, for example, John P. Maggard, "Positioning Revisited," *Journal of Marketing,* January 1976, pp. 63–66.
9.   "Ads Start to Take Hold in the Professions," *Business Week,* July 24, 1978, p. 124. Excellent discussions of advertising by professionals appear in Michael D. Bernacchi and Ken Kono, "The Public Interest Marketplace of Professional Service Advertising: A Case of Consumer Rights and Duties," in *Research Frontiers in Marketing: Dialogues and Directions, 1978 Educator's Conference,* ed. Subhash C. Jain (Chicago:

American Marketing Association, 1978), pp. 292–294; Ronald B. Marks and Larry P. Long, "An Empirical Investigation of the Effect of Advertising on the Demand for Legal Services," in *Proceedings of the Southern Marketing Association,* ed. Robert S. Franz, Robert M. Hopkins, and Al Toma, New Orleans, Louisiana, November 1978, pp. 119–122; John R. Darling and Donald W. Hackett, "The Advertising of Fees and Services: A Study of Contrasts between, and Similarities among, Professional Groups," *Journal of Advertising,* November 2, 1978, pp. 23–34; and Paul N. Bloom, "Advertising in the Professions: The Critical Issues," *Journal of Marketing,* July 1977, pp. 103–110.

10. This section is based on information in Aimee L. Morner, "It Pays to Knock Your Competitor," *Fortune,* February 13, 1978, pp. 104–106, 110–111. Comparative advertising is also discussed in Peter M. Ginter and Jack M. Starling, "The Comparative Advertising Controversy," *Proceedings of the Southwestern Marketing Association,* ed. John E. Swan, Robert A. Peterson, and G. Edward Kiser, 1977, p. 1; William L. Shanklin and Gerald L. Schroder, "The Effects of Comparison and Noncomparison Advertisements on Television Viewers," *Pittsburgh Business Review,* June 1978, pp. 5–8; Stephen W. Brown and Donald W. Jackson, Jr., "The Current Status of Comparative Advertising," *Arizona Business,* February 1979, pp. 3–9; V. Kanti Prasad, "Communications-Effectiveness and Comparative Advertising: A Laboratory Analysis," *Journal of Marketing Research,* May 1976, pp. 128–137; Terrell G. Williams, "An Experiment in the Effects of Comparative Advertising on Brand Awareness, Comprehension and Preference," *Southern Business Review,* Spring 1978, pp. 30–42; Charles W. Lamb, Jr., William M. Pride, and Barbara A. Pletcher, "A Taxonomy for Comparative Advertising Research," *Journal of Advertising,* November 1, 1978, pp. 43–47; and Linda Swayne and Jack Starling, "Comparative Advertising: The Retaliation Issue," *Proceedings of the Southwestern Marketing Association,* ed. Robert C. Haring, G. Edward Kiser, and Ronnie D. Whitt, Houston, Texas, 1979, pp. 89–90.

11. Morner, "It Pays to Knock Your Competitor," p. 104.

12. An interesting article is S. Prakash Sethi, "Institutional/Image Advertising and Idea/Issue Advertising as Marketing Tools: Some Public Policy Issues," *Journal of Marketing,* January 1979, pp. 68–78.

13. Ellen Graham, "The Dewar's Do'ers: Young, Ambitious, Instantly Famous," *Wall Street Journal,* August 1, 1978, pp. 1, 13.

14. Daniel Machalaba, "Municipalities Step Up Image-Building Aimed at Firms and Tourists," *Wall Street Journal,* October 4, 1977.

15. Reported in "Business Bulletin," *Wall Street Journal,* October 19, 1978, p.1.

16. The discussion of various advertising media is adapted from material in Dunn and Barban, *Advertising,* pp. 535–606. The advertising volume percentages for the four major media (newspapers, television, magazines, and radio) are reported in *Advertising Age,* November 17, 1975, p. 35.

17. Patrick Dunne, "Some Demographic Characteristics of Direct Mail Purchasers," *Baylor Business Studies,* July 1975, pp. 67–72.

18. Reported in *Direct Marketing,* October 1978, p. 6.

19. This section is based on Dunn and Barban, *Advertising,* pp. 287–310.

20. Employment in various types of advertising organizations is explored in Jack A. Gottschalk, "Industrial Advertising Management: The Gloomy Side of the 'Glamour' Business," *Fairleigh Dickinson University Business Review,* Summer 1975, pp. 20–25.

21. John E. Cooney, "Food Marketers Spend Billions Persuading Us to Buy Their Products," *Wall Street Journal,* June 24, 1977.

22. William M. Carley, "Gillette Co. Struggles as Its Rivals Slice at Fat Profit Margin," *Wall Street Journal,* February 2, 1972, p. 1.

23. This section is based on information in John Emmerling, "Want a Celebrity in Your Ad? O.K., but Watch Your Step," *Advertising Age,* November 1, 1976, pp. 63–64; "Greenbacks for Ol' Blue Eyes," *Newsweek,* October 9, 1978, p. 37; John Cooney, "Celebrities Brighten More Ad Campaigns—and Darken a Few," *Wall Street Journal,* August 15, 1978, pp. 1, 16; Charles W. Theisen, "More Stars Are Dazzling Commercials," *Detroit News,* August 17, 1978; and "Let the Steller Seller Beware," *Time,* May 22, 1978, p. 66.

24. Dunn and Barban, *Advertising,* p. 638.

25. Joseph N. Fry and Gordon H. McDougall, "Consumer Appraisal of Retail Price Advertisements," *Journal of Marketing,* July 1974, pp. 64–67.

26. This definition is adapted from *How to Play Championship Specialty Advertising* (Chicago: Specialty Advertising Association International, 1978).

27. Walter A. Gaw, *Specialty Advertising* (Chicago: Specialty Advertising Association, 1970), p.7.

28. "Reminders from the IRS," *Specialty Advertising Report* 7, no. 4, p. 4.

29. William H. Bolen, "Consumer Attitudes toward Specialty Advertising," *Atlanta Economic Review,* August 1971, p. 35. See also William H. Bolen, "Specialty Advertising: Its Effect on the Retail Image," paper presented to the Southwestern Federation of Administrative Disciplines, Houston, Texas, March 6–8, 1975.

30. Trading stamps are discussed in Louis E. Boone, James C. Johnson, and George P. Ferry, "Trading Stamps: Their Role in Today's Marketplace," *Journal of the Academy of Marketing Science,* Winter/ Spring, 1978, pp. 70–76.

31. Buddy Hackett's experience is described in Urban C. Lehner, "Tuxedo Firm Thrives by Promoting Apparel That Most Men Dislike," *Wall Street Journal,* October 14, 1975, pp. 1, 21.

32. Gene Harlan and Alan Scott, *Contemporary Public Relations: Principles and Cases* (Englewood Cliffs, N.J.: Prentice-Hall, 1955), p. 36.

CHAPTER 14
ELEMENTS OF
PROMOTIONAL STRATEGY:
PERSONAL SELLING

Key Terms

personal selling
missionary sales
prospecting
qualifying
presentation
canned approach
closing

follow-up
selling up
suggestion selling
sales management
commissions
salaries
quota

Learning Goals

1. To explain the three basic sales tasks: order processing, creative selling, and missionary sales.
2. To describe the sales process.
3. To differentiate retail selling from field selling.
4. To examine the roles and tasks of the sales manager.

14

The firm's engineering department had a problem. Its engineers required welding specifications and related information for welding a low-carbon, heat-treated tubing to a material that was thought to be incompatible with the tubing. When none of the engineers could come up with the solution, someone suggested contacting H. L. Tyree, a salesman for Bass-Saunders, a wholesaler of pipes, valves, and fittings. Tyree promptly solved the engineering dilemma. He also showed the same customer how to save $30,000, cut waiting time by over 60 percent, and improve quality by switching from a foreign to a domestic valve. Sales professionalism of this caliber led *Purchasing* magazine to choose Tyree as one of the nation's ten leading salespeople.[1] Salespeople like Tyree are an important ingredient of any firm's marketing mix.

This chapter will examine how personal selling is employed in contemporary marketing. **Personal selling** was defined in Chapter 12 as *a seller's promotional presentation conducted on a person-to-person basis with the buyer.* It is an inherent function of any business enterprise. Accounting, engineering, personnel management, and other organizational activities are useless unless the firm's product can be sold to someone. Millions of sales employees bear witness to selling's importance in the U.S. economy.

Evolution of Personal Selling[2]

Selling has been a standard part of business for thousands of years. The earliest peddlers were traders who had some type of ownership interest in the goods they sold after manufacturing or importing them. In many cases, selling was viewed as a secondary industry for these people.

Later, selling became a separate function. The peddlers of the eighteenth century sold to the farmers, planters, and settlers of the vast North American continent. In the nineteenth century, salespeople called "drummers" sold to both consumers and marketing intermediaries. These early sellers sometimes employed questionable sales practices and techniques and earned an undesirable reputation for themselves and their firms.

Some of this negative stereotype remains today.[3] But for the most part, selling is far different from what it was in the early years. The sales job has evolved into a professional occupation. Today's salesperson is more concerned with helping customers select the right product than with simply selling whatever is available. Modern professional salespeople advise and assist customers in their purchase decisions. Where repeat purchases are common, the salesperson must be certain that the buyers' purchases are in their best interests or else no future sales will be made. The interests of the seller are thus tied to those of the buyer.

Sales Tasks

Not all selling activities are alike. While all sales activities assist the customer in some manner, the exact types of activities performed vary from one position to another.[4] Nonetheless, three basic sales tasks can be identified: order processing, creative selling, and missionary selling.

While these tasks can form the basis for a sales classification system, most salespeople do not fit into any single category. Instead, they often perform all three tasks to a certain extent. A sales engineer for a computer firm may spend 50 percent of the time at missionary sales, 45 percent at creative sales, and 5 percent at order processing. Most salespeople engage in a variety of sales activities, even though a sales job may be classified on the basis of the primary selling task.

Order Processing

Selling at the wholesale and retail levels is often characterized by *order processing.* Sales people who handle this task:

1. *Identify customer needs.* A hosiery salesperson may determine that an in-store display should be restocked.
2. *Point out the need to the customer.* The salesperson may inform the store manager of the hosiery situation.
3. *Complete the order.* The store manager may acknowledge the inventory need, and the salesperson may fill the display.

Order processing, which is part of most selling jobs, becomes the primary task where needs can be readily identified by the salesperson and acknowledged by the customer. Route drivers, rack jobbers, and many retail sales personnel are examples of sellers primarily involved in order processing.

Creative Selling

Some purchases require considerable review and analysis by prospective buyers, and the salesperson must skillfully solicit orders from such prospects. To do so, creative selling techniques must be used. New products, for example, often require a high degree of creative selling. The seller must persuade the buyer of the worth of the item.

Missionary Sales

Missionary sales are an indirect type of selling; *people who handle them sell the goodwill of a firm, often by providing the customer with product use assistance.* The maintenance of goodwill has always been an important sales function. In recent times, product use assistance such as that provided by a systems specialist has become a critical part of missionary selling.

Detailers are the missionary salespeople of the health care industry.[5] They do not sell drugs, medicines, and the like to patients but instead concentrate their efforts on intermediaries like physicians and hospitals. Detailers attempt to get medical practitioners to use their products when prescribing treatment. Detailers are an important source of product information in the health care industry. Their employers—the manufacturers and distributors—depend on them to keep the goodwill of physicians, nurses, and medical technicians.

The Qualities of a Successful Salesperson

Selling is not an easy job; it involves a great deal of practice and hard work. While some individuals adapt to selling more easily than others, most people have some degree of sales ability. Each of us is called upon to sell others on our ideas, philosophies, or personalities at some time.

As Table 14–1 indicates, one survey of top-ranking sales executives found that enthusiasm was the most important quality in new salespeople. Being "well organized" and possessing "obvious ambition" were ranked second and third by these marketers. "Apparent sociability" was ranked last, in marked contrast to many of the myths surrounding sales.

Effective salespersons are self-motivated individuals who are well prepared to meet the demands of the competitive marketplace. The continuing pressure to solve buyers' problems requires that salespeople exhibit considerable enthusiasm and self-motivation. Bob Hutton, a salesman for Capp Homes—a maker of "finish-it-yourself" houses—puts it this way: "Any job I've ever had, I couldn't stand it if I wasn't the best. The harder it is, the better I like it."[6]

Women in Selling. The sales field offers excellent career opportunities to women. Selling has been a nontraditional occupation for women, but the field is opening rapidly. Marcia Davis is one example of a woman who has found success in one of the toughest of all sales fields—retail automobile

Table 14–1
Desirable Attributes in New Sales Personnel

Rank	Attribute
1	Enthusiasm
2	Organization
3	Obvious ambition
4	High persuasiveness
5	General sales experience
6	High verbal skill
7	Specific sales experience
8	High recommendation
9	Following of instructions
10	Apparent sociability

Source: Adapted from Stan Mose, "What Sales Executives Look for in New Salespeople," *Sales & Marketing Management,* March 1978, p. 47. Reprinted by permission from *Sales & Marketing Management* magazine. Copyright 1978.

sales. After her divorce, Davis went to work for the post office. She later left to enter selling—first in real estate, then insurance. Now she sells Hondas, Audis, Mercedes, Porsches, and Volkswagens for Wood Motors in Detroit. Davis reports, "I really think I've found my niche."[7]

Considerable research has been done on women in selling.[8] While the evidence is often confusing and contradictory, the general conclusions are that this is an area in transition and that considerable opportunities for women now exist in field selling. Traditional biases and misconceptions are disappearing as more and more women prove themselves in sales.

Feedback: The Responsibility of Every Salesperson

There is one function that all sales personnel perform—providing sales intelligence to the marketing organization. Chapter 12 noted that field sales reports were part of the feedback generated within the marketing system. Since the sales force is in continuing contact with the market, it is often the best and most reliable source of the current marketing information upon which management decisions are based.[9]

The marketing intelligence provided by field sales personnel is varied. Salespeople can supply timely, current assessments of competitive efforts, new product launches, customer reactions, and the like. Marketing executives should nurture these valuable sources of information.

Sales personnel must be thoroughly familiar with the policies and internal operations of their company. Nothing is more embarrassing than a customer who knows more than the salesperson about how the company operates. Successful sales representatives are experts in their field. Knowledge of the customer is also extremely important in effective selling. Good salespeople keep accurate written records on their customers and update and review them periodically.

The salesperson's knowledge must extend to competitors and their products. Both the strengths and the weaknesses of the competition must be known.

Salespeople should know their own strengths and weaknesses. They should make a periodic critical assessment of their attitudes, temperament, and ability. They should objectively evaluate their own sales record and make necessary corrections.

A knowledgeable salesperson must also be able to plan work schedules, selling strategies, and presentations. Good planning allows the representative to budget selling time effectively. Setting sales objectives is another critical aspect of sales planning. The objectives should flow logically from the goals of the sales force, which should in turn be a function of the organization's overall objectives. As Figure 14–1 reveals, all marketing, sales force, and individual goals must be based on the general organizational objectives.

**Figure 14–1
Hierarchy of
Objectives**

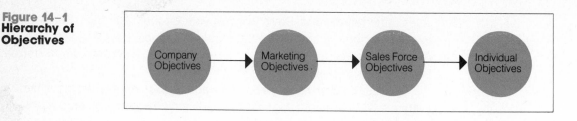

The Sales Process

What, then, are the steps involved in selling? While the terminology may vary, most authorities agree on the following sequence: (1) prospecting and qualifying, (2) approach, (3) presentation, (4) demonstration, (5) handling of objections, (6) closing, and (7) follow-up.

Prospecting and Qualifying

The identifying of potential customers, which in sales parlance is called **prospecting,** is difficult work that involves many hours of diligent effort.[10] Prospects may come from many sources: previous customers, friends, other vendors, and suppliers, among others. New sales personnel often find prospecting frustrating, since there is usually no immediate payback. But there are also no future sales unless the salesperson begins prospecting. Many sales management experts consider prospecting the very essence of the sales process. Certainly, it is the source of most customers.

Prospecting is crucial in selling.

Source: Reprinted by permission. ©1978 NEA, Inc.

Qualifying—*determining that the prospect is really a potential customer*—is another important sales task. As Chapter 4 pointed out, qualified customers are people with both money and the authority to make purchase decisions. A person may wish to embark on an around-the-world trip, but the person's financial position may make the trip unlikely. Similarly, a child may desire the latest toy but may lack the authority or the funds to make such a purchase.

Approach

Once the salesperson has identified a bona fide prospect, he or she should collect all available information about the potential buyer and plan an *approach*—the initial contact of the salesperson with the prospective customer. Approaches can vary. Some will be aggressive and some very low key, but all should be based on comprehensive research. The salesperson should find out as much as possible about the prospect. Retail salespeople often cannot do this, but they can compensate by asking leading questions to get a feel for the prospect's purchase preferences. Industrial marketers have far more data available, and they should make use of it before scheduling the first interview.

Presentation

When the salesperson gives the sales message to a prospective customer, he or she makes a *presentation*. The **presentation** *describes the product's major features and relates them to the customer's problems or welfare.* The seller's objective is to talk about the product or service in terms meaningful to the buyer—benefits rather than technical specifications. The presentation is thus the stage where the salesperson relates product features to customer needs.

The presentation should be clear, concise, and positive. One type of presentation is the canned approach, developed in the late 1800s by John H. Patterson of National Cash Register Company. The **canned approach** is *a memorized sales talk used to ensure uniform coverage of the points deemed important by management.*[11] While canned presentations are still used in such areas as door-to-door cold canvassing, most professional sales forces have long since abandoned their use. The prevailing attitude is that the salesperson should be allowed to take account of differences among prospects. Proper planning is an important part of tailoring the presentation to the customer.

Demonstration

Demonstration plays a critical role in a sales presentation. A demonstration ride in a new automobile, for example, allows the prospect to become involved in the presentation of the car. Demonstrations awaken customer interest in a manner that no amount of verbal presentation can achieve. They add to and highlight what the sales representative has already told the prospect. The key to a good demonstration is planning. A unique demonstration is more likely to gain a customer's attention than is the usual kind of sales presentation. A demonstration must also be well planned and executed if a favorable impression is to be made. The importance of planning cannot be overemphasized.

Handling Objections

A vital part of selling involves handling objections. It is reasonable to expect a customer to say "well, I really should check with my wife" or "perhaps I'll stop back next week" or "I like everything except the price." A good salesperson uses each objection as an opportunity to provide additional information to the prospect. In most cases, an objection such as "I don't like the bench-type seats" is really the prospect's way of asking what other choices or product features are available. Customers' questions generally reveal their interest in the product and allow the seller a chance to provide more information.

Closing

The moment of truth in selling is the **closing,** for this is *when the salesperson asks the prospect to conclude the purchase.* The sales representative should not hesitate during the closing. If he or she has made an effective presentation, the closing should be the natural culmination of the process.

The number of salespeople who have difficulty actually asking for an order is surprising. But to be effective, they must overcome the difficulty. Following are some basic techniques for closing a sale:

1. The *alternative-decision technique* poses choices to the prospect that are all favorable to the salesperson.
2. The *SRO (standing room only) technique* involves telling the prospect that the sales agreement should be concluded immediately because the product may not be available later.
3. *Emotional closes* attempt to get the prospect to buy through appeal to such factors as fear, pride, romance, or social acceptance.
4. *Silence* is another closing technique, since the discontinuance of a sales presentation forces the prospect to take some type of action (either positive or negative).
5. *Extra-inducement closes* are also designed to motivate a favorable buyer response. The extra inducements may include quantity discounts, special servicing arrangements, or a layaway option.[12]

Follow-up

The post-sales activities that often determine whether a person will become a repeat customer *constitute the sales* **follow-up.** To the greatest extent possible, sales representatives should contact their customers to determine if they are satisfied with the purchase. This step allows the salesperson to reinforce the purchaser's original decision to buy. It also gives the seller an opportunity to deal with any sources of discontent about the purchase, to secure important market information, and to make additional sales. Major appliance dealers sometimes keep elaborate records on their customers so they can promote new products to people who have already shown a willingness to buy from them.

Effective follow-up is a logical part of the selling sequence. As part of it, the salesperson should evaluate every call made to purchasers. Assessing sales successes and failures can help improve sales effectiveness.

Retail Selling

For the most part, the public is more aware of retail selling than of any other form of personal selling. In fact, many writers have argued that people's basic attitudes toward the sales function are determined by their impression of retail sales personnel.[13]

Retail selling has some distinctive features that require its consideration separately from other forms. The most significant difference between it and its counterparts is that the customer comes to the retail salesperson. This requires that retailers effectively combine selling with a good advertising and sales promotion program—one that will draw customers into the store. Another difference is that while, in one sense, store employees are sales personnel, they are also retailers in the broader dimension. Selling is not their only responsibility.

Retail sales personnel should be well versed in store policy and procedures. Credit, discounts, special sales, delivery, layaway, and return policies are examples of the type of information the salesperson should know. Uninformed salespeople are a major complaint of today's customer.

Two selling techniques particularly applicable to retailing are selling up and suggestion selling. **Selling up** is *the technique of convincing the customer to buy a higher priced item than he or she originally intended to buy.* An automobile salesperson, for example, may convince a consumer to buy a more expensive model car than the person originally wanted. The practice of selling up should always be used within the constraint of the customer's real needs. Many times, the salesperson can demonstrate that the more expensive item will better fit the customer's needs. If the salesperson sells the customer something that he or she really does not need, the potential for repeat sales to that customer is substantially diminished.

Suggestion selling *seeks to broaden the customer's original purchase with related items, special promotions, and holiday or seasonal merchandise.* Here too the sales efforts should be based on the idea of helping the customer recognize his or her needs rather than on selling the person unwanted merchandise. Suggestion selling is one of the best methods of increasing retail sales and should be practiced by all sales personnel.

Sales Management

Contemporary selling requires **sales management**—*the management activities of securing, maintaining, motivating, supervising, evaluating, and* *controlling an effective sales force.* As Figure 14–2 shows, sales management can be divided into several administrative levels, often on a geographical basis. For instance, field sales personnel may report to a district sales manager, who reports to a regional sales manager, who reports to a general sales manager. The chief sales executive then reports to general marketing management, such as a vice-president of marketing.

Sales management is the administrative channel for sales personnel; it links the individual salespersons to general management. The sales manager performs six basic managerial functions: (1) recruitment and selection, (2) training, (3) organization, (4) supervision, (5) compensation, and (6) evaluation and control.

Recruitment and Selection

The initial step in building an effective sales force involves recruiting and selecting good personnel.[14] New salespeople may come from community colleges, trade and business schools, colleges and universities, and other firms.

A successful career in sales offers several opportunities that people generally look for when deciding on a profession:

1. *Opportunity for advancement.* Successful sales representatives advance rapidly in most companies. Advancement can come either within the sales area or in some other functional area of the firm.
2. *High earnings.* The earnings of successful salespeople compare favorably to the earnings of successful people in other professions. In fact, over the long run, sales earnings usually exceed those of most other professional occupations.
3. *Security.* Contrary to what many college students believe, selling provides a high degree of job security. There is a continuing need for good sales personnel, and thousands of openings exist annually for those who want to enter the competitive sales arena.
4. *Independence and variety.* Most often, salespersons really operate as "independent" businesspeople or as managers of sales territories. Their work is varied and provides an opportunity for involvement in numerous business functions.

The careful selection of salespeople is important because it requires sub-

Figure 14–2
Typical Sales Management Organization

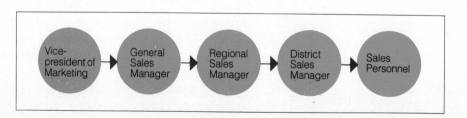

stantial amounts of money and management time and because mistakes will be detrimental to customer relations and sales force performance as well as costly to correct. Sales managers use several tools in selecting new sales personnel. A study of eighty-four large industrial firms reported their rankings of selection tools on the basis of helpfulness in selecting salespeople, order of use in the selection process, and relative cost. These rankings are summarized in Table 14–2.

Interviews were considered the most helpful selection tool despite the fact that they were the most costly. They were second in the order of use in the selection process, following completion of application forms. In contrast, references and intelligence, aptitude, and personality tests received relatively poor scores in terms of helpfulness.

Training

To shape new sales recruits into an efficient sales force, management must conduct an effective training program. The principal methods used in such programs are lectures, role playing, on-the-job training, training films, and experiential exercises.

Sales training is also important for veteran salespeople. Most of this type of training is done in an informal manner by sales managers. A standard format is for the sales manager to travel with a field sales representative periodically, then critique the person's work afterwards. Sales meetings are also an important part of training for experienced personnel.

Organization

Sales managers are responsible for the organization of the field sales force. General organizational alignments, which are usually made by top management, can be based on geography, products, customers, or some combination of these factors. A geographical organization might be set up like the one in Figure 14–2. A product sales organization would have specialized sales forces for each major category of products offered by the firm. A customer organization would use different sales forces for each major type of customer served. For instance, a plastics manufacturer selling to the auto-

---

Table 14–2
Rankings of Selection Tools on Helpfulness, Order of Use, and Relative Cost

Selection Tool	Rankings on		
	Helpfulness	Order of Use	Relative Cost
Interviews	1	2.0	1.0
Application blanks	2	1.0	6.5
Physical exams	3	6.5	2.0
References	4	4.5	6.5
Intelligence tests	5	3.0	3.5
Aptitude tests	6	4.5	3.5
Personality tests	7	6.5	5.0

Source: Thomas R. Wotruba, "An Analysis of the Salesmen Selection Process," *Southern Journal of Business,* January 1970, p. 47. Reprinted by permission.

mobile, small appliance, and defense industries might decide that each type of customer requires a separate sales force.

The individual sales manager then has the task of organizing the sales territories within his or her area of responsibility. Generally, the territory allocation decision should be based on company objectives, personnel qualifications, and equality of workloads.[15]

Supervision

A constant source of debate among sales managers is the supervision of the sales force. It is impossible to pinpoint the exact amount of supervision that is right for each situation, since the amount varies with the individuals involved. Sales personnel are generally self-motivated persons who require only moderate supervision. Sales management must therefore be willing to provide helpful advice, encouragement, and discipline only when necessary.

The key to good supervision seems to be open communication with the sales force. This, of course, involves effective listening on the part of the sales manager. Sales personnel who clearly understand messages from management and who have an opportunity to express their concerns and opinions to their supervisors are usually easy to supervise and motivate.[16]

Some sales managers are tough supervisors.

"Here's a one-way ticket. Land the order and I'll wire you return fare."

Source: Reprinted by permission of Masters Agency.

Compensation

Since monetary rewards are an important factor in motivating subordinates, compensation of sales personnel is a critical matter to managers.[17] Basically, sales compensation can be determined on either a straight salary plan, a commission plan, or some combination of the two.[18]

Commissions are *payments directly tied to the sales or profits achieved by a salesperson.* For example, a salesperson might receive a 5 percent commission on all sales up to a specified quota, then 7 percent on sales beyond the quota. Commission plans offer the following advantages:

1. The pay relates directly to performance and results achieved.
2. The system is easy to understand and compute.
3. Salespeople have the greatest possible incentive.
4. Unit sales costs are proportional to net sales.
5. The company's selling investment is reduced.

The disadvantages are:

1. Emphasis is more likely to be on volume than on profits.
2. Little or no loyalty to the company is generated.
3. Wide variations in income of sales personnel may occur.
4. Salespeople are encouraged to neglect nonselling duties.
5. Some salespeople may be tempted to "skim" their territories.
6. The service aspect of selling may be slighted.
7. Problems may arise in cutting territories or shifting people or accounts.
8. Pay is often excessive in periods of expansion and very low in recession periods.
9. Salespersons may sell themselves rather than the company and stress short-term rather than long-term relationships.
10. Highly paid salespeople may be reluctant to move into supervisory or managerial positions.
11. Excessive turnover of sales personnel may occur when business declines.

Salaries are *fixed payments made on a periodic basis to employees, including some sales personnel.* A firm that has decided to use salaries rather than commissions might pay a salesperson a set amount every other week, for example. Benefits of using salaries exist for both management and sales personnel. Among the advantages are that salaries:

1. Assure a regular income.
2. Develop a high degree of loyalty.
3. Make it simple for managers to switch territories or change quotas or reassign sales personnel.
4. Ensure that nonselling activities are performed.
5. Facilitate administration.
6. Provide relatively fixed sales costs.

Disadvantages also exist. Salaries may:

1. Fail to produce a balanced sales mix if salespeople concentrate on the products with greatest customer appeal.
2. Provide little, if any, financial incentive for sales personnel.
3. Offer few reasons for putting forth extra effort.
4. Protect the salespeople who are least productive.
5. Tend to increase direct selling costs over other types of plans.
6. Create the possibility of salary compression where new trainees earn almost as much as experienced sales personnel.

The third alternative, *combination plans,* use a base salary along with a commission incentive. For instance, a salesperson might receive $800 per month plus 2 percent commission on all sales. The benefits associated with a combination plan are:

1. It offers participants the advantages of both salary and commission.
2. It provides a greater range of earnings possibilities than does straight salary.
3. It gives salespeople greater security because of the steady base income.
4. It makes possible a favorable ratio of selling expense to sales.
5. It compensates sales personnel for all activities.
6. It allows a greater latitude of motivation possibilities so that goals and objectives can be achieved on schedule.

Disadvantages of the combination plan are:

1. It is often complex and difficult to understand.
2. When the salary is low and the bonus or commission high, the bonus may be too great a percentage of earnings; then, when sales fall, the salary may be too low to retain the sales personnel.
3. It is sometimes costly to administer.
4. It can result in a "windfall" of new accounts and runaway earnings unless there is a decreasing commission rate for increasing sales.
5. It has a tendency to offer too many objectives at one time so that important ones can be neglected, forgotten, or overlooked.

Evaluation and Control

Perhaps the most difficult of the tasks required of sales managers are evaluation and control.[19] The basic problem is in finding an instrument to measure sales performance. Sales volume, profitability, and investment return are the usual means of evaluating sales effectiveness. They typically involve the use of a **quota**—*a specified sales or profit target a salesperson is expected to achieve.* A particular sales representative might be expected to sell $300,000 in Territory 414 during a given year, for example. In many cases, the quota is tied to the compensation system. Maryland Cup is an example of a firm that has integrated its quota, evaluation, and compensation programs.

No Paper Tigers Need Apply

> Maryland Cup's sales compensation program has the same goals as its marketing program: to sell every product possible and to increase dollar volume. Full-line salespeople, who make up over three-fourths of the four hundred-person sales force, earn a salary plus a bonus on their sales over quota. Moreover, the bonus paid this year becomes the salesperson's salary increase for the next year.
>
> The hitch is that if a salesperson fails to meet his or her quota, the salary for the following year is cut accordingly. "It's a funny thing," says national sales administrator Bill Blake, "but people will work harder to avoid a cut than to get a raise." Naturally, the company wants its new salespeople to be the kind who work for raises, people who come from industries where, as Blake puts it, "if you don't close, you don't eat." Thus the company takes a hard line on hiring and firing. New salespeople are evaluated quickly; those who are not deserving of a raise within six months are let go.
>
> The company believes that the person responsible for training and supervision—the district manager—should also handle recruitment. Because of the heavy responsibility of this job, it tries to have one district manager for every seven salespeople. District managers frequently go on calls with salespeople to help them learn about the ever-growing product line. In addition, the company holds training and manpower development seminars, district and regional managers hold their own seminars, and there is an annual one-week training program for district managers.

Source: Adapted from Rayna Skolnik, "Maryland Cup's Not Just Whistlin' Dixie," *Sales & Marketing Management,* August 1978, p. 39. Reprinted by permission from *Sales & Marketing Management* magazine. Copyright 1978.

Summary

Personal selling is the seller's promotional presentation conducted on a person-to-person basis with the buyer. It is inherent to all business enterprises. The earliest sellers were known as peddlers, and some of the negative stereotyping associated with them remains today.

Three basic selling tasks exist: order processing, creative selling, and missionary selling. The successful salesperson is self-motivated and prepared to meet the demands of the competitive marketplace.

The basic steps involved in selling are (1) prospecting and qualifying, (2) approach, (3) presentation, (4) demonstration, (5) handling of objections, (6) closing, and (7) follow-up.

Retail selling is different from other kinds of selling, primarily in that the customer comes to the salesperson. Also, salespeople in stores are concerned with responsibilities other than selling. Two selling techniques particularly applicable to retailing are selling up and suggestion selling.

Sales management involves six basic functions: (1) recruitment and selection, (2) training, (3) organization, (4) supervision, (5) compensation, and (6) evaluation and control. Sales compensation can be on a straight salary plan, a commission plan, or a combination of the two. Each type of compensation has numerous advantages and disadvantages.

Questions for Discussion

1. Explain the following terms:

personal selling	follow-up
missionary sales	selling up
prospecting	suggestion selling
qualifying	sales management
presentation	commissions
canned approach	salaries
closing	quota

2. Trace the evolution of personal selling.
3. Cite examples of salespeople who are engaged primarily in performing the following sales tasks:
   a. order processing
   b. creative selling
   c. missionary selling
4. What sales tasks are involved in selling the following products:
   a. Burroughs computer equipment
   b. a fast-food franchise
   c. the United Fund to a local union meeting
   d. used cars
   e. cleaning supplies for plant maintenance
5. Identify the attributes new salespeople should have.
6. Comment on the following statement: Salespeople play a crucial role in providing management with marketing information.
7. Discuss the importance of planning to a salesperson.
8. Outline the seven basic steps involved in effective selling.
9. Develop a sales presentation for the following items.
   a. an expensive line of women's apparel
   b. a set of reference books
   c. a new Ford
   d. a group life insurance policy to the personnel director of a firm
10. What role do flight crews play in an airline's promotional effort?
11. How is retail selling different from field selling?
12. How would you describe the job of each of the following:
    a. a real estate agent
    b. a salesperson in a retail furniture store
13. Outline the basic functions of a sales manager.
14. Discuss the benefits of a sales career.
15. As marketing vice-president of a large paper company, you are asked to talk to a group of college students about selling as a career. What will you say?
16. What are the advantages and disadvantages of commission, salary, and combination compensation plans?
17. Who was the best salesperson you ever encountered? What made this person stand out?
18. There have been proposals for stringent regulations of telephone sales solicitations. What arguments can be made for and against such regulations?
19. Suppose that you are the sales manager for an office supply firm employing six salespeople who call on local firms. What type of compensation system will you employ?
20. How will you evaluate the salespeople described in Question 19?

Notes

1. Janet Key, "Tack of a Salesman's Salesman," *Chicago Tribune,* October 4, 1978.
2. This section is based on David L Kurtz, "The Historical Development of Selling," *Business and Economic Dimensions,* August 1970, pp. 12–18. A good historical account of personal selling is contained in Henry W. Nash, "Origin and Development of Personal Selling," *Mississippi Business Review,* January 1977, pp. 6–8.

3. See Conway Rucks, "It's Time for Salespeople's Lib," *Sales & Marketing Management,* March 1978, pp. 51–52, 54, 58.
4. An interesting discussion of selling is presented in Benson R. Shapiro and Ronald S. Posner, "Making the Major Sale," *Harvard Business Review,* March–April 1976, pp. 68–78.
5. Detailers are discussed in Louis J. Haugh, "Detailmen—Salesmen Who Don't Sell," *Advertising Age,* February 13, 1978, pp. 67–68, 70.
6. Quoted in James Kenyon, "Have Houses, Will Travel: Salesman's a Hard-driven Man," *Detroit News,* August 21, 1978.
7. Luther Keith, "A Woman's Touch Helps Her Sell Cars," *Detroit News,* June 12, 1978.
8. Two excellent articles on the subject of women in selling appeared in the January 1978 issue of the *Journal of Marketing:* Leslie Kanuk, "Women in Industrial Selling," pp. 87–91; and John E. Swan, Charles M. Futrell, and John T. Todd, "Same Job, Different Views: Women and Men in Industrial Sales," pp. 92–98. Also see Cecil V. Hynes, "Women in the Sales Force—Some Perceptions of Sales and Marketing Executives," *Proceedings of the Southwestern Marketing Association,* ed. John E. Swan and Robert C. Haring, Dallas, Texas, March 1978, p. 58; John E. Swan and G. E. Kiser, "Industrial Purchasers' Attitudes toward Men vs. Women as Salespeople," *Proceedings of the Southern Marketing Association,* ed. Robert S. Franz, Robert M. Hopkins, and Al Toma, New Orleans, Louisiana, November 1978, pp. 188–191; and Dan H. Robertson and Donald W. Hackett, "Saleswomen: Perceptions, Problems, and Prospects," *Journal of Marketing,* July 1977, pp. 66–71.
9. An interesting discussion of Pillsbury's computer-based salesperson reporting system and its use in implementing marketing strategies is presented in Lloyd M. Deboer and William H. Ward, "Integration of the Computer into Salesman Reporting," *Journal of Marketing,* January 1971, pp. 41–57. See also James M. Comer, "The Computer, Personal Selling, and Sales Management," *Journal of Marketing,* July 1975, pp. 27–33.
10. Some of the problems involved in prospecting are reported in Gordon L. Wise, "Automobile Salesman's Perceptions of New-Car Prospects," *Bulletin of Business Research,* February 1971, pp. 2–6.
11. This approach is discussed in Marvin A. Jolson, "The Underestimated Potential of the Canned Sales Presentation," *Journal of Marketing,* January 1975, pp. 75–78.
12. These and other closing techniques are outlined in David L. Kurtz, H. Robert Dodge, and Jay E. Klompmaker, *Professional Selling* 2d ed. (Dallas: Business Publications, 1979), pp. 202–208.
13. An interesting discussion is contained in Gilbert A. Churchill Jr., Robert H. Collins, and William A. Strang, "Should Retail Salespersons Be Similar to Their Customers?" *Journal of Retailing,* Fall 1975, pp. 29–42, 79.
14. Salesperson selection is discussed in Fred J. Krutz, W. Austin Spivey, and George D. Williams, "Validity and the Selection of Sales Personnel," *Santa Clara Business Review,* Summer 1978, pp. 13–23; Robert J. Small and Larry J. Rosenberg, "Appraising Job Performance in the Industrial Sales Force: An Application of a Partial Model," *Fairleigh Dickenson Business Review,* Fall 1976, pp. 18–25; William L. Shanklin, "Is Psychological Testing in Sales Selection Passé?" *Proceedings of the Southern Marketing Association,* ed. Henry W. Nash and Donald P. Robin, Atlanta, Georgia, November 1976, pp. 137–138.
15. Territory decisions are discussed in Michael S. Heschel, "Effective Sales Territory Development," *Journal of Marketing,* April 1977, pp. 39–43.
16. The need for positive reinforcement is pointed out in Rom J. Markin and Charles M. Lillis, "Sales Managers Get What They Expect," *Business Horizons,* June 1975, pp. 51–58.
17. An interesting discussion appears in Gilbert A. Churchill, Jr., Neil M. Ford, and Orville C. Walker, Jr., "Personal Characteristics of Salespeople and the Attractiveness of Alternative Rewards," *Journal of Business Research* 7 (1979): 25–50.
18. The advantages and disadvantages of the commission, salary, and combination plans are adapted by permission from John P. Steinbrink, "How to Pay Your Sales Force," *Harvard Business Review,* July–August 1978, p. 112. Copyright © 1978 by the President and Fellows of Harvard College; all rights reserved.
19. The need for careful evaluation is suggested in William P. Hall, "Improving Sales Force Productivity," *Business Horizons,* August 1975, pp. 32–42. See also Donald W. Jackson, Jr., and Ramon J. Aldag, "Managing the Sales Force by Objectives," *MSU Business Topics,* Spring 1974, pp. 53–59; and Porter Henry, "Manage Your Sales Force as a System," *Harvard Business Review*, March–April 1975, pp. 85–95.

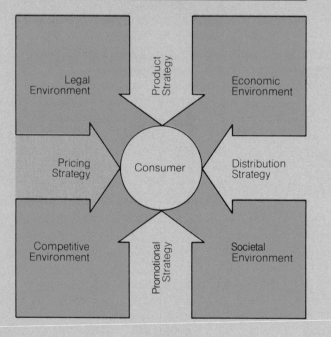

CHAPTER 15
INTRODUCTION TO PRICING

Key Terms

price
profit maximization
target return
objective
sales maximization
market share
objective
social and ethical
considerations
status quo objective
prestige goals

customary prices
pure competition
monopolistic
competition
oligopoly
monopoly
cost-plus pricing
breakeven analysis
markup
mark-on
stock turnover

Learning Goals

1. To explain the concept of price and its importance to society.
2. To identify the major pricing objectives used by firms.
3. To distinguish between price determination in theory and in practice.
4. To explain the concept of breakeven analysis
5. To show the relationship between markup and turnover.

15

Pricing, the fourth variable in the development of a marketing strategy, may be the most complex aspect of the marketing manager's job. Consider the case of International Desserts from the Kitchens of Sara Lee. When Sara Lee began test-marketing its new line, management realized that the International Desserts cakes would have to be priced about a dollar higher than its regular cheesecakes and those of its nearest competitor. Sara Lee also had to contend with the $2 barrier—the absolute limit the industry felt customers would pay for frozen bakery goods. In addition, the economy appeared to be heading for a recession. How did Sara Lee overcome these monumental problems?

The new line was test-marketed at three prices—$2.29, $1.99, and $1.89—in order to determine the correctness of the $2 barrier theory. The price differences had little impact on sales, so Sara Lee marketers chose $2.19 retail price. International Dessert's price disadvantage was occasionally reduced by the use of cents-off coupons of as much as $.60. Supported by reliable market research findings, a promotional campaign aimed at the over $25,000 income group, and an effective sales effort, International Desserts went on to become one of Sara Lee's greatest successes.[1]

The firm's experience with the new dessert line illustrates the difficulty of determining the right price for a product. But an even greater difficulty is determining the meaning of *price* and its role in society.

The Concept of Price

Price is *the exchange value of a good or service;* and the *value of an item* is what it can be exchanged for in the marketplace. In earlier times, the price of a pair of sandals might have been five yards of cloth, a piece of pottery, or two chickens. Price is a measure of what one must exchange in order to obtain a particular good or service. When the barter process was abandoned in favor of a monetary system, price became the amount of money (dollars, pesos, pounds, rubles, francs, marks) required to purchase an item.

All products have some degree of *utility*—want-satisfying power. An individual might be willing to exchange the utility derived from a color television for that of a vacation. Prices are a mechanism that allows the consumer to make such a decision. In contemporary society, of course, prices are translated into monetary terms. Consumers evaluate the utility derived from a range of possible purchases and then allocate their exchange power (in monetary terms) so as to maximize satisfaction.

The Importance of the Price Variable

Ancient philosophers recognized the importance of price to the functioning of the economic system. Some of their early written accounts refer to attempts to develop a fair, or *just,* price. Their limited understanding of time, place, and possession utilities, however, thwarted such efforts.

Today, price still serves as a means of regulating economic activity. The employment of any or all of the four factors of production (land, labor, capital, and entrepreneurship) depends on the prices received by each. For an individual firm, prices and the corresponding quantity to be sold represent the revenue to be received. Prices therefore influence a company's profit as well as its employment of the factors of production.

A widely cited 1964 study by Jon G. Udell found that executives ranked pricing sixth in a long list of factors leading to marketing success.[2] When Udell's factors are reorganized into the four major marketing mix variables, price ranks third—ahead only of distribution.

But times have changed. A 1979 study of marketing executives found that pricing ranked as the single most important marketing mix variable.[3] Product planning and management was a close second, while distribution strategy and promotional decisions ranked third and fourth, respectively. Table 15–1 compares Udell's 1964 rankings to the findings of the study conducted fifteen years later.

The question of what is the correct price to charge still remains a perplexing problem in modern marketing management. Some say it is whatever the consumer will pay. Others believe it should be low enough to permit everyone the opportunity to buy the product. The determination of market prices within the context of the contemporary business environment is the subject of this chapter. The understanding of this complex topic will be enhanced by reviewing pricing legislation in Chapter 2.

Pricing Objectives

Pricing objectives are a crucial part of the means-end chain from overall company objectives to specific pricing policies and procedures (see Figure 15–1). The goals of the firm and the marketing organization provide the basis for the development of pricing objectives, which must be clearly established before pricing policies and procedures are implemented.

A firm might have as its primary objective the goal of becoming the dominant factor in the domestic market. Its marketing objective might then be to achieve maximum sales penetration in all sales regions. The related pricing

Table 15–1
The Importance of the Pricing Variable: A Comparison of the 1964 and 1979 Studies

Rank	1964 Study[a]	1979 Study[b]
1	Product	Pricing
2	Promotion	Product
3	Pricing	Distribution
4	Distribution	Promotion

[a]Adapted from Jon G. Udell, "How Important Is Pricing in Competitive Strategy?" *Journal of Marketing*, January 1964, pp. 44–48. Reprinted from the *Journal of Marketing* published by the American Marketing Association.
[b]*Pricing Objectives and Practices in American Industry: A Research Report.* © 1979 by Louis E. Boone and David L. Kurtz; all rights reserved.

Figure 15–1
The Role of
Pricing Objectives
in Contemporary
Marketing

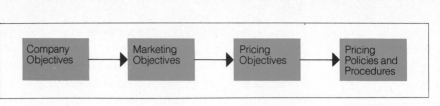

goal would be sales maximization. This means-end chain might lead to the adoption of a low-price policy implemented by the highest cash and trade discounts in the industry.

Pricing objectives can be classified into three major groups: (1) profitability objectives; (2) volume objectives; and (3) social and ethical considerations, status quo objectives, and prestige goals. Profitability objectives include profit maximization and target return goals. Volume objectives can be categorized as either sales maximization or market share goals.

As one would expect, pricing objectives vary from firm to firm. Xerox wants its earnings to grow 15 percent annually. Eaton Corporation aspires to rank either first or second in market share in each market within which it operates. Burroughs has targeted a 15 percent increase in revenue each year.[4]

A recent study of U.S. businesses asked marketers to identify both the primary and secondary pricing objectives of their companies. Meeting competitive prices was most often mentioned as a primary or secondary pricing objective. It was followed closely by two profitability oriented objectives: a specified rate of return on investment and specified total profit levels. These two objectives ranked first and second, respectively, as primary pricing objectives.[5] The findings are shown in Table 15–2.

Predatory pricing
can be disastrous.

"You said you'd ruin me, Featherson. How far do you intend to go?"

Source: Reprinted by permission of Charles Rodrigues and *Saturday Review*.

Table 15-2
Primary and Secondary Pricing Objectives of Firms

Pricing Objective	Percentage of Respondents Ranking the Item		
	As Primary Objective	As Secondary Objective	As Either Primary or Secondary Objective
Meeting of competitive price level	38.3	43.0	81.3
Specified rate of return on investment	60.9	17.2	78.1
Specified total profit level	60.2	17.2	77.4
Increased market share	31.3	42.2	73.5
Increased total profits above previous levels	34.4	37.5	71.9
Specified rate of return on sales	47.7	23.4	71.1
Retaining of existing market share	31.3	35.9	67.2
Serving of selected market segments	26.6	39.1	65.7
Creation of a readily identifiable image for the firm and/or its products	21.9	41.4	63.3
Specified market share	15.6	40.6	56.2
Other	5.5	—	5.5

Source: *Pricing Objectives and Practices in American Industry: A Research Report.* © 1979 by Louis E. Boone and David L. Kurtz; all rights reserved.

Profitability Objectives

The traditional pricing objective in classical economic theory has been that of maximizing profits.[6] The concept of microeconomics is based on certain assumptions—that buyers and sellers are rational and that rational behavior is an effort to maximize gains and minimize losses. In terms of actual business practice, this means that profit maximization is assumed to be the basic objective of individual firms.

Profits are a function of revenue and expenses:

Profits = Revenues − Expenses.

Revenue is determined by the selling price and quantity sold:

Total revenue = Price × Quantity sold.

Price should therefore be increased up to the point where it causes a disproportionate decrease in the number of units sold. A 5 percent price increase that results in only a 3 percent cut in volume adds to the firm's revenues. However, a 5 percent hike that causes a 6 percent sales decline reduces revenues.

Economists refer to this approach as *marginal analysis.* They identify **profit maximization** as *the point where the addition to total revenue is just balanced by the increase in total cost.* The basic problem is how to achieve this delicate balance between marginal revenue and marginal cost. Relatively few firms actually achieve the objective of profit maximization. A significantly larger number prefer to direct their efforts toward goals that are more reasonably implemented and measured.

Consequently, target return objectives have become common in industry, particularly among the larger firms, where public pressure typically prohibits consideration of the profit maximization objective.[7] Automobile companies are examples.[8] **Target return objectives** are *either short-run or long-run goals usually stated as a percentage of sales or investment.* A company may, for instance, seek a 15 percent annual rate of return on investment or an 8 percent rate of return on sales. A specified rate of return on investment was the most commonly reported primary pricing objective in Table 15–2. Goals of this nature also serve as useful guidelines in evaluating corporate activity. As one writer has aptly expressed it: "For management consciously accepting less than maximum profits, the target rate can provide a measure of the amount of restraint. For firms making very low profits, the target rate can serve as a standard for judging improvement."[9]

Target return objectives offer several benefits to the marketer. As noted above, they serve as a means for evaluating performance. They also are designed to generate profits judged to be fair by management, stockholders, and the general public as well.

Volume Objectives

Some writers argue that a better explanation of actual pricing behavior is William J. Baumol's belief that firms attempt to **maximize sales** within a given profit constraint.[10] In other words, they set *a minimum at what they consider the lowest acceptable profit level and then seek to maximize sales (subject to this profit constraint) in the belief that the increased sales are more important than immediate high profits to the long-run competitive picture.*[11] The companies continue to expand sales as long as their total profits do not drop below the minimum return acceptable to management.

Another pricing objective is based on the firm's **market share objective**—the goal set for *the control of a portion of the market for the firm's product.* The company's specific goal can be to maintain or increase its share of a particular market, say from 10 percent to 20 percent.[12]

Table 15–3 shows when it is best to use a pricing strategy to gain market share, how it should be applied in the marketplace, and what its cost implications are. Gaining market share is a common pricing objective in U.S. business. A firm's marketing plans must be adapted to its market share position in a particular market.[13]

Some firms with high market shares may even prefer to reduce their share at times because of the possibility of government action in the area of monopoly control. Courts have often used market share figures in their evaluation of cases involving alleged monopolistic practices.

Market share objectives can be critical to the achievement of other objectives. High sales, for example, may mean more profit. The extensive Profit Impact of Market Strategies (PIMS) project conducted by the Marketing Science Institute found a link between market share and profitability.[14] Pretax profits as a percentage of sales were 3.4 percent for firms with 10 to 20

Table 15–3
Pricing Strategy for Gaining Market Share

When to Use	How to Apply in Marketplace	Cost Implications
1. To gain a share in a product line where there is room for growth.	1. Set the general market price level below average.	1. Will lower gross margin by decreasing spread between cost and price for a period of time.
2. To gain a share in a new product, preferably in a growth market.	2. Lower prices for specific target customers where reduced prices will capture high volume accounts and where competition is vulnerable on a price basis.	2. Will lower cost as cumulative volume increases and costs move down the experience curve.
	3. Lower prices enough to keep the business.	
	4. Lower prices against specific competitors who will not or cannot react effectively.	

Source: Adapted from C. David Fogg, "Planning Gains in Market Share," *Journal of Marketing*, July 1974, pp. 30–38. Reprinted from the *Journal of Marketing* published by the American Marketing Association.

percent market shares, but they climbed steadily to 13.2 percent for firms with market shares above 40 percent.[15] Achievement of market share objectives places the firm in a much stronger competitive position within the industry.

Other Objectives

Some pricing objectives are not related to either profitability or sales volume, but they are extremely important in the pricing behavior of many firms. These objectives include (1) social and ethical considerations, (2) status quo objectives, and (3) prestige goals.

Social and ethical considerations are *the determining factors in certain pricing situations.* For years, some medical doctors used a sliding scale based on relative income to set patient fees. Essentially, these doctors used an ethical evaluation of *ability to pay* as an input into their pricing formula.

But a recent survey of physicians indicated that they were not the only sellers who priced on an ability to pay basis. Two-thirds of the physicians questioned by *Medical Economics* believed they had paid higher prices for such services as home and auto repairs because of their occupation! And only about 20 percent had complained about the alleged overcharging.[16] Social and ethical considerations are playing a larger role in the pricing policies of all marketers.

Status quo objectives—*objectives based on the maintenance of stable prices*—are the crux of the pricing philosophy for many enterprises. They usually stem from a desire to minimize competitive pricing action in order to be able to concentrate efforts in other areas of marketing, such as product improvement or promotion. For a long time, the automobile producers deemphasized price competition in their advertisements in favor of devel-

The Clenet Roadster – For Drivers Who Have Everything

Clenet Coachworks of Santa Barbara, California, is a small auto manufacturer by Detroit standards. But when it comes to pricing, Clenet is an industry leader. Its founder and president, Alain J-M Clenet—a French-born former American Motors Corporation designer—permits a production run of only 250 cars, each with its own number recorded on a silver plaque attached to the door. The current model, a handcrafted roadster, is already sold out at $67,500 per copy—even though it has never been advertised. Clenet explains: "We have discovered a microscopic market of successful, self-made business men and women who are not too well known beyond their own circles of friends and associates. The Clenet provides instant celebrity status. Everywhere the Clenet is driven, it draws attention and provides actual and vicarious recognition for the owner."

Clenet roadsters are handcrafted by a ninety person work force. Standard features include power steering, power brakes, air-conditioning, cruise control, automatic transmission, AM-FM stereo radio, English leather upholstery, English carpeting, a solid walnut dashboard, hand rubbed paint, teakwood body accents, and a leather-wrapped steering wheel.

After production of the roadster is completed, Clenet plans to produce five hundred four-passenger convertibles.

Source: Adapted by permission from Charles W. Theisen, "No Advertising Needed to Sell Out Clenet Roadster," *Detroit News,* July 26, 1978. Updated information provided by Clenet Coachworks. Photo courtesy of Clenet Coachworks.

oping features that differentiated their products from competitors'. Even today, status quo objectives remain a significant factor in pricing.

Prestige goals—*goals based on setting relatively high prices so as to maintain a quality image*—are another type of objective unrelated to either profitability or sales volume. While some marketers set relatively high prices so as to maintain a prestige image with their consumers, others prefer to have a "low-price" image among customers.

How Are Prices Determined?	There are two ways to look at the determination of price: (1) theoretical concepts of supply and demand and (2) the cost oriented approach that characterizes current business practice. During the first part of this century, most considerations of price determination emphasized the classical concepts of supply and demand. Since World War II, the emphasis has shifted to a cost oriented approach. Hindsight allows us to see that both concepts have certain flaws.

Another aspect of price determination is often overlooked. *Custom, tradition, and social habit* also play an important role in price determination. Numerous examples of **customary,** or *traditional,* **prices** exist. The candy makers' attempt to hold the line on the traditional five-cent candy bar led to considerable reductions in the size of the product. Eventually, almost all vending machines were supplied with larger ten-cent bars, and the shrinking process began again. Similar practices have prevailed in the marketing of soft drinks. There has been a reduction in the number of first-class seats on some airplanes, and the amount of leg room has been cut for some coach seats.[17]

A slightly different approach was taken by Hershey Food Corporation in late 1978. Hershey raised its price and size simultaneously. Cost increases for raw materials forced Hershey to increase the price of its candy bar from twenty cents to twenty-five cents. At the same time, the company increased the product's weight from 1.05 ounces to 1.2 ounces. The 14.3 percent size increase partially compensated for the 25 percent price increase for the long-time favorite candy.[18]

The division of the U.S. beer market into *premium* and *popular* price levels is another example of a traditional pricing system. In the 1930s several major brewers were faced with excess capacity that could not be absorbed by their local markets. These brewers began to ship their product to distant markets. The freight charges were covered by retail prices higher than those charged for local beers. And the higher prices were justified by the marketers' claims that their beers were of higher quality than the local beers. The "imports," classified as premium by their marketers, often actually were better than the numerous local brands. Today, any quality differences among beers are probably slight, and there is little difference in the production costs of premium and popular beer. However, the traditional pricing system continues to exist.[19]

At some point in time, someone had to set *initial* prices for products. Sustained inflation has also created a need for periodically reviewing firms' price structures. The rest of this chapter will discuss the traditional and current concepts of price determination. It will also raise the question of how best to tie the concepts together in order to develop a realistic approach to pricing.

Price Determination in Economic Theory

The microeconomic approach to price determination assumes a profit maximization objective and leads to the derivation of correct equilibrium prices in the marketplace. It considers both supply and demand factors and is therefore a more complete analysis than that typically used by business firms.

There are four types of market structures: pure competition, monopolistic competition, oligopoly, and monopoly. **Pure competition** is *a market structure in which there are such a large number of buyers and sellers that none of them has a significant influence on price.* Other characteristics of pure competition are *a homogeneous product and an ease of entry for sellers that results from low start-up costs.* The closest examples of this marketing structure exist in the agricultural sector.

Monopolistic competition, which typifies most retailing, *is a market*

Some prices change very quickly.

"Well, it may have been 68 cents when you got in line, but it's 74 cents now!"

structure with large numbers of buyers and sellers. However, it involves a heterogeneous product and product differentiation that allow the marketer some degree of control over prices. In **oligopolies,** *there are relatively few sellers; and, because of high start-up costs, there are significant entry barriers to new competitors.* Oligopolies occur frequently in the automobile, steel, tobacco, and petroleum refining industries. **Monopolies** *are market structures with only one seller of a product and no close substitutes for it.*

Antitrust legislation has nearly eliminated all but temporary monopolies such as those provided by patent protection and regulated monopolies such as the public service companies—telephone, electric, and gas utilities. Regulated monopolies are allowed by government in markets where competition would lead to an uneconomic duplication of services. In return for this license, government reserves the right to regulate the monopoly's rate of return.

The demand side of price theory is concerned with revenue curves. *Average revenue (AR) is obtained by dividing total revenue (TR) by the quantity (Q) associated with these revenues:*

$$AR = \frac{TR}{Q}$$

The average revenue line is actually the demand curve facing the firm. *Marginal revenue (MR) is the change in total revenue (ΔTR) that results from selling an additional unit of output (ΔQ):*

$$MR = \frac{\Delta TR}{\Delta Q}$$

The demand curves—average revenue lines—and marginal revenue curves for each market are shown later in the chapter in Figure 15–3.

Average cost (AC) is obtained by dividing total costs (TC) by the quantity (Q) associated with these costs:

$$AC = \frac{TC}{Q}$$

Total costs are composed of both fixed and variable components. *Fixed costs (FC)* are costs that do not vary with differences in output, while *variable costs (VC)* are those that change when the level of production is altered. Examples of fixed costs are executive compensation, depreciation, and insurance. Variable costs include raw materials and the wages paid operative employees.

Average variable cost (AVC) is simply the total variable costs (TVC) divided by the related quantity (Q):

$$AVC = \frac{TVC}{Q}$$

Figure 15–2
Cost Curves

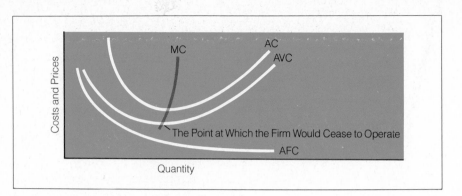

Similarly, *average fixed cost (AFC)* is determined by dividing *total fixed costs (TFC)* by the related quantity (Q):

$$AFC = \frac{TFC}{Q}$$

Marginal cost (MC) is the change in total cost (ΔTC) that results from producing an additional unit of output (ΔQ):

$$MC = \frac{\Delta TC}{\Delta Q}$$

Marginal costs are therefore similar to marginal revenue—the change in total revenue resulting from the production of an incremental unit. The point of profit maximization is where marginal costs are equal to marginal revenues. The cost curves of the equations shown above appear in Figure 15–2. The marginal cost (MC) curve intersects the average variable cost (AVC) curve and average cost (AC) curve at the minimum points.

In the short run, a firm will continue to operate even if the price falls below AC, provided it remains above AVC. Why is this rational market behavior? If the firm were to cease operations after the price fell below AC, it would still have some fixed costs, but it would have *no* revenue. Any amount received above AVC can be used to cover at least part of the fixed costs. The manager is acting rationally by continuing to produce as long as price exceeds AVC, since this minimizes losses. If price falls below AVC, the manager should cease operations because continued operation begins to maximize losses. The *supply curve,* therefore, is the marginal cost curve above its intersection with AVC, since this is the area of rational pricing behavior for the firm.

How are prices set in each of the product market situations? Figure 15–3 shows how prices are determined in each of the four product markets. The point of profit maximization (MC = MR) sets the equilibrium output (Point A), which is extended to the AR line to set the equilibrium price (Point

Figure 15–3
Price Determination in the Four Product Markets

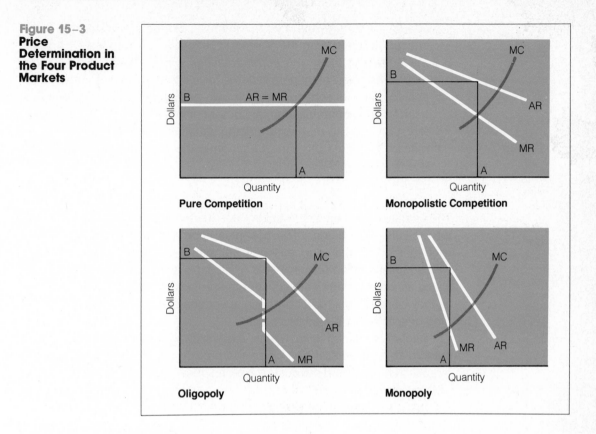

B). In the case of pure competition, AR = MR, so price is a predetermined variable in this product market.[20]

Practical Problems in Applying Price Theory

From the viewpoint of the marketer, price theory concepts are sometimes difficult to apply in practice. What, then, are their practical limitations?

1. *Many firms do not attempt to maximize profits.* Economic analysis is subject to the same limitations as the assumptions on which it is based—for example, the proposition that all firms attempt to maximize profits.

2. *It is difficult to estimate demand curves.* Modern accounting procedures provide managers with a clear understanding of cost structures. The managers can therefore readily comprehend the supply side of the pricing equation. But it is difficult to estimate demand at various price levels. Demand curves must be based on market research estimates that are often not as exact as cost figures. Over time, however, these problems may be eliminated by the use of advanced research meth-

odology. Although the demand element can be identified, it is often difficult to measure in the real world setting.[21]

3. *Inadequate training and communication hinders price theory in the real world.* Many managers lack the formal training in economics to be able to apply its concepts to their own pricing decisions. On the other hand, many economists remain essentially theorists, devoting little interest or effort to real world pricing situations. This dual problem significantly hinders the use of economic theory in actual pricing practice.[22]

Price Determination in Practice

The practical limitations inherent in price theory have forced practitioners to turn to other techniques. The cost-plus approach is the most commonly used method of setting prices today. For many years, government contracts with suppliers called for payments of all expenses plus a set profit usually stated as a percentage of the cost of the project. These *cost-plus contracts,* as they were known, have now been abandoned in favor of competitive bidding or specifically negotiated prices.

Cost-plus pricing *takes some base cost figure per unit and adds a markup to cover unassigned costs and provide a profit.*[23] The only real difference in the multitude of cost-plus techniques is the relative sophistication of the costing procedures employed. For example, a local apparel shop may set prices by adding a 40 percent markup to the invoice price charged by the supplier. The markup is expected to cover all other expenses and permit the owner to earn a reasonable return on the sale of the clothes.

In contrast to this rather simple pricing mechanism, a large manufacturer may employ a pricing formula that requires a computer to handle the necessary calculations. But while the advanced calculations are for a sophisticated costing procedure, in the end, the formula still requires someone to make a decision about the markup. The apparel shop and the large manufacturer may be vastly different with respect to the *cost* aspect, but they are remarkably similar when it comes to the *plus* (markup) side of the equation.

This discussion demonstrates one of the problems associated with cost oriented pricing: "Costs do not determine prices, since the proper function of cost in pricing is to determine the profit consequences of pricing alternatives."[24] Unfortunately, this point is not always understood by marketers.

The two most common cost oriented pricing procedures are the full cost method and the incremental cost method. *Full cost pricing* uses all relevant variable costs in setting a product's price. In addition, it allocates the fixed costs that cannot be directly attributed to the production of the specific item being priced. Under the full cost method, if job order 515 in a printing plant amounts to 0.000127 percent of the plant's total output, then 0.000127 percent of the firm's *overhead* expenses are allocated to that job. This approach allows the pricer to recover all costs plus the amount added as a profit margin.

The full cost approach has two basic deficiencies. First, there is no consideration of the demand for the item or its competition. Perhaps no one wants to pay the price the firm has calculated! Second, any method of allocating overhead (fixed expenses) is arbitrary and may be unrealistic. In manufacturing, overhead allocations are often tied to *direct labor hours.* In retailing, the mechanism is sometimes *square footage* of each profit center. Regardless of the technique, it is difficult to show a cause-effect relationship between the *allocated* cost and most products.

One way to overcome the arbitrary allocation of fixed expenses is by *incremental cost pricing,* which attempts to *use only those costs directly attributable to a specific output in setting prices.* For example, consider a small manufacturer with the following income statement:

Sales (10,000 units at $10)		$100,000
Expenses:		
Variable	$50,000	
Fixed	40,000	90,000
Net profit		$ 10,000

Suppose the firm is offered a contract for an additional 5,000 units. Since the peak season is over, these items can be produced at the same average variable cost. Assume that the labor force would be idle otherwise. In order to get the contract, how low could the firm price its product?

Under the full cost approach, the lowest price would be $9 per unit. This figure is obtained by dividing the $90,000 in expenses by an output of 10,000 units.

The incremental approach, on the other hand, could permit a price of $5.10, which would significantly increase the possibility of securing the additional contract. This price would be composed of the $5 variable cost related to each unit of production plus a 10 cents per unit contribution to fixed expenses and overhead. The income statement for these conditions of sale is:

Sales (10,000 at $10; 5,000 at $5.10)		$125,500
Expenses:		
Variable (15,000 × $5)	$75,000	
Fixed	40,000	115,000
Net profit		$ 10,500

Profits are increased under the incremental approach. Admittedly, the illustration is based on two assumptions: (1) the ability to isolate markets so that selling at the lower price will not affect the price received in other markets; and (2) the lack of legal restrictions on the firm. The example, however, does show that profits can sometimes be enhanced by using the incremental approach.

Limitations of Cost Oriented Pricing

While the incremental method eliminates one of the problems associated with full cost pricing, it fails to deal effectively with the basic malady: *Cost oriented pricing does not adequately account for product demand.* The problem of demand estimation is as critical to these approaches as it is to classical price theory. To the marketer, the challenge is to find some way of introducing demand analysis into cost-plus pricing. Marketers must look at pricing from the buyer's perspective.[25] It cannot be done in a management vacuum.

Toward Realistic Pricing

Pricing is one of those gray areas in marketing management where the participants struggle to develop a theory, policy, procedure, technique, or "rule of thumb" on which they can depend. There is no simple solution to the dilemma. Pricing is a complex variable because it has both objective and subjective aspects. It is an area where exact decision tools and executive judgment meet.

Breakeven Analysis

Breakeven analysis is *a tool that allows decision makers to compare the profit consequences of alternative prices.* Figure 15–4 presents a breakeven chart where a single price is assumed. The total cost curve includes both fixed and variable segments, and total fixed cost is represented by a horizontal line. Average variable cost is assumed to be constant per unit—as it was in the example for incremental pricing.

The *breakeven point* is the point where total revenue (TR) just equals total cost (TC). It can be found by using the following formula:

$$\frac{\text{Breakeven point}}{\text{(in units)}} = \frac{\text{Total fixed cost}}{\text{Per unit contribution to fixed cost}}.$$

In our earlier example, a selling price of $10 and an AVC of $5 resulted in a per unit contribution to fixed costs of $5. This figure can be divided into total fixed costs of $40,000 to obtain a breakeven point of 8,000 units:

$$\text{Breakeven point (in units)} = \frac{\$40,000}{\$5} = 8,000.$$

Breakeven analysis is a valuable pricing tool. It allows marketers to test the financial implications of price decisions before they are actually implemented. For example, if the price were to change to $9 in the situation above, the breakeven point would be 10,000 units. If the price were $11, the breakeven point would be 6,667 units.

Figure 15–4
Breakeven Chart

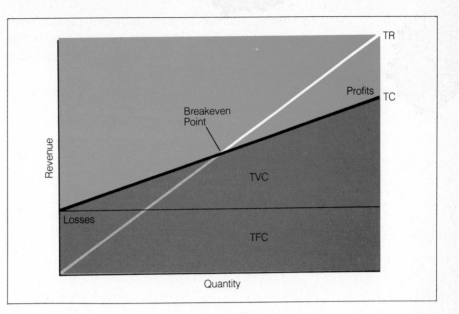

One criticism that can be leveled at all approaches to pricing is that the decision makers have consistently attempted to develop rigid procedures by which prices can be derived. Their efforts have often produced incorrect prices for a given market situation, because they ignored the creative aspects of pricing. Markup policies are an example of this problem.

A **markup** is *the amount added to cost to determine the selling price.* It is stated as a percentage of the selling price:

$$\text{Markup percentage} = \frac{\text{Amount added to cost}}{\text{Price}}$$

A closely related item is the **mark-on,** which is *the markup based on cost:*

$$\text{Mark-on percentage} = \frac{\text{Amount added to cost}}{\text{Cost}}$$

Consider an example from retailing. Suppose an item selling for $1 has an invoice cost of $.60. The total markup is $.40; that is, the markup percentage is 40 percent (0.40/1.00), and the mark-on percentage is 66⅔ percent (0.40/0.60). To determine selling price when only cost and markup percentage are known, use the following formula:

$$\text{Price} = \frac{\text{Cost in dollars}}{100 \text{ percent} - \text{Markup percentage}}$$

Too many times, traditional markup percentages lead to competitive inertia within an industry.[26] Standard markups are applied to all items in a given category regardless of other factors, such as demand.

Markups, Mark-ons, and Turnover *(margin heading)*

One way to overcome this problem is to use flexible markups that vary with **stock turnover**—*the number of times the average inventory is sold annually.* This figure can be calculated by one of the following formulas. When inventory is recorded at retail:

$$\text{Stock turnover} = \frac{\text{Sales}}{\text{Average inventory}}$$

When inventory is recorded at cost:

$$\text{Stock turnover} = \frac{\text{Cost of goods sold}}{\text{Average inventory}}$$

Store A, with $100,000 sales and an average inventory of $20,000 (at retail), would have a stock turnover of 5. Store B, with $200,000 sales, a 40 percent markup, and an average inventory of $30,000 (at cost), would have a stock turnover of 4.

Store A

$$\text{Stock turnover} = \frac{\$100,000}{\$20,000} = 5$$

Store B

$200,000 Sales
−80,000 Markup (40 percent)
$120,000 Cost of goods sold

$$\text{Stock turnover} = \frac{\$120,000}{\$30,000} = 4$$

While most businesses realize the importance of turnover, they often use it more as a measure of sales effectiveness than as a pricing tool.[27] Flexible markups should vary in accordance with stock turnover (see Table 15–4). This assures at least a minimum consideration of demand within the cost oriented concept of pricing. High (above average) turnover, such as for grocery products, means a lower markup, while low turnover, such as for jewelry, means a higher markup.

Pricing Criteria

Turnover is not the only criterion that must be considered in pricing decisions. Product type, mode of manufacture, market coverage, amount of pro-

Table 15–4
Relationship between Markup and Stock Turnover

Stock Turnover in Relation to the Industry Average	Markup in Relation to the Industry Average
High	Low
Average	Average
Low	High

Table 15–5
Pricing Criteria

Low	Criteria	High
Little	**Promotion**	Much
Commodity	**Product type**	Proprietary
Mass-produced	**Manufacture**	Custom-made
Intensive	**Market coverage**	Selective
Long-lived	**Product obsolescence**	Short-lived
Slow	**Technological changes**	Rapid
Capital intensive	**Production**	Labor intensive
Large	**Market share**	Small
Short	**Channels of distribution**	Long
Mature	**Stage of market**	New or declining
Long-term	**Profit perspective**	Short-term
Single-use	**Product versatility**	Multiple-use
Much	**Promotional contribution to line**	Little
Few or none	**Ancillary services**	Many
Short	**Product life in use**	Long
Fast	**Turnover**	Slow

Source: William Crissy and Robert Boewadt, "Pricing in Perspective," *Sales Management,* June 15, 1971, p. 44. Reprinted by permission of *Sales Management,* the Marketing Magazine, Copyright 1971.

motion, degree of product obsolescence, technological changes, type of production, market share, length of distribution channels, stage of market, profit perspective, product versatility, promotional contribution to line, extent of ancillary services, and length of use also affect prices. These pricing criteria are summarized in Table 15–5.

Effective pricing is influenced by a variety of factors and circumstances and involves far more than the rigid application of a pricing formula. The starting point is the careful analysis of the influences on pricing decisions as they fit into an overall marketing strategy.

Summary

Price—the exchange value of a good or service—is important because it regulates economic activity as well as determining the revenue to be received by a specific enterprise.

Pricing objectives should be the natural consequence of company and marketing goals. They can be classified under three headings:

1. Profitability objectives, including profit maximization and target return.
2. Volume objectives, including sales maximization and market share.
3. Objectives not related to either profitability or sales volume, including social and ethical considerations, status quo objectives, and prestige goals.

Prices can be determined by theoretical or cost oriented approaches. Economic theorists attempt to equate marginal revenue and marginal cost, while businesses tend to rely on cost-plus approaches. Both methods have practical limitations.

Breakeven analysis, the relationship between markup and turnover, and other pricing criteria are all directed toward the improvement of contemporary pricing behavior.

1. Explain the following terms:

price	pure competition
profit maximization	monopolistic competition
target return objective	oligopoly
sales maximization	monopoly
market share objective	cost-plus pricing
social and ethical considerations	breakeven analysis
	markup
status quo objective	mark-on
prestige goals	stock turnover
customary prices	

2. How important is pricing to the success of a marketing strategy?
3. Examine the role of pricing objectives in contemporary marketing.
4. What does the economist mean by *marginal analysis*? Discuss.
5. Do you share Baumol's conceptualization of pricing behavior? Explain.
6. Why would a firm choose to have a reduced market share? What are the policy implications of this situation?
7. Identify the main determinants of price discretion. Cite specific examples of each.
8. How are prices set in each of the four product markets: pure competition, monopolistic competition, oligopoly, and monopoly?
9. Describe cost oriented pricing. Include both full cost and incremental approaches.
10. Discuss the limitations of both theoretical and cost oriented pricing.
11. What is the breakeven point for a product with a selling price of $25, an average variable cost of $16, and related fixed costs of $126,000?
12. How can the derivation of the breakeven point assist in price determination? Comment.
13. Describe the relationship between markup and stock turnover.
14. Comment on the various criteria that must be considered in pricing decisions.
15. What market situations exist for the following products:

    a. telephone service   e. wheat
    b. U.S.-made cigars   f. refrigerators
    c. tennis rackets   g. cameras
    d. aluminum   h. skis

16. Give examples of pricing situations where social and ethical considerations are important. Are there any general conditions that characterize these situations? Discuss.
17. How are the following prices determined and what do they have in common:

    a. a ticket to a movie theater
    b. your tuition fee
    c. the local property tax rate
    d. the printing of graduation announcements

18. Calculate the markup and mark-on percentage for an item that costs a retailer $4 and is sold by the retailer for $5.
19. What is the stock turnover for a store with $350,000 in sales and an average inventory of $50,000 (at retail)?
20. What is the stock turnover for a store with sales of $1 million, a 50 percent markup, and an average inventory of $125,000 (at cost)?

Notes

1. The pricing of International Desserts is described in Kevin V. Brown, "Pricing: Sara Lee Beats the Recession with Costly Cakes," *Product Marketing,* April 1977, pp. 21–24.
2. Jon G. Udell, "How Important Is Pricing in Competitive Strategy?" *Journal of Marketing,* January 1964, pp. 44–48.
3. Price was also found to rank first in a study by Robert A. Robicheaux. See "How Important Is Pricing in Competitive Strategy? Circa 1975," in *Proceedings of the Southern Marketing Association,* ed. Henry W. Nash and Donald P. Robin, Atlanta, Georgia, November 1976, pp. 55–57.
4. These objectives are reported in Bro Uttal, "Xerox Is Trying Too Hard," *Fortune,* March 13, 1978, p. 84; Ralph E. Winter, "Corporate Strategists Giving New Emphasis to Market Share, Rank," *Wall Street Journal,* February 3, 1978, p. 1; and Bro Uttal, "How Ray MacDonald's Growth Theory Created IBM's Toughest Competitor," *Fortune,* January 1977, p. 96.
5. Research by Saeed Samiee ranked "satisfactory return on investment" first among a similar list of objectives. Samiee correctly points out the difficulties in making the "meeting competition" objectives operational. See "Pricing Objectives of U.S. Manufacturing Firms," *Proceedings of the Southern Marketing Association,* ed Robert S. Franz, Robert M. Hopkins, and Al Toma, New Orleans, Louisiana, November 1978, pp. 445–447.
6. An alternative to the profit maximization concept is suggested in Bruce Gunn, "Profit Optimization: A Paradigm for Risk Reduction," *Akron Business and Economic Review,* Spring 1977, pp. 14–22.
7. Target rate-of-return pricing is discussed in Douglas G. Brooks, "Cost-Oriented Pricing: A Realistic Solution to a Complicated Problem," *Journal of Marketing,* April 1975, pp. 72–74.
8. See James E. Hansz and Kenneth P. Sinclair, "Target Return Pricing: Panacea or Paradox?" in Franz, Hopkins, and Toma, eds., *Proceedings of the Southern Marketing Association,* pp. 441–444.
9. Robert A. Lynn, *Price Policies and Marketing Management* (Homewood, Ill.: Richard D. Irwin, 1967), p. 99.
10. See William J. Baumol, "On the Theory of Oligopoly," *Economica,* August 1958, pp. 187–198. See also William J. Baumol, *Business Behavior, Value, and Growth* (New York: Macmillan, 1959).
11. The importance of volume objectives is pointed out in Robert A. Lynn, "Unit Volume as a Goal for Pricing," *Journal of Marketing,* October 1968, pp. 34–39.
12. Various market share strategies are discussed in Paul N. Bloom and Philip Kotler, "Strategies for High Market Share Companies," *Harvard Business Review,* November–December 1975, pp. 63–72.
13. This is pointed out in Bernard Catry and Michael Chevalier, "Market Share Strategy and the Product Life Cycle," *Journal of Marketing,* October 1974, pp, 29–34.
14. Robert D. Buzzell, Bradley T. Gale, and Ralph G. M. Sultan, "Market Share—A Key to Profitability," *Harvard Business Review,* January–February 1975, pp. 97–106.
15. Some contradictory evidence was reported in Richard T. Hise and Robert H. Strawser, "The Validity of Market Share as a Marketing Objective: Some Disconcerting Evidence," *Southern Journal of Business,* August 1972, p. 14.
16. Reported in "Labor Letter," *Wall Street Journal,* August 29, 1978, p. 1.
17. Customary pricing is described in Stanley C. Hollander, "Customary Prices," *MSU Business Topics,* Summer 1966, pp. 45–56.
18. Reported in "Candy Fans Get Sour Price News," *Detroit News,* November 9, 1978, p. 1.
19. Charles G. Burck, "While the Big Brewers Quaff, the Little Ones Thirst," *Fortune,* November 1972, p. 106.
20. For a thorough discussion of price determination in economic theory, see Edwin G. Dolan, *Basic Economics,* 2d ed. (Hinsdale, Ill.: Dryden Press, 1980).
21. Experimental methods for estimating demand curves are discussed in Edgar A. Pessemier, *Experimental Methods of Analyzing Demand for Branded Consumer Goods* (Pullman: Bureau of Economic and Business Research, Washington State University, 1963). See also William J. Kehoe, "Demand Curve Estimation and the Small Business Managers," *Journal of Small Business Management,* July 1972, pp. 29–31.
22. Some problems of using economic models in practice are discussed in Kent B. Monroe and Albert J. Della Bitta, "Models for Pricing Decisions," *Journal of Marketing Research,* August 1978, pp. 413–428.
23. Interesting discussions of how costs can be used in pricing appear in David R. Rink, "What Every Businessman Should Know about the Direct Costing Approach," *In-Sights,* November 1973, pp. 1–8; Len F. Minars, "Management Accounting and Product Costs for Pricing Decisions," *Baylor Business Studies,* July 1975, pp. 55–66; and, Joseph P. Guiltinan, "Risk-Aversion Pricing Policies: Problems and Alternatives," *Journal of Marketing,* January 1976, pp. 10–15.
24. Theodore E. Wentz, "Realism in Pricing Analysis," *Journal of Marketing,* April 1966, p. 26.
25. This is suggested in Benson P. Shapiro and Barbara B. Jackson, "Industrial Pricing to Meet Customer Needs," *Harvard Business Review,* November–December 1978, pp. 119–127.
26. Hollander, "Customary Prices," pp. 53–54.
27. For an interesting discussion of the use of markups, see Roger Dickinson, "Markups in Department Store Management," *Journal of Marketing,* January 1967, pp. 32–34.

CHAPTER 16
ELEMENTS OF PRICING STRATEGY

Key Terms

list price
market price
cash discount
trade discount
quantity discount
trade-in
promotional
allowance
rebate
FOB plant
freight absorption
uniform delivered
price

zone pricing
basing point system
psychological pricing
odd pricing
unit pricing
skimming pricing
penetration pricing
price flexibility
price lining
promotional price
loss leader
transfer price
profit center

Learning Goals

1. To outline the organization for pricing decisions.
2. To explain price quotations.
3. To discuss why pricing policies are the foundation on which pricing decisions are made.
4. To relate price and the consumer's perception of a product's quality.
5. To examine negotiated prices and competitive bidding, transfer pricing, and pricing in the public sector.

16

United States airlines carried a record number of passengers—275 million—in 1978. Revenue for the twenty-three major carriers topped $23 billion, of which about $1 billion was profit. Most of the increase was attributed to substantial price discounting by the carriers. In fact, the Civil Aeronautics Board estimated that half of all airlines passengers received some type of price discount.

Jammed flights led to a near rebellion by businesspeople, who usually paid full fare rates. Flight time that used to be devoted to reading reports and doing paperwork was made unproductive by the crowding. Some of the airlines responded to complaints by issuing three classes of tickets: first class, full price coach class, and discount class. TWA, American Airlines, British Airways, and Pan Am all offered some version of this plan. Typically, full fare coach passengers received faster check-in and baggage pick-up services, advance seat selection, allocation of all empty seats to their section, and, in some cases, better food and beverage service than did discount passengers. United Airlines took a somewhat different approach. It cut the premium for first class tickets from 30 percent to 20 percent.

How is the new pricing strategy working? If Continental Airlines is an example, perhaps not as well as planned. Continental was the first to set up a special discount section in the rear of the plane—its so-called Chickenfeed fare program. But the airline soon found that many cost-conscious firms were snapping up its Chickenfeed tickets and putting their executives in the crowded discount section.[1]

As the airline example suggests, there are numerous elements to consider in setting a pricing strategy. This chapter will expand the concepts developed in Chapter 15 by considering the organization for pricing decisions, pricing policies, price-quality relationships, negotiated prices, competitive bidding, transfer pricing, and pricing in the public sector.

Organization for Pricing Decisions

Pricing objectives must be translated into pricing decisions. But how? There are basically two major steps to follow. First, the overall pricing structure must be set. Then, someone must be assigned responsibility for administering the pricing structure.

Setting Price Structures. A 1979 survey of marketing executives found that the people or groups most commonly chosen to set price structures were (1) a pricing committee composed of top executives, (2) the president of the company, and (3) the chief marketing officer (see Table 16–1).

Administering Price Structures. According to the same survey, the pricing structure is administered most often by marketers. As Table 16–2 indicates, the chief marketing officer was the responsible person in 51 percent

Table 16–1
Executives Responsible for Setting Price Structures

Executive Category	Percentage
Pricing committee composed of top executives	35.2
President	21.1
Chief marketing officer	14.1
Corporate vice-president	7.0
Board of directors	4.7
Executive vice-president	4.7
Pricing committee composed of middle level executives	3.9
Product or brand manager	3.1
Other	6.4

Source: *Pricing Objectives and Practices in American Industry: A Research Report.* © 1979 by Louis E. Boone and David L. Kurtz. All rights reserved.

Table 16–2
Executives Responsible for Administering Price Structures

Executive Category	Percentage
Chief marketing officer	51.0
Product or brand manager	14.3
Pricing committee composed of top executives	11.2
President	8.2
Corporate vice-president	8.2
Chief financial officer	4.1
Regional or zone sales manager	3.1

Source: *Pricing Objectives and Practices in American Industry: A Research Report.* © 1979 by Louis E. Boone and David L. Kurtz. All rights reserved.

of the firms surveyed. In all, marketers administered the pricing structure in over 68 percent of the companies.

How Are Prices Quoted?

The method for quoting prices depends on many factors, among them cost structures, the traditional practices in the particular industry, and the policies of individual firms. In this section, the reasoning and methodology behind price quotations will be examined.

List Prices. The basis on which many price structures are built is the **list price**—*the rate normally quoted to potential buyers.* List prices are usually determined by some type of cost-plus procedure. The sticker prices on new automobiles are one example of list prices. They show the price for the basic model and that for each of the options on the particular car being sold.

Discounts and Allowances. The **market price**—*the amount the consumer or middleman pays*—may or may not be the same as the list price, since discounts or allowances can reduce the list price. Discounts can be classified as cash, quantity, or trade.

Cash discounts, probably the most commonly used variety, are *price* *reductions that are made for prompt payment of bills.* They usually specify an exact time period in the form of, say, 2/10, net 30. This means that the bill is due within thirty days and that if it is paid in ten days, the buyer can deduct 2 percent from the amount due. Cash discounts are a traditional pricing practice in many industries. They are legal if they are granted to everyone on the same terms. The discounts were originally instituted to improve the cash position of sellers, to lower bad-debt losses, and to reduce the sellers' collection expenses. But whether these advantages outweigh the disadvantage of the relatively high cost of capital involved depends on the buyer's need for cash as well as alternative sources and costs of funds.

Trade discounts, also called **functional discounts,** are *payments to channel members or buyers for performing some marketing function normally required of the manufacturer.* They too are legal as long as all similar buyers (such as all wholesalers or all retailers) receive the same discount schedule. Trade discounts were initially based on the operating expenses of each trade category but have now become more a matter of custom in some industries (although they are not as common as they once were).[2] An example of a trade discount is "40 percent, 10 percent off list price" for wholesalers. In other words, the wholesaler passes the 40 percent discount on to the customers (retailers) and keeps the 10 percent discount as payment for activities such as storing and transporting goods.

Quantity discounts are *price reductions granted for large purchases.* They are given because large volume purchases reduce selling expenses and may shift part of the storing, transporting, and financing functions to the buyer. Quantity discounts are legal provided they are offered to all customers and do not infringe on the provisions of the Robinson-Patman Act limiting the discount to the amount of cost savings associated with selling in large quantities.

Quantity discounts are either noncumulative or cumulative. *Noncumulative quantity discounts* are one-time reductions in list price, such as the one shown in Table 16–3. *Cumulative quantity discounts* are reductions determined by purchases over a stated time period. Annual purchases of $25,000 might entitle the buyer to an 8 percent rebate, while purchases exceeding $50,000 may mean a 15 percent rebate. These price reductions are sometimes termed *patronage discounts,* since they tend to bind the customer to the seller.

Table 16–3
A Firm's Discount Schedule

Units Purchased	Price
1	List price
2–5	List price less 10 percent
6–10	List price less 20 percent
More than 10	List price less 25 percent

Allowances also reduce the price the purchaser must pay. The major categories of allowances are trade-ins, promotional allowances, and rebates. **Trade-ins,** often used in the sale of durable goods such as automobiles, *preserve the list price of the new item while cutting the amount the customer actually has to pay by allowing the customer credit on a used object, usually of the kind being purchased.* **Promotional allowances** are *attempts to integrate promotional strategy in the channel.* For example, manufacturers often provide advertising and sales support allowances for other channel members.

Rebates are *refunds by the sellers of a portion of the purchase price.* They have been used most prominently by automobile manufacturers eager to move models during periods of slow sales. Other recent users have included "Mr. Coffee" coffee makers and "First Alert" smoke detectors. One of the most interesting rebates has been given by Nguyen Huy Han, a Vietnam refugee who now runs a restaurant in Pontiac, Michigan. Han gives his customers a rebate at the end of each year on the basis of his profits. His first-year rebate was 30 percent, and one customer received $300.[3]

Transportation Costs

Shipping costs are important in pricing when the movement of heavy, bulky, low unit-cost materials is involved. In such cases, transportation is a relatively high portion of a product's total cost and must be carefully considered when the firm's market is spread over a wide geographic area. Prices may be quoted where either the buyer or the seller pays all transportation charges or there is some type of expense sharing.

The way in which this problem is handled can greatly influence the success of a firm's marketing program by helping to determine the scope of the geographic market area the firm is able to serve, the vulnerability of the firm to price competition in areas located near its production facilities, the net margins earned on individual sales of the product, the ability of the firm to control or influence resale prices of distributors, and how difficult it is for salesmen in the field to quote accurate prices and delivery terms to their potential customers.[4]

The seller has several alternatives in handling transportation costs: FOB plant, freight absorption, uniform delivered price, zone pricing, and basing points.

FOB Plant. *When a price does not include any shipping charges, it is shown as* **FOB plant.** In this situation, the buyer must pay all the freight charges. The seller is responsible only for the cost of loading the merchandise aboard the carrier selected by the buyer. (The abbreviation *FOB* means "free on board.") Legal title and responsibility pass to the buyer once the purchase is loaded and the receipt is obtained from the carrier.

Freight Absorption. Prices may also be shown as *FOB plant—freight allowed.* In this situation—known as **freight absorption**—*the seller permits the buyer to subtract transportation expenses from the bill.* The amount the seller receives varies with the freight charges absorbed. This method is commonly used by firms seeking to extend their market area since it permits the same price to be quoted regardless of shipping costs.

Uniform Delivered Price. *The same price (including transportation expenses) is quoted to all buyers* when a **uniform delivered price** is the firm's policy. This kind of pricing is the opposite of FOB pricing. The system is often compared to the pricing of mail service and is therefore sometimes called *postage stamp pricing.* The price quoted includes an average transportation cost per buyer, which means that distant customers actually pay a lesser share of selling costs while customers near the source pay more. The customers paying more are said to be paying *phantom freight*—that is, the average transportation charge exceeds the actual cost of shipping.

Zone Pricing. In **zone pricing,** which is simply a modification of the uniform delivered pricing system, *the market is divided into different regions, and a price is set within each one.* United Parcel Service's system depends on zone pricing. The primary advantage of this pricing policy is that it allows the seller to compete better in distant markets.

Basing Points. When a **basing point system** was used—it no longer is—*the price to the customer included the price at the factory plus freight charges from the basing point nearest the buyer.* The basing point was the point from which freight charges were determined; it was not necessarily the point from which the goods were shipped. There were both single and multiple basing point systems. In either case, the actual shipping point was not considered in the price quotation.

During the 1940s, several legal cases involving the steel, glucose, and cement industries were brought against users of basing point pricing systems. The outcomes of the proceedings themselves were confusing, but the result was the discontinuance of these systems as a basis for pricing.

The best-known basing point system was the *Pittsburgh-plus pricing* procedure that was used in the steel industry for many years. *Steel price quotations contained freight charges from Pittsburgh regardless of where the steel was produced.* As the industry matured, other steel centers, such as Chicago, Gary, Cleveland, and Birmingham, emerged. Pittsburgh, however, remained the basing point for steel pricing. This meant that a buyer in Terre Haute, Indiana, who purchased steel from a Gary mill had to pay phantom freight from Pittsburgh.

Psychological
Pricing

Psychological pricing is *based on the belief that certain prices or price ranges are more appealing than others to buyers.* There is, however, no consistent research-based foundation for such thinking, since studies often report mixed findings.[5] Prestige pricing, mentioned in Chapter 15, is one of the many forms of psychological pricing.

Under **odd pricing**—a good example of the application of psychological pricing—*prices ending in numbers not commonly used for price quotations are set.* A price of $16.99 is assumed to be more appealing than $17 because it is a smaller-appearing figure.

There are many explanations of the origin of odd pricing. One popular account is that it was used to force clerks to make change, thereby serving as a cash control device within stores.[6] Now it has become a customary feature of contemporary price quotations. For instance, one discounter uses prices ending in 3 and 7 rather than 5, 8, or 9 because of a belief that customers regard price tags such as $5.95, $6.98, and $7.99 as *regular* retail prices and price tags such as $5.97 and $6.93 as *discount* prices.[7]

Unit Pricing

Consumer advocates have often pointed out the difficulty of comparing consumer products that are available in different size packages. Is a 28-ounce can selling for $.75 a better buy than two 16-ounce cans priced at $.81? Is it a better buy than another brand's three 16-ounce cans for $.89? The critics argue that there should be a common way of pricing consumer products.

Unit pricing is a response to this problem. Under **unit pricing,** *all prices are stated in terms of some recognized unit of measurement (such as a pound or a quart) or standard numerical count.* Mandatory unit pricing has been legislated in some places; and many firms, particularly grocery store chains, have adopted it voluntarily. The American Marketing Association's board of directors has endorsed the concept for grocery products in all large stores.[8]

Some supermarket chains have come to regard the adoption of unit pricing as a competitive tool on which to base extensive advertising. Others have argued that unit pricing significantly increases retail operating costs.

The real question, of course, is whether unit pricing helps consumers make good decisions.[9] One study found that the availability of unit prices resulted in consumer savings and that retailers also gained when unit pricing led to greater purchases of store brands. The study concluded that unit pricing was valuable to both buyer and seller and that it merited full-scale usage.[10]

Pricing Policies

Pricing policies, the basis on which pricing decisions are made, are an important ingredient in the firm's total image. Many businesses would be well advised to spend more managerial effort in their establishment and periodic review.

Pricing policies must deal with varied competitive situations. The type of policy chosen by an individual firm depends on the environment within which pricing decisions must be made. The types of policies considered in this chapter are new-product pricing, price flexibility, relative price levels, price lining, and promotional prices.

New-Product Pricing

The pricing of new products presents a peculiar problem to marketers.[11] The initial price quoted for an item may determine whether the product will eventually be accepted in the marketplace. It also may affect the amount of competition that will emerge.

Consider the options a company might follow in pricing a new product. While many firms choose to price at the level of comparable products, some select other alternatives (see Figure 16-1). The **skimming pricing** policy is that of *a relatively high entry price.* The name is derived from the term *skim-the-cream.* One purpose of this strategy is to allow the firm to recover its new-product costs quickly, on the assumption that competition will eventually drive the price to a lower level. Such was the case with electric toothbrushes.

A skimming policy therefore attempts to maximize the revenue received from the sale of a new product before the entry of competition. Management takes the viewpoint that it is easier to lower the price than to raise it. Ballpoint pens were introduced shortly after World War II at a price of about $20. Today, the best-selling ballpoint pens are priced at less than $1. Other examples of products that have been introduced under a skimming policy are cellophane, television sets, and Polaroid cameras.[12]

During the late growth and early maturity stages of the product life cycle, the price is reduced for two reasons—the pressure of competition and the desire to expand the product's market. While 10 percent of the market for Product X might buy the item at $10, another 20 percent might buy at $8.75. Successive price declines will expand the firm's market as well as meet new competition.

The skimming policy has one chief disadvantage; it attracts competition. Potential competitors that see the innovating firm's profit also enter the market, and this forces the price even lower. Figure 16-1 indicates that 14.4 percent of the respondents in a 1979 pricing study used a skimming price policy. Skimming also appears to be more common in industrial markets than in consumer markets.

Penetration pricing, the opposite policy in new-product pricing, results in *an entry price lower than what is intended as the long-term price.* The pricing study shown in Figure 16-1 suggests that penetration pricing is used

Figure 16-1
Use of New-
Product Pricing
Strategies

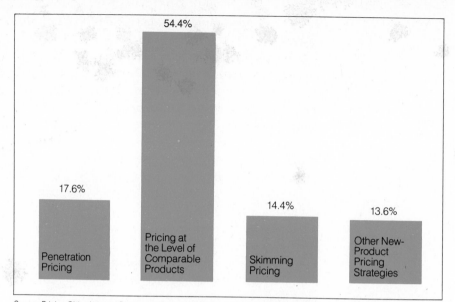

54.4%

17.6%

Penetration
Pricing

Pricing at
the Level of
Comparable
Products

14.4%

Skimming
Pricing

13.6%

Other New-
Product
Pricing
Strategies

Source: *Pricing Objectives and Practices in American Industry: A Research Report.* © 1979 by Louis E. Boone and David L. Kurtz.
All rights reserved.

more often in consumer markets than in industrial markets. Soaps and toothpastes are good examples of this kind of pricing.

The premise of penetration pricing is that an initially lower price will help secure market acceptance. Since the firm intends to increase the price later, brand popularity is crucial to the success of this policy. One advantage of the penetration policy is that it discourages competition, since the prevailing low price does not suggest the attractive returns associated with the skimming policy.

The key decision is when to move the price up to its intended level. Consumers tend to resist price increases; therefore, correct timing is essential. The solution depends on the degree of brand loyalty achieved. Brand loyalty must be at the point where a price increase will not cause a disproportionate decrease in customers. A series of modest price changes, rather than a single large hike, also can keep customers.

Price Flexibility

Marketing executives must determine company policy with respect to **price flexibility**—*whether to have just one price or to pursue a variable price policy in the market.* Generally, *one-price policies* characterize situations where mass selling is employed, while *variable pricing* is more common where individual bargaining typifies market transactions.

A one-price policy is common in retailing since it facilitates mass merchandising. For the most part, once the price is set, the manager can direct attention to other aspects of the marketing mix. Variable prices are found more in industrial markets. This does not mean that price flexibility exists only in manufacturing industries. A study of the retail home appliance market concluded that price differentials were common for consumers purchasing identical products from the same dealer. The primary reasons for the price differences were customer knowledge and bargaining strength.[13]

While variable pricing allows flexibility in selling situations, it may conflict with provisions of the Robinson-Patman Act (see Chapter 2). It may also lead to retaliatory pricing on the part of competitors, and it may not be well received by those who have paid the higher prices.

Relative Price Levels

An important pricing policy decision concerns the relative price level. Are the firm's prices to be set above, below, or at the prevailing market price? In economic theory this question would be answered by supply and demand analysis. However, from a practical viewpoint, marketing managers *administer* prices. In other words, cost oriented pricing allows them the option of subjectively setting the markup percentages.[14] Chapter 15 provided a framework for determining markups, but the decision maker must still develop a basic policy in regard to relative price levels.

Following the competition is one method of negating the price variable in marketing strategy, since it forces competitors to concentrate on other factors. Some firms choose to price below or above competitors. These decisions are usually based on a firm's cost structure, overall marketing strategy, and pricing objectives.

Price Lining

Most companies sell varied lines of products. An effective pricing strategy should consider the relationships among the firm's products rather than viewing each one in isolation. **Price lining** is *the practice of marketing merchandise at a limited number of prices.*[15] For example, a clothier might have a $150 line and a $225 line of men's suits. Price lining is used extensively in retail selling—witness the original five-and-ten-cent stores.

Price lining requires that the market segment to which the firm is appealing be identified. For example, "Samsonite sees its market not as all luggage, but as the 'medium-priced, hard side' portion of the luggage trade."[16] A dress manufacturer may have lines priced at $49.95, $69.95, or $89.95. Price lining not only simplifies the administration of the pricing structure but also alleviates the confusion that can occur when all products are priced separately.

One problem with a price line decision is that once it is made, retailers and manufacturers may have difficulty adjusting it. Rising costs, for example, may put the seller in the position of either changing the price lines—with its resulting confusion—or reducing production costs—which opens the firm to the complaint that "XYZ Company's merchandise certainly isn't what it used to be."

Promotional Prices

A **promotional price** is *a lower-than-normal price used as an ingredient in a firm's selling strategy.* Texas International employed a unique promotional price—$.39 for a roundtrip ticket on its new Dallas–Las Vegas route. The exact amount was chosen to highlight the airline's regular $39 roundtrip rate, a rate far lower than the $114 charged by its competitors. Only the first 39 buyers qualified for the $.39 promotional price, and even these people had to bring items like 39 peanuts, proof of marriage or divorce in 1939, or a photo of the person standing on the 39-yard line of the Dallas Cowboys.[17]

Most promotional pricing is done at the retail level.[18] **Loss leaders** are *retail goods priced at less than cost so as to attract customers who will then buy other regularly priced merchandise.* The use of loss leaders can be effective. For example:

Probably one of the best innovators of this pricing method was Cal Mayne of Dorothy Lane Food Store, Des Moines, Iowa. He was one of the first men to systematically price specials and to evaluate their effect on gross margins and sales. Mayne increased sales substantially by featuring coffee, butter, and margarine at 10 percent below cost. Ten other demand items were priced competitively and at a loss when necessary to undersell competition. Still another group of so-called secondary demand items were priced in line with competition. Mayne based his pricing policy on the theory that a customer can only remember about 30 prices. Keep prices down on these items and the customer will stay with you.[19]

A low price suggests low quality to many consumers.

"He's looking right at you, too. I hope you're proud of yourself for saving eight cents on that brand."

Source: *New Yorker*, February 5, 1979, p. 33. Drawing by Modell; © 1979 The New Yorker Magazine, Inc.

Some studies, however, have reported considerable price confusion on the part of consumers.[20] One study of consumer price recall reported that the average person missed the price he or she paid for coffee by over 12 percent, toothpaste by over 20 percent, and green beans by 24 percent. While some people named the prices exactly, others missed by several hundred percent.[21]

Three possible pitfalls should be considered in making promotional pricing decisions:

1. Promotional pricing may violate some state unfair trade laws (see Chapter 2).
2. Continuous use of an artificially low rate may result in its acceptance as customary for the product. Poultry, which was used as a loss leader during the 1930s and 1940s, has suffered from this phenomenon.
3. Some consumers are little influenced by price appeals, so promotional pricing will have minimal impact on them.[22]

Price-Quality Relationships

One of the most researched aspects of pricing is the relationship between price and consumer perception of the product's quality.[23] In the absence of other cues, price is an important indication of the way the consumer perceives the product's quality.[24] The higher the price, the better the buyer perceives the quality of the product. One study asked four hundred people what terms they associated with the word *expensive*; two-thirds of the replies—such as *best* and *superior*—dealt with high quality.[25] The relationship between price and perceived quality is a well-documented fact in contemporary marketing.

Probably the best price-quality conceptualization is the idea of *price limits*.[26] It is argued that consumers have limits within which product quality perception varies directly with price. A price below the lower limit is regarded as too *cheap*, while one above the higher limit is too *expensive*.

This concept provides a reasonable explanation of the price-quality relationship. Most consumers do tend to set an acceptable price range when purchasing goods and services. The range, of course, varies among consumers, depending on their socioeconomic characteristics and buying disposition.

Negotiated Prices and Competitive Bidding

Many government and industrial procurement situations are not characterized by set prices, particularly for nonrecurring purchases such as a defense system for the armed services. Such markets are growing at a fast pace. For instance, government units now spend about one-third of the U.S. GNP, and this portion will probably rise in the years ahead.

Competitive bidding involves buyers requesting that potential suppliers make price quotations on a proposed purchase or contract.[27] *Specifications* give a description of the item (or job) that the government unit or industrial firm wishes to acquire. One of the most important tasks in modern purchasing management is to adequately describe what the organization seeks to buy. This effort generally requires the assistance of the firm's technical personnel, such as engineers, designers, and chemists.

Competitive bidding strategy should employ the concept of *expected net profit,* which can be stated as:

Expected net profit = P (Bid − Costs)

where

P = The probability of the buyer accepting the bid.

Consider the following example. A firm is going to submit a bid for a job that it estimates will cost $23,000. One executive has proposed a bid of $60,000, another a bid of $50,000. There is a 40 percent chance of the buyer accepting the first bid ($60,000) and a 60 percent chance of accepting the second bid ($50,000). The expected net profit formula indicates that the second bid will be best, since its expected net profit is the highest:

Bid 1
ENP = 0.40 ($60,000 − $23,000)
    = 0.40 ($37,000)
    = $14,800.

Bid 2
ENP = 0.60 ($50,000 − $23,000)
    = 0.60 ($27,000)
    = $16,200.

The most difficult task in applying this concept is estimating the probability that a certain bid will be accepted. But this difficulty is not a valid reason for failing to quantify an estimate. Prior experience can provide the foundation for such estimates.

In some cases, industry and government purchasers use *negotiated contracts* instead of having competitive bidding on a project. In these situations, terms of the contract are set through talks between the buyer and a seller.

Some Bids Are Very Low

The Army Corps of Engineers needed to refit two pier barges. According to established procedures, it requested bids on the project. Three firms entered competitive bids. The first was for $20,000, the second was for $19,000, and the third was for $.01. Needless to say, the government quickly accepted the $.01 bid.

But why did the company submit such a low bid? It turned out that the firm was interested in the trestle bridges that topped the 165-foot pier barges. Under government procedures, these would be declared salvage and would become the property of the successful bidder.

Source: Adapted from "Bidder Gets 1-Cent Contract," *Detroit News,* September 27, 1978. Used by permission of UPI.

Where there is only one available supplier or where contracts require extensive research and development work, negotiated contracts are likely to be employed. These cases can be described as situations where competitive bidding would be the more expensive method of securing the product. For example, some state and local governments permit their agencies to negotiate purchases under a certain limit, say $500 or $1,000. This policy is an attempt to eliminate the economic waste involved in obtaining bids for relatively minor purchases.

Transfer Pricing

One pricing problem peculiar to large-scale enterprises is that of determining an internal **transfer price**—*the price for sending goods from one company profit center to another.*[28] As companies expand, they need to decentralize management. They set up profit centers as a control device for the new operation. **Profit centers** are *any part of the organization to which revenue and controllable costs can be assigned, such as a department.*

In large companies, the centers can secure many of their resource requirements from within the corporate structure. The pricing problem becomes: What rate should Profit Center A (machining department) charge Profit Center B (assembly department) for machining the materials used by B? Should the price be the same as it would be if A did the work for an outside party? Should B receive a discount? The answer to these questions depends on the philosophy of the firm involved.

The transfer pricing dilemma is an example of the variations that a firm's pricing policy must deal with. Consider the case of UDC-Europe, a Universal Data Corporation subsidiary that itself has ten subsidiaries. Each of the ten is organized on a geographic basis, and each is treated as a separate profit center. Intercompany transfer prices are set at the annual budget meeting. Special situations, like unexpected volume, are handled through negotiations by the subsidiary managers. If complex tax problems arise, UDC-Europe's top management may set the transfer price.[29]

Pricing in the Public Sector

The pricing of public services has become an interesting and sometimes troublesome aspect of contemporary marketing. Traditionally, government services were priced using the full cost approach; users paid all costs associated with the service. In more recent years, there has been a move toward incremental or marginal pricing, which considers only those expenses specifically associated with a particular activity. However, it is often difficult to determine the costs that should be assigned to a particular activity or service. Government accounting problems are often more complex than those of private enterprise.

Another problem in pricing public services is that taxes act as an indirect price of a public service. Someone must decide the relationship between the direct and indirect prices of such a service. A shift toward *indirect* tax charges (where an income or earnings tax exists) is a decision to charge on the *ability-to-pay* rather than the *use* principle.

The pricing of any public service involves a basic policy decision as to whether the price is an instrument to recover costs or a technique for accomplishing some other social or civic objective. Public health services, for example, may be priced near zero so as to encourage their use, while parking fines in some cities are so high as to discourage the use of private automobiles in the central business district. Pricing decisions in the public sector are difficult because of their many noneconomic objectives.

Summary

The main elements to consider in setting a pricing strategy are the organization for pricing decisions, pricing policies, price-quality relationships, negotiated prices, competitive bidding, transfer pricing, and pricing in the public sector. Methods for quoting prices depend on factors such as cost structures, traditional practices in a particular industry, and policies of individual firms. Prices quoted can be list prices, market prices, cash discounts, trade discounts, quantity discounts, and allowances such as trade-ins, promotional allowances, and rebates.

Shipping costs are often important in the pricing of goods. There are a number of alternatives for dealing with these costs: FOB plant, when the price does not include any shipping charges; freight absorption, when the buyer can deduct transportation expenses from the bill; uniform delivered price, when the same price—including shipping expenses—is charged to all buyers; zone pricing, when a set price exists within each region; and basing points, when the buyer pays a set price from a particular point, regardless of whether the goods are shipped from that point.

Psychological pricing, a method of determining prices that will be appealing to buyers, includes odd pricing.

Some people confuse price, quantity, and quality.

Source: Copyright, 1978, Universal Press Syndicate.

Pricing policies vary among firms. Among the most common are new-product pricing, which includes skimming pricing and penetration pricing; price flexibility; relative pricing; price lining; and promotional pricing.

A heavily researched area of pricing is the relationship between price and consumer perception of quality. A well-known and accepted concept is that of price limits—limits within which the perception of product quality varies directly with price.

Sometimes, prices are negotiated through competitive bidding, a situation where several buyers quote prices on the same service or good. At other times, prices depend on negotiated contracts, a situation where the terms of the contract are set through talks between a particular buyer and seller.

A phenomenon of large corporations is transfer pricing, where a company sets prices for transferring goods or services from one company profit center to another.

Pricing in the public sector has become a troublesome aspect of marketing. It involves decisions on whether the price of a public service is an instrument to recover costs or a technique for accomplishing some other social or civic purpose.

Questions for Discussion

1. Explain the following terms:

list price	basing point system
market price	psychological pricing
cash discount	odd pricing
trade discount	unit pricing
quantity discount	skimming pricing
trade-in	penetration pricing
promotional allowance	price flexibility
rebate	price lining
FOB plant	promotional price
freight absorption	loss leader
uniform delivered price	transfer price
zone pricing	profit center

2. Contrast the freight absorption and uniform delivered pricing systems.
3. Who is responsible for setting a price structure?
4. Who is responsible for administering a price structure?
5. Comment on the policy implications of the basing point system.
6. Prepare a list of arguments that might be used in justifying a basing point pricing system.
7. List and discuss the reasons for establishing price policies.
8. What is meant by price lining?
9. When does a price become a *promotional price?* What are the pitfalls in promotional pricing?
10. Discuss the relationship between price and the consumer's perception of product quality.
11. Contrast negotiated prices and competitive bidding.
12. Explain the expected net profit concept.
13. What types of decisions must be made in the pricing of public services?
14. At a recent meeting of a state highway commission, one member suggested that the pricing of new highways is inadequate. She pointed out that the pricing of highway construction has traditionally been based on the *direct* costs of land acquisition, site prepa-

ration, and actual construction. She noted that such calculations should include *indirect* costs, such as interest on debt and the property taxes lost when the highway land is no longer taxed. What is your opinion of this line of thought? Can you think of any other indirect costs that might be considered?

15. What type of new-product pricing would be appropriate for the following items:
    a. a new ultra-sensitive burgler and fire alarm
    b. a new pattern in a line of fine china
    c. a new deodorant
    d. a new doll

16. American Motors offered a 1979 AMC Spirit DL for $4,199. Was this an example of odd pricing? Promotional pricing? Psychological pricing? Comment.

17. How are prices quoted for each of the following:
    a. A Pan Am ticket to Australia
    b. a new Dodge Diplomat
    c. an aluminum siding installation by a local contractor
    d. a new sport shirt from a men's store
    Discuss why the methods of quoting prices are different.

18. Comment on the following statement: Unit pricing is ridiculous because everyone ignores it.

19. A metropolitan newspaper showed firms advertising prices such as $9.98, $4.44, and $2.27. Why would businesses use price quotations ending in 8, 4, and 7?

20. What criteria should be considered for transfer pricing in a large corporation like General Motors?

Notes

1. Vincent Coppola, John Walcott, and Pamela Abramson, "Airlines: Fare Play," *Newsweek,* October 16, 1978, pp. 92–94.

2. See Louis P. Bucklin, "The New Math of Distribution Channel Control," in *Review of Marketing, 1978,* ed. Gerald Zaltman and Thomas V. Bonoma (Chicago: American Marketing Association, 1978), pp. 453–470.

3. Reported in "Saying Thank You with Rebates," *Time,* June 12, 1978, p. 34. See also Clark Hallas, "More You Eat, More You Earn," *Detroit News,* May 29, 1978.

4. Donald V. Harper, *Price Policy and Procedure* (New York: Harcourt Brace Jovanovich, 1966), p. 204.

5. See, for example, Zarrel V. Lambert, "Perceived Prices as Related to Odd and Even Price Findings," *Journal of Retailing,* Fall 1975, pp. 13–22, 78.

6. See David M. Georgoff, "Price Illusion and the Effect of Odd-Even Retail Pricing," *Southern Journal of Business,* April 1969, pp. 95–103. See also Dik W. Twedt, "Does the '9 Fixation in Retailing Really Promote Sales?" *Journal of Marketing,* October 1965, pp. 54–55; Benson P. Shapiro, "The Psychology of Pricing," *Harvard Business Review,* July–August, 1968, pp. 14–16; and David M. Georgoff, *Odd-Even Retail Price Endings: Their Effects on Value Determination, Product Perception, and Buying Propensities* (East Lansing: Michigan State University, 1972).

7. Mark I. Alpert, *Pricing Decisions* (Glenview, Ill.: Scott, Foresman, 1971), pp. 112–113.

8. Hans B. Thorelli, "AMA Board Approves Unit Pricing in Taking First Public Policy Stand," *Marketing News,* August 1, 1972, p. 1.

9. Two excellent articles appeared in the July 1972 issue of the *Journal of Marketing:* Kent B. Monroe and Peter J. La Placa, "What Are the Benefits of Unit Pricing?" pp. 16–22; and Michael J. Houston, "The Effect of Unit Pricing on Choices of Brand and Size in Economic Shopping," pp. 51–54. See also Carl E. Block, Robert Schooler, and David Erickson, "Consumer Reaction to Unit Pricing: An Empirical Study," *Mississippi Valley Journal of Business and Economics,* Winter 1971–72, pp. 36–46; William E. Kilbourne, "A Factorial Experiment on the Impact of Unit Pricing," *Journal of Marketing Research,* November 1974, pp. 453–455; and J. Edward Russo, Gene Krieser, and Sally Miyashita, "An Effective Display of Unit Price Information," *Journal of Marketing,* April 1975, pp. 11–19.

10. J. Edward Russo, "The Value of Unit Price Information," *Journal of Marketing Research,* May 1977, pp. 193–201.

11. See, for example, G. Clark Thompson and Morgan B. MacDonald, Jr., "Pricing New Products," *Conference Board Record,* January 1964, pp. 7–9.

12. Robert A. Lynn, *Price Policies and Marketing Management* (Homewood, Ill.: Richard D. Irwin, 1967), p. 137.

13. Walter J. Primeaux, Jr., "The Effect of Consumer Knowledge and Bargaining Strength on Final Selling Price: A Case Study," *Journal of Business,* October 1970, pp. 419–426. Another excellent article is James R. Krum, "Variable Pricing as a Promotional Tool," *Atlanta Economic Review,* November–December 1977, pp. 47–50.

14. A survey technique for testing price levels above and below current levels is described in D. Frank Jones, "A Survey Technique to Measure Demand under Various Pricing Strategies," *Journal of Marketing,* July 1975, pp. 75–77.

15. See Alfred R. Oxenfeldt, "Product Line Pricing," *Harvard Business Review,* July–August 1966, pp. 137–144.

16 Lynn, *Price Policies and Marketing Management,* p. 143.

17. Reported in "Business Bulletin," *Wall Street Journal,* September 21, 1978, p. 1.

18. An interesting study of consumer response to promotion prices is outlined in Norman D. French and Robert A. Lynn, "Consumer Income and Response to Price Changes: A Shopping Simulation," *Journal of Retailing,* Winter 1971–72, pp. 21–23.

19. Bernie Faust, William Gorman, Eric Oesterle, and Larry Buchta, "Effective Retail Pricing Policy," *Purdue Retailer* (Lafayette, Ind.: Department of Agricultural Economics), p. 2.

20. Sidney Bennett and J. B. Wilkinson, "Price-Quantity Relationship and Price Elasticity under In-store Experimentation," *Journal of Business Research,* January 1974, pp. 27–38.

21. Karl A. Shilliff, "Determinants of Consumer Price Sensitivity for Selected Supermarket Products: An Empirical Investigation," *Akron Business & Economic Review,* Spring 1975, pp. 26–32.

22. John F. Willenborg and Robert E. Pitts, "Perceived Situational Effects on Price Sensitivity," *Journal of Business Research,* March 1977, pp. 27–38.

23. See, for example, Nessim Hanna, "Can Effort/Satisfaction Theory Explain Price/Quality Relationships?" *Journal of the Academy of Marketing Science,* Winter 1978, pp. 91–100; Barry Berman, "The Effects of Socioeconomic and Attitudinal Variables upon the Price-Quality Association," *Proceedings of the Southwestern Marketing Association,* ed. Robert C. Haring, G. Edward Kiser, and Ronnie D. Whitt, Houston, Texas, 1979, pp. 46–47; and Barry Render and Thomas S. O'Connor, "The Influence of Price, Store Name, and Brand Name on Perception of Product Quality," *Journal of the Academy of Marketing Science,* Fall 1976, pp. 722–730.

24. J. Douglass McConnell, "An Experimental Examination of the Price-Quality Relationship," *Journal of Business,* October 1968, pp. 439–444.

25. James H. Myers and William H. Reynolds, *Consumer Behavior and Marketing Management* (Boston: Houghton-Mifflin, 1967), p. 47.

26. See Kent B. Monroe and M. Venkatesan, "The Concepts of Price Limits and Psychophysical Measurement: A Laboratory Experiment," in *Marketing Involvement in Society and the Economy: Proceedings of the American Marketing Association,* ed. Phillip R. McDonald (Cincinnati: American Marketing Association, 1969), pp. 345–351.

27. See, for example, Kenneth J. Roering and Robert J. Paul, "An Appraisal of Competitive Bidding Models," *Marquette Business Review,* Summer 1977, pp. 57–66; and Douglas G. Brooks, "Bidding for the Sake of Follow-on Contracts," *Journal of Marketing,* January 1978, pp. 35–38.

28. See Paul E. Dascher, "Some Transfer Pricing Standards," *Pittsburgh Business Review,* November–December 1971, pp. 14–21; Thomas S. Goho, "Intracompany Pricing Strategy for International Corporations," *Business Studies,* Spring 1972, pp. 5–9; David Granick, "National Differences in the Use of Internal Transfer Prices," *California Management Review,* Summer 1975, pp. 28–40; and Peter Mailandt, "An Alternative to Transfer Pricing," *Business Horizons,* October 1975, pp. 81–86.

29. M. Edgar Barrett, "Case of the Tangled Transfer Price," *Harvard Business Review,* May–June 1977, p. 22.

PART SEVEN
FURTHER PERSPECTIVES

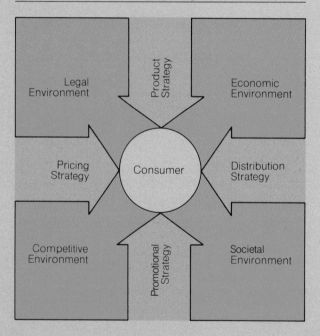

CHAPTER 17
INTERNATIONAL MARKETING

Key Terms

exporting
importing
balance of trade
balance of payments
exchange rate
floating exchange
rate
devaluation
revaluation
absolute advantage
comparative
advantage
multinational
corporation

tariff
General Agreement
on Tariffs and Trade
(GATT)
import quota
embargo
Tokyo Round
exchange control
dumping
cartels
friendship,
commerce, and
navigation (FCN)
treaties

Learning Goals

1. To describe the importance of international marketing today.
2. To explain the basic concepts of international marketing and trade.
3. To identify the various levels of involvement in international marketing.
4. To describe the international aspects of marketing strategy.
5. To describe the environment for international marketing.
6. To list the three basic formats for economic integration.
7. To show how the United States is an attractive market target for foreign marketers.

17

Budget Rent A Car may be number four in the United States (behind Hertz, Avis, and National), but it is number one in Canada and Australia. Budget moved into thirty-seven countries in a five-year period and gained at least a third-place ranking in every nation. In fact, nearly one-third of Budget's fleet is based in foreign countries.[1]

Budget's overseas success illustrates the opportunities that exist abroad. But not all U.S. firms are successful outside the United States, and even the best of them have had to learn the difficulties and pitfalls of doing business abroad.

McDonald's put its first European outlet in a suburb of Amsterdam, following a pattern the firm had originally established in Chicago. But the giant fast-food franchisor found that most Europeans still reside in the cities and lack the mobility of people in the United States. McDonald's soon moved into the city.[2]

Hong Kong provided the locale for a mistake by another fast-food retailer. All of Kentucky Fried Chicken's eleven Hong Kong outlets failed within two years. Fried chicken apparently conflicted with the cultural upbringing of Hong Kong residents, who typically receive hot hand towels with their meals.[3]

The International Sector of Contemporary Marketing

International marketing is obviously of considerable importance to Budget Rent A Car. It is also important to Chas. Pfizer, since it generates over 50 percent of the company's total revenues abroad. The importance of international marketing for selected U.S. firms is shown in Table 17–1. But just as some firms depend on foreign sales, others depend on purchasing raw materials to use in their manufacturing operations at home. A furniture company's need to purchase South American mahogany is an example.

International trade is vital to a nation and its marketers for several reasons. It expands the market for a country's or firm's products and thus makes production and distribution economies feasible. It can also mean more jobs at home. Some 30,000 to 40,000 new jobs are supported by each billion export dollars.[4]

Foreign trade can be divided into **exporting**—*selling goods abroad*—and **importing**—*buying foreign goods and raw materials.* While the United States is both the largest exporter and the largest importer in the world, foreign trade is still less critical to it than to such countries as Belgium and West Germany, where exports account for 46 percent and 23 percent of gross national product (GNP), respectively. U.S. exports account for only about 6.4 percent of U.S. GNP.[5] The leading export for the United States is motor vehicles and parts, and the leading import is petroleum.[6]

Some of the discussion in Chapter 17 follows that in Vern Terpstra, *International Marketing,* 2d ed. (Hinsdale, Ill.: Dryden Press, 1978); and in Louis E. Boone and David L. Kurtz, *Contemporary Business,* 2d ed. (Hinsdale, Ill.: Dryden Press, 1979).

**Table 17–1
Importance of
Foreign Markets
to Some U.S.
Companies in
1978**

Company	Percentage of 1978 Sales Abroad
Abbott Laboratories	34.5
AMF Incorporated	20.1
Caterpillar Tractor	48.1
Chesebrough-Pond's International	29.0
Dresser Industries	35.0
Du Pont	28.3
Emhart Corp.	44.3
General Electric	18.1
H. J. Heinz	37.4
Chas. Pfizer	55.9
Raytheon Company	33.6
Warner-Lambert	43.0

Sources: 1978 annual reports of the listed companies.

**Scorekeeping in
the International
Sector**

Since imports and exports are important contributors to a country's economic welfare, governments and other organizations are concerned about the status of various components of international marketing. The concepts of balance of trade and balance of payments are a good starting point for learning about international business.

Balance of Trade

A nation's **balance of trade** is *determined by the relationship between its exports and imports.* A favorable balance of trade occurs when a nation's exports exceed its imports. This means that, other things being equal, new money comes into the country via foreign sales. An unfavorable balance of trade, by contrast, results when imports exceed exports. The net money flow then is outward, other things being equal. The 1978 U.S. balance of trade was a negative $34 billion, a record deficit.[7]

**Balance of
Payments**

A country's balance of trade accounts for a major portion of its **balance of payments**—*the flow of money into or out of a country.* However, other factors are also important. A favorable balance of payments indicates there is a net money inflow, while an unfavorable balance of payments means there is a net money outflow.

The balance of payments is also affected by such factors as tourism, military expenditures abroad, investment abroad, and foreign aid. A money outflow caused by these factors may exceed the money inflow from a favorable balance of trade and leave a nation with an unfavorable balance of payments.

**Exchange Rate
Adjustments.**

It is sometimes necessary for a nation to adjust its **exchange rate**—*the rate at which its currency can be exchanged for other currencies or gold.* These adjustments have a significant impact on both the balance of trade and the balance of payments. **Floating exchange rates**—*those that are allowed to* *adjust to market conditions*—are now prevalent. The United States, among other countries, uses a floating exchange rate.

Devaluation occurs *when a nation reduces the value of its currency in relation to gold or some other currency.* Devaluation of the dollar has the effect of making U.S. products less expensive abroad and trips to the United States cheaper for foreign visitors. **Revaluation**—a less typical case—occurs *when a country adjusts the value of its currency upward.* Either of these actions may force firms to modify their world marketing strategies.

Basic Concepts in International Marketing

The Pacific island republic of Nauru has only four thousand citizens, but one of the richest deposits of phosphate in the world covers 85 percent of its land area.[8] Japan's large population lives on a relatively small land mass, and the island nation is chronically deficient in some raw materials. Forced to depend on foreign trade, Japan has become a premier international marketer.

These situations suggest that nations are usually better off if they specialize in certain products or marketing activities. By doing what they do best, they are able to exchange the products not needed domestically for foreign-made goods that are needed. Nauru could attempt to develop a tourist trade, but it has opted for specializing in phosphate mining. This allows it a higher standard of living than would be possible through diversified business enterprises.

Specialization by countries sometimes produces odd situations. Consider, for example, the "Buy American" stickers that can be found on the rear bumpers of some Datsuns and Toyotas owned by steelworkers.

An understanding of the concepts of absolute and comparative advantage is vital to the study of world marketing. These concepts explain why

The "buy American" sentiment is evident in various sectors of the U.S. economy — even among buyers of imported goods.

Source: Copyright © 1980 by Sidney Harris. Reprinted by permission.

countries specialize in the marketing of certain products. A nation has an **absolute advantage** in the marketing of a product *if it is the sole producer or can produce the product for less than anyone else.* Since few nations are sole producers, and since economic conditions rapidly alter production costs, examples of absolute advantage are rare. The concept of **comparative advantage** is a more practical approach to international trade specialization. This concept says that *a nation has a comparative advantage in an item if it can produce it more efficiently than it can produce alternative products.* Nations usually produce and export those goods in which they have the greatest comparative advantage (or the least comparative disadvantage) and import those items in which they have the least comparative advantage (or the greatest comparative disadvantage). The United States tends to export manufactured items, such as machinery, and natural resources, such as coal. By contrast, countries with lower labor costs tend to specialize in products that require a significant labor content, such as textiles, shoes, and clothing.

Of course, there are noneconomic reasons for specializing in certain

Comparative advantage is a key concept in international marketing.

"I see no reason why we can't work out a mutually satisfactory trade policy. Both our countries are rich in some of life's necessities and poor in others. For instance, we have our oil and you have your blue jeans. . . ."

Source: *Wall Street Journal*, May 3, 1978. Reprinted by permission of the cartoonist, Bruce Cochran, and the *Wall Street Journal;* © 1979.

items. The United States, for example, is attempting to reduce its dependence on foreign oil for various political and strategic, as well as economic, reasons.

Competing in the World Marketplace

Many U.S. firms never venture outside their own domestic market. They feel they do not have to, because the U.S. market is huge. Even today, only about 8 percent of domestic manufacturing firms export their products.[9] Those that do venture abroad find the international marketplace far different from the one to which they are accustomed. Market sizes, buyer behavior, and marketing practices all vary, which means that the international marketer must carefully evaluate all market segments in which he or she expects to compete.

Market Size

A prime ingredient of market size is population growth, and every day the world's population increases by about 200,000 people. By the year 2000, the world's population may be in the range of 6.5 to 7 billion, compared to the current 4 billion. A review of these projections produces some important contrasts. Average birthrates are dropping, but death rates are declining even faster. Population growth has fallen in industrialized nations, but it has increased in the less-developed countries.

Many of the world's new inhabitants end up living in large cities. By the year 2000, these urban dwellers are expected to account for half the world population instead of the current 39 percent. Today, twenty-one cities have a population of 5 million or more. In 2000, sixty such cities will exist. Mexico City, which now ranks third in population, is expected to grow to 31.5 million, making it the world's largest city.[10]

Statistical data indicate that the international marketplace will continue to grow in size and that it will become increasingly urbanized. This does not mean, however, that all foreign markets will have the same potential. Income differences, for instance, vitally affect any nation's market potential. India has a huge population of about 600 million, but its per capita income is very low. Canada, on the other hand, has only a small fraction of India's population, but its per capita income is nearly as high as that in the United States.

It might surprise many people to know that the United States is no longer the world's wealthiest industrialized nation. According to University of Pennsylvania economists, Kuwait ranks higher on a per capita output basis. But the United States is still ahead of other industrialized nations—like West Germany, Japan, the United Kingdom, France, and Italy.[11]

Effective marketing often greatly increases a company's share of a foreign market. Coca-Cola, which already holds a 90 percent share of the Brazilian cola market, is seeking to increase that nation's annual per capita consumption of ninety-five 6.5-ounce bottles. A Coca-Cola executive claims that,

**China
Recognition —
Effect on Trade?**

Recognition of the People's Republic of China has been hailed as a step toward world peace by many—and a sell-out of Taiwan by others. But formal recognition of the world's largest nation (with its 900 million inhabitants) will definitely affect international marketing.

Coca-Cola has already been granted the sole privilege of selling cola drinks in the Chinese market. Coke, which was sold in China from 1928 to 1949, will initially be distributed in tourist spots and cities such as Peking, Kwangchow, Hangchow, and Shanghai. Pan Am and United Airlines have requested routes to China, and Inter-Continental Hotels has announced plans to construct a number of hotels there.

Even though an expansion of trade between the two countries is expected, trade growth will not be spectacular. Trade between the United States and China was approximately $1 billion last year and is expected to double this year. Most of this trade was in the form of U.S. agricultural products and sophisticated machinery, and this pattern is expected to continue for the immediate future. The Chinese exports include textiles, foodstuffs, and non-ferrous metals. U.S. importers point out that the name of the leading brand of men's cotton underwear would have to be changed in order to find a market abroad. The brand—"Pansy."

Taiwan is currently the United States' eighth leading trade partner, with a level of $7.5 billion. The absence of normal diplomatic relations is expected to have only a slight effect on trade.

Sources: Background information from "Recognition Stirs Visions of Ripe China Market," *Advertising Age,* December 25, 1978, pp. 1, 29; and "A Slow Boat to China," *Sales & Marketing Management,* February 5, 1979, p. 20.

in some areas, sales of soft drinks decline when the temperature drops, so the firm sees a tremendous potential off-season consumption. The soft drink market could also be expanded if Brazilians could be persuaded to drink less mineral water at home and less coffee at work.[12]

When color television transmission began in Australia in late 1974, the total 1975–1976 market for color sets was forecast at 380,000 units. Actual sales were double that figure. Color television achieved a 25 percent market penetration within one year of its introduction in Australia; it took fourteen years to reach a comparable figure in the United States. The leading market share in Australia has been held by a firm jointly owned by the United Kingdom's Rank International group and the Nippon Electric Corporation of Japan.[13]

Buyer Behavior

Buyer behavior differs from one country to another. Therefore, marketers should carefully study each market before implementing a marketing strategy. Not all marketing strategies that prove successful at home can be exported to other parts of the world. Consider the problems associated with using the "Body by Fisher" slogan for General Motors cars. In some translations, it comes out "Corpse by Fisher." Similarly, Pepsi Cola's "come alive" theme can be translated "come out of the grave!"[14]

Marketers must also be careful that their marketing strategies comply with local customs, tastes, and buying practices. In some cases, even the product itself has to be modified. General Foods, for instance, offers different blends of coffee to each of its overseas markets. One variety goes to

British consumers, who prefer to use considerable amounts of milk with their coffee; another goes to the French, who usually drink coffee black; still another mix goes to Latin Americans, who prefer a chicory taste.[15]

Different buying patterns mean that marketing executives should do considerable research before entering a foreign market. Sometimes, the research can be done by the marketer's own organization or a U.S.-based research firm. In other cases, a foreign-based marketing research organization should be used. Foreign research firms are often innovative. For example, Audits, Ltd., of Great Britain, was an innovator in the field of home audits of package goods. The British firm provides its respondents with a special trash container rather than relying on a diary of purchases. Discarded packages are then studied to determine consumer buying patterns.[16]

Marketing Practices

Marketing practices vary the world over.[17] These practices must be taken into consideration when an ''outside'' firm decides to launch a marketing campaign. A high illiteracy rate, for example, may substantially limit the types of advertising campaigns employed. Aggressive sales efforts may be regarded negatively in some foreign cultures. Business customs and traditions may restrict a firm's distribution strategy to certain marketing channels. A brief consideration of each marketing strategy component will illustrate the differences that exist in marketing practices overseas.

Product Strategy

A midwestern power tool manufacturer had to change its products in order to sell them in Australia, New Zealand, and South Africa. These nations mandate that all power tools have equipment to prevent them from interfering with radio and television transmissions.[18] Packing modifications were necessary for an electric motor exporter before the firm could sell its product in Mexico, since Mexico does not permit packaging parts and motors together.[19] According to one report, Holiday Inn plans to make its European hotels look less ''American'' and more ''European'' so as to better compete in the European marketplace.[20]

All these examples illustrate that it is often necessary to adapt products to foreign markets. Successful adaptation can significantly extend the market for a product. Sometimes, the product itself has to be modified; in other cases, it is the packaging; in still others, it is the product's identification. Consider the many products that might use the word *mist* as part of their name. But imagine the difficulty of marketing a consumer product using this name in Germany, where *mist* means ''manure.''[21]

Distribution Strategy

Sears, Roebuck—one of the most effective retailers in the United States—found its match in Seibu, a large Japanese retailer with six hundred outlets. So Sears turned to Seibu to sell its catalog merchandise in Japan. The venture was so successful that a Sears subsidiary, Allstate Insurance, now markets its life insurance policies through Seibu's retail locations.[22]

Nissan Motors' Datsun is the leading seller in oil-rich Saudi Arabia (where gasoline sells at 12 cents per gallon). Its large market share is credited to the excellent organization of local distributors, who were recruited in the early 1960s. The Japanese firm sought out Saudi entrepreneurs who had sufficient investment capital and who were skilled managers and marketers.[23] The strategy was obviously effective.

Distribution is a vital aspect of overseas marketing. Proper channels must be set up and extensive physical distribution problems handled. Transportation systems and warehousing facilities may be unavailable or of poor quality. International marketers must adapt speedily and efficiently to these situations if they are to profit from overseas sales.

Promotional Strategy

Bribery, payoffs, and the sometimes dubious use of sales agents in foreign markets have received considerable publicity in recent years. People are usually shocked by a firm that violates either U.S. or foreign laws. All overseas marketing practices must be evaluated in terms of standards and practices in the United States and abroad. Many organizations have taken a firm stand against any illicit business practices.

While effective personal selling continues to be vital in foreign markets, advertising has gained in importance. The wider availability of media such as radio and television has enhanced advertising's contribution to the overall promotional effort. In fact, the Japanese are now the world's leading television viewers. Their television sets are on for some seven hours and seventeen minutes each day, and 70 percent of their sets are operating by 8 A.M. U.S. and Canadian households, by comparison, watch television approximately six hours and eleven minutes daily.[24]

Pricing Strategy

Pricing in foreign markets can be a critical ingredient in overall marketing strategy. One study found that export pricing was the marketing variable requiring the greatest degree of adaptation and change. Nearly 73 percent of the respondents reported that such adaptation was of importance in export markets.[25]

Pricing practices in overseas markets are subject to considerable competitive, economic, political, and legal constraints. International marketing managers must clearly understand these requirements if they are to succeed.

It seems certain that prices will continue to be a hotly debated subject in international marketing circles. Resource-rich developing nations complain that industrialized nations have traditionally been able to obtain their raw materials at low prices. The advanced economies then sell their manufactured products to the less fortunate nations at high prices.[26] This balance seems to be shifting as more and more materials suppliers have turned to collective export organizations. OPEC (the Organization of Petroleum Exporting Countries) was able to bring about a considerable restructuring in some traditional trade balances. Other export organizations are now following similar practices.

Levels of Involvement in International Marketing

Several levels of involvement in international marketing can be identified: casual or accidental exporting, active exporting, foreign licensing, overseas marketing, and foreign production and marketing.

Casual or accidental exporting is a passive level of involvement in international marketing. A U.S. company may export goods without even knowing it if its goods are bought by resident buyers for foreign companies. In other cases, a firm may export only occasionally when surplus or obsolete inventory is available.

When the firm actually makes a commitment to seek export business, it engages in *active exporting.* While the exact extent of the commitment may vary, the term implies that the firm is making a continuing effort to sell its merchandise abroad.

Foreign licensing occurs when a firm permits a foreign company to produce and distribute its merchandise under a formal agreement. Licensing has several advantages over exporting, among them the availability of local marketing information and distribution channels and protection from various legal barriers. However, conflicts between the parties involved cause three of every ten licensing agreements to fail. Another two or more are unsatisfactory to at least one of the participants.[27]

A firm that maintains a separate marketing or selling operation in a foreign country is involved in *overseas marketing.* Examples are foreign sales offices and overseas marketing subsidiaries. The product may be produced by domestic factories, foreign licensees, or contract manufacturers; but the company always directly controls foreign sales.

Foreign production and foreign marketing, the ultimate degree of company involvement in the international market arena, can be accomplished in the following ways:

1. The firm can set up its own production and marketing operation in the foreign country.
2. It can acquire an existing firm in the country in which it will do business.
3. It can form a joint venture, sharing the risks, costs, and management of the foreign operation with a partner who is usually a national of the host nation.

**Maquiladoros —
An Alternative to
Foreign
Production**

Maquiladoros is a Mexican term for the U.S. factories that operate on the Mexican side of the border. People in the United States call these operations *in-bond* or *twin* plants, since counterpart operations exist on nearby U.S. soil. U.S. firms are allowed to import raw materials into Mexican plants, where the product is substantially produced, and then to ship them back across the border to a twin plant where U.S. labor finishes the job. Only modest customs charges are involved.

The program was designed to reduce unemployment in the Mexican border towns. While labor has objected to this program, companies argue that it leads to more jobs in the United States because it prevents buyers from switching to foreign-made goods. The firms reason that the products involved would not be competitive with foreign goods without the *maquiladoros.*

Source: Adapted from Kenneth G. Slocum, "U.S. Concerns Worry That Soaring Wages in Mexico May Hurt Border-Plant Profit," *Wall Street Journal*, November 21, 1975. Reprinted by permission of The Wall Street Journal, © Dow Jones & Company, Inc., 1975. All rights reserved.

**Organizing for
Multinational
Marketing**

Switzerland's Nestlé now operates in fifty national markets with 137,000 employees and three hundred plants. Total sales are approximately $10 billion. Nestlé gets 47 percent of its revenue from Europe, 20 percent from Third World nations, and the remainder primarily from the United States and Japan.[28]

Multinational corporations *operate in several countries and literally view the world as their market.* Nestlé is an example of an effective multinational corporation. The company is thoroughly international in perspective. The board chairman is French; the president is Swiss; one executive vice-president is French, and another is Italian. The senior vice-presidents include a U.S. and a Spanish citizen. Nestlé executives are regularly rotated to different assignments between the "center" (company headquarters at Vevey on Lake Geneva) and the "markets" (as the foreign operations are known). In the United States, Nestlé's brands and acquisitions include Nestea, Taster's Choice, Stouffer Foods, Crosse & Blackwell, and Libby, McNeill, & Libby.

Multinationals have been the subject of considerable public scrutiny both in the United States and abroad. Some U.S. multinationals have been criticized for their involvement in South Africa. These firms typically respond that they are contributing to social and economic progress in all the nations in which they operate. Some nations—Australia and Canada, for example—have occasionally expressed concern about the multinationals' domination of some domestic markets. Similar complaints have been expressed in the United States about the inroads made by Japanese firms in the consumer electronics industry. While criticism of multinational practices is likely to continue, it is obvious that multinational corporations have become fixtures in the international marketplace.

The Environment for International Marketing

Various environmental factors can influence international marketing strategy. Marketers should be as aware of these influences as they are of those in domestic markets.

Cultural, Economic, and Societal Blocks

International marketing is often influenced by cultural, economic, and societal factors. The economic status of some countries makes them less or more likely candidates for international business expansion. Nations with low per capita income may be poor markets for expensive industrial machinery but good markets for agricultural hand tools. These nations cannot afford the technical equipment necessary in an industrialized society. Wealthier countries can prove to be prime markets for the products of many U.S. industries, particularly those involved with consumer goods and advanced industrial products.

Many a product has failed abroad simply because the producing firm tried to use the same marketing strategy that was successful in the United States. Phillip Morris introduced its blended tobacco cigarettes in Canada in an attempt to benefit from its U.S. television advertising, which was seen by many Canadians who picked up the telecasts. Market research showed that Canadians preferred straight tobacco rather than blends, but Phillip Morris disregarded the research and went ahead with its Canadian marketing program. Canadians failed to switch their cigarette buying attitudes, and Phillip Morris had to abandon its effort.[29]

U.S. products sometimes face consumer resistance abroad. U.S. automobiles, for example, have traditionally been rejected by European drivers, who complain of poor styling, low gasoline mileage, and poor handling. But the new, smaller cars from Detroit are making inroads into European markets—with a major assist from the declining value of the dollar.[30] This reversal suggests that it is not always possible to determine whether cultural, economic, or societal factors exist before entering a foreign market. The Japanese, tea drinkers for centuries, have always preferred natural tea. But Boston Tea Company's blended, spiced, and herbed tea is now selling well in Japan.[31]

Trade Restrictions

Assorted trade restrictions also affect world trade. These restrictions are most commonly expressed through **tariffs**—*taxes levied against imported products*. Some tariffs are based on a set tax per pound, gallon, or unit; others are figured on the value of the imported product. They can be classified as either revenue or protective tariffs. *Revenue tariffs* are designed to raise funds for the government. Most of the revenue of the infant U.S. government came from this source. *Protective tariffs* are designed to raise the retail price of imported products to that for a similar domestic product—or higher. They are usually higher than revenue tariffs. In the past, it was believed that a country should protect its infant industries by using tariffs to keep out foreign-made products. Some foreign goods would enter, but the addition of a high tariff payment would make domestic products competitive. Recently, it has been argued that tariffs should be raised to protect employment and profits in domestic U.S. industry.

The **General Agreement on Tariffs and Trade (GATT)**—*an international trade accord*—has sponsored several tariff negotiations that have reduced the overall level of tariffs throughout the world. The latest series, the so-called **Tokyo Round,** began in 1974 and concluded in 1979. The trend has been toward tariff reductions among nations.

There are also other forms of trade restriction. An **import quota** *sets limits on the amount of products in certain categories that can be imported.* The objectives of import quotas are to protect local industry and employment and to preserve foreign exchange. The ultimate quota is the **embargo**—*the complete ban on importing certain products.* In the past, the United States has prohibited the import of products from some Communist countries.

Foreign trade can also be regulated by exchange control through a central bank or government agency. **Exchange control** means that *firms gaining foreign exchange by exporting must sell this exchange to the central bank, or agency, and importers must buy foreign exchange from the same organization.* The exchange control authority can then allocate, expand, or restrict foreign exchange according to existing national policy.

Dumping – A Contemporary Marketing Problem[32]

Bethlehem Steel ran advertisements to protest what it viewed as an economic injustice. The Bethlehem action was symbolic of the public outcry against **dumping**—*selling a product at a lower price in a foreign market than it sells for in the producer's domestic market.* It is often argued that foreign governments give substantial export support to their own companies. Such support may permit these firms to extend their export markets by offering lower prices abroad.

Products that have been dumped on U.S. markets can be subjected to additional import tariffs to bring their prices into line with domestically produced products. For instance, a 32 percent dumping duty was assessed against five Japanese steel sellers. However, businesses often complain that charges of alleged dumping must go through a lengthy investigative and bureaucratic procedure before duties are assessed. In an attempt to speed up the process in the steel industry, the Carter administration adopted a *trigger pricing system,* which established a set of minimum steel prices. Japanese production costs, the world's lowest, were used in these calculations. Any imported steel selling at less than these rates triggers an immediate Treasury Department investigation. If dumping is substantiated, additional duties are imposed.

The Tokyo Round

The Tokyo Round was named for the city where it was decided to start the talks, but the negotiations actually took place in Geneva. Ninety-nine nations participated in this complex debate.

The following figure shows that the Tokyo Round will result in considerable tariff reductions throughout the world. These cuts, expected to average 33 percent during the next eight years, will affect about 5,700 products.

Numerous nontariff barriers have also been reduced. With the exception of Japan, the participating governments agreed to change their procurement regulations to allow foreign marketers to bid on government purchases. The new pact reduced each nation's ability to use custom valuations or product standard regulations to discriminate against foreign goods. It also reduced restrictions on the international sale of civil aircraft and restricted government subsidies to exporters.

Early assessments of the Tokyo Round suggest that it could lead to a considerable increase in international trade. A Brookings Institution representative estimated that the United States will gain $4.5 billion in exports annually—which will help offset the nation's enormous trade deficit.

Cuts in tariffs and nontariff barriers...

**Total trade between industrial
countries covered by tariff cuts** .... **$200 billion**

Tariffs	Average reduction
Between the U.S. and EC	35% each way
Between the U.S. and Canada	40% each way
On U.S. imports into Japan	40%
On Japanese imports into the U.S.	30%

Nontariff barriers	New rules
Government procurement code	Opens $20 billion annually in foreign official purchasing to bids by U.S. suppliers
Customs valuation code	Establishes the invoice price as basis for valuing imports
Product standards code	Requires public procedures and encourages uniformity in setting standards and certifying products
Civil aircraft code	Eliminates 5% U.S. import tariff; eases government preferences, "offsets," and other restrictions by other countries
Subsidies and countervailing duties code	Requires governments to take account of trade effects of domestic subsidies and authorizes countermeasures by injured countries

...should spur continued growth in trade

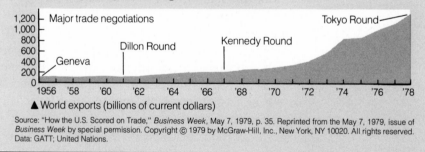

▲ World exports (billions of current dollars)

Source: "How the U.S. Scored on Trade," *Business Week,* May 7, 1979, p. 35. Reprinted from the May 7, 1979, issue of *Business Week* by special permission. Copyright © 1979 by McGraw-Hill, Inc., New York, NY 10020. All rights reserved. Data: GATT; United Nations.

Sources: Information from Peter Nulty "Why the 'Tokyo Round' Was a U.S. Victory," *Fortune,* May 21, 1979, pp. 130–132, 134–135; "A Smooth End to the Tokyo Round," *Business Week,* April 9, 1979, pp. 32–33; "How the U.S. Scored on Trade," *Business Week,* May 7, 1979, pp. 34–35; "Can World Head Off a Trade War?" *U.S. News & World Report,* April 23, 1979, pp. 43–44; and "Significant Trends," *Sales & Marketing Management,* May 14, 1979, p. 82.

Steel is not the only product to involve allegations of dumping. Similar allegations have been leveled against foreign makers of products as diverse as hockey sticks, cement, and motorcycles.

Demands for protection against foreign imports are common in all countries, particularly during periods of economic uncertainty. Firms ask for protection against sales losses, and unions seek to preserve their members' jobs. Overall, however, the long-term trend is in the direction of free trade among nations.

Political and Legal Factors in International Marketing

Political factors greatly influence international marketing. Colgate's popular Irish Spring soap was introduced in England with a political name change. The British know the product as Nordic Spring.[33] India once told Coca-Cola that it could not continue to operate unless it gave the government its syrup formula. Coca-Cola declined, and the government began marketing a drink called "77," using the same bottlers.[34]

Many nations try to achieve political objectives through international business activities. Japan, for instance, has openly encouraged its firms' involvement in international marketing, because much of the nation's economy is dependent on overseas sales.

Legal requirements complicate world marketing.[35] Quebec's requirement that all firms have a French identity has caused some firms to change the "Ltd." typically used in Canada to "Inc." The reason? "Inc." can be either English or French.[36] Some nations have *local content laws* that specify the portion of a product that must come from domestic sources. These examples suggest that managers involved in international marketing must be well-versed in legislation affecting their specific industries. The legal environment for U.S. firms operating abroad can be divided into three dimensions: (1) U.S. law, (2) international law, and (3) legal requirements of host nations.

International marketing is subject to various trade regulations, tax laws, and import/export requirements. One of the best-known U.S. laws is the *Webb-Pomerene Export Trade Act* of 1918, which exempted from antitrust laws various combinations of U.S. firms acting together to develop foreign markets. The intent was to give U.S. industry economic power equal to that possessed by **cartels**—*the monopolistic organizations of foreign firms.* Companies operating under the Webb-Pomerene act cannot reduce competition within the United States and cannot use "unfair methods of competition." Today, Webb-Pomerene associations account for less than 2 percent of U.S. exports. The U.S. Commerce Department has recommended that the act be expanded to include services as well as products.[37]

The most important new legislation is the *Foreign Corrupt Practices Act,* which makes it illegal to bribe a foreign official in an attempt to solicit new or repeat sales abroad. The act also specifies that adequate accounting controls be installed to monitor internal compliance. Violations can result in a $1 million fine for the firm and a $10,000 fine and five years imprisonment for individuals involved.[38]

International law can be found in the treaties, conventions, and agreements that exist among nations. The United States has many **friendship, commerce, and navigation (FCN) treaties** *that deal with many aspects of commercial relations with other countries,* such as the right to conduct business in the treaty partner's domestic market.

Other international business agreements concern international standards for various products, patents, trademarks, reciprocal tax treaties, export control, international air travel, and international communications. The International Monetary Fund has been set up to lend foreign exchange to nations that require it to conduct international trade. These agreements facilitate the whole process of world marketing.

The legal requirements of host nations affect foreign marketers. For example, some nations limit foreign ownership in their business sectors. Inter-

Figure 17-1
U.S. Goods and Services Produced by Foreign-Owned Companies

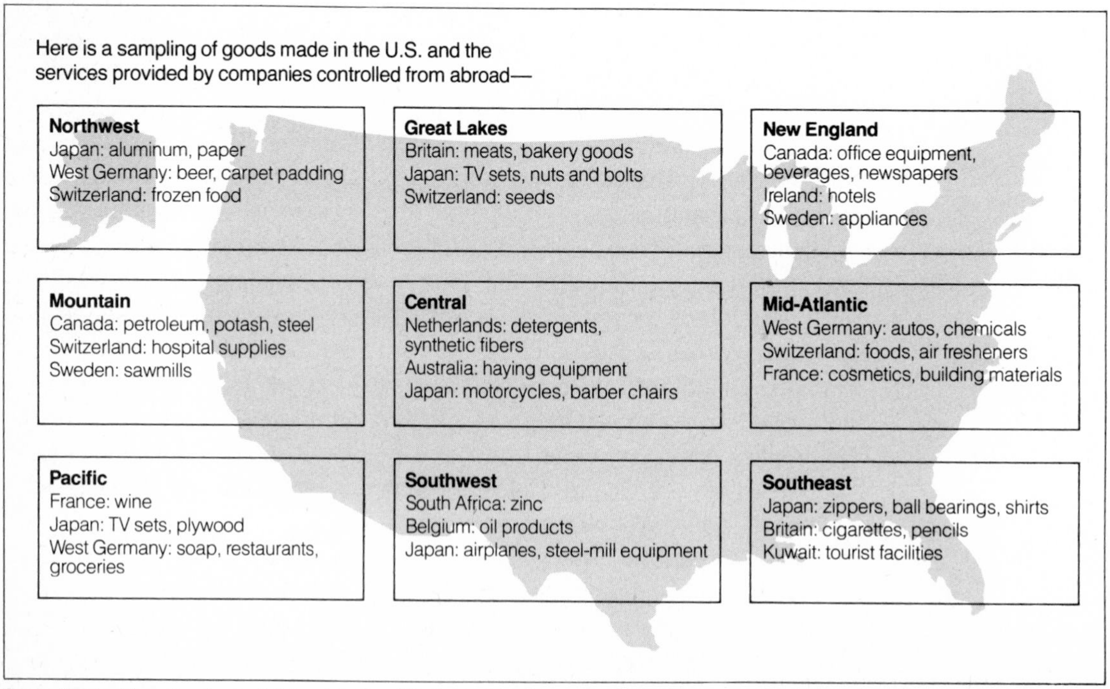

Here is a sampling of goods made in the U.S. and the services provided by companies controlled from abroad—

Northwest
Japan: aluminum, paper
West Germany: beer, carpet padding
Switzerland: frozen food

Great Lakes
Britain: meats, bakery goods
Japan: TV sets, nuts and bolts
Switzerland: seeds

New England
Canada: office equipment, beverages, newspapers
Ireland: hotels
Sweden: appliances

Mountain
Canada: petroleum, potash, steel
Switzerland: hospital supplies
Sweden: sawmills

Central
Netherlands: detergents, synthetic fibers
Australia: haying equipment
Japan: motorcycles, barber chairs

Mid-Atlantic
West Germany: autos, chemicals
Switzerland: foods, air fresheners
France: cosmetics, building materials

Pacific
France: wine
Japan: TV sets, plywood
West Germany: soap, restaurants, groceries

Southwest
South Africa: zinc
Belgium: oil products
Japan: airplanes, steel-mill equipment

Southeast
Japan: zippers, ball bearings, shirts
Britain: cigarettes, pencils
Kuwait: tourist facilities

Source: "Foreign Firms: Covering the U.S.," reprinted from *U.S. News & World Report,* July 24, 1978, p. 54. Copyright 1978 U.S. News & World Report, Inc.

national marketers in general recognize the importance of obeying the laws and regulations of the countries within which they operate. Even the slightest violations of these legal requirements are setbacks for the future of international trade.

Multinational Economic Integration and World Marketing

A noticeable trend toward multinational economic integration has developed since the close of World War II. The Common Market, or European Economic Community (EEC), is the best known of these multinational economic communities.

Multinational economic integration can be set up in several ways. The simplest approach is a *free trade area,* where the participants agree to free trade of goods among themselves in a particular area. All tariffs and trade restrictions are abolished between the nations involved. A *customs union* establishes a free trade area, plus a uniform tariff for trade with nonmember nations. The EEC is the best example of a customs union. A true *common market* or *economic union,* involves a customs union and also seeks to bring all government regulations affecting trade into agreement. The EEC has been moving in the direction of an economic union.

Multinational economic communities have played a significant part in international business. United States firms invested heavily in Western Europe in the 1960s basically because of the attraction of larger markets offered by the EEC. Multinational economic integration is forcing management to adapt its operations abroad, and it is likely that the pace will accelerate.

The United States: An Attractive Market for International Marketers

The United States has become an increasingly inviting target for foreign marketers. It has a large population, high levels of discretionary income, political stability, an attitude generally favorable to foreign investment, and economic ills that are relatively controlled in comparison to many other countries. Figure 17–1 shows U.S. goods and services produced by foreign-owned companies.

A number of foreign-owned competitors are also finding the United States an attractive market. The Atlanta Hilton is Kuwaiti-owned. Volkswagen Rabbits are made in New Stanton, Pennsylvania. Many Sony television receivers are assembled in San Diego. Popular U.S brands such as Alka-Seltzer, Pepsodent, Baskin-Robbins, Wisk, and Calgon are owned by foreign-controlled firms.[39]

Many foreign nations actually conduct or coordinate their marketing efforts in the United States through agencies or corporations of their own government. Agricultural and primary products are often marketed in this way.

Some people have shown a preference for foreign products over domestic competitors. Foreign sports cars, English china, and French wine all have sizable shares of the U.S. market. Some foreign products—such as Porsche sports cars—are sold in the United States because of their quality image. Others sell on the basis of a price advantage over domestic competition.

U.S. marketers must expect to face substantial foreign competition in the years ahead. The United States' high levels of buying power are sure to continue their considerable appeal abroad, and the reduction of trade barriers and expanded international marketing seem to be long-run trends.

Summary

International marketing has become increasingly important to the United States. Many U.S. firms depend on their ability to market their goods abroad, while others depend on buying raw materials from other countries.

International marketing is often considered in terms of a nation's balance of trade (the relationship between exports and imports) and balance of payments (flow of money into or out of the country). Countries must sometimes adjust their exchange rates (the rates at which their currency can be exchanged for others or for gold).

Two of the basic concepts in international marketing are absolute advantage and comparative advantage. An absolute advantage exists if a nation is the sole producer of an item or can produce it for less than any other nation. A comparative advantage exists if a country can produce an item more efficiently than it can produce alternate ones.

Competing in overseas markets is often considerably different from competing at home. Market size, buying behavior, and marketing practices may all differ. International marketers must make significant adaptations in their product, distribution, promotion, and pricing strategies to fit different markets abroad.

Several levels of involvement in international marketing can be identified: casual or accidental exporting, active exporting, foreign licensing, overseas marketing, and foreign production and marketing.

The world's largest firms are usually multinational in their orientation. Such companies operate in several countries and view the world as their market.

Various environmental factors can influence international marketing strategy. Cultural, economic, and societal factors can hinder international marketing. So can assorted trade restrictions and some political and legal factors.

Since the end of World War II, there has been a noticeable trend toward multinational economic integration. Three basic formats for integration are free trade areas, customs unions, and common markets.

The United States is now viewed as an attractive market target for marketers from abroad. Thus U.S. firms can expect to face stiff foreign competition in their own domestic market.

Questions for Discussion

1. Explain the following terms:

exporting	multinational corporation
importing	tariff
balance of trade	General Agreement on Tariffs and Trade (GATT)
balance of payments	import quota
exchange rate	embargo
floating exchange rate	Tokyo Round
devaluation	exchange control
revaluation	dumping
absolute advantage	cartels
comparative advantage	friendship, commerce, and navigation (FCN) treaties

2. Comment on the following statement: International business offers both opportunities and challenges to contemporary marketers.

3. How important is exporting and importing to the United States?

4. France's Perrier water has become very popular in the United States. Research the marketing program used to sell water to people in the United States.

5. How could a nation have both a favorable balance of trade and an unfavorable balance of payments?

6. Trace the recent experience of the United States in the balance of trade and balance of payments accounts.

7. What effect does the reduction of a nation's exchange rate have on international marketing?

8. Differentiate between the concepts of absolute advantage and comparative advantage. List other factors that can influence what a nation produces and markets.

9. Describe the existing trends in world population. How do these trends affect international marketing?

10. Discuss this statement: It is sometimes dangerous for a firm to attempt to export its marketing strategy.

11. Describe the types of adaptations that international business forces firms to make in their marketing strategies.

12. What is your opinion of existing U.S. policy toward dumping?

13. Identify and explain the different levels of involvement in international marketing.

14. Should the U.S. government take action to restrict *maquiladoros*?

15. Outline the basic premises behind the operation of a multinational corporation.

16. What environmental factors influence international marketing?

17. Do you agree with the general movement toward reduced trade restrictions among nations? Explain.

18. How has multinational economic integration affected international marketing?

19. Why is the United States such an attractive market target for foreign marketers? What does this mean for U.S. firms?

20. Some people argue that foreign investment in the United States should be limited. Would you agree with a plan that would limit such investment in a particular company to some specified amount? Explain.

Notes

1. Christy Marshall, "Budget: Pass the Keys 'n Pizza, Please," *Advertising Age,* February 13, 1978, p. 89.
2. "Not for Export?" *Forbes,* October 15, 1975, p. 24.
3. Kentucky Fried Chicken's failure in Hong Kong is reported in "Colonel's Chicken Flops in Hong Kong," an AFP wire story, and in *International Newsletter,* May 5, 1975.
4. "Trying to Right the Balance," *Time,* October 9, 1978, p. 84.
5. Eva Cullen, "United States Foreign Trade," *Conference Board Economic Roadmaps,* August 1978, p. 1.
6. U.S. Department of Commerce, Bureau of Economic Analysis, *Survey of Current Business,* July 1978, pp. S–22 to S–24.
7. Lawrence Minard, "Is Free Trade Dead?" *Forbes,* May 14, 1979, p. 67.
8. Charles Hillinger, "Nauru Is Killing the Bird That Laid the Golden Guano," *Detroit News,* April 2, 1978.
9. Lindley H. Clark, Jr., "More U.S. Companies Begin to Sell Abroad as Sales at Home Slip," *Wall Street Journal,* April 4, 1975, p. 1.
10. World population growth is traced in Jonathan Spivak, "Population of a World Growing Faster than Experts Anticipated," *Wall Street Journal,* April 12, 1976, pp. 1, 15.
11. Michael Doan, "In Spite of Its Troubles, U.S. Ranks as Second Richest Nation," AP story, November 24, 1978.
12. Ramona Bechtos, "Coke Tries to Widen Brazil Market," *Advertising Age,* August 11, 1975, pp. 3, 6.
13. Roland Burgman, "Product Managers Should Know How Consumers Will See New Products, but They Don't Always Guess Right," *Marketing News,* April 9, 1976, p. 4.
14. S. Watson Dunn, "Effect of National Identity on Multinational Promotional Strategy in Europe," *Journal of Marketing,* October 1976, p. 50.
15. David A. Ricks, Marilyn Y. C. Fu, and Jeffrey S. Arpan, *International Business Blunders* (Columbus, Ohio: Grid, 1974), pp. 17–18.
16. Ralph Z. Sorenson, II, "U.S. Marketers Can Learn from European Innovators," *Harvard Business Review,* September–October 1972, p. 97.
17. Some interesting viewpoints on varied marketing practices and environments abroad are presented in Dean M. Peebles, John K. Ryans, and Ivan R. Vernon, "Coordinating International Advertising," *Journal of Marketing,* January 1978, pp. 28–34; James Kilbough, "Improved Payoffs from Transnational Advertising," *Harvard Business Review,* July–August 1978, pp. 102–110; Jack G. Kaikati, "How Multinational Corporations Handle the Arab Boycott," *Columbia Journal of World Business,* Spring 1978, pp. 98–111; and Susan Douglas and Bernard Dubois, "Looking at the Cultural Environment for International Marketing Opportunities," *Columbia Journal of World Business,* Winter 1977, pp. 102–109.
18. Clark, "More U.S. Companies Begin to Sell Abroad," p. 25.
19. J. Donald Weinrauch and C. P. Rao, "The Export Marketing Mix: An Examination of Company Experiences and Perceptions," *Journal of Business Research,* October 1974, p. 451.
20. "An Idea That Didn't Travel Well," *Forbes,* February 15, 1976, pp. 26–27.
21. William Mathewson, "Trademarks Are a Global Business These Days, but Finding Registerable Ones Is a Big Problem," *Wall Street Journal,* September 4, 1975, p. 26.
22. "Sears Adds Insurance to Its Line of Exports," *Business Week,* August 4, 1975, p. 39.
23. "Nissan Competes with the Camel," *Business Week,* May 26, 1975, p. 44.
24. "Japanese Are Top TV Watchers," *Tulsa Tribune,* December 4, 1975.
25. Weinrauch and Rao, "The Export Marketing Mix," pp. 448–449.
26. This argument is described in Everett Martin and Roger Ricklefs, "'Third World' Presses to Stabilize the Prices of Its Raw Materials," *Wall Street Journal,* July 3, 1975, pp. 1, 15.
27. These failure rates are reported in Erwin H. Klaus, "How to Negotiate International Licensing Agreements and Keep Smiling," *Marketing News,* December 5, 1975, p. 8.
28. Robert Ball, "Nestlé Revs Up Its U.S. Campaign," *Fortune,* February 13, 1978, pp. 80–83.
29. Reported in Warren J. Keegan, "Multinational Product Planning: Strategic Alternatives," *Journal of Marketing,* January 1969, p. 58.
30. Reported in "GM's Big Push to Sell U.S.-Built Cars," *Business Week,* July 31, 1978, p. 45; and "Europe Takes to U.S. Autos," *Detroit News,* October 29, 1978.
31. "Business Bulletin," *Wall Street Journal,* September 28, 1978, p. 1.
32. This section is based on Robert Z. Chew, "U.S. Steel Makers Mostly Mum on Volatile Issue of Import 'Dumping,'" *Advertising Age,* October 24, 1977, pp. 28, 112; Greg Conderacci, "'Trigger-Price' System to Help Steel Industry Triggers Much Dismay," *Wall Street Journal,* September 26, 1978, pp. 1, 19; and "Mounting Clamor for Trade Barriers," *U.S. News & World Report,* February 6, 1978, p. 57.
33. "Off the Record," *Detroit News,* February 28, 1975, p. 1.
34. Richard Manville, "33 Caveats for the Prospective Overseas Marketer," *Marketing News,* March 10, 1978, p. 6. Excerpted and abridged from *Selling Overseas Successfully.* Copyright © 1978 by Richard Manville, Westport, CT 06880.

35. Legal risks are discussed in Sandra McRae Huszagh, "Reducing Legal Risks to Marketing in Multiple Country Operations," *Columbia Journal of World Business,* Spring 1978, pp. 50–58.
36. "Business Bulletin," *Wall Street Journal,* March 23, 1978, p. 1.
37. "Webb-Pomerene: Washington Sends Business Mixed Signals," *Forbes,* July 24, 1978, p. 44.
38. "The Antibribery Bill Backfires," *Business Week,* April 17, 1978, p. 143.
39. These examples are from "The Selling of America," *Time,* May 29, 1978, pp. 70–71, 73.

CHAPTER 18
MARKETING AND SOCIETY: CONTEMPORARY ISSUES

Key Terms

public responsibility
committee
Green River
ordinances
consumerism
class action suit
ecology

planned
obsolescence
pollution
recycling
open dating

Learning Goals

1. To describe how external relationships form the basis of the societal issues confronting contemporary marketing.
2. To explain the need for better measures of marketing performance.
3. To categorize the current issues in marketing.
4. To list the alternatives for resolving the societal issues facing contemporary marketing.

18

AT&T, Dow Chemical, General Electric, J. C. Penney, Pillsbury, and Westing-house, among others, have set up **public responsibility committees**—*permanent committees of the firms' boards of directors that consider matters of corporate social responsibility.*[1] All these firms are acting responsibly to contemporary business and societal issues. And marketing has a key role to play in the resolution of these matters. Marketing's relationship to society in general and to specific public issues is subject to constant change. Marketing typically mirrors changes in the entire business environment. As a result, the marketer usually carries much of the responsibility for dealing with the various societal issues affecting any firm.

Marketing's Contemporary Environment

Marketing operates in an environment that is external to the firm. It reacts to its environment and is, in turn, acted upon by it. The environmental relationships include those with customers, employees, the government, vendors, and the society as a whole. While they are often a product of the exchange process, they are coincidental to the primary functions of marketing.

External relationships form the basis of the societal issues confronting contemporary marketing. A firm's marketing relationship to its external environment has a significant effect on the degree of success it achieves. Marketing must always find new ways to deal with the social issues facing the competitive system.

Historically, marketing has neglected some environmental relationships. The so-called **Green River ordinances** were enacted *to limit door-to-door selling,* which had become excessive in some areas. Corrective advertisements were ordered for Profile Bread's diet claims. The government has had to ban some children's toys because of their dangerous and harmful qualities. And alleged payoff scandals involving firms like Lockheed stunned the populace in the mid-1970s.

The competitive marketing system is a product of the drive for materialism. Similarly, materialism developed from society itself. People in the United States usually view the acquisition of wealth favorably. Their motto seems to be "more equals better." They have defined a *better* life in terms of *more* physical possessions—although that attitude may be changing.

Adam Smith, the father of capitalism, argued that people's desire to serve their own best interest would act as an "invisible hand" in guiding the economy. The resulting maximization of output would improve life and society by improving the standard of living. Smith saw competition as the watchdog that kept the economy on the correct course. The materialism explicit in his thoughts has continued to serve as the economic philosophy of U.S. society.

One theme runs throughout the arguments of marketing's critics: Material-ism as exemplified by the competitive marketing system is concerned only with the *quantities* of life and ignores the *quality* of life. Traditionally, a firm was considered socially responsible in the community if it provided employ-ment to its residents, thereby contributing to its economic base. Employ-ment, wages, bank deposits, and profits—the traditional measures of soci-etal contribution—are quantity indicators. But what of air, water, and cul-tural pollution? What of the boredom and isolation associated with mass assembly lines? And what of the depletion of natural resources? The charges of neglect in these areas often go largely unanswered simply be-cause reliable indices by which to measure a firm's contribution to the qual-ity of life have not been developed.

Several attempts have been made to develop a *quality index*. Environ-mentalists, for instance, have made efforts in this area for several years. The U.S. Congress's Joint Economic Committee has used a *Misery Index*—the total of the unemployment and inflation rates—in its deliberations. A com-mittee member, the late Hubert Humphrey, used to check what was selling at his drug store in Huron, South Dakota. Humphrey reported "When there is stress, they buy bromides and laxatives. . . . In good times, it vanishes."[2]

A Japanese bank has developed a *Happiness Index* based on thirty-three factors, including income, crime, paved roads, parks, and suicide rates. Even though some of its measures are admittedly subjective, the index does show that people in the United States are 2.53 times happier than those in Japan.[3]

A major government-funded study by the Midwest Research Institute measured the quality of life in 243 U.S. cities of over 50,000 population. The study, which considered 123 statistical variables, rated each city on five fac-tors: economic, environmental, political, social, and health and educational.[4] The rankings for metropolitan areas with populations of 500,000 or more are shown in Table 18–1.

Obviously, these attempts need to be refined further, but they do repre-sent a step toward solving a pressing national need. The development of *quality indicators* is a matter deserving the increased attention of marketers. A multidisciplinary approach—with a substantial contribution from market-ing—is called for if society is ever to be able to assess its quality content.

Individual companies are becoming more concerned about reporting societal behavior. Various firms—such as General Motors—have made at-tempts at corporate reports on social performance. These efforts go under a variety of names; among them are social audits, consumer affairs audits, and reports on social responsibility.[5] Marketers are not the dominant factors in all areas of social responsibility, but they play a role in many aspects of the issue.[6]

Table 18–1
Ranking U.S. Cities of 500,000 and Over for Quality of Life

Outstanding	Excellent	Good	Adequate	Substandard
1. Portland, Ore.*	14. Anaheim, Calif.*	26. San Bernardino, Calif.*	38. Newark, N.J.	56. Tampa, Fla.*
2. Sacramento, Calif.	15. Buffalo	27. Houston	39. Paterson, N.J.*	57. Philadelphia*
3. Seattle*	16. Oklahoma City	28. Phoenix	40. Springfield, Mass.*	58. Memphis*
4. San Jose, Calif.	17. Omaha*	29. Akron	41. Youngstown, Ohio*	59. Norfolk*
5. Minneapolis*	18. Albany, N.Y.*	30. Cincinnati*	42. Detroit	60. Greensboro, N.C.*
6. Rochester	19. Syracuse	31. Honolulu	43. Richmond	61. Jacksonville
7. Hartford, Conn.	20. Washington, D.C.*	32. Dayton	44. Fort Worth	62. San Antonio
8. Denver	21. Los Angeles*	33. New York	45. Atlanta	63. New Orleans
9. San Francisco*	22. Columbus	34. Dallas	46. Fort Lauderdale*	64. Birmingham
10. San Diego	23. Boston	35. Kansas City*	47. Miami	65. Jersey City
11. Grand Rapids	24. Cleveland	36. Indianapolis	48. Nashville*	
12. Milwaukee	25. Toledo*	37. Chicago	49. Pittsburgh	
13. Salt Lake City			50. Allentown, Pa.*	
			51. St. Louis*	
			52. Gary, Ind.*	
			53. Louisville*	
			54. Providence*	
			55. Baltimore	

*Metropolitan areas that include more than one city or cross state lines.
Source: "Ranking the Cities," *Time*, September 29, 1975, p. 83. Reprinted by permission of TIME, The Weekly Newsmagazine; Copyright Time Inc. 1975. Data from Ben-chieh Liu, *Quality of Life Indicators in U.S. Metropolitan Areas, 1970* (Washington, D.C.: Government Printing Office, 1975).

Current Issues in Marketing

Marketing faces numerous and diverse social issues. They range from consumerism to the pricing practices of retailers in low-income areas to the cultural pollution caused by some television advertisements.

The current issues in marketing can be divided into three major subjects: *consumerism, marketing ethics,* and *social responsibility.* While the overlap and classification problems are obvious, the framework provides a foundation for systematically studying the issues.

Consumerism

Marketers, industry, government, and the public are all aware of the impact of consumerism on the nation's economy and general well-being. **Consumerism** is *the demand that marketers give greater attention to consumer desires in making their decisions.* It is a protest against abuses and malpractice in the marketing system and often is seen as part of a broader movement that seeks increased social responsibility in many sectors of society.[7]

Prior to the emergence of the current consumerism movement in the late 1960s, state and federal laws designed to maintain a competitive environment were the primary protection afforded consumer interests. The underlying assumption was that a highly competitive environment provided adequate safeguards for customers and the general public. Consumer protection was viewed as a by-product of the regulation of competition.

Many academicians and practitioners have argued that the rise in consumerism is proof that the marketing concept has failed. Their reasoning is based on two premises:

1. Not enough firms have adopted the marketing concept to provide adequate consumer safeguards.
2. The concept itself has not made firms more responsive to consumer desires in such areas as product safety, guarantees, warranties, and service.

These arguments seem unnecessarily critical. Consumerism does not mark the end of the marketing concept. Instead it introduces a new era in marketing responsibility.

The advent of consumerism provides marketers with new opportunities. Generally, marketers support its philosophy. The Social Concerns Survey, a study of 1,400 members of the American Marketing Association, asked respondents to indicate their attitude toward the following statement: "The 'consumer movement' is likely to result in more harm than good for society." Of the members responding, 80 percent disagreed with the statement, and only 16 percent agreed.[8] Admittedly, consumerism will require changes in some aspects of business life. It will, for example, force companies to be more responsible to their constituents. But this is all to the good. Consumerism is heralding an era of increased importance for the marketing concept.

Consumerism's Indictment of the Competitive Marketing System	Consumerism's indictment of marketing lists six separate charges:

1. **Marketing costs are too high.**[9] The charge is that distribution costs, which average about 50 percent of the selling price, are unjustified.
   Marketing's Plea: Innocent. This charge ignores the effect that efficient distribution has on the total cost structure. The competitive system has expanded the market for most products so that the production costs per unit have declined in amounts exceeding the cost of the marketing system. While distribution costs per se are high, products are cheaper under the competitive system than they would be under alternative methods. The negative implication of the charge is therefore unfounded.

2. **The marketing system is inefficient.** The premise is that the competitive marketing system often does not respond promptly to consumer dictates.
   Marketing's Plea: Guilty, with mitigating circumstances. The charge is

true. Not all firms have adopted the consumer orientation explicit in the marketing concept. These *individual* marketing systems are often inefficient and unresponsive. However, when they are judged and found wanting by the impersonal forces of the competitive market, they soon disappear or are modified so as to become effective.

3. **Marketers are guilty of collusion and price fixing.** Such restraints of trade are direct affronts to all consumers.

    Marketing's Plea: No contest. Yes, some firms have been convicted of such violations. However, some legislators have been accused of accepting bribes, a few ministers have been charged with "having their hand in the church till," and some members of the medical profession have been involved in insurance, Medicaid, and Medicare scandals. The point is that individual examples of unethical practices are regretable, but when compared in size and number to the vast volume of transactions in the market, they are also relatively few. There is no evidence for a general indictment of *all* marketers, but there are areas needing careful attention.

4. **Product quality and service are poor.** Consumer advocates point to numerous examples of faulty products supported by worthless warranty programs administered through incompetent service departments. These critics say that one need only buy a new car, washing machine, or television to prove their point.

    Marketing's Plea: Guilty. No industry has been able to escape the problems of poor product quality and service. A survey of 2,400 households found that only one-fourth of them were satisfied with companies' resolutions of nonprice problems. A substantial part of the dissatisfaction comes from people who do not even bother to register their complaints. One suggestion resulting from the study was that companies should make greater efforts to inform consumers of their ability to handle complaints and of the procedures consumers should follow. Toll-free telephone lines are one way of helping achieve this objective.[10] It

Faulty products are a common frustration of consumers.

Source: "Broom Hilda," June 7, 1979. Reprinted by permission of the Chicago Tribune–New York News Syndicate, Inc.

is clear that marketers should pay more attention to consumer complaints in the future.

5. **The marketing system has produced health and safety hazards.** Critics point to examples such as the numerous toys that have been labeled hazardous by a government regulatory agency, the reported dangers and side effects of using various pharmaceuticals, and the health dangers of several forms of pollution.

Marketing's Plea: No contest. The previously mentioned Social Concerns Survey showed that 72 percent of the marketers polled disagreed with the statement that "consumers are adequately protected against health hazards." Furthermore, 94 percent agreed with the statement that "when public health or safety are involved, compulsory product and service standards should be established by the government unless voluntary standards are established and adhered to."[11] It is interesting to note that while auto safety was the basis for Ralph Nader's original consumer campaign, when Ford offered seatbelts as optional equipment in the 1950s, there were few takers. No-lead gasoline was initially rejected by consumers despite an extensive marketing effort, and the elimination of lead in gasoline required mandatory legislation at the federal level. The American Marketing Association study suggests that marketers are at least as concerned with these dangers as is the average citizen.

6. **Consumers do not receive complete information.** Proponents of consumerism argue that purchase decisions are often unnecessarily complicated because the consumer does not receive adequate information. Trade and legal jargon sometimes makes warranties confusing. Computer-based checkouts have eliminated individual price marking in many stores. As a result of these and other practices, consumers sometimes lack important information in their buying decisions.

Marketing's Plea: Guilty, with reservations. Marketing pleads guilty with some reservation about the amount of information required. Yes, it is difficult to compare alternative products without complete information. However, reports on the truth-in-lending legislation (see Chapter 2) suggest that more complete information has not significantly altered consumer handling of credit purchases. Studies about other areas of consumer information show similar results. It seems that the degree of information required depends on the item involved, its price, and the available alternatives. The real question appears to be: How can society best provide information of lasting value to the consumer?

Rights of the Consumer

Not all consumer demands are met. A competitive marketing system is based on individualistic behavior of competing firms and requires that reasonable profit objectives be achieved. Given these constraints, what should the consumer have the right to expect from this system?

One of the clearest policy statements on the rights of the consumer was issued by President John F. Kennedy in a speech to Congress on March 15, 1962. He delineated the following rights:

1. The consumer has the right to safety.
2. The consumer has the right to be informed.
3. The consumer has the right to choose.
4. The consumer has the right to be heard.

These rights have formed the conceptual framework of much of the consumer legislation passed since 1962. However, the question of how best to guarantee them remains unanswered.

Responses to Consumerism

The public response to consumerism has been varied in both orientation and relative achievement. Essentially, the consumer movement has brought four primary reactions:

1. Passage of more legislation designed to aid the consumer.
2. Creation of additional consumer protection agencies.
3. The concept of class action suits.
4. Improved consumer education.

Hundreds of pieces of consumer legislation have been introduced not only in Congress but also in state legislatures and city halls. Consumer protection agencies with varying responsibilities and authority now proliferate at all levels of government. Consumer legislation and the edicts of various consumer protection agencies form a patchwork of regulations that are often confusing and that sometimes work at cross-purposes.

But consumerism may not have quite the political clout it once had. Many people now realize that increased consumer protection comes at a cost. This cost may be reflected in higher prices or increased taxes to support more regulatory efforts. A 1978 bill to create a federal level Office of Consumer Representation was defeated. In voting for its defeat, many members of Congress noted that their constituents—consumers all—were opposed to more government regulation and agencies.[12]

Another potent consumer weapon is the **class action suit**—*a suit brought by private citizens on behalf of any group of consumers for damages caused by unfair business practices.* Such suits give consumers a process by which to seek corrective action in cases of marketing abuses. One proposal to modify class action suits generally would speed up the suits, cut legal fees, and involve the U.S. Attorney General in suits where individual damages were small.[13] Litigation, however, is not always the best way to correct society's problems. The recent medical malpractice crisis illustrates some unpleasant side effects of corrective actions based largely on litigation. Many physicians, for example have dropped malpractice insurance altogether. Others have raised their fees substantially to offset spiraling malpractice insurance premiums.

Perhaps the most promising long-term solution to the questions raised by the consumer movement is an expanded educational program.[14] Such an effort would be concentrated in primary and secondary schools as well as in adult education classes. One current effort in this area is being made by the Boy Scouts; they have added a merit badge for consumer buying.[15] Mass media could also be employed to improve consumer decision making through education. In the long run, the best customer safeguard is a well-informed consumer!

Most companies have taken a progressive attitude toward consumerism. While individual strategies vary, all firms have had to adapt to the consumerism movement in some way. Their most important action has been that of giving consumer affairs and customer relations a more important role in the organization.[16] In other words, business is responding by assigning greater weight to consumer needs and opinions.

Marketing Ethics

Another widely debated aspect of the contemporary social environment is marketing ethics.[17] It is a subject that is receiving increased attention in an era characterized by a general questioning of business and marketing procedures.

Individuals develop their own standards of ethical behavior. This *individual ethic* helps each person deal with the various ethical questions in his or her personal life. However, a serious role conflict may materialize for the individual in a work situation. Individual ethics sometimes differ from the *organizational ethic* of the employer. An individual may, for example, personally believe that industry participation in redeveloping the inner city is highly desirable, but if the firm takes the position that such a venture is unprofitable, the individual may experience role conflict. Similar conflicts are not difficult to imagine.

How can this situation be resolved? The development of and adherence

Consumer Education May Be One of the Most Pressing National Needs

The need for improved consumer education was clearly pointed out by a government financed study of 34,000 people aged seventeen and 4,200 people in the twenty-six to thirty-six age bracket. The survey was designed to assess how well people could solve basic consumer mathematics problems. The majority of the respondents could not calculate the most economical size of a product, determine a correct taxi fare, or balance a checkbook. Upon learning the study's results, the presidential consumer adviser remarked that it was little wonder a record number of consumers had gone bankrupt the previous year.

Sources: Information from "Survey Flunks Americans on Consumer Math Test," *Detroit News*, July 24, 1975; and "Study Says Students of New Math Flunk Consumer Problems," *Wall Street Journal*, July 25, 1975, p. 28.

Table 18–2
**American
Marketing
Association
Code of Ethics**

Our Code of Ethics

As a member of the American Marketing Association, I recognize the significance of my professional conduct and my responsibilities to society and to the other members of my profession:

1. By acknowledging my accountability to society as a whole as well as to the organization for which I work.
2. By pledging my efforts to assure that all presentations of goods, services and concepts be made honestly and clearly.
3. By striving to improve marketing knowledge and practice in order to better serve society.
4. By supporting free consumer choice in circumstances that are legal and are consistent with generally accepted community standards.
5. By pledging to use the highest professional standards in my work and in competitive activity.
6. By acknowledging the right of the American Marketing Association, through established procedure, to withdraw my membership if I am found to be in violation of ethical standards of professional conduct.

Source: American Marketing Association, *Constitution and Bylaws*, rev. ed. (Chicago: American Marketing Association, 1977), p. 20. Reprinted by permission.

to a *professional ethic* may provide a third basis of authority.[18] This ethic should be based on a concept of professionalism that transcends both organizational and individual ethics. It depends on the existence of a professional peer association that can exercise collective sanctions over a marketer's professional behavior. The American Marketing Association, for example, has developed a code of ethics that includes a provision to expel members who violate its tenets (see Table 18–2).

A variety of ethical problems face the marketer every day. While promotional matters have received the greatest attention recently, ethical questions concerning research, product management, channel strategy, and pricing also arise.

**Ethical Problems
Related to
Research**

Marketing research has been castigated because of its alleged *invasion of personal privacy.* Citizens of modern urban society seek identity as individuals rather than as members of homogeneous groups. They often resist others' efforts to make information about their personal lives public. Personal privacy has therefore become a public issue for many.

**Some
Hypothetical
Situations
Involving Ethical
Questions**

A study conducted by the Bureau of Business Research at the University of Michigan posed a series of "action" situations to a sample of 401 marketing research directors and chief marketing executives. The respondents were told that the marketing research director of a company had taken some particular action. The participants were then asked, "Do you approve or disapprove of the action taken?" A sample of these situations and the resulting responses are shown below. How would you have replied?

One-Way Mirrors

One product of the X Company is brassieres, and the firm has recently been having difficulty making some decisions on a new line. Information was critically needed concerning the manner in which women put on their brassieres. So the marketing research director designed a study in which two local stores cooperated in putting one-way mirrors in their foundations dressing rooms. Observers behind these mirrors successfully gathered the necessary information.

	Approve	*Disapprove*
Research directors	20%	78%
Line marketers	18	82

Advertising and Product Misuse

Some recent research showed that many customers of X Company are misusing Product B. There's no danger; they are simply wasting their money by using too much of it at a time. But yesterday, the marketing research director saw final comps on Product B's new ad campaign, and the ads not only ignored the problem of misuse but actually seemed to encourage it. The director quietly referred the advertising manager to the research results, well known to all people involved with B's advertising, and let it go at that.

	Approve	*Disapprove*
Research directors	41%	58%
Line marketers	33	66

General Trade Data to Citizens' Group

The marketing research department of X Company frequently makes extensive studies of its retail customers. A citizens' group working to get a shopping center in their low-income area wanted to know if they could have access to this trade information. But since the firm had always refused to share this information with trade organizations, the marketing research director declined the request.

	Approve	*Disapprove*
Research directors	64%	34%
Line marketers	74	25

Source: Based on and quotes from C. Merle Crawford, "Attitudes of Marketing Executives toward Ethics in Marketing Research," *Journal of Marketing*, April 1970, pp. 46–52. Reprinted from the *Journal of Marketing* published by the American Marketing Association. Another excellent discussion of marketing research ethics is found in Robert Bezilla, Joel B. Haynes, and Clifford Elliott, "Ethics in Marketing Research," *Business Horizons*, April 1976, pp. 83–86.

Ethical Problems Related to Product Management

Chevrolet motors were installed in 128,000 Oldsmobiles, Buicks, and Pontiacs as a result of unexpected demand for the medium priced models. General Motors reasoned that the Chevrolet engines were the same size and horsepower and that a switch of this nature was an acceptable marketing practice. But buyers were not informed of the switch, and consumer complaints and legal cases resulted. General Motors may eventually have to make a multimillion-dollar settlement in what the media labeled the "Chevymobile case."[19] This incident suggests the changing nature and growing importance of ethical decisions in product management. Accepted marketing practice in this case was no longer acceptable to consumers.

Product quality, planned obsolescence, brand similarity, and packaging present ethical problems to product management. The packaging question

Chelsea: The Baby Beer Controversy

Anheuser-Busch wanted to introduce a premium-priced soft drink to appeal to the urban adult. The product it developed had a ginger, lemon, and apple flavoring and a malt-type base. It also had a 0.4 percent alcoholic content—compared to 6 percent in most beers. The new product, Chelsea, was to be priced at about $2 per six-pack.

Chelsea was test-marketed in late 1978 in Richmond and Staunton, Virginia, as well as in Massachusetts, Louisiana, and Illinois. Its introduction led to widespread protests by church groups, nurses, and educators. It was labeled "Baby Beer" by its critics, who claimed it would condition children to drink beer when they became older. They pointed out that Chelsea was advertised as "the not-so-soft soft drink" and that it foamed like beer. The amber color product, sold in clear bottles, also looked like beer.

Anheuser-Busch quickly stopped marketing Chelsea because of the protests. The product had by then already exceeded the 1 percent market share figure commonly used in the beer industry to assess new product viability.

Anheuser-Busch had had previous experience with a similar product. Its "Bevo" brand had failed after being introduced during Prohibition. Competition from bootleggers was too much for it.

In December 1978, after consulting with the many critics of the original product, Anheuser-Busch began testing a new version of Chelsea. The new Chelsea had only a trace of alcohol, was similar to other citrus-flavored beverages, and no longer had the foam. It was sold in green bottles to mask the product's amber color. The company's new advertising slogan was "the natural alternative." When Chelsea's product manager was asked what would be done with the original Chelsea, he replied, "We may dig a hole somewhere and bury it." Instead, Anheuser-Busch's marketers have been successful in establishing a market for the original Chelsea in Africa. And the St. Louis firm is now negotiating to market it in Western Europe as well.

Sources: Information from "Battle Brews over 'Near Beer,'" *Detroit News*, October 18, 1978; and Jeffrey Mills, "'Baby Beer' Is Being Replaced," *Mobile Register*, December 13, 1978. Updated information and ad from Anheuser-Busch. Used with permission.

is a significant concern of consumers, management, and the Federal Trade Commission. Competitive pressures have forced marketers into packaging practices that can be considered misleading, deceptive, and unethical in some quarters. Larger than necessary packages are used to gain shelf space and customer exposure in the supermarket. Odd-size packages make price comparisons difficult. Bottles with concave bottoms give the impression that they contain more liquid than is actually the case. The real question seems to be whether these practices can be justified in the name of competition. Growing regulatory mandates, however, appear to be narrowing the range of discretion in this area.

Ethical Problems Related to Distribution Strategy

A firm's channel strategy is required to deal with ethical questions such as:

1. What is the appropriate degree of control over the channel?
2. Should a company distribute its products in marginally profitable outlets that have no alternative source of supply?

The question of control typically arises in the relationship between a manufacturer and its franchised dealers. Should an automobile dealership, a gas station, or a fast-food outlet be forced to purchase parts, materials, and supplementary services from the parent organization? What is the proper degree of control in the channel of distribution?

Furthermore, should marketers serve unsatisfied market segments even if the profit potential is slight? What is marketing's ethical responsibility in serving retail stores in low-income areas, users of limited amounts of the firm's product, or a declining rural market?

These problems are difficult to resolve because they often involve individuals rather than broad segments of the general public. An important first step is to assure that channel policies are enforced on a consistent basis.

Ethical distribution practices usually return a dividend—but seldom to the extent of one received by a suburban Oklahoma City automobile dealer. Fifteen years earlier, the dealer sold a car to an Iranian student at Central State University. The student—Bob Azarmi—remembered that the dealer had given him a fair deal. Later, Azarmi, by then the sole purchasing agent for the Iranian Contractors Association, placed an order for *1,100 trucks* with the honest dealer he remembered from his college days.[20]

Ethical Problems Related to Pricing

Pricing is probably the most regulated aspect of a firm's marketing strategy. As a result, most unethical price behavior is also illegal. When asked to identify unethical practices they wanted eliminated, fewer executives specified issues such as price collusion, price discrimination, and unfair pricing in a 1976 survey than a similar group did in a 1961 study. This suggests that tighter government regulations exist in these areas now than in the past.[21]

There are, however, some grey areas in the matter of pricing ethics. For example, should some customers pay more for merchandise if distribution costs are higher in their areas? Do marketers have an obligation to warn customers of impending price, discount, or returns policy changes? All these questions must be dealt with in developing a professional ethic for marketing.

Ethical Problems Related to Promotion

Promotion is the component of the marketing mix where the majority of ethical questions arise. Personal selling has always been the target of ethically based criticism. The early traders, peddlers, and drummers and the twentieth century used-car sellers have all been accused of marketing malpractice ranging from excessive product claims to outright deceit. Gifts, bribes, and the like were identified as the primary ethical abuses in both the 1961 and 1976 studies discussed in the last section.[22]

Advertising, however, is even more maligned than sales. It is impersonal and hence easier to criticize. But there are also several legitimate concerns regarding advertising. For instance, ethical questions about advertising aimed at ethnic groups, women, and children have arisen. Black awareness has made the mass media particularly sensitive to promotions with such an orientation. Other ethnic groups have also begun to monitor advertising. For example, some Polish-Americans launched a nationwide campaign to improve the cultural image of this large segment of the U.S. population. Effective advertising requires that all promotional appeals be carefully reviewed so as to eliminate any ethical problems.

The portrayal of women in advertising has been of particular concern to marketers. Too often, it is argued, women have been assigned stereotyped housewife roles in television commercials and other media. Advertisers are now making a concerted effort to show women in varied situations, such as professional work environments.

Another ethical concern surrounds advertising aimed at children.[23] Some critics fear that television advertising exerts an undue influence on children—that children are easily influenced by toy, cereal, and snack food commercials. Correspondingly, they assume that children then exert substantial pressure on their parents to acquire these items. It has been estimated that children spend or influence their parents to spend $29 billion annually.[24]

A study published in the *Harvard Business Review* found that children in different age groups react to advertising in varying ways.

Reactions of Children to Advertising

Five- and six-year-olds. Children five to six years old largely ignore advertising, viewing it as irrelevant to their lives. Although they sometimes recognize that it can be misleading, they usually enjoy it as part of the programming.

Seven- to ten-year-olds. From seven to nine, children attempt with great difficulty and little success to integrate advertising into their lives; at age ten, they resolve the conflict temporarily through an overgeneralization that all advertising is misleading.

Eleven- and twelve-year-olds. Children eleven to twelve years old resolve conflicts more satisfactorily as they refine their early impressions and can identify both the good and the bad aspects of advertising.

Source: Adapted from T. G. Bever, M. L. Smith, B. Bengen, and T. G. Johnson, "Young Viewers' Troubling Response to TV Ads," *Harvard Business Review*, November–December 1975, p. 119. Copyright © 1975 by the President and Fellows of Harvard College; all rights reserved.

Children's advertising has been a regular target of the Federal Trade Commission, which made various attempts to improve this area of advertising throughout the 1970s. The so-called *Kid-Vid Rule of 1978* was one of its most extensive proposals. It would:

1. Prohibit advertising during times when certain ages of children make up a specified proportion of the viewers, perhaps 20 percent or more.
2. Prohibit advertising of products that exceed a specified maximum sugar content level.
3. Require advertisers to underwrite health announcements and nutri-

tional disclosures to the same extent as their expenditures for sales oriented advertising directed toward children.[25]

Social Responsibility

The third contemporary issue affecting marketing is social responsibility. This issue may be the most difficult to define since it involves so many aspects of modern society.[26] Two crucial matters are (1) the relationship between social responsibility and the profit motive and (2) the process for making socially responsible decisions in the organization.

The pressing need for socially responsible marketing decisions is readily agreed to by both critics and defenders of contemporary marketing. Marketers and consumers now accept the viewpoint that business should be concerned with the quality of life as well as with the quantities by which market performance was previously measured. Determining the quality dimension of marketing decisions, however, is likely to remain a problem in the decade ahead.

Social decision making within the organization has always been an important ethical consideration. Who should be specifically accountable for the social considerations involved in marketing decisions: A district sales manager? A staff marketing department? The marketing vice-president? The president? The board of directors? Probably the most valid assessment is that *all marketers,* regardless of their station in the organization, should be accountable for the social aspects of their decisions.

A related question is: How should socially responsible decisions be made? Figure 18–1 presents a flowchart that illustrates the types and levels

Children's programs – and advertising – dominate Saturday morning television schedules.

"Dammit, don't they think anyone over ten years old gets up on Saturday morning?"

Source: *Wall Street Journal,* November 8, 1978. Reprinted by permission of the cartoonist, Schochet, and the *Wall Street Journal.*

Figure 18–1
Decision-Making
Flowchart

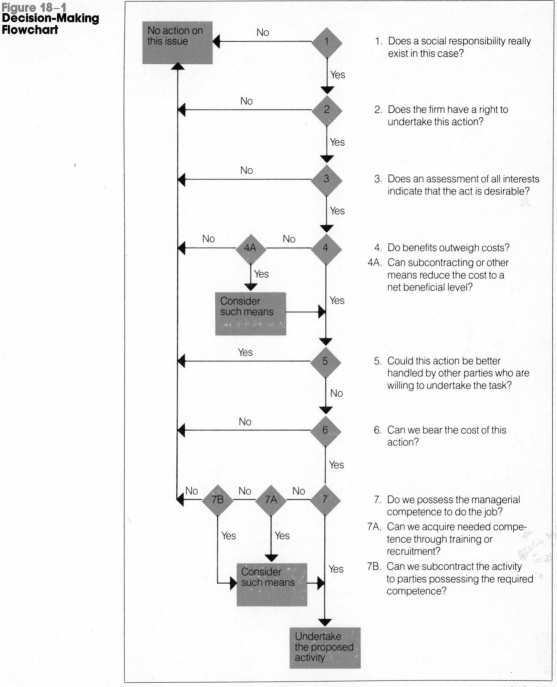

1. Does a social responsibility really exist in this case?

2. Does the firm have a right to undertake this action?

3. Does an assessment of all interests indicate that the act is desirable?

4. Do benefits outweigh costs?
4A. Can subcontracting or other means reduce the cost to a net beneficial level?

5. Could this action be better handled by other parties who are willing to undertake the task?

6. Can we bear the cost of this action?

7. Do we possess the managerial competence to do the job?
7A. Can we acquire needed competence through training or recruitment?
7B. Can we subcontract the activity to parties possessing the required competence?

Source: Ramon J. Aldag and Donald W. Jackson, Jr., "A Managerial Framework for Social Decision-Making," *MSU Business Topics,* Spring 1975, p. 34. Reprinted by permission of the publisher, Division of Research, Graduate School of Business Administration, Michigan State University.

of social responsibility decision making. It also provides a framework for dealing with these critical issues.

Marketing's
Responsibilities

The concept of business responsibility has traditionally concerned the relationships between managers and their customers, employees, and stockholders. Management has had the responsibility of providing customers with a quality product at a reasonable price, of providing adequate wages and decent working environment for employees, and of providing an acceptable profit level for stockholders. Only on occasion has the concept involved relations with the government—and only rarely with the general public.

Today, the responsibility concept has been extended to the entire social framework. A decision to continue operation of a profitable but air-polluting plant may be responsible in the traditional sense. Customers receive an uninterrupted supply of the plant's products, employees do not face layoffs, and stockholders receive a reasonable return on their investment in the plant. But from the standpoint of contemporary business ethics, it is not a socially responsible decision.

Similarly, a firm that markets foods with low nutritional value may satisfy the traditional concept of responsibility, but its behavior is less acceptable in the contemporary perspective. This is not to say that the firm should distribute only foods of high nutritional value; it means only that the previous framework for evaluation is no longer considered comprehensive in terms of either scope or time.

Contemporary marketing decisions must now regularly involve consideration of the external social environment. Decisions must also account for eventual long-run effects. Socially responsible marketing decisions must consider future generations as well as existing people.

In no other area is marketing's responsibility more obvious than in its dealing with blacks, women, Indians, Orientals, and Spanish-speaking people in the United States. The marketing system has sometimes denied these consumer segments the level of product quality, the price structure, or the employment opportunities available to other parts of society. Each of the subcultures has its own distinctive set of marketing problems.

The sometimes discriminatory operation of the marketing system has been clearly pointed out in the debate over whether the urban poor (primarily blacks) pay higher prices than their more affluent counterparts in the suburbs.[27] This issue is the subject of continual discussion in the marketing literature.[28] The conclusions of various studies have been mixed, however. The urban poor typically do pay more for merchandise, but it is often the result of service and quality differences among retail stores, not of a specific policy. This situation has led to a growing business concern over the marketing problems of low-income areas. Many retailers, for instance, have expanded their operations in these areas with better merchandise at prices comparable to those found in suburban stores.

Marketing and Ecology

Ecology is an important aspect of marketing.[29] The concept of **ecology**—*the relationship between humanity and the environment*—appears to be in a constant state of evolution.

There are several aspects of ecology that marketers must deal with: planned obsolescence, pollution, recycling waste materials, and preservation of resources.

The original ecological problem facing marketing was **planned obsolescence**—*a situation where the manufacturer produces items with limited durability.* Planned obsolescence has always represented a significant ethical question for the marketer. On the one side is the need for maintaining sales and employment; on the other is the need for providing better quality and durability.

A practical question is whether the consumer really wants or can afford increased durability. Many consumers prefer to change styles often and accept less durable items. Increased durability has a cost associated with it. It may mean fewer people can afford the product.

Pollution is a broad term that can be applied to a number of circumstances. It usually means *making unclean.* Pollution of such natural resources as the water and the air is of critical proportions. But there are definite signs of progress. Over $74 billion has been spent since 1973 to clean up the rivers and lakes of the United States. And while the federal government projects that another $174 billion will be required to meet "fishable" and "swimmable" goals by 1984, there are some successes to report. Salmon, which had not spawned in the Connecticut River since the mid-1800s, are back now. Even the Potomac is nearing recovery. But when a swim-in was suggested as a means of demonstrating the Potomac's progress, police evoked an ordinance that forbids people from making "deliberate contact" with the river.[30]

Recycling—*the reprocessing of used materials for reuse*—is another important aspect of ecology. The marketing system annually generates billions of tons of packaging materials, such as glass, plastics, metal, and paper, that add to the nation's growing piles of trash and waste. The theory behind recycling is that if these materials could be processed so as to be reusable, they would benefit society by saving natural resources and energy as well as by alleviating a major factor in environmental pollution.

U.S. tire manufacturers have built artificial fish reefs out of used tires.[31] Minnesota Mining and Manufacturing Company has put outlines for splints on the corrugated shipping cartons destined for hospitals. The cartons are then used by emergency and rescue teams for temporary splints.[32]

The burning of trash as a fuel substitute will become more attractive in the years ahead. One important factor will be the *Resource Conservation Recovery Act* that requires all dumps to be closed by 1983.[33]

Recovery rates for reusable materials vary by industry. For instance, the rate for copper is 50 percent, for iron and steel 30 percent, for paper and paper products 20 percent, and for glass only 4 percent. In many instances, the recovery rates are now less than they were in the mid-1950s. Yet it is estimated that extensive recycling could produce 40 percent of the materials needed by U.S. manufacturers.[34]

The biggest problem in recycling is getting the used materials from the consumer back to the manufacturer that will handle the technological aspects of recovery. These *backward channels* are limited, and those that do exist are primitive and lack adequate financial incentives.[35] Marketing can play an important role by designing appropriate channel structures.

Another ecological problem concerns the *preservation of natural resources.* The natural gas and fuel oil shortages during the 1970s illustrate the urgent need for effective policies for both conserving and finding new sources of these resources.

Some critics point out that business spends more money publicizing its ecological expenditures than it does meeting the specific ecological problems. In many cases, the criticism is valid, but experience has shown that consumers are also at fault in that they sometimes fail to support ecology inspired products.

Toward the Resolution of Contemporary Issues in Marketing

Dealing with the contemporary issues of consumerism, social responsibility, and marketing ethics is probably one of the most crucial tasks facing marketing. Progress in these areas is essential if the competitive marketing system is to survive at all.

Three courses of action are available to resolve the vital questions in these areas: increased regulation, better public information, and a more responsible marketing philosophy.

Few marketers doubt that *increased regulation* will become a reality in the marketplace if reforms are not instituted. History has shown that the government, responding to consumer pressures, has always moved to fill voids created by business apathy and neglect. Expanded and improved self-regulation by marketers is mandatory if stricter government controls are to be avoided.

Better public information is a solution applicable to all contemporary issues. In many cases, issues arise simply because the public is not informed or is mistakenly misinformed about something. Package labeling is a good example of where improvement is needed. Consumers complain that current labeling omits or disguises important product information. Once again, the case for voluntary industry action is urgent. Unit pricing, a widely debated method of providing better information, was explained in Chapter 16.

Open dating, which *sets the last date a perishable or semiperishable food can be sold,* involves similar questions.[36] To what type of information should consumers be entitled? Is better public information worth the cost? How can marketers improve the information consumers receive? Many of these questions will have to be answered in the decades ahead.

A more responsible marketing philosophy is also needed in contemporary society. Incidents like the following one cast a poor reflection on marketers and their firms:

One unhappy patron who discovered bedbugs in his hotel bed and complained bitterly in writing to the company received a mollifying reply to which had been attached, accidentally, a scribbled note from some executive to his secretary that said: "Alice, send this guy the bedbug letter."[37]

A responsible marketing philosophy should encourage consumers to voice their opinions. These comments can result in significant improvements in the products and services offered by the seller. For instance, White Truck Division of White Motor Corporation in Cleveland has incorporated 140 improvements in its Road Commander truck, all the result of user complaints.[38]

The marketing concept must include social responsibility as a primary function of the marketing organization. Social and profit goals are compatible, but they require the aggressive implementation of an expanded marketing concept. This is truly marketing's greatest challenge!

Summary

There are many important issues in contemporary marketing's societal environment. Marketing's environmental relationships have expanded in scope and importance. In fact, some companies have even set up public responsibility committees at the board level to deal with some of these issues.

The current issues in marketing can be categorized as (1) consumerism, (2) marketing ethics, and (3) social responsibility. Consumerism is a protest against abuse and malpractice in the marketing system as well as a plea for greater attention to consumer wants and desires. Marketing ethics is a complex subject since it can be considered from the viewpoints of individual, organizational, or professional ethics. Ethical problems exist in marketing research, product management, distribution strategy, pricing, and promotion. Another issue is the relationship between social responsibility in marketing and the profit motive and process for making socially responsible decisions in the organization.

Increased regulation, better public information, and a more responsible marketing philosophy are possible alternatives for resolving these issues. All are expected to play a greater role in the years ahead.

1. Explain the following terms:
   public responsibility committee
   Green River ordinances
   consumerism
   class action suit
   ecology
   planned obsolescence
   pollution
   recycling
   open dating

2. Examine Adam Smith's thoughts on competition. How have they affected the competitive marketing system?

3. Explain the causes of the consumerism movement. Does the rise of consumerism suggest that the marketing concept has failed?

4. Evaluate consumerism's indictment of the competitive marketing system.

5. Comment on President John F. Kennedy's declaration that the consumer has the right to safety, the right to be informed, the right to choose, and the right to be heard.

6. What can be learned from the Chevymobile case?

7. Discuss the problems involved in setting up "backward" channels of distribution for the recycling of used packages.

8. Distinguish among individual, organizational, and professional ethics.

9. Describe the ethical problems of:
   a. marketing research
   b. product management
   c. channel strategy
   d. pricing
   e. promotional strategy

10. Do you agree with the proposed Kid-Vid rules? Explain.

11. Describe the main avenues open for the resolution of the contemporary issues facing the marketing system.

12. Some have suggested that the majority of people are consumer illiterates. How would you alleviate this problem?

13. How would you have responded to each of the situations described in the section on ethical problems related to research? Explain.

14. Describe the conflict that exists between the consumer demand for product durability and the ecology movement.

15. The need for developing a reliable measure on the quality of life is well recognized. Suppose that you were in charge of a federally funded project of this nature. How would you go about your task?

16. Comment on the following statement: The marketing concept marked the advent of the age of consumerism.

17. List examples of business practices that you feel are not socially responsible. What factors went into deciding to include each item on your list?

18. In 1978, the U.S. Supreme Court decided that Tennessee's Tellico Dam, then nearing completion, might destroy the remaining snail darters, a fish only three inches long. The Court ruled that the $116 million project should be stopped because the snail darter was an endangered species and therefore protected by the Endangered Species Act. Relate this incident to the material in this chapter.

19. Paul Oreffice, president and chief executive officer of Dow Chemical Company, has observed:

    We are not saying government should not regulate. We say the regulations should be reasonable. I think a speed limit of 55 miles an hour on a freeway is a reasonable regulation; a speed limit of 20 miles—I think we all would agree—would be unreasonable. Government is imposing some regulations on business which are the equivalent of a 20-mile speed limit.[39]

    Comment on Oreffice's viewpoint.

20. What can be learned from Anheuser-Busch's experience with Chelsea?

Notes

1. Michael L. Lovdol, Raymond A. Bauer, and Nancy H. Treverton, "Public Responsibility Committees on the Board," *Harvard Business Review,* May–June 1977, p. 40.
2. "U.S. 'Misery Index' Posts Slight Decline from a Year Earlier," *Wall Street Journal,* December 10, 1975, p. 18.
3. "A Happiness Index," *Wall Street Journal,* January 20, 1972, p. 1.
4. This study is described in "Portland, Oregon Is Rated Best U.S. City in Survey," *Detroit Sunday News,* September 21, 1975.
5. Good articles include Frederick D. Sturdivant and James L. Ginter, "Corporate Social Responsiveness," *California Management Review,* Spring 1977, pp. 30–39; John Robertson, "Corporate Social Reporting by New Zealand Companies," *Journal of Contemporary Business,* Winter 1978, pp. 113–133; and Larry J. Rosenberg, John A. Czepial, and Lewis C. Cohen, "Consumer Affairs Audits," *California Management Review,* Spring 1977, pp. 12–20.
6. See A. H. Kizilbash, Carleton Maile, William Hancock, and Peter Gillett, "The Marketing Manager's Role in the Corporate Social Audit," *Bulletin of Business Research,* April 1978, pp. 4–7.
7. For an excellent anthology of the literature in this field, see David A. Aaker and George S. Day, *Consumerism: Search for the Consumer Interest,* 3rd ed. (New York: Free Press, 1978).
8. This AMA survey is the subject of "Consumers Not Well Protected, Back Standards If Safety Periled," *Marketing News,* Mid-November 1971, p. 2.
9. This issue has been widely debated in the marketing literature. Good summaries of the debate are contained in William J. Stanton, *Fundamentals of Marketing,* 5th ed. (New York: McGraw-Hill, 1978), pp. 581–582; and E. Jerome McCarthy, *Basic Marketing: A Managerial Approach,* 6th ed. (Homewood, Ill.: Richard D. Irwin, 1978), pp. 656–681.
10. Alan R. Andreasen and Arthur Best, "Consumers Complain—Does Business Respond?" *Harvard Business Review,* November–December 1977, pp. 93–101.
11. "Consumers Not Well Protected," p. 1.
12. See Malcolm Forbes, "Fact and Comment," *Forbes,* March 6, 1978, p. 23. An interesting discussion of the current status of consumerism is reported in "Consumerism at Bay?" *Dun's Review,* May 1978, pp. 96–98.
13. "Clash over Class Action," *Detroit News,* November 1978, p. 73.
14. Consumer education programs are discussed in Paul N. Bloom and Mark J. Silver, "Consumer Education: Marketers Take Heed," *Harvard Business Review,* January–February 1976, p. 32. Also see James U. McNeal, "Consumer Education as a Competitive Strategy," *Business Horizons,* February 1978, pp. 50–56.
15. The new merit badge is reported in "Business Bulletin," *Wall Street Journal,* November 6, 1975, p. 1.
16. "Consumer Affairs Climbs Corporate Ladder," *Industry Week,* July 10, 1978, pp. 55–58.
17. Ethical standards are discussed in James Owens, "Business Ethics: Age-Old Ideal, Now Real," *Business Horizons,* February 1978, pp. 26–30; and O. C. Ferrell and K. Mark Weaver, "Ethical Beliefs of Marketing Managers," *Journal of Marketing,* July 1978, pp. 69–73. Also see Frederick D. Sturdivant, *Business and Society* (Homewood, Ill.: Richard D. Irwin, 1977).
18. The discussion of individual, organizational, and professional ethics is based on Henry O. Pruden, "Which Ethic for Marketers?" in *Marketing and Social Issues: An Action Reader,* ed. John R. Wish and Stephen H. Gamble (New York: Wiley, 1971), pp. 98–104.
19. Terry P. Brown, "GM, State Aides Due to Disclose Accord for $200 Rebates in 'Chevymobile' Case," *Wall Street Journal,* December 19, 1977, p. 16.
20. "Honesty Pays," *Detroit News,* February 15, 1975, p. 1.
21. See Steven N. Brenner and Earl A. Mollander, "Is the Ethics of Business Changing?" *Harvard Business Review,* January–February 1977, pp. 61–62; and Jeffrey Sonnenfeld and Paul R. Lawrence, "Why Do Companies Succumb to Price Fixing?" *Harvard Business Review,* July–August 1978, pp. 145–157.
22. Brenner and Mollander, "Is the Ethics of Business Changing?" p. 62.
23. Recent discussions of advertising aimed at children are found in Bruce L. Stern and Alan J. Resnik, "Children's Understanding of Television Commercial Disclaimer," in *Research Frontiers in Marketing,* ed. Subhash C. Jain (Chicago: American Marketing Association, 1978), pp. 332–336; Ronald S. Rubin, "Children's Responses to TV Advertising: Product versus Premium Orientation," *Journal of the Academy of Marketing Science,* Fall 1976, pp. 742–752; and Thomas E. Barry and Anees A. Sheikh, "Race as a Dimension in Children's TV Advertising: The Need for More Research," *Journal of Advertising,* Fall 1977, pp. 5–10.
24. See "Use More Care on Kiddie Ads, Professor Asks," *Advertising Age,* February 3, 1975, p. 51.
25. Scott Ward, "Compromise in Commercials for Children," *Harvard Business Review,* November–December 1978, p. 128.

26. The concept of social responsibility is examined in such articles as Thomas J. Steele, "Social Responsibility in Business—Its International Dimensions," *Business Ideas and Facts,* Winter 1974, pp. 37–42; Michael M. Pearson, "The Motivation of Social Responsibility," *Bulletin of Business Research,* May 1975, pp. 1–3, 6; Ronald J. Dornoff and Clint B. Tankersley, "Do Retailers Practice Social Responsibility?" *Journal of Retailing,* Winter 1975–76, pp. 33–42; and Lyman E. Ostlund, "Are Middle Managers an Obstacle to Corporate Social Policy Implementation?" *Business and Society,* Spring 1978, pp. 5–20.

27. Most authorities date the debate from David Caplovitz's *The Poor Pay More* (New York: Free Press, 1963). Charles Goodman published a classical article on the subject in 1968: "Do the Poor Pay More?" *Journal of Marketing,* January 1968, pp. 18–24.

28. This research has been described in Alan R. Andreason, "The Ghetto Market Life Cycle: A Case of Underachievement," *Journal of Marketing Research,* February 1978, pp. 20–28.

29. Ecological aspects of marketing are discussed in Patrick E. Murphy and Gene R. Laczniak, "Marketing and Ecology: Retrospect and Prospect," *Business and Society,* Fall 1977, pp. 26–34.

30. "Now We Can See through Water," *Detroit News,* November 1, 1978.

31. Ralph E. Winter, "The Tiremakers Try All Sorts of Methods to Destroy Old Tires but Not Environment," *Wall Street Journal,* April 27, 1972, p. 30.

32. "Business Bulletin," *Wall Street Journal,* December 11, 1975, p. 1.

33. Liz Roman Gallese, "Art of Turning Waste into Useful Fuel Gains in Popularity Rapidly," *Wall Street Journal,* August 4, 1977, pp. 1, 20.

34. Edward M. Syring, "Realizing Recycling's Potential," *Nation's Business,* February 1976, pp. 68, 70.

35. William G. Zikmund and William J. Stanton, "Recycling Solid Wastes: A Channels-of-Distribution Problem," *Journal of Marketing,* July 1971, pp. 34–39. Also see Donald A. Fuller, "Recycling Consumer Solid Waste: A Commentary on Selected Channel Alternatives," *Journal of Business Research,* January 1978, pp. 17–31; and Peter M. Ginter and Jack M. Starling, "Reverse Distribution Channels: Concept and Structure," in *Proceedings of the Southern Marketing Association,* ed. Robert S. Franz, Robert M. Hopkins, and Al Toma, New Orleans, Louisiana, November 1978, pp. 206–208.

36. Open dating is examined in Prabhaker Nayak and Larry J. Rosenberg, "Does Open Dating of Food Products Benefit the Consumer?" *Journal of Retailing,* Summer 1975, pp. 10–20.

37. A. T. Baker, "Louder!—The Need to Complain More," *Time,* July 3, 1972, p. 33.

38. "Using Consumer Gripes to Improve the Product," *Industry Week,* November 20, 1972, pp. 34–36.

39. Quoted in Charles W. Theisen, "Dow Enters Stage of Social Sensitivity," *Detroit News,* May 28, 1978.

CHAPTER 19
INTEGRATING THE
MARKETING PROGRAM

Key Terms

marketing strategy
planning
market planning
ROI (return on
investment)

PERT (program
evaluation and review
technique)
critical path
marketing audit

Learning Goals

1. To determine the strategic requirements for effective marketing.
2. To explain the role of marketing strategy in contemporary business.
3. To describe the planning process.
4. To examine positioning strategies for marketing organizations.
5. To list the variables that affect strategy formulation.
6. To describe the importance and use of marketing audits.

19

Hewlett-Packard Company has adopted a competitive strategy emphasizing technologically advanced products that sell at a premium price.[1] This strategic decision can be considered a brave stance, since Hewlett-Packard competes in industries such as calculators, the scene of some extensive price competition.

Other organizations employ varied marketing strategies. The president of Colgate-Palmolive describes new product competition with Procter & Gamble as follows: "Procter & Gamble has a textbook style—we really know how they're going to operate. No point in bucking them in their initial launch. You might as well save your money, come in later and give them a crack."[2]

Effective marketing requires strategic decisions that successfully integrate all the components of the firm's marketing program. Once these decisions are made, the marketer must be prepared to meet competitors' counterstrategies, and the battle begins. The Tylenol-Datril competitive clash is a classic example. Eastman Kodak's invasion of the instant photography mar-

Tylenol versus Datril

Johnson & Johnson first introduced Tylenol in 1961 as an aspirin substitute for people who experienced unpleasant side effects from aspirin. Tylenol, which was promoted to physicians and druggists, proved to be a tremendously profitable item for Johnson & Johnson. For years, until 1974, Tylenol faced no substantial competition in the nonaspirin field. Its profit margin was estimated at 30 to 40 percent of each sales dollar during this period. Sales grew to $50 million yearly, or approximately 12 percent of the total analgesic market. The Johnson & Johnson product captured about 85 percent of nonaspirin sales.

Then competition moved in. In 1974 Bristol-Myers test marketed Datril in Albany, New York, and Peoria, Illinois. Datril included acetaminophen, the pain reduction ingredient used in Tylenol. On the basis of its field tests, Bristol-Myers decided to introduce Datril nationwide. The new product was sold by Bristol-Myers' large consumer products sales force and was promoted as being less costly than Tylenol. Millions of dollars were spent on television advertising of Datril.

Johnson & Johnson protested the use of these advertisements to the television networks and the Council of Better Business Bureaus' National Advertising Division. The Bristol-Myers ads were later revised. Johnson & Johnson also did more than protest. It slashed the Tylenol retail price to counter the Datril move. Tylenol sales efforts were supplemented by additional personnel loaned by other Johnson & Johnson units. Rebates were given to retailers who had bought Tylenol before the price cuts, which protected the merchants' investment in floor stocks.

The competitive battle escalated with both firms making extensive use of special deals. In some locations the price went down to 79 cents per 100-tablet bottle, less than a third of Tylenol's earlier price. Bristol-Myers introduced a nonaspirin children's liquid (grape-flavored) to counter a Johnson & Johnson item. The Tylenol line expanded with the introduction of "extra strength" Tylenol and 50-tablet bottles designed to increase its retail shelf space.

As a result of this classic confrontation, Datril now holds a 14 percent share of the nonaspirin market, with approximately one-sixth of Tylenol's sales. Several other companies are joining the fray by introducing nonaspirin pain relievers. It is apparent that this competitive struggle is far from over.

Source: Adapted from Bernard Wysocki, Jr., "Punching Is Furious in Tylenol-Datril Fight for Non-Aspirin Users," *Wall Street Journal*, May 24, 1976, p. 1, 17. Reprinted with permission of *The Wall Street Journal*, © Dow Jones & Company, Inc., 1976. All rights reserved.

Polaroid versus Eastman Kodak

Polaroid Corporation introduced instant photography in 1948 and enjoyed a monopoly position in this segment of the photographic market until 1976, when industry giant Eastman Kodak entered the field. Polaroid annual sales were then $813 million as compared to Kodak's $5 billion yearly volume.

The mass market has always been Kodak's target. The firm has maintained excellent dealer relations with camera retailers. The strategy has resulted in a favorable reception to Kodak at this level of distribution. Polaroid, on the other hand, has relied on technologically advanced products.

Faced with a pending product entry by Kodak, Polaroid had to gird to meet the challenge. The company brought out new models and successfully reduced prices in an attempt to gain maximum market share before Kodak's launch. Polaroid also introduced special edition versions of its cameras with five-year rather than one-year guarantees. The special edition models provided better dealer margins. A toll-free service and a distribution center were established, and bonuses were promised to dealers who exceeded Polaroid sales quotas.

Kodak, by contrast, had to develop marketing strategies for the new instant cameras that would not hurt the sales of its conventional product line. The new cameras also required some changes in Kodak's relations with camera retailers.

The competitive action grew furious as the two firms jockeyed for position in the marketplace. New products were introduced. Price competition was intense; some earlier vintage Polaroids eventually sold for only $20. But by 1979, both contestants seemed satisfied. Kodak and Polaroid had increased their annual revenues to $6.8 billion and $1.4 billion, respectively.

How was this possible? The competition had generated a far larger instant camera market than had existed when the battle began. This market was now 15 million units annually as compared to 7.4 million in 1976. Forty-five percent of new camera buyers chose an instant model in 1979 versus 25 percent in 1975. Polaroid held a 65 percent market share but had increased its unit sales by over 50 percent in a two-year period. Kodak, on the other hand, was pleased with its 35 percent share. Kodak's instant camera business became profitable in 1979, and management knew that this was a growth market.

Source: Adapted from William M. Carley, "Polaroid Seen Wary, Worried as It Girds for Kodak Arrival in Instant-Photo Field," *Wall Street Journal,* April 16, 1976, p. 4. Reprinted by permission of *The Wall Street Journal,* © Dow Jones & Company, Inc., 1976. All rights reserved. Information in last two paragraphs from James O'Hanlon, "Bedlam in Photoland," *Forbes,* February 5, 1979, pp. 35–36.

ket and Polaroid Corporation's response provide another excellent illustration of marketing strategy at work.

The examples cited clearly show the importance of developing effective marketing strategies. These firms and their counterparts in other industries realize that a firm's marketing strategy may well determine whether the company survives in the business world.

The Role of Marketing Strategy in Contemporary Business

Marketing strategy is *the general term used to describe the overall company program for selecting a particular market segment and then satisfying the consumers in that segment through careful use of the elements of the marketing mix.* In short, a marketing strategy is an organization's plan for reaching the consumer. It has to be resource efficient, flexible, and adaptable. Phillip E. Benton, Jr., a top Ford executive, stated it aptly:

Sound marketing must start from a basic game plan. Although the ability to deviate effectively from that plan is essential—it is also essential that the long-term consequences of that deviation be thoroughly understood in terms of basic strategy, particularly in a period such as the present, when swift and drastic changes in direction are the name of the game.[3]

Comprehensive Program: The Essential Requirement for Marketing Strategy

A productive marketing strategy requires that all aspects of the marketing mix be considered. The components of an overall marketing strategy are product planning, distribution, promotion, and pricing. An advertising strategy by itself is not a marketing strategy; nor is a pricing strategy. Marketing mix components are subsets of the overall marketing strategy.

A strategy may emphasize one mix component more than others. For example, a discount store may depend primarily on its pricing strategy, but it must also maintain adequate product selection and efficient distribution and promotion. One industrial goods manufacturer may emphasize its advanced product technology, while a competitor may stress its superior field sales force. But neither can totally neglect the other elements of marketing strategy.

Marketers must also be prepared to alter their strategies. When S. C. Johnson introduced Pledge, the first aerosol furniture polish, most competitors felt certain that it would fail because its quality was believed lower than some competitive products, including Johnson's own Old English brand. But Pledge proved a major sales success when Johnson carefully positioned it as an easy-to-use dusting product rather than a furniture polish. Johnson succeeded because it adapted its marketing strategy with the "waxed beauty instantly as you dust" advertising theme.[4]

Organizational Strategies: The Basis for Marketing Strategies

Just as the mix components are a subset of marketing strategy, an organization's marketing plan is the result of a strategic planning process that begins with the formulation of a corporate mission. For example, the Carborundum Company has traditionally marketed an extensive line of coated abrasives, abrasive grain, and grinding wheels. Carborundum therefore has set its corporate mission as the provision of a comprehensive system for metal polishing, cleaning, and removal.[5]

Figure 19–1 shows the overall strategic planning process. Once the corporate mission has been determined and the objectives specified, the process goes through a series of planning stages until actual administrative plans, such as the one for marketing, emerge.

Marketing Strategy: An Art and a Science

Is marketing an art or a science? Debates on this subject usually conclude that marketing strategy involves aspects of both. At times—such as in customer and dealer relations—strategists must rely on their own creative and

Figure 19–1
The Strategic
Planning Process

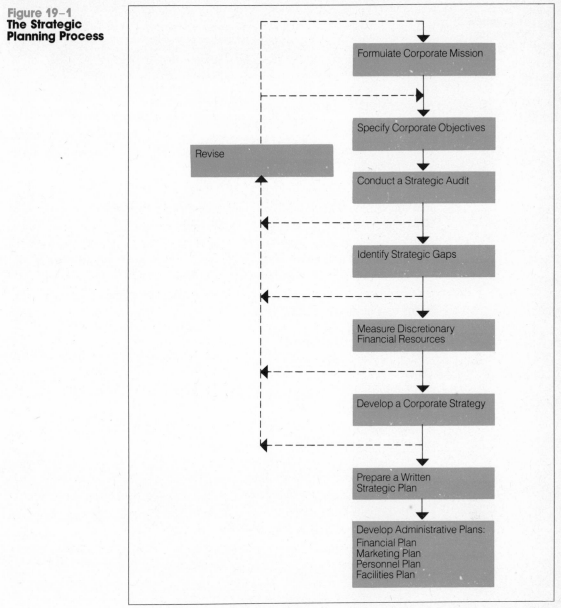

Source: David T. Kollat, Roger D. Blackwell, and James F. Robeson, *Strategic Marketing* (New York: Holt, Rinehart and Winston, 1972), p. 13. Copyright © 1972 by Holt, Rinehart and Winston. Reprinted by permission of Holt, Rinehart and Winston.

innovative intuition; at other times—such as in examining marketing research reports—they must rigidly follow the dictates of scientific inquiry.

One study of marketing executives found that their answers to the art versus science question vary for different aspects of marketing strategy. As Figure 19–2 indicates, personal selling was viewed primarily as an art, while

Figure 19–2
An Art-Science Continuum for Marketing

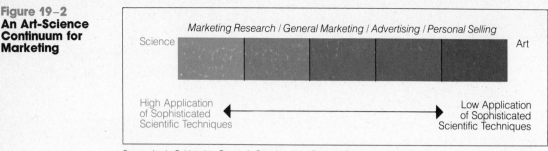

Marketing Research / General Marketing / Advertising / Personal Selling

Science   Art

High Application
of Sophisticated
Scientific Techniques

Low Application
of Sophisticated
Scientific Techniques

Source: Jac L. Goldstucker, Barnett A. Greenberg, and Danny N. Bellenger, "How Scientific Is Marketing? What Do Marketing Executives Think?" *MSU Business Topics*, Spring 1974, p. 42. Reprinted by permission of the publisher, Division of Research, Graduate School of Business Administration, Michigan State University.

marketing research was at the opposite end of the continuum. The probable reasoning behind this ranking is that the respondents see a positive relationship between science and the use of sophisticated scientific techniques.

Successful implementation of a marketing strategy requires sound, innovative management. No single strategy is always correct even under similar circumstances. Marketers must make carefully balanced analyses prior to making strategic decisions and then must use their best judgment about the appropriate steps to take.

The use of marketing research is just one aspect of the art-science continuum for marketing.

"This car is not for everyone, sir. Would you care to take our aptitude test?"

Source: Copyright © 1980 by Sidney Harris. Reprinted by permission.

Market Planning

In 1970, General Electric (GE) underwent a major reorganization by separating planning and policy oriented activity from administration. The former is long-term in nature, while the latter tends to involve shorter times. GE is now regarded as having one of the best long-range planning functions in the United States.[6] Its efforts suggest the importance that its chief executives assign to planning.

Planning is the basis of all strategy decisions. It is the underlying foundation for general corporate strategy as well as for strategy in functional areas such as marketing. **Planning** is *the function of anticipating the future and determining the courses of action to achieve company objectives.* It is managerial activity that must be performed by all units of the organization. Personnel and production executives, as well as marketers, have planning responsibilities.

Market planning—*the implementation of planning activity as it relates to the achievement of marketing objectives*—is the basis for all marketing strategies. Product lines, distribution channels, prices, and promotional campaigns all depend on the plans that are formulated within the marketing organization.

The Planning Process

All planning, including market planning, follows the same general sequence. The steps in the planning process are shown in Figure 19–3.

Planning first involves a recognition of the problems and opportunities in any situation. An analysis of sales data, for example, may indicate that a certain market segment is not being served by the company. Next, alternative courses of action must be developed. Perhaps an existing product can be adapted to the needs of an unfulfilled consumer segment or a new product can be developed. An evaluation of these alternatives may suggest that product adaptation is the best course of action. Once this alternative has been selected, a plan must be chosen to implement it. Finally, the planning should include some evaluation and feedback mechanism to assess the effectiveness of the decision.[7] All planning involves these basic steps in some fashion.

Figure 19–3
Steps in the Planning Process

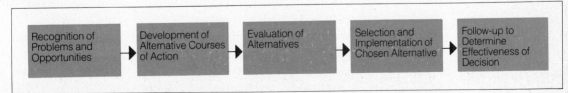

Source: Louis E. Boone and David L. Kurtz, *Contemporary Business*, 2d ed. (Hinsdale, Ill.: Dryden Press, 1979), p. 80. Copyright © 1979 by Dryden Press, a division of Holt, Rinehart and Winston. Reprinted by permission of Holt, Rinehart and Winston.

Planning has become increasingly sophisticated. Marketing decision making is too crucial an activity—often involving millions of dollars—to leave the planning phase to chance. ROI and PERT are examples of sophisticated planning and evaluative tools.

ROI — A Technique for Evaluating Alternatives

Evaluating alternative courses of action is one of the most challenging tasks facing the marketing manager. The basic problem is to find an instrument capable of measuring marketing performance—actual and planned. Historically, sales volume was first used in this capacity; later, profitability became the accepted yardstick. More recently, return on investment (ROI) has gained popularity as an effective evaluative device.

ROI is *a quantitative tool that seeks to relate the activity or project's profitability to its required investment.* Simply stated, return on investment is *equal to the rate of profit multiplied by the turnover rate.* ROI can be calculated as follows:

$$ROI = \frac{Net\ profit}{Sales} \times \frac{Sales}{Investment}.$$

In other words:

ROI = Rate of profit × Turnover.

A brief example shows how ROI can be used as an evaluative device in planning. Consider a new product idea for which the firm estimates that a $200,000 investment will be required. The company expects to reach $500,000 in sales, with a net profit of $40,000. The proposed project's ROI is calculated in the following manner:

$$ROI = \frac{\$40,000}{\$500,000} \times \frac{\$500,000}{\$200,000}$$
$$= 0.08 \times 2.5 = 20\ percent.$$

Whether or not this expected performance is acceptable depends on the ROI of alternative uses of corporate funds. It would not be viewed favorably at Gould, Inc., for instance. This major industrial goods manufacturer wants all new products to generate a return on investment of 40 percent before taxes.

ROI is often used in conjunction with other evaluative tools. For example, Gould also specifies that its new products should generate profits of 30 percent before taxes and 15 percent annual sales and profit growth. It also insists on a $20 million sales potential within five years following introduction and a total market potential of about $50 million.[8]

PERT — A Useful Planning and Evaluative Tool

PERT (program evaluation and review technique) is *a commonly used planning and scheduling technique.* Originally developed for defense projects, PERT is now widely applied in a variety of industries to minimize project completion time. PERT diagrams outline the **critical path** for the project— *the sequence of tasks that requires the longest total completion time.* Other tasks can be performed early or postponed until later in the sequence. Organizational resources can thereby be concentrated on critical path tasks and then later returned to other work.

Consider the following illustration. The H. S. Daugherty Company is considering the introduction of Porta-Vac, a cordless vacuum cleaner powered by a rechargeable battery.[9] Daugherty management has initiated a feasibility study to evaluate Porta-Vac; it wants the study to indicate the action that should be taken with respect to the product. Figure 19–4 offers a PERT diagram for the project. The diagram shows the activities that must be accomplished in order to complete the overall project. For instance, the market research plan (B) and the marketing brochure (E) must precede the market survey (H).

Positioning Strategies for the Marketing Organization

Few companies have experienced the changes in their business mix that W. R. Grace and Company has been through since 1950. At that time Grace was essentially a steamship line operating in Latin America. Today W. R. Grace is a diversified multinational corporation with substantial investments in natural resource industries and consumer products and services; it is also ranked fifth among U.S. chemical companies. The Grace organization's repositioning of the company is shown in Table 19–1.

Figure 19–4
PERT Network of the Porta-Vac Project

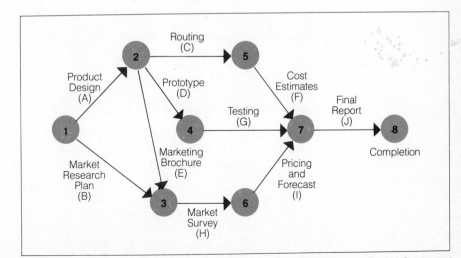

Table 19-1
W. R. Grace & Company's Composition of Operating Capital (in Millions)

Industry	1950	1975
Chemicals	$ 5	$958
Oil, gas, and coal	—	237
Consumer products and services	—	770
Steamship (Grace Line) and other businesses	121	37

Source: Adapted by permission from W. R. Grace & Company, *A Management Perspective* (New York: W. R. Grace & Company, 1976), p. 4.

Alternative positioning strategies are available to marketers. The selection of any given one is based on market and product factors, competition, and other environmental influences. Five alternative positioning strategies can be identified: (1) balancing strategy, (2) market retention strategy, (3) market development strategy, (4) growth strategy, and (5) new venture strategy.[10] Examples of businesses employing the five strategy positions are given in Table 19-2.

Balancing Strategy. The approach used for mature products in established markets where the competition is well known is generally the balancing strategy. The company seeks to balance revenues and costs and empha-

Table 19-2
The Five Alternative Strategy Positions Put to Use

Balancing Strategy
Strategy position occupied by railroads, electric utilities, and various other mature industries.
Holiday Inn's provision of motel services to its existing markets.

Market Retention Strategy
Annual model changes of appliance manufacturers aimed at retaining market share.
Introduction of ribs to the Kentucky Fried Chicken food line.
Modification of styles and models by automobile manufacturers.

Market Development Strategy
Procter & Gamble's development of "Pringles" potato chips.
Efforts of public transportation firms to lure people away from use of the automobile through modification of services.
Movement of the large aluminum companies into automobile and beverage can markets for their products.

Growth Strategy
Offering first-run movies at a fee on private TV channels in hotels and motels.
Texas Instruments' move into consumer electronic calculator markets.
Designing and marketing of a low premium $1 million umbrella personal liability insurance policy for individuals.

New Venture Strategy
Polaroid's introduction of the original Land camera.
Xerox's pioneering development and marketing of copying equipment.
Initial publication and marketing of *Playgirl* magazine.

Source: Adapted from David W. Cravens, "Marketing Strategy Positioning," *Business Horizons,* December 1975, p. 57. Copyright 1975 by the Foundation for the School of Business at Indiana University. Reprinted by permission.

sizes control rather than planning. The marketing program is well set and seldom revised extensively

Market Retention Strategy. Established firms usually favor a market retention strategy in their approach to the market. The company seeks to implement product adaptations or expand its markets. Many of the decisions are similar to those employed in a balancing strategy.

Market Development Strategy. The alternative strategy positioning of market development requires a major effort on the part of the organization. Resources, personnel, product lines, organizational structure, and the like may have to be altered. The strategy emphasizes new markets and new product requirements.

Growth Strategy. A growth strategy is riskier than the alternatives already described. The company offers a new product or enters a new market along with expanding its market or adapting its products. Texas Instruments' decision to move into consumer electronic calculators is an illustration.

New Venture Strategy. When a firm decides to follow a new venture strategy, it is making an effort in an entirely new area for the company. While risks are high, so are business opportunities. Competition is usually limited. The development of an effective marketing program is a difficult aspect of this strategy.

Influences on Marketing Strategy	Holiday Inn offers a "family plan" that allows children under twelve to sleep and eat free. Howard Johnson owns a subsidiary motel chain called 3 Penny Inn that features budget priced rooms.[11] Why have these big motel chains implemented such strategies?

    The probable reason is the growth of the budget motel chains such as Red Roof Inns, Motel 6, Dollar Inns of America, Regal Eight Inns, and Days Inn of America. Such motels offer considerable travel savings to consumers who are not concerned about all the amenities offered by the large nationwide chains. Located primarily along major travel routes, these firms have drastically altered the competitive environment in some geographical areas.

An Overview

Competition seems to be a major influence on the Holiday Inn and Howard Johnson strategies reported above. But other factors could be involved. Actually, at any one time, a strategy can be influenced by a variety of variables.

    Figure 19–5 presents a basic model for the study of strategic decision making. Strategy formulation requires consideration of three primary vari-

Figure 19-5
A Conceptual Framework for Strategic Analysis

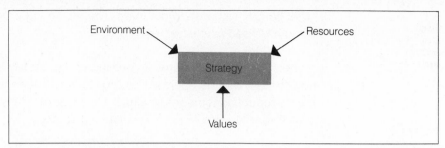

Source: Renato Mazzolini, "European Corporate Strategies," *Columbia Journal of World Business,* Spring 1975, p. 99. Reprinted by permission from the Spring 1975 issue of the *Columbia Journal of World Business.* Copyright © 1975 by the Trustees of Columbia University in the City of New York.

ables: (1) corporate environment, (2) company resources, and (3) management values.

Corporate Environment. On some travel routes, Days Inn of America is certainly part of Holiday Inn's corporate environment and vice versa. But competition is only one aspect of a firm's corporate environment. Consider the newspaper business.

When was the last time you read *Chicago Today,* the *Chicago Daily News,* the *New York Journal-American,* the *Detroit Times,* or the *Cleveland News?* Probably not recently, since all are no longer published.[12] These papers were all PMs—afternoon newspapers—and this segment of the industry has fallen on hard times. PMs were very popular when people went to work in the predawn hours and returned home sometime in the afternoon. But the PM environment has changed in recent times. The white-collar labor force now reports for work at 9 A.M. rather than 6 A.M.

An increase in employment among married women means that families now shop during the evening hours, when they used to read PMs. Furthermore, the Roper Organization now reports television to be the most popular source of news. Environmental factors seem to be favoring the AMs—morning newspapers—in their competitive confrontation with the once powerful PMs. But the afternoon newspapers are fighting back by beefing up their suburban, entertainment, and special interest sections and coverage. Clearly, the environment is playing a major role in the strategy decisions of the PMs.

One method of evaluating the corporate environment is to employ an industry assessment form such as the one that appears in Figure 19-6. An industry's financial and operating flexibility and demand stability are two important aspects of the corporate environment. By plotting these characteristics as shown in the figure, one can fairly assess the summary position of the industry.[13]

Figure 19-6 shows health related products to be in a strong industry position because of high demand stability and high financial and operating

Figure 19–6
Factors Determining the Status of an Industry

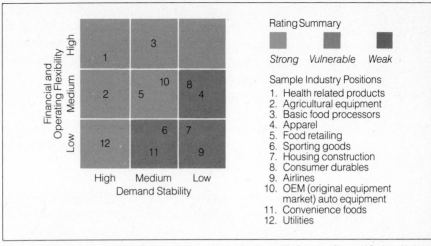

Source: B. A. Bridgewater, Jr., Donald Clifford, Jr., and Thomas Hardy, "The Competition Game Has Changed," *Business Horizons,* October 1975, p. 14. Copyright 1975 by the Foundation for the School of Business at Indiana University. Reprinted by permission.

flexibility. Housing construction and the airlines, on the other hand, are in a weak position because of low rankings on both factors.

Company Resources. An organization's resources also influence the corporate strategy employed. Resources include marketing strengths, production strengths, financial position, research and development capability, and quality of management.[14] Bic, a French manufacturer of inexpensive ballpoint pens, apparently needed to acquire an effective distribution setup in the United States, so it purchased Waterman, a U.S. firm that made fountain pens. Four years later, it discontinued the line of fountain pens.[15]

A company's position within an industry can be assessed in much the same way as the industry is assessed, as Figure 19–7 indicates. Competi-

Figure 19–7
Factors Determining the Status of a Company

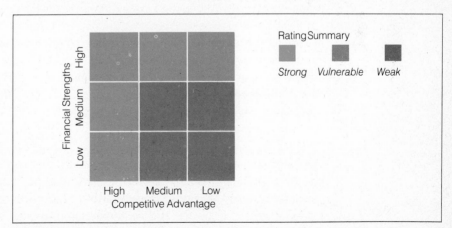

Source: B. A. Bridgewater, Jr., Donald Clifford, Jr., and Thomas Hardy, "The Competition Game Has Changed," *Business Horizons,* October 1975, p. 14. Copyright 1975 by the Foundation for the School of Business at Indiana University. Reprinted by permission.

tive advantage and financial strength should be considered. Competitive advantages include a large market, cost efficiency, superior product and service technology, and brand insistence. Financial strengths are particularly important during economic downturns. For instance, during a recent credit squeeze, financially strong companies like Du Pont and 3M were still able to raise new capital.[16]

Figure 19–7 illustrates one method of assessing a company's position within an industry. Strong organizations are those with financial strength and competitive advantage. Weak companies receive low rankings in both areas.

Management Values. Strategic planning can also be affected by management values, which vary among different cultures. Japanese managers, for example, rely on consensus to make critical decisions, despite the time involved. Japanese executives, accustomed to working with lifetime employees, actively encourage proposals from subordinates.[17]

Closed Door versus Open Door

The compulsion for orderliness and formality is an ingredient of the German culture, and their offices reflect these national characteristics. For one thing, the Germans take their office doors very seriously. They are heavy, solid, soundproof. A German executive assigned to an office will . . . . test the click of the latch just as Americans kick a tire or slam the door of a car to listen for a tinny rebound. American companies which have opened branch offices or subsidiaries in Germany have had to act as arbiters of clashes between U.S. executives and German managers over the issue of the "closed door vs. the open door." Americans keep their doors open; Germans, solidly shut. A whole generation of American businessmen has grown up in a tradition that the "open door" is a democratic virtue. To Germans, open doors are sloppy and disorderly and reflect an unbusinesslike air, where to the Americans, the closed door conveys a conspiratorial atmosphere.

Source: Lawrence Stessin, "Incidents of Cultural Shock among American Businessmen Overseas," *Pittsburgh Business Review,* November–December 1971, p. 19. Reprinted by permission of the University of Pittsburgh Graduate School of Business.

A marketer's personal or corporate value system may have a sizable impact on the strategies that are developed and implemented. For instance, ethical standards may be considered in determining a promotional strategy. Certainly, management values can have as profound an influence on marketing strategy as environmental and resource factors.

The Marketing Audit

All marketing organizations need to evaluate their operations and performance periodically. Such a review is invaluable not only in identifying the tasks that the organization does well but also in highlighting its failures. Periodic review, criticism, and self-analysis are crucial to the vitality of any organization. They are particularly critical to a function that is as diverse and dynamic as marketing.

**The Persian
Messenger
Syndrome**

William S. Woodside, the President of American Can Company, has been quoted as saying: "The roughest thing to get rid of is the Persian Messenger Syndrome, where the bearer of bad tidings is beheaded by the king. You should lean over backward to reward the guy who is first with the bad news. Most companies have all kinds of abilities to handle problems, if they only learn about them soon enough."

Source: Quoted in Arthur R. Roalman, "Why Corporations Hate the Future," *MBA*, November 1975, p. 37. © 1975 MBA Communications, Inc. Reprinted by permission.

**The Marketing
Audit Defined**

If the marketing organization is to avoid the Persian Messenger Syndrome, it must not only institute periodic program reviews, but must also be willing to accept the objective results of such evaluations. For most organizations, this means the use of a **marketing audit**—*a thorough, objective evaluation of an organization's marketing philosophy, goals, policies, tactics, practices, and results.*[18]

The marketing audit goes beyond the normal control system. The control process for marketing essentially asks: Are we doing things right? The marketing audit extends this question to: Are we also doing the right things?[19]

Marketing audits are applicable to all organizations—large or small, profitable or profitless, and nonprofit or profit-oriented. Audits are particularly valuable when they are done for the first time or when they are conducted after a long absence from the managerial process. Not all organizations have implemented marketing audits, but the number of firms using them is expected to grow. One study found that 28 percent of the firms surveyed had used a marketing audit. Table 19–3 reflects the use of audits in different industries.

**Selecting the
Marketing Auditors**

Selection of the auditors is a crucial aspect of conducting a marketing audit. Three potential sources of auditors can be identified: regular corporate executives, special marketing audit staffs, and outside marketing consultants.[20]

Some firms prefer to assign selected executives to perform marketing audits on a periodic basis. The difficulties in such an arrangement include

**Table 19–3
Marketing Audit
Usage by Industry**

Type of Company	Percentage Conducting Marketing Audits
Industrial goods manufacturers	36
Consumer goods manufacturers	19
Manufacturers of consumer and industrial goods	22
Service related firms	28
Total of all firms	28

Source: Adapted from Louis R. Capella and William S. Sekely, "The Marketing Audit: Usage and Applications," in *Proceedings of the Southern Marketing Association*, ed. Robert S. Franz, Robert M. Hopkins, and Al Toma, New Orleans, Louisiana, November 1978, p. 412. Used by permission of the Southern Marketing Association. Copyright © 1978 by the Southern Marketing Association. All rights reserved.

the time pressure of the executives' regular duties and the problem of maintaining impartiality. Other organizations set up a separate marketing staff if their size permits such a structure. This arrangement can provide an excellent balance between impartiality and extensive in-house knowledge. Marketing consultants are often recommended for marketing audits because they enter the evaluation with an independent viewpoint that is often valuable. Consultants may also be able to offer the most up-to-date evaluation methodology.

How to Conduct a Marketing Audit

Marketing audits are probably as diverse as the people who conduct them. Some auditors follow only informal procedures. Others have developed elaborate checklists, questionnaires, profiles, tests, and related research instruments. Regardless of the tools employed, all marketing audits have four major steps.

1. Securing agreement between the auditor and the organization on the audit's objectives and scope.
2. Developing a framework for the audit.
   a. Studying the company's external environment.
   b. Profiling the major elements of the marketing system.
   c. Examining the key marketing activities.
3. Preparing an audit report with findings and recommendations.
4. Presenting the report in a manner that will lead to action.[21]

These steps can be implemented in a variety of ways. Certainly, some basic questions can be raised under each topic, and they must be answered

Not all marketing strategies are successful.

"Miss Grimsby, send in a scapegoat."

Source: *Wall Street Journal*, October 16, 1978, p. 24. Reprinted by permission of the cartoonist, C. E. Vadun, and the *Wall Street Journal.*

if a proper audit is to be made. For instance, during the initial stage, the auditor and the organization involved should agree on the goals to be achieved by the audit, its coverage and depth, and the provision of data sources for it. Similar vital questions can be raised during each of the other stages of the marketing audit.

The real value of a marketing audit may not emerge until considerably after the final report has been prepared and presented. Philip Kotler has pointed out:

> The marketing audit can function as a catalyst to start management discussion as to where the company should be going. The final actions taken may vary from those recommended but the audit has served its purpose in starting the needed dialogue about the company's marketing strategy.[22]

Such an audit can make a significant contribution to improved marketing productivity in virtually all organizations. The starting point, as noted earlier, is to stop beheading the Persian Messenger.

Future Perspectives for Marketing Strategy

A static marketing strategy is one doomed to failure in the long run. Marketers must constantly reassess their positions and revamp their strategies. It is therefore useful to consider some future perspectives for marketing strategy.[23]

Forecasting the Future: A Risky Venture

In the mid-1960s the National Planning Association estimated that by the year 2000 the United States would have a GNP of $2,280 billion in 1960 prices and a population of 340 million people. Ten years later, the forecasts had to be revised sharply downward. The average family had at that time only 2.1 children, as compared to the 3.1 figure used in the earlier projections. The U.S. population had risen to only 214 million by the mid-1970s rather than the 226 million forecast a decade earlier.[24]

Population and GNP are broad aggregate figures that can be estimated from numerous data sources. The difficulty in setting these forecasts suggests the problems that marketers face in predicting future events of a smaller nature. Often business forecasters face a high degree of uncertainty and insufficient information. Marketing forecasts are risky and should be considered as such by the managers who use them.

R. J. Reynolds introduced its low tar Real cigarettes in 1977 after Phillip Morris had achieved considerable success with Merit. Reynolds did not test market Real, choosing instead to move quickly into a national rollout—a nationwide launch of the product. Merit's success in the low-tar market and the "natural ingredients" fad that had stimulated the sales of a number of packaged goods led Reynolds management to conclude that the Real brand would prove a major winner. Instead, the brand failed dismally. Reynolds had spent an estimated $60 million promoting Real, but its market share never exceeded 0.4 percent—far below the 1 percent level necessary to induce vending machine operators to stock the brand in their machines. The Real failure is one more example of the difficulty of predicting marketing success.[25]

Adaptable Marketing Strategies a Must

The need for adaptable marketing strategies is evident in the abundant examples provided by a variety of industries and firms. Toyota's management recognizes the challenge faced by the company in the U.S. market. The highly profitable Japanese firm knows that several factors are working against increased automobile sales for both itself and the other makers of imports. Slower domestic sales are expected in the near future. Detroit now offers small cars to compete with the Japanese compacts. And the rising value of the yen relative to the U.S. dollar forced Toyota to raise its retail prices by more than 20 percent in a recent year.

What has Toyota done to counter the possibility of a slowdown in new car sales? It has begun to produce and market prefabricated houses and commercial buildings through its strong domestic dealer network. Although the new products represent a very small percentage of total sales, the move into a completely different industry illustrates Toyota's marketing adaptability.[26]

When a Kentucky Fried Chicken outlet opened in Harlan, Kentucky (population 3,300), some customers waited in line 1½ hours to purchase their chicken.[27] Over a ton of fried chicken was sold on the opening day despite the fact that the store did no advertising. Kentucky Fried Chicken's move to a community of 3,300 people illustrates a dramatic change taking place in fast-food franchising. Until recently, KFC Corporation preferred *not* to operate in areas of under 35,000 population. Now, 890 of its 4,000 units are located in towns with fewer than 10,000 residents.

Other fast-food franchisers are also revamping their distribution strategies. Pizza Hut is considering areas of under 4,000 population, and Burger King has plans for reduced-size units for smaller towns. These fast-food franchisers have found that smaller communities sometimes offer less competition than do larger areas. The franchise operators also benefit from changed consumer preferences and national advertising. The move to smaller towns illustrates how fast-food franchisers have modified their marketing strategies to cope with the modern business environment.

Strategy adaptations should be based on careful evaluation of marketing programs and results. Changes in strategy should be subject to the same careful analysis that characterized the original decision. Marketers must be careful to avoid ill-conceived or hasty strategy adaptations.

Various factors will influence marketing strategy in the future. Some current trends will likely accelerate in the years ahead and will play a critical role in new marketing strategies. Other anticipated changes will cease to be factors in marketing decision making. It seems likely that many potential influences on future marketing strategies will cluster around a few basic areas: structural changes in the marketing system, public and legal pressures, market changes, and technological changes.

Structural Changes. Some structural changes in the marketing system have had a pronounced effect on marketing decisions. The franchise system has altered concepts of small business ownership. Collective marketing organizations such as OPEC have certainly influenced the world markets for their products. Executives must constantly evaluate the changes taking place in the marketing system. Even slight and gradual changes can have a profound effect on sales and profits.

Public and Legal Pressures. Future marketing strategies could be most affected by public and legal pressures. Actions such as the proposed restructuring of the petroleum industry may shake many of the basic foundations upon which marketers have always operated. Further legislation seems likely as all levels of government strive to fill what some critics see as loopholes in the system. The need for self-regulation in marketing is greater than ever before. Effective self-regulation is probably the best response to marketing's critics.

Market Changes. Perhaps the most obvious potential influence on strategic decisions are market changes. Market potentials for various goods and services shift with changes in geographical patterns of population and income. Life-style preferences also influence marketing. The trends toward shorter workweeks, longer vacations, and earlier retirements affect marketers of recreational equipment, travel services, real estate, and leisure-time activities. Monitoring market shifts is vital to successful marketing.

Technological Changes. The goods and services that are marketed in the free competitive system of the United States are affected by technological changes. Since technological shifts can make a product obsolete overnight, marketers must be assured of a constant new product development effort. Marketing strategy requires that products and services be effectively matched with consumer desires.

Change is inevitable. A permanent part of contemporary marketing, it must be dealt with constantly. Marketers know that changes in the structure of the marketing system, the public and legal framework, markets, and technology can alter the very foundation of today's marketing discipline. Successful future marketers will be those who are best able to cope with these changes.

Summary

Marketing strategy is the general term used to describe the overall company program for selecting a particular market segment and then satisfying its consumers through careful use of the elements of the marketing mix. Effective marketing requires strategic decisions that successfully integrate a firm's marketing program. Marketing strategies, which involve aspects of both art and science, are derived from overall organizational strategies.

Planning is the basis of all strategy decisions. The planning process begins with a recognition of problems and opportunities. Subsequent steps are the development of alternative courses of action, the evaluation of alternatives, the selection and implementation of chosen alternatives, and the following up to determine the effectiveness of the decision. ROI and PERT are illustrations of planning tools.

Five positioning strategies are: balancing, market retention, market development, growth, and new venture. Three primary variables influencing strategy formulation are the corporate environment, company resources, and management values.

A marketing audit is a thorough, objective evaluation of an organization's marketing philosophy, goals, policies, tactics, practices, and results. Marketing audits are applicable to all organizations. They are particularly valuable because they extend beyond the normal control system.

Potential influences on future marketing strategy include structural changes in the marketing system itself, public and legal pressures, market changes, and technological changes.

Questions for Discussion

1. Explain the following terms:

   marketing strategy PERT (program evaluation and review technique)
   planning critical path
   market planning marketing audit
   ROI (return on investment)

2. Assume that you were responsible for the Datril launch. Would you have used a low price strategy to enter the market against Tylenol? Explain.

3. What is the current status of the Polaroid-Kodak instant photography competition? Do you agree with the marketing strategies that have been used?

4. Comment on the following statement: A productive marketing strategy requires that all aspects of the marketing mix be considered.

5. Describe the relationship between marketing strategies and organizational strategies.

6. Outline the strategic planning process, beginning with the formulation of a corporate mission.

7. Is marketing an art or a science? Explain.

8. Why is planning the basis for all strategy decisions?

9. List and discuss the steps in the planning process.

10. What is the ROI for a new product in which the firm expects to invest $400,000 and to generate $800,000 in sales and $40,000 in net profits?
11. How are PERT diagrams used in planning?
12. Develop a hypothetical PERT chart for the introduction of Datril. Specify any necessary assumptions.
13. Differentiate among balancing, market retention, market development, growth, and new venture strategies.
14. What are the primary variables influencing strategy formulation?
15. Pick an industry with which you are familiar. How would you rate it on the industry status chart shown in Figure 19–6? Explain.
16. Pick a company with which you are familiar. How would you rate it on the company status chart presented in Figure 19–7? Explain.
17. Why are marketing audits important?
18. Identify the major sources of auditors for marketing audits in organizations. What are the advantages and disadvantages of each source?
19. Outline the major steps in a marketing audit.
20. What is your perspective on the future direction of marketing strategy?

Notes

1. Hewlett-Packard's marketing strategy is reviewed in "Hewlett-Packard: Where Slower Growth Is Smarter Management," *Business Week,* June 9, 1975, pp. 50–54, 56, 58.
2. Quoted in "Inside Colgate Marketing Policy: How It Looks from the Top," *Advertising Age,* December 2, 1974, p. 40.
3. Phillip Benton's remarks were presented in an address to the Detroit chapter of the American Marketing Association and were quoted in "Ford Exec Says Auto Industry Rules, Marketing Strategies Keep Changing," *Marketing News,* August 1, 1975, p. 8.
4. Robert S. Wheeler, "Marketing Tales with a Moral," *Product Marketing,* April 1977, p. 43.
5. David T. Kollat, Roger D. Blackwell, and James F. Robeson, *Strategic Marketing* (New York: Holt, Rinehart and Winston, 1972), p. 15.
6. "Does G. E. Really Plan Better?" *MBA,* November 1975, p. 42.
7. The need to periodically evaluate plans is noted in J. Donald Phillips, Lyndon E. Dawson, and William A. Hedges, "A Dual Approach to Managerial Decision-Making: A Pragmatic View," *Idaho Business and Economic Journal,* January 1975, pp. 16–23. Excellent discussions of planning appear in Keith T. Stephens and Edward M. Mazze, "Planning: The Marketing Skill You Must Master," *Product Management,* September 1976, pp. 55–59; Derek F. Abell, "Metamorphosis in Marketing Planning," in *Research Frontiers in Marketing: Dialogues and Directions,* ed. Subhash C. Jain (Chicago: American Marketing Association, 1978), pp. 257–259; W. J. E. Crissy and Frank H. Mossman, "Matrix Models for Marketing Planning: An Update and Expansion," *MSU Business Topics,* Autumn 1977, pp. 17–26; and two papers in Barnett A. Greenberg and Danny N. Bellenger, eds., *Contemporary Marketing Thought* (Chicago: American Marketing Association, 1978): Robert J. Williams and Colin Neuhaus, "A Model for a Strategic Marketing Plan," p. 523; and Noel Capon and Joan Robertson Spogli, "Strategic Marketing Planning: A Comparison and Critical Examination of Two Contemporary Approaches," pp. 219–223.
8. The Gould example is reported in "Industrial Newsletter," *Sales & Marketing Management,* April 3, 1978, p. 32.
9. The Porta-Vac example is taken from David R. Anderson, Dennis J. Sweeney, and Thomas A. Williams, *An Introduction to Management Science* (St. Paul: West Publishing, 1976), pp. 295–310.
10. The discussion of these strategies is based on David W. Cravens, "Marketing Strategy Positioning," *Business Horizons,* December 1975, pp. 53–61. Cravens notes that other arrays of strategy positions are presented in H. Igor Ansoff, *Corporate Strategy* (New York: McGraw-Hill, 1965), pp. 122–138; John W. Humble, *How to Manage by Objectives* (New York: American Management Association, 1973), p. 75; and Kollat, Blackwell, and Robeson, *Strategic Marketing,* pp. 21–23.
11. These examples and the discussion of budget motels in the following paragraph are based on Leonard Yourist, "Budget Motels Spur Space Race along Freeways," *Detroit Sunday News,* May 9, 1976.
12. This discussion is based on Frederick C. Klein, "Big Afternoon Papers Still Losing Readers; Many Factors Blamed," *Wall Street Journal,* May 25, 1976, pp. 1, 28.
13. See B. A. Bridgewater, Jr., Donald K. Clifford, Jr., and Thomas Hardy, "The Competition Game Has Changed," *Business Horizons,* October 1975, pp. 13–14.

14. These resources are suggested in Renato Mazzolini, "European Corporate Strategies," *Columbia Journal of World Business,* Spring 1975, pp. 102–105.
15. Arnold C. Cooper and Dan Schendel, "Strategic Responses to Technological Threats," *Business Horizons,* February 1976, p. 68.
16. Bridgewater, Clifford, and Hardy, "The Competition Game Has Changed," pp. 14–17.
17. Louis Kraar, "The Japanese Are Coming—With Their Own Style of Management," *Fortune,* March 1975, p. 117.
18. An excellent discussion of marketing audits appears in Kollat, Blackwell, and Robeson, *Strategic Marketing,* pp. 498–500, and forms the basis of this and the next section.
19. Ibid., p. 500.
20. Ibid., pp. 499–500, for this section.
21. This section is adapted from an address by Philip Kotler to the Chicago chapter of the American Marketing Association. Reported in "Kotler Presents Whys, Hows of Marketing Audits for Firms, Nonprofit Organizations," *Marketing News,* March 26, 1976, p. 21. Measurement of marketing effectiveness is also discussed in Philip Kotler, "From Sales Obsession to Marketing Effectiveness," *Harvard Business Review,* November–December 1977, pp. 67–75.
22. "Kotler Presents Whys, Hows of Marketing Audits," p. 21.
23. Future perspectives for marketing strategy are discussed in Gene R. Laczniak, Robert F. Lusch, and Jon G. Udell, "Marketing in 1985: A View from the Ivory Tower," *Journal of Marketing,* October 1977, pp. 47–56; and William Lazer, "The 1980s and Beyond: A Perspective," *MSU Business Topics,* Spring 1977, pp. 21–35.
24. Alfred L. Malabre, Jr., "U.S. Unlikely to Be as Big—or as Rich—as Analysts Thought," *Wall Street Journal,* March 15, 1976, pp. 1, 23.
25. "When Marketing Takes Over at R. J. Reynolds," *Business Week,* November 13, 1978, p. 84.
26. "Toyota Motor: Hedging Autos with a Move into Housing," *Business Week,* November 13, 1978, pp. 162–165.
27. The move of fast-food franchises to smaller communities is described in David P. Garino, "Fast-Food Chains Deserve a Break Today, So They Are Moving into Smaller Towns," *Wall Street Journal,* April 21, 1976, p. 36.

CASES

PART 1

THE CONTEMPORARY MARKETING ENVIRONMENT

**Case 1
King-Cola, Inc.**

Most people who have celebrated their eighty-second birthday do not think of forming new businesses. But Walter Mack, who once led Pepsi-Cola, Coca-Cola, and several other firms, has joined some former soft drink industry executives to establish King-Cola, Inc. Mack is the president of the firm, where the average age of management is sixty-two.

How do Mack and his associates expect to compete with the soft drink giants? By using the time-tested formula of offering a quality product and low prices. Pepsi-Cola's former chief chemist came up with the King-Cola formula.

Mack plans to dispense with the industry practice of using local bottlers. King-Cola will have only twenty-nine plants—labeled "Kingdoms"—which will market to the centralized warehouses of major supermarket chains. The retailers will then be responsible for distributing the cola to individual stores, much like grocery items.

The only soft drink firm using a similar system is C&C Cola, a regional brand that Mack once set up—and later sold—to test his concept. King-Cola will sell for $1.09 to $1.19 a six-pack, considerably less than its major competitors. It was scheduled to be launched with the promotional theme "Twice as nice! Less in price!"

Source: "Older Execs Aim for Cola Prize," *Chicago Tribune,* October 6, 1978. Used by permission of Associated Press.

**Discussion
Questions**

1. What is the current status of King-Cola?
2. What is your opinion of King-Cola's marketing mix?

3. What other marketing suggestions could you offer Mack and his associates?

Case 2
Heller-Allen Co. —
Marketing an
Alternative Energy
Source

In 1886, a Napoleon, Ohio, blacksmith came up with the idea that steel could be used in place of wood for windmill blades—and Heller-Allen Co. was born. Farmers were the firm's biggest customers. They used windmills to pump water from their wells.

Windmills experienced declining sales for many years. President Roosevelt's rural electrification program put many firms out of business. Heller-Allen remained solvent by diversifying into pumps, watering tanks, fountains, and a variety of water related items.

Today, windmills are once again popular items. Business has doubled in recent years at Heller-Allen, and 60 percent of the firm's revenues now come from windmills. Farmers are using the windmills for irrigation and even for their wells once again. Heller-Allen has also built windmill towers for firms that want to generate electricity with them. The firm's product line ranges from a model with a six-foot leader to a twelve-foot windmill. Prices begin at $800.

Source: "He Rides the Winds of Fortune," *Mobile Press*, December 6, 1978. Used by permission of Associated Press.

Discussion
Questions

1. What does the history of Heller-Allen suggest about the environment for marketing decision making?
2. Devise a marketing strategy for Heller-Allen.

Case 3
Generic Drug
Substitutes

Since Kentucky passed the first generic drug law in 1972, twenty other states have come up with some version of a law that permits the substitution of generic drugs for brand name products. Exact wording of the laws varies from state to state. In some states, pharmacists can automatically substitute a generic drug for a brand name drug unless the physician specifically indicates that this is not to be done. In other states, substitution is not permitted unless the physician specifically authorizes it.

Consumer advocates hope that these laws will reduce prescription costs. The pharmaceutical manufacturers, who make both brand name and generic products, argue that generic drugs are not therapeutically interchangeable with the brand name products.

A list of states allowing generic substitutes is shown in Table 1.

Source: Information from Nancy F. Millman, "Battle Lines Harden in Fight over Generics," *Advertising Age*, February 13, 1978, p. 76.

Discussion
Questions

1. Do you support this type of legislation?
2. Relate the generic substitution laws to the changing legal environment for marketing decisions.

Table 1
**States Allowing
Generic
Substitutes**

	Year Enacted	Notice to M.D. Required After Substitution	Prior Authorization Required	Preventing Substitution
Alaska	1976	Yes	Yes	C
Arkansas	1975	No	No	B
California	1975	No	No	B
Colorado	1976	No	No	B
Connecticut	1976	No	No	B
Delaware	1976	No	Yes	A
District of Columbia	1976	No	No	B
Florida	1976	No	No	B
Georgia	1977	No	Yes	A
Illinois	1977	No	Yes	A
Iowa	1976	No	No	B
Kentucky	1972	No	No	B
Maine	1975	No	No	B
Maryland	1977	No	No	B
Massachusetts	1976	No	Yes	A
Michigan	1974	No	No	B
Minnesota	1974	No	No	B*
Montana	1977	No	No	B
Nebraska	1977	No	No	B
New Jersey	1977	No	Yes	B
New York	1977	No	Yes	A
New Mexico	1976	Yes	Yes	B
Ohio	1977	No	No	B
Oregon	1975	No	No	B
Pennsylvania	1976	No	Yes	A
Rhode Island	1976	No	Yes	A
Tennessee	1977	No	Yes	A
Utah	1977	No	No	B
Virginia	1977	No	Yes	A
Washington	1977	No	Yes	A
Wisconsin	1976	No	No	B

A–Substitution occurs only if M.D. expressly gives prior approval by signing on the appropriate line on the prescription.
B–Pharmacist is automatically authorized to substitute unless M.D. indicates disapproval.
C–In Alaska, M.D. must expressly permit or deny substitution; if he fails to indicate, authority to substitute is denied.
*When the manufacturer of the substitute product is the same as the manufacturer of the prescribed brand name, M.D. may not prevent substitution.
Source: Pharmaceutical Manufacturers Assn. Reprinted by permission.

PART 2   IDENTIFYING CONSUMER NEEDS

**Case 4
Cal Design
Construction**

Cal Design is a major tract home builder with annual sales exceeding $250 million. Its home office is in southern California. Typically, the firm buys several hundred acres of land at a time, usually at the outer edge of the suburban area of a major city. It develops a master plan, including plans for all roads, utilities, parkways, drainage systems, and homes.

Cal Design assumes responsibility for the total development of the area from the initial work through the actual building and selling of the homes. Historically, the firm has concentrated its building activity west of Denver, although it plans to expand geographically. The houses it builds usually have between 1,800 and 2,200 square feet of floor space and three or four bedrooms. The prices of such houses generally are from $75,000 to $90,000. The houses are sold almost exclusively to white-collar families in which the husband is in a middle management position.

The company has been growing steadily and has been consistently profitable. This success has come only through careful market analysis and excellent engineering and construction know-how. The president, Arthur Riggsby, recently became concerned over the implications of the following statement in *Marketing News:*

One- and two-person households—the single, the widowed, the empty nesters, childless and unmarried couples, and young couples planning to have children later—now account for 59 percent of United States households.[1]

Cal Design typically builds houses that are larger than the average in the local community and that include a variety of luxury options. In addition, the cost per square foot of these houses has been rising faster than the cost-of-living index and the overall national rate of inflation.

Given the information in *Marketing News,* some members of Cal Design's management have strongly suggested that the firm move into the construction of low-cost, no-frills houses. These houses generally have fewer square feet of floor space than usual, can be put on smaller lots, and can be completed much more rapidly than the kind of house Cal Design has been building.

The market for the no-frills house seems to be larger than that for the house of Cal Design's present focus, and it is growing. Furthermore, financing for the smaller houses may be more easily arranged, given their lower price and the fact that several federal assistance programs offer aid to low- and middle-income buyers.

At this time, Cal Design is formulating its marketing strategy for next year. Its management needs help in analyzing the market trends that may affect its future.

[1]"New Minority: The 'Average American Family,'" *Marketing News,* February 24, 1978, p. 3
Source: Adapted from Carl E. Block and Kenneth J. Roering, *Essentials of Consumer Behavior,* 2d ed. (Hinsdale, Ill.: Dryden Press, 1979), pp. 92–93. Copyright © 1979 by Dryden Press, a division of Holt, Rinehart and Winston. Adapted by permission of Holt, Rinehart and Winston.

Discussion Questions

1. What aggregate market trends, if any, will affect the plans that Cal Design is now formulating?
2. Even if some indicators suggest a changing market composition, is it really necessary for Cal Design to respond to them in order to maintain its level of profitability? Explain.

Case 5
The United States Army Recruiting Program

Since the onset of the all-volunteer armed forces, all the services have strengthened their recruiting organizations and have undertaken large-scale advertising efforts. Research has shown that more than 80 percent of prime prospects between the ages of seventeen and twenty-one and 60 percent of the influencers, such as parents and guidance counselors, can accurately recall the theme "Today's Army Wants to Join You." The total campaign is designed to stimulate both initial enlistment and reenlistment among men and women.

The primary male audience for enlistment is the high school graduate, aged seventeen to twenty-one. Other key targets are college dropouts, junior college students, and vocational students. A second major audience category is the influencers—parents, guidance counselors, other educational influencers, and peer groups. The objective of the advertising is to enhance the knowledge of the general public.

An extensive series of interviews was undertaken with prospects during past years, and research into recruitment motivation is an ongoing process. From these interviews it appears that the following advertising themes will be most fruitful:

1. *Jobs and on-the-job training:*
   a. A wide variety of jobs, now; immediate employment
   b. Over two hundred excellent job-training courses
   c. Civilian negotiable jobs
   d. Guaranteed choice of training, if qualified
   e. The opportunity to earn while you learn
   f. "Hands-on" on-the-job training
2. *Combat arms enlistments:*
   a. A test of personal courage
   b. Physical development
   c. Opportunity to be part of a team
   d. The chance to use athletic prowess
   e. The chance to live a rugged outdoor life
   f. Adventure training
3. *Overseas enlistments:*
   a. Working abroad
   b. Travel and adventure
4. *Pay and benefits:*
   a. A good salary plus attractive additional compensations
   b. Salaries competitive with industry for high school graduates
5. *In-service education:*
   a. Today's army encouraging and rewarding education
   b. The variety of army schools
   c. The quality of instruction

    d. Financial aid for civilian correspondence courses

    e. Financial aid for college degrees at off-post universities

    f. The G.I. Bill or any new educational option replacing it

6. *Enlistment guarantee:*

    a. The wide variety of insured choices open to qualified prospects.

    b. Evidence of a changing army

    c. A powerful appeal for the skeptical influencer

7. *Pride in serving:*

    a. Patriotism

    b. Pride in uniform

    c. Family pride

    d. Service to one's country

Source: Case adapted from Roger D. Blackwell, James F. Engel, and W. Wayne Talarzyk, *Contemporary Cases in Consumer Behavior* (Hinsdale, Ill.: Dryden Press, 1977), pp. 96–99. Copyright © 1977 by Dryden Press, a division of Holt, Rinehart and Winston. Adapted by permission of Holt, Rinehart and Winston.

Discussion Questions

1. Has the army correctly identified the motivations of prospects for possible military service?

2. Relate the army's efforts to recruit volunteers to the consumer behavior concepts presented in the text.

**Case 6
McDonald's Corporation**

In 1975, one of the younger major corporations in the United States celebrated its twentieth birthday. In the first two decades of its operation, McDonald's served 16 billion hamburgers and had sales of more than $7.7 billion from 3,343 outlets operated throughout the world. In 1974, sales by all licensed and company-owned restaurants were a record $1,943 billion, up 29 percent from the 1973 total and almost twice the sales in 1972. Computed on an average per day basis, the total represents a daily hamburger, soft drink, and order of french fries for every person in the cities of Chicago and Detroit—and every town in between.

    The architect of the McDonald's concept and one of the pioneers of the modern franchising development is Ray Kroc, the chairman of the board of McDonald's. At the age of 52, Kroc was a moderately successful salesman of malted milk machines. He became interested in a particularly successful restaurant in San Bernardino, California, that was using eight of his milkshake machines. In 1954, Kroc visited this restaurant, which was owned and managed by Richard and Maurice McDonald. After observing its success and its method of operation, he proposed a program for selling franchises for the McDonald concept of service to the customer.

    Kroc had observed that major changes were occurring in the United States in the mid-1950s. These changes centered on the movement of the middle-class population to the suburbs. Kroc had noted that massive numbers of middle-income families were moving, and they all had one thing in common—lots of children. Actually, they had a number of things in common, such as the possession of automobiles, a casual life-style, time to be spent on travel, and frequent family trips to shopping centers.

Another phenomenon was occurring at the same time as the migration from the city: a massive increase in discretionary dollars for the average suburban family. Although this proliferation of affluent households was occurring at an unprecedented rate, the offerings of U.S. marketers were also proliferating at a rapid pace.

To Kroc, all these market factors indicated the need for a series of restaurants that would provide uniform quality and the assurance of cleanliness—wherever and whenever a family might choose to eat—at an affordable price. In addition, Kroc observed that one of life's frustrating experiences for a family with children was to enter the typical restaurant and wait for service.

From all these factors, McDonald's developed the concept of QSC—quality, service, and cleanliness. To all McDonald's personnel:

1. *Quality* means that meals are hot, fresh, and good-tasting and that only the best products are used in preparing them.
2. *Service* means quick, courteous service by friendly McDonald's personnel.
3. *Cleanliness* means neat, clean surroundings, both inside and outside—including personnel, equipment, and presentation.

The history of McDonald's is a record of the most successful growth ever of a restaurant business. At the inception of McDonald's, Kroc stated that the marketing environment included massive numbers of families and young people across the country who would constitute a large market for budget-priced hamburgers produced at a fast rate. In the 1960s and early 1970s, McDonald's advertising was specifically targeted to these consumers. During these years, consumer research disclosed that nearly 80 percent of McDonald's sales were made to families influenced by children.

Kroc credits McDonald's success to "finding something the public wants, something basic and simple, something that can be sold in volume and sold fast." He adds, "What could be more natural than meat and potatoes—and that's what we're selling at McDonald's." The company's first menu was centered around the hamburger, and the emphasis twenty years later is still on hamburgers.

Source: Case adapted from Roger D. Blackwell, James F. Engel, and W. Wayne Talarzyk, *Contemporary Cases in Consumer Behavior* (Hinsdale, Ill.: Dryden Press, 1977), pp. 59–66. Copyright © 1977 by Dryden Press, a division of Holt, Rinehart and Winston. Adapted by permission of Holt, Rinehart and Winston. Information courtesy of McDonald's.

Discussion
Questions

1. Do you agree with Ray Kroc's explanation of McDonald's success?
2. What aspects of the changing marketing environment are likely to af-

fect McDonald's in the next five years? How should McDonald's respond to the changing environment?

Case 7
Lite versus Natural Light: The Battle of the Brewers

In 1977, Anheuser-Busch introduced its Natural Light brand in an attempt to match the success of the Miller Brewing Company, whose Lite beer had catapulted it into second place in the brewing industry. Anheuser-Busch was faced with a difficult assignment, since Miller was firmly entrenched with a 75 percent share of the light beer market. Miller had appealed to the so-called macho segment; it featured in its television commercials retired athletes and other rugged-looking individuals enjoying good times over cold Lites. Anheuser-Busch's difficulties were compounded by the fact that Miller's brand name, consisting of just four letters, had become virtually the generic name for this product, due in large part to its descriptive nature and early entry into the market.

By the time Natural Light was introduced, several other companies had introduced their own brands of light beer. One competitor, Schlitz, had used a promotional strategy that appeared to be aimed at outdoing Miller Lite's macho appeal. Schlitz had enjoyed limited success, however, which suggested that such a strategy would not prove successful for Natural Light. One study revealed that people could remember the macho image of the Schlitz Light ads but could not recall the name of the beer being promoted.

A major problem for Anheuser-Busch was competing with Miller's brand name. One executive remarked, "A four-word name is a killer. Not many people are going to walk into a bar and say, 'gimme an Anheuser-Busch Natural Light.'" Another executive pointed out, "When someone orders a light beer in a restaurant, he is automatically brought a Miller Lite."

There were, however, several factors working in Anheuser-Busch's favor. The firm had an excellent reputation as a producer of quality beers. It also had a highly developed distribution network, which enabled it to move rapidly into the market at a time when other brewers were preparing to market their own light beers. Both Miller and Schlitz had been cultivating the male market for light beer, but Anheuser-Busch saw an excellent opportunity to market the beer to women. Research had indicated that women constituted 50 percent of the light beer market and 35 percent of all beer drinkers. In addition, 60 percent of all beer purchases were made in supermarkets, largely by women. These facts, as well as the rapidly climbing sales in the light beer market, dispelled all fears at Anheuser-Busch that the demand for this product was nothing more than a fad.

Source: Adapted from Carl E. Block and Kenneth J. Roering, *Essentials of Consumer Behavior*, 2d ed. (Hinsdale, Ill.: Dryden Press, 1979), pp. 67–69. Copyright © 1979 by Dryden Press, a division of Holt, Rinehart and Winston. Adapted by permission of Holt, Rinehart and Winston.

1. Suggest a basis for market segmentation among light beer drinkers. Use market target decision analysis to show how you would go about segmenting this market.
2. What should Anheuser-Busch do about the problem of its brand name, Natural Light, and about the association of Miller's Lite with light beer?

PART 3   PRODUCT STRATEGY

**Case 8
Imaginetics
International**

Imaginetics International is ecstatic about its recent product development—a toy Volkswagen van named George that "hears" and responds to voice commands. The toy's overwhelming success at trade shows across the nation has inspired confidence about its market potential. Imaginetics marketers have predicted that virtually everyone who sees the toy will want it, despite its $30 price tag.

A recent development in the economics of voice control has made such an invention feasible. The toy obeys a predetermined sequence of commands, such as "Turn left," "Go straight," "Turn right," and "Stop." But since George is programmed to respond only to this fixed sequence of motions, the user must issue the commands in the proper sequence in order to obtain a correct response. One way of overcoming this drawback is for the user to extend the sounds in the command, which will cause George to skip a step or two in the sequence. For example, if George is stopped and the user wants him to turn right, the person can say, "Ple-e-ease go right," and the left and straight sequences will be passed over. One advantage of George's design is that the toy actually responds to sounds rather than words. This design feature will enable Imaginetics to market George in foreign countries as effectively as in the United States.

Source: Adapted from Carl E. Block and Kenneth J. Roering, *Essentials of Consumer Behavior*, 2d ed. (Hinsdale, Ill.: Dryden Press, 1979), pp. 563–564. Copyright © 1979 by Dryden Press, a division of Holt, Rinehart and Winston. Adapted by permission of Holt, Rinehart and Winston.

1. Suggest methods Imaginetics International might employ to speed the rate of adoption.
2. What other products might the firm consider if it chooses to develop a product line?

**Case 9
Developing New
Product Ideas
from Existing
Products**

Most new products are not "new" in the sense of such major breakthroughs as microwave cooking, instant photography, or air transportation. Many represent adaptations of present products to new uses or users. As such, the basis of many new additions to a firm's product line already is in evidence in the form of existing products. Alex Osborn, an expert on the subject of creativity, proposes the following checklist for use in generating new product ideas:

Put to other uses?	New ways to use as is? Other uses if modified?
Adapt?	What else is like this? What other idea does this suggest? Does past offer parallel? What could I copy? Whom could I emulate?
Modify?	New twist? Change meaning, color, motion, sound, odor, form, shape? Other changes?
Magnify?	What to add? More time? Greater frequency? Stronger? Higher? Longer? Thicker? Extra value? Plus ingredient? Duplicate? Multiply? Exaggerate?
Minify?	What to subtract? Smaller? Condensed? Miniature? Lower? Shorter? Lighter? Omit? Streamline? Split up? Understate?
Substitute?	Who else instead? What else instead? Other ingredient? Other material? Other process? Other power? Other place? Other approach? Other tone of voice?
Rearrange?	Interchange components? Other pattern? Other layout? Other sequence? Transpose cause and effect? Change pace? Change schedule?
Reverse?	Transpose positive and negative? How about opposites? Turn it backward? Turn it upside down? Reverse roles? Change shoes? Turn tables? Turn other cheek?
Combine?	How about a blend, an alloy, an assortment, an ensemble? Combine units? Combine purposes? Combine appeals? Combine ideas?

Source: The checklist is reprinted from Alex F. Osborn, *Applied Imagination* (New York: Charles Scribner's Sons, 1963), pp. 286–287.

Discussion
Questions

1. List an example of a product or service that illustrates the use of each item on Osborn's checklist.
2. What disadvantages exist in the use of such a list for new-product ideas?

**Case 10
Warner
Communications,
Inc.**

The idea of a television service that charges subscribers for programs they view was conceived in 1929. Since that time, a number of companies have lost millions of dollars in an effort to develop a profitable system. In recent years, however, pay-TV systems charging customers a flat monthly rate to view recent movies and sports events with no commercial interruptions have encountered some success. Of the approximately 11 million viewing homes that pay a monthly rate of $7 to $10 for the clear reception offered by cable TV, slightly more than 1 million are subscribing to the movie service. Home Box Office, the Time, Inc., subsidiary that supplies pay-TV programs to some 900,000 homes, has subscribers among more than two hundred different cable systems.

The young industry has been split over whether to charge a flat rate per month or by the program. One advocate of the per program charge is Warner Communications, Inc., which has developed a new kind of cable system called QUBE (pronounced "cube"). QUBE subscribers pay an installation fee and then purchase "on impulse" programs that are of interest to them. They make their purchases by pressing buttons on a small control unit that relays a message to a central computer to transmit a specific movie, play, educational course, audience participation quiz show, or public affairs lecture to the television set. Different prices are charged for the various programs. For example, the opera *Cavalleria Rusticana* costs $2.50, a Frank Sinatra concert is $2, and movies range from $1 for *High Noon* to $3.50 for *Network.*

Although a few similar systems are operating in other test markets, Warner feels that its system offers features not present in the others. For instance, QUBE allows viewers to "talk back" to the studio by pushing certain buttons on their control devices. These buttons enable them to place bids for items shown at an auction, select optional football plays that a quarterback should run, "vote" on civic questions, or choose answers in courses given for school credit.

Source: Adapted from Carl E. Block and Kenneth J. Roering, *Essentials of Consumer Behavior,* 2d ed. (Hinsdale, Ill.: Dryden Press, 1979), pp. 257–258. Copyright © 1979 by Dryden Press, a division of Holt, Rinehart and Winston. Adapted by permission of Holt, Rinehart and Winston.

Discussion Questions

1. Suggest methods for increasing the rate of adoption for QUBE.
2. What other applications can you see for such a system? How might it affect marketing programs of different firms?

PART 4   DISTRIBUTION STRATEGY

**Case 11
The Japanese Distribution System**

Marketers in developing countries view Japan as an example of how *not* to set up a distribution system. This highly developed, industrialized nation has one of the most inefficient distribution structures in the world. One U.S. marketer referred to it as "marketing in a maze." What went wrong?

Japan appears to have a market tailor-made for short channel structures: a huge population, about half as large as that in the United States, concentrated in an area only 4 percent as large as that of the United States. Yet channels are anything but short. Direct sales from the manufacturer to the consumer are virtually unheard of, and a three-level structure—manufacturer to retailer to consumer—is almost as rare.

Much more common are several levels of wholesalers intervening between the manufacturer and the retailer, which results in channel structures of four levels. For instance, the tortured journey of imported consumer products through the Japanese distribution system—customs to importer to national wholesaler to local wholesaler to retailer to consumer—may result in a final retail price twice that in the United States.

The reasons for such long channel structures even in the face of dense markets are traceable to two basic phenomena: the market behavior of the Japanese consumer and the historical background of Japanese society. In commenting on the first phenomenon, a market research study of Japanese buyer behavior stated: "The average Japanese housewife shops every day within 500 yards of her home. . . . You must have a great number of points of supply for this; it is the logistics of bits and pieces."

The second phenomenon? Historically the long, complex channel structures grew from the early development of Japanese villages, which commonly distrusted each other. Many neutral middlemen were needed to sell goods from one village to the next. Then, as trading companies began to appear in the late nineteenth century, they became so prominent in buying and selling that many manufacturing companies never bothered to develop sales staffs.

Sources: Case adapted from Bert Rosenbloom, *Marketing Channels: A Management View* (Hinsdale, Ill.: Dryden Press, 1978), pp. 168–169. Copyright © 1978 by Dryden Press, a division of Holt, Rinehart and Winston. Adapted by permission of Holt, Rinehart and Winston. Based on William D. Hartley, "Cumbersome Japanese Distribution System Stumps U.S. Concerns," *Wall Street Journal*, March 2, 1972, pp. 1, 12. See also Masayoshi Kanabayashi, "Japan's Complex Distribution System Hinders Foreign Companies' Efforts to Sell Goods There," *Wall Street Journal*, May 3, 1978, p. 1.

Discussion Questions

1. What can be learned from studying the Japanese distribution system?
2. How would the Japanese distribution system affect U.S. firms wishing to market their goods in Japan?

Case 12
The Death of Robert Hall

Another retail failure occurred shortly after the demise of W. T. Grant. This time the unlucky party was a chain of discount clothiers, founded four decades ago, that aimed at a market target seeking low prices and almost no retail services. Even its name, Robert Hall, was chosen to suggest a mythical blue-collar bargain hunter. The stores' interiors were designed to emphasize the no-frills image, with clothing hung on gas-pipe racks. The only store employees were those who operated the cash register.

For years, this low-service, low-price chain produced heavy profits for its parent firm, United Merchants and Manufacturers. But the 1960s and 1970s saw major changes in retailing—a movement from downtown locations to the suburbs, the addition of new lines of merchandise to cater to consumer demands for one-stop convenience, and a trading up of product quality to keep pace with ever-changing fashions. Robert Hall's management ignored these changes and saw the company's sales erode.

By 1977, the chain had lost $100 million, and UM & M began bankruptcy proceedings. Inventory at the Robert Hall stores was sold at auction, and by 1980 Robert Hall was only a memory.

Discussion
Questions

1. Suggest methods by which Robert Hall's management might have prevented the company's demise.
2. Are you aware of other firms that appear to be making similar mistakes in their retail marketing strategy? How are their decisions different from or similar to Robert Hall's?

Case 13
B. F. Goodrich:
Developing a
New Physical
Distribution
Strategy

A double problem faced the management of B. F. Goodrich Tire Company in the mid-1970s. President Patrick C. Ross stated the problem this way: "How can we improve responsiveness to customer requirements while holding down distribution costs?" Ross pointed out that the challenge was great: "The cost of distributing many products has become such a large proportion of the product's total cost that a sluggish distribution system is a luxury few can afford."

To attack the problem, a new corporate position was created: vice-president of distribution and supply. The new vice-president had to deal simultaneously with the twin objectives of controlling skyrocketing increases in freight costs while maintaining—and preferably increasing—the overall level of customer service standards. The first objective was accomplished by an intensive analysis of transport scheduling. Large volume shipments are now made by independent transport firms, which has lowered the freight rates per product shipped. Next, Goodrich purchased a fleet of company trucks for use in emergencies. The company owned trucks can leave at any time and deliver to any warehouse in under twenty-four hours. Use of the company trucks has reduced the average transit time between warehouses and customers' receiving docks.

As a result of these changes, customer service standards have improved while transportation costs have dropped. The average time between the receipt of an order and its delivery to the customer has been reduced from seven to four days. In addition, order placement has been made more convenient. Customer orders to Goodrich can be placed through a twenty-four-hour, toll-free telephone service. As the order is taken, the customer is immediately told whether the product is in inventory and what the expected delivery date will be.

Source: Adapted from Patrick C. Ross, "Distribution Costs and Customer Service: Do We Have to Trade Off?" *Handling and Shipping*, 1975 Presidential Issue, pp. 7–9. Reprinted from Handling & Shipping Magazine's 1975 Presidential Issue. Copyright 1975 Industrial Publishing Company.

Discussion
Questions

1. Relate the decisions made by B. F. Goodrich management to the three elements of the physical distribution concept.
2. What other activities should be included in the position of vice-president of distribution and supply?

PART 5   PROMOTIONAL STRATEGY

Case 14
Victor Borge and the Bosendorfer

Austrian-made Bosendorfer, the world's biggest and most expensive piano, was virtually unknown. Then Kimball Industries, Inc., of Jasper, Indiana, acquired the 150-year-old product and began to build up the brand. In the process, the company ran into some tough competition. Steinway, a CBS affiliate, has been a dominant U.S. firm for decades. Baldwin is also a strong brand.

Kimball first raised production from 200 pianos a year to 620 by opening a new plant and importing 100 pianos a year from Austria. Kimball then started to line up distributors in the 25 largest U.S. cities. The manufacturer wanted each dealer to keep one Bosendorfer ready at all times for traveling concert pianists. At first, many dealers refused to take on the new brand. But Kimball was gradually able to set up a national distribution system.

The promotional strategy for Bosendorfer has been to get many of the concert pianists to abandon the use of Steinway and to switch to the Austrian make. Kimball provides a Bosendorfer at all concerts without charge to these artists. It also promotes the artist and the piano in return for the pianist's agreement to use Bosendorfer.

Classical pianists Michael Block and Garrick Ohlsson and jazz pianist Oscar Peterson use Bosendorfer. And comedian-pianist Victor Borge has also switched to it. Borge calls the Bosendorfer the "Rolls-Royce of pianos."

Endorsements like Borge's are a major part of Kimball's promotional strategy. The Indiana firm's objective is to sell Bosendorfer to universities, orchestras, and concert halls. But it also hopes the promotion will assist its own Kimball brand piano, which sells for up to $7,000. The Bosendorfer costs $45,000—and "that's without the stool," according to Borge.

Source: Adapted from Bernard Wysocki, Jr., "Piano Peddler Seeks Musicians' Loyalty in Battle for Sales," *Wall Street Journal*, September 28, 1978, pp. 1, 26. Reprinted by permission of *The Wall Street Journal*, © Dow Jones & Company, Inc. 1978. All rights reserved.

Discussion
Questions

1. Evaluate the promotional strategy for Bosendorfer pianos.
2. What other means of promotion might be available to Kimball Industries?

**Case 15
Tiffany & Co.**

A major retail diamond shortage had developed by early 1978. Dealers and others began hoarding diamonds because of a variety of economic factors. Diamond prices had proved a traditional hedge against inflation, and many Western nations were experiencing substantial inflation. Israel, a major demand center, had inflation running at 42.5 percent annually. The decline of the U.S. dollar also contributed to the hoarding since international diamond trading is done in U.S. dollars. The United States accounts for 52 percent of all diamond sales. Dealers and speculators felt they would gain by holding their diamonds rather than selling them for lower-valued U.S. dollars. The net result was that retail diamond prices soared.

At the peak of the diamond speculation, Tiffany & Co., one of the nation's most prestigious jewelers, placed the following ad in the *New York Times*:

Diamonds Are Too High!

This may be an unusual statement by an organization like Tiffany & Co.

But some speculators have driven diamond prices too high.

We suggest you look before you leap!

TIFFANY & CO.
FIFTH AVENUE & 57TH STREET
NEW YORK

The Tiffany warning echoed one by de Beers, the firm that controls 80 percent of all diamond output in the world. It was probably the most unusual advertisement ever run by anyone in the diamond industry.

Source: Information from "A Diamond is Forever . . . Rising in Price," *Forbes*, April 17, 1978, pp. 38–39. Ad courtesy of Tiffany & Co.

1. What is your opinion of the Tiffany ad?
2. What do you think Tiffany's objectives were in running this ad?
3. Identify similar examples of private firms presenting advertising messages they deem socially responsible.

Case 16
Listerine versus the FTC

In late 1975, the Federal Trade Commission ordered Warner-Lambert Company to include the following statement in Listerine advertisements funded by the next $10.2 million it spent on advertising:

Contrary to prior advertising, Listerine will not help prevent colds or sore throats or lessen their severity.

This order reaffirmed the decision of an FTC administrative law judge. It was the first case where the FTC had required corrective advertising (discussed in Chapter 2) after a full hearing before a law judge.

Listerine is the most popular mouthwash in the United States; it has about 40 percent of a $275 million annual market. Warner-Lambert's advertising budget for it has been about $10 million per year.

The FTC reported that Listerine had been advertised as a cold remedy since 1921 but that the commission had heard contradictory medical testimony and for that reason had ordered the corrective advertising. The FTC decision was called "unfounded and without legal authority or precedent" in a Warner-Lambert statement. The firm appealed the case.

In 1977, the U.S. Circuit Court of Appeals upheld the FTC order but eliminated the "contrary to prior advertising" part of the statement. Warner-Lambert then appealed to the U.S. Supreme Court. In 1978, the Supreme Court decided against reviewing the case. The FTC order stood except for the revised wording of the corrective advertising statement.

Sources: Most of case is adapted from "FTC Upholds Decision That Warner-Lambert Ads Were False," *Wall Street Journal*, December 19, 1975, p. 4. Reprinted with permission of *The Wall Street Journal*, © Dow Jones & Company, Inc., 1975. All rights reserved. The recent information is from "Court Reaffirms FTC on Ordering Listerine Corrective Ads," *Advertising Age*, October 3, 1977, p. 6; George E. Hartman, "Courts Affirm, Spell Out Rules for Corrective Ads," *Marketing News*, October 21, 1977; and "Taking It Back," *Time*, April 17, 1978, p. 83.

1. Evaluate the concept of corrective advertising.
2. Is corrective advertising an effective way for the FTC to deal with deceptive advertising?

Case 17
AT&T Realigns Its Sales Force

AT&T sales personnel were traditionally responsible for two often competing functions—selling and servicing. A study by McKinsey and Company, a consulting firm, found that AT&T salespeople spent about 70 percent of their time on their service function and only 30 percent of their time selling.

AT&T marketers decided to reorganize the sales force in hopes of doubling the amount of actual selling time. The service function was given to a new position in the sales organization—sales assistant. Salespeople were thereby released to concentrate on new sales opportunities. The sales assistants were made responsible for most of the post-order activity required in the sale of communications systems. Order-handling procedures were also modernized to cut the sales force's paperwork.

Source: Adapted from Thayer C. Taylor, "AT&T Is on the Line—at Last," *Sales Management,* March 3, 1975, pp. 29–34. Reprinted by permission from *Sales Management* magazine. Copyright 1975.

Discussion
Questions

1. What are the advantages and disadvantages of AT&T's revised sales force organization?
2. Can you identify other firms or selling situations that use an approach similar to that employed by AT&T?
3. Should AT&T continue to use this type of sales organization?

PART 6   PRICING STRATEGY

Case 18
The Pricing of Color Televisions

Few remember TV brands like Teletone, Tele King, Air King, Emerson, DuMont, Stromberg-Carlson, Hallicrafters, Raytheon, and Capehart-Farnsworth. All of these brands have long since disappeared from the color television market. Back in 1950, there were over a hundred U.S. manufacturers of televisions. Today, there is just a handful. Zenith and RCA lead the rest with market shares slightly over 20 percent.

While the output of televisions has grown from 2.97 million sets in 1949 to about 17 million per year in this decade, prices have declined drastically. Average prices have dropped 38 percent since 1950. Escalating costs of labor and materials mean that some television sets are now priced at $10 to $20 less than cost, according to one widely accepted estimate.

The pricing of televisions has also been affected by a flood of imports from Japanese manufacturers. Indeed, the Japanese have taken over much of the private brand business. Even Sony, which once priced its sets at the high end, has come under increased price pressure with the end of fair trade laws (see Chapter 2). A retail price war in Sony models has caused some dealers to stop carrying the brand. Meanwhile, Zenith and RCA have been cutting their prices to fend off the cheaper imports. Zenith cut its work force by 25 percent and shifted some production to overseas plants. A recent Japanese–United States agreement offered some hope of relief. The Japanese agreed to export only 1.75 million color televisions annually to the United States, down about 30 percent from their record high.

Sources: Adapted primarily from David Lachenbruch, "The Customer Gets a Break," TV Guide, July 12, 1975, pp. 24–28. Reprinted by permission from TV Guide® Magazine. Copyright © 1975 by Triangle Publications, Inc., Radnor, Pennsylvania. Information also from Paul Ingrassia, "In a Color-TV Market Ruled by Price Wars, Sony Takes a Pounding," Wall Street Journal, March 16, 1978, pp. 1, 27.

Discussion Questions

1. Why has television manufacturing become an often profitless enterprise?
2. How can prices decline at the same time industry output is rising and the number of competitors is falling?
3. How can television manufacturers escape their current pricing dilemma?
4. How might the television industry's pricing structure affect its research and development efforts?

Case 19
Pricing in the Automobile Industry

Donaldson Brown, a vice-president of General Motors in the 1920s, developed a pricing concept that still exists in the automobile industry. Brown used an annual sales projection, called "standard volume," that represents 80 percent of capacity. The standard volume has to be large enough to cover all fixed and variable costs, be priced at an acceptable level, and produce the appropriate target return, since only variable costs may be covered once standard volume is obtained. Profits mount rapidly beyond this point, but they decline sharply if standard volume is not achieved.

Source: Information from "Detroit's Dilemma on Prices," Business Week, January 20, 1975, p. 82.

Discussion Questions

1. What is your opinion of Brown's pricing formula?
2. Do other industries use similar approaches to pricing their products?
3. Why would Ford, Chrysler, and American Motors use the same type of pricing scheme?

Case 20
U.S. Postal Service

The Continental Congress accepted Benjamin Franklin's proposal for setting up the Post Office Department on July 26, 1775. Early postage rates were high even by today's standards. A 1792 law based postal charges on distance. Letters going fewer than 30 miles carried a six-cent rate, those going 60 to 100 miles were ten cents, and those going more than 450 miles were twenty-five cents.

Postal rate criteria have varied through the years. Sometimes rates have been based on distance, weight, or destination (local or out-of-town). Finally, in 1944, the postal rate was set at three cents for all letters. The rate was raised to four cents in 1958. Since then, rates have risen rapidly. Stamp prices were increased to five cents in 1963, six cents in 1968, eight cents in 1971, ten cents in 1974, thirteen cents in 1975, and fifteen cents in 1978. Yet the U.S. Postal Service continues to run large deficits. The frequent price increases were aimed at reducing—and hopefully eliminating—the continuing operation deficits that have long plagued the U.S. postal service.

Source: Most of case adapted by permission from "Rising Postal Rates Are Reviewed in Armand Gerbert, Blame It on Ben Franklin," *Detroit News*, July 25, 1975.

Discussion
Questions

1. Why have postal rates tripled since 1963?
2. What should be the pricing objectives of the U.S. Postal Service?
3. Can postal rates ever reach a point where people will refuse to use the mails? Explain.

PART 7   FURTHER PERSPECTIVES

Case 21
The Lada 2106–1

The Lada 2106–1 sold well in Canada, so the international marketers began plotting their assault on the U.S. markets. Who are these marketers, and what is a Lada 2106–1? The 2106–1 is a four-door sedan produced in Togliatti, USSR. The car is the export version of the Russian Lada 1500S, which in turn is a modified Fiat 124. Fiat helped build the Togliatti plant. It also discontinued its 124 model in 1974.

Ladas are now marketed in seventy countries outside the Soviet Union. A hundred thousand were sold in West Germany alone. The Lada 1500S is a four-cylinder subcompact. It has a beefed-up suspension system, bumpers, and seats higher off the road than the Fiat. It comes equipped with a twenty-one-piece tool kit and a system for crank-starting the motor. All these features are required by the USSR's poor roads and lack of service facilities. The Lada has a Canadian combined city-highway mileage rating of thirty miles per gallon.

Satra Corporation will handle U.S. distribution. The new import is expected to be priced at under $4,000, and Satra expects first-year sales of 15,000 cars. A survey has indicated that over 90 percent of the automobile dealers contacted are interested in selling the Lada. Possible problems include union opposition to the import and consumer resistance to Soviet-made products.

Source: Adapted by permission from Clark Hallas, "They Want to Sell a 'Lada' Cars in the U.S.," *Detroit News*, September 24, 1978.

Devise a marketing program for the Lada in the United States.

Dinner theater has become very popular in many areas of the country, particularly near medium-sized cities. Consider the case of Dick Carrouthers and Dennis Hennessy of Kansas City. The two University of Missouri drama graduates first met while working in a little-theatre production. But they soon discovered there were few employment opportunities for drama majors.

Carrouthers and Hennessy took a chance and converted a commercial laundry into a 276-seat dinner theater, which they named "Tiffany's Attic." Their theater featured low-budget comedies and was an immediate success. A year later, the firm's stockholders agreed to convert a 1920-era burlesque and movie house into a larger theater, which Carrouthers and Hennessy called the "Waldo Astoria."

It has been estimated that the nation's dinner theaters gross three times Broadway's annual revenue and employ more actors than the New York stage. They have also provided the first live theater experience for many people.

Dinner theaters usually charge less than $15 for dinner and the show. Drinks are extra and carry the biggest profit margins for most theaters; the average customer consumes 2.5 drinks. Jay Barney of Actors' Equity Association says, "A good dinner can carry a bad show, but a lousy dinner will ruin a hit." Dinner theaters place considerable emphasis on their decor. For instance, it cost $900,000 to convert a barn and adjoining brick building into the rustic "Hayloft" dinner theater near Washington, D.C.

Staging costs run from about $3,500 for a straight drama to $6,000 for a musical. Advertising is usually a major expense. The Carrouthers/ Hennessy theaters, for example, spend $5,000 to $8,000 monthly for advertising.

While some critics downgrade dinner theater, Giles M. Flower, drama editor of the Kansas City Star, says:

It's not a subtle thing, and it's not going to give you a transcendent theatrical experience, but there are times when dinner theater entertains the hell out of me. It's the closest thing to mass entertainment theater that we've had in this country.

Source: Adapted from Stephen Sansweet, "Restaurant Theaters Thrive When Owners Get Formula Right," *Wall Street Journal*, May 15, 1974, pp. 1, 14. Reprinted by permission of *The Wall Street Journal*, © Dow Jones & Company, Inc., 1974. All rights reserved.

1. What factors seem to be important to the success of a dinner theater?
2. Devise a comprehensive marketing strategy for a dinner theater in your area.

Case 23
Bankers Discover Marketing

Not too many years ago, banks were stodgy places with steel cages, armed guards, austere furnishings highlighted only by an oil painting of the bank's founder, and pompous-looking financiers sitting behind large mahogany desks. Banks were then viewed solely as financial institutions that accepted deposits and loaned money. Banking was a prestigious occupation in the community. It was the epitome of conservative business practices.

This stereotype is a far cry from today's bright, colorful, open banks with their drive-up windows, discreet security cameras, and personnel in contemporary attire. Most consumers will agree that the revolutionary changes in banking practices are for the better.

The banking industry discovered marketing when it realized that banks existed to provide consumer services. Computer banking, extended service hours, attempts to eliminate long lines at teller windows, and courteous service—often the result of a customer relations training program—are all examples of how banks have become more consumer oriented in

Figure 1
Advertising Is an Important Part of Bank Marketing

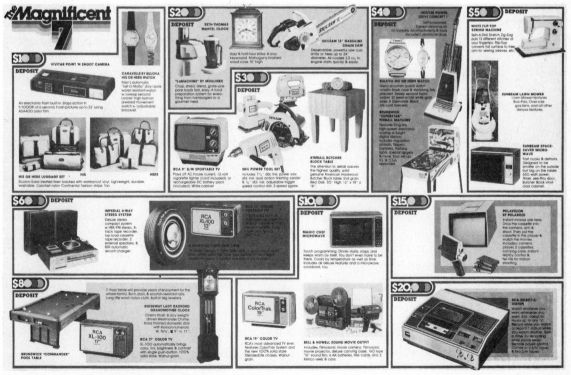

Source: Courtesy of the First National Bank of Mobile.

recent years. Bank marketing specialists have become an important part of banks' competitive strategies.

The tight money supply conditions of 1978 and 1979 saw the prime interest rate—the rate charged to banks' most creditworthy customers, such as major corporations—rise to above 13 percent. Banks had to go out and aggressively seek funds that could then be loaned. New products were made available. Among them were six-month deposit certificates and plans that automatically switched money from savings into checking accounts so people could earn interest on all their deposited funds. Banks and other savings institutions had to call their new products to the attention of savers by extensive advertising campaigns. Figure 1 illustrates this kind of advertising.

Discussion Questions

1. Why have banks become more marketing oriented?
2. Visit some local banks. Then prepare a list of their good marketing practices and a list of improvements they could make.
3. Ask a bank marketing executive to describe this field to your class.

Case 24
IBM's Business Conduct Guidelines

IBM publishes a booklet, entitled *Business Conduct Guidelines,* which summarizes the computer giant's rules for ethical behavior. An opening letter from board chairman Frank Cary emphasizes: "If there is a single, overriding message in this book, it is that IBM expects every employee to act, in every instance, according to the highest standards of business conduct."

The guidelines consider such topics as respect for IBM's assets; political contributions and questionable payments; financial interests and insider information; tips, gifts, and entertainment; information about customers, prospects, and suppliers; fair competition; unannounced products; selling against competitive orders; information about competitors; getting the best price, but not a preferential one; reciprocity; the Sherman Act; and the Clayton and Robinson-Patman Acts.

IBM acknowledges that the booklet cannot cover all eventualities. It suggests that if an ethical dilemma does occur, "Ask yourself: If the full glare of examination by associates, friends, even family were to focus on your decision, would you remain comfortable with it? If you think you would, it probably is the right decision."

Source: *Business Conduct Guidelines* (New York: International Business Machines, n.d.). Quotes are from pp. 5 and 6. Courtesy IBM Corporation.

Discussion Questions

1. Discuss IBM's concept of ethical business conduct.
2. Identify other firms that have similar guidelines.

Case 25
Reaching the Hispanic Market

General Motors has produced a new advertisement for its Chevrolet Monza. The ad features a Mexican *charro* (cowboy) and is narrated in Spanish. It may eventually be translated into English too. The Monza commercial illustrates that the nation's biggest automobile manufacturer is committed to reaching the Hispanic market.

Other firms have also created original commercials for Spanish-speaking consumers. General Foods, Greyhound, Bank of America, Warner Bros., and Schlitz have adopted similar promotional strategies. The firms all conclude that English language advertisements and Spanish dubbings are ineffective in reaching the U.S. market of an estimated 20 million Hispanics, 2.5 million of whom live in the Los Angeles metropolitan area alone. Latinos tend to maintain their Spanish rather than switching to the majority language. The increased attention to the Hispanic market is suggested by the fact that *Noble y Asociados,* Mexico's largest advertising agency, now has a U.S. operation and serves such clients as General Foods. In addition, a number of U.S. radio and television stations are broadcasting in Spanish at least some of the time.

Source: Information from John Revett, "GM Joins Swing to Latin-Oriented Campaigns," *Advertising Age,* May 23, 1977, pp. 6, 103.

1. What other adjustments should U.S. firms make to their marketing mix in order to better serve the Hispanic market?
2. Do marketers have a social obligation to make such adjustments?

Case 26
A. G. Edwards & Sons

St. Louis–based A. G. Edwards & Sons is one of the most profitable brokerage firms in the securities industry. Its 114 offices produce an average annual return on equity of 17 percent, a figure that leads the industry. Edwards has about nine hundred account representatives, each averaging about $60,000 a year in commissions. E. F. Hutton's $74,000 average leads the securities industry. Edwards usually reports 8 percent aftertax margins; this rate of profit has brought the company a tenfold increase in its capital in a decade. Why is A. G. Edwards & Sons so successful?

Edwards decided several years ago to concentrate on retail buyers rather than on the large institutional trades by mutual funds, pension funds, insurance companies, and financial institutions. It also has tended to shy away from investment banking and bond trading. Unlike Merrill Lynch and E. F. Hutton, Edwards does not use major advertising campaigns to attract customers.

A. G. Edwards & Sons' offices are half the size of some of its major competitors and are concentrated in smaller towns and suburbs, where competition is not very intense. The company has employed a strategy counter to that of some of the bigger brokerage houses. While they were scrambling to serve wealthy retirees on Florida's East Coast, Edwards set up eleven offices on the state's West Coast, where the company was sometimes the only stockbrokerage firm in the community.

Source: Adapted from "The Quiet One," *Forbes*, October 1, 1977, p. 76. Reprinted by permission of *Forbes* magazine from the October 1, 1977, issue.

Discussion Questions

1. Evaluate the overall marketing strategy employed by A. G. Edwards & Sons. This may require further research on the company.
2. What other markets might be appropriate for expansion by Edwards?

APPENDIX
CAREERS IN MARKETING

The United States, with its trillion-dollar-plus economy, continues to be a consumption dominated society in which the marketing of goods and services plays a vital role in economic activity and progress. The marketing occupations—necessary to get the marketing tasks done—constitute a significant and interesting aspect of the overall employment scene. This appendix discusses marketing careers. It emphasizes:

1. The kinds of positions available, offering brief descriptions of the responsibilities attached to each.
2. The necessary academic and other preparation for marketing employment.
3. Marketing employment trends and opportunities.
4. Marketing employment for women and minorities.

Marketing Positions

The text has examined the great extent and diversity of the components of the marketing function. The types of marketing occupations required to fulfill these tasks are just as numerous and diverse. Indeed, with the growth of industrial society, marketing occupations have become more complex and specialized. Students intending to pursue a marketing career may be bewildered at the range of employment opportunities in marketing. How can they find their way through the maze of marketing occupations and concentrate on the ones that best match their interests and talents? A convenient starting point is an understanding of the different positions and the duties required of each.

This appendix was prepared by Dinoo T. Vanier of San Diego State University.

Marketing personnel are described as either sales force personnel or marketing staff personnel. They are persons employed in such service and staff functions as advertising, product planning, marketing research, purchasing, and public relations. The precise nature of their responsibilities and duties varies among organizations and industries. Marketing tasks may be undertaken in-house by company marketing personnel or subcontracted to outside sources. Indeed, a large number of agencies are available to support in-house marketing efforts. Among them are advertising agencies, public relations firms, and marketing research agencies. Marketing employment can be found in a variety of organizations: manufacturing firms, distributive enterprises such as retailers and wholesalers, service suppliers, and research agencies.

All these organizations have managerial positions. The specific duties of the positions vary with the size of the organization, the nature of its business, and the extent to which marketing operations are departmentalized or centralized. Marketing management jobs generally require the individual to formulate and assist in the formulation of the organization's marketing policies and to plan, organize, coordinate, and control marketing operations and resources. Some of the typical management positions (the particular titles of which may differ) and descriptions of their responsibilities follow.

The Chief Marketing Executive. The person who oversees all the marketing activities and is ultimately responsible for the success of the marketing function is the chief marketing executive. All other marketing executives report through channels to this person.

The Product Manager. The person in charge of marketing operations for a particular type of product—such as clothing, building materials, or appliances—is the product manager. This person also assumes responsibilities for some, or all, of the functions of the marketing executive—but only insofar as they pertain to particular products.

The Brand Manager. The brand manager performs functions similar to those of the product manager—but only with regard to a specific brand.

The Marketing Research Director. The marketing research director determines the marketing research needs of the organization and plans and directs various stages of the marketing research projects—formulation of the problem, research design, data collection, analysis, and interpretation of results. On the basis of his or her marketing research, the director also helps formulate marketing policy and strategies pertinent to any of the marketing variables

The Sales Manager. The person responsible for managing the sales force is the sales manager. Some of the manager's specific duties are establishing sales territories; deploying the sales force; recruiting, hiring, and training salespeople; and setting sales quotas.

The Advertising Manager. The person who plans and arranges for the promotion of the company's products or services is the advertising manager. Among that person's duties are formulating advertising policy, selecting advertising agencies, evaluating creative promotional ideas, and setting the advertising budget.

The Public Relations Officer. The public relations officer directs all the activities that project and maintain a favorable image for the organization. This person arranges press conferences, exhibitions, news releases, and the like.

Purchasing or Procurement Manager. The purchasing manager controls all purchasing and procurement activities involved in acquiring merchandise, equipment, and materials for the organization.

The Retail Buyer. The retail buyer is responsible for the purchase of merchandise from various sources—manufacturers, wholesalers, and importers, among others—for resale through retail outlets.

The Wholesale Buyer. The person who buys products from manufacturers, importers, and others for resale through wholesale outlets is the wholesale buyer. This buyer's duties are similar to those for the retail buyer but within the specific context of wholesale distribution.

The discussion so far has spotlighted the top management level of each type of work. Depending on company size, however, there may be several other levels within each of the categories described. For every management position, there are several other marketing occupations that involve the "doing" of specific tasks that are supervised and controlled by the managers; their exact number varies considerably from organization to organization. In the area of marketing research, for instance, employees engage in field work, information collection, editing, coding, tabulation, and other statistical analyses of data.

In advertising, the copywriter assimilates information on the products and customers or likely customers and then writes copy—creating headlines, slogans, and text for the advertisements. The media planner is often a time and space buyer who specializes in determining which advertising media will be most effective. The advertising layout person decides the exact layout of illustrations and copy that comprise the finished advertisement.

The majority of people in marketing are in the area of sales. Sales representatives sell at the manufacturing, wholesale, or retail level. Their job description varies somewhat with the types of products and customers. Sales positions are a common entry point for people desiring promotion to marketing management positions.

Academic and Other Preparation

What are the requirements necessary for obtaining a marketing job? What are the typical positions at which marketing careers begin? What are the usual patterns of progression to the top spots in marketing management?

A survey conducted by the Conference Board found that education and experience were important criteria in corporate hiring for marketing positions.[1] It determined that a college education is now required by most companies for marketing positions. It also revealed that industrial manufacturers give greater preference to technological rather than business education.

While companies consider experience another major criterion for hiring sales or marketing people, they also rely on company training programs to equip them with a knowledge of the company's products and policies. It is not unusual for trainees to start their marketing careers in sales and later shift to staff positions.

Another study conducted by the Conference Board showed that a large majority of chief marketing executives are in their forties and fifties; a minority are under age forty. Over 70 percent of these executives have worked for only one or two companies, and most have averaged twenty years with a single company. Chief executives with the title of divisional marketing head generally moved up from the position of sales manager or some other closely related position. There are more than three times as many chief executives with bachelor's degrees as with advanced degrees.[2]

All these findings suggest that undergraduate education is significant and that any experience the marketing student has or can acquire in business or in specific marketing fields will be of decided benefit in launching a marketing career. The usual starting point is sales, but movement into marketing staff and managerial positions is common. Moreover, marketing executive positions can be reached at a relatively young age.

Trends and Opportunities

The U.S. Department of Labor, through its Bureau of Labor Statistics, furnishes data on employment in different occupations. While marketing staff positions are, with few exceptions, grouped within an overall administrative category (including business functions other than marketing), the data do delineate sales workers as well as buyers of farm products and buyers in other wholesale and retail trades. Table A–1 shows employment, average annual job openings, and median earnings in these job categories.

Table A–1

Selected Marketing Occupations: Employment, Average Annual Growth Rate, and Average Annual Job Openings, 1970–1985

Occupation	Employment (in Thousands)			Average Annual Growth Rate (Percent)			Average Annual Job Openings		
	1970	1980	1985	1970–1980	1970–1985	1980–1985	Total	Due to Growth	Due to Attrition
Sales workers	4,608	5,862	6,107	2.4	1.9	0.8	316,500	99,900	216,600
Insurance agents, brokers, and underwriters	412	523	576	2.4	2.3	1.9	23,700	10,900	12,800
Real estate agents and brokers	316	414	450	2.7	2.4	1.7	26,900	8,900	18,000
Sales representatives, manufacturing	394	476	493	1.9	1.5	0.7	16,800	6,600	10,200
Sales representatives, wholesale	635	810	837	2.5	1.9	0.6	31,200	13,500	17,700
Sales clerks, retail trade	2,190	2,782	2,825	2.4	1.7	0.3	175,500	42,300	133,200
Sales workers, retail trade	407	497	523	2.0	1.7	1.0	21,400	7,700	13,700
Salespersons, service and construction	151	219	250	3.8	3.4	2.7	14,000	6,600	7,400
Stock and bond sales agents	103	141	153	3.2	2.7	1.7	7,000	3,400	3,600
Sales managers and department heads, retail	275	391	428	3.6	3.0	1.8	18,900	10,200	8,700
Buyers and shippers, farm products	25	20	20	-2.1	-1.5	-0.1	400	-300	700
Buyers, wholesale and retail trade	155	210	226	3.1	2.6	1.5	11,800	7,100	4,700

Source: Adapted from Conference Board, *Changes in Occupational Characteristics: Planning Ahead for the 1980's* (New York: Conference Board, 1976). Used by permission.

The data show that the largest class of employees is that of retail sales clerks; they are followed by sales representatives at the wholesale and manufacturing levels and retail sales workers. The highest average annual growth rate over the period up to 1985, however, will be in sales jobs in service and construction industries and in stock and bond sales. The number of buyers of farm products will decline during this period, while wholesale and retail trade buyer jobs will increase. By far the highest number of annual job openings (some 175,500) will be in retail sales clerk positions. The next greatest demand will be for wholesale sales representatives, real estate agents, and insurance agents, respectively. In the sales worker category, the highest median earnings will be for stock and bond salespersons. Retail sales clerks will earn the least in the entire category. Sales occupations and buyer positions will have higher median earnings than in the economy as a whole. The median income for all occupations in the United States is projected at $15,260 by 1985.

Table A–2
Average Salary for Marketing Positions, 1978

Job Title	Construction Products Marketers	Industrial Products Marketers	Construction Service Marketers	Industrial Service Marketers	Retailers
Chairman/president	$93,725	$135,091	$100,000	$94,300	$143,333
Executive vice-president	70,600	—[a]	65,000	85,000	—[a]
General manager	66,750	50,000	40,000	40,000	45,000
Vice-president/ director of marketing	55,463	45,667	37,357	47,800	—[a]
Vice-president/ director of sales	53,083	45,000	—[a]	72,500	49,000
Vice-president/ director of advertising	45,469	31,569	41,488	—[a]	40,386
Vice-president/ director of marketing services	53,857	32,729	36,500	—[a]	—[a]
Vice-president/ director of public relations	40,667	43,333	43,167	40,000	—[a]

[a]Not available (returns insufficient to provide representative sample).
Source: *Gallagher Report*, vol. 27 (supplement to March 26, 1979). © 1979 The Gallagher Report Inc. All rights reserved. Reprinted by permission.

Table A–2 depicts the average annual salary for marketing management positions. The total compensation of these executives is not entirely reflected by this information, since they usually receive bonuses and participate in corporate profit-sharing. The data do, however, illustrate the earnings potential in marketing careers. A more pertinent question, perhaps, from the student's viewpoint is: What are the beginning salary levels in marketing? According to the College Placement Council, the following types of companies generally pay higher salaries to new marketing graduates than do other employers: public utilities; tire and rubber; chemical, drug, and allied products; petroleum and allied products; automotive and mechanical equipment; and aerospace, electronics, and instruments.

Marketing Employment for Women and Minorities

In recent years, strong nondiscriminatory legislation and supportive societal commitment have begun protecting the employment rights of women and minorities. The Supreme Court of the United States, for example, has emphatically held that the consequences of an employer's actions—not the intent—determine whether discrimination has occurred.[3] As a result, companies have been actively attempting to fill positions with women and minorities. To illustrate: A survey of 110 companies showed that a substantial proportion of them were taking specific steps to encourage the employment of women and minorities. They were, for example, interviewing and recruiting at predominantly black and women's schools, enlisting special personnel firms and community organizations to locate minority applicants, and providing intensive on-the-job training to minorities.[4] These efforts have

The prediction of future employment trends is a difficult undertaking.

"That's our daughter the doctor. That's our daughter the lawyer. But this is the one who really made good—she runs an auto body repair shop."

Source: *Wall Street Journal*, May 10, 1979. Reprinted by permission of the cartoonist, Edwin Lepper, and the *Wall Street Journal*.

Table A–3
Marketing Occupations: Percent Distribution of Employment by Sex and Race, 1970–1985

Occupation	1970 Male	1970 Female	1980 Male	1980 Female	1985 Male	1985 Female	1970 White	1970 Non-white	1980 White	1980 Non-white	1985 White	1985 Non-white
Sales workers	61.8	38.2	59.4	40.6	58.6	41.4	96.4	3.6	95.1	4.9	94.4	5.6
Insurance agents, brokers, and underwriters	87.5	12.5	84.6	15.4	83.1	16.9	96.4	3.6	95.1	4.9	94.4	5.6
Real estate agents and brokers	67.7	32.3	68.2	31.8	55.1	44.9	97.8	2.2	97.7	2.3	97.6	2.4
Sales representatives, manufacturing	91.5	8.5	93.4	6.6	94.3	5.7	98.2	1.8	97.3	2.7	96.8	3.2
Sales representatives, wholesale	93.6	6.4	91.3	8.7	90.1	9.9	98.0	2.0	97.1	2.9	96.6	3.4
Sales clerks, retail trade	35.2	64.8	33.7	66.3	32.9	67.1	95.3	4.7	93.5	6.5	92.6	7.4
Sales workers, retail trade	87.2	12.8	85.1	14.9	84.0	16.0	97.3	2.7	96.3	3.7	95.8	4.2
Salespersons, service and construction	65.9	34.1	55.7	44.3	51.4	48.6	95.9	4.1	93.7	6.3	92.6	7.4
Stock and bond sales agents	91.4	8.6	88.8	11.2	87.5	12.5	97.8	2.2	96.8	3.2	96.3	3.7
Sales managers and department heads, retail	75.9	24.1	75.2	24.8	74.8	25.2	92.8	7.2	92.5	7.5	92.3	7.7
Buyers and shippers, farm products	97.9	2.1	96.9	3.1	96.4	3.6	98.8	1.2	99.0	1.0	99.1	0.9
Buyers, wholesale and retail trade	70.6	29.4	76.7	23.3	79.7	20.3	97.5	2.5	97.4	2.6	97.3	2.7

Source: Conference Board, *Changes in Occupational Characteristics: Planning Ahead for the 1980's* (New York: Conference Board, 1976). Reprinted by permission. Data from U.S. Department of Labor, Bureau of Labor Statistics.

produced marked increases in the employment options available to women and minorities.

Advertising, marketing research, and retailing are marketing occupations in which women have traditionally held jobs. Most women enter the fields by way of retail sales, where they outnumber men by a ratio of almost two to one (as shown by Table A–3). Women also account for approximately one-third of the total employees in real estate sales, service, construction sales, and wholesale and retail trade buying. But less than 10 percent of manufacturing and wholesale sales representatives and stock and bond agents are women. The percentage of women in all but one of the marketing occupations indicated in Table A–3 is expected to increase by 1985. The exception is manufacturers' sales representatives, a group that is actually expected to lower its percentage of women employed.

Women are numerically underrepresented in managerial positions. Except for the retail field, in which 24 percent of the sales managers and department heads are women, very few sales or marketing managers are women. The few women in these positions work primarily for advertising agencies and consumer products companies.

Although there have been gains in women's employment, an earnings gap between men and women employees still exists. The average pay for women is still lower than that for men in most fields, according to recent data from the U.S. Departments of Labor and Commerce.[5] For example, the typical woman sales worker in general earned only 43 percent of what the typical male sales worker was paid. In retail sales, the median full-time annual earnings of women sales workers were 54 percent of the earnings of full-time male sales workers.

Nonwhite employment in marketing is typically less than 5 percent of any particular marketing job category, as illustrated by Table A–3. Similar to the female marketing employment situation, a higher proportion of nonwhites are employed as retail sales clerks (4.7 percent) or as salespersons in service and construction (4.1 percent) than in any other category of sales workers; and approximately 7 percent of sales managers or department heads in retailing are nonwhites. Few nonwhites hold other marketing managerial positions, but, as is the case with women, nonwhite participation in marketing employment is expected to grow.

Notes

1. See David L. Hurwood, *The New Generation of Marketers: A Management View* (New York: Conference Board, 1973).
2. See David Hopkins, *The Chief Marketing Executive: A Profile* (New York: Conference Board, 1971).
3. *Griggs v. Duke Power Co.*, 401 U.S. 424 (1971).
4. David L. Hurwood, "More Blacks and Women in Sales and Marketing?" *Conference Board Record*, February 1973, pp. 38–44.
5. "Working Women," *U.S. News & World Report*, January 15, 1979, p. 67.

GLOSSARY

The terms in this section are followed by the chapter number (or numbers) in which they are explained.

Absolute advantage (17) The position of a nation in international marketing if it is the sole producer of a product or can produce the product for less than anyone else.

Accessory equipment (6) Capital items that are usually less expensive and shorter-lived than installations; includes items such as typewriters, hand tools, and adding machines.

Administered vertical marketing system (8) A VMS in which channel coordination is achieved through the exercise of economic and political power by the dominant channel member. *See also* Channel captain.

Adoption process (6) The various decisions a consumer makes about a new product. The consumer adoption process has several identifiable stages: awareness, interest, evaluation, trial, and adoption.

Advertising (12, 13) A nonpersonal sales presentation usually directed to a large number of potential customers.

Agent wholesaling middleman (8, 9) A middleman who performs wholesaling functions but does not take title to the goods handled. Also simply called *agent*.

AIO statements (5) *See* Psychographics.

APACS (12) The abbreviation for the Adoptive Planning and Control Sequence, formulated in the Marketing Science Institute's study of promotional decision making. APACS provides an analytical framework, consisting of eight steps, for reaching promotional decisions.

Approach (14) The initial contact between the salesperson and the customer, an important step in the sales process.

Area sampling (3) A method of obtaining a random sample, used when population lists are unavailable. Blocks instead of individuals are selected; then, everyone on the designated block is interviewed. In some cases, respondents are randomly selected from each designated block.

Attitude (5) A person's enduring favorable and unfavorable evaluations, emotional feelings, and pro or con tendencies in regard to some object or idea.

Auction house (9) An agent wholesaling middleman who brings buyers and sellers together in one location and allows potential buyers to inspect the merchandise before purchasing it.

Automatic vending machines (10) Robot retail stores that provide maximum convenience for a wide variety of convenience goods.

Average cost (15) Total cost divided by the quantity associated with this cost.

Average fixed cost (15) Total fixed cost divided by the related quantity.

Average revenue (15) Total revenue divided by the quantity associated with that revenue; the average revenue line is actually the demand curve facing the firm.

Average variable cost (15) Total variable cost divided by the related quantity.

Balance of payments (17) The flow of money into or out of a country.

Balance of trade (17) The relationship between a nation's exports and imports.

Basing point system (16) A pricing procedure in which the price quoted to the customer included the price at the factory plus freight charges from the basing point nearest the buyer.

Battle of the brands (7) Competition between national brands and private brands offered by wholesalers and large retailers.

Birdyback (11) A term used to describe the intermodal coordination of motor carriers with air carriers. The birdyback combination allows the shipper to obtain the benefits of both transportation modes.

Brand (7) A name, term, sign, symbol, design, or some combination used to identify the products of one firm and to differentiate them from competitive offerings.

Brand insistence (7) The last stage in brand acceptance when consumers will accept no alternatives and will search extensively for the product.

Brand name (7) That part of the brand consisting of words or letters that comprise a name used to identify and distinguish the firm's offerings from those of competitors; the brand name is the part of the brand that can be vocalized.

Brand preference (7) The second stage of brand acceptance. Based on previous experience with the product, consumers will choose it rather than its competitors—if it is available.

Brand recognition (7) A company's first objective for its newly introduced products—to make them familiar to the consuming public.

Breadth (10) *See* Width.

Break-bulk center (11) A central distribution center where economical carload and truckload shipments are disassembled and then redistributed to numerous customers over shorter distances at higher than carload or truckload rates.

Breakeven analysis (15) A tool that allows decision makers to compare the profit consequences of alternative prices. The *breakeven point* (in units) equals total fixed cost divided by the per unit contribution to fixed cost.

Broker (9) An agent wholesaling middleman who facilitates marketing operations by bringing together small, geographically dispersed buyers and sellers.

Buyer's market (1) A market with an abundance of goods and services.

Canned approach (14) A memorized sales talk used to ensure uniform coverage of the points deemed important by management.

Cartels (17) Monopolistic organizations of foreign firms. One example of a cartel is OPEC (the Organization of Petroleum Exporting Countries).

Cash-and-carry wholesaler (9) A merchant wholesaler who provides most services, with the exception of financing and delivery.

Cash discounts (16) Price reductions that are made for prompt payment of bills.

Catalog retailer (10) A mass merchandise retail store that mails catalogs to its customers and operates from a showroom displaying single units of each item listed in the catalog; orders are filled from a backroom warehouse.

Celebrity testimonial (13) A type of promotion in which a particular product, service, idea, or institution is praised or recommended by a big-name personality in order to attract consumer attention.

Celler-Kefauver Antimerger Act (1950) (2) A federal statute that amended the Clayton Act to include restrictions on purchases of assets where such purchases would decrease competition. Previously, only "acquiring of stock" of another firm was prohibited if it lessened competition.

Census (3) The collection of data from all possible sources.

Chain stores (10) Groups of retail stores that are centrally owned and managed and that handle the same lines of products.

Channel captain (8) The dominant and controlling member of each channel who assumes the responsibility for obtaining cooperation among the individual channel members.

Civil Aeronautics Board (11) The agency that regulates U.S. air carriers.

Class action suit (18) A legal suit brought by private citizens on behalf of any group of consumers for damages caused by unfair business practices.

Class rate (11) The standard rate established for shipping various commodities.

Clayton Act (1914) (2) A federal statute that strengthened antitrust legislation by restricting practices such as price discrimination, exclusive dealing, tying contracts, and interlocking boards of directors.

Closed sales territories (8) A practice in which some manufacturers restrict the geographic territories for each of their distributors.

Closing (14) The step in the sales process when the salesperson asks the customer to conclude the purchase.

Cognitive dissonance (5) The postpurchase anxiety that occurs when an imbalance exists among a person's cognitions (knowledge, beliefs, and attitudes).

Combination plan (14) A method of compensation that combines a base salary along with a commission incentive.

Commission merchant (9) An agent wholesaling middleman who takes possession of and negotiates the sales of the goods handled. Commission merchants predominate in the marketing of agricultural products such as grain, produce, and livestock.

Commissions (14) Payments directly tied to the sales or profits achieved by a salesperson.

Commodity rate (11) A special rate granted by carriers to shippers as a reward for either regular use or large quantity shipments.

Common carrier (11) A regulated carrier that offers transportation services to all shippers.

Communications (12) The transmission of a message from a sender to a receiver.

Comparative advantage (17) The position a nation in international marketing has if it can produce a product more efficiently than it can produce alternative products.

Comparative advertising (13) A type of persuasive product advertising that makes direct promotional comparisons with leading competitive brands.

Competitive bidding (16) A process by which buyers request potential suppliers to make price quotations on a proposed purchase or contract.

Competitive environment (2) The process of interaction that occurs in the marketplace.

Concentrated marketing (7) The practice of firms that select a small segment of the total market and devote all their marketing resources to satisfying this single segment.

Concept testing (7) The evaluation of a product idea prior to the actual development of the product in the new-product development process.

Consumer behavior (5) The acts of individuals in obtaining and using goods and services, including the decision processes that precede and determine these acts.

Consumer Credit Protection Act (1968) (2) Also known as the Truth-in-Lending Act, the statute that requires disclosure of the annual interest rates on loans and credit purchases in order to make it easier for consumers to compare sources of credit.

Consumer goods (4, 6) Products purchased by the ultimate consumer for personal use and not intended for resale or further use in the production of other goods.

Consumer Goods Pricing Act (1975) (2) Legislation that halted all interstate usage of resale price maintenance agreements.

Consumer innovators (6) The first purchasers of new products and services.

Consumerism (18) The demand that marketers give greater attention to consumer wants and desires in making their decisions.

Consumer Product Safety Act (1972) (2, 7) Legislation that established the Consumer Product Safety Commission (CPSC) and granted it authority to specify safety standards for most consumer products, except those already regulated by other agencies.

Consumer rights (18) A statement of rights, delineated by John F. Kennedy, that have formed the conceptual framework for much of the consumer legislation passed since 1962. They include the rights to be safe, to be informed, to choose, and to be heard.

Containerization (11) The combination of several unitized loads of products into a single load in order to facilitate intertransport changes in transportation modes.

Contest (13) A sales promotion technique that seeks to attract additional customers by offering substantial cash or merchandise prizes.

Contract carrier (11) A carrier that establishes specific contracts with a few customers and does not offer its services to the general public.

Contractual vertical marketing system (8) A VMS in which channel coordination is achieved through formal agreements between channel members. The three types are wholesaler-sponsored voluntary chains, retail cooperatives, and franchise operations.

Controlled experiment (3) A direct test for results and a method of collecting information carried out under controlled conditions.

Convenience goods (6) Products that consumers want to purchase frequently, immediately, and with a minimum of effort, such as milk and bread.

Cooperative advertising (13) The sharing of advertising costs between the retailer and the manufacturer or vendor.

Corporate vertical marketing system (8) A VMS created through single ownership of each stage of the marketing channel.

Corrective advertising (2) A policy of the Federal Trade Commission under which companies found to have used deceptive advertising are required to correct their earlier claims with new promotional messages.

Cost-plus pricing (15) An approach to price determination that takes some base cost figure per unit and adds a markup to cover unassigned costs and provide a profit. The two most common cost-plus procedures are full cost pricing and incremental cost pricing.

Cost trade-offs (11) A concept in the total systems approach to physical distribution whereby some functional areas of the firm will experience cost increases while others will have cost reductions, but the result will be that total physical distribution costs will be minimized.

Coupon (13) A sales promotion technique that offers a discount on the next purchase of a product.

Creative selling (14) A basic sales task used when purchases require considerable analytical decision making on the consumer's part; the salesperson must skillfully solicit orders from such prospects through the use of creative selling techniques.

Creeping inflation (2) Modest increases in the general price level.

Critical path (19) The sequence of tasks in a PERT network that require the longest total completion time.

Cues (5) Any objects existing in the environment that determine the nature of the response to a drive.

Culture (5) The complex of values, ideas, attitudes, and other meaningful symbols created by people to shape human behavior and the artifacts of that behavior as they are transmitted from one generation to the next.

Customary price (15) A price that tends to be set by custom or tradition in the marketplace.

Customer service standards (11) The quality of service that a firm's customers will receive.

Decoding (12) The receiver's interpretation of the sender's message in a communications system.

Demand curve (15) A schedule relating the quantity demanded to specific prices; it is the average revenue line.

Demarketing (2) The process of cutting consumer demand for a product back to a level that can reasonably be supplied by the firm.

Demographics (13) Characteristics, such as the age, sex, and income level, of potential buyers.

Demonstration (14) The step in the sales process when the salesperson involves the potential customer in the presentation by allowing him or her to use, test, or experiment with the product.

Department store (10) A large retail store organized into departments for the purposes of promotion, service, and control. A department store typically stocks a wide variety of shopping and specialty goods that may include men's and women's clothing and accessories, linens and dry goods, appliances, and home furnishings.

Depth (10) The number of sizes, colors, and other characteristics carried by the retailer in a single product line.

Detailers (14) Missionary salespeople of the health care industry.

Devaluation (17) An official reduction in the value of a nation's currency in relation to some other currency or to gold.

Differentiated marketing (7) The practice of firms that produce numerous products with different marketing mixes to satisfy smaller market segments.

Diffusion process (6) The acceptance of new products and services by the members of a community or social system.

Direct-sales results test (12) A test that measures the effectiveness of promotion. It ascertains for each dollar of promotional outlay the corresponding increase in revenue.

Discount house (10) A store that charges lower than usual prices and does not offer such traditional retail services as credit, sales assistance by clerks, and delivery.

Distribution strategy (1) An element of marketing decision making that deals with the physical distribution of goods and the selection of marketing channels.

Distribution warehouse (11) A place to assemble and then redistribute products. The objective of the distribution warehouse is to facilitate rapid movement of products to the purchasers rather than to serve as a storage facility.

Distributor (8) *See* Wholesaler.

Drive (5) Any strong stimulus that impels action.

Drop shipper (9) A merchant wholesaler who receives orders from customers and forwards them to producers, who ship directly to the customers; although drop shippers take title to the goods, they do not carry inventories.

Dumping (17) Selling a product at a lower price in a foreign market than it sells for in the producer's domestic market.

Ecology (18) The relationship between humanity and the environment.

Economic environment (2) Complex and dynamic business fluctuations that tend to follow a four-stage pattern: (1) recession, (2) depression, (3) recovery, and (4) prosperity.

Embargo (17) The complete ban on importing certain products, especially from certain countries.

Encoding (12) The translation of a message into understandable terms and its transmittal through a communications medium.

Energy crisis (2) The general realization that energy resources are not limitless.

Engel's laws (4) Statements published in an early study of spending behavior by German statistician Ernst Engel. His three generalizations about spending predict that as family income increases: (1) a smaller percentage of expenditures go for food; (2) the percentage spent on housing and household operations and clothing remains constant; and (3) the percentage spent on other items increases.

Environmental pollution (18) Contamination of natural resources such as water or air.

Environmental Protection Act (1970) (2) Legislation that established the Environmental Protection Agency (EPA) and gave it the power to deal with major types of pollution.

EOQ (economic order quantity) model (11) A technique devised to determine the optimum order quantity of each product; the optimum point is determined by balancing the costs of holding inventory and the costs involved in placing orders.

Equal Credit Opportunity Act (1975–1977) (2) Legislation that banned discrimination in lending practices on the basis of sex, marital status, race, national origin, religion, age, or receipt of payments from public assistance programs.

Exchange control (17) A method of regulating foreign trade in which firms gaining foreign exchange by exporting must sell this exchange to the central bank or a control agency, and importers must buy foreign exchange from the same organization.

Exchange rate (17) The rate at which a nation's currency can be exchanged for other currencies or gold.

Exclusive dealing agreement (8) An agreement that prohibits a middleman from handling competing products.

Exclusive distribution (8) An extreme form of selective distribution wherein the manufacturer grants exclusive rights to a wholesaler or retailer to sell in a geographic region.

Expected net profit (16) A concept employed in competitive bidding strategy. Expected net profit equals the probability of the buyer accepting the bid times the bid price minus related costs.

Exploratory research (3) Research designed to give the researcher an understanding of the problem area and insight into its causes and effects through discussion with informed sources both within and outside the firm and through examination of secondary sources of information.

Exporting (17) The sale of goods and services abroad.

Fabricated parts and materials (6) The finished industrial goods that actually become part of the final product.

Facilitating agencies (8) Organizations, such as marketing research firms, transportation and storage companies, advertising agencies, insurance companies, and financial institutions, that provide specialized assistance for the regular channel members in moving products from producer to consumer.

Fair Credit Reporting Act (1970) (2) Legislation that gives individuals access to credit reports prepared about them and that permits them to change information that is incorrect.

Fair Debt Collection Practices Act (1978) (2) Legislation that outlawed harassing, deceptive, or unfair collection practices by debt-collecting agencies. In-house debt collectors such as banks, retailers, or attorneys are exempt from the act.

Fair Packaging and Labeling Act (1967) (2, 7) Legislation requiring disclosure of product identity, name and address of manufacturer or distributor, and information about the quality of the contents.

Fair trade laws (2) State laws, passed during the depression of the 1930s, that allowed a manufacturer to stipulate a minimum retail price for a product and to require retailers to sign contracts stating that they would abide by such prices. The Consumer Goods Pricing Act (1975) ended all interstate usage of these agreements.

Family brand (7) One brand name used for several products made by the same firm, such as Johnson & Johnson or General Electric.

Family life cycle (4) The process of family formation and dissolution. The stages of the cycle include bachelor, young married couple with no children, young married couple with children, older married couple with dependent children, older married couple with no children at home, and solitary survivor.

Federal Maritime Commission (11) The agency that regulates U.S. ocean carriers.

Federal Trade Commission Act (1914) (2) Legislation that prohibited "unfair methods of competition" and established the Federal Trade Commission (FTC) as an administrative agency to oversee the various laws dealing with business.

Feedback (12) Information about a receiver's response to a message that is returned to the sender.

Fishyback (11) A term used to describe the intermodal coordination of motor carriers with water carriers. The fishyback combination allows the shipper to obtain the benefits of both transportation modes.

Fixed costs (15) Costs that do not vary with differences in output, such as depreciation and insurance.

Flammable Fabrics Act (1953) (2) Legislation outlawing the interstate sale of flammable fabrics.

Floating exchange rates (17) Exchange rates that are allowed to fluctuate to adjust to market conditions.

FOB (16) "Free on board," a price quotation that does not include any shipping charges; the buyer must pay all freight charges.

Focus group interview (3) Group interview in which small numbers of individuals are brought together in one location to discuss a subject of interest.

Follow-up (14) The step in the sales process that concerns post-sales activities. Follow-up provides information on sales successes and failures and often determines whether a person will become a repeat customer.

Food and Drug Administration (FDA) (2) The agency authorized to regulate such matters as product development, branding, and advertising.

Food, Drug, and Cosmetic Act (1938) (2) Legislation prohibiting adulteration and misbranding of food, drugs, and cosmetics in interstate commerce.

Foreign Corrupt Practices Act (1977) (17) Legislation making it illegal to bribe a foreign official in an attempt to solicit new or repeat sales abroad.

Form utility (1) A kind of utility that is created when raw materials are converted into finished products.

Franchise (8) An agreement whereby dealers (franchisees) agree to meet the operating requirements of a manufacturer or other franchisor.

Freight absorption (16) A pricing system under which the seller permits the buyer to subtract transportation charges from the bill. Also known as *FOB plant—freight allowed.*

Freight forwarder (11) A wholesaling middleman who consolidates shipments of several shippers in order to enable them to achieve the cost savings of truckload or carload shipments.

Friendship, commerce, and navigation (FCN) treaties (17) Treaties between the United States and many other countries that deal with various aspects of commercial relations, such as the right to conduct business in the treaty partner's domestic market.

FTC (2) *See* Federal Trade Commission Act.

Full cost pricing (15) A cost-plus pricing procedure that uses all relevant variable costs in setting a product's price.

Full-function merchant wholesaler (9) A wholesaling middleman who provides a complete assortment of services for retail customers, including storage, regular contacts through a sales force, delivery, credit, returns privileges, and market information.

Fur Products Labeling Act (1952) (2) Legislation requiring labels on products made with fur to identify the name of the animal from which the fur came.

General Agreement on Tariffs and Trade (GATT) (17) An international trade accord that has sponsored various tariff negotiations that have reduced the overall level of tariffs throughout the world.

General merchandise store (10) A retail store that carries a wide variety of product lines, all of which are stocked in some depth.

General store (10) A general merchandise store stocked to meet the needs of a small community or rural area.

Generic name (7) A brand name that has become a generally descriptive term for a product (for example, nylon, zipper, and aspirin). When this occurs, the original owner loses exclusive claim to the brand name.

Generic products (7) Food and household staples characterized by plain descriptive labels, little or no advertising, and no brand name. Such products compete with branded items on the basis of price.

Goods-services continuum (6) A method for visualizing the differences and similarities of goods and services.

Green River ordinances (18) Local laws enacted to limit door-to-door selling.

Gross national product (3) The market value of all final products produced in a country in a given year.

Handling objections (14) The step in the sales process when the salesperson responds to the potential customer's questions and concerns.

Highway Beautification Act (1965) (13) Legislation regulating the use of outdoor advertising near interstate highways.

House-to-house retailing (10) Direct contact between the seller and the customer at the customer's home.

Hypermarket (10) A giant mass merchandising retail outlet that operates on a low-price, self-service basis and carries lines of soft goods and groceries.

Importing (17) The purchase of foreign goods and raw materials.

Import quota (17) A restriction on the amount of products in certain categories that can enter a country.

Impulse goods (6) Products for which the consumer spends little time in conscious deliberation in making a purchase decision. These products, such as candy and cigarettes, are often displayed near store cash registers to induce spur-of-the-moment purchases.

Incremental cost pricing (15) A cost-plus pricing procedure that attempts to use only those costs directly attributable to a specific ouptut in setting a product's price.

Individual brand (7) A product known by its own brand name, such as Tide or Crest, rather than by the name of the company producing it.

Industrial distributor (6) A wholesaling middleman who operates in the industrial goods market and typically handles small accessory equipment and operating supplies.

Industrial goods (4, 6) Products purchased for use either directly or indirectly in the production of goods for resale.

Inflation (2) A rising price level that results in reduced purchasing power for the consumer.

Informative institutional advertising (13) A type of promotion concerned with increasing public knowledge of a concept, political viewpoint, industry, or company.

Informative product advertising (13) A type of promotion that seeks to develop initial demand for a product. It is used in the introduction phase of the product life cycle.

Input-output models (3) Models used in economic forecasting that depict the interactions of various industries in the production of goods.

Installations (6) A firm's major capital assets such as factories and heavy machinery; they are expensive and relatively long-lived, and their purchase represents a major decision for the company.

Institutional advertising (13) A type of advertising that is concerned with promoting a concept, an idea, a philosophy, or the good will of an industry. It is often closely related to the public relations function of an enterprise.

Intensive distribution (8) A practice by manufacturers of convenience goods who attempt to provide saturation coverage of their potential markets.

Interstate Commerce Act (1887) (11) Legislation that established the first regulatory body in the United States, the Interstate Commerce Commission (ICC), and gave it the power to regulate interstate transportation systems such as railroads, pipelines, motor carriers, and inland water carriers.

Jobber (8) *See* Wholesaler.

Job-order production (8) A production system in which products are manufactured to fill customers' orders.

Joint venture (17) A type of international enterprise in which a company shares the risks, costs, and management of the foreign operation with a partner who is usually a national of the host nation.

Just and reasonable rates (11) A term used in the regulation of transportation modes. It means that rates must be just to shippers and provide a reasonable rate of return to the transporter.

Just price (15) A concept held by early philosophers that there was one fair price for each good or service.

Kefauver-Harris Drug Amendments (1962) (2) Amendments to the Pure Food and Drug Act that mandated generic labeling of drugs and a summary of adverse side effects.

Label (7) The descriptive part of the package that usually contains the brand name or symbol, the name and address of the manufacturer or distributor, the product composition and size, and the recommended uses for the product.

Lanham Act (1946) (7) Legislation requiring that registered trademarks must not contain words in general use—such as automobile or suntan lotion. These *generic words* are descriptive of a particular type of product and thus cannot be granted exclusively to any company.

Learning (5) Any change in behavior as a result of experience.

Legal environment (2) The numerous, often vague, laws passed by a multitude of authorities that regulate marketing activities.

Life-style (2) The way people decide to live their lives. It concerns the family, job, social activities, and consumer decisions.

Limited-function merchant wholesaler (9) A wholesaling middleman who reduces the number of services provided to retail customers and also reduces the costs of servicing these customers. The three types include cash-and-carry wholesalers, truck wholesalers, and drop shippers.

Limited line store (10) A retail store that competes with larger stores by offering a complete selection of a few related lines of merchandise, such as clothing, hardware, or sporting goods.

List price (16) The rate normally quoted to potential buyers. It is the basis on which most price structures are built.

Loss leader (16) A retail good priced at less than cost so as to attract customers who possibly will then buy other regularly priced merchandise.

Magnuson-Moss Warranty Act (1975) (6) Legislation giving the Federal Trade Commission power to develop regulations affecting warranty practices for any product costing more than $15 that is covered by a written warranty. It is designed to assist consumers in comparison shopping.

Mail-order retailing merchandiser (10) A retail outlet that makes use of catalogs and allows customers to order merchandise by mail, by telephone, or by visiting the mail-order desk of a retail store. Goods are then shipped to the customer's home or the local retail store.

Make-bulk center (11) A central distribution center where small shipments of products shipped over a short distance are consolidated into economical carload or truckload quantities, then shipped over longer distances to a customer or storage warehouse.

Manufacturers' agents (8, 9) Independent salespeople who work for a number of manufacturers of related but noncompeting products and who receive a commission based on a specified percentage of sales. Also called *manufacturers' representatives*.

Marginal analysis (12, 15) The balancing of marginal revenues and marginal costs.

Marginal cost (15) The change in total cost that results from producing an additional unit of output.

Marginal revenue (15) The change in total revenue that results from selling an additional unit of output.

Market (4) Customers who possess purchasing power and both the willingness and the authority to buy.

Marketing (1) The development and efficient distribution of goods and services for chosen consumer segments.

Marketing audit (19) A thorough, objective evaluation of an organization's marketing philosophy, goals, policies, tactics, practices, and results.

Marketing channels (1, 8) The paths that goods or services, and title to them, follow from producer to final consumer.

Marketing communications (12) The messages that deal with buyer-seller relationships.

Marketing concept (1) A consumer oriented managerial philosophy based on the premise that planning begins with an analysis of the consumer and that company objectives involve satisfying consumer wants and achieving long-run profits.

Marketing cost analysis (3) The evaluation of such items as selling costs, billing, warehousing, advertising, and delivery expenses in order to determine the profitability of particular customers, territories, or product lines.

Marketing information system (MIS) (3) A designed set of procedures and methods for generating an orderly flow of pertinent information for use in making decisions, providing management with the current and future states of the market, and indicating market response to company and competitor actions.

Marketing mix (1) The blending of the four strategy elements of marketing decision making (product planning, distribution, promotion, and price) to satisfy chosen consumer segments.

Marketing research (3) The systematic gathering, recording, and analyzing of data about problems relating to the marketing of goods and services.

Marketing strategy (19) The general term used to describe the overall company program for selecting a particular market segment and then satisfying the consumers in that segment through the careful use of the elements of the marketing mix.

Market planning (19) The implementation of planning activity as it relates to the achievement of marketing objectives.

Market price (16) The amount the consumer or middleman pays. It may or may not be the same as the list price, since discounts and allowances can reduce the list price.

Market segmentation (4) The production of separate products and design of different marketing mixes to satisfy smaller homogeneous segments of the total market.

Market share objective (15) The goal set for the control of a portion of the market for the firm's product.

Market target (4) A specific segment of the overall potential market that has been analyzed and selected by the firm. The firm's marketing mix will be directed toward satisfying this chosen consumer segment.

Market target decision analysis (4) The evaluation of potential market segments by dividing the overall market into homogeneous groups. Cross-classifications may be based on variables such as type of market, geographic location, use frequency, or demographic characteristics.

Mark-on (15) Markup based on cost.

Markup (15) The amount that is added to cost to determine the selling price.

Maslow's hierarchy of needs (5) A classification whereby priority is assigned to the basic needs that must be at least partially satisfied before proceeding to the next order of needs. The hierarchy proceeds from physiological to safety to social to esteem to self-actualization needs.

Mass merchandisers (10) Major retailers such as discount houses, hypermarkets, and catalog retailers who compete by stocking a wider line of products than most department stores, although usually not in as great a depth. They emphasize low prices, high turnover, and reduced services.

Materials handling (11) All the activities involved in moving products within the manufacturer's plants, warehouses, and transportation company terminals.

Megalopolis (4) An extensive contiguous urban-suburban strip of population. The largest megalopolis extends from Boston to Washington, D.C.

Merchandise mart (9) A permanent exhibition facility where manufacturers rent showcases for their product offerings and display them for visiting retail and wholesale buyers.

Merchant wholesaler (8, 9) A wholesaling middleman who takes title to the goods handled.

Message (12) Information transmitted by a communications system.

Metric system (7) The standard of weights and measures based on the decimal system of ten and its multiples and used throughout most of the world.

Middleman (8) A business firm operating between the producer and the consumer or industrial purchaser. The term includes both wholesalers and retailers.

Miller-Tydings Resale Price Maintenance Act (1937) (2) Legislation exempting interstate fair trade contracts from compliance with antitrust requirements.

Missionary sales (14) An indirect type of selling; people who handle this task sell the goodwill of a firm, often by providing the customer with product use assistance.

Missionary salesperson (8) Special representative who helps wholesalers and retailers become familiar with the firm's products.

Monopolistic competition (15) A market structure with large numbers of buyers and sellers that involves a heterogeneous product and product differentiation and in which the marketer has some degree of control over prices. This situation is characteristic of most retailing.

Monopoly (15) A market situation in which there is only one seller of a product and no close substitutes for it. Antitrust legislation has effectively eliminated all but *temporary monopolies,* such as those provided by patent protection, and *regulated monopolies,* such as the public service companies (telephone, electric, and gas utilities).

Motive (5) An inner state that directs people toward the goal of satisfying a felt need.

MRO items (6) *See* Supplies.

Multinational corporation (17) A firm that operates in several countries and literally views the world as its market.

National brands (7) Brands offered by manufacturers; sometimes called *manufacturer's brands.*

Need (5) The lack of something useful.

Negotiated contract (16) A situation in which the terms of a contract are set through talks between the buyer and the seller rather than through competitive bidding on a project. Industry and government purchasers use negotiated contracts when there is only one available supplier or when extensive research and development work is involved.

New product committee (7) A common organizational arrangement for new-product development. The committee is usually composed of representatives from top management in such areas as marketing, finance, manufacturing, engineering, research, and accounting.

New product department (7) A separate, formally organized division within the firm that is involved with new-product development on a permanent, full-time basis.

Noise (12) Interruption that interferes with the transmission of a message in a communications system.

Observational study (3) A study conducted by actually viewing (either by visual observation or through mechanical means such as hidden cameras) the overt actions of the respondent.

Odd pricing (16) A type of psychological pricing that uses prices with odd endings, such as $16.95, $17.99, or $18.98, under the assumption that these prices appear lower and therefore more appealing. Originally, odd pricing was initiated to force sales clerks to make change, thus serving as a cash control device within the firm.

Oligopoly (15) A market situation with relatively few sellers; because of high start-up costs, there are significant entry barriers to new competitors. Oligopolies occur frequently in the steel, petroleum refining, and automobile industries.

Open dating (18) A practice in the marketing of perishable or semiperishable food in which the last date that the item can be sold is shown on the package.

Opinion leader (5) The individual in any group who is a trend-setter; the opinions of such an individual are respected and often sought. Opinion leaders serve as information sources about new products.

Order processing (14) A basic sales task at the retail and wholesale level where needs are readily identified by the salesperson and acknowledged by the customer.

Ownership utility (1, 8) A kind of utility created by marketers when title to products is transferred to the customer at the time of purchase.

Pallet (11) A platform, usually made of wood, on which products are transported.

Party-plan selling (10) A variation of house-to-house selling in which a customer hosts a party to which neighbors and friends are invited, and a company representative than makes a presentation of the firm's products. The host usually receives a commission based on the amount of products sold.

Penetration pricing (16) A new-product pricing policy that uses an entry price lower than what is intended as the long-term price. The premise is that the initially lower price will help secure market acceptance.

Perception (5) The meaning that each person attributes to incoming stimuli received through the five senses.

Personal selling (12, 14) A seller's promotional presentation conducted on a person-to-person basis with the buyer.

Persuasive institutional advertising (13) A type of promotion used to advance the interests of a particular institution within a competitive environment.

Persuasive product advertising (13) A competitive type of promotion that attempts to develop demand for a particular product or brand. It is used in the growth phase and to some extent in the maturity phase of the product life cycle.

PERT (7, 19) The designation for Program Evaluation and Review Technique, a commonly used planning and scheduling technique applied in a variety of industries to minimize project completion time.

Phantom freight (16) The amount in a uniform delivered price system by which the average transportation charge exceeds the actual cost of shipping for customers near the supply source.

Physical distribution (11) The broad range of activities concerned with efficient movement of finished products from the end of the production line to the consumer. These activities include freight transportation, warehousing, materials handling, protective packaging, inventory control, order processing, plant and warehouse site selection, and market forecasting, organized as a system to produce customer service.

Physical distribution concept (11) The integration of the three basic concepts of physical distribution—the total cost approach, avoidance of suboptimization, and cost trade-offs.

Piggyback (11) A term used to describe the intermodal coordination of truck trailers on railroad freight cars. The piggyback combination allows the shipper to obtain the benefits of both transportation modes.

Pittsburgh-plus pricing (16) A well-known basing point system that was used in the steel industry for many years. Steel price quotations contained freight charges from Pittsburgh, regardless of where the steel was produced.

Place utility (1, 8) A kind of utility created by marketers who have products available where the consumers want to buy.

Planned obsolescence (18) A situation where the manufacturer produces items with limited durability.

Planned shopping center or **planned retailing center** (10) A geographical cluster of retail stores, collectively handling a varied assortment of goods, designed to satisfy the purchase needs of consumers within the area of the center. There are neighborhood, community, and regional planned shopping centers.

Planning (19) The function of anticipating the future and determining the courses of action to achieve company objectives.

Point-of-purchase advertising (13) Displays, demonstrations, and other promotions located near where a buying decision is actually made.

Pollution (18) A broad term that is usually defined as "making unclean."

Positioning (13) The development of a marketing strategy aimed at a particular segment of the market. The strategy is applicable primarily to products that are not leaders in their particular fields and often attempts to introduce the product as an alternative to a competitive product.

Posttesting (13) The assessment of advertising copy after it has been used.

Premium (13) A bonus item given free with the purchase of another product.

Presentation (14) The step in the sales process when the salesperson gives the sales message to the prospective customer. The presentation describes the product's major features and relates them to the customer's needs.

Prestige goals (15) Pricing objectives based on setting relatively high prices so as to maintain a quality image.

Pretesting (13) The assessment of an advertisement's effectiveness before it is actually used.

Price (15) The exchange value of a good or service.

Price flexibility (16) A company policy decision that involves whether to have just one price or to pursue a variable price policy in the market. Generally, a *one-price policy* is common in retailing because it facilitates mass merchandising, while *variable pricing* is more common in industrial markets, where individual bargaining typifies transactions.

Price limit (16) The price range within which a consumer's product quality perception varies directly with the price. A price below the lower limit is regarded as *too cheap,* while one above the higher limit is *too expensive.*

Price lining (16) The practice of marketing merchandise at a limited number of prices.

Pricing objectives (15) The goals a company seeks to reach through implementation of its pricing strategy. Pricing objectives can be divided into three types: profitability objectives; volume objectives; and social and ethical considerations, status quo objectives, and prestige goals.

Pricing strategy (1, 16) An element of marketing decision making that deals with the methods of setting profitable and justified prices.

Primary data (3) Data collected for the first time during a marketing research study.

Private brand (7) A line of merchandise offered by a wholesaler or retailer with its own label, such as Sears Kenmore washing machines.

Private carrier (11) A freight carrier that transports products only for a particular firm and cannot legally solicit other transportation business.

Product (6) A bundle of physical, service, and symbolic attributes designed to produce consumer want satisfaction.

Product advertising (13) The nonpersonal selling of a particular good or service.

Product deletion (7) The elimination of marginal items from a firm's product line.

Product liability (7) The responsibility of the producer or seller for damage or injury caused by unsafe or defective products.

Product life cycle (6) The path of a product through four stages—introduction, growth, maturity, and decline—before its death.

Product line (7) A series of related products—for example, a line of grooming aids including shaving cream, razors, deodorant, and hair spray.

Product manager (7) The management official assigned to one product or product line who has complete responsibility for determining objectives and establishing marketing strategies for it.

Product strategy (1) An element of marketing decision making comprising decisions about package design, branding, trademarks, warranties, guarantees, product life cycles, and new product development.

Profit center (16) Any part of the organization to which revenue and controllable costs can be assigned, such as a department.

Profit maximization (15) The traditional pricing objective in classic economic theory; the assumption that all firms need to maximize their gains or minimize their losses.

Profits (15) Revenues minus expenses.

Promotion (12) The function of informing, persuading, and influencing the consumer's purchase decision.

Promotional allowance (16) An advertising or sales promotional grant by a manufacturer to other channel members in an attempt to integrate promotional strategy in the channel.

Promotional price (16) A lower-than-normal price used as an ingredient in the firm's selling strategy.

Promotional strategy (1) An element of marketing decision making that comprises personal selling, advertising, and sales promotion tools.

Prospecting (14) The step in the sales process that involves the identification of prospective customers.

Psychographics (5, 13) Psychological profiles of different consumer types developed from quantitative research; sometimes referred to as *AIO (attitudes, interests, and opinions) statements*.

Psychological pricing (16) A pricing procedure based on the belief that certain prices or price ranges are more appealing than others to buyers.

Psychophysics (5) The relationship between the actual physical stimulus and the corresponding sensation produced in the individual. *See also* Weber's law.

Public Health Cigarette Smoking Act (1971) (2) Legislation restricting tobacco advertising on radio and television.

Publicity (12, 13) The part of public relations that is most directly related to promoting a company's products or services.

Public relations (12, 13) A firm's communications and relationships with its various publics, including customers, suppliers, stockholders, employees, the government, and the society in which it operates.

Public responsibility committees (18) Permanent committees of a firm's board of directors that consider matters of corporate social responsibility.

Public warehouse (9) An independently owned storage facility that will store and ship products for a rental fee.

Pulling strategy (12) A promotional effort by the seller to stimulate final user demand; this demand exerts pressure on the distribution channel. The plan is to build consumer demand for a product that is recognizable to channel members who will then seek to fill this void.

Pure competition (15) A market structure in which there are such a large number of buyers and sellers that none of them has a significant influence on price. Other characteristics of pure competition include a homogeneous product and an ease of entry for sellers that results from low start-up costs.

Pure Food and Drug Act (1906) (2) Legislation prohibiting adulteration and misbranding of food and drugs in interstate commerce. The legislation was enacted in response to unsanitary meat-packing practices in the Chicago stockyards.

Pushing strategy (12) The promotion of the product to the members of the marketing channel through cooperative advertising allowances, trade discounts, and other dealer support.

Qualifying (14) The step in the sales process that seeks to determine whether a prospect is a customer with both money and the authority and willingness to buy.

Quantity discount (16) A price reduction granted for large purchases. Such a discount can be either *cumulative* (based on purchases over a stated period of time) or *noncumulative* (a one-time reduction in list price).

Quota (14) A specified sales or profit target a salesperson is expected to achieve. *See also* Import quota and Sales quota.

Rack jobber (9) A wholesaler who markets specialized lines of merchandise to retail stores and provides the services of merchandising and arrangement, pricing, maintenance, and stocking of display racks.

Raw materials (6) Industrial goods such as *farm products* (wheat, cotton, soybeans) and *natural products* (coal, lumber, iron ore) used in producing final products. Most raw materials are graded, which assures the purchaser of a standardized product with uniform quality.

Rebate (16) A refund by the seller of a portion of the purchase price.

Receiver (12) The person or persons a message is directed to in a communications system.

Reciprocity (4) The practice of giving favorable consideration to suppliers who are also purchasers of the firm's products.

Recycling (18) The reprocessing of used materials for reuse. Recycling provides a new source of raw materials and alleviates a major factor in environmental pollution.

Reference group (5) A group with which an individual identifies to the point where the group becomes a standard toward which the individual orients his or her behavior patterns.

Reinforcement (5) The reduction in drive that results from a proper response.

Remainder oriented institutional advertising (13) A type of promotion used to reinforce previous promotional activity on behalf of an institution, concept, political viewpoint, industry, or company—for example, the reminder oriented advertising in the closing weeks of a political campaign.

Reminder oriented product advertising (13) A type of promotion that seeks to reinforce previous promotional activity by keeping the product name in front of the public. It is used in the maturity stage as well as throughout the decline stage of the product life cycle.

Research design (3) A series of advanced decisions that, taken together, comprise a master plan or model for the conduct of an investigation.

Response (5) The individual's reaction to cues and drives.

Retail advertising (13) All advertising by stores that sell goods or services directly to the consuming public.

Retail cooperative (8) A contractual agreement between a group of retailers in which, in order to compete with chain operations, each retailer purchases stock in a retail-owned wholesaling operation and agrees to purchase a minimum percentage of supplies from the operation.

Retailer (8) A middleman who sells products that are purchased by individuals for their own use and not for resale.

Retailing (10) All of the activities involved in the sale of products and services to the ultimate consumer for his or her own use.

Return on investment (9) *See* ROI.

Revaluation (17) An official upward adjustment in the value of a nation's currency in relation to other currencies or to gold.

Revenues (15) The price of a product multiplied by the quantity sold.

Reverse reciprocity (4) The practice of giving favorable consideration to purchasers who supply the firm with needed supplies and raw materials.

Robinson-Patman Act (1936) (2) Technically an amendment to the Clayton Act, this legislation prohibited price discrimination not based on a cost differential. It also disallowed selling at an unreasonably low price in order to eliminate competition.

ROI (return on investment) (19) A quantitative tool that seeks to relate the activity or project's profitability to its investment. ROI is equal to the rate of profit multiplied by the turnover rate.

Role (5) What the other members of a group expect of the individual who is in any particular position within the group.

Sales agent (9) *See* Selling agent.

Sales analysis (3) The in-depth evaluation of a firm's sales. It involves breaking aggregate data down into component parts to obtain more meaningful information.

Sales branch (9) An establishment maintained by a manufacturer that serves as a warehouse for a particular sales territory, thereby duplicating the services of independent wholesalers. Sales branches carry inventory and process orders to customers from available stock.

Sales forecast (3) The estimate of a company's sales for a specified future period under a proposed marketing plan and under an assumed set of economic and other influences. The forecast may be for an individual product or for an entire line of products.

Sales management (14) The management activities of securing, maintaining, motivating, supervising, evaluating, and controlling an effective sales force.

Sales maximization (15) A pricing philosophy analyzed by economist William J. Baumol. In this approach, firms set a minimum at what they consider the lowest acceptable profit level and then seek to maximize sales in the belief that the increased sales are more important than immediate high profits to the long-run competitive picture.

Sales office (9) An establishment maintained by a manufacturer that serves as a regional office for salespeople. Unlike a sales branch, it does not carry inventory.

Sales promotion (12, 13) Those marketing activities other than personal selling, advertising, and publicity that stimulate consumer purchasing and dealer effectiveness; they include displays, shows and exhibitions, demonstrations, and various nonrecurrent sales efforts not in the ordinary routine.

Sales quota (3) A standard of comparison used in sales analysis; the level of expected sales by which actual sales are compared.

Sample (3) A representative group.

Sampling (13) The free distribution of a product in an attempt to obtain future sales for it.

Scrambled merchandising (10) The practice of carrying dissimilar lines of products in an attempt to generate added sales volume—for example, the carrying of antifreeze in a supermarket.

SCSA (4) *See* Standard Consolidated Statistical Area.

Secondary data (3) Information that has been previously published.

Selective distribution (8) The selection of a small number of retailers to handle a firm's product or product line.

Selective perception (5) The idea that consumers are consciously aware of only those incoming stimuli they wish to perceive.

Self-concept theory (5) The theory that the way people picture themselves influences the manner in which they act as consumers.

Seller's market (1) A market with a shortage of goods and services.

Selling agent or **sales agent** (9) An agent wholesaling middleman who is responsible for the total marketing program of a firm's product line. The selling agent has full authority over pricing decisions and promotional outlays and often provides financing for the manufacturer.

Selling up (14) The technique of convincing the customer to buy a higher priced item than he or she originally intended to buy. The practice of selling up should always be used within the constraint of the customer's real needs.

Semantic differential (5) A scaling device that uses a number of bipolar adjectives—such as hot and cold—to rank consumer attitudes.

Sender (12) The source of a communications system.

Services (6) Intangible tasks that satisfy consumer and industrial user needs when efficiently developed and distributed to chosen market segments. Services are included in the marketing definition of *product.*

Sherman Antitrust Act (1890) (2) Federal antitrust legislation that prohibits restraint of trade and monopolization and subjects violators to civil suits as well as to criminal prosecution.

Shopping center (10) *See* Planned shopping center.

Shopping goods (6) Products purchased only after the consumer has made comparisons of competing goods in competing stores on bases such as price, quality, style, and color. Shopping goods can be classified as either *homogeneous* (in which the consumer views them as essentially the same) or *heterogeneous* (in which the consumer sees significant differences in quality and style).

SIC codes (4) *See* Standard Industrial Classifications.

Simple random sample (3) A sample chosen in such a way that every member of a representative group has an equal chance of being selected.

Single line store (10) A retail store that competes with larger stores by offering a complete selection of one line of products.

Skimming pricing (16) A new-product pricing policy that uses a relatively high entry price. The name is derived from the term *skimming the cream.*

SMSA (4) *See* Standard Metropolitan Statistical Area.

Social class (5) The relatively permanent divisions of a society into which individuals or families are categorized on the basis of prestige and community status.

Societal environment (2) The marketer's relationships with society in general.

Specialty advertising (13) A sales promotion medium that utilizes useful articles carrying the advertiser's name, address, and advertising message to reach the target consumer. These items include calendars, pens, and matchbooks.

Specialty goods (6) Products that possess some unique characteristics that cause the buyer to prize them and to make a special effort to obtain them. Specialty goods are frequently branded and are typically high-priced.

Specialty store (10) A retail store that handles only part of a single line of products, although this part is stocked in considerable depth. Examples of specialty stores include meat markets, bakeries, and men's shoe stores.

Specifications (16) Written descriptions of items or jobs that the government unit or industrial firm wishes to acquire for use in competitive bidding.

Speculative production (8) Production based on the firm's estimate of the demand for its product.

SSWD (4) A term applied to single-person households; it stands for single, separated, widowed, and divorced.

Stagflation (2) A kind of inflation that is characterized by high unemployment and a rising price level at the same time.

Standard Consolidated Statistical Area (SCSA) (4) A large population concentration that contains an SMSA with a population of at least 1 million and one or more SMSAs that are related to it by high-density population centers and intermetropolitan commuting of workers.

Standard Industrial Classification (SIC) (4) A series of industrial classifications developed by the federal government for use in collecting detailed statistics for each industry. These classifications are called *SIC codes.*

Standard Metropolitan Statistical Area (SMSA) (4) An integrated economic and social unit containing one city of 50,000 inhabitants or twin cities with a combined population of at least 50,000.

Status (5) The relative position in the group of any individual member.

Status quo objectives (15) Pricing objectives based on the maintenance of stable prices.

Stock turnover (15) The number of times the average inventory is sold annually.

Storage warehouse (11) The traditional warehouse where products are stored prior to shipment. Storage warehouses are often used to balance supply and demand for producers and purchasers.

Subculture (5) Subgroups with their own distinguishing modes of behavior that exist within the prevailing culture.

Subliminal perception (5) Communication at a subconscious level of awareness.

Suboptimization (11) A condition in which individual objectives are accomplished at the expense of accomplishing the broader objectives of the total organization.

Suggestion selling (14) A retail sales technique that seeks to broaden the customer's original purchase with related items, special promotions, or holiday and seasonal merchandise.

Supermarket (10) A large-scale departmentalized retail store offering a variety of food products such as meat, dairy products, canned goods, produce, and frozen foods in addition to various nonfood items. Supermarkets operate on a self-service basis and emphasize low prices and adequate parking facilities.

Supplemental carriers (11) Freight carriers that specialize in transporting small shipments, such as United Parcel Service (UPS).

Supplies (6) Regular expense items necessary in the daily operation of the firm but not part of the final product, including maintenance, repair, and operating (MRO) items.

Supply curve (15) A schedule relating the quantity offered for sale to specified prices. It is the marginal cost curve above where it crosses the average variable cost curve.

Survey (3) A study that asks respondents to answer questions in order to obtain information on attitudes, motives, and/or opinions. There are three types of surveys: telephone, mail, and personal interview.

Systems (11) A set of objects with relationships between the objects and between their attributes.

Target return objectives (15) Either short-run or long-run profit goals usually stated as a percentage of sales or investment.

Tariff (17) A tax levied against products that are imported from abroad. The two types of tariffs are *revenue tariffs,* those designed to raise funds for the government, and *protective tariffs,* those designed to raise the retail price of imported products to that for similar domestic products (or higher) for the purpose of protecting profits and employment in domestic industry.

Tariffs (11) Books of official publications listing the rates for shipping various commodities. These tariffs take on the force and effect of statutory law when they are filed with the appropriate regulatory body.

Task objective method (12) A sequential approach to the development of a firm's promotional budget. The organization must (1) define the particular goals that it wants the promotional mix to accomplish and (2) determine the type and the amount of promotional activity required to accomplish each of the objectives that have been set.

Teleshopping (10) A new type of shopping made possible by cable television whereby consumers can order merchandise that has been displayed on their television sets.

Test marketing (3, 7) The introduction of a product into a particular city or area considered typical of the total market and the observation of the results of the promotional campaign in that area. The results largely determine whether the product will be introduced on a larger scale.

Time utility (1, 8) A kind of utility created by marketers having products available *when* consumers want to buy them.

Tokyo Round (17) A series of international trade negotiations, started in 1974 and concluded in 1979, that, among other things, will result in considerable tariff reductions throughout the world.

Ton-mile (11) The moving of one ton of freight one mile.

Top-down method (3) A method that starts with a forecast of general economic conditions that is then used to forecast industry sales and develop a forecast of company and product sales.

Total cost approach (11) The premise that all relevant factors in physically moving and storing products should be considered as a whole, not individually.

Trade discount (16) A payment to channel members for performing some marketing function normally required of the manufacturer. Also called *functional discount*.

Trade fairs or **trade exhibitions** (9) Periodic shows where manufacturers in a particular industry display their wares for visiting retail and wholesale buyers.

Trade-in (16) A type of price allowance that preserves the list price of the new item while cutting the amount the customer actually has to pay by allowing the customer credit on a used object, usually of the kind being purchased.

Trademark (7) A brand that has been given legal protection; the protection is granted solely to the brand's owner. The term *trademark* includes not only the pictorial design but also the brand name.

Trade show (13) *See* Trade fair.

Trading stamps (13) Sales promotion premiums offered by some retailers with a purchase. These stamps can be exchanged for items of value at stamp redemption centers.

Transfer price (16) The charge for sending goods from one company profit center to another.

Trigger pricing system (17) Minimum price levels for imported steel set by the U.S. government. Such prices are based on costs, and any sales at prices below these levels bring an immediate investigation of dumping.

Truck wholesaler or **truck jobber** (9) A wholesaler who specializes in marketing perishable food and in making regular deliveries to retail stores.

Truth-in-Lending Act (2) *See* Consumer Credit Protection Act.

Tying agreement (8) An agreement that requires a dealer who wishes to become the exclusive dealer for a manufacturer's products to also carry other of the manufacturer's products in inventory. The legality of a tying agreement is based on whether it restricts competitors from major markets.

Undifferentiated marketing (7) The practice of firms that produce only one product and market it to all customers with a single marketing mix.

Unfair trade laws (2) State enactments requiring sellers to maintain minimum prices for comparable merchandise.

Uniform delivered price (16) A pricing practice under which the same price (including an average transportation charge) is quoted to all buyers; sometimes called *postage stamp pricing*.

Unitizing (11) The combination of as many packages as possible into one load, preferably on a pallet. Unitizing promotes faster product movement, requires less labor in materials handling, and reduces damage and pilferage.

Unit pricing (16) The pricing of items in terms of some recognized unit of measure (such as a pound or quart) or a standard numerical count (such as a dozen).

Utility (1) The want-satisfying power of a product or service.

Variable costs (15) Costs that change when the level of production is altered, such as raw materials and the wages paid operative employees.

Variety (10) The number of product lines carried by the retailer.

Venture team (7) An organizational strategy for developing new-product areas through combining the management resources of technological innovations, capital, management, and marketing expertise. Venture teams, composed of specialists from different areas of the organization are physically separated from the permanent organization and linked directly with top management.

Vertical marketing system (VMS) (8) A professionally managed and centrally programmed network engineered to achieve operating economies and maximum impact in the channel.

Warranty (6) The guarantee to the buyer that the manufacturer will replace the product or refund its purchase price if it proves to be defective during a specified period of time.

Webb-Pomerene Export Trade Act (1918) (2) Federal legislation that excluded voluntary export trade associations from the Sherman Act restrictions—but only in their foreign trade dealings. The act was designed to allow U.S. firms to compete with foreign cartels.

Weber's law (5) The proposition that the higher the initial intensity of a stimulus, the greater the amount of change in intensity necessary for a difference to be noticed.

Wheeler-Lea Act (1938) (2) Legislation amending the Federal Trade Commission Act so as to ban deceptive or unfair business practices per se.

Wheel of retailing (10) A hypothesis by M. P. McNair that attempts to explain patterns of change in retailing. According to the hypothesis, new types of retailers gain a competitive foothold by offering lower prices to their customers through the reduction or elimination of services. Once they are established, however, they add more services and their prices gradually rise. They then become vulnerable to a new low-price retailer who enters with minimum services—and the wheel turns.

Wholesaler (9) A wholesaling middleman who takes title to the goods handled. The terms *jobber* and *distributor* are synonymous with wholesaler.

Wholesaler-sponsored voluntary chain (8) A contractual agreement between a group of retailers and an independent wholesaler that enables the retailers to compete with chain operations and that preserves a market for the wholesaler's products.

Wholesaling (8) The activities of persons or firms who sell to retailers, other wholesalers, and industrial users but who do not sell in significant amounts to ultimate consumers.

Wholesaling middlemen (9) A broad term that describes not only wholesalers (those middlemen who take title to the goods they handle) but also agents and brokers who perform important wholesaling activities without taking title to the goods.

Width (10) The complementary products carried by the retailer within a merchandise line.

Wool Products Labeling Act (1939) (2) Legislation requiring that labels must identify the kind and percentage of each type of wool used in making a product containing wool.

Zero population growth (4) The point at which the number of live births equals the current death rate.

Zone pricing (16) A modification of the uniform delivered price system in which the market is divided into different regions and a price is set within each one.

NAME INDEX

Dubois, Bernard, 414 n.17
Dunn, Dan T., 193 n.7
Dunn, S. Watson, 301 n.13; 308; 315; 330 n.1, n.5; 331 n.16, n.24; 414 n.14
Dunne, Patrick M., 37 n.15, 71 n.6
Durand, Richard M., 134 n.19

Egan, Richard, 85
Elliott, Clifford, 426
Ellis, Dean S., 17 n.1
Emmerling, John, 331 n.23
Engel, Ernst, 90
Engel, James F., 128; 133 n.4; 134 n.26, n.29; 135 n.33
Engledow, Jack L., 18 n.19
Enis, Ben M., 162 n.4
Erdos, Paul, 57
Erickson, David, 390 n.9
Etgar, Michael, 301 n.13
Ettkin, Lawrence P., 194 n.22

Farris, Martin T., 279 n.19
Faust, Bernie, 391 n.19
Ferber, Robert, 71 n.10
Fernandez, José, 100 n.6
Ferrell, O. C., 437 n.17
Ferry, George P., 332 n.30
Festinger, Leon, 135 n.43
Field, George A., 104
Finkelman, Bernice, 18 n.24
Finney, E. Robert, 100 n.10
Fogg, C. David, 359
Forbes, Malcolm, 437 n.12
Ford, Henry, 11, 106
Ford, Neil M., 349 n.17
Franklin Benjamin, 305
Franz, Robert S., 37 n.8; 71 n.4; 100 n.10; 133 n.2; 194 n.25; 217 n.7; 234 n.5; 278 n.4; 301 n.13; 331 n.8; 349 n.8; 373 n.5, n.8; 438 n.35; 453
Frazier, Gary L., 217 n.7
French, Norman D., 391 n.18
French, Warren A., 37 n.18
Frink, George, 310
Fry, Joseph N., 331 n.25
Fu, Marilyn Y. C., 414 n.15
Fuller, Dennis, 71 n.9
Fuller, Donald A., 255 n.8, 438 n.35
Fulmer, Robert M., 100 n.12
Futrell, Charles M., 349 n.8

Gale, Bradley T., 373 n.14
Gallese, Liz Roman, 438 n.33
Gamble, Stephen H., 437 n.18
Gandz, Jeffrey, 72 n.22
Gardner, David M., 37 n.18
Garino, David P., 460 n.27
Gates, Roger, 71 n.14
Gaulden, Corbett, 133 n.2
Gaw, Walter A., 331 n.27
Gecowitz, George A., 278 n.14

Gelb, Betsy D., 100 n.6
Gemmill, Henry, 57
Gentry, Dwight L., 72 n.22
George, Claude S., 18 n.13
George, William R., 163 n.14
George, William W., 193 n.7
Georgoff, David M., 390 n.6
Getschow, George, 247
Giges, Nancy, 5
Gilbreth, Frank, 11
Gilbreth, Lillian, 11
Gillett, Peter L., 255 n.10, 437 n.6
Gilson, Christopher C., 134 n.20, n.23
Ginter, James L., 193 n.10, 437 n.5
Ginter, Peter M., 331 n.10, 438 n.35
Glaskowsky, Nicholas A., Jr., 37 n.14, 270
Goeldner, C. R., 71 n.7
Goho, Thomas S., 391 n.28
Goldstucker, Jac L., 444
Good, Robert E., 72 n.25, n.27
Goodman, Charles, 438 n.27
Gorman, William, 391 n.19
Gottschalk, Jack A., 331 n.20
Graham, Ellen, 330 n.1, 331 n.13
Granick, David, 391 n.28
Green, Paul E., 72 n.21
Greenberg, Barnett A., 18 n.19; 37 n.20; 99 n.2; 100 n.7; 134 n.24, n.27; 194 n.24; 217 n.8; 254 n.2, n.15; 301 n.13; 444; 459 n.7
Greene, Bob, 14
Gross, Charles W., 38 n.28
Gross, Daniel, 71 n.4
Grubb, Edward L., 133 n.9
Gubar, George, 88
Guffey, Hugh J., Jr., 72 n.15
Guiltinan, Joseph P., 373 n.23
Gunn, Bruce, 373 n.6
Guzzardi, Walter, Jr., 194 n.24

Haas, Robert W., 100 n.7
Hackett, Donald W., 217 n.12 n.13; 331 n.8; 349 n.8
Haire, Mason, 114, 134 n.16
Hall, Arthur D., 278 n.7
Hall, Edward T., 135 n.39
Hall, William P., 349 n.19
Hallas, Clark, 390 n.3
Hancock, William, 437 n.6
Hanna, Nessim, 37 n.26, 391 n.23
Hansen, Harry L., 18 n.26
Hansen, Robert A., 163 n.11
Hansz, James E., 373 n.8
Hardy, Thomas, 451, 459 n.13, 460 n.16
Hargrove, Earnestine, 18 n.19
Haring, Robert C., 37 n.16, 255 n.8, 331 n.10, 391 n.23
Harlan, Gene, 332 n.32
Harness, Edward G., 38 n.32
Harper, Donald V., 390 n.4
Harris, James R., 71 n.15

SUBJECT INDEX

Key terms and their page numbers appear in boldface type for convenience in locating them.